THE BLACK CROSS

THE
BLACK CROSS

A HISTORY OF THE BALTIC CRUSADES

Aleksander Pluskowski

YALE UNIVERSITY PRESS
NEW HAVEN AND LONDON

Published with assistance from the foundation established in memory of Oliver Baty Cunningham of the Class of 1917, Yale College.

Copyright © 2026 Aleksander Pluskowski

All rights reserved. This book may not be reproduced in whole or in part, in any form (beyond that copying permitted by Sections 107 and 108 of the U.S. Copyright Law and except by reviewers for the public press) without written permission from the publishers.

All reasonable efforts have been made to provide accurate sources for all images that appear in this book. Any discrepancies or omissions will be rectified in future editions.

For information about this and other Yale University Press publications, please contact:
U.S. Office: sales.press@yale.edu   yalebooks.com
Europe Office: sales@yaleup.co.uk   yalebooks.co.uk

Set in Van Dijck MT by IDSUK (DataConnection) Ltd
Printed and bound in the UK using 100% renewable electricity at CPI Group (UK) Ltd

Library of Congress Control Number: 2025942014
A catalogue record for this book is available from the British Library.
Authorized Representative in the EU: Easy Access System Europe, Mustamäe tee 50, 10621 Tallinn, Estonia, gpsr.requests@easproject.com

ISBN 978-0-300-27906-1

10 9 8 7 6 5 4 3 2

For Melissa

Contents

List of Plates and Maps	ix
A Note on People and Places	xi
Acknowledgements	xii
Introduction	1

Holy War in Northern Europe

1. Confronting Paganism: Territorial Christianity in the North — 27
2. The First Crusade in the North: Conquering the Wends — 54
3. Precarious Frontiers: From the Oder to the Vistula — 81
4. From Pagans to Crusaders: Scandinavian Expansion in the Baltic — 108

Militarised Christianity in the North

5. Terra Mariana: Creating Livonia — 137
6. Black Cross Ascendant: Conquering Prussia — 163
7. Fortresses of Heaven: Religious Rule in the Medieval Baltic — 188
8. Apocalypse Then? The 'Eternal Crusade' against Lithuania — 214

CONTENTS

Worlds in Transition

9. The Hanseatic World: Migrants and Indigenes in the Medieval Baltic — 243
10. Old Gods, New Gods: Religion and Indigenous Resilience — 269
11. Holy War in Crisis: Rebellion and Reformation — 296

From Black Cross to Iron Cross

12. Ancestral Struggles: Reimagining the Baltic Crusades — 325
13. From Aryan Crusaders to European Heritage: The Baltic Crusades Rehabilitated — 352

Notes — 379
Bibliography — 397
Index — 426

PLATES AND MAPS

PLATES

1. Aerial view of Malbork Castle, Poland. NetVideo / Shutterstock.
2. Virgin and Child, St Mary's Church, Malbork Castle, Poland. Author's photo.
3. Obermarsberg (formerly Eresburg), North Rhine-Westphalia, Germany. mauritius images GmbH / Alamy.
4. Martyrdom of St Adalbert, Gniezno Cathedral bronze doors. Alizada Studios / Shutterstock.
5. Reconstructions of early medieval Western Slavic buildings, Archäologisches Freilichtmuseum Groß Raden, Mecklenburg-Western Pomerania, Germany. Author's photo.
6. Excavated late twelfth-century timber building, Gründungsviertel, Lübeck, Germany. Courtesy of Lübeck Archaeological Service.
7. Carved stone possibly depicting Otto of Bamberg. LAKD M-V, Landesarchäologie, Andreas Paasch (with permission).
8. Horses buried in the north Sambian cemetery of Kholmy, Kaliningrad Oblast, Russia. Photo by Roman Shiroukhov and Andrei Zinoviev (with permission).
9. Remains of Slavic religious centre at Arkona, Mecklenburg-Western Pomerania, Germany. Author's photo.

10. *The Taking of Arkona by Valdemar the Great and Bishop Absalon in 1169* by Laurits Tuxen, 1894. Museum of National History, Frederiksborg Castle, Hillerød, Denmark.
11. Reconstruction of the church excavated on Ristimäki, Ravattula, Finland. Photo by Samuli Holopainen. Copyright Samuli Holopainen.
12. Excavations at 33 Kalēju iela, Riga, Latvia. Photo by Uldis Kalējs (with permission).
13. Monument inside the stronghold on Muhu, Estonia. Author's photo.
14. Excavated greyware pots. Author's photos.
15. Brandenburg Castle, Kaliningrad Oblast, Russia. Digital model by Paweł Moszczyński (with permission); author's photo.
16. Malbork Castle's 'golden gate', Pomerania, Poland. Author's photo.
17. Castle and cathedral at Kwidzyn, Pomerania, Poland. Patryk Kosmider / Shutterstock.
18. Kuressaare Castle, Saaremaa, Estonia. trabantos / Shutterstock.
19. Reconstruction of one of the Teutonic Order's campaigns. Photo by Magnus Elander (with permission).
20. Lifting the wreck of the Lootsi cog, Tallinn, Estonia. Mere Muuseum.
21. Sacred oak near the village of Laumėnai, Samogitia, Lithuania. Photo by Vykintas Vaitkevičius (with permission).
22. Cēsis Castle, Vidzeme, Latvia. trabantos / Shutterstock.
23. *The Battle of Grunwald* by Jan Matejko, 1878. National Museum in Warsaw, MP 443.
24. *Alka* monument by Ieva Vasauskienė and Gytis Tiškus, 2007. Author's photo.
25. Alexander Nevsky monument, Samolva, Russia. Karasev Viktor / Shutterstock.

MAPS

1. The Baltic Sea region today.
2. The expansion of Frankish territory in the north.
3. The expansion of the Piast state.
4. The Baltic Sea region in the mid-twelfth century.
5. Routes of the Baltic Crusades, 1147–1293.
6. Medieval Prussia, Livonia and Swedish Finland.
7. The Baltic Sea region in 1910.

A NOTE ON PEOPLE AND PLACES

THIS BOOK IS INTENDED for an English-speaking readership, and so personal names have been anglicised in many cases. Where names are better known in their native form – particularly those of historical figures (e.g. Jan Matejko, Paweł Włodkowic, Heinrich von Treitschke) – these have been retained for clarity and consistency. At times, I have also included original terms to provide readers with a better sense of the historical context. Variations in some names, such as Perkun, Perkuno, and Perkūnas, have been preserved to reflect the linguistic and cultural settings of the sources in which they appear. There are many variants of regional names applied to the numerous territories of the eastern Baltic, and I have aimed for consistency. In many national scholarly traditions, modern place names are used even when referring to historical contexts, whilst international scholarship tends to use historical names. I have chosen to use both historical and modern place names where appropriate. At times, I have switched between different names when referring to their specific linguistic context and hopefully this, along with the repeated use of paired place names, will reinforce their interchangeability rather than confuse readers.

ACKNOWLEDGEMENTS

THE IDEA FOR THIS book emerged during the course of an International Visitor Fellowship at the Stanford Humanities Center (SHC) in the winter of 2016. I am extremely grateful to Krish Seetah and Stanford University for sponsoring this, and to my colleagues at the SHC for their encouragement and feedback at the time. I would also like to thank all my colleagues and team members who I've had the privilege of working with over the last twenty years, giving me invaluable opportunities to familiarise myself with the sources, historical monuments and landscapes around the Baltic. Many of these people worked on the 'Ecology of Crusading' project which I directed between 2010 and 2014. These are, in Poland: Daniel Makowiecki, Zbigniew Sawicki, Waldek Jaszczyński, Marcin Wiewióra, Adam Chęć, Dariusz Poliński, Maciej Karczewski, Małgorzata Karczewska, Seweryn Szczepański, Maria Kasprzycka, Mirosław Marcinkowski, Joanna Fonferek, Monika Badura, Małgorzata Latałowa, Beata Możejko, Katarzyna Pińska, Mirosława Zabilska-Kunek, Gregory Leighton and Janusz Trupinda; in Estonia: Heiki Valk, Juhan Kreem, Lembi Lõugas, Eve Rannamäe, Martin Malve, Liivi Varul, Juhan Kari, Ragnar Saage, Anti Selart, Lembi Siim Veski and Normunds Stivriņš; in Latvia: Kaspars Kļaviņš, Gundars Kalniņš, Zigrīda Apala, Oskars Uspelis, Anda Dripe, Eva Eihmane, Laimdota Kalniņa, Māris Zunde, Agris Dzenis, Uldis Kalējs, Arnis Mugurēvičs, Artūrs Tomsons and Rūta Vecmuktāne; in Lithuania: Linas Daugnora, Miglė Stančikaitė, Vykintas Vaitkevičius and Vladas Žulkus; in Germany: Roman Shiroukhov,

ACKNOWLEDGEMENTS

Marc Jarzebowski, Timo Ibsen, Udo Arnold, Jürgen Sarnowsky and Jörn Staecker (unfortunately no longer with us); in Denmark: Janus Møller Jensen, Jette Linaa, Christer Carlsson and Marianne Hem Eriksen; in Sweden: Anders Andrén, Magnus Elander, Per Lagerås, Nanouschka Myrberg Burström, Jonas Monié Nordin, Mats Roslundand, Neil Price; in Hungary: József Laszlovszky, Alice Choyke and Laszlo Bartosiewicz. I'd also like to thank Katherine French for bringing me back to the Baltic in recent years as part of her project on horses in pre-crusade burial rites.

I would also like to thank my colleagues in the UK who have been involved in varying ways with my work in the Baltic, both directly and indirectly, over the years, especially at the University of Reading: Alexander Brown, Rowena Banerjea, Kevin Hayward, David Thornley, Grenville Astill, Gundula Müldner, Stuart Black, Charlotte Scull, Roberta Gilchrist, Mark Maltby, Gary King, Richard Madgwick, David Orton, Chris Gerrard, Catherine Hills, Martin Carver, Ivy Yeh, Piers Mitchell and Jonathan Phillips. I would like to extend my thanks to the staff of the British Library, UCL and the Warburg Institute in London, the libraries of the Castle Museum in Malbork, the Museum of Warmia and Masuria in Olsztyn, and the University of Nicolaus Copernicus in Toruń, for their help with accessing relevant source material. I would like to thank Heather McCallum and the team of Yale University Press London for giving me the opportunity to finally bring this book into the world, the two reviewers who provided invaluable comments on the manuscript, and Robert Sargant for his exemplary copy-editing skills.

My family, as always, have been tremendously supportive, and I'd like to thank my mother Irena and my sisters Klara and Helena in particular. Early discussions with Krys Plucinsky also helped shaped the text for a broader readership, and I'm grateful for her thoughts and ideas. The writing of this book has also taken place in the company of two cats – Bruno, who tragically passed away not long before I had completed the first draft, and Jack, who came into our lives during the preparation of the final manuscript. Last but not least, I would like to thank my partner Melissa for her tireless support throughout the writing of this book, for sacrificing numerous weekend and evening plans so I could get it done, and for driving me hundreds of kilometres through blizzards in northern Germany to get photos of archaeological sites! This book is dedicated to her.

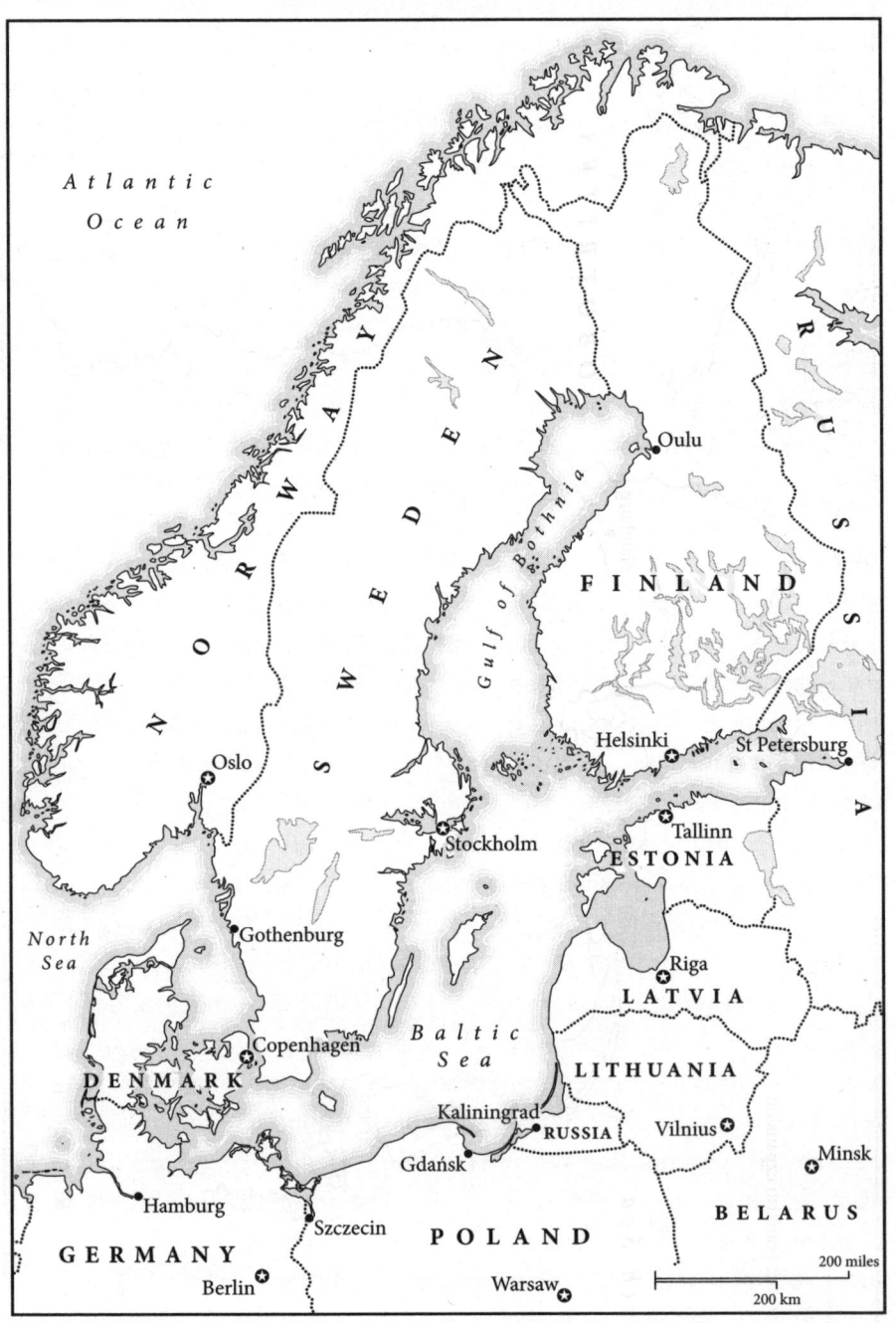

Map 1. The Baltic Sea region today.

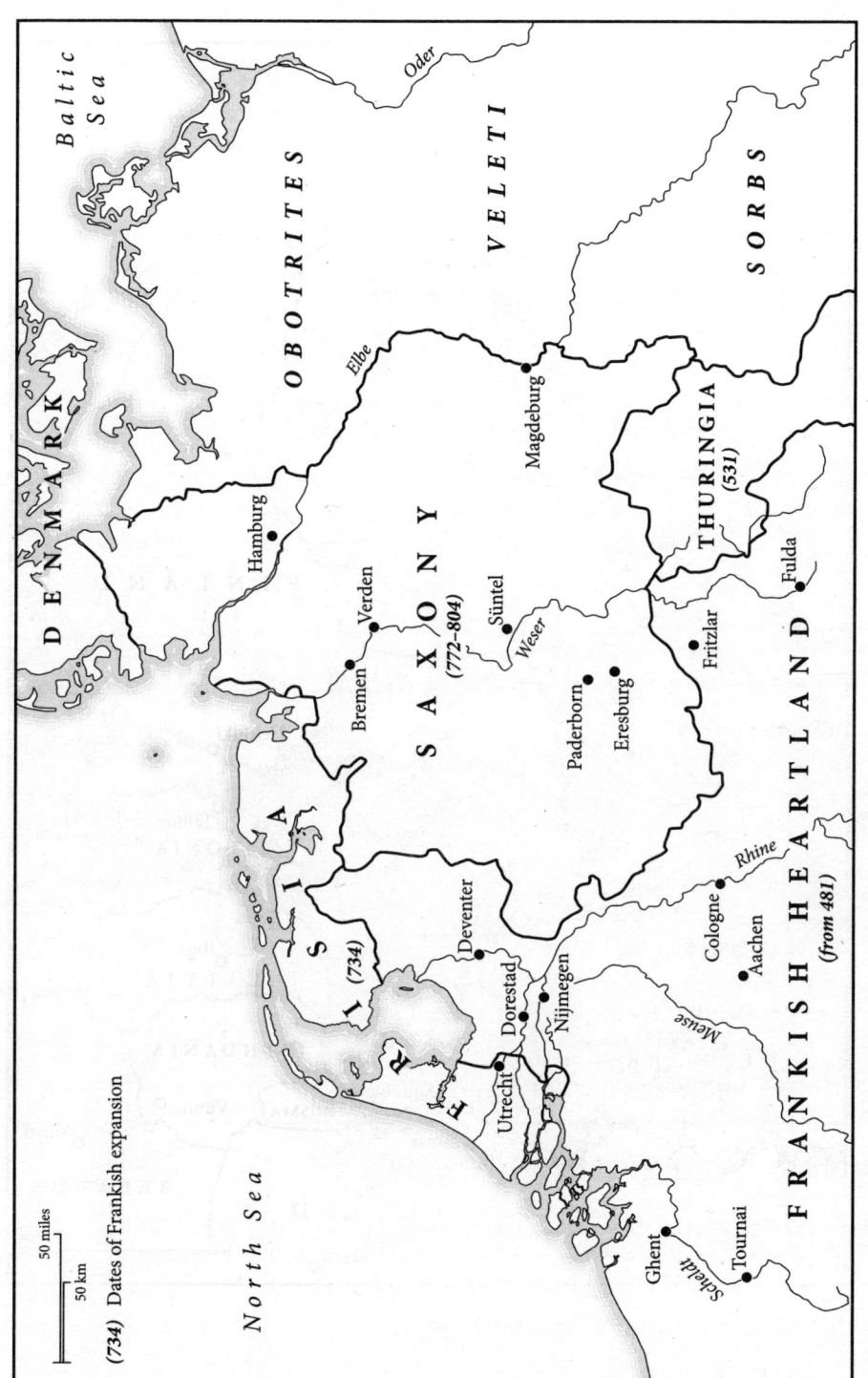

Map 2. The expansion of Frankish territory in the north.

Map 3. The expansion of the Piast state.

Map 4. The Baltic Sea region in the mid-twelfth century.

Map 5. Routes of the Baltic Crusades, 1147–1293.

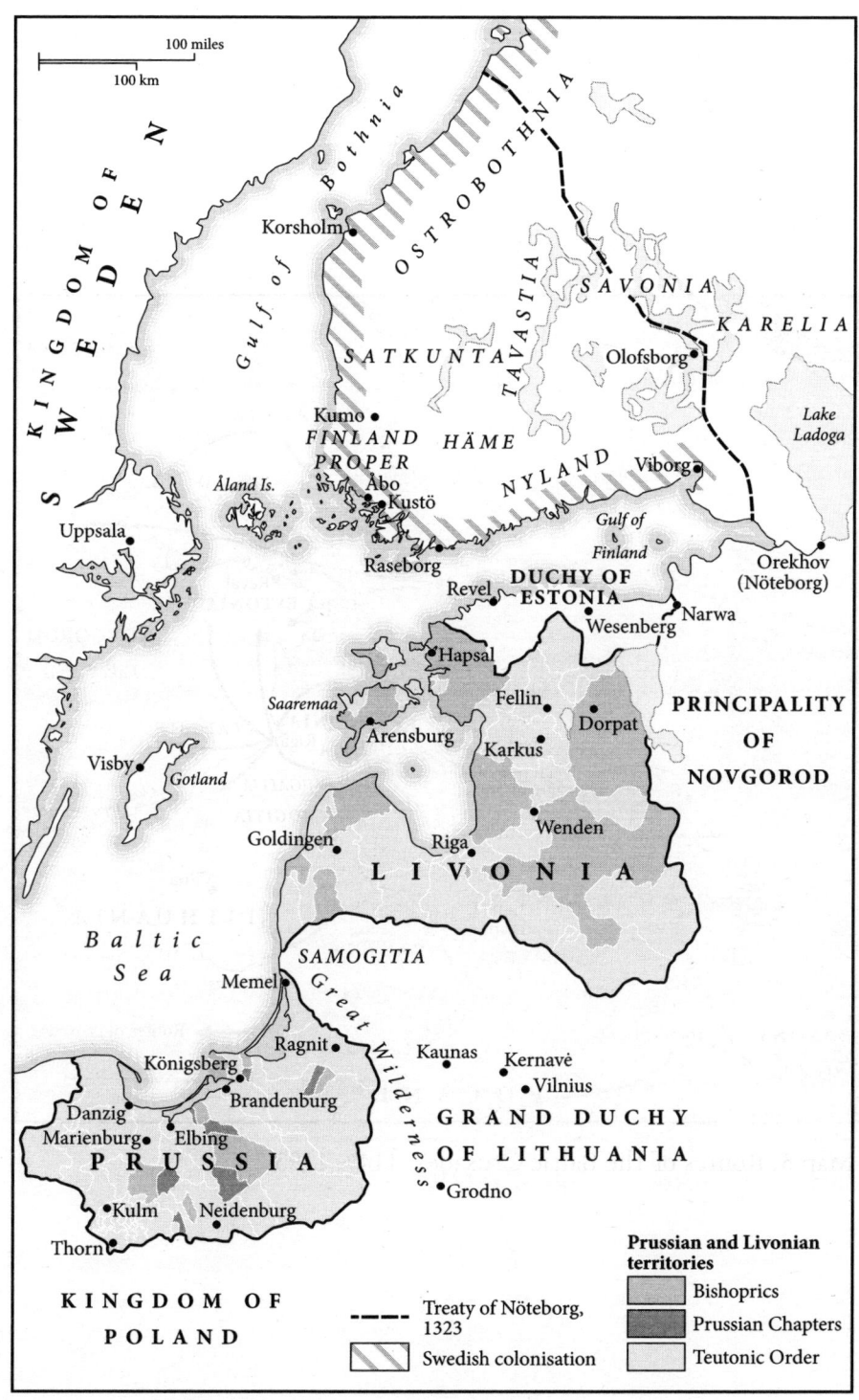

Map 6. Medieval Prussia, Livonia and Swedish Finland.

Map 7. The Baltic Sea region in 1910.

INTRODUCTION

The white snow was like blood, and the entire field turned red . . .
Livonian Rhymed Chronicle[1]

A CASTLE IN NORTH POLAND

In 2004, when I first visited the largest castle in the world, I was completely unprepared for what I saw. Growing up in the UK with history-obsessed parents, I had seen a lot of castles and been impressed by the grandeur of Windsor, Dover and Caernarfon. My 'local', the Tower of London, still fills me with awe. As an archaeology student I had travelled around Europe and seen numerous other citadels and crumbling fortified residences. I even had the opportunity and privilege to work for a brief time within the majestic castle complex in Prague, with its cathedral, churches, palaces and hidden alleyways. But even this did not prepare me for the experience of Malbork, located in the far east of Pomerania in northern Poland.

The castle was easy to reach. From Gdańsk I caught the train to Malbork, some 40 kilometres to the south-east, on the far side of the expansive floodplain of the Vistula river and its eastern tributary, the Nogat. As we crossed the floodplain, the castle, still many kilometres away, gradually came into view. First it appeared as a small speck on the horizon, rising above the rows of trees that interrupted the surrounding low-lying fields and meadows. Then, gradually, its features became more pronounced. A tall red tower dominated the skyline, emerging from a long line of brick buildings. I was only able to catch glimpses as clusters of trees lining the rail tracks repeatedly obscured the view. It was only when we reached the west bank of the Nogat that the fortress suddenly appeared in full. Its crowded array of towers and walls, all built from brick, vividly reflected in the river below, contrasted dramatically with the blue sky. Since then, I've seen this view countless times, in all seasons, and it never fails to impress.

The train crossed the river and suddenly we were inside the castle, as the railway cut through the outer wall. Was that deliberate? It seemed a careless oversight. I later found out the bridge was constructed in the mid-nineteenth century, one of two crossing the Nogat. At that time, the castle was only just beginning to be appreciated as a historical monument, and a direct route through the outer ward provided the easiest solution for connecting both ends of the line. But my surprise was quickly overwhelmed by the castle itself which completely dominated my field of view to the south, an ascending cascade of red buildings, seemingly piled one on top of the other. We sped past multiple rows of walls, studded with towers and interspersed with deep moats. The castle vanished as suddenly as it had appeared, concealed by rows of modern buildings – dreary blocks from the Communist era that fill the suburbs of all Polish towns. The train finally came to a grinding halt. We had arrived in Malbork. The station was itself like a miniature castle, built from red bricks with a high tiled roof. Inside, the walls were decorated with coats of arms. This building, since renovated, had been constructed in 1890 in a neo-gothic style clearly inspired by the castle. Here were also visible reminders of a more recent history – bullet holes in the walls, traces of a desperate firefight in the final stages of the Second World War. I would later learn how this was entangled in the biography of the castle and town, a stark chapter in the ethnic upheavals that in 1945 had completely transformed the region – Prussia, then a part of Germany. The rail tracks that cut through the castle had originally connected Berlin with Königsberg; both had been the capitals of Prussia at different times.

Walking through more recently built suburbs I finally reached the castle on foot from the east. The whole structure was impossible to take in with one glance. By the measure of the surface area enclosed within its outermost historical bounds, it encompassed some 21 hectares. Millions of bricks had been used in its construction and restoration. Here and there sections of wall were visible beyond the trees lining the road. I crossed the bridge over the canal that had originally fed the castle's inner moats before draining out into the river. Passing by the outer walls and crossing a deep moat, dry and grassy, I reached the first substantial line of defences, following the road that led to the centre of the castle's first ward. Once the trees parted, I was greeted by the sight of the tall tower I had seen from the train, now clearly defined with a Polish flag fluttering from its pinnacle. Beneath was a shorter tower with large gothic-arched windows of what was evidently a church, protruding out beyond the inner battlements. There was no window in its eastern end. Instead, there was a large empty alcove which I soon learned had housed a striking sculpture of the Virgin Mary wearing a gold crown and holding the Christ Child in her arms. Standing at over 8 metres, the figure had been destroyed along with much of the church in 1945. It would be reconstructed a decade after my first visit. At first glance, it seemed unusual for such a large religious sculpture to decorate the exterior of a castle.

I crossed the covered wooden bridge over a wide moat and passed through another two sets of gates. They were guarded by iron portcullises that hung menacingly above. The passage narrowed as the cobbled expanse and green lawns of the inner ward slowly came into view. Then the space opened up and the true heart of the castle became visible, towering over the surrounding buildings. As I walked alongside its brick ranges, I glimpsed numerous holes which peppered the walls – more bullet holes. I passed through a heavy wooden door into a vast hall with a vaulted ceiling and stained-glass windows. The south-facing wall was covered in paintings. The scenes included mounted knights with shields, some decorated with red eagles, others with black crosses. These had been painted in the early twentieth century during the castle's first phase of restoration, and had only been uncovered recently. Leaving the hall, I crossed a wooden bridge over another moat into the oldest and most important part of the complex – the so-called 'upper castle'. Passing through a broad gothic arched gate, I stepped into the courtyard of the strangest castle interior I had ever seen. Surrounded by multiple storeys of arcades, with pointed arches and gothic windows, I suddenly felt like I was inside the cloister of a monastery.

In fact, the castle in its heyday could have been likened to a fortified monastery. Its first name was recorded in Latin as Castrum sanctae Mariae – Mary's Castle. In German, this was rendered as Marienburg.[2] The Polish name Malbork, a sixteenth-century Germanism, was finally adopted as the official place name when the town, castle and its district, along with most of Prussia, came into Poland's possession in 1945. The castle was by far the largest of almost fifty similar structures referred to as convents, built across the eastern Baltic region by one of the most remarkable religious organisations of the Middle Ages. A corporation of warrior monks, whose emblem was a black cross. They were the Ordo Teutonicus or German Order, more familiar to English readers as the Teutonic Order or Teutonic Knights. The Latin word *Teutonicus* was used by medieval writers as a synonym for German people, and thanks to persistent habit this archaic rendering continues to be used in modern English.[3] In fact, their full name was much longer – the Hospital of St Mary of the Germans in Jerusalem. This alludes to their humble origins in the Holy Land, as a German brotherhood who manned a field hospital at the port of Acre (today in Israel) at the end of the twelfth century. But within a few decades of their foundation, the Teutonic Order had become the dominant force leading military campaigns which would completely reshape the societies of north-eastern Europe. Historians would later call these the Northern or Baltic Crusades.

CRUSADING

When you think of the crusades, you're probably imagining those that focused on the Levant. After all, what would later become known as the 'First Crusade' was a penitential war initiated by Pope Urban II in 1095 with the aim of seizing Jerusalem, then under the control of the Islamic Fatimid Caliphate. Those answering the pope's call for holy war sewed crosses onto their clothes to publicly show they had taken the oath to fight. As such they were 'marked with a cross' – *crucesignatus* – which provided the basis for the later term 'crusader'.[4] Against all the odds and after three gruelling years fighting Seljuk forces, the remnants of the crusader armies succeeded in capturing Jerusalem on 15 July 1099. Some of the European lords involved also carved out their own territories in the Levant. This resulted in the creation of three additional 'crusader states', alongside that centred on Jerusalem.[5] You might also draw similarities with the Christian conquests of Muslim Iberia and Sicily. Both of these began earlier than the First Crusade and received papal support. In time, these all came to be seen as part a broader existential struggle for the survival of Catholic Christendom.[6]

The military successes of the First Crusade, an unprecedented event in European history, were never repeated, but the establishment of Catholic states in the Levant and the subsequent upsurge in pilgrimage breathed new life into the Christian idea of the Holy Land.[7] This ultimately changed how Christians experienced religious devotion, particularly as pilgrims. It also accelerated the institutionalisation of Christian holy war which would have profound consequences for Catholic Europe and its neighbouring regions. Described by some historians as 'ecclesiastical statecraft', crusading became a powerful political weapon in the hands of later popes: a means of raising armies, funding and moral support.[8] It provided an attractive incentive that could appeal to all, irrespective of social background, occupation and income. This was the spiritual reward. Half a century after crusaders took Jerusalem, when the fiery Cistercian orator Bernard of Clairvaux preached what historians have called the 'Second Crusade', he presented this incentive in clear and unambiguous terms, reinforcing the message of the papacy: 'Take the sign of the cross and you shall gain pardon for every sin that you confess with a contrite heart. The material itself [referring to the cloth cross sewn onto the garments of crusaders], being bought, is worth little; but if it be placed on a devout shoulder, it is, without doubt, worth no less than the kingdom of God.'[9]

The actual mechanism for conferring this reward was called an indulgence. The system of indulgences issued by the Church was not fully established until the thirteenth century, and it enabled individuals to remit the temporal punishment for committing sins. In medieval (and in fact modern) Catholic theology, there were two categories of sin. The most grievous were mortal sins, popularly known as the Seven Deadly Sins. They could be forgiven by receiving absolution from God, mediated by a priest during confession. However, this would not erase all the sins which had accumulated during one's lifetime. To purify the soul completely required further atonement, both in this world and immediately after death, in a temporary hell called Purgatory. In the Christian West, popular belief in Purgatory had developed by the eleventh century, along with the notion that good deeds in life could reduce your penance after death. The indulgence became the official recognition of those deeds, bestowed by the pope or a delegated clerical authority. The most common was a partial indulgence, which marked a reduction in the time spent suffering in Purgatory. There was also a posthumous indulgence which could be granted to the dead. Or there was a full pardon, erasing an entire lifetime of sin. This would be offered to crusaders.

The Holy See would provide a receipt – a sheet of parchment outlining the terms of the spiritual pardon. This would be sealed with a small lead bulla, stamped with the name and symbols of the pope in whose name it was issued. These objects became regarded as powerful amulets and sometimes they were even buried with individuals, perhaps as a guarantee of swifter passage to heaven.[10] For most crusaders, however, the oath to participate in a holy war sanctioned by the pope was enough. To die on crusade was the closest most could get to leading the life of a saint. A martyr's death guaranteed direct entry into heaven, in a way that was extremely difficult with other forms of penance. There were also a number of lesser and more easily attainable indulgences issued by the papacy that gradually built a solid base of support for the crusading movement. At the Fourth Lateran Council in 1215, Pope Innocent III declared that those unable to fight could exchange their crusading vows for payments. In this way, everyone could contribute and this purchasable indulgence would play a major role in financing later crusades. Later on, Pope Gregory IX would add release from excommunication to the bundle of privileges which crusaders could enjoy.[11] Sermons that were intended to inspire congregants to join crusades were not solely calls to arms, but emphasised moral obligations, the nature of sin and the role of penance. Preachers sought to highlight not just the benefits to the individual but the value of crusading to the defence of Christians, and to divine salvation for all.

Whilst the remission of sins provided a powerful incentive for individuals to become crusaders, political allegiances and potential material gains resulting from territorial conquests also played a role in motivating participants. In a world where religious identity was entangled with a person's social status and where the Church played a fundamental social and political role, these were not mutually exclusive motivations, as evident in the earlier Christian conquests of Sicily and northern Iberia. Both were accompanied by the building of churches and monasteries, and lauded as the restoration of the Christian community, whilst the conquerors also benefited from material gains and personal prestige. However, crusading was an expensive, and at times financially ruinous (not to mention lethal), activity. This prompts us to carefully consider the motivations of its participants. Some, if not many, who promoted and participated in crusades must have genuinely believed they were building a better world by defending Christendom against its enemies – real and perceived. Indeed, crusading became far more than just a struggle between Christianity and Islam in the Levant: it provided a means to expand and defend Catholic Christendom across a much broader frontier.

THE PAGAN FRONTIER

As Christianity advanced northward, new frontiers arose along the borders of emerging and expanding Catholic states. Beyond them lay the lands inhabited by what Christian commentators called pagans. Originating from Latin *paganus*, the term first gained popularity in the Christian West in the fourth and fifth centuries as a way of mocking religious outsiders (Jews were exempted from this branding due to their shared biblical heritage).[12] Pagans were imagined as naive rustics, simpletons living in the countryside – at the opposite end of the civilising spectrum to that of Roman and by then largely Christian cities. As Christianity spread to Northern Europe, the term became used to refer to indigenous peoples who worshipped a variety of different gods and who recognised spiritual meaning and power in certain aspects of the natural world.[13] Of course, none of the people branded in this way thought of themselves as pagan. This was a collective and derogatory term which never described any one religion per se, and could even be used to refer to other Christians.

By the time of the crusades the word pagan was being used to describe *all* the enemies of Christendom, including Muslims. Indeed, in every version of the reported speech at Clermont which instigated the First Crusade, Pope Urban II had referred to the Seljuk Turks who held Jerusalem at the time as pagans.[14] He was also said to have evoked the glorious reputation of Charlemagne and other ancestral Frankish kings who 'destroyed the pagan kingdoms and brought them within the bounds of Christendom'.[15] Carolingian churchmen had promoted campaigns against Muslims in Iberia as religious wars aimed at protecting Frankish Christians and expanding Christianity,[16] but Charlemagne's armies had also targeted the Saxons, a group with polytheistic beliefs living in what is today largely northwest Germany. In this respect, the wars being fought for the Holy Land and against Muslims in Iberia became connected to those against non-Christian societies in Northern Europe. They were perceived as part of the same struggle for the survival of Catholic Christendom against a hostile pagan 'other'.[17]

Christian chroniclers, who were mostly clerics, used the term pagan liberally. Those writing in German, a language which became widespread across the Baltic Sea region by the end of the thirteenth century, would use its equivalent *Heide* or heathen. Despite its derogatory origins, pagan remains a useful label when trying to explain the encounters between Christians and non-Christians in the North. There is a clear sense that a real distinction was made at the time between these different religions, although with a more objective lens we can see that beliefs and practices were more complex, fluid and adaptable. With this caveat in mind, I have chosen to use the term throughout this book as a handy and familiar label for the polytheistic societies of Northern Europe.

By the twelfth century, the Baltic Sea region was home to the last indigenous pagan societies of Europe. This small body of water, although less than a quarter of the Mediterranean in size, separated – and connected – three worlds. Catholic Europe, firstly, where most of the Christians on the planet resided at this time. A large proportion of the rest, who belonged to the Eastern Orthodox Church, lived in the lands between the Baltic and Black seas. Theirs was a world of city states, a hybrid of Slavic and Scandinavian cultures referred to as Rus' (or by its Latinised exonym Ruthenian), the precursor to 'Russian', although historians have used both terms interchangeably. For centuries this had been dominated by Kyiv but, when this realm fragmented into independent principalities, the north-west came to be ruled by the cities of Polotsk, Pskov and Novgorod. Caught between these two worlds – in what is today Finland, Estonia, Latvia, Lithuania, part of Belarus, the Russian Kaliningrad Oblast, north Poland and north-east Germany – were a number of pagan societies where Finnic, Baltic and Slavic languages were spoken. In contrast to their Christian neighbours, they were organised into smaller political groups governed by local aristocratic dynasties. Many scholars have referred to these societies as 'tribal', a problematic term with colonial overtones that nonetheless highlights the importance of extended kinship groups in their social organisation. Of these, only the Lithuanians developed a centralised political structure that had crystallised into a powerful state by the mid-thirteenth century – the grand duchy.

The creation of Western European territories in the Levant had been an unintended consequence of the First Crusade. But in Northern Europe, crusading became twinned with the seizure of land from the outset. There was already some historical precedent for this. The emergence of a Catholic political community in the latter centuries of the first millennium had added a new dimension to the territorial conquests of non-Christian regions. Allegiance to dominant Christian regimes required adopting the religion of its rulers, at the very least in principle (and in public), if not in practice. This became a measure of trust. The template for this had been established by the symbolic inheritor of Roman rule in the West – the Carolingian Empire and its eastern Ottonian splinter state, forerunner of what later became known as the Holy Roman Empire. In this respect, when rulers extended their territorial control, they also pushed the boundaries of Christendom. The influential historian Robert Bartlett argued these conquests laid the foundations for Europe as we know it today, through a process of cultural replication at its expanding borders, or 'Europeanisation'.[18]

The expansion of states in the Christian West was endorsed by the ambitions of the Catholic Church. This was growing into a vast, transnational institution, with the pope at its head, simultaneously a spiritual leader and powerful statesman. The Church underpinned the authority of Christian rulers within Catholic Europe, but it also had its own agenda – to expand Christendom, to protect Christians and to save the souls of those it considered spiritually ignorant or misguided. Those who were lost had fallen prey to the Devil and were a threat to true Christians, as well as to each other. If persuasion did not work, violence became a valid means of protecting 'God's vineyard': a Biblical turn of phrase, popular at the time, which signified the global Christian community. In fact, Christians on Earth were believed to be waging an ongoing spiritual war against evil, what became collectively referred to as *ecclesia militans* – the Church Militant. Monastic institutions exemplified the commitment of the Church Militant to combating evil through prayer, discipline and works of charity. The invention of crusading added a new dimension to the communal struggle against evil, one that fused physical and spiritual warfare. This became embodied in new organisations that arose in the Levantine crusader states – the military orders, of which the Teutonic Order would play a defining role in the Baltic Crusades.

THE MILITARY ORDERS

Most crusaders who survived the siege of Jerusalem in 1099 returned home, leaving only a small number behind – some 300 knights – to consolidate the territorial gains that had been made. Pilgrims began flocking to the Holy Land, eager to visit the Holy Sepulchre and other sacred sites now accessible under Catholic control. However, travel remained perilous. The crusader states faced challenges in maintaining order, with banditry on the roads, especially near frontier areas. In Easter of 1119, hundreds of pilgrims visiting the reputed site of Christ's baptism on the Jordan river were massacred. Then on 28 June, the army of the crusader state of Antioch was destroyed by the Muslim ruler of Aleppo. The battle became known as 'the field of blood', after the catastrophic Christian losses. These events were a wake-up call for a small group of knights in Jerusalem. Later that year, they decided to band together to protect the pilgrim routes and shrines that had come under Christian control. This 'new knighthood', as Bernard of Clairvaux described them, took the crusading vow of secular knights to a completely new level. Adopting the model of the Cistercians and committing to a monastic life of individual poverty, celibacy and obedience, the Templars set the precedent for the militarisation of other religious institutions based in the Holy Land. Three other hospital orders would take up arms over the course of the twelfth century: the Order of St John (the Hospitallers), the Order of St Lazarus (the so-called Leper Knights) and the Teutonic Order.[19]

The wealth amassed by the military orders surpassed that of many royal treasuries, enabling them to fund the construction of the largest castles in Christendom. They were at the cutting edge of military engineering and logistics, and from the mid-twelfth century the orders amassed huge estates in both the Levant and Europe, with the result that their officials also became capable and experienced administrators, financiers and diplomats. They planned and built towns, mills, sugar refineries and glass factories, intensifying production in the eastern Mediterranean far beyond the level achieved in earlier centuries.[20] The aim of all this investment was, above all, to sustain the defence of the crusader states and to keep the Holy Land in the hands of Catholics. Living as both monks and warriors, they were the soldiers of Christ par excellence, forever committed to the struggle against the pagan 'other'.

At this point it is worth briefly sketching out the history of the Teutonic Order.[21] In September 1189, a large contingent of crusaders from Bremen and Lübeck reached Acre, where they joined the other crusading forces besieging the city. This was part of the 'Third Crusade', aimed at retaking Jerusalem from Saladin. As casualties started piling up, it became clear the Hospitallers, who were primarily responsible for caring for the sick and injured, were overstretched. Moreover, the German crusaders, many of whom needed care but spoke only their own language, must have faced difficulties communicating with the predominantly French-speaking Hospitallers. To remedy this situation, the Germans set up a makeshift hospital outside the city walls, consisting of a simple tent made from a ship's sail. As was common with all such foundations, the hospital was staffed by a religious brotherhood. Wounded and infirm German crusaders must have been grateful they were being looked after by their own.

When the German brethren were given permission to administer last rites and bury the dead, this angered the Hospitallers. Until then, they had held a monopoly over burial in the crusader states. This was a lucrative business, especially if you were providing aftercare for the souls of wealthy nobles, who were keen to offer suitable renumeration. A petty rivalry developed, but the German hospital attracted powerful patrons. After the surrender of Acre to the crusaders, the brethren were granted buildings within the city, which steadily grew into a substantial complex. In the meantime, they were given properties and trading privileges by the Holy Roman Emperor, Henry VI. The Third Crusade failed in the end to take Jerusalem, but it had secured what was left of the crusader states, a series of castles and towns which clung on to the Levantine coast. When the emperor planned a further campaign, those German crusaders who reached the Holy Land realised they needed more soldiers, and called for the hospital in Acre to be militarised. The German brethren were given the rule of the Templars to structure their military organisation, whilst the provision of care was informed by the rule of the Hospitallers – the best of both worlds. In fact, the Hospitallers were now more intent than ever on absorbing this new upstart military order into their own ranks, and so the German brethren asked the Templars for their protection. As a result, they were permitted to wear the Templars' characteristic white mantles, and to use the symbol of a 'wheel' (a circle) with a black half cross. The new Teutonic Order was inaugurated in a ceremony at the Templars' palace in Acre, and the following year its status was confirmed by the pope. Although still a hospital, the German brethren were now also charged with waging holy war against the enemies of Christendom. Within a couple of decades, the Order had shaken off the influence of both the Templars and Hospitallers, and adopted its own, familiar emblem.

In a world where clothing communicated your social identity, the military orders were distinguished by their insignia – the red cross of the Templars, the white cross of the Hospitallers and the green cross of the Lazarites. The Teutonic Order adopted a full black cross as its own. When on the Order's business or in battle, the brethren's rule specified the black cross must remain visible at all times on their garments, whether on mantles, surcoats worn over armour or on headgear. New members admitted into the Order had their mantles ceremonially sprinkled with holy water. As such, the black cross was not just a brand: it

INTRODUCTION

was also spiritual protection. In time, although none could have foreseen it then, this simple insignia would come to symbolise one of the most powerful and controversial forces in the history of Europe.

THE TEUTONIC ORDER GOES INTERNATIONAL

The German brethren's meteoric rise in the early decades of the thirteenth century was largely thanks to their fourth master, an inspirational and talented leader called Herman of Salza. A lesser noble from Thuringia (today, central Germany), Herman was a brilliant politician and tactful diplomat, and developed close ties with both the emperor and the pope. He led the Order's involvement in the 'Fifth Crusade' (1217–21) which sought to reclaim Jerusalem by first targeting the Ayyubid Sultanate of Egypt. The brethren fought and provided hospital care for their fellow German crusaders, buried the fallen and ministered to their souls with prayers. Inspired by their example, many crusaders joined the Order. They also lavished the brethren with gifts, which included properties and land in Europe, especially within the empire. The Order's membership increased, along with a regular stream of income from its growing estates. Although dominated by men, its hospitals were also staffed by women who were admitted as sisters.

But Herman realised his German brethren needed to find their place in a crusading world dominated by the Templars and Hospitallers. His first opportunity to diversify the Order's activities came just a year after his appointment as master. In 1211, he agreed to defend the eastern frontier of the Hungarian kingdom, in exchange for some land there. But why would an institution founded in the Holy Land and dedicated to crusading become involved in defending some remote part of Eastern Europe? This was made clear in the prologue to the Order's Rule, which stated that 'the Church now shall have knights sworn to drive out the enemies of the Church by force'.[22] This was the greater struggle of the Church Militant. When the brethren agreed to defend the eastern frontier of the Hungarian kingdom, they were fulfilling their role as defenders of the Christian community. Here, the threat came from a pagan Turkic nomadic group known as the Cumans. The Hungarian king Andrew II granted the brethren various privileges to set them up in the territory at the forefront of Cuman attacks, referred to in documents as the Terra Bursa or Borsa. This was situated in south-eastern Transylvania, and bordered by the Carpathians. This privilege included permission to build castles and, in little over a decade, they would construct five. The most important and the probable centre of their domain was called Marienburg. This was the first time the brethren had named one of their strongholds as 'Mary's castle', after the Mother of Christ and their main patron saint. Once constructed, Marienburg acted as a stabilising force on its surroundings, and the Order encouraged German settlers to establish new villages in the vicinity. As the brethren took the battle to the Cumans beyond the Carpathians, they began to build castles outside the lands granted to them by the king. This proved to be a step too far for the Hungarian king and nobility expelled the brethren from Transylvania by force.[23]

Despite their northern foray, the Order remained committed to the defence of the Holy Land. In the same years as fighting the Cumans they had participated in the Fifth Crusade. In 1226, they began to construct their own castle in the Levant in a secluded location up in the Galilean hills, a healthy distance from Acre and far enough from the prying eyes of the Templars and Hospitallers. The castle was called Montfort or, in German, Starkenberg – Strong Mountain. At this time, another ruler began courting the Order. This was Conrad of Masovia, one of the most ambitious dukes in Poland, whose gaze was set upon the vacant Polish throne in Cracow. But in order to be able to fully dedicate himself to claiming the crown, Conrad needed to secure the northern border of his lands, which was threatened by the pagan Prussians. Echoing Andrew's invitation to Transylvania, he attempted to woo the Order's master with a substantial grant of land which had once been under his control. After protracted negotiations, the Order's brethren arrived at the Masovian frontier – within a few years, they had become the leading protagonists in a series of violent conquests of large swathes of north-eastern Europe.

FIELDS OF BLOOD

Although pagans in Northern Europe had been targeted by military campaigns with religious overtones in the decades following the conquest of Jerusalem, the first papally sponsored crusade took place here in 1147.[24] It was aimed at Western Slavic groups living between the Oder and Elbe rivers (today north Germany), collectively referred to by German and Scandinavian chroniclers as Wends. They neighboured the lands of the Saxons, by then the most prominent group within the northern stretches of the Holy Roman Empire. The proposed military campaign was approved by the pope, but instigated by Saxon nobles who sought to exchange the obligation to crusade in the Holy Land for something more relevant to their immediate interests. This crusade was about the seizure of territory, and it was part of an ongoing regional struggle between Catholic and pagan rulers in the southern Baltic for power and influence. Bernard of Clairvaux, who preached the crusade once it had met with papal approval, realised that territorial gain was the driving motivation behind the proposed 'Wendish Crusade'. Framing the campaign as a war to protect Christendom, he attempted to persuade its participants to convert the Wends, rather than just seize their land.[25] Several bishops did end up participating in the campaign, hoping to extend the bounds of their dioceses.

The Wendish Crusade amounted to little on the ground, but with hindsight it became a historical turning point. Within a few decades, the lands of the Wends were carved up between German, Danish and Polish lords and became fully incorporated into the Catholic world. In a series of papal bulls issued in 1171 and 1172, the pope offered an indulgence to all those in Denmark, Norway and Sweden who would participate in a crusade against the pagan Estonians. This was still not as spiritually attractive as the privileges and rewards offered for crusading in the Holy Land, and in the end, the call did not result in anything.[26]

The event that was fated to mark the beginning of a *sustained* era of crusading in the North was the arrival of an army from Saxony on the eastern shores of the Baltic in 1198. There was already a Catholic foothold here. A German Augustinian canon named Meinhard had followed merchants down the Daugava (or the Düna as the Germans called it), just upstream of Riga in modern Latvia, and established a missionary outpost in the Liv village he called Üxküll (Latvian Ikšķile). The Livs were a Finnic group who inhabited what is today the north-western part of Latvia. The merchants advised Meinhard to first gain the consent of the Rus' prince of Polotsk, Vladimir, who claimed authority over the region, which he did. He then managed to convert the local Livs after promising to build them a stone fortification to protect them from Lithuanian raiders. This was the first mortared building the Livs had ever seen, and it allegedly impressed them so much that the neighbouring community on the island of Holm wanted their own. Archaeologists would later discover the impressive remains of this structure: a square, stone walled enclosure with a tower. Meinhard obliged, but in exchange, they had to be baptised and accept the authority of the bishop. Many did, but later changed their mind and sought to wash off the baptism in the river. Others were openly hostile to the idea from the start.

The mission received the support of Archbishop Hartwig II of Hamburg-Bremen who, sensing an opportunity to extend his see's influence, elevated Meinhard to the position of Bishop of the Livs. This was standard protocol for incorporating a territory into Christendom and, from the Church's perspective, it also meant this could now be legitimately defended from the forces that threatened to destroy the Catholic world. The pope also became interested in the mission, as it seemed that Meinhard was challenging the spiritual authority of the Rus' Orthodox Church. When Meinhard returned to the eastern Baltic in 1187, he brought a group of missionaries with him which included Cistercians. One of these monks named Theoderic began preaching to the Livs in Treiden (Latvian Turaida) on the Gauja river, and baptised their leader, Kaupo. After Meinhard's death in 1198, the mission would be taken over by a Cistercian monk named Berthold, hailing from the abbey of Loccum in Lower Saxony.

Berthold began by showering the Livs with gifts, and he was at first grudgingly accepted. But it soon became apparent that acceptance of baptism was accompanied by a whole list of expectations which threatened the Livs' way of life. The most offensive demand was the payment of a new religious tax – the tithe – to support the mission, which would be collected by force if necessary. Things soon escalated. After Berthold consecrated a new Christian cemetery on Holm, 'some conspired to burn him in the church, others to kill him, and others to drown him'.[27] Terrified, the bishop slipped away on a ship and returned to Saxony. In order to save the mission in Livonia, he persuaded the pope to grant him a crusading bull to raise an army. This became the first successful crusade to the eastern Baltic. Once in Livonia, the two forces confronted each other in a battle where Berthold died in spectacular fashion, worthy of a medieval Christian martyr. Unable to control his horse, the bishop found himself right in the midst of the battle where he was seized, speared and torn limb from limb. What happened next is described by a chronicler named Henry, who documented the early crusades in Livonia:

> The army, having lost its leader, was naturally wrought up, and with both horses and ships, fire and sword, laid waste the crops of the Livs. When they had seen this, the Livs renewed the peace in order to avoid greater damage, and called the clergy to them. About fifty were baptised at Holm on the first day, and about a hundred were converted at Üxküll on the following day.[28]

Mass baptisms were the staple climax of all such missionary narratives, but they rarely seemed to be effective. The priests left behind to minister to the new congregation were soon driven out. The Livs once again washed themselves in the river, believing this would remove any traces of their baptism. When the next bishop, a monk from Bremen called Albert who was also Archbishop Hartwig's nephew, arrived with a fleet of twenty-three ships in 1200, he brought with him another crusading army. These were the sparks that ignited military confrontations across the eastern Baltic region, which rapidly transformed into wars of conquest.

Today, the Baltic Crusades are largely known to the world as a series of military campaigns that resulted in the conquests of pagan lands around the southern and eastern edges of the Baltic Sea. Readers unfamiliar with the intricacies of the region's history would be forgiven for thinking that it was in a state of continuous warfare over the last millennium. Wendish lands were conquered in the middle decades of the twelfth century. When the Teutonic Order initiated the conquest of Prussia in 1230 and joined the fray in Livonia seven years later, it became the dominant military power in both regions. Prussian lands (within modern north-east Poland, the Russian Kaliningrad Oblast, south-western

Lithuania and part of western Belarus) took over fifty years to conquer. It was here that the Order eventually decided to establish their headquarters at Marienburg, after being driven out of the Levant. The castle was expanded over the course of the fourteenth century to become the largest fortified structure in Christendom. The violent creation of Catholic Livonia (most of modern Latvia and Estonia) was not fully complete until 1310, although significant resistance had ended two decades earlier. In the meantime, Swedish crusaders conquered the southern part of what is today Finland and pushed the frontier of the Catholic world to Karelia, up against the lands of Novgorod.

The Teutonic Order then waged war on the last pagan state in Europe, the Grand Duchy of Lithuania. This continued throughout the fourteenth century and eventually morphed into a regional power struggle with the Catholic Polish-Lithuanian union that lasted throughout much of the fifteenth century. The rise of another superpower – Moscow – set the scene for an escalation in the regional power struggle which ultimately saw Sweden, Poland-Lithuania and Russia fighting for dominion of the eastern Baltic. The seventeenth century was marked by a series of wars which saw large parts of the Polish-Lithuanian Commonwealth occupied by Russian armies to the east, and Swedish forces to the west. Russia came to dominate much of the eastern Baltic after the Great Northern War which broke out in 1700, Sweden retained control over Finland, and the Commonwealth would be incrementally partitioned from 1772. In the twentieth century, the Eastern Front during both world wars stretched across the fields, forests and lakes of the historical territories of Livonia and Prussia. The castle and town of Marienburg, then within Nazi Germany, would find itself on the front line. The Red Army reached it in January 1945, as it pushed towards Berlin. The town was obliterated; the castle, garrisoned by German soldiers, partially destroyed. Soon after, it passed into Polish ownership and the official name was changed to Malbork. The bullet holes in its walls remained.

Across the eastern Baltic, archaeologists, after sinking their spades a few centimetres into the ground, routinely find shrapnel, cartridges, barbed wire, fragments of military uniform such as belt buckles, buttons and insignia, and even human remains. It seems that the landscapes here, with their seasonal capping of snow and ice, have been soaked in blood for centuries. This vivid imagery, quoted at the start of this chapter, is taken from the *Livonian Rhymed Chronicle* – an account of the conquest and colonisation of the lands rebranded in Latin as Livonia. Written in Middle High German in the last decade of the thirteenth century, it is the first piece of literature produced by a member of the Teutonic Order, drawing in part on the author's personal experiences. The image it conjures in the mind has resonated through time.

A NEW HISTORY

It is therefore no surprise that the struggle between the conquerors and the conquered defined the national histories of the Baltic countries in the nineteenth and twentieth centuries. These narratives were also mobilised to serve the needs of the ancestral conquerors of these regions, primarily in the Kingdom of Prussia from which the German Empire would emerge in 1871. The medieval Teutonic Order would become reframed in ethno-historical terms, as the principal representative of German power in the 'Barbaric East'. The Order's flared black cross would first be reimagined as a military decoration – the Iron Cross. This, in turn, would become connected to the identity of the new German Empire, and with it the militarism and horror of both world wars.

After the defeat of Nazi Germany, it would take another five decades before a new public conversation about the past could begin in Central-Eastern Europe. In the Soviet-dominated, so-called 'Eastern Bloc', nationalist narratives continued to emphasise the ancestral struggle against the Germans. The dissolution of the Soviet Union made it possible to begin detaching the history and heritage of the Baltic Crusades from these narratives. This is a process that is still continuing, as a new generation of historians, archaeologists, art historians and museum curators re-examine old sources with updated methodologies, uncover new data and challenge traditional conceptions. Before the 1990s, scholarship in the Baltic Sea region had been confined to national silos, and the dissemination of knowledge was restricted by political and language barriers. Today, the cultural heritage of the region is studied internationally. It is no coincidence that, with the integration of many of the former Eastern Bloc countries into the European Union (and also into NATO), Baltic history has become recognised as a fundamental part of European history.

This book is not intended to be a military history, although it contains numerous and sometimes detailed references to military events. For anglophone readers, these have been covered far more comprehensively by others.[29] Instead, my aim is to provide a broader context for the Baltic Crusades and to show how our understanding of these events has changed. It is of course a truism that history is written by the victors, and that written sources are also the product of a relatively small elite group. Baltic pagan societies and migrating Catholic peasants did not produce any texts offering alternative perspectives. We can still extract many important details about them from the written sources produced by the elites, particularly in regions like Prussia where the Teutonic Order developed an incredibly fastidious bureaucracy. Large numbers of documents have survived into the present day and provide us with detailed glimpses into life under the brethren's rule. But to better understand the lived experiences of the larger number of people involved in the transformation of the medieval Baltic world, we also have to turn to the physical traces they left above and below ground.

Coming from an archaeological background, my perspective has always been more focused on the broader societal trends that are visible in the multiplicity of material traces from sites built and occupied by people, as well as the palaeoenvironmental record of the landscape. This is not to say that archaeologists shy away from individuals. They are physically represented by their skeletal remains, and their agency can also be highly visible in buildings and artefacts. I have therefore sought to maintain a balance between the biographical details of different individuals who participated in and shaped the world of the Baltic Crusades, the historically documented events that drove societal transformations in the conquered regions and the thousands of material traces that, taken together, can provide us with glimpses of life at varying resolutions. The lives of individuals are set alongside the biographies of whole towns, villages and castles. This represents a different approach to the Baltic Crusades to the one found in more conventional histories. I have intended this book to be as much a cultural history as a reflection of the military impact of crusading. The stories of each society have their own particular features, but all were composites of migrants, their descendants (who then regarded themselves as native) and indigenous people, with contrasting worldviews, languages and customs. Whilst the shadow of war was never far away in the medieval Baltic, there were, in fact, decades of peace, stability and prosperity which saw population growth, trade and the flourishing of new, distinctive cultures.

These stories are organised into four parts and follow on from each other more or less chronologically. The first part considers how crusading came to accentuate the expansion of Christian territories in the North. We begin a few centuries before the First Crusade. At this time the most powerful state in Western Europe – the Carolingian Empire and its eastern splinter, the Ottonian Empire – exerted a tremendous political and cultural influence on its neighbours. Both would provide a compelling model for rulership where territorial conquests became twinned with religious conversion. This established a tradition of religious warfare that pre-dated the papal vision of crusading. It served as a model for the fledgling Polish state, whose expansion would continue the territorialisation of Catholic Christianity, laying the groundwork for the later crusades against the Prussians. The following chapters explore the conquest of Wendish lands, which saw the first official crusade in the North, the adoption of crusading ideology by the Polish state and the creation of a religious borderland in its north-eastern corner, and finally Scandinavian expansion across the Baltic which later becomes framed in the rhetoric of crusading.

The second part of the book focuses on the establishment of militarised Christianity in the Baltic Sea region, and particularly in Livonia and Prussia. Missions turned into crusades, at first led by bishops, but within decades the dominant force in the region became the Teutonic Order. Regular military campaigns led to permanent conquests which pushed the north-eastern edge of the Catholic world as far as it would go – to the borders of the Eastern Orthodox Rus' lands, a cultural and political frontier that has endured into the present day. In the process, indigenous societies were irrevocably transformed and a new world was created, one largely governed by militarised religious authorities. These authorities coexisted alongside each other, at times jostling for power, which in Livonia broke out into open warfare. They promoted themselves as the defenders of Christendom in the North, and secured their rule with impressive castles which projected both power and faith. We will take a closer look at Marienburg which grew in size over the course of the fourteenth century to reflect its new role – as the Order's headquarters, and the ultimate symbol of their crusading mission. This was an unfinished mission from the Order's perspective. Lithuania and Samogitia remained defiantly pagan, and the Order spent over a century forcibly attempting to bring them into the Catholic fold. In doing so, their campaigns became *the* place for the nobility of Europe to experience crusading. Knights from across Europe would undertake the expensive and at times perilous journey to the pagan frontier, a treacherous, marshy wilderness home to wolves, bison and aurochs, where they could attain both spiritual rewards and renown.

The third part of the book is concerned with the world transformed by the Baltic Crusades, and one that would continue to change. Encounters between migrants and indigenous peoples resulted in as much a synthesis as a clash of cultures. The first melting pots were towns, established during the crusades as Christian footholds in pagan lands. These became populated by merchants, whose actions contributed to the development of the Hanse – a mighty trading confederation which connected the regions around the Baltic Sea with the rest of Christendom, crossing religious and political divides. Timber, fur, wax, grain and luxury commodities became the staples moved around the Hanseatic network, generating unprecedented levels of wealth. However, this wealth was unevenly distributed, largely along the lines of the migrant/indigenous divide which remained more visible in some places than others. The new regime and towns depended on access to natural resources, and so rural communities, both indigenous and migrant, were mobilised to exploit the countryside. Here, far from the gaze of the religious authorities, indigenous beliefs endured the longest, keeping alive a sacred landscape with unbroken customs and oral traditions, whilst absorbing Christian elements. This world would be transformed yet again by another revolution in religious thinking, one which challenged the hegemony of the Church – the Reformation. In the sixteenth century, the brethren of the Teutonic Order in Prussia and Livonia finally abandoned their vows and crusading insignia in favour of a secular life.

Lutheranism would proliferate in their former territories, confronting the composite religious practices of the indigenous peasantry. Politically and culturally, the eastern Baltic would then be shaped by two centuries of conflict between Poland-Lithuania, Russia and Sweden.

The final part of the book deals with the legacy of the Baltic Crusades. The birth of national identities, or 'national awakenings' as they are called in the eastern Baltic, breathed new life into the fading memories of the crusades. But now these were not the exclusive preserve of the ruling elite, the inheritors of the conquerors. Indigenous writers and artists, for the first time, documented their own histories. The past became a battleground for identity – the culture wars of the nineteenth and twentieth centuries. As the Teutonic Order's black cross was reinvented as the Iron Cross, the memories of the Baltic Crusades were mobilised to serve the present. The black cross became more feared than it had ever been, as it became synonymous with the aggression of the Nazi regime. After the Second World War, nationalist narratives were reframed once again, this time under Soviet influence. They would persist beyond the dissolution of the Soviet Union and have left a lingering influence on popular historical memory.

In recent decades, the traditional narratives have begun to be unpicked. For even as the spectre of Russian imperialism hangs over the eastern Baltic countries and invokes historical struggles, there is a sense of reconciliation with the medieval past – an era of military conquests and cultural transformations that left a profound legacy which shaped the Europe we know. This book is called 'Black Cross' because this symbol connects the most notorious actors in the Baltic Crusades with the reimaginings of the past in the modern era. It is a symbol that has been variously admired, feared, hated and now increasingly rehabilitated. The crusades have cast a long shadow across Northern Europe for almost nine centuries. As this shadow recedes and we increasingly understand the past on its own terms, their story deserves to be told afresh.

HOLY WAR IN
NORTHERN EUROPE

CHAPTER 1

CONFRONTING PAGANISM
Territorial Christianity in the North

> ... he decided to attack the treacherous and treaty-breaking tribe of the Saxons and to persist in this war until they were either defeated and forced to accept the Christian religion or entirely exterminated ...
> *Royal Frankish Annals*, 775[1]

THE NEW CHRISTIAN EMPIRE

On Christmas Day in 800, the ruler of the Frankish kingdom, Charles – more familiar as Charlemagne – was crowned as 'Emperor of the Romans' by Pope Leo III in old St Peter's Basilica in Rome. At that moment his kingdom, already the first Christian superpower in the West, was symbolically transformed into something far more grandiose – the successor of Ancient Rome.

Charlemagne was given the sobriquet 'Father of Europe' by an anonymous poet who composed an epic in his honour,[2] hailing the Christian empire, one that would unite the faithful under its banner and the spiritual leadership of the papacy. The new emperor and his successors claimed a divine right to rule, a position legitimised by the Church which organised their public anointing and crowning. Charlemagne was undoubtedly a devout Christian and, in addition to supporting the foundation of monasteries and the implementation of religiously informed laws and education, he led the way in furthering the Christianisation of the territories under his rule. His state ideology, which combined royal and later imperial authority with Christian identity, was promoted in grand architectural projects. The most famous would be the palatial complex at Aachen, a fusion of Roman, Byzantine and Frankish design, with its chapel intended to symbolise the heavenly Jerusalem. Coins minted towards the end of Charlemagne's reign were also emblazoned with the inscription *'Christiana religio'* – a proclamation of Christianity as the state religion in emulation of earlier Roman imperial coinage.[3]

During the forty-six years of Charlemagne's reign, the Carolingian state continued to expand east of the Rhine, absorbing Bavaria, Alemannia, Hessia, Thuringia and Lombardy. These regions already had variously established Christian communities, supported by diocesan organisations. Under Frankish rule, these were partially reorganised and strengthened. To the north-east, Frisia had been conquered before Charlemagne came to power and its bishopric at Utrecht was an established centre for missionary activity, but parts of the region remained something of a frontier which would see occasional rebellions and persistent pagan practices. The Frisians allied themselves on a number of occasions with their neighbours, the Saxons. The term 'Saxon' was used by Carolingian writers as a catch-all for several different groups – Westphalians, Eastphalians, Angarians and Nordliudi – inhabiting a large part of what is today north-western Germany.

In contrast to neighbouring Frisia which was ruled over by a king, Saxon society was governed by an oligarchy, where regional groups were headed up by nobles. This fragmented structure meant that it was more difficult to conquer, and so when Charlemagne's initial campaign in 772 transformed into a territorial war, it would take three decades to complete. Contemporaries framed this as a war of religious conversion, the culmination of decades of attempts to bring the true faith to the fringes of the Frankish state.[4] At the same time, the conflict played out a regional power struggle which drew in many different groups allied to the Franks and Saxons, including Frisians, Danes and Slavs. The Christianised Saxons, in turn, played a significant role in the formation of what would later become the Ottonian Empire, as Carolingian influence waned in East Francia in the late ninth and early tenth centuries.

The expansion of the Carolingian and Ottonian realms provided a blueprint for the territorialisation of Christianity in the North, one that would also be adopted by other rising Christian states, most notably the Piasts in what became Poland. This would help lay the groundwork for the Baltic Crusades.

CONQUERING THE SAXONS

There was a long history of tensions between the Franks and Saxons. In the late seventh century, the Franks had refortified several prehistoric hillforts on the frontier with Saxon lands. These functioned as administrative centres, but also defined the borderland as a militarised zone, facing off Saxon strongholds further east. The Frankish statesman Charles Martel and his sons, Pippin and Carloman, had led campaigns against the Saxons with the aim of extracting tribute. Martel had also provided the missionary Boniface with protection during his travels into pagan lands, perhaps the first mention of a military force accompanying an evangelising expedition.[5] Then in 744, Pepin III's campaign against the Saxons allegedly resulted in many being baptised. This is the first of several references connecting Christian conversion with fealty to the Carolingian state. This entanglement between political authority and religion was probably why a Saxon incursion into Frankish territory several years later destroyed some thirty churches. Missionary efforts directed from Utrecht continued in the following decades, this time led by another English monk, Lebuinus (aka Liafwin or Lebwin). The mid-ninth-century account of his life described how he had entreated the Saxons to accept Christianity to protect them against foreign rule – an ominous, if retrospective, foreshadowing of the later conquest.[6]

Charlemagne's first campaign followed the pattern of earlier Carolingian attacks across the frontier. The trigger may have been the destruction of the church at Deventer, which had been built on the east bank of the IJssel (today in the Netherlands) by Lebuinus as a missionary base a few years earlier. Charlemagne's army seized the Saxon stronghold of Eresburg and then marched on the pagan sanctuary where the Irminsul – a sacred tree trunk representing the axis of the world – was housed. They destroyed the trunk and looted the sanctuary, taking away the votive offerings of gold and silver they found there. This was a swift victory that gained Charlemagne both prestige and war booty.

The intention to actually conquer the Saxons only became evident after Charlemagne's military triumph over the Lombards in 773. In his absence, the Saxons had attacked Frankish territory, much like they had done before, where they sought to destroy Boniface's church at Fritzlar. This provoked a Carolingian reprisal, but things would be different this time. Perhaps emboldened by his victory in Italy, Charlemagne's campaign against the Saxons in 775 would herald the start of a war of conquest. At this point the words of the *Royal Frankish Annals*, quoted at the start of this chapter, presented the king's determination to convert or exterminate the pagan Saxons. Later Saxon chroniclers would play down the worldly elements of the conquest and celebrate the triumph of Christianity, ascribing Charlemagne the role of an apostle. By all accounts the battles were brutal, with high casualties on all sides. Control of strongholds such as Eresburg, which served as political and religious centres, remained the strategic focus, but the spiritual dimension of the conquest was elevated to new heights.

Carolingian writers viewed the wars against the Saxons through a religious lens; the accounts ascribed Frankish victories to divine support and referred to miraculous happenings that terrified the Saxons. The mass baptisms of subjugated enemies in 776 and 777 were dramatic set pieces of political theatre that served as public demonstrations of allegiance to both the Carolingian regime and the Christian community. Conversion through violence was celebrated by contemporaries. The anonymous *Poem Concerning the Conversion of the Saxons*, written in around 777, spoke of how Charlemagne subjected the Saxons to himself 'with a glittering sword, and dragged the legions of forest-worshippers to the heavenly kingdom'.[7] With Christianity so firmly wedded to Frankish authority, dissent became connected with its rejection. When Saxon defiance became centred on Wittekind (aka Widukind), who encouraged both Saxons and Frisians to rebel against Charlemagne's rule, he may even have acted in the manner of a religious leader, heading a pagan resistance. Wittekind had initially taken shelter in the Danish court, but returned in 782, when the Saxons rebelled whilst Charlemagne was preoccupied fighting Muslims in Iberia. After a Frankish army was defeated at Süntel, Charlemagne rushed back with his soldiers and the Saxons submitted to him. According to several contemporary chroniclers, he then ordered

4,500 Saxons connected with the rebellion to be executed at Verden. This actual figure was probably an invention – medieval chroniclers did not provide accurate estimates. Verden was also not that exceptional, as references to massacres pepper the accounts of the Saxon Wars, but many centuries later it would be singled out for memorialisation by the Nazis, with lasting influence into the present.[8]

Wittekind fled back to Denmark, but three years later surrendered and converted to Christianity in what was a public relations triumph for the Carolingian state.[9] He joined those Saxon nobles who converted and filled the ranks of Charlemagne's *fideles* – faithful subjects, a term used to convey that blend of political and religious allegiance. They were rewarded with land, political offices and opportunities to marry into Frankish families, quickly becoming an integral part of the new regime. With Wittekind's baptism, the Saxons were now understood to have officially joined the Christian fold en masse. This view of an entire people becoming Christian overnight is a recurring feature of medieval clerical accounts of religious conversion.[10] When a revolt broke out in 792 and marked the start of another lengthy conflict, the Franks were quick to condemn what they saw as *perfidia* – infidelity – an offence against both the king and God which justified the retribution that followed.

This time the rebelling Saxons would be fighting the Saxon faithful, and against the Carolingians' new allies, the pagan Obotrites. In 789, this confederation of Western Slavic groups, inhabiting what are today the German states of Mecklenburg and parts of Schleswig-Holstein, had joined the Carolingians in a military campaign against a mutual foe in Western Pomerania – the Veleti. The Obotrites were also enemies of the Saxons and aided Charlemagne's efforts to suppress resistance. The conflict was largely confined to the eastern parts of Saxony,[11] and the written sources no longer emphasise the importance of conversion, almost certainly because the Saxons were considered to be officially Christian by this time, despite their lapses.[12] The Obotrites themselves were attacked by the pagan Danes, allies of the Saxons, and their leader Witzan, a vassal of Charlemagne, would be assassinated in 795, but following a few decisive battles, the war ended with the suppression of Saxon resistance. In his biography of Charlemagne, the Frankish courtier Einhard described how in 804 the emperor forcibly expelled 10,000 Saxon families from

Wigmodia, a region between the Weser and Elbe rivers, and from the lands beyond the Elbe. They were relocated to other parts of the Frankish empire. He then granted the lands east of the Elbe to the Obotrites.[13] Charlemagne had already begun to deport large numbers of Saxons from 794, and had ordered hostages to be sent to monasteries throughout the Frankish realm in order to expedite their conversion to Christianity. These converts would become the first Saxon monks, perhaps even acting as missionaries themselves amongst their own people. But the clearance of Wigmodia was the largest episode of resettlement. The cumulative effect of these deportations was to break the social cohesion of Saxon society and facilitate the imposition of Frankish governance. Less than two decades later these lands would be granted back to loyal Saxons.

RELIGIOUS TRANSFORMATION

Charlemagne's conquest was widely regarded at the time as the enabler of Saxon Christianity. It was marked by the imposition of laws that sought to impose Christian behaviour on the conquered population – the *Capitulary for the Saxon Regions*. Issued most likely as a response to the Saxon insurrection of 792, these were notoriously harsh in their attitude to paganism.[14] They included the death sentence for a whole list of transgressions, including for those who remained unbaptised, observed pagan customs or ignored fasting at Lent. A second cartulary issued a few years later was more lenient. However, the notion that Christianity was rapidly imposed from above, during and after the conquest, is misleading. The tempo of religious transformation was much slower. It had begun before the destruction of the Irminsul and continued long after Charlemagne's reign.

The Saxons and other neighbouring pagan societies first came into contact with Christian ideas through trade, earlier conflicts and even marriage. Some may have converted or incorporated Christian figures into their own pantheons, enabling the new religion to gain a foothold long before its official and highly politicised introduction. Indeed, it was usually local elites who adopted the official trappings of Christian identity, as these typically came with political advantages. This was Christianity as performance, and only later would this be followed by profound changes in worldviews. The pace of religious change would vary between individuals, their kinship groups and larger communities, and its impact on children – the future propagators of any new religion – would also vary depending on their educational environment. If the old gods were still worshipped within the family, in private, that could perpetuate earlier beliefs and customs amongst younger generations. But it is also evident that Christian ideas were themselves modified in the process by those adopting them: merged with existing beliefs, simplified, misunderstood and reworked.[15]

From an archaeological perspective, the gradual adoption of Frankish-style burial rites within Saxon communities provides the earliest evidence for the adoption of customs connected with Christian notions of the life course. The treatment of the dead, as well as the locations of burial grounds can illustrate cultural change, as they represent the meeting between public expressions of social identity, power dynamics, ancestral memory and eschatological beliefs – those concerning the fate of the dead in the afterlife, which are informed by religion.[16] Cremation, that quintessential pagan mortuary custom, had been abandoned in the heartlands of Saxony long before Charlemagne's conquest – by the early eighth century.[17] The same is true of burials in mounds. Instead, the dead began to be inhumed laid out on their backs in rows, with burials aligned either along a north–south axis or, following the prevailing custom in Christian cemeteries, increasingly east–west. By the early ninth century, mortuary rites in the Saxon heartlands were pretty indistinguishable from those in the rest of the Frankish realm. Cremation and mound burials continued in the north and east of Saxony, at the fringes of imperial control.

Despite this, Carolingian authorities were evidently concerned with the correct treatment of the dead when it came to the Saxons. The *Capitulary* singled out the practice of cremation as punishable by death, along with burials near ancestral burial mounds instead of churches and their associated cemeteries. Given the abundance of archaeological evidence for a variety of burial locations and the growing prevalence of inhumation burials, some have argued the laws were singling out an imagined and outdated paganism in order to define, for the very first time, correct Christian behaviour. But they may also have been targeting the continued veneration of ancestors and, with them, claims to territory and political sovereignty, as well as those who would use or revive pagan identity as a means of defying Carolingian rule.[18] When churchyard burial began, it was most likely practised by members of the noble families who owned the churches. Only later would parish church cemeteries become the normal place for burying everyone else.

Outward expressions of Christian identity are more evident from the end of the eighth century, when people in Frisia and Saxony adopted the custom of wearing cross-shaped brooches or ones decorated with crosses, a bust of a saint or a dove. These have been found in excavations of graves and settlements, and they have often been interpreted as reflecting the presence of missionaries who would have encouraged their production and use as public statements of Christian identity. The designs were inspired by objects produced in neighbouring Frankish areas – the Central Rhine, Moselle and Main regions. Perhaps the most elaborate object associated with Christian identity is a walrus ivory pendant decorated with the scene of the crucifixion, discovered in the fill of a sunken house in Balhorner Feld near Paderborn. Manufactured in northern England in the early eighth century, it has been connected with the presence of missionaries in Saxon Westphalia.[19]

The new religion would only become embedded with the introduction of an ecclesiastical administration and, with it, a new system of taxation – tithes. Within a few years of the start of the conflict with the Saxons, Charlemagne purportedly divided their lands into districts that would serve as missionary zones, the basis for future dioceses. But as the wars dragged on, the conquerors had to keep returning to the drawing board. In Paderborn, the royal palace which was built to serve as a centre for administration and missionary activity was destroyed by the Saxons in 778, a year after its construction. It would only be permanently reinstated on the map of the conquered territory by the end of the century, and a new church was constructed in time for the pope Leo III's visit in 799. Leo donated the relics of St Stephen to the newly completed church, hoping their spiritual protection would ward against future attacks. This church was a huge, three-aisled building, and would be replaced by an even larger church in the ninth century. Most of Paderborn's early bishops, hailing from the British Isles, Hesse or the Rhineland, were missionaries, and drove efforts to Christianise the local population.

The appointment of the first indigenous bishops of Paderborn – Hathumar and Badurad – prompted a new wave of investment in churches, monasteries and religious education.[20] Later chroniclers would exaggerate the speed at which the new dioceses were set out, often as a means of justifying the legitimacy and rights of their own institutions. In fact, few churches were constructed during the time of the Saxon Wars. Monastic foundations were risky ventures. Not all were sustainable, and some had to be relocated when local resources could not support them. But by the end of the ninth century, some forty religious houses – cathedrals, monasteries, churches – had been built across Saxony, reflecting the reach of missionaries as far east as the Lower Elbe and as far north as Holstein. Alongside the bishoprics, towns had developed, stimulated by their wealth and financial privileges. Interestingly, this growth in religious houses did not reflect much investment from the Carolingian state. Instead, this was largely the initiative of local Saxon patrons. Strikingly, despite the dominance of men in setting up the initial infrastructure of the Saxon Church, the majority of monastic houses were small foundations, established by the local nobility for their female relatives. Women who founded monasteries may have also been safeguarding their property rights.[21]

Yet even if Carolingian and Saxon chroniclers declared that Charlemagne's conquest had made the Saxons Christian, what did that actually mean? It almost certainly did not mean a complete rejection of the earlier worldview, and it invariably resulted in a spectrum of beliefs and practices that ranged from the Christian mainstream to those which became branded as superstition with echoes of heathenry. The Saxon elites who survived the Frankish conquest became heavily invested in the new religion and when indigenous writers eventually penned their thoughts on the conquest, they viewed it in a positive light. This is perhaps unsurprising, given they were all members of the new religious class with a clear stake in the empire. They downplayed the violence and humiliation of the conquest and framed Charlemagne's triumph as a spiritual one, which freed the Saxons from 'the devil's tyranny'. But they also emphasised indigenous agency in driving the conversion – the Saxons had chosen their rightful destiny. Dissenting voices are of course absent from the indigenous written record, as those who had resolutely opposed Carolingian rule had been killed or disenfranchised.[22]

Religious transformation took longer and was more complex than the picture painted in the written sources, but actual written references to paganism are few and far between. Archaeological traces of identifiable pagan practices are also ambiguous. Here it becomes difficult to separate religion from magic. If magic was a substrate of religion — a controversial argument proposed by some scholars — was the continued deposition of objects in the peat bogs, forests and hills of Frisia and Saxony now tethered to a new belief system or did it reflect the invocation of older supernatural forces?[23] Christianity was itself reimagined by, and for, the indigenous population. In the absence of an indigenous Christian heritage, missionaries became adopted as saints, relics were imported to fill the new churches, and new local religious histories were produced (one might even say manufactured) by Saxon clerics. Importantly, the message of Christianity was filtered through the indigenous language and mindset. Perhaps the best example of this is the *Heiland*, an anonymous poetic reworking of the Gospel written in Old Saxon at some point between 821 and 850, most probably at the monastery of Fulda. The text includes references to local customs and portrays Christ as a chieftain born in a hillfort, with his disciples as armed thanes. The poem, intended for public performance, was designed to teach the newly converted Saxon elite how to embrace Christian values in a manner that resonated with their own cultural traditions.

The conquest of Saxony and its transformation into an imperial province have been compared to later colonial processes: a global superpower with a monotheistic religion confronting and overwhelming a smaller society with decentralised social organisation and polytheistic beliefs. Cast in this light, the Saxon experience was comparable to that of indigenous societies impacted by later colonialism around the world.[24] At the same time, indigenous agency is clearly visible in the long-term adoption of Christian elements and eventually in political autonomy. Saxony developed its own Germanised Christianity and, more than that, its own Christendom.

Ultimately, the expansion of the Frankish empire proved to be unmanageable. Following its partitions in the ninth century, the political centre of its easternmost fragment — East Francia — became centred on Saxony. In an ironic twist, the new ruling dynasty, the Ottonians, promoted the Saxon rebel Wittekind as a heroic ancestor. In doing so they proclaimed their independence and distanced themselves from the remnants of the Frankish empire. Yet the Carolingians had set an inspiring precedent. The Saxon rulers as inheritors of the Roman Empire now turned to the lands of their old pagan enemies for further territorial gains, and with them the proliferation of Christianity.

CONQUEST AND CHRISTIANISATION AT THE OTTONIAN FRONTIER

In the heart of the Ottonian realm, clerics continued to despair over misunderstandings of the key tenets of Christianity, and at how much their congregants clung on to old beliefs, now branded as superstitions. A fascinating glimpse of this is provided by a Hessian bishop named Burchard. Following his appointment to the episcopal see of Worms in around 1000, Burchard compiled twenty books on canon law. Intended for the instruction of local priests, these outlined the codes of behaviour the Ottonian Church sought to encourage, almost four centuries after the bishopric's foundation. The nineteenth book, known as the *Corrector*, dealt with penances for misdemeanours connected with what may have once been beliefs and practices embedded within a pre-Christian worldview. Although some of these appear to have been clerical inventions copied over from earlier texts, a number of the entries were written by Burchard himself. They appear to be personal observations. The *Corrector* refers to magical practices, some of which were harmful, to werewolves, night flights by witches with retinues of female demons, augury involving spirits, the healing of the dead and warding against revenants. Women were particularly singled out for their superstitious and maleficent behaviour, although what this may reveal, aside from Burchard's inherent misogyny, is the pivotal role of women as stewards of ancestral customs, especially those connected with the dead.[25]

Burchard was referring to goings-on in the Rhineland. Further north, the Saxon priest Helmold of Bosau writing in the later twelfth century described how Vicelin (later the Bishop of Oldenburg) undertook missionary activity amongst the Holsteiners – Saxons living in the Danish–German frontier region of Nordalbingia – and discovered they were Christian in name only.[26] Clearly it would take generations for the

Saxons and their neighbours to internalise the Christian message in a way that profoundly changed their perception of reality. Conflating imagined pagan religious practices with local customs, clerics complained about widespread ignorance and the persistence of 'sacrilegious' behaviour. For even as the worship of pagan deities was abandoned, elements of pagan and Christian religious beliefs were incorporated into magical practices that proliferated across the empire.[27]

Imperial expansion in the north-east began in earnest from the mid-tenth century. During the reign of Charlemagne, the neighbouring Obotrites had been allies against the Saxons and they had also been the first of several Western Slavic groups to embrace Christianity. These groups inhabited the lands between the Elbe and Lower Vistula rivers: from Holstein and Pomerania in the north to alpine Carinthia and Silesia in the south. Some were organised as regionally distinct federations: the Lutici and Pomeranians, for example, were each composed of four principal groups, whilst the Hevelli, Sprevani and Rani were smaller, individual groups. Their names were provided by Latin writers, who also collectively referred to them as Slavs. But to differentiate them from neighbouring Slavic societies, they used the exonym Veneti or Venedi – Wends.[28] Proximity to the Carolingian Empire had stimulated the political and economic development of Wendish society, which underwent dramatic changes from the end of the ninth century.[29] Impressive strongholds with associated settlements began to be constructed at the behest of new local dynasties, some of which came to wield power over other Wendish groups, who would pay them tribute. Contemporary Latin sources referred to the largest Wendish agglomerations as *civitates*, on a par with German towns.[30] These settlements attracted artisans, and became important centres of manufacturing, reflected in the specialisation of craft activities. Located at key points on communication networks consisting of interconnected rivers and lakes, they became involved in long-distance trade and attracted foreign merchants.[31] Along the coast, maritime trading centres had developed under Scandinavian influence. To feed the growing populations of these settlements, a complex rural economy developed around them, with grain and meat brought in from varying distances.[32] Some of these *civitates* also contained important pagan shrines, whose priests wielded significant political power.

The Ottonians regarded the lands of the Wends as strategically important for commerce, communication and their own political influence. The Elbe, which represented the eastern frontier between Saxon and Wendish lands, provided access to the sea, and to the lucrative trade routes and resources beyond. But it is virtually impossible to untangle the Ottonian state's territorial ambitions from the religious motivations of its ruling class, especially given the close relationship with its Church. Territorial annexations of pagan lands also enlarged the Christian community, for like the Carolingians, submission to Ottonian authority became synonymous with the acceptance of a Christian identity. The expansion of the empire into Wendish lands began in the early decades of the tenth century under the leadership of Henry I 'the Fowler' – the founder of the Ottonian dynasty. In 929, responding to a massacre by the Redarians (part of the Lutici) at Walsleben, a Saxon stronghold on the frontier, and an Obotrite uprising, Henry defeated the Wendish alliance, forcing them to pay tribute and convert to Christianity. During the same campaign, he raided the lands of the Hevelli and seized their stronghold at Brenna (later called Brandenburg). This key regional centre would change hands thirteen times between Henry's conquest and the mid-twelfth century, when it came under lasting German rule and was reorganised into two towns. Only then were enduring Christian monuments constructed, and it became possible to begin a sustained programme of religious education aimed at changing the belief system of the conquered Hevelli.

Henry's conquests reached as far as Danish territory around Schleswig, and the seized lands were reorganised as frontier lordships, here collectively referred to as the northern marches.[33] Governance over these was delegated to margraves (marcher counts), who became powerful rulers in their own right. They exacted tribute payments from the Wends and were responsible for ensuring they remained obedient to the empire. The conquered lands were also subdivided into dioceses, whose bishoprics, just as in Carolingian times, became centres of missionary activity. The bishops sometimes came into conflict with the margraves, who were often accused of being more interested in obtaining tribute from the subjugated Wends than in their spiritual wellbeing. Indeed, the chronicler Adam of Bremen would later blame the use of force and the greed of the Saxon marcher lords in preventing the conversion of the Slavs.[34] However, from the Wendish perspective, both margraves and bishops, and the fortified towns they resided in, must have represented Ottonian colonial rule. This is also evident from how Christian writers like Adam portrayed the Wends – as dangerous and barbaric. The political histories they produced were framed in the rhetoric of dichotomies, as the clash of Saxons or Danes and Wends, Christians versus pagans.

The reality on the ground was of course far more complex, but for clerics and those writing dynastic histories, the actions of Ottonian rulers were above all judged by their advancement of the Christian cause. So, whilst the reign of Henry's son Otto is associated with a flourishing artistic culture, contemporaries measured his success by victories against pagans at the frontiers of the empire. Imperial expansion went hand in hand with religious conversion. Instrumental to this was the development of the cult of St Maurice, powerfully symbolised by the relic of the saint's lance which Otto had inherited from his father and was credited with using in battle against the enemies of the faith. The iconic spearhead, housed today in the Kunsthistorisches Museum in Vienna, has been dated to the last quarter of the eighth century. By the mid-tenth century it had been transformed into a relic, with the centre of its blade hollowed out where a pointed iron object, believed to be a nail which had pierced Christ on the cross, was inserted. Small brass crosses were also added to mark places where fragments of the nail had been embedded. Several centuries later its association with St Maurice would be replaced with that of Longinus, who in the biblical narrative of the Passion had pierced Christ's side whilst he hung from the cross.[35]

Otto was celebrated for halting the advance of the pagan Magyars – whose armies had swept into the Carpathian Basin in the last years of the ninth century – in 955; he had carried the Holy Lance into battle with him. Before then, the early decades of his reign were marked by ongoing conflicts with the Wends who regularly tested the rule of the northern margraves. The Obotrites turned for aid to their old enemies the Danes, allying with King Gorm and later his son Harald (known as Bluetooth from c. 1140). Otto confronted and routed the Danish-Wendish army, forcing Harald to become his vassal and reasserting control over the rebellious territories. The conquered Wends, in turn, had to pay tribute to the empire, accept the reimposition of ecclesiastical administration and construct churches. Denmark would remain a fief of the empire until King Canute VI refused to swear allegiance to Emperor Frederick Barbarossa in 1182. However, even many decades before this, the great defensive earthwork known as the Danevirke, stretching from the River Treene to the Baltic Sea and marking the Saxon–Danish borderland, was reinforced. Its origins in the eighth century attest to the longevity of this frontier.

Christianity had not properly rooted in Denmark, despite the baptism of King Harald Klak over a century earlier. Gorm was a pagan by all accounts. His son would convert in around 965 as an expression of his submission to the empire, and Otto, in turn, demonstrated his overlordship by granting privileges to bishoprics in Denmark. Indeed, the Danish Church remained under the authority of the Saxon archbishops of Hamburg-Bremen until 1103, when a new see uniting the Scandinavian churches was established in Lund. Harald lived in a world where his politicised action had to be reinforced with physical symbols, and so he chose to express his new allegiance at the royal burial ground at Jelling where his parents were interred. The focus of the site consists of two monumental mounds, in between which stands a stone church dating to the early twelfth century. Excavations under the church in 1947 and in the late 1970s uncovered traces of three successive timber churches, the earliest of which was attributed to Harald's politicised actions. Within this church, archaeologists also discovered the burial of a middle-aged man, interpreted as Gorm, who had been exhumed from the northern mound where he had been buried only a few years earlier.[36] Re-dating of the southern mound indicated that it had been built in the 970s, after Harald's conversion. Its function remains unknown, but it covered the lower part of a huge setting of stones in the outline of a ship, and perhaps this was a way of neutralising a monument so dramatically associated with the pagan past.

Saxon chroniclers such as Widukind of Corvey naturally assumed the Danes were already Christians and Harald's actions were simply a reassertion of faith and political allegiance. His coins were decorated with crosses, a design repeated in the layout of his Trelleborg-type fortresses which some have suggested emulated a Christian world map with Jerusalem at its centre. Their construction can be connected to the expansion of Harald's realm, which was accompanied by public acts of

Christianisation. In 974, Haakon Sigurdsson, who ruled southern Norway and had previously aided Harald against the Ottonians, accepted baptism in exchange for his support. At Jelling, Harald set up a rune stone in memory of his parents, and also proclaimed his triumphant conquest which was both territorial and spiritual – he had won Denmark and Norway, and converted the Danes. In contrast to other rune stones, the lines of text on the Jelling stone were arranged horizontally, as they were in a Christian religious text. The stone was also decorated with a lion grasping a snake and the crucified Christ, the pairing suggesting a biblical reference to divine approval of secular rule. This was a statement of legitimacy for Harald's annexation of the neighbouring pagan petty kingdoms, and it would set the tone for future royal expansion. After relocating the royal residence from Jelling to Roskilde, he sponsored the construction of a church in the new centre where he would later be buried.[37] His son Sweyn 'Forkbeard' led a pagan rebellion against both Harald and the Ottonians, although later chroniclers would denounce him as an apostate for, by all accounts, he was a Christian and would go on to sponsor the construction of several churches. Again, the archaeological evidence suggests the pace of religious transformation in Denmark was slower than chroniclers imagined.

Otto would go on to transform the trading centre of Magdeburg on the Elbe into a stronghold that served as a missionary outpost for converting the Wends. After he married the English princess Edith, who traced her ancestry to St Oswald, martyred in battle against the pagan Mercians, the couple took a keen interest in the cult of St Maurice. In 937, on the eve of St Maurice's feast day, 21 September, Otto and Edith dedicated the newly constructed Benedictine monastery at Magdeburg to the saint and his companions. When Edith died, she was buried in the monastic church. In the wake of his victory against the Magyars, Otto had the monastery rebuilt as a cathedral, where Edith was reinterred. Six years later he would bequeath its community the relics of St Maurice given to him by Conrad of Burgundy. Otto's coronation as 'Emperor of the Romans' by the Pope on 2 February 962 was followed by the elevation of Magdeburg to the status of an archbishopric, in a papal bull that noted Otto's victories over pagans and his sponsorship of missionary activities. The first Archbishop of Magdeburg, Adalbert, had been previously involved in a failed mission to disseminate Latin Christianity to the Rus' in Kyiv. In his new role he would train other missionaries, including one Vojtěch (Polish Wojciech) who would adopt his mentor's name and eventually die whilst trying to evangelise the pagan Prussians. By this time Magdeburg embodied the Ottonian struggle against paganism.

Otto's son fared less well against the empire's pagan enemies. He lost the lands acquired by his father in southern Italy to Fatimid armies and in 983 faced a Wendish rebellion which overwhelmed the fragile Christian authority in the northern marches. According to Christian chroniclers, this was led by the Lutici, but in fact there were many different groups involved and they all had the same axe to grind. In attacking German Christianity, they targeted churches, killed priests and desecrated Christian symbols. The loss of imperial dominion – and the reach of the Ottonian Church – over lands east of the Elbe lasted for more than a century. Bishops continued to be appointed to these sees but they held only titular positions, residing in centres safely within secure Christian territory. The frontier became more sharply defined as new fortifications were constructed against the threat of the Wends.[38] For the Saxon monk Bruno of Querfurt, later martyred by the pagan Prussians, the rebels were despicable apostates – far worse in the eyes of the Church than pagans, for they had rejected the authority of the empire and thereby severed themselves from the Christian community.[39] Bruno believed that violence was a justifiable means of bringing them back to the fold. This would take time, but the early history of the northern marches provides a vital context for the later motivation to crusade against the Wends and the subsequent conquests of their lands. The attitude of Ottonian rulers and churchmen emulated that of the Carolingians. This, in turn, influenced another pagan dynasty, situated beyond Wendish lands to the east of the Oder river, who adopted Christianity in their rise to power. Their story is also important, as it provides the background to what would later become one of the most important crusading frontiers in Northern Europe.

THE VIOLENT RISE OF POLAND

There is a rich mythology associated with Mieszko, the acclaimed founder of Catholic Poland and his family, the Piasts.[40] However, in recent years archaeologists and historians have provided an increasingly nuanced understanding of how Poland came into existence as a distinct political and cultural entity, and how Christianity became an integral part of the identity of its rulers and their expanding dominion.[41] During the early decades of the tenth century, the majority of strongholds in what is today Greater Poland were destroyed or abandoned, as the political system they represented was violently dismantled and reorganised. They were replaced by a smaller number of heavily fortified settlements, attributed to a Slavic group referred to in later sources as Polanie or Polans, led by the Piasts. Decades of excavations have demonstrated how several of these new strongholds developed into multi-zonal complexes spread across hills and promontories, protected by substantial timber and earth ramparts, ditches and timber palisades. They were built at the behest of the Piasts and their allies, whose presence is evident from finds of luxury artefacts, including gold jewellery, fashionable dress accessories and feasting vessels.

The new regime built up significant military power. Excavations at one such stronghold on the lake island of Ostrów Lednicki have uncovered one of the largest assemblages of early medieval weapons found in Europe: over 300 artefacts including 159 axes, 60 spearheads, several swords, fragments of chain mail, equestrian equipment and a rare find of a helmet – the majority dating from the second half of the tenth century through to the mid-eleventh century. Large numbers of boats were also discovered in the lake, with one whose length spanned over 10 metres and which may have been used for combat. Its timbers were dated by dendrochronology to 966. Such impressive military assets reflect the Piasts' affluence, and a contemporary account by the Sephardi Jewish traveller Ibn Ya'qub describes how Mieszko paid his retinues – kinsmen and mercenaries – salaries.[42] These retinues were cosmopolitan in character, with warriors hailing from neighbouring regions or further afield.[43]

The Piasts' original base may have been the stronghold at Giecz, which was constructed in the second half of the ninth century,[44] but within a few decades, the stronghold at Gniezno became promoted above all other centres. According to a story written down at the end of the thirteenth century and subsequently popularised, the site was chosen by an ancestor of the Piasts called Lech who, wandering in search of new lands, witnessed a white eagle settling into her nest against the red hue of the setting sun. Taking it as a sign, he chose to establish his first settlement there, naming it after the eagle's nest – *gniazdo*. This is more likely to be an apocryphal explanation for the Polish crest, and the white eagle has remained a powerful and emotive symbol of Poland's sovereignty. Recently, it has been argued that the Piasts may have originally migrated to the Polish lowlands across the western Carpathians from Great Moravia, bringing with them experiences of territorial organisation, governance, stronghold construction and perhaps even an understanding of Christianity.[45]

The earliest account of the history of Poland was written by an anonymous cleric visiting Boleslaus III's court in the early twelfth century, named Gallus by historians. He described how Gniezno supplied Mieszko's son, Boleslaus 'the Brave', with the highest number of warriors in the Piast state, whilst ranking the other major centres in terms of military assets. Boleslaus's reign (992–1025), which culminates in his coronation as King of the Poles, certainly coincides with further investment in the dynasty's legendary centre; Gniezno's ramparts were extended across the northern part of the hill and the associated settlement to the south grew in size. Here, and in similar settlements associated with the Piast strongholds, archaeologists have identified evidence for intensive manufacturing, long-distance trade, regimented food preparation and stabling. The building and extension of these complexes required substantial amounts of timber and earth, as well as labour, and their communities depended on significant quantities of food and fuel. These were supplied by villages and farmsteads within their immediate territories, where a growing population is evident in the decades of the new state's rise. The economic prosperity of the Piast state was powered by conquest, as much as trade and eventually taxation, and military incursions enabled the seizure of booty, the inducement of tributary payments and in some areas, particularly where rival rulers had been defeated, the enslavement of the subjugated population.[46]

The trading activities of the early Piasts brought them into contact with the two great Christian power blocks flanking their lands: the Ottonian Empire, with its allies in Bohemia, and Kyivan Rus' aligned with the Byzantine Empire. The Piasts must have recognised the benefits – or perhaps the inevitability – of aligning with one or other of these international Christian confederations. That choice was ultimately determined by events in the mid-tenth century. The Bohemian duke Boleslaus I 'the Cruel' had expanded his territory across the western Carpathians into Silesia and Lesser Poland. There is little if any evidence of the Bohemian impact in these regions, and the gains may have been tenuous at best. But perhaps because of this, Boleslaus arranged for his daughter Doubravka to marry the pagan Mieszko in 965, who was then allegedly baptised the following year. The year 966, although only noted in later sources and not always consistently, is still widely regarded as the symbolic beginning of Poland's national history. This is also why Mieszko remains a far more important figure than any of his ancestors who had actually laid the foundations for the early Piast state.

In his account of Polish history, Gallus described how Mieszko was blind until his seventh birthday, when God returned his sight, foreshadowing the end of Poland's moral 'blindness' with the acceptance of Christianity.[47] Gallus also emphasised Doubravka's role in persuading Mieszko to abandon paganism, and although initially reluctant to marry into the Piast family, she relented and made the journey across the mountains to the lands of the Polans with a substantial entourage of Christian followers. For Mieszko, the symbolic act of baptism was politically astute as this meant his family immediately signed up to a powerful international community, headed by the pope and Ottonian emperor. This provided a certain legitimacy for their rule, as well as support for further territorial expansion, and particularly the expectation of a Bohemian military alliance against Gero, the ambitious margrave of the Saxon Eastern March. According to Widukind of Corvey, Mieszko's earlier territorial ambitions in Pomerania, at the north-western edges of the Piast realm, had clashed with those of Gero's kinsman, Wichman, who had allied with the pagans of Wolin, an island just off the coast. They faced each other in battle with the result that Mieszko's brother was killed. But in 976, following Mieszko's marriage to Doubravka, a joint Polish–Bohemian force confronted Wichman in battle, where he was slain.[48] In the eyes of the Piasts, the adoption of Christianity had clearly paid off. Mieszko soon realised that the spiritual leader of the Christian West had sway over the Ottonian Empire, and in a politically astute move offered his vassalage directly to the papacy.

CONFRONTING PAGANISM

THE FIRST POLISH CHURCHES

In Piast mythology, Christianity was synonymous with the dynasty's rise to power. But in the decades after Mieszko's conversion, any visible Christian identity was restricted to the ruler's inner circle.[49] Gerhard of Augsburg relates in his biography of St Ulrich of Augsburg how Mieszko was wounded by a poisoned arrow in battle with the Wends, after which he made a vow to the saint that he would offer him a shoulder fashioned from silver if he survived. It is easy to imagine how supernatural support in battle — from what was perceived to be an evidently more powerful deity — would have appealed to the Piasts in a world where military achievements defined political success, and this became part of their identity.[50] The family invested in monuments expressing their new religious allegiance, with architectural projects drawing inspiration from the Ottonians, whilst at the same time reflecting local experimentation in new building forms.[51] Although traces of the earliest church at Gniezno can perhaps be dated to Mieszko's reign, the first Christian buildings took the form of chapels.

One of the most striking examples was attached to the large palatial building within a stronghold on the riverine island of Ostrów Tumski. Some 15 kilometres to the west of Gniezno, on the lake island of Ostrów Lednicki, a similar palatial residence with an attached chapel contained a structure interpreted by some as a baptistry, dated to the second half of the tenth century.[52] Monumental churches at these sites would be built later, in the reign of Boleslaus. At Giecz, the only two unmistakable Christian objects associated with the early Piast state — part of a reliquary and a bell — were also found. But the church here was never finished and the whole complex was abandoned around the time of a widespread rebellion against Piast rule in 1038–9 described in Gallus's chronicle, referred to by historians as a 'pagan reaction' to Christian rule.

In the latter half of the tenth century, the Piasts expanded their territorial rule in all directions through military conquests, which snaked out along the riverine arteries emanating from the Gniezno region. They all followed a similar pattern. Existing centres of power were either appropriated or destroyed. At the same time, an influx of silver from these territories reflected either a sudden boom in trade, or the extraction of tribute from the subjugated Slavic groups, or perhaps both. The conquered populations were supplemented by migrants, a policy of colonisation deliberately encouraged by the Piasts, particularly Boleslaus. In some cases, these population movements appear to have been forced, a pragmatic if callous way of breaking up earlier power structures that was straight out of the Frankish playbook.[53] What about the new religion the Piasts had adopted to consolidate their political and military position in Central Europe? The evidence suggests this was in fact a much slower process.

The region to the north-east of the Piast heartland, later more commonly known as the Kulmerland (Polish Ziemia Chełmińska), had been nominally incorporated into the expanding state in the mid-tenth century, before Mieszko's conversion. This saw the replacement of the early Slavic settlement near the present-day village of Kałdus with a new regional power centre, a stronghold which has been identified with later Culm. The site, which has been the focus of many decades of excavation, is famous for the discovery of the foundations of a substantial stone church, similar in style to the early cathedrals in Gniezno and Poznań.[54] Its construction has been dated to the first half of the eleventh century and its altar was placed over a large boulder interpreted as a pre-Christian offering site. Given its location, on the frontier with pagan Prussian lands, some have speculated the church was intended as a base for missionary activity. However, as at Giecz, the building was never finished and its abandonment has been associated with the same rebellion. After the Piasts reasserted their control, the stronghold continued to function as a frontier outpost with neighbouring pagan Prussian lands and the idea of investing in a monumental Christian structure was scrapped.

Directly to the north-west of the Piast heartlands, bordered by the Vistula and the Oder, lay the Wendish territory named in Latin sources as Pomerania. Here, a number of settlements with access to the coastline had developed into major trading centres during the Viking Age, particularly Wolin, Gdańsk and, in the Pomeranian–Prussian borderlands, Truso. Their prosperity attracted the attention of the Piasts, who focused their campaign in the 960s on the Lower Vistula, eventually conquering Gdańsk. But here there is no evidence for monumental Christian structures before the eleventh century.[55] The prevalent burial rite – cremation – had been supplemented by inhuming bodies in the same cemeteries already from the ninth century, and both rites continued to be used alongside each other into the tenth century. Cremation was finally abandoned in the following century.[56] By this time, a Christian administration had been more firmly established in the region, following Boleslaus's conquest of Western Pomerania. A bishopric was founded in Kolberg (Polish Kołobrzeg), providing a missionary base not just for evangelising the Pomeranians but also other Wendish groups.

In the 970s, Piast expansion in the south-east was intended to reach Cracow, which was under the control of the Bohemian Přemyslids. Mieszko finally seized the centre in c. 990, where archaeologists have discovered more early medieval monumental structures within the fortified settlement on Wawel Hill than anywhere else in Poland. Most recently it has been argued these stone buildings date to the first quarter of the eleventh century, following Cracow's elevation to a bishopric in 1000. At the easternmost frontier of the Piast realm bordering with Kyiv's territory, a centre was established at Przemyśl where a stone palatial residence with a rotunda was built at the start of the eleventh century, again resembling those constructed in the Gniezno heartland. Here the church may have been intended to serve the broader community, rather than simply as the private chapel of the local elites. When the Piasts took control of Silesia in the 980s, they inherited the existing pastoral infrastructure established by Byzantine and later Catholic missionary activity associated with the expansion and contraction of Greater Moravia. This had seen the construction of several stone churches. Half a century later, there is some evidence from Wrocław of the 'pagan reaction' to Piast rule, where alongside the destruction of the settlement's rampart, a new timber building was constructed with its interior space subdivided into four chambers. Here, fragments of linen, silk and gold cloths were found, with a sacral area identified in association with what has been interpreted as a statue of a deity, reminiscent of other pagan Wendish shrines. As the building was being constructed, a horse skull was placed as a foundation deposit. The cathedral that had been built in the town during the reign of Boleslaus was destroyed at this time. It would be rebuilt as a larger structure following the restoration of Piast authority. If there was indeed a religious dimension to the short-lived rebellion against their rule, which we largely see through Gallus's exaggerated narrative, it was because Christianity was so closely tied to the Piasts' political identity and authority.

To the east of the early Polish heartland stretched the vast territory of Masovia, bordering to the north with Prussian lands and further east with Kyiv's territory. Masovia did not correspond to a homogenous cultural zone but encompassed a variety of regions with their own distinctive characters. Here, the presence of the early Piasts is difficult to detect. Strongholds destroyed by fire in the mid-tenth century may reflect the initial conquest, but there was little investment in a regional centre before the 990s. At that point Płock was chosen and its loose cluster of settlements was replaced by a denser concentration of housing, along with the construction of a new stronghold on the previously unoccupied Tum Hill, the highest point overlooking the Vistula. The fortified complex was expanded in the late eleventh century and a cathedral is documented there in 1075.[57] This was a comparatively late development but Masovia was a frontier for the Piasts. Situated between the cultures of the pagan Prussians, Orthodox Kyiv and Latin Poland, absorbing an influx of refugees from other parts of Poland in the 1030s during Bretislav of Bohemia's invasion, the region become something of a cultural melting pot. Christianity would also take time to become firmly established here, particularly in its northern fringes where the cremation of the dead continued to be practised into the mid-twelfth century.[58]

As we have seen, the construction of churches coincides with the consolidation of Piast rule in the conquered territories during Boleslaus's reign. This also saw the church in Gniezno elevated to the status of the cathedral of the first Polish archbishopric in the year 1000. Gniezno would become the centre for promoting the Piasts' ideology of evangelisation, centred on the figure of Adalbert, who had been killed whilst trying to convert the Prussians in 997. Adalbert was canonised by the pope and Boleslaus purchased the saint's bones from the Prussians for, as the story goes, an equivalent weight in gold. The young German emperor Otto III, who had been a close friend of Adalbert, travelled to Gniezno, where as a pilgrim he walked barefoot to the church and placed the saint's bones in the altar with his own hands.[59] Archaeologists excavating under the later gothic cathedral at Gniezno uncovered traces of the first church, a rotunda which had two annexes added to it after its initial construction, one of which was presumably built to accommodate Adalbert's relics. After its status was elevated, the old church was expanded into a large basilica which was rebuilt again from the mid-eleventh century. The first archbishop was not named 'of Gniezno' but rather 'of St Adalbert', stressing the bond with the saint. Otto himself presided over the summit that conferred this status and effectively guaranteed the independence of the newly founded Polish Church. There were multiple political reasons why he was moved to do this, including seeking to develop an alliance in opposition to Kyiv and Constantinople, but Adalbert's influence was undeniable, something that Boleslaus may have recognised and acted upon in obtaining the relics from the Prussians.[60] Otto commissioned the saint's first *vita* (written by an anonymous author) and ordered a church dedicated to him built on Tiber Island in Rome, where he deposited a relic of Adalbert's arm. He would go on to establish a collegiate church in Aachen dedicated to St Adalbert which was completed after his death, where the monks would receive a relic of the saint's skull.

Thanks to Otto, Adalbert's cult was established in major religious centres beyond Gniezno,[61] but for Boleslaus, who had obtained the relics, it elevated Poland to the status of a true Christian kingdom. His coins, struck after 1003, referred to his subjects as Poles (*Polonie*) – a political identity that gradually merged with an ethnic one.[62] When Bretislav raided the town in 1039, he seized Adalbert's relics and took them to Prague, where they became the focus of a parallel cult. However, Polish sources claimed the duke had taken the wrong relics, and that St Adalbert had in fact remained in Gniezno. Irrespective of who had the possession of the saint's actual bones – and both Gniezno and Prague maintained their claim – Adalbert retained his status as patron of the Piast state. A century later, after the events of the First Crusade, the conversion of pagans had become inextricably tied to the northward expansion of Poland. Boleslaus III 'Wrymouth' would invoke St Adalbert in his 'holy war' against the Pomeranians, and his own coins minted from 1107 depicted the Polish ruler being blessed by the saint.[63] Two decades later, the saint's head was miraculously discovered and brought to Gniezno, and in 1147, Mieszko III 'the Old' added the final touches to the monumentalisation of Adalbert's cult by sponsoring the construction of an elaborate set of bronze doors depicting the saint's life, martyrdom and entry to paradise. They were eventually installed in the rebuilt cathedral at Gniezno, a reminder of both the Piast claim to the saint's body and the deadly threat of pagans on the frontiers of Polish lands.

CHRISTIANITY TERRITORIALISED

Charlemagne is undoubtedly one of the most influential figures in European history and has been widely praised as the ideal Christian ruler, warrior and patron of learning.[64] His forebears had forged the link between loyalty to the state and Christian identity – symbolically marked by baptism. Charlemagne would take this to a new level, where the conquest of the Saxons, in particular, became linked to the simultaneous expansion of the Carolingian Empire and the Christian community. After his death, Charlemagne quickly attained legendary status. His achievements were exaggerated and the extent of his empire was reimagined to span the entirety of the Christian world – from Jerusalem to Rome to Iberia.[65] The emperor's body was even thought to be asleep in his tomb, waiting to emerge one day as a messianic ruler to unite all Christians in a final apocalyptical struggle against the enemies of God. When Urban II called for the First Crusade, he invoked the memory of Charlemagne and appealed directly to those living within the former Carolingian Empire, breathing new life into the idea of the Franks as the quintessential defenders of Christianity. By the mid-twelfth century, Charlemagne was widely idealised as the model crusader and his campaigns against Muslim Al-Andalus – which aimed to expand both the Carolingian state and the Christian community – were reimagined as crusades.[66]

Inspired by the Carolingians and Ottonians, the military successes of the leading dynasties of Central Europe – the Premyslids, Piasts and Arpads – were framed by their promoters as the result of divine aid. From their perspective, the territorial expansion of the western empires had been evidently supported by a powerful deity. In pragmatic terms, adopting Christianity opened political and commercial doors to powerful allies. Papal endorsement of newly created sovereign states became an indispensable and internationally recognised badge of legitimate government across Catholic Europe. As a result, the expansion of these states became both a political and religious act, where loyalty to the new regime became attached to the public adoption of a Christian identity. The foundation of bishoprics became the most visible expression of territorialised Christianity, and in these new states, bishops were more than drivers of missionary activity. They also came to play important roles as administrators, which included leading armies and organising military support.[67] Over time, the integrity of Catholic states became defined in opposition to their pagan neighbours. This provides the essential background for understanding how and why crusading in Northern Europe, when locally adopted over the course of the twelfth century, became twinned with the expansion of Catholic German, Polish and Scandinavian states.

CHAPTER 2

THE FIRST CRUSADE IN THE NORTH
Conquering the Wends

> . . . going against the Slavs and other pagans living in the north and, with the help of God, subjugating them to the Christian religion . . .
>
> Crusade bull issued by Eugenius III, April 1147[1]

PRELUDE TO CRUSADE

In 1108, a letter penned in the name of Adelgoz, Archbishop of Magdeburg, along with several bishops, priests and Saxon magnates, called for a holy war against the pagans living east of the Elbe.[2] These were groups of Western Slavs collectively referred to as Wends. The letter described the Wends as beheading Christians and filling chalices with their blood to honour their god Pripegala, and urged Christian lords – and naming, amongst others, Count Robert II of Flanders, one of the leaders of the First Crusade – to seize the lands of the pagans. The letter stated, as an added incentive, that these were plentiful in natural resources:

> And so, most renowned Saxons, French, Lorrainers and Flemings and conquerors of the world, this is an occasion for you to save your souls and, if you wish it, acquire the best land in which to live.[3]

Nonetheless, the reward would be primarily spiritual, and the letter referred to the lands of the pagan Wends as 'our Jerusalem'.[4] In its structure and content, it sought to emulate Pope Urban's call to holy war thirteen years earlier. The intention was clear – the success of the First Crusade was to be repeated against the enemies of the Catholic community in the North. The letter also reiterated the support of the Danish king for this righteous war, the Saxons and Danes aspiring to overcome their earlier hostilities to bring about the destruction of a common enemy. In the light of the Ottonian conquests which had created the northern marches, expanding the empire in step with Christianity, this was nothing new, and whilst it seemingly contradicted the ethos of Urban's call for the liberation of Jerusalem, the creation of Catholic states in the Levant meant that crusading and the seizure of territory were not, in fact, incompatible.[5]

There was already a long tradition of framing the Wends as the pagan 'other' – a threat to their Christian neighbours, particularly after the rebellion in 983 which had seen the collapse of Ottonian rule east of the Elbe. Thietmar, the Bishop of Meresburg and an avid supporter of the empire, was the first to write about the uprising, a few decades later. For him, the Wends were treacherous, barbaric and prone to violence. But his most pointed criticisms focused on their religious practices. He described their worship of multiple gods, idols and nature-based rituals, which he saw as directly opposed to Christianity. He also provided the first detailed description of a Wendish religious centre, that of Riedegost, whose priesthood had assumed important political roles within the Lutici union. Thietmar described the fortified temple as a triangular building situated within a vast sacred forest, inside of which stood imposing idols of pagan deities clothed in armour. Behind the shrine, accessible through a small, eastern-facing door, was a sacred lake. The temple served as the meeting spot for war councils, whose decisions were informed by divination using a sacred white horse which was led over two crossed spears placed on the ground. Depending on how the actions of the horse were interpreted, the priests would offer up the blood of humans and animals to appease their gods. The sanctuary also served as a mustering point for the Lutici's armies, and warriors would take up the banners from the shrine in times of war.[6]

Adam of Bremen, writing over fifty years later, echoed Thietmar's criticisms, and was also disturbed by the pagan practice of animal and especially human sacrifice. He too described the religious centre of Riedegost, which he called Rethra, but he was far more scathing, branding it as a temple of demons.[7] Neither Thietmar nor Adam had seen the temple, and both differed in the details to the extent that some scholars have suggested they were referring to two different places. Later in the twelfth century, the Saxon priest Helmold of Bosau would continue in the same vein, describing how the pagan Wends regularly sacrificed and tortured Christians to appease their gods, including crucifying them to mock their religion.[8] Archaeological excavations at Wendish religious centres have indeed uncovered evidence for the ritual killing of livestock, which was probably consumed in special feasts. Human remains have also been found in some sites, indicating that ritual deposition if not sacrifice was practised.[9]

The rulers of the Ottonian Empire and their successors – the Salians and the Hohenstaufens – viewed Wendish lands as a frontier where the Catholic world reached its limit. This borderland had been pushed northwards through the actions of missionaries and the policies of rulers, a process that came under the supervision of the archbishops of Hamburg-Bremen, who claimed credit for evangelising several Wendish groups, as well as the Scandinavian kingdoms. Of these groups, the Obotrites emerged as a cohesive Christian state headed from the late tenth century by a royal dynasty – the Nakonids. The first and second generations of the dynasty had joined the rebellion against Ottonian rule, and were condemned for having abandoned Christianity. But in the mid-eleventh century, the Obotrite king Gottschalk would ally with the Saxon duke Bernard II and Adalbert, the Archbishop of Hamburg-Bremen, having set his sights on expansion into the lands of the Lutici. This involved setting up new, fortified diocesan centres and sending out missionaries. For the Lutici, Christianity was perceived as a form of political subjugation which came with forced payment of tribute to Ottonian rulers and tithes to the Saxon Church. Resistance against foreign rule also meant a rejection of Christianity, or at least its political trappings.

In 1066, the Obotrites, encouraged by the Lutici, rose up against their own Christian ruler and the insurrection destroyed the recently established dioceses. Priests and monks were slain, Gottschalk was murdered and his sons fled into exile. The elderly Bishop of Mecklenburg, John, was captured and, according to Adam's chronicle, sacrificed at the shrine of Rethra – his head offered up to the pagan gods. One of the Obotrites leading the rebellion, Kruto, assumed control. He established his stronghold on an island in the Baltic Sea (most likely modern-day Großenbrode or an island in Wismar Bay), from where he ruled, resisting both Saxon and Christian influence. Two years later, a Saxon army led by Bishop Burchard II of Haberstadt marched on Rethra. The bishop allegedly seized the sacred horse kept at the temple and rode it back to his see, a symbolic act of triumph over the pagan priesthood in what had previously been one of the most important Wendish religious centres.[10] Rethra's final fate is unknown, as it is no longer named in the historical record. Its memory was, however, preserved in the folktales of the Mecklenburg region, which were documented in the early twentieth century. In these the temple is attacked by Germans, and the Slavs escape with an idol of their deity, which is usually fashioned from gold, after which they bury it or throw it into a lake. The temple itself has never been convincingly located, although archaeologists have made several attempts to find it.[11] As the political significance of the Lutici faded in the northern marches, Henry, one of Gottschalk's sons, returned from Denmark in 1090, and a few years later killed Kruto and then defeated pagan Obotrite forces. The Nakonid Christian kingdom was restored. Henry then set about attacking his Wendish neighbours to extract tribute, and raiding Danish lands. Although a Christian, he allegedly permitted his subjects to continue their former religious practices.

Meanwhile, German influence over Denmark waned in the early twelfth century, when a new archdiocese was established at Lund with ecclesiastical jurisdiction over the entirety of Scandinavia. With the added loss of control over its Wendish dioceses following the earlier insurrection, Hamburg-Bremen's authority and financial basis – derived from the payment of tithes – declined. As Danish rulers began to consolidate their power by expanding into the lands of the Wends, Magdeburg, the other German archdiocese situated on the frontier of the Elbe, now sought to assert its spiritual jurisdiction over the northern marches. This is the context for Adelgoz's letter, written barely a decade after the capture of Jerusalem by crusaders. Much like Pope Urban's imagined description of Muslims (also framed as pagans) spreading the blood of circumcised Christians on their altars, which was clearly intended to provoke outrage with its lurid details,[12] the archbishop's letter followed a long tradition of depicting the enemies of the faith as blasphemous and barbaric.

The sanctioning of the first crusades in Northern Europe marked a turning point in the conquest and assimilation of Wendish lands into the Holy Roman Empire, and initiated a wave of settlement – or colonisation, as it has long been called by historians and archaeologists – which would be repeated in other regions targeted by crusades. The end result was a gradual, and not wholly complete, ethnic transformation of the conquered population, a process referred to as Germanisation. This would play a foundational role in shaping the historical and cultural landscape of the German-speaking world. In this respect, the story of the Wends is also an integral part of German history, even though the concept of a unified Germany did not exist for many centuries after these events.

THE WENDISH CRUSADE

The outcome of Magdeburg's call to holy war in 1108 almost certainly did not result in anything. The historical record is silent on this. However, in the following years there were documented military incursions into Wendish lands accompanied by the destruction of pagan religious sites. In 1114, the nominal Bishop of Brandenburg, Hartbert, attacked his designated see which lay in Wendish territory and claimed to have destroyed many pagan idols. He also appears to have converted some local Wendish leaders, most notably Widukind in Havelberg and Pribislav in Brandenburg, who became political allies of the Saxon Church. A decade later, Lothar, Duke of Saxony, along with an army of Christian Obotrites, most probably attacked and finally destroyed the sanctuary at Rethra. He would have continued on to the religious centre of the Rani at Arkona on the island of Rügen, if the thawing ice had not prevented his army from crossing the narrow stretch of sea separating it from the mainland.

The convening of the First Lateran Council in 1123 by Pope Calixtus II was an epoch-making event, where the superiority of the pope's spiritual authority was confirmed. This was the culmination of a protracted dispute known as the 'investiture controversy', which split the empire from Rome and established the pope, rather than the emperor, as the true head of the Western Christian community. The council also explicitly connected the war against Muslims in Iberia with crusading in the Holy Land. This laid the groundwork for the sanction of future crusades in other regions where the Catholic community was perceived to be threatened. In the North, attacks and raids led by Scandinavian and Polish rulers which included a religious motivation are documented around this time.[13] Their targets included Wendish regions. By 1123, the Polish duke Boleslaus III 'Wrymouth' had subjugated Western Pomerania and hoped to conquer Rügen, but was unable to do so. King Eric II 'the Memorable' would then attack the island in 1136 to reassert Danish authority. Pledges of loyalty from the conquered Rani were reinforced by compulsory baptism, although according to the chronicler Saxo Grammaticus they promptly lapsed back into their former ways once the Danish army departed. This trope of the Wends as deceitful and apostatising was regularly used by Christian writers, echoing how the Saxons had been described in earlier centuries, and how their eastern neighbours, the Prussians, would also be framed. Once oaths of loyalty had been sworn by the subjugated groups, any resistance to Christian authority was seen as beyond contempt.

Following the death of Henry, the Obotrite prince, the German emperor named his Danish vassal Canute Lavard as the overlord of the western Wends. Not long after, Canute was murdered by a rival and now Obotrite lands were subdivided between two pagan rulers, Pribislav and Nyklot. In the meantime, German lords jostled for control over the Duchy of Saxony, which briefly fell into the hands of the Margrave of Lusatia, Albert the Bear, before coming under the control of Henry the Lion. During these years, raids and military campaigns were organised against the Wends in the northern marches. But rather than exacting tribute and leaving local power structures intact, as was the policy of earlier Carolingian and Ottonian rulers, these now became wars of territorial expansion. Wendish leaders were deprived of their lands, and the German lords secured their presence by constructing new fortifications and inviting settlers to populate the conquered territories. They were followed by bishops, priests and monks, reviving missionary activity amongst Wendish groups regarded as either still pagans or apostates who, in their eyes, needed to be brought back into the fold of the Church.

It was in this context of territorial expansion, settlement and conversion, during the call for what became known later as the Second Crusade, that the ideology of papally sanctioned holy war became officially extended to Northern Europe. In 1147, whilst touring to promote the papal call to crusade against the Seljuk Turks, Bernard of Clairvaux had met with a group of Saxon nobles in Frankfurt. They refused to join the crusade to the Holy Land and instead suggested an alternative target that was much closer to home – those rebellious 'idolatrous pagans', the Wends. The Saxon nobles' plea was therefore not a spontaneous response to Bernard's visit, but part of the ongoing military and religious struggle for control of the northern marches. Whilst the influence of the emperor had diminished since the time of the Ottonians, the fight against the Wends had been taken up by the margraves and supported by leading prelates keen on extending the influence of their sees. Both groups imagined they were, by their actions, expanding the bounds of Christendom. Bernard's statements regarding the Wends suggests that conversion was in fact of secondary importance, and what was more pressing was the defence of Christian territory and the preservation of peace, but his visit provided a new opportunity to re-establish control over the marches.

Bernard pre-empted the pope's approval and verbally agreed to the Saxon nobles' request, subsequently persuading Eugenius III – previously his novice at Clairvaux – to authorise this first official crusade in the Baltic region.[14] In April 1147, the crusading bull was issued, but with an added caveat, quoted at the start of this chapter. Unlike those armies heading towards the Holy Land to reclaim Christian territory, the pope declared that the condition of what became later known as the 'Wendish Crusade' was to convert pagans to Christianity. This contradicted canon law which prohibited conversion by force, but not only was the concept of armed missions already familiar in the North: conversion was envisaged as a means of achieving a lasting peace – ending the cycle of wars with the Wends.[15] The point was reiterated by Bernard to the Saxon magnates. For the first time, crusading had been twinned with missionary activity, but the campaign was plagued with doubts over its purpose, conflicting agendas, competing claims to territory and military failures. Indeed, the pope may not have trusted the motivations of the Saxon lords and appointed Bishop Anselm of Havelberg as his official legate to manage the crusade.

The campaign can be summarised very briefly. In July, a Saxon army led by Henry the Lion and Archbishop Adalbero of Bremen, along with the forces of the rival Danish kings Canute V and Sweyn III, besieged but failed to capture the Obotrite stronghold at Dobin on Lake Schwerin. Following an attack on the Danish fleet by the Rani, the two rival kings left to continue their own conflict. When token promises of conversion were offered by the Obotrite leader Nyklot to Henry and Adalbero, the Saxon army withdrew. Later that month, a Saxon army led by the papal legate Bishop Anselm and which included six other bishops, two margraves – Conrad and Albert the Bear – and most probably a Polish contingent led by Mieszko III, marched out from Magdeburg, destroyed the pagan religious centre at Malchow and besieged the Lutici stronghold of Demmin. At the margraves' instigation, the army then moved on to Stettin (Polish Szczecin) only to discover it was already a Christian town – the inhabitants hung crosses on its walls. The crusaders reluctantly withdrew.[16]

Historians have traditionally viewed the Wendish Crusade as a cynical use of religion to validate the political and economic agendas of the various Saxon, Danish and Polish lords involved. In the background raged the protracted battle for control over the dioceses east of the Elbe.[17] Contemporaries, however, did not criticise the Crusade's objective per se, but lamented its failure to convert the Wends effectively, and in the context of the crusading movement (as will become evident) it is difficult to disentangle religion from other motivations.[18] The crusading bull officially conferred spiritual rewards upon its participants – the remission of sins. This was an effective way of raising a substantial army for a war that may have been otherwise difficult to justify, let alone finance. It also sanctioned violence as a means of protecting the Catholic community through what was framed as a defensive war. Although no further crusading bulls were issued against the Wends, Pope Eugenius III had inadvertently set a new precedent for religious conversion by force.

In the wake of the Wendish Crusade, a German version of the famous Frankish tale of Roland – *Rolandslied* – was written by a priest named

Conrad. The story reimagined Charlemagne's conflict with Andalusi Muslims (somewhat removed from the actual events), where the legendary ruler was presented as an idealised crusader. Conrad's work was most likely patronised by Henry the Lion and his English wife Matilda, and must have provided a source of inspiration for the Saxon duke. Henry emphasised his own personal connection to Charlemagne through his grandfather Lothar II, the German emperor, and aspired to lead his own crusade against the pagans in the North. But such sentiments were widely held, and the *Rolandslied* gave a new poetic voice to a popular German conception linking imperial holy war and crusading. The Wendish Crusade may have failed as an enterprise, but it laid the groundwork for envisaging future conquests of Wendish territories as unofficial crusades.[19]

FOOTHOLDS IN THE NORTHERN MARCHES

The year after the Wendish Crusade, Bishop Anselm relocated to his see at Havelberg together with his canons, adopting what he envisaged as a lifestyle imitating that of Christ and his apostles. In a letter to the abbot of Corvey, he described the dangerous conditions they were living in; some of his brethren were even anticipating martyrdom at the hands of the pagans. This embrace of mission had become a feature of the north Saxon houses of the Premonstratensians. Anselm had been one of the protégés of the order's founder, Norbert of Xanten, who had been appointed as Archbishop of Magdeburg in 1126. Norbert was a controversial figure, a preaching hermit who had given up his privileges and wealth to pursue the apostolic life through rigorous asceticism. When his licence to preach had been renewed, Norbert was placed under the watchful eye of Bishop Bartholomew of Laon, who encouraged him to set up a religious community in Prémontré. Papal approval of the Premonstratensians in the same year that Norbert was appointed to the see of Magdeburg was a means of taming what was perceived as a radical and potentially dangerous movement. With Norbert reluctantly taking on the appointment and quickly facing hostility and even attempts on his life when he tried to tackle corruption in Magdeburg, the fledgling order was obliged to gradually take on a pastoral role which included administering sacraments and managing parishes.

Norbert had appointed Anselm to the see of Havelberg and introduced him to the imperial and papal courts, where both became important figures. The order's institutionalisation and its general chapter's imposition of gender segregation bitterly divided Norbert's followers, some of whom would reject the order and in later years face dramatic accusations of heresy. The Premonstratensian circary (or province) of Saxony, however, embraced missionary activity as a feature of apostolic life, which invariably meant suffering for the faith. This was a major factor in Anselm's decision to relocate to Havelberg, where a Premonstratensian community was established with the cathedral as its church, following the model established by Norbert in Magdeburg. The cathedral building itself, initially constructed from stone sourced from the Magdeburg region, would not be consecrated until its completion two decades later, in 1170.[20] Anselm did not remain there for long: after two years he moved his community on to the estates granted by King Conrad III (who was never crowned emperor), and adopted the most effective strategy for Christianising the region – encouraging its settlement by Christian migrants.

Some Wends did convert. These were typically members of the elite, who bolstered their own positions by allying with their powerful Christian neighbours. For example, Pribislav, the ruler of the Hevelli, had asked to be baptised and took the Christian name Henry (Heinrich), agreeing to build churches and pay tithes. In 1156, he participated in the Bishop of Oldenburg's mission to eastern Holstein, following the invitation of another Wendish ruler, Thessemar. The party included Helmold who described the pagan religious site they encountered en route – a sacred grove with oak trees and idols dedicated to the god Prove – as a 'refuge of unholiness'.[21] The grove was marked and protected by a fence with two gates, and it was forbidden for anyone but priests and those seeking sanctuary within to enter. Missionaries, believing it was their duty to cleanse these places of demons (as they regarded pagan deities), would of course ignore any such prohibitions and, according to his biographers, Adalbert had been executed by the pagan Prussians for entering and thereby desecrating such a sacred place. The bishop ordered his men to destroy the grove, and led the way by striking the elaborately decorated gate with his staff. The sacred trees were cut down and burned.

However, this symbolic victory was bittersweet. Upon reaching Thessemar who hosted a lavish banquet for the missionaries, they discovered enslaved Danish Christians who had been tortured and the priests had become emaciated from hunger. The missionaries were powerless to help them and focused instead on preaching to the Slavs in Lübeck.

Pribislav, as a Christian ruler, sought to emulate the trappings of power of his Christian neighbours. He was the first Wendish ruler to issue coins. These took the form of double-sided pennies decorated with a mounted warrior and cross on one side, and a representation of Brandenburg on the reverse, accompanied by Latin inscriptions. A second variant represents Pribislav in armour holding a sword and a standard, and on the reverse an image of his wife, Petrissa, shown with long, flowing hair, wearing a dress and flanked by an eight-pointed star and a cross. Such conjugality was not typical of how medieval Christian rulers portrayed themselves, and can only speak of the esteem Petrissa was held in as, at the very least, a figure of political authority. Pribislav's own image imitates that used by the German margraves, symbolising their ability to muster and command armies.[22]

Pribislav's death without issue in 1150 provoked a rebellion against the German claimant to his stronghold at Brandenburg, Albert the Bear, one of the leaders of the Wendish Crusade. Albert is regarded as one of the greatest German statesmen of his era, partly due to his diplomacy which unified the conflicting worlds of the Saxons and Wends. Albert and Petrissa had allegedly come to a secret agreement over the succession, which in any event was challenged by the Slav Jaxa of Köpenick, whose religious identity as either a pagan or Christian is disputed in contemporary accounts.[23] Indeed, Jaxa's rebellion was supported by both Christian and pagan Wends, as well as Germans. He also received military support from the Poles, who saw the region as an essential buffer against the expansionist ambitions of Emperor Frederick Barbarossa. Bolstered by imperial military support, which led to the withdrawal of the Polish contingent of Jaxa's army, Albert seized Brandenburg and established his residence there as the centre of the new margraviate. The Slavic settlements of Brandenburg were reorganised into two independent towns, the old town emerging from the earlier foreign merchant's district and the new town founded on an adjacent, previously unoccupied site. As in the case of Havelberg, a cathedral was built within the former stronghold, completed in 1165. The Slavic temple dedicated to the three-headed deity Triglav was converted into a church and rededicated to the Blessed Virgin.

Albert, like Jaxa and Pribislav before him, issued coins depicting an armed warrior: an emphasis on military authority drawing on a common design from the coins of Magdeburg which represented St Maurice, the protector of the city and patron saint of the empire. Jaxa had included the Slavonic word for 'prince' (*kniaz*) on one of his bracteates, where he is shown in full armour carrying a spear and shield, alongside a palm branch which can be interpreted as a Christian symbol of eternal life. In contrast to earlier coins including those of Pribislav, Jaxa and Albert's coins were bracteates, that is they were composed of thinner and flimsier silver blanks with a single image beaten into them using an iron die, leaving a negative impression on the reverse. They became the popular form of coinage amongst territorial German lords in the twelfth and thirteenth centuries, and were very much a sign of their time.[24] Constrained by the decreasing availability of silver and produced for local rather than international markets, their proliferation also reflected the weakening of the emperor's authority and the rising power of the margraves. These were the defining features of the twelfth-century frontier, and similar minting practices would be adopted by crusading institutions during the conquests of the eastern Baltic. The adoption of coins was the first step in the development of a monetary system which accompanied the integration of Wendish lands into the empire. However, Wendish society would begin to profoundly change with the coming of foreign settlers.

MECHANISMS OF SETTLEMENT

Territorial gains at the fringes of the Holy Roman Empire would be followed by an influx of settlers, who came from both neighbouring lands and much further afield. Migration itself was nothing new, and the First Crusade was itself a mass movement of people from Western Europe to the Levant. By the twelfth century, the combination of rising populations, increasing prices of farmland and crops, and territories devastated by warfare that needed repopulating resulted in convoys of migrants becoming a familiar sight. Catholic lands in the Levant, Iberia and the southern Baltic became attractive destinations for Western migrants. Moreover, these were organised migrations, part of a successful strategy for manging newly acquired territories, including those conquered during crusading campaigns. In this respect, the crusader and the settler, if not one and the same person, became close associates.

The most powerful drivers of migration were imperial magnates seeking to sustain their own power bases, central to which was the procurement of new lands through marriage, inheritance, purchase or conquest. These magnates included both secular and ecclesiastical lords, but also monastic orders, particularly the Cistercians and Premonstratensians, who were regularly granted estates within newly acquired or annexed territories to manage and cultivate. They, in turn, invited migrants to work on their lands. This was not solely a top-down process: migrants were incentivised rather than coerced, and more often than not the choice to relocate was theirs. This approach to economically developing the land was not confined to the actions of German magnates, but was also widely adopted by neighbouring rulers in Poland, Bohemia and Hungary.[25] These migrants were often referred to in documents as *hospites* or 'guests', a term that was used for those invited to both towns and villages; the former became populated by merchants and artisans, whilst the countryside was settled by peasants and knightly families.

The term 'colonisation' is still widely used to describe the settlement of the conquered lands of the medieval Baltic Sea region by immigrants, who are framed as 'colonists', a legacy of nationalist and then more recent scholarship which has drawn comparisons with later colonial enterprises. The term implies political subordination to the 'mother country', which some have argued was not a feature of the expansion of medieval states, nor of the creation of new ones.[26] But its usage does draw attention to the relationship between the migrant and indigenous populations, which was an unequal one where power and privilege lay predominantly in the hands of the former group. Indeed, this was the case for the Wends in the twelfth century. The model for this was established in the previous century with the drainage of the Flemish coastal zone, where the local counts brought in migrants to reclaim the land by constructing canals and dykes. This necessitated the formulation of laws governing the settlements inhabited by the incoming peasants, which included both the migrants' own legal customs and the privileges they were granted. Dutch settlers would be invited in the early twelfth century by the Archbishop of Hamburg-Bremen to drain the wetlands of the lower Wester, and subsequently Dutch and Flemish migrants were invited by German lords to drain the marshes in the conquered Wendish territories. The privileges granted to them, which became codified as Flemish and Dutch settlement laws, were influential in formulating subsequent rural settlement legal structures, particularly the German Law, which became the gold standard for organising villages outside of the core imperial lands in Central and Eastern Europe.[27] These privileges included personal freedom (the right to leave at will), the hereditary ownership of the granted land with a fixed rent in agrarian produce or money, often with an initial period of exemption from payments, the right to self-governance and access to their own court, which meant immunity from local jurisdiction. Tithes would be payable to the Church as usual. Although these communities were ultimately answerable to their territorial overlords, in spirit they were co-operatives. From the twelfth century, marcher lords extending their territories into Wendish lands would also encourage large numbers of Saxon migrants to relocate, offering the same privileges and favourable conditions. Some would have come from their lords' existing estates, but it became increasingly necessary to rely on agents to recruit them from other parts of the empire.[28]

These middlemen, acting on behalf of an overlord – later referred to as 'locators' and the settlements as 'located', with *locatio* used in Latin charters and rendered into Low German as *setting* or *besettinge* – were crucial to the success of the colonising venture. Their additional incentives typically included a generous plot of land, double that of other peasants, and the hereditary position of village headman or *Schultheiss*. The locators took significant risks in organising and populating the settlement of unknown, potentially dangerous lands, but if successful the rewards were extensive and could be passed down to later generations. For large expanses of land requiring a significant level of recruitment, locators might band together to form consortia. Some even made a family business of it. They would travel to towns and villages to recruit settlers, promising a new life of opportunity. The famous story of the Pied Piper of Hamelin has been interpreted by some scholars as representing the activities of such a locator, highlighting the detrimental impact of these migrations. The Piper notoriously led away the children of Hamelin in 1284, echoing the fact that communities targeted by locators could be depleted of their younger generations – those strong and intrepid enough to uproot and resettle far from home.[29] But sometimes people relocated without any intermediaries. The preparation of a new village could take six months to a year, concluding with the careful subdivision of its associated fields into units which had been specified in the location privileges. These defined the amount of land that could be ploughed, and so located settlements in the countryside became the economic engines of the reorganised marches.[30]

This was clearly noted by the chronicler Helmold when describing Albert the Bear's policy of encouraging migrants, including Dutch and Flemish settlers, to relocate to Brandenburg. This impacted not only on the growth of towns, villages and the drainage of the marshlands, but also on bolstering the presence of Christianity:

> The bishopric of Brandenburg, and likewise that of Havelberg, was greatly strengthened by the coming of the foreigners, because the churches multiplied and the income from the tithes grew enormously.[31]

Further west, between the northernmost stretch of the Elbe and the Danevirke, the same process is evident in the lands claimed by the dukes of Saxony, the counts of Holstein and the Danish kings. In north-eastern Holstein, Count Adolf's army had destroyed the Slavic stronghold on the island of Olsborg in Lake Plön in 1139 and a couple of decades later, together with Bishop Gerold, invested in shifting the trading focus to the mainland where a town was founded at Plön. This decision may have been prompted by rising water levels in the wetlands as the climate became increasingly wetter, resulting in the shrinkage of the region's lacustrine islands. According to Helmold, the Wendish population in the surrounding countryside which had boomed from the tenth century with the establishment of the centre at Olsborg, declined and eventually disappeared, whilst Saxon migrants came in and settled in their place. However, their impact would not become significant until the mid-thirteenth century, when the regional pollen record attests to large-scale woodland clearance and expanding cultivation.[32]

Henry the Lion subsequently continued the process, refounding the episcopal see of Ratzeburg in 1154 and relocating the bishopric of Oldenburg to Lübeck in 1160, as well as encouraging Saxon migrants to settle in the region. As a result, the religious landscape dramatically transformed. Before the twelfth century, there were only four churches and two monasteries precariously located in Holstein, in contrast to the much higher density in neighbouring Danish and Saxon regions. By the 1170s, numerous parish churches had been built here, part of a general pattern across the northern marches.[33] They are associated with the introduction of burial grounds in the centres of settlements, with graves containing few if any artefacts.[34]

This transformation of the religious elements of Wendish lands cannot be untangled from its economic counterpart; in fact, both can be understood as superimposed layers of a new cultural landscape. In his description of the flourishing of Brandenburg and Havelberg quoted above, Helmold's detail about tithe income is highly significant, as it reflects the economic incentive for settlement which appealed to both German and Wendish magnates alike. Key to this was the cultivation of land, and the differences in farming practices between Wendish and Saxon, Danish and Dutch peasants. The Wends used ards for ploughing – these were light, with ploughshares that loosened the top of the soil, all that was required to meet the needs of a relatively less dense population. In contrast, peasants coming in from neighbouring western regions used a heavier plough which included a mouldboard and coulter. The latter, a vertical cutting blade positioned in front, loosened the soil which the mouldboard lifted and turned over, enabling deeper tillage. This meant that heavier, more fertile soils could be ploughed, and at a faster rate. The end result was larger fields and a marked increase in cultivated produce. The adoption of the mouldboard in north-western Europe was once thought to have triggered an agricultural revolution at the start of the second millennium. In fact, archaeologists have demonstrated this was a much slower and more varied process. In parts of Denmark, for example, the mouldboard plough was already being used as early as the third century AD. In England, its use as a rare high-status tool is evident only from the seventh century. Recent research also suggests that Carolingian northern France, once thought to be characterised by intensive crop rotation, saw more regional diversity in agricultural practices.[35]

Aside from archaeological finds of ploughshares, the tell-tale signs of the heavy plough are indicated by deep ridged furrows in the fields, a smaller number of grain species being identified in excavations of settlements and evidence for crop rotation. At the same time, there is a marked increase in cultivated species and deforestation in regional pollen records. Between the Oder and Vistula, this suite of evidence begins to appear later than in neighbouring German and Danish regions. It coincides with the documented presence of German settlers, who not only disseminated the use of the heavy plough, but also a new economic template for maximising produce from the land. This was represented by the new units of land allocated to villages that were much larger than those given to the Wends. Coupled with the use of the heavy plough, it enabled a higher return on grain for the landowner and, importantly, for the Church in terms of tithes – a tenth of the produce.

Settlements organised under German laws were therefore much more profitable and attractive to elite institutions, whether they were German or Wendish. This, more than any other motive, drove their proliferation. Payment of taxes and tithes prompted the development of a surplus, one that was managed with the construction of mills. These were expensive to build and became important and closely regulated economic structures. The reorganisation of estate ownership and agricultural land resulted in profound changes in Wendish social structures. Some historians have called this a 'feudal revolution', which saw the transformation of rural society based on free peasants to one dominated by a landed aristocracy. Both migrant and indigenous populations must have regarded each other as culturally and even religiously distinct, and, in contrast to the incomers perceived by the new authorities as partners in settlement, Wendish peasants were rarely granted comparable privileges and were often viewed as a troublesome, subject population to be controlled. This *was* colonisation.

URBANISING THE MARCHES

Almost all the Wendish territories between the Oder and Elbe would eventually be incorporated into the Holy Roman Empire, but Danish political interests in the region did not wane. In the late 1180s, King Canute VI declared himself 'King of the Slavs', making a direct claim to Wendish lands down to the Elbe and challenging the rule of the German marcher lords. His policy of territorial expansion was promoted by his heirs and in the early thirteenth century Valdemar II would temporarily seize Holstein after defeating its count, Adolf III, in battle. In 1216, the Danes would go on to capture Hamburg, and the German emperor even acknowledged Danish lordship over the Wendish territories. This was short-lived and, after a decade, Holstein was reincorporated back into the empire. Only the Wendish rulers of the island of Rügen remained vassals of Denmark.

As territories were reorganised following either the conquest or the acquisition of land, changes on the ground were driven by both rural and urban settlers.[36] The establishment of planned towns resulted in the abandonment of several Wendish centres, which gradually became overgrown earthworks. In some cases, the new towns directly replaced the old, as evident from a number of archaeological investigations demonstrating continuity in their locations. New or reorganised towns were founded with similar principles to those used for settling the countryside. Their privileges attracted foreign merchants and artisans, as well as indigenous Wends who quickly adopted urban lifestyles, albeit with economic inequality often split along ethnic lines. Some migrants who populated towns were also affluent peasants, with a stake in the ownership of land in the surrounding countryside.[37] With the settlers came new administrative languages – Latin and Low German – and a different type of architecture consisting of timber-framed houses with stone foundations, later referred to in German as *Ständerhäuser*.[38] The imported architectural fashion prevailed and was gradually adopted by the indigenous population. The construction of dwellings built from cross-logs in the so-called 'blockhouse' style, prevalent in earlier Slavic settlements, ended. The settlers also brought with them new technologies, customs and, of course, religion.

Perhaps the best-known example of the reworking of a Slavic centre is Lübeck, a town which would become a widely copied template for urbanism and play a pivotal role in the north European crusading movement.[39] Lübeck is, without doubt, one of the most archaeologically researched towns in Germany.[40] The preservation of the timber structures of the earliest phases of the town is remarkable and has given the city its fabled reputation amongst urban archaeologists; the oldest wooden cellars have been dated by dendrochronology to circa 1166. Its historic centre was designated a World Heritage Site by UNESCO in 1987 for its exceptionally preserved merchant houses, warehouses, churches and civic buildings, largely dating to the fifteenth and sixteenth centuries. During the Second World War, Lübeck was targeted by British bombers, most notably in 1942 during one of the first major air raids on a German civilian centre. Many historical structures were heavily damaged or destroyed, but large parts of the medieval city layout remained intact or repairable, and later reconstruction was meticulous. The preserved street plan is even earlier than its iconic brick buildings, reflecting the new paradigm of urban planning introduced in the mid-twelfth century that would influence the design of towns in Central and Eastern Europe for centuries to come.

Lübeck was founded, along with several other planned towns constructed on the lands of the Wends in the twelfth century, by the deliberate actions of magnates. The first of these was Adolf II, Count of Schauenburg and Holstein, who established the settlement in 1143, a few miles south of the former Slavic town of Liubice (referred to as 'Old Lübeck'), abandoned five years earlier. Archaeologists have discovered the peninsula of the later town already had sporadic traces of Slavic occupation before the establishment of the new urban settlement. These were largely focused on the area of what became the castle, first reported by the chronicler Helmold in 1147. Strategically located in the narrow corridor linking the peninsula to the mainland, its earlier defences were rebuilt almost certainly on Adolf's orders, and new timber buildings were erected. Here there is evidence for the continuity of earlier architectural forms, specifically wattle and daub houses and 'blockhouses', as well as log-and-sill-beam constructions with sunken cellars representing a composite of architectural traditions. At this time, at least a third of the peninsula was covered by peaty marshes liable to flooding and therefore unsuitable for occupation. But all this would change.

In 1158, Adolf had to relinquish the stronghold to Henry the Lion. Henry's importance is difficult to exaggerate: he accumulated vast amounts of land through a combination of military campaigns and diplomacy and was a major player in imperial politics, supporting and later clashing with Emperor Frederick Barbarossa. In 1147, he had been one of the leading participants in the crusade against the Wends. Within a couple of years of acquiring Lübeck, Henry established a bishopric there, relocated from Oldenburg. He encouraged Saxon settlers to move in to augment the Wendish population still clinging to their old religion. Helmold describes how the bishop spoke to the local Slavs in the marketplace and exhorted them to renounce their idols, to desist from killing Christians and embrace the true God.[41] Henry's authority over the region was secured with strongholds which still litter the countryside in the form of overgrown earthen mounds. At the time of their use in the twelfth century these mounds would have been topped with timber fortifications – the residences of German knights and Slavic vassals who enforced ducal authority in their assigned territories. The Wendish population remained but quickly adopted the customs of the conquerors, including the new kitchenware that flooded local markets as potters moved in and set up kilns firing ceramics at a much higher temperature.

Just as Wendish potters had influenced southern Scandinavian ceramic technology in the eleventh and twelfth centuries, so German artisans would come to dominate the production of ordinary cooking vessels across swathes of the southern Baltic in the thirteenth century.[42] The dominant form that was widely disseminated has been labelled 'greyware' because of its colour, and whilst this may conjure up an image of drab mass-produced pots, their proliferation is one of the clearest indicators of the cultural changes that swept across the frontier. One of the best examples of such a kiln from the Margraviate of Brandenburg was discovered at Göttin, 5 kilometres south of Brandenburg's new town. The settlement here dated from the tenth century, but the new pottery began to be produced from the late twelfth century. The village most likely provided Brandenburg with ceramic vessels, as similar potsherds with the same fabric composition were also found there. The nationalist archaeologist Gustaf Kossina had notoriously promoted the idea of German settlers introducing superior technology and aesthetics to the Slavs, and archaeologists continue to attach ethnic significance to contrasting styles of pottery in the southern Baltic, but with the recognition that technologies can be adopted without population replacements, that are not exclusively tied to a single group, and having abandoned notions of cultural superiority.[43] Greyware vessels are found across the region at Wendish settlements dating to the twelfth century, including the town refounded by Henry.

Archaeologists have discovered that Henry's town was established as a planned settlement in the area between the historic market and the harbour — the linear streets leading down to the waterfront becoming fossilised in the later urban landscape. Indeed, the new town was founded with trade in mind as Henry offered privileges to new settlers, granted Scandinavian and Rus' merchants free access to trade, and Gotlandic merchants in particular were provided with attractive regulatory conditions in a charter. The harbour was upgraded to accommodate cogs, a new type of ship that were revolutionising the movement of people and commodities across the sea. Due to their steep bows, cogs required a draught (the distance between the waterline and the keel) of up to a metre to dock. With the increased volume in trade, and the construction of bigger ships designed to hold more cargo, Lübeck's engineers rose to the challenge and extended the quay out into the river to accommodate ships with a draught of up to 2 metres.

The impact on the cityscape was completely transformative. In the last quarter of the twelfth century, the quality and density of housing dramatically improved — the old posthole-and-log construction dwellings became largely replaced by expansive, multi-storeyed, fully timber-framed buildings with substantial basements for storage. Along with shifts in ceramic technology, these architectural trends have been associated with the influx of migrant artisans and merchants.[44] Some of these timbers, sturdy oak planks, had been shipped in from the eastern side of the Baltic. They represent the earliest known traces of a north European trade in timber that would intensify in the centuries to come, in part to meet the needs of the flourishing ship-building industry which saw the construction of increasingly larger cogs. Alongside merchants, there is archaeological evidence for the presence of artisans producing tools, vessels and containers for cooking and dining, clothing and game pieces, butchers, fishmongers, millers and grocers provisioning the growing population, and of course a burgeoning construction industry providing work for carpenters, sawyers and masons.

Henry the Lion remained dedicated to the crusading cause. In 1172, he travelled to the Holy Land as a pilgrim and met with the Templars and Hospitallers. But after failing to support the Emperor Barbarossa in his territorial ambitions in Lombardy, Henry was stripped of his estates and title and exiled. He would seek to take back his lands by force in subsequent years, but his role in shaping Lübeck was over. Under the emperor's rule, the city was granted the right to appoint a council. This consisted of some nobles, but largely merchants, reinforcing the focus on commerce. They were, for all intents and purposes, a new kind of nobility, and indeed adopted many of the recognised trappings of power: a grandiose hall was constructed for their meetings with an adjoining chapel. This was both a practical space and a symbol of civic authority. In the first decades of the thirteenth century, the first brick buildings with vaulted cellars were constructed, at which point this became the building material of choice. It was far more durable, especially with recurring fires that could devastate towns largely constructed of timber. Not everyone could afford the upgrade, of course, and wooden buildings continued to be a feature of the city. But as the town's merchants prospered with the increasing volume of commerce, the density of brick buildings increased. Brick walls were added around the town in the 1180s but, as the city grew, these had to be dismantled and a new circuit was built in 1217. At this time the marshes surrounding the peninsula were drained and the land reclaimed, enlarging the town's inhabitable area by some 50 per cent and prompting the walls to be rebuilt yet again by the end of the century. Some central authority drove this enterprise, perhaps the town council or even the Danish king. As with the rest of the northern marches, the city was at the frontier with the expanding Danish realm and had come under King Valdemar's control in 1216, although his hold over the region barely lasted a decade.

The growth of new towns in the marches had a knock-on effect on the countryside. Village economies became increasingly tied to grain production or livestock rearing for urban markets.[45] The growing demand for grain was met by the intensified exploitation of larger fields, facilitated by the new, heavier ploughs. From the mid-thirteenth century, enough of a grain surplus was produced in Brandenburg that it began to be shipped out to Flanders and England. But this was not the case everywhere and some Wendish communities continued to rely on traditional methods of farming. The Wends themselves were not often physically replaced by incoming migrants, whose numbers were comparatively limited, and they retained a distinct identity.[46] Some indigenous power structures clearly endured as Wendish nobles continue to be mentioned in written sources into the fourteenth century, and presumably the social dynamics of village communities were also maintained. Both Germans and Wends had separate legal systems and, where disputes involved both, the newly introduced German laws specified exactly how these would be dealt with and even which language was to be used. Select communities were even initially exempt from tithes. This has cast descriptions of the clearance or decline of Wendish communities in a sinister light, for there was a clear financial incentive to replace them with migrant settlers whose lands would be subject to tithes. In some regions, additional taxes were nonetheless extracted from Wendish communities, as evident in Henry the Lion's edicts which specified sums for the upkeep of parish priests.[47]

During the thirteenth century, Wends became subject to the same judicial procedures as Germans, a reflection of increasing cultural assimilation – Germanisation. This term is widely used by scholars to describe the adoption of German cultural traits by the Wendish population, including language, customs, personal names and material culture. But what did it mean to be German? First and foremost, this was a political identity. East Francia, the eastern part of the Carolingian Empire, had been recast as the Kingdom of Germany (Regnum Teutonicum, a term adopted from Classical writers) and the revived title of 'Emperor of the Romans', bestowed upon Charlemagne, was subsequently granted to the German king Otto in 962, after which both titles were typically held together into the eighteenth century. Not all kings of Germany held the imperial title: some died before being elected, others were never chosen for election. There were also times when there were multiple claimants to the imperial title, leading to rival emperors or anti-kings. What became later referred to as the Holy Roman Empire was not a single nation with a sense of shared destiny, but reflected the relationship between the ruler and those people considered to be their subjects within a territory with fluctuating boundaries. The empire itself was a dynamic mosaic composed of nested polities inhabited by different populations, with its outer borders expanding even as the overarching authority of the emperor gradually diminished over time. This expansion incorporated the Wends in the north, but also other Slavic groups like the Czechs in Bohemia and the Carantanians in Carinthia, what is today southern Austria and northern Slovenia.

The empire's political decentralisation resulted in the emergence of four or five varieties of spoken German, and in written form these became standardised within specific regions. In the Baltic, Low German (derived from Old Saxon) was the prevalent form and connected migrant communities across the sea. In the Middle Ages, regional identity was therefore more pronounced than any sense of shared national feeling. Whilst the proliferation of the printing press in the sixteenth century led to further linguistic standardisation, the form of German used by the educated classes would not be lauded as a 'national language' until the seventeenth and eighteenth centuries, whilst a German 'national consciousness' was not promoted until the Napoleonic Wars.[48] Language certainly does become increasingly relevant as an identifier during the time of the Baltic Crusades, but there is no evidence for a co-ordinated 'German agenda' of eastward colonisation in the Middle Ages and certainly not one targeting specific ethnicities in a war of cultural superiority or economic aggression. Instead, the eastward movement of German migrants should be understood as driven by the varying agendas of powerful secular and religious elites. These agendas twinned territorial conquest with the expansion of Christianity. In the process, German cultural traits were variously disseminated, adopted, transformed, ignored or resisted. Migrant communities, in turn, developed their own, distinct, regional identities.

By the fifteenth century, there are fewer references to Slavic villages in the northern margraviates, but Wendish communities were still noticeably present. In Lower Lusatia, for example, Wends constituted just over 50 per cent of the population in the mid-fifteenth century. A hundred years later, that figure was reduced to just over a third, coinciding with the proliferation of German texts and increasing literacy.[49] But even then, evidence for Wendish interpreters in towns indicates the indigenous language continued to thrive. Traces survived in place names and personal names which retained Slavic elements, but also within part of the population. The Western Slavic ethnic group residing today in eastern Germany, particularly in the regions of historical Lusatia (spanning parts of Saxony and Brandenburg), traces its ancestry back to the Wends. We will pick up their story again later.

TERRITORIAL OR SPIRITUAL CONQUEST?

In the decades after the end of the Second World War, the narrative regarding the Germanisation and subjugation of the Wends shifted, especially in the German Democratic Republic. The Nazi regime's atrocities led to a greater sensitivity toward issues of imperialism, racism and the oppression of minorities. At the same time, a Pan-Slavic agenda promoted by Soviet Russia influenced the framing of historical events. Cast in this light, the medieval expansion of Germans into Wendish lands was rebranded as an oppressive feudal process which resulted in ethnic and cultural destruction. Today, a less brutal interpretation of the incorporation of Wendish lands into Latin Christendom is generally accepted. But as we have seen, there is a valid argument to be made for describing the settlement of these territories as a form of colonisation, which brought with it cultural and economic dominance. In this light, Christianity, embedded into the identity of the conquering regime, can in turn be perceived as a colonial religion. Crusading with the aim of forcibly converting pagans, once officially sanctioned by the papacy, was then readily mapped onto the rapid expansion into Wendish lands in the second half of the twelfth century. Yet the origins of this alliance between Church and State in the expansion of the Christian *imperium* can be traced back to the Ottonians and Carolingians.

German, Polish and Danish territorial conquests (as well as conflicts between Wendish rulers), resulted in the incremental transformation of the cultural landscape at this time, with the destruction of Wendish strongholds and their replacement by a smaller number of fortified residences associated with the new authorities. This was accompanied by the establishment of planned or reorganised towns and numerous villages with new field systems.[50] In some areas the Wendish population was displaced, but in others it remained substantial and visible. Not everything was achieved through military conquest: Wendish princes also chose to accept German overlordship along with Christianity out of political expediency. Dynastic interests came to the fore, for both German and Wendish rulers. Regime change reconfigured the region's political identity. By the start of the fourteenth century, the western stretches of the former Nordmark (Northern March) were now referred to as the Altmark (Old March), with the new frontier east of the Oder River defined as the Neumark, and the lands in-between as the Mittelmark (Middle March). Long after these lands stopped functioning as borders, their names continued to preserve this memory.

Even if we accept political motivations as the key drivers of these conquests, or the Wendish Crusade itself, this territorial expansion became inextricably linked with missionary activity, which its proponents argued was necessary to save the souls of the colonised, and which was met with both enthusiastic acceptance of the new faith or stubborn resistance that was eventually overcome. Moreover, from the Ottonian conquests through to the final victories of the margraves against the Wends, the promotion of the cult of St Maurice is ever present, centred on the missionary powerhouse of Magdeburg. Pagan religious sites were destroyed and, in some cases, replaced with churches. There is a tone of Christian triumphalism in the descriptions of these events, and this is also occasionally visible in the material traces of the spiritual conquest. In the choir of Lehnin Abbey in Brandenburg, founded by the Cistercians in the late twelfth century, an ancient oak stump was embedded into the brick steps leading up to the altar. Here, the preservation and display of the stump – most likely the remains of a felled sacred tree strategically placed so that it could be regularly trodden underfoot – comes across as a very clear statement of the victory over Wendish heathenism. This abbey's purpose was made clear in its foundational directives, which included the eradication of 'the Slavs, the heathens, and all enemies of the cross of Christ'.[51] Other sacred trees were not felled but were marked with crosses, designating the presence of the new religion in the landscape.[52]

The dioceses sketched out in previous centuries gradually solidified and newly constructed or enlarged cathedrals became the lynchpins of the revamped sacred landscape. But the process of religious transformation was slow and uneven, nor was the end result some pristine model of Catholicism that everyone adhered to. At the turn of the thirteenth century, a priest in Holstein wrote down the visions described to him by Godskalk, a local peasant. They speak of the blended religious world of the frontier, with a vivid description of an otherworld that was not in tune with the Church's teachings on the afterlife. By this time, not all the Wendish lands had been incorporated into Christendom. In the expanding Polish and Scandinavian Christian realms, the embrace of crusading ideology would not only invigorate ambitions to seize the remaining pagan Wendish lands, but also those of groups residing on the eastern side of the Baltic Sea.

CHAPTER 3

PRECARIOUS FRONTIERS
From the Oder to the Vistula

> ... it [Poland] has as neighbours three most savage nations of pagan barbarians, Selencia, Pomerania, and Prussia, and the duke of the Poles is constantly at war with these countries, fighting to convert them to the faith. But neither has the sword of preaching been able to sway their hearts from faithlessness, nor the sword at their throats wipe out this generation of vipers in its entirety.
>
> *The Deeds of the Princes of the Poles*, Gallus Anonymous[1]

REVIVING CHRISTIANITY IN POMERANIA

The Polish city of Szczecin in Western Pomerania is one of the largest in the country. Rebuilt after the Second World War, it has become a major cultural centre and an increasingly popular tourist destination. Both the city and region's branding are dominated by a red griffin derived from the heraldic emblem of Szczecin's historical ruling dynasty, who also adopted it for their family name from the twelfth century. In the Middle Ages, the Griffins (Polish Gryfici) were the de facto power in a frontier region where the Pomeranians, the easternmost group of Slavic Wends, were caught between the political spheres of Poland, Denmark and the Holy Roman Empire, and where the Polish and German churches competed for supremacy, whilst simultaneously aiming to combat indigenous paganism. These various influences have been connected with the sporadic presence of Christians in Pomerania already in the ninth century.² In the last few decades of the tenth century, Mieszko's armies had swept into the region and nominally established the authority of the rising Piast state. Pomerania's centres had subsequently rebelled against Polish rule, and it was only under the leadership of Boleslaus III 'Wrymouth' (controlling the overlordship of Poland between 1107 and 1138) that Piast control was more visibly asserted. Along with the conquest of Wendish lands by German marcher lords and the territorial reorganisation that followed, this finally broke apart the Lutici federation which had united the peoples of Western Pomerania against their Christian overlords.

Boleslaus's military campaigns, which began in 1109, would be framed as a protracted holy war, tying the Piasts to the crusading movement only a decade after the storming of Jerusalem. In his history of Polish rulers, written a few years after Boleslaus's invasion, the chronicler Gallus presented the campaigns as righteous wars with divine support characterised by the intervention of saints. Both the conversion and destruction of Pomeranian pagans were presented as laudable outcomes, analogous to the actions of crusaders during the First Crusade.³ Boleslaus maintained close links with the Danish king Niels who was keen on crusading against the Wends, and perhaps Danish and Polish attacks on Pomerania were even co-ordinated. Following a well-established precedent, Boleslaus would use religious conversion as a means of securing political submission, sponsoring a mission by Otto, the Bishop of Bamberg, to ensure the public evangelisation – and loyalty – of the Pomeranian elites. There was some urgency to this as he intended to lay spiritual claim to the region before the Archbishop of Magdeburg could. The earliest accounts of Otto's life, written in the decades after his death in 1139, provide vivid accounts of the campaigns and describe how the groundwork for subsequent missionary activity was laid. Polish forces destroyed towns and massacred civilians to essentially terrorise the Pomeranians into submission but also, equally importantly, to ensure the allegiance of their leaders who could then host and protect missionaries.⁴ Whilst written sources glorifying Boleslaus's holy wars contain invaluable details of how the religious and political struggle played out through the eyes of clerics, archaeologists have also shed important light on the nature and tempo of cultural change associated with the volatile politics of this frontier.[5]

Archaeological excavations in the region had already taken place in the nineteenth and early twentieth centuries, but the allocation of parts of previously German-held Western Pomerania to Poland in 1945 heralded a new era of research. This was driven by a government-sponsored programme on the origins of the Polish state, an ideological exercise in post-war national reconstruction which included consolidating the country's historical links with what became known as the 'Recovered Territories'. The programme would culminate with celebrations in 1966 marking a thousand years of the Polish state, as well as the resilience of the Polish nation in the face of external aggressors. As part of the process of restoring the management of heritage in the war-torn territories, archaeologist Tadeusz Wieczorowski arrived in Szczecin in 1946 as a representative of the state museum in Warsaw, and became the director of the former town museum, now rebranded as the Museum of Western Pomerania. He spearheaded efforts to uncover traces of the region's Slavic history, which led to excavations in the other early medieval centres in the region with historical connections to the Piast state alongside Szczecin – Wolin, Kołobrzeg and Kamień Pomorski.[6] The excavations funded by the Millennium of the Polish State programme, with its clear political agenda, focused on the strongholds in these towns and their associated settlements. In the process, they uncovered new evidence for their origins and development. This lay the foundations for more critical research, even as this fed the myths endorsed by the post-war Polish state which connected the 'Recovered Territories' with the Piast conquests.[7]

More recent excavations, alongside critical reappraisals of the written sources, have provided a more nuanced picture of how Pomerania was gradually incorporated into Latin Christendom over the course of the twelfth century. The region was split into two duchies, each run by powerful local dynasties based in the largest towns. Whereas Western Pomerania's story then became one of a complex frontier between jostling Catholic states, Eastern Pomerania, also known as Pomerelia, became embroiled with a very different borderland. To the east of the Vistula lay the lands of the pagan Prussians, where the Piasts' favoured saint, Adalbert, had been martyred. From the tenth century, Pomeranian settlers had crossed the floodplain of the Vistula and established settlements in a region named Pomesania, coexisting alongside Prussian communities. This had led to the region's Latin moniker 'Terra Pacifica' or 'Land of Peace', where flourishing trade was centred on the emporium of Truso. Further up the Vistula, the territorial ambitions of Masovia's dukes were also accompanied by the establishment of new settlements in closer proximity to Prussian lands. But the Piasts had neither forgotten nor forgiven the pagans. Prussia was *'terram satis barbaram'*, a barbarous land, where Polish armies sought to repeat their earlier successes in Pomerania – subdue the pagans with the sword before preaching to them the word of God.[8] In this, they failed. Prussian armies, in turn, and for different reasons, would cross into Masovia and Pomerelia, killing, looting and enslaving. By the early thirteenth century, these Vistula borderlands had become the vulnerable edge of Catholic Christendom, preparing the stage for the onslaught to come.

The story of the two northern frontiers of Piast Poland is therefore tied to the gradual adoption of crusading culture in the Baltic, when in the twelfth and early thirteenth centuries they became important settings for the broader Catholic struggle against paganism.

CONQUEST AND CULTURAL CHANGE IN WESTERN POMERANIA: AN URBAN BIOGRAPHY

In Western Pomerania, the largest settlements which can be characterised as early towns emerged and prospered in the late Viking Age. They benefited from the natural advantages of their locations, which had direct access to the trade routes connecting the ports around the Baltic littoral. Szczecin, first named in Latin sources as Sedinum or Stetinum and in German as Stettin, lay on the west bank of the Oder river which fed into a nearby lake and vast lagoon connected with the sea.[9] On the northern side of the lagoon was Wolin, situated on an island in the Dziwna river and further up the coast was another Wendish centre located on the Parseta river, its Latinised name Colobrega eventually rendered as German Kolberg and Polish Kołobrzeg. By the twelfth century these were impressive towns with vibrant communities of artisans and merchants, the latter forming powerful oligarchies whose commercial influence gave them political authority. Much like their counterparts in the western Wendish regions, groups of pagan priests who maintained the region's shrines also wielded significant influence from these centres.

Over the course of the twelfth century, Western Pomerania was transformed by conquest accompanied by regime change and missionary activity. As with the gradual incorporation of the northern marches into the empire, scholars have characterised this as the reorganisation of Pomeranian society into a 'feudal' structure under the Piasts. A new dynasty of indigenous rulers emerged to replace the urban oligarchies – the Griffins. It was their acceptance of the new political order, and the religious allegiance that went with it, which eventually transformed life for indigenous Pomeranians. This acceptance was not simply replacing one religion with another, swapping the popular three-headed Slavic deity Triglav for Christ. Pomeranian pagan religion was closely connected with social identity, with ancestral laws, ways of life as well as a profound relationship with the land, and its abandonment was nothing less than a cultural revolution.[10]

The story of Western Pomerania's transformation can be told through the biography of the region's ducal seat, Szczecin. Decades of excavations in the town have revealed layer upon layer of timber buildings and roads, repeatedly built up, cleared and rebuilt. They tell a story of enduring resilience in the face of recurring catastrophes. The earliest settlement, established in the second half of the eighth century, was situated on the hill overlooking the Oder. On the highest part of the hill, an area segregated by a shallow ditch from the surrounding spread of wattle-work houses with sunken floors has been identified as the first temple to Triglav, the largest and most lavishly decorated of the four pagan shrines in the town mentioned by Otto's biographers in the twelfth century. A settlement was also established at the foot of the hill near the river, with many of its inhabitants engaged in farming and fishing.[11] A hundred years later, this had developed into a densely packed urban centre with timber-paved streets, enclosed by fortifications on its upland side. It became populated by artisans, particularly blacksmiths and glass makers as well as merchants. With the establishment of a new settlement between the hill and river in the first half of the tenth century, a port developed alongside it and trade flourished. Judging by the provenance of some of the traded artefacts, the rising fortunes of the town reflected trading connections with the emerging Piast state to the south. A share of the wealth generated by trade ended up in the hands of the priests of Triglav, although some of this was also derived from war spoils, of which a proportion would customarily be given to the temple. Within a few decades, the hill was fortified with ramparts, marking the presence of a more consolidated authority visibly connected with Triglav's shrine, which remained segregated from the rest of the hillside settlement. When the threat from the Piasts became more apparent, additional fortifications were constructed around the settlement at the foot of the hill.

These investments in the town's defences did not stop the region of the Lower Oder falling under Piast control in the late 960s. The stronghold in Szczecin was destroyed and then rebuilt by the new regime. The town's strategic location was clearly recognised, as what followed the conquest was an economic boom: the settlement around the river was reorganised, trade intensified, particularly with Scandinavian regions, and an influx of Polish coins is evident in the town's archaeological record. What of Christianity? It would take a few decades before a bishopric with jurisdiction over the newly formed Pomeranian diocese was established in Kolberg in 1000, during the same congress where the German emperor laid the bones of Adalbert to rest in Gniezno. A Saxon, Reinbern, was appointed bishop and symbolically poured holy oil and water into the sea to mark the baptism of Pomerania. He then set about destroying pagan sanctuaries, eventually provoking a rebellion that drove out the Christian authorities. Reinbern would never return, and an ongoing conflict between Poland and the empire, which dragged on until 1018, saw Piast influence wane in Western Pomerania. In Szczecin, as in the other regional centres, the town's governance came to rest in the hands of an urban oligarchy. There is evidence for significant investment in infrastructure from the mid-eleventh century and, with the settlement spilling out onto the Oder's floodplain, a dyke was constructed to protect the town from flooding. By the end of the 1080s, the northern part of the town was encircled with a defensive rampart, effectively forming a separate, fortified district. Meanwhile the area of the stronghold saw the construction of massive horizontal log buildings, in stark contrast to the smaller wattle-work houses in the rest of the town, reflecting the power of the new elite. The shrine next to the stronghold also came back into use, with Christianity evidently rejected by Szczecin's rulers.

In the second quarter of the twelfth century the stronghold's rampart, along with many of the buildings on the hill, including the shrine, were destroyed by fire. These archaeological traces of the destruction of Szczecin's elite settlement can be connected with the invasion and occupation of the region by Boleslaus's army. The town appears to have been depopulated for a time, but soon began to prosper again as a commercial centre, as evident from large numbers of imported commodities, as well as quantities of balance weights and scales – the hallmarks of merchants and a reflection of the intensity of trade. Despite the destruction of Triglav's shrine, paganism appears to have remained entrenched in the population and perhaps with it a certain reluctance to accept Polish rule. In 1124–5 and 1128, Otto of Bamberg and his entourage of clerics led missions to several of the towns of Western Pomerania, including Szczecin. They received full co-operation from the most powerful indigenous leader in the region, Wartislaw, the progenitor of the ruling Griffin family and, following a period in Saxon captivity, an alleged convert to Christianity. Wartislaw had opposed Polish rule, but his forces were defeated at the decisive battle of Naklo in 1109. Swearing allegiance to Boleslaus, he agreed to help Christianise the region and so when the missionaries eventually came, they were welcomed and provided with an armed escort. The recent discovery of a carved stone in the village of Klotzow, on the edge of the Szczecin Lagoon in north-eastern Germany, has been connected with Otto's mission. The carving appears to depict the figure of a Christian bishop – perhaps even Otto himself – and has been dated to the twelfth century.

Although Otto's biographers characteristically describe him as baptising thousands in dramatic episodes of instant conversion, as well as removing idols and destroying pagan sanctuaries, judging by all accounts his initial efforts to convert the population were not very successful. The failure to train local Pomeranians as clergy meant that pastoral provision for new converts remained limited, and the ongoing power struggle between the archbishops of Magdeburg and Gniezno for spiritual hegemony over Pomerania stifled any sustained investment in evangelising indigenous communities, especially beyond the region's few towns. Nonetheless, the inhabitants of Szczecin, reeling from the carnage of the Polish assault and under the threat of further military action, were obliged to abandon their pagan idols and build churches – at the very least out of political pragmatism. As such, a church was constructed on top of Triglav's hill and dedicated to St Adalbert, the patron of the Piasts and a clear symbol of the new regime.[12] In the end, Otto was successful in undermining and eventually crippling the power of the pagan priesthood in Western Pomerania, paving the way for its replacement with a Christian equivalent. In this respect, the 1120s were a turning point in Pomerania's history. Traces of public pagan religious activity begin to vanish from the archaeological record across the region at this time. Finds of animal remains and anthropomorphic figures in lakes – interpreted as ritual acts – are dated to no later than the twelfth century, and the deposition of whole horses in Pomeranian cemeteries also ceased at this time, with the abandonment of public animal sacrifice marking a major cultural shift.[13]

The inhumation burial rite had already become prevalent in the region in the ninth century, coinciding with the beginnings of Scandinavian settlement in Pomerania, although cremations continued into the eleventh century and there were many instances where both rites were practised in the same cemeteries. Most animal bone deposits found by archaeologists are associated with cremation burials and many represent debris left over from feasts or offerings by the graveside. Fragments of ceramics found in cemetery excavations have been connected with this, although they may have also played a role in apotropaic practices associated with the dead.[14] Visibly pagan mortuary practices were targeted by missionaries. In Otto's biography, written by the monk Ebo in the mid-twelfth century, the bishop forbade Pomeranian converts to bury their dead with those of pagans in woods or fields and to place sticks on their graves, which may have been connected to beliefs concerning the soul. Indeed, over the course of the twelfth century, cremation was abandoned and burials became standardised in terms of their character and location, as cemeteries attached to churches replaced the traditional places for internment. Yet the custom of eating meals within cemeteries continued in Pomerania and was documented in detail in the sixteenth century. Contemporary accounts described how it was believed the dead would eat any leftovers placed in the grave. The practice lingered even as its original function faded from memory, and in the southern part of the region authorities fought to suppress it even in the early twentieth century.

More concerted efforts to establish Christianity came when Wartislaw's brother, Ratibor, transformed Szczecin from an urban republic into the centre of the West Pomeranian duchy. The region's location meant that it remained contested between competing Christian powers throughout the twelfth century. Boleslaus paid tribute to the German emperor who nominally controlled Western Pomerania, with the result that the Griffins essentially became autonomous rulers. As with the conquered Wendish lands further west, it was not unusual for marcher lords to govern frontiers which lay at the fringes of central political control. Wartislaw adopted Polish legal, military and judicial customs, but his descendants would also invite German settlers and introduce practices from the empire. A further obstacle which frustrated external control over the region came with the re-established Pomeranian diocese in 1140, whose independence from both Magdeburg and Gniezno was formally granted by the pope a few decades later. This ultimately made its bishops powerful rulers in their own right, and they would come to wield secular power over several towns from the thirteenth century. The political struggle was acutely visible during the Wendish Crusade in 1147, when the townspeople prevented Szczecin from falling into the hands of Saxon crusaders. A few years later Ratibor together with his Rus' wife Pribislava, continued to promote missionary activity by founding the first monastery in Pomerania at Stolpe, which became populated by Saxon monks from Berge. The location had been chosen to mark the site where Wartislaw had been assassinated by a pagan. His martyrdom was commemorated by a monument inscribed with a cross referred to much later as 'Wartislaw's Stone'. Shortly before Ratibor and Pribislava's death, the couple founded a Premonstratensian monastery on the island of Usedom at the northern edge of the lagoon.

Western Pomerania gradually became politically tied to the empire; however, it was recognised as a frontier and referred to as the Neumark (the 'New March'), where Pomeranian, Polish, German and Danish magnates fought for control in the early decades of the thirteenth century, and where military incursions and episodes of localised violence were commonplace.[15] In 1164, Bogislaw, the Duke of Szczecin, had joined his brother to aid the Wendish Obotrites in their rebellion against Henry the Lion. Henry was supported by the Danish king Valdemar and defeated the Slavic coalition, and the Pomeranian duchy became a vassal state of Saxony. Henry would later elevate the defeated Obotrite leader Pribislav to rule over Mecklenburg, having executed his brother for rebelling. The new generation of Slavic rulers became committed to the forceful suppression of paganism. Pribislav, together with Bogislaw, would go on to help Valdemar in his attack on Rügen and the destruction of the pagan religious centre at Arkona.[16] Pribislav's son Henry Borwin, who married Henry the Lion's daughter Matilda, continuing the Mecklenburg dynasty established by his father, would later join the Danish crusades into Estonia. However, Bogislaw turned against the Danes in a conflict that would drag on for another decade. This saw Szczecin besieged by a Danish army in 1173 and then destroyed by fire in 1189. The stronghold and town were quickly rebuilt, and archaeological finds attest to its growing prosperity under Danish overlordship. This was the result of a boom in commerce, with a vibrant trade in silver, amber and imported glassware. In contrast, Wolin, on the other side of the lagoon, was fighting against growing inundations from the rising waters of the Baltic Sea. Economic decline, Danish raids and the relocation of Western Pomerania's episcopal see from here in 1150 prompted the abandonment of the old settlement and its refoundation as a planned town, although by this point it had been completely eclipsed by the region's other centres.

In 1227, control over Western Pomerania was finally wrested from the Danes by Emperor Frederick II, who delegated its governance to the Ascanian margraves of Brandenburg. This revived the conflict between the Ascanian and Griffin families, and their fluctuating territorial gains and losses defined the political history of the region for the rest of the century. Ultimately, the Griffins assumed full control again, but in those decades the demographic composition of the town, and the wider region, began to change. The last Polish bishop of West Pomerania, fittingly named Adalbert, had died in 1160 and was succeeded by a series of

German bishops, accompanied by an influx of German clerics who then influenced the character of the West Pomeranian Church. Some have suggested this caused a rift with the indigenous Slavic population, and the Polish claim to the region would be reiterated in later centuries. The Griffins, argued the Polish chronicler Jan Długosz, had familial ties with the Piasts, a connection that was revived in Poland's cultural memory after the Second World War. German identity was certainly recognised as distinct from Slavic in medieval Western Pomerania, but it was not connected with any notion of an ethnically defined 'Germany' at the time.

German merchants were already settled in Szczecin when, in 1237, the privileges granted to them by the duke were extended to the rest of the town, which a few years later were formally codified as the Magdeburg Law.[17] This prompted the gradual replanning of the townscape and the construction of the first timber-framed houses, replacing the earlier preference for horizontal cross-log and wattle-work structures. This was Germanisation in action, and saw the introduction of new customs, architectural styles and, most importantly, language into the lives of Pomeranians. But these things were taken up because they were advantageous and fashionable, rather than imposed by force. As with the territories conquered by the Saxon Margraves to the west, the demographic composition of Pomerania's towns and villages, as well as the organisation of farmland, would begin to shift over the course of the thirteenth century with increasing numbers of German migrants who flocked in from the expanding Margraviate of Brandenburg.

As they settled, they introduced German place names into the landscape; Szczecin's name derives from a Slavic word variously interpreted as referring to the marshes or hill on which the settlement was founded. Slavic toponyms in West Pomerania were gradually superseded and outnumbered by German place names, a process that was completely reversed after 1945 with the redrawing of Poland and Germany's national borders. By the fourteenth century, as elsewhere across the Wendish region, there was a differentiation between Pomeranians who had Germanised and those who maintained a distinctive Slavic identity, defined above all by language. The latter came to be represented by the Kashubs, a gradually diminishing population and, particularly after Pomerania's Reformation in

1534, experiencing increasing marginalisation. Some have argued the Kashubs and Slavic Pomeranians were the same group of Wends, but the former became distinctive enough by the thirteenth century that the dukes of Pomerania referred to themselves as *dux Slavorum et Cassubie* – claiming overlordship over both Slavs and Kashubs. By the mid-nineteenth century, when the Kashubs experienced their own national awakening, they had become largely confined to the province of West Prussia within the Kingdom of Prussia. Kashubian would be officially recognised as a regional language within Poland in 2005.[18]

POMERELIA AND GDAŃSK/DANZIG

The story of Eastern Pomerania, or Pomerelia, also begins with a city – Gdańsk, rendered in Latin sources from the Slavic name for the local river, Gdania. Due to the difficulty of pronouncing the consonants 'gd' in German, following the influx of German merchants in the thirteenth century the name was simplified as Danzk in 1263, which a few centuries later evolved into Danzig.[19] This city would not only come to dominate the region in terms of politics, religion and social organisation, but also become one of the most important centres in Northern Europe. There is some debate concerning its precise origins, but the earliest known settlement, which was located near the confluence of the Motława and Vistula rivers, came under Mieszko's rule in the 960s. A stronghold was constructed on a hill overlooking the estuary. Excavations here uncovered Arabic dirhems dating to the ninth and tenth centuries, as well as pre-Christian burials. Investment in this otherwise obscure settlement was strategic: the Piasts gradually took control of the entire Lower Vistula which connected their heartland with the Baltic, and tapped into the trade networks with Scandinavian regions. Across from Gdańsk on the other side of the Vistula Delta, the trading emporium of Truso, identified with the archaeological site of Janów Pomorski,[20] was probably set up on the initiative of a Scandinavian diaspora community working with local Prussian merchants, supplied by settlements in the vicinity and visited by Slavic merchants. Although the Piasts did not extend their political influence into Prussian lands, their investment in Gdańsk most probably resulted in competition between the two trading centres.

Gdańsk's fortunes would rise as Truso's declined, and the latter was abandoned in the eleventh century.

The Christianisation of Gdańsk was similar to the proliferation of the new religion in Western Pomerania – it was gradual and driven by the initiatives of ambitious rulers and clerics. Missionary activity followed in the wake of the initial Piast conquest, and in fact the first mention of the settlement is in St Adalbert's life written at the end of the tenth century. He allegedly visited in April 996, but there is little evidence for Christianity in what was the north-eastern frontier of the Piast state, and the town's growing population proved to be persistently rebellious, with several documented uprisings against Polish rule. Casimir I 'the Restorer' was able to regain control of Pomeranian lands, and it was probably under his orders than a new stronghold was constructed at the mouth of the Motława. Archaeologists have identified a timber and earthen structure which was built in the second half of the eleventh century, and in the base of its ramparts the body of a horse had been deposited. Based on the skeletal pathology, the horse had been suffering from a debilitating disease, most likely tuberculosis. Horse skulls have been found buried in the foundations of other Western Slavic strongholds. Here, the killing and deposition of an individual animal may have been prompted by its visible lameness; diseased animals appear to have been regarded as particularly suitable for apotropaic offerings.[21] At the time, this magical ritual may have evoked elements of a pre-Christian worldview, but such practices would continue following the widespread acceptance of Catholicism. The stronghold functioned as the residence of a Polish official, and soon a settlement of artisans, merchants and fishermen grew up in the vicinity – by the eleventh century it had an estimated 1,500 inhabitants. Pomeranians rebelled against Polish rule again in 1069 when Boleslaus II 'the Bold' was in control. His younger brother Duke Ladislaus Herman's failure to retain control over Pomerelia prompted orders to destroy all of its strongholds, but his son Boleslaus would go on to conquer Gdańsk in 1119 and reassert control over the entire region.[22]

Following the conquest, Boleslaus appointed officials from prominent Polish noble families to govern the region's centres on his behalf, as stewards. In Gdańsk, this became a hereditary post held by the Samboride family, passed down from father to son. When referring to the appointment of the first of the line, Vincentius, the Bishop of Cracow, described the territory as *Gdanensi marchia* – a march, a frontier. The Samborides quickly became politically assertive, seeking independence from both Polish and Danish rulers who were confronting each other over the control of Pomerania. Little is known of the first documented member of this family in the late twelfth century, Sobieslaw, although his son Sambor – the earliest named ruler of Gdańsk – is credited with founding the Cistercian monastery at Oliwa in 1186, built some 10 kilometres to the north-west. Its first abbot Dithardus and the dozen monks who formed the early community were Danes, brought over from Kolbatz (Polish Kołbacz), located south-east of Szczecin between the edge of a vast forest and lake. Kolbatz was connected with the cult of St Otto of Bamberg, who was canonised by the papacy in 1189. Otto's elevation may have been harnessed by Sambor in his aspirations for autonomy, materialised in that portable material culture of political and economic power – coinage.

During recent excavations in Gdańsk on the site of a twelfth-century urban settlement area, some 500 coins and jettons were discovered, which included an extraordinary set of twenty-five bracteates. These were found placed alongside each other as if they had been rolled up in cloth, now long decayed, and appear to have been struck by the same die. They were decorated with a cross-shaped monogram interpreted as most likely representing St Otto, with the name Sambor inscribed on their margins. This suggests the first named ruler of Gdańsk asserted his authority by using his own name on the earliest known (although probably not the first minted) coins in the city, alongside a recently canonised saint connected with Pomerania, rather than the patron of the Piasts, St Adalbert.[23] Sambor chose his timing well – the Polish dukes were fighting each other over the throne of Cracow, and with the Danish king over Pomerania. The Duchy of Pomerelia briefly came under the overlordship of Denmark in 1210, before returning to Polish control the following year. After the assassination of the Polish High Duke Leszek 'the White' in 1227, Swietopelk II divided Pomerelia in two, granting a part to his brother whilst retaining Gdańsk's territory where he exercised autonomous rule. Tensions between Pomerelia and Brandenburg resulted in the brief occupation of Gdańsk by the Margrave's forces in 1272 which destroyed part of the stronghold. Polish rule would be reasserted again, briefly, with the death of the last Samboride duke, Mestwin II, in 1294.

Under the Samborides, Gdańsk developed into a significant urban centre, with the emergence of four distinct settlement areas. The first was the ducal stronghold, with its own church dedicated to the Virgin Mary, of which only a few column bases from this early Romanesque structure are known. Nearby was a settlement inhabited by fishermen and amber gatherers. A new urban district was also established, with its own circuit of walls and timber streets. This was later referred to as the 'Main Town' and, over the decades, it became filled with multi-storey houses occupied by artisans, as domestic craft activities gave way to mass production. It was served by a parish church dedicated to St Mary. Merchants from Lübeck settled west of the stronghold in the late twelfth century, establishing an affluent community around a church dedicated to St Catherine in what later became known as the 'Old Town'.[24] The wealthiest invested in substantial buildings reflecting architectural fashions popular in towns like Lübeck, particularly large oak-framed houses with brick hearths. They imported stoneware ceramics, hand-painted glass vessels and even popularised footwear fashions from the West. They also brought with them new ideas of self-governance, as the duke would eventually grant their settlement autonomy and privileges under the Lübeck Law.[25] Trade poured into the city from all directions, vividly represented by archaeological finds of Danish, Bohemian, English, Hungarian, German and Polish coins, and even fragments of vessels used for transporting wine from Rus' lands. The surrounding landscape became increasingly deforested as land was cleared to feed the growing population and supply timber for ship building, although substantial tracts of woodland remained.[26]

When a parish church was built in the central market by the end of the twelfth century to serve both locals and merchants, it was dedicated to St Nicholas. His cult had been spreading amongst both Catholic and Orthodox communities around the Baltic alongside the explosion in maritime shipping. The German community invariably contributed to the presence of Catholics within the city, and perhaps those Pomeranians and Prussians documented living there had also adopted mainstream Christian practices. Nonetheless, some have argued that Christianity would not be firmly established here until the arrival of the Dominicans from Cracow in early 1227. Swietopelk II granted them St Nicholas's Church and it became the focus of a new friary. Only a few years later, crusading armies would sweep down the Vistula into Prussian lands.[27]

CROSSING THE PRUSSIAN BORDERLANDS

The quote from Gallus's chronicle at the start of this chapter referred to the three pagan peoples that Boleslaus sought to conquer and Christianise. It's not clear where Selencia was, as it is not mentioned by other contemporaries, but it may have been the territory of a Wendish group west of Pomerania. The third group, the Prussians, were not Slavs, but Western Balts. The Piast conquests which followed the Vistula to the north and east, incorporating Pomerania and Masovia into the early Polish state, did not reach their lands. But the river itself, which connected the Carpathians with the Baltic Sea, was not a barrier to political expansion. A broad frontier developed to the east and north of the Vistula where the construction of strongholds by the rulers of Pomerelia and Masovia – and the settlements that developed in their vicinity – reflected the intent to extend their territorial hold into pagan Prussia.

To the east of the Vistula, archaeological evidence suggests the first Pomerelian strongholds had been constructed between the eighth/ninth and early tenth centuries, and they were associated with a growing population in the surrounding landscape. These were centres of local authority, governing and protecting the villages and farms built by migrant families and, as elsewhere, they are associated with forest clearance and the expansion of cultivated land. However, with the rise of the Piast state, settlement intensified, reflecting a deliberate policy to colonise the delta region.[28] By the twelfth century, the largest strongholds were the residences of castellans, officials who governed districts called castellanies on behalf of the dukes of Gdańsk, emulating a system of territorial organisation used by the Piasts. The borderlands were not fixed lines etched into the landscape, but slowly expanding territories marked by the construction of new settlements and their fields. In other words, there were large numbers of migrants continuously redefining what was regarded as Polish territory – or, more accurately, the semi-autonomous territories of Pomerelia and, where the Vistula snaked to the south-east, the corner of Kuyavia and the northern stretch of Masovia, which encompassed smaller frontier provinces such as the Kulmerland.

By the twelfth century, written sources certainly make a sharp distinction between Christian Poland and pagan Prussia and, in terms of language, customs, religious practices, organisation and of course political fealty, the differences would have been pronounced. Moreover, Polish dukes would lead armies across these frontiers in attacks that nominally had a missionary purpose. Their lands were to be defined by the presence of Christian subjects, which in their minds would include Prussian converts. Everything written about the indigenous Prussians derives from external sources – there was no indigenous literary culture. Amidst the moralising, confusion, misunderstandings and stereotyping that permeates these narratives are occasional details which complement the substantially larger body of archaeological information recovered from Prussian sites, as well as a range of environmental data that provides an invaluable record of human activities across Prussian lands.[29]

By the tenth century, the Prussian peoples – traditionally referred to as 'tribes' in the scholarly literature (like the Wends), defined by extended kinship groups which recognised both paternal and maternal lineage – were governed by a decentralised, militarised aristocracy. Power lay in the hands of local aristocratic families, which Christian chroniclers recognised as akin to their own nobility. Like the Western Slavs, they too resided within strongholds built from timber and earth, what Latin chroniclers would commonly refer to as *castra*, and archaeologists have also identified smaller elite residences, most likely inhabited by family groups at the lower end of the aristocratic social ladder. As in the case of Wendish and Polish strongholds, settlements of variable size were laid out alongside them, the largest of which appear to have had flourishing communities of merchants and artisans.[30] The rest of the population lived in villages consisting of clusters of farmsteads occupied by extended families, which written sources suggest could be quite large, and which would have also housed communities of slaves.

Although the trading centres at Truso and Wiskiauten had been abandoned in the eleventh century, regional commerce became focused on major strongholds and their associated settlements. These centres continued to trade in amber, fur and slaves, and imported in raw metals such as bronze, alongside jewellery, weapons and armour from neighbouring regions – Scandinavia, Poland, Lithuania and Rus' lands. The Prussians did not produce their own coinage, but readily incorporated money from their neighbours into their system of exchange, which was largely centred on silver ingots. Burials which included a set of weights and scales appear with greater frequency in the Sambian Peninsula than anywhere else in Prussia, and attest to the importance of merchants here as a distinct social group.[31] But Sambians are more frequently described in German and Scandinavian chronicles as pirates raiding the coastlines of the western Baltic.

Descriptions of Prussian religion are few and far between, and were produced by clerics with all their inherent problems and biases. The priest of the Teutonic Order who chronicled the events of the later crusades against the Prussians, Peter of Dusburg, summarised it like this:

> And because God was unknown to them [the Prussians], this gave rise to the error of foolishly worshipping every creature as a god: thunder, sun, stars and moon, birds, animals and even toads were gods to them. Fields, rivers and forests were also sacred according to their beliefs, so they were not allowed to plough them or fish in them or cut down trees in the forests.[32]

In viewing the Prussians as simple, rustic and spiritually ignorant, Peter was falling back on the well-established Christian construct of what it meant to be a pagan. Nonetheless, some aspects of indigenous Prussian religion are consistently mentioned across different types of sources, including the charters of the Christian regime issued after the crusades which recorded toponyms and boundary markers.

As such, we know the Prussians, like pagan peoples across the Baltic Sea region, attributed religious importance to specific trees, woods, hills, fields, rivers, lakes and marshes. Some of these sacred natural sites were located at the edges of settlements, on or near territorial boundaries, and may have been a way of organising the landscape in the pre-crusade period.³³ As suggested by Peter above, these places would have been untouchable, and the reluctance of Prussians to dig up tree stumps, even if they presented an obstacle for ploughing, was also noted by the Teutonic Order.³⁴ Archaeological investigations of some of the massive glacial erratic boulders which litter the landscapes of historic Prussia confirm these were also used for some form of religious activity. Several are marked with hollows on their topmost surface, which may have been used for the placement of offerings and libations. Others have had artefacts, including weapons, buried around them. Better known are a number of granite boulders carved with human forms in low reliefs, which may have served as images of deities. Those that have been preserved are found within the bounds of present-day Poland, where they are called '*Baby*'.³⁵ Although many have been moved from their original location, they would have originally been located on the edges of settlements, in woods and wetlands, functioning as territorial markers connected with sacred natural sites.³⁶ The incorporation of one of these sculptures into the church walls at Prątnica demonstrates just how they were perceived by Christian migrants in the decades after the crusades.

There is no compelling evidence for what Peter described as a major religious centre called Romow with a 'pagan pope', whose authority was recognised by every Prussian group. But there were ritual specialists – priests – who played important roles at funerals, as well as those who were believed to be able to commune with the gods.³⁷ The names of these gods are largely known from much later sources and may represent borrowings from neighbouring cultures or reimaginings. The only one that is named during the crusading period is featured in the Treaty of Christburg, which was drawn up between members of the Prussian nobility and the Teutonic Order in 1249. This is the deity Kurke, rendered in Latinised form as Curche. Some scholars have associated this deity with linden trees, and the name features in a number of toponyms, particularly in Galindia.³⁸ The Dominican Simon Grunau, writing in the early sixteenth century, was the first to describe this figure in more detail, specifying how the Prussians burnt offerings of grain, wheat, flour, honey and milk in front of the deity's image standing before an oak tree, which Anselm, the later Bishop of Warmia, would cut down.

Fishermen in the western Prussian region of Pogesania would also burn their first catch for Kurke on a sacred stone.[39] Simon, rendering the name in Early New High German as Curcho, included this deity within a list of five others – Patollo, a fearful god of night and the dead, to whom human blood was offered; Potrimppo (first named in a document in 1418), a god of the harvest and luck in conflict, to whom children were sacrificed; Perkuno, the storm god; and two brothers who had become deities following their sacrificial self-immolation: Wurschayto, a former pagan priest, and Szwaybrotto, a former Prussian ruler.[40] How much of this was invention or exaggeration remains debated, especially given the persistent demonisation of pagan religions by Christian chroniclers, but variants of these names crop up in toponyms and other sources.

Indigenous cemeteries have also been widely understood as sacred sites by scholars. Ancestral memory was certainly important and there is archaeological evidence for the reopening and sealing of graves in parts of Prussia, as well as the continued use of cemeteries over many centuries. Burial rites were quite diverse, and by the twelfth century included both cremations and inhumations. Like Christianity for the Piasts, Prussian religion appears to have provided ideological reinforcement for elite dynasties. The presence of weapons and horses in graves was a particularly striking feature of early medieval Prussian funerary culture. In Sambia, where the majority of these cemeteries have been excavated, on average some 40–50 per cent of graves dated between the late tenth and early thirteenth century contained weapons. A small number, which contained swords, maces, imported weapons and those inlaid with bronze and silver, as well as horse harnesses, can be attributed to the warrior elite. More recent, careful analysis of the findings from these cemeteries has revealed that horses were the most frequently occurring feature associated with Prussian graves.

The ritualistic deposition of horses was already evident from the first century AD in the Masurian region and from the following century in Sambia,[41] but from the end of the fifth century, horses were laid out in pits – or rather coaxed into them and in some cases bound, given that many appear to have been buried alive – and then cremated human remains would be placed on top of them, along with weapons, armour, equestrian equipment and a range of jewellery and other objects. Some sixty cemeteries are known from Sambia where human burials are associated with around 750 horses, dating between the eighth and thirteenth centuries. Around half of these graves include weapons, but they were not exclusively male – a number of women were also buried in this way. Recent isotopic and genetic analysis has revealed that both mares and stallions were ritually killed in cemeteries, and that some had been brought over considerable distances – from as far afield as Scandinavia, perhaps the spoils of a raid or diplomatic gifts between warlords.[42]

By the twelfth century, these had become clustered in cemeteries, with large numbers of cremated individuals placed above deposits of weapons and multiple horses. Later written sources, including the Treaty of Christburg, consistently point to an eschatological role for the deposition of both objects and horses – they would accompany the dead to the afterlife. The same commentators also spoke of (and ridiculed) the Prussian belief in reincarnation, including the transference of souls into animals.[43] But at the same time these burial rites have also been interpreted as reflecting the emergence of a more professional warrior class, serving an increasingly powerful militarised artistocracy. Peter of Dusburg would later note that the Sambians could muster several thousand horsemen.[44] During this time of increasingly visible militarism in funerary culture, various Prussian groups – not just the Sambians – were raiding their neighbours, especially in the latter decades of the twelfth century.

These raids crossed the borderlands into the lands of the Pomerelian dukes. The stronghold at Węgry, strategically located overlooking the Nogat to control river traffic linked to the most important waterway passing through the Polish principalities, had been constructed in the early eleventh century. However, in the 1160s it was destroyed and almost all the settlements within its vicinity were abandoned. The most likely explanation is Prussian raids, which eventually reached as far as Gdańsk itself.[45] This marked the beginning of increasing hostilities across the borderlands, particularly with Masovia, one that was provoked, in part, by a renewed commitment from the Piasts to missionary warfare.

THE MASOVIAN FRONTIER

To the south of Prussian lands lay the sprawling territory of Masovia. When Boleslaus III, the subjugator of Pomerania, died in 1138, the Polish state was subdivided between his sons, and the frontier principality of Masovia was redefined as a duchy under the governance of Boleslaus 'the Curly' (so-called after his curled locks of hair). Predictably, within a few years, fighting broke out between the brothers, as well as the Grand Duke of Kyiv whose daughter was married to Boleslaus 'the Tall', the Duke of Wrocław. The involvement of the Saxons in the negotiations which ended the civil war between the Piasts in 1146 almost certainly led to Polish participation in the Wendish Crusade. Yet the gains for the Piasts were ephemeral: at best, the short-lived campaign reminded the Pomeranian nobility who was in control. In the winter of the same year, Boleslaus, now High Duke of Poland, led an army into Prussia, taking advantage of the indulgences offered by the papal bull in April to recruit crusaders. This may have been motivated by the need to defend the Masovian border against Prussian raids, but contemporary sources indicate this was also a missionary war, where the Prussians were offered the choice between baptism or death.

The war was therefore intended both for the protection of Polish Christians in the borderland and the salvation of the Prussians. The pope had, after all, given his blessing to conversion by force or the eradication of pagan enemies. This, and the campaign against the Wends, can be understood as part of a diffused crusading endeavour that historians have called the Second Crusade. Contemporaries understood this as a universal enterprise against the dark forces threatening Latin Christendom from all sides.[46] Later that year, Duke Mieszko 'the Old' commissioned the great bronze portal for Gniezno, a reminder of the Piast commitment to the evangelisation of the Prussians. It would appear the crusading movement had found widespread support amongst the Piast dukes by the mid-twelfth century. This is not so surprising, given the presence of papal legates and German clerics in Poland had contributed to disseminating the culture of Latin Christianity in the courtly circles of the Piasts, which included crusading ideology.[47]

The northern stretch of ducal Masovia was a more complex borderland than the windswept fens of the Vistula Delta. In its western part, which incorporated Kuyavia, it bordered Pomerelia, and its eastern flank met the lands of Eastern Orthodox Kyivan Rus'. In between, lay the territories of pagan Prussian groups. The heartland of Masovia, centred on Płock, was the most densely settled. Płock had become the ducal seat under Ladislaus Herman and, when the Piast complex was destroyed by fire in 1126 or 1127 during a Pomeranian raid, it prompted a complete replanning of the town. Under the leadership of its bishops, particularly Alexander of Malonne, it became a major centre for flourishing art and architecture in the Piast state. Alexander acted as a lord in his own right, wielding considerable secular power in the name of the Masovian dukes. He was responsible for introducing the religious norms of the Latin Church to Płock, establishing a collegiate church and developing an episcopal suburb around the new cathedral which was finally consecrated in 1144. The bishop commissioned artisans in Magdeburg to cast an impressive bronze door for the cathedral, imitating the doors of Hildesheim and Mainz, with representations of the Church's missionary activity alongside scenes from the Old and New Testaments.[48] Alexander was one of the north European 'warrior clerics' of the twelfth century – religious statesmen who pressed for the use of force in the expansion and defence of Christendom – who supported crusading against pagans.[49]

In those decades, the Prussian frontier had steadily attracted Masovian knightly and peasant families. The territory was managed as a series of smaller provinces, of which the Kulmerland, bordered on its southern and western side by the Vistula, was ringed with formidable strongholds described as *castra* in contemporary sources. These strongholds with their garrisons provided security, but also fulfilled administrative functions and were supported by a network of villages, as elsewhere in the Piast state. At the centre of the castellany was Culm, identified with the settlement complex uncovered by archaeologists at Kałdus. To the east of this region lay small territories known as Dobrzyń Land and Lubavia, and beyond that, substantial belts of woodland separated the vast Prussian territory of Galindia from north Masovia, with settlements on either side of the frontier located some 40 kilometres apart. Parts of this borderland were even walled with timber palisades, statements of territorial claims from the Piasts which are still visible in the landscape today as substantial linear earthworks.[50] Further east, in what was the wildest part of the frontier, the castellans at Wizna guarded the confluence of the Narew and Biebrza rivers. This was the last Masovian regional centre before pagan Sudovia, which lay to the north down the Biebrza.

The Masovians and Prussian Galindians had not always been enemies. Within a few years of the death of the Polish king Mieszko II, the lord of Masovia, Mieclaw, led a rebellion against the late king's son Casimir which drew in the Galindians, who came to the aid of the Masovians. Mieclaw's catastrophic defeat in battle in 1047 by a Polish–Rus' coalition weakened the Galindians and prompted – according to Peter of Dusburg's much later account – other Prussian groups to pillage their territory. This resulted in a decline in some of the power centres in Galindia but, whilst archaeologists have shown the region was not completely depopulated, it seems to have been of little concern to the Masovians in the twelfth century. During the civil war between the Piasts in the 1140s, High Duke Ladislaus II had even recruited Prussians as allies against his brother, the Duke of Masovia, an act that was denounced by the Archbishop of Gniezno. But even though pagan practices had lingered in those parts of Masovia which were far from the reach of episcopal authorities, the political border with Prussian lands visibly hardened in the decades after Boleslaus's missionary war.[51]

Boleslaus's attempt to convert the Prussians and bring them under his rule ended ignominiously. The Prussians allegedly rejected Christianity as soon as the Polish army left, but it is questionable whether they had really adopted it in the first place. Boleslaus seems to have ignored this and continued to accept their tribute payments. Acceptance of Polish political suzerainty and Christianity was a familiar post-conquest package, but one that required sustained investment to reshape religious beliefs and practices. Eventually, an insurrection prompted Boleslaus to return in October 1166 at the head of an army with his younger brother Henry of Sandomierz, the famed Piast crusader who had fought in the Holy Land. The Polish army was routed during an ambush and Henry was killed – a martyr's death in the eyes of his compatriots.[52]

The threat to the Masovian borderland at this time was certainly credible, and the fact that the Prussians were pagans or worse – apostates – must have amplified the sense of danger from the perspective of Christian communities that were targeted by their attacks. According to the Polish sources, when the Prussians raided in the late twelfth and early thirteenth centuries, they did so to loot, pillage and to enslave. It is difficult to measure the true impact of these raids. Archaeologically, the damage is clearly visible – the stronghold at Grudusk was abandoned, although the nearby church continued to be used, that of Serock was destroyed by fire three times and rebuilt twice between the ninth and thirteenth centuries, whilst at Ciechanów the fortified centre was destroyed in the twelfth century and would only be reoccupied 200 years later.[53] In the climate of mounting hostility between Poles and Prussians, Duke Boleslaus appointed Hugo Butyr as castellan of the Kulmerland. Hugo came from a crusading family – his father had participated in the First Crusade and died in the Holy Land in 1112. Hugo had also commanded Masovian forces when defending the frontier and leading attacks against the Prussians, and his reputation endured into the fourteenth century when Peter of Dusburg mentioned his role in the defence of the Polish borderland. The Kulmerland became the main frontline against the Prussians, and the entry point for future crusades.

TOWARDS A NEW HOLY WAR

No further Polish incursions are documented across the Masovian frontier until almost three decades later in 1192, when Casimir II 'the Just' led an army against the 'Pollexians', a Prussian group residing somewhere between Galindia and Sudovia. This endeavour may have been inspired by the preaching of the Third Crusade within the courtly and familial circles of the Piasts. Describing this episode, the Bishop of Cracow, Vincentius, drew direct parallels between the Pollexians and the Muslims in the Levant. In his eyes, the Prussians were a bestial race of persistent sinners, with converts to Christianity quickly lapsing into apostasy. The acceptance of Polish rule and Christianity were synonymous, and so he perceived the wars led by the Polish dukes against the Prussians in the twelfth century as righteous. His intention was to raise the profile of the wars against the Prussians to the level of a crusade in defence of the Holy Land, even though there was no papal authorisation for these campaigns.[54] The 1192 expedition was allegedly successful at subduing some Prussian groups, but the ensuing conflicts amongst the Piasts following the death of Casimir in 1194 resulted in the abandonment of further ducal campaigns of evangelisation.

In this climate of increasing enthusiasm for holy war, it is not surprising to see ducal investment in the international representatives of the crusading movement – the military orders. Within the duchy of Gdańsk, three Hospitaller houses were founded by the end of the twelfth century at Starogard, Lubiszewo and Skarszewy, whilst the Iberian Order of Calatrava held property at the Vistula crossing in Tymawa. The presence of the latter is interesting – the Order of Calatrava had been founded by the Cistercians (who had also endorsed and shaped the first military order, the Templars) and was officially militarised with papal approval in 1164. The Pomeranian borderland was also a region of expansion for the Cistercians, who built abbeys and were involved in missions to the neighbouring Prussians. The deployment of the military orders in this region was therefore to be expected, but the overall distribution of their foundations across the Polish principalities suggests their introduction was not solely concerned with securing the frontier of Christendom.

In the Holy Roman Empire, support for the military orders was increasing from the last decades of the twelfth century, as more Germans participated in crusades to the Levant. An early supporter of the Templars was none other than Henry the Lion, who had visited the Levant in 1172, but the later Slavic rulers of Mecklenburg also supported the Hospitallers. Their rivals, the Margraves of Brandenburg, focused their donations on the Templars, except for some land given to the Hospitallers at Werben by Albert the Bear in 1160. Again, these foundations were not linked to the security of the northern marches but followed the general pattern of endowments by ruling families to religious institutions, especially those with a history of crusading and pilgrimage in the Holy Land.[55] Even on the Pomerelian frontier with Prussia, it is not clear whether the military-order communities were engaged as combatants or whether they were just managing estates.[56] But the military orders were not ordinary monastic communities and their presence demonstrates popular support for crusader ideology amongst the ruling Christian elites of Northern Europe. In a short period of time, they would come to define the crusading culture of the medieval Baltic world.

The coronation of Pope Innocent III in January 1198 heralded the start of a new crusading era in Northern Europe. The new pope devoted his attention to fighting heretics in southern France and crusading in the eastern Mediterranean, but also sanctioned crusades into the territory of the Livs and supported Bishop Albert's foundation of the Sword Brothers, as well as their early campaigns. Their stated aim had been to protect Christian converts, a role for crusading formalised by the Fourth Lateran Council in 1215. This would inspire the crusading movement in Poland, which became tethered to the territorial ambitions of the Piast dukes. The archdiocese of Gniezno, the mythical home of the Piast dynasty, became the principal spiritual centre for promoting the crusade against the Prussians – the reliefs on the great bronze doors of its cathedral serving as a constant reminder of St Adalbert's mission and martyrdom at the hands of the pagans. With the crusades in Livonia in full swing, it would only be a matter of time before a holy war – in the name of defending Christians – was unleashed on Prussia.

CHAPTER 4

FROM PAGANS TO CRUSADERS
Scandinavian Expansion in the Baltic

Afterwards our troops went about the double task of burning down the temple and building a church from the wood of their siege engines, thus transforming their instruments of war into an abode of peace. So the machines they had designed for crushing the bodies of their adversaries were now devoted to saving their souls.

Saxo Grammaticus, *History of the Danes*[1]

BALTIC VIKINGS

Between the eighth and eleventh centuries, what is today referred to as the Viking Age, Scandinavian groups – from present-day Norway, Sweden and Denmark – settled in diverse regions, from the British Isles and parts of the European mainland, through to Iceland, Greenland and even as far as North America. In the eastern Baltic, their presence is evident at trading centres, the earliest of which has been identified at Grobiņa, located in the estuary of the Ālande river in modern southwestern Latvia. Occupied from the mid-seventh to ninth centuries, its material culture and that of the surrounding area suggests little interaction between the migrants from Sweden and Gotland, and the local Curonians. This contrasts with the trading centres which emerged along the southern Baltic coast in the eighth century, where Scandinavian merchants, artisans and warriors settled in larger numbers, living alongside other migrant and indigenous groups. This included the urbanised settlement at Janów Pomorski in the Pomerelian–Prussian borderland, identified as the port of Truso described by the voyager Wulfstan, Bardy-Świelubie near Kołobrzeg on the Pomeranian coast, and Wolin, which by the eleventh century, before its relocation, may have been the largest town in the Baltic Sea region. As Grobiņa was abandoned, the settlement at Kaup in Wiskiauten on the northern coast of the Sambian Peninsula becomes visible. It would outlast all the other Baltic trading centres associated with a Scandinavian presence. On the basis of the material culture found in graves, it has been connected with migrants from Gotland, and subsequently Danes, living alongside the local Prussians. It endured perhaps as late as the mid-eleventh century and, as such, was exceptional.[2] The other trading settlements had disappeared by then, along with a noticeable decrease in Scandinavian artefacts in the eastern half of the Baltic Sea region.

Scandinavian presence in these settlements has sometimes been framed in the language of colonialism, but these trading settlements were not Scandinavian 'colonies' in the sense of extensions of Danish or Swedish sovereign territories. They are better understood as diaspora communities. Nonetheless, overseas claims to such lands did develop as political authority in the southern and western Baltic became more concentrated, as regional chiefdoms transformed into kingdoms.[3] Central to this process was the adoption of Christianity, where rulers led the way in their public allegiance to the new religion – Harald Klak and later Harald Gormsson (Bluetooth) in Denmark, Olaf Tryggvason in Norway, Olof Skötkonung in Sweden, and their successors. Churchmen, such as Adam of Bremen, often remarked on whether these rulers were truly good Christians and, as elsewhere, there was a performative, political dimension to their religious allegiance. But the new religion was also embraced at the grassroots level. The quickest to convert were Scandinavian migrant communities who had settled in Christian lands – in Britain, Ireland, Normandy and Brittany, as well as in the territories of Kyiv and Novgorod. The diasporas on Iceland and Greenland adopted Christianity in the eleventh century. The populations in the Scandinavian heartlands took longer to abandon their earlier beliefs and associated customs, including animal sacrifice, but despite some dramatic accounts of forced baptisms the process was generally one of gradual acceptance, rather than singularly imposed from the top through coercion.[4]

The first attempts at expanding the Danish realm in the northern fringes of the Ottonian Empire were led by pagan rulers, but with Harald Gormsson's defeat and subsequent public proclamation of his Christian allegiance, territorial expansion began to take on a religious dimension. Subsequent rulers would target pagan groups in what later historians dubbed as 'missionary wars', where conquest was accompanied by conversion and the building of churches. The sharpening of religious identities is particularly evident in descriptions of the conflicts with the pagan Wends, who were pitched as the scourge of the Danish maritime kingdom. Crucially, the concept of martyrdom, dying for the faith, became adopted in both Denmark and Norway, and readily mapped onto warfare against pagan neighbours. Earlier notions of the afterlife reserved for warriors who fell in battle – the halls of Valhöll and Sessrúmnir – were replaced by aspirations to enter heaven. This was made clear in the mid-eleventh century when the Archbishop of Hamburg-Bremen encouraged the Danish king Sweyn II and the Obotrite Christian ruler Gottschalk to convert Wendish pagans, with promises of martyr's crowns and celestial rewards. The pope would make similar promises to those fighting Muslims in Iberia.

In Sweden, the last of the Scandinavian kingdoms to maintain public pagan religious centres, Christian institutions were already present in the tenth century, after a false start with Ansgar's short-lived mission in 829 to the trading centre of Birka and the Mälaren Valley. Its fate tied to the initiatives of the ruling dynasties and their inner circles, the new religion would not become widely accepted in the most important Swedish province, Uppland, where the great pagan centre of Uppsala was located, until the end of the eleventh century. Even then, the abandonment of earlier practices amongst rural communities took longer: some of the old deities endured in folk magic, and further north, in the vast and sparsely populated region of Norrland, Christianity failed to take root amongst the Saami. By the later twelfth century, Greenland represented the westernmost edge of Christendom, where the ice fields separated the Catholic settlements from the Inuit, who were also regarded as pagans. This did not stop trade across the religious divide, and Scandinavian merchants remained as pragmatic and flexible as they had been in earlier centuries. Yet the ideology of holy war did become increasingly attractive to Scandinavian rulers and nobles, inspired by the events of the First Crusade. The adoption of crusading in Scandinavia would, in turn, become twinned with territorial expansion.

SCANDINAVIANS AS CRUSADERS

During the Viking Age, Scandinavians – primarily Swedes – settled in the lands between the eastern Baltic and the Black Sea occupied by Eastern Slavic groups, in what are today western Russia, Belarus and Ukraine. Referred to as Rus' in the local Slavonic languages, they came to define the ruling class of the constellation of states which gradually centred on a powerful dynasty in Kyiv. Whilst they maintained strong links with their Scandinavian homelands, particularly in terms of alliances, the Rus' gradually assimilated into the indigenous Slavic cultures. Kyiv's ascension was due to trading in valuable woodland products, furs, wax and honey, which were widely available in its territories and could be shipped down the Volga and Dnieper rivers to north European, Middle Eastern and Mediterranean markets. The route to the Mediterranean across the Black Sea passed through Constantinople, the capital of one of the great superpowers of the early Middle Ages – the Eastern Roman Empire, more familiarly the Byzantine Empire. In 989, Anna Porphyrogenita, the sister of Emperor Basil II, married the pagan Grand Prince of Kyiv, Vladimir 'the Great'. A condition of the marriage was Vladimir's adoption of Eastern Orthodox Christianity, something he had allegedly been contemplating already. As with all politically motivated conversions, this was accompanied by public spectacle – mass baptisms in the Dnieper river, the destruction of pagan idols and the building of churches. These events, taking place in 988–9, firmly aligned Kyiv with the Eastern Empire, which provided the model for religious architecture, as well as the form of Christian worship and the organisation of monastic life.

Scandinavian mercenaries joined some of the empire's military divisions and, following the marriage alliance with Kyiv, became a formally organised imperial bodyguard called the Varangians. Old Norse *Væringjar* had originally been used to describe men who joined a mercantile company and, given their prevalence in the East, the local Slavs adopted the term to refer to all Scandinavian migrants. In Constantinople, the ranks of the Varangians were initially dominated by Swedes, but also included Danes and Norwegians.[5] Here, they encountered the ongoing confrontation between Christianity and Islam, mapped onto the territorial struggles between competing empires. Scandinavians carrying out raids on the Iberian Peninsula – against both Christians and Muslims – also encountered similar religious tensions.[6]

When the First Crusade was announced, requests for military aid to defend the Eastern Empire as well as the route to Constantinople were already familiar to Scandinavians, along with papal calls to defend the Church. In 1073, Gregory VII had written to the Danish king Sweyn II to ask for military aid against heretics (those within the Church who opposed his reforms) and the enemies of God (Muslims).[7] Sweyn was one of several rulers who had become vassals of the Holy See, part of a network developed by the papacy to counter the power of the German emperor. Given this, it is not surprising that Danes readily participated in the expedition to the Levant in 1095. Five years later, a Norwegian fleet set out to aid the fledgling Kingdom of Jerusalem but failed to reach it, and three years after that the Danish king Eric I 'the Good' died en route to the Holy Land. In 1107, a much larger fleet assembled by the Norwegian king Sigurd set off for Acre to help Baldwin I, the King of Jerusalem, take Sidon from the Fatimids. On the way, the royal fleet had raided the Muslim-held Portuguese coast and Balearic Islands.[8] Sigurd would return to earn his sobriquet '*Jórsalafari*' ('Jerusalem farer') and brought with him a relic of the True Cross which he donated to a church in the town of Konghelle (near present-day Gothenburg), along with an elaborate tabernacle built in Constantinople and a missal gifted by its patriarch. At the time, Konghelle was on the frontier with the pagan lands of Västergötland, and Sigurd believed the presence of the relic would protect his kingdom. When Pomeranians raided Konghelle in 1135, they destroyed the church and the tabernacle, but the relic and missal were miraculously saved.[9]

With the exception of Sigurd's expedition to the Holy Land, Norwegian engagement with the crusading movement is otherwise sporadic, with two further expeditions documented in the twelfth century as well as participation in the Fifth Crusade.[10] But they did help to popularise the cult of St Olaf. Reigning as King of Norway from 1015, Olaf Haraldsson had been driven into exile and then died at the hands of his own subjects in 1030. Later, as part of his informal canonisation by the Bishop of Nidaros (today Trondheim), Olaf would be framed as a martyr who fell valiantly in battle. The pope would recognise him officially as a saint in 1164, after elevating Nidaros – the centre of his cult – to an archdiocese. Olaf quickly became a role model for Norwegian kings and, more broadly, Scandinavian crusaders. They would disseminate his cult around the Baltic, whilst the Varangians would adopt him as their saint in Anatolia. The restoration of the Church of the Nativity in Bethlehem in the 1160s was accompanied by new paintings which included St Olaf and the Danish king St Canute – a reflection, perhaps even an acknowledgement, of the role played by crusaders and pilgrims from both Scandinavian kingdoms in the Holy Land. In contrast, Swedish crusaders had little direct engagement with the Levant, instead focusing on the eastern Baltic as we shall see later.[11]

The Scandinavian kingdoms have sometimes been viewed as peripheral in the history of medieval Europe, but it is clear that their churches were major players in European ecclesiastical politics, in part due to the relations between their leading clerics and the papal curia, particularly the archbishops of Lund – Eskil (1137–77) and Anders Sunesen (1201–28) – who were instrumental in popularising the crusading movement in Denmark.[12] Traditionally, historians regarded these local crusades as merely a pretext for aggressive foreign policies of territorial expansion. In recent years, the pendulum has swung the opposite way, with some even describing medieval Denmark as a 'crusader state', part of a broader re-examination of the religious motivations behind crusading. It is difficult to untangle religion from politics and commerce in the Middle Ages, and all three were features of the Baltic Crusades. When situated within the longer history of encounters between Scandinavians and the societies around the Baltic Sea, the crusades mark a shift in attitudes based on religious differences. Scandinavian rulers and clerics would come to see their corners of Christendom as under threat from the same forces that were thought to imperil the rest of the Catholic world.[13]

SUPPRESSING WENDISH PAGANISM

The Danes played a key role in the events that reshaped the geopolitics of the south-western Baltic over the course of the twelfth century, variously fighting against pagan Wends and Christian Saxons. In 1108, the Danish king Niels had been named in the Archbishop of Magdeburg's plan to crusade against the Wends for 'Jerusalem in the North'. This was a murky episode in a protracted conflict that also saw Niels's nephew, Canute Lavard, Duke of Schleswig, lead assaults against the Obotrites in the following decade. In 1123 or 1124, Niels had invited Sigurd '*Jórsalafari*' to campaign with him against the pagans in the southern Swedish province of Småland, perhaps eyeing the opportunity to control the trade route that passed through the Kalmar Sound, although only the Norwegian army set out in the end. The brief accounts of the campaign state that the Swedes were converted and Sigurd returned with booty and 1,500 cattle. The attack on Småland was encouraged by the Archbishop of Lund in what appears to have been pitched as an armed mission, but the details are obscure and, as with many of these events, elaborated in later sources.[14] In any case, the Norwegian king's attitude to confronting pagans was noticed. Peter the Venerable, the influential abbot of Cluny, praised Sigurd for fighting the enemies of the Church both at home and at the frontier.

It was during this time that crusading was being officially expanded to Iberia, paving the way for its deployment at the other permeable edges of Christendom. After the muted outcomes of the 'Wendish Crusade' in 1147 which had involved a German–Danish–Polish coalition, military campaigns against the Wends intensified under the leadership of King Valdemar. He strengthened the authority of the Danish crown and was able to muster military resources far more effectively than any of his predecessors. In preparing for assaults against the Wends, each district within the kingdom was obliged to provide ships and men. This, and the attraction of martyrdom with the promise of spiritual salvation, resulted in impressive mobilisations that enabled the Danes to engage with multiple pagan enemies.

Valdemar's wars were a turning point in a much longer history of conflict and coexistence between Danes and Wends.[15] From the end of the tenth century, Danish rulers had been allied with the Obotrites against their Slavic neighbours. Wendish prisoners taken during these conflicts appear to have been transported to Danish Scania (today southern Sweden) to work as labourers on estates. These included potters, whose presence has been connected with the discovery of ceramics reminiscent of those found on the island of Rügen and within its vicinity. The firing techniques and vessel designs introduced by Wendish potters clearly inspired local artisans and, within a generation, Scandinavian potters would begin to imitate Slavic ceramic forms and disseminate them widely to rural communities across Denmark and parts of Sweden. Wendish slaves remained a noticeable part of Danish farming households into the twelfth century, and eventually would have merged into the mainstream population. But there was also tolerated, perhaps even encouraged, migration from Wendish regions. Obotrites settled freely on Danish lands and some may have even held fiefs there.[16] Permanent Wendish communities cohabiting with or alongside Danes are suggested by place names in southern Denmark bearing Slavic elements.[17]

Wendish pirates also developed alliances and friendships with various Danish island communities, leaving some unscathed, even as others were raided. Careful analysis of ship parts, excavated on the banks of the River Fribrødre on the island of Falster and dated to the mid-eleventh century, has indicated these were Scandinavian-style boats repaired by craftsmen familiar with Wendish shipbuilding technology. Contemporary accounts certainly speak of widespread Slavic piracy involving the collaboration of Danish islanders,[18] but the picture painted by chroniclers such as Saxo and endorsed by fiery churchmen like Absalon – the Bishop of Roskilde and later Archbishop of Lund – was of an ideological divide between Danes and Wends.[19] This was part of the same attitude shift that transformed Scandinavian perceptions of peoples in the eastern Baltic. Moreover, from the perspective of Danish rulers, these island communities with their variable cultures of coexistence, at the edges of the realm already threatened by Germans and Slavs alike, presented a challenge to their authority and to their essentialist vision of their Christian kingdoms.

One response to this challenge was to secure the islands with castles, and a boom in the construction of fortifications is evident during the twelfth century. A number served the interests of the crown, but others were built by local communities who genuinely feared raiders. Amongst the largest were Gammelborg on Bornholm and Virket on Falster, both mentioned by Saxo as the target of Wendish raids in 1158. More detailed insights into these raids have been discovered by archaeologists on the island of Langeland. On its southern side, just outside the village of Magleby, excavations of the overgrown semicircular embankment at Borrebjerg uncovered disarticulated human remains and associated artefacts. The bodies, of which the identifiable included a child, three women and three men, had been dumped into the fill of the rampart when it was rebuilt in the early twelfth century. Not long after, the reinforced defences were breached once more, at which point the site was abandoned, this time with the dead left unburied. A poignant find from this final phase was a gilt-silver pendant, newly acquired as it lacked any evidence of wear, and inscribed by its maker Alfwine, who was active in Lund in the 1130s. Borrebjerg's builders had taken full advantage of the defensive opportunities provided by the landscape. The embankment had been constructed on a natural island within a cove, which today has dried up and vanished. Lacking structures within its enclosed area, the site was never meant for permanent occupation. Instead, like others built by local farming communities, it was intended as a temporary refuge in the event of an attack. When the attack came, the refuge's natural and artificial defences failed the sheltering islanders – twice.[20]

Further north on Langeland, archaeologists made a chilling discovery at the overgrown remains of another small, fortified refuge of Guldborg. Amidst the destroyed earthen banks of the stronghold, they uncovered the scattered remains of arrowheads, javelins and lances: traces of the final assault that overwhelmed the defenders in the mid-twelfth century. The remains of a number of women, men and children were found gathered together by the entrance and behind the burnt palisade, together with objects that must have been their personal possessions. In front of the gate, the bodies of a man and a twelve-year-old child had been carefully buried, and a flayed horse's head had been hung above them. Although it is difficult to conclude whether these two individuals had been deliberately killed for this purpose or if they had died during the siege and then been repositioned, the arrangement could certainly be described as ritualistic.

The destroyed refuges and mass graves tally with accounts of Wendish raids around the Danish straits in the twelfth century. We can imagine that a fear of attacks from any number of aggressors, coupled with perceptions of pagan religious practices – however exaggerated – pervaded some of these communities. But these attacks were also part of the region's political vicissitudes; several Wendish groups were allied with German magnates against Danish interests, some also sought retribution for Danish incursions and, in the case of the Rani, they reflected exertions of power in an ongoing struggle for regional influence. In the background, trading and the movement of Wendish merchants, if not slaves, continued, as suggested by finds of temple rings (a type of jewellery worn by women on or around the head), spindle whorls and mounts for knife scabbards of Wendish manufacture.

A turning point in the regional dynamics came with the Danish conquest of the island of Rügen. Its inhabitants, the Rani, had first come under Danish rule during the reign of Eric I (1095–1103), with their spiritual welfare assigned to the newly established archbishopric of Lund. But in time they had shrugged off Danish control, and another attempt was made to subjugate the island in 1136. Valdemar attacked Rügen several times, even with the support of the Saxon duke Henry the Lion, having agreed to split the island's taxes between them. Each attempt had failed. Then in 1168, the campaign, which also involved Bishop Absalon, culminated with the destruction of the pagan religious centre at Arkona.[21] On the king's orders, the many-headed idol of the Slavic god, Svantovit, was cut down. Saxo describes this moment in great detail – the gigantic idol fell with a crash, swathed in rotting purple drapery that still glittered, and a devil in the form of a black animal was seen fleeing from the innermost shrine.[22] For the Danes this was not just about correcting ignorance of the true faith: it was also an exorcism. The idol was chopped up and used as fuel for cooking the crusaders' soup. Saxo continued to describe, in a passage quoted at the start of this chapter, how the temple was set ablaze, and a church built in its place from the timbers of dismantled siege engines. This was a justification of the destruction of Arkona – the Danes were saving the souls of the Rani. Absalon then moved onto Karenz, which held as much religious importance as Arkona on the island, where his men likewise cut down and burnt the idols of the pagan deities.

The toppling of Svantovit's imposing idol would later be immortalised by the Danish court painter Laurits Tuxen in 1894, celebrating a pivotal event in the national history of Denmark. The focus of attention in Tuxen's painting is the black-clad figure of Absalon who holds out his pastoral staff and looks on with stern approval, whilst Valdemar stands calmly behind him – the union of Church and State in the triumph over Slavic heathenry and the ascendancy of the Danish kingdom. Historically, Absalon's fearsome reputation was said to have terrified the Wends. If we are to believe Saxo's account, the bishop had once ordered that all Wendish men were to be killed and, during one campaign, he allegedly interrupted a mass to continue fighting, proclaiming that 'no sacrifice can be more pleasing to the Almighty than the killing of the wicked'.[23] Eskil, the Archbishop of Lund, who had recently returned from exile, also participated in the island's conquest. In contrast to the Danish nationalist celebration of the island's conquest, the Czech artist Alphonse Mucha painted *The Celebration of Svantovit on Rügen* in 1912, as part of his Slav Epic series. It depicts an imaginary celebration at Arkona filled with white-clad pilgrims as the pagan gods become embroiled in a struggle with a pack of wolves in the sky above, foreshadowing the destruction of the sanctuary in what was regarded as an iconic event in Slavic history.

In the early twentieth century, archaeologists eagerly hunted for the destroyed temple, inspired by Saxo's detailed account of the sanctuary and its religious practices, as well as the Danish siege.[24] The remains of the complex are situated on the edge of a chalk cliff which has gradually crumbled into the sea: an estimated 100–200 metres have vanished over the last thousand years. The first serious excavations took place in 1921 under Carl Schuchardt, then director of the Department of Prehistory in Berlin's Ethnological Museum. The island of Rügen had changed hands many times since the Danish conquest, becoming part of Germany after being assigned to Prussia in the aftermath of Napoleon's defeat. Schuchardt imagined he had found the remains of the sanctuary and even the stone foundations which had supported Svantovit's idol, but subsequent investigations in 1969 cast doubt on this, uncovering a much larger area around the earthen rampart and inside the stronghold. These, and later excavations in the 1990s, revealed pits that appear to have been used for ritual depositions, containing arrowheads, knives, glass beads and coins, with some completely filled up with stones. Archaeologists also discovered human remains from the earliest use of the site in the ninth century, but in larger quantities from the eleventh- and twelfth-century phases. Some remains, which displayed cut marks and were interpreted as human sacrifices, had been placed in a pit together with arrowheads, beads, ceramics and animal bones. Analysis of the latter revealed a prevalence of young cattle, pigs, sheep and goats, as well as adult horses, suggesting many were slaughtered in the late summer and most likely for the purposes of ritual feasting. Saxo's account describes how people from across the island participated in annual festivals at the end of the summer, involving feasting and sacrifices to Svantovit. He also mentioned offerings of coins, food and war booty. However, clear traces of the temple building have remained elusive.

Though not a papally sanctioned crusade, the subjugation of Rügen continued the trend of earlier campaigns, where allegiance to the Danish crown was coupled with the formal acceptance of Christianity.[25] In 1169, Valdemar sought and obtained papal recognition of the authority of the see of Roskilde over the conquered island, and the Danish Church set about establishing its infrastructure, which included the foundation of a dozen churches and several monasteries. The destruction of Arkona and the surrender of Karenz ended the power of the island's pagan priesthood. The two brothers who had ruled Rügen – Tezlaw and Jaromar – swore fealty to their new overlord and dutifully converted to Catholicism. As with baptised vassals elsewhere, they led the way in the sponsorship of church and monastery construction. The first was Dargun, founded by monks from the Danish house at Esrum and allegedly built on a levelled pagan temple in 1172, although the earliest monastery here was destroyed during a conflict between Denmark and Brandenburg in 1198. Jaromar, then the sole ruler of Danish Rügen, relocated the monks of Dargun to Eldena. He also sponsored the construction of a church dedicated to the Virgin Mary in his stronghold at Rugard which, soon after its consecration, became part of another Cistercian monastery.

Danish and German settlers were actively encouraged to settle the island, particularly with the establishment of planned towns, but the Rani's distinctive identity appears to have persisted for several centuries. This is evident in the continued use of Slavic personal names, but also in material culture. Wendish-style pottery continued to be produced until the fourteenth century, in contrast to the changes in ceramic production evident on the conquered mainland, and perhaps reflected the deliberate assertion of a local identity. In any event, the island's population became a composite society and, much like in the German marches, Christianity proliferated with the new settlers, who were particularly encouraged by the island's monasteries.[26] One of the oldest surviving churches on Rügen is at Bergen, founded by Jaromar in c. 1180 and granted to Benedictine nuns in the following decade. The earliest parts of the structure, still visible, were constructed from brick on top of a level of fieldstones. This and the Church of Altenkirchen near Arkona dating to c. 1200, which must have acted as a replacement for the former pagan centre, are built in a style reminiscent of contemporary Danish architecture, suggesting Danish masons were responsible. The latter includes a granite block decorated with a representation of a moustached man holding a drinking horn. Popularly known as the 'Svantovit Stone', it has been identified as Tezlaw's tombstone or perhaps a representation of a pagan Slavic priest. If the latter, and given the figure's horizonal positioning in the church wall, it may echo the treatment of visibly pagan monuments following the Danish conquest.[27]

DENMARK AS A 'CRUSADING STATE'

The drawn-out conflict with pagans saw Danish rulers and churchmen shape the kingdom into what some historians have called a 'crusader state'.[28] Even if this label seems like an exaggeration, the second half of the twelfth century saw the political culture of Denmark become aligned with a new chivalric ethos, at the heart of which was pilgrimage and crusading. It was particularly marked, as elsewhere, by support for the military orders. In the 1160s, Valdemar gave the Hospitallers substantial estates in Denmark, with the consent of the realm's leading nobles, and also granted them a tax from every household, perhaps the first example of a national tax supporting a military order. The Hospitallers established their principal house at Antvorskov on the island of Zealand, and it would remain the headquarters of their Scandinavian province through to the Reformation. The Templars never became established on Danish territory, or in any of the Scandinavian countries. Why exactly is not clear, although the Hospitallers also appear to have been a consistently popular choice in the Holy Roman Empire. Whilst they acquired lands in the frontier duchy of Schleswig, which was created and expanded during the conflict with the Saxons and the Wends, they did not establish themselves in the ducal capital. Perhaps Schleswig itself was already too heavily militarised, or the town's lords, keen on maintaining their independence, were not interested in favouring an organisation so closely connected with the crown. A Hospitaller house would be established on Rügen at Maschenholt, although the date of its foundation is unclear, and it may have been long after the Danish conquest. When considering their limited role in military campaigns in the North, it appears that investment in the order was more ideological than driven by the intention of securing frontiers with hostile pagans. The Hospitallers contributed to the preaching of crusades in the Danish realm, as well as recruiting for the ongoing defence of Christian territory in the Levant. But they were also part of a more substantial investment by Valdemar and his successors which emphasised connections between the Danish crown and the Holy Land.

Pilgrimage to Jerusalem in the wake of the First Crusade inspired the construction of churches around Europe in imitation of the Holy Sepulchre, the holiest place in the Christian world. Some of these round churches were famously built by the Templars and Hospitallers, but others were sponsored by other religious groups and magnates. In the Danish kingdom, the early spate of building round churches from the 1120s may have been inspired by Polish and Bohemian rotundas built in the eleventh and twelfth centuries. A new wave of round church building in Denmark in 1171–4 appears to have been connected to Archbishop Eskil's pilgrimage to Jerusalem, with the majority built on Zealand. They were most likely sponsored by the powerful Hvide family who were part of Valdemar's inner circle and filled the leading ranks of the Danish Church, as well as leading the military campaigns against the Wends. Valdemar himself had introduced coins which depicted him grasping a banner with a cross and holding a palm frond – symbols of the pilgrimage to Jerusalem.[29] Yet Eskil was almost certainly the driving force behind the rebuilding of churches imitating the Holy Sepulchre in two of the most important cities in the Danish realm – Schleswig and Ribe.

The round church in Schleswig, which served as the king's permanent residence and where he promoted the cult of his slain father, Canute, was rebuilt to emulate elements of the Holy Sepulchre. A few years later, in 1175, the eastern part of the cathedral in Ribe was also rebuilt with reference to the architecture of the Sepulchre. At a time when tensions between the Church and secular rulers across Europe were heightened – Thomas Becket had been murdered in Canterbury Cathedral in December 1170 – the visual connection with Jerusalem in two of the most important towns within the Danish realm emphasised the long-standing connections with the papacy. They may also have been triumphalist monuments celebrating the conquest of the Wends, drawing parallels with crusading in the Holy Land; indeed, the rebuildings not only coincided with Eskil's pilgrimage, but also with the granting of indulgences by Pope Alexander III for crusades against the Estonians. Eskil's reconciliation with Valdemar only lasted a short period and he went into voluntary exile in 1174, before finally relinquishing his office to Absalon three years later. With him, the impetus for crusading in the eastern Baltic faded, at least for a while. The Scanians and Zealanders contemplated a military campaign against the Estonians a decade later, but they were instead mobilised by Absalon to counter the threat of the Pomeranian attack on the island instigated by the German emperor.

Crusading fervour would be revived when Saladin took Jerusalem from the Franks on 2 October 1187, after destroying the crusader army at Hattin. These events shook Christendom. In the Danish realm, the fall of the holy city was also met with grief, and a fleet led by Danish and Frisian nobles set sail, arriving in Acre in 1189. According to several contemporary sources, it was substantial, consisting of some fifty cogs and 12,000–14,000 men.[30] It is possible their participation inspired some of the murals painted in Danish churches in the following decades which depicted knights and martyred saints.[31] We can certainly imagine how they could have served to vividly illustrate sermons and inspire recruitment for the ongoing holy war which, from 1198, was being promoted by Pope Innocent III. Yet a proportion of the taxes collected for crusading in the Holy Land ended up in the royal Danish coffers, and contributed to financing the expansion of the kingdom through warfare against pagans in the Baltic. Around this time, there were Danish campaigns organised against the Finns and, in the early decades of the thirteenth century, Danish crusading endeavours, twinned with the overseas expansion of the kingdom, became focused, above all, on the Estonians.

The fashion for building round churches in Denmark returned, although it appears they were now constructed as part of a preconceived network, perhaps serving as regional mustering points for crusaders, as the renewed fervour for holy war became connected with the expansion of the Danish kingdom under Valdemar II, who took the throne in 1202.[32] As he conquered more lands in Holstein, and Lübeck came under Danish rule, Valdemar built a round church at Schlamesdorf, replacing an earlier structure, a visible assertion of Danish authority in the southern frontier. The construction of the round church at Kalundborg, under the auspices of Absalon's brother Esbern Snare, resembled a fortress with its striking towers. These churches provided clear reminders of Jerusalem, although the largest of their kind in Scandinavia was not constructed in Denmark, but on the western coast of the Oslo Fjord in Norway, at Tønsberg. Dedicated to St Olaf, the crusading saint, its original investor remains unknown, and it would soon come into the possession of the Premonstratensians, an order associated with promoting Christianisation in the North.[33] The Cistercians, who had established themselves in Denmark with Eskil's encouragement, also influenced the dissemination of the ideological programme of crusading through baptismal fonts produced in Danish and Gotlandic workshops. Some 150 of these were made in the late twelfth and early thirteenth centuries, decorated with scenes of martyrdom, military saints, the symbols of the military orders and representations of physical and spiritual warfare. They have recently been interpreted as advocating for the eradication of paganism in the Baltic, a deliberate strategy to promote 'Jerusalem in the North'. Armed pilgrims had received their 'first cross' at baptism, and now would receive a second with the public consecration of their status as crusaders.[34]

But while the Danish conquests clearly had a religious dimension connected with a vision of Christian kingship, they were also financially important. The annexation of Wendish lands had resulted in the seizure of tribute, livestock and slaves; indeed, Danish provincial laws had to introduce new regulations on slaves as a result and the practice persisted in the kingdom into the mid-thirteenth century.[35] At a time when the

Danish crown owned as little as 5 per cent of land in the realm, taxation, replacing the earlier custom of exacting tribute, became an important source of revenue. According to Saxo, before the Danish conquest each man on Rügen paid a single coin to the shrine at Arkona every year. After the conquest, they had to pay forty silver coins for each plough, although as the island and its revenue had been granted to local vassals as a fief, what the Danish king could essentially call upon was military aid.[36] Tezlaw's forces participated in the Danish assault on Stettin in 1170, whilst Jaromar and Hildegard's son and later ruler of Rügen, Witslaw, would, in turn, aid his overlord Valdemar II in his crusade against the Estonians in 1219. Rügen marked a watershed in the long war with the Wends, although the Danish kings would only claim full overlordship over the conquered (and converted) pagans after Canute VI's naval victory against Bogislaw of Pomerania in 1184, part of a larger conflict with Emperor Frederick Barbarossa who had demanded recognition of his supremacy from the Danish king. The rulers of Denmark were not the only ones to combine crusading with their long-held territorial ambitions. Swedish kings also set their sights on lands in the eastern Baltic which their ancestors had been familiar with for centuries, and which offered lucrative opportunities for expanding their realm.

CRUSADING AGAINST THE FINNS

In 1157, the Swedish king Eric Jedvardsson allegedly landed with an army on the south-western shores of the Finnish Peninsula, the midpoint of what is still regarded today as the 'crusading period' in Finland, spanning some 150–200 years and linking the Viking Age with the Middle Ages in the country's historical periodisation.[37] Or so claims the first known account of the event which survives in a manuscript written almost 200 years later, although scholars now believe it was written in the 1270s (with the earliest known manuscript dating to 1344). What later became known as the 'First Swedish Crusade' is the most intangible of all the northern holy wars of the twelfth century. Most historians regard it as an invented narrative used to justify subsequent Swedish rule, for there is virtually no contemporary evidence for this 'crusade', nor any papal bulls supporting crusades against the Finns at this time.³⁸ An integral part of this fabrication was the supposed involvement of the Bishop of Uppsala, an English cleric named Henry. His role would have been to organise the newly established Church in Finland, an essential reinforcement of royal authority and a vital requisite for further missionary efforts. However, there are no contemporary references to Henry, whose supposed martyrdom in the process of converting the Finns was in all likelihood a creation of the canons of Åbo (Finnish Turku) – the centre of the later medieval Finnish Church – to validate their claim on his saintly cult. Henry became Sweden's Adalbert, far more effective in death than he had been in life. The authority of the Finnish Church was bound up in the heritage of the Swedish conquest, and Eric Jedvardsson would later be venerated as the patron saint of Sweden, whilst Henry would become the equivalent for Finland.³⁹

The shadowy origins of the Swedish crusades nonetheless take place against a culture shift in the kingdom, which saw chivalric, legal and religious norms increasingly adopted from the Continent. Participation in crusading became regarded as a desirable quality for a ruler, a visible demonstration of military prowess and piety. As in Denmark, this was accompanied by a change in how neighbouring groups were perceived, based on their religious differences. During the late Viking Age, it is possible that Swedish raids targeted the Finnish coastline, but the greater prize would have been northern Estonia and its islands.⁴⁰ Nonetheless, the large quantities of Viking Age weapons decorated in Scandinavian styles found in south-west Finland point to close ties with eastern Sweden, with transported ceramics indicating commercial contacts with the trading centre of Birka. The most sought-after commodity would have been furs harvested from the wilderness of the Finnish Peninsula. The growing demand for these in European markets had a massive impact on those living in the interior who switched from a life of subsistence farming to commercial hunting and trapping. Coastal communities became the intermediaries between the trappers and foreign merchants. When Gotland took over as the main commercial hub for the Baltic in the eleventh and twelfth centuries, it facilitated the movement of commodities between Central Europe and the Finnish coast. Even as Swedish rulers continued to take an interest in the trade route that connected the Baltic to Rus' markets, what evidently changed (as for the other parts of the eastern Baltic) was the adoption of a frontier mentality. Now the various groups inhabiting the region of modern Finland (which the Swedes called Österland (East Land)) – Finns, Tavastians, Saami and Karelians – were framed as pagans who threatened Christendom. Under Pope Innocent III, this threat would be extended to 'bad Christians', in this case the neighbouring Orthodox Rus' of Novgorod.[41]

Swedish raids in the eastern Baltic are documented a couple of times in the twelfth century by Rus' chroniclers, reaching as far as Lake Ladoga. In the early 1170s, Pope Alexander III wrote to Scandinavian rulers and prelates asking them to crusade against the pagans in Estonia and others who threatened Christians, with offers of indulgences. In a letter to the Archbishop of Uppsala and Earl Guttorm, the pope demanded that the Swedes should take over strongholds in Finland and take hostages to ensure that the converted Finns did not apostatise as soon as the Christian army left. He complained the Finns only sought the Christian faith when they needed protection from their enemies, mocking God and the Christian religion.[42] It appears that the Swedish king Canute later took up the call as, in 1193, the pope sent him a letter, thanking him for his continued efforts to expand Christendom and wage war against the pagans. In the meantime, the Danes organised crusades against the Finns in 1191 and 1202. In the early decades of the thirteenth century, there may have been several Swedish military campaigns which have been merged into a singular 'Second Swedish Crusade', as the imposition of Swedish royal rule over southern-central Finland – with papal approval – is certain by the mid-thirteenth century.[43] There had even been an attempt to establish a permanent military presence in Estonia at Lihula in 1220, but the Swedes were beaten back.

Once the inhabitants of the south-western parts of the Finnish Peninsula had been subjugated – that is, they were paying taxes and tithes to the Swedes – the perceived threat to this new corner of Catholic Christendom shifted to Karelia, the frontier region with Novgorod. Complaints of Karelian piracy prompted the pope to demand the Archbishop of Uppsala preach a crusade against them in 1274, offering the same indulgences as for those fighting in the Holy Land. The actual campaigns took place much later after a Novgorodian raid on Häme in

1292. The response to this attack, the following year, came to be referred to as the 'Third Swedish Crusade'. This saw the construction of the stronghold at Viborg (Russian Vyborg), and the region would continue to draw the attention of Swedish rulers. King Birger Magnusson declared that the Karelians had been converted and Viborg had been built for the glory of God and the Virgin Mary, but many scholars remain sceptical of the underlying agenda behind this eastward extension of Swedish rule.[44]

In the absence of indigenous written accounts and the limited Swedish ones (due to various later fires that destroyed archives), archaeology offers an alternative perspective on the impact of the events of the twelfth and thirteenth centuries. Given the material evidence for the dramatic cultural transformations associated with conquest and regime change in the southern Baltic, is there anything comparable in Finland? There is in fact very little clear archaeological evidence of Swedish military activities. Royal castles started to be built only from the end of the thirteenth century, although two early military garrisons may have been based at the prehistoric hillfort of Vanhalinna near Lieto and further inland, at Hakoinen. Yet the crusading period does not coincide with the abandonment of indigenous hillforts, which continued to be used. Was the conquest then as violent as the later written sources suggest? Given the decentralised social organisation of the various groups inhabiting the Finnish Peninsula, as well as the scattered nature of the population, the introduction of new structures of governance would have taken some time. But the relatively smooth introduction of Swedish rule may have been aided by the region's early exposure to Christianity. Again, hints of this are visible archaeologically.

Throughout the Iron Age, over many centuries, complex, staged and choreographed cremation rites defined the funerary culture of the Finns, where the bones of most of the dead were commingled with those buried previously – the ancestors – losing their individuality in a collective grave. Some people were cremated and then buried individually, and these included men, women and children. From the early eleventh century, inhumation burials begin to appear within the cremation cemeteries of south-western Finland, a funerary rite adopted first by local elites. These become increasingly prevalent until they define the norm by the mid-twelfth century, and this coincides with a decline in the quantity of objects deposited with the dead, particularly weapons. Cross pendants, largely deriving from Scandinavia (and particularly Gotland), become increasingly common finds within these inhumation burials. Structures found in a few cemeteries have also been interpreted as bell towers or perhaps small chapels. In some places the dead continued to be buried with lavish grave goods, including weapons, and the process of change is best understood at the regional and local levels, even varying between neighbouring villages. Many Finnish archaeologists have interpreted this variation as reflecting the gradual influence of Christian customs, but also of the acceptance of new beliefs concerning death and resurrection.[45]

Exposure to Christianity before the arrival of Swedish crusaders and settlers was most likely the result of increasing Finnish engagement with maritime trade in the eleventh and twelfth centuries. This created a new social class whose wealth and status were drawn from their involvement in commerce, which in turn drove competition that appears to have also manifested in how the dead were memorialised. In the cemetery at Rikalanmäki, within the town of Salo in the Halikko municipality of south-west Finland, archaeologists discovered numerous swords deposited in graves dating to the crusading period. These were interpreted as markers of wealth and prestige. The community of Rikalanmäki was associated with a nearby hillfort, and had grown wealthy following the establishment of trade routes in the eleventh century. The newly acquired purchasing power of this regional centre's leading families would have prompted dramatic changes in social ranking and may explain why collective cremation burials were abandoned in favour of more individualistic inhumations. Here the deposition of weapons reflected the wealth of the elites linked to commerce, although it is also likely that beliefs concerning the afterlife and the attributes of the ancestors became attached to such deposits.[46] This may have kick-started a fashion for inhumation, as others sought to emulate those who had become affluent from trade. But even if there was a new eschatological element in such burials, there is nothing to say these individuals were the right type of Christians in the eyes of Swedish clerics, or that they considered themselves Christian in the first place. In all probability, the Christian god was added alongside Finnish pagan deities and only gradually became the dominant supernatural force in the indigenous belief system.

We are on firmer ground with the construction of churches and their associated cemeteries, which eventually resulted in the abandonment of the more traditional places of burial in south-western Finland. Some of these early churches were built at the initiative of indigenous elites, already familiar with Christianity, most evident where they were constructed on ancestral burial grounds. Others were built by Swedish migrants, who came over and settled in droves during the crusading period. The earliest archaeologically attested church was discovered in 2013 on a wooded hill called Ristimäki ('Cross Hill') in the village of Ravattula in Kaarina, close to the Aura river and the later ecclesiastical centre at Koroinen. The communities in the Aura Valley here had been long connected to maritime trading networks and with them exposure to Christian ideas, so it was an obvious place for missionaries to begin their work.

The timber building which stood on a coarse stone setting, almost 10 metres in length, consisted of a nave, with a doorway on its south side, and a narrow chancel. It most likely had a wooden floor which rested on stones placed underneath. Around twenty coins, mostly of Gotlandic origin, were also found inside the building and, based on their dates, appear to have accumulated under the church floor in a short period of time. Many are dated to the last quarter of the twelfth century. The hill surrounding the church was used for burials, where the dead were inhumed in traditional dress and accompanied by small valuables, and their graves oriented south-west–north-west. The cemetery appears to have been in use from the mid-twelfth century through to the first two decades of the thirteenth century, when its abandonment coincides with the establishment of parishes. A new church would have been allocated, serving a larger district increasingly populated with farms and villages.

This creation of a new Christian landscape followed the establishment of an episcopal centre at Koroinen, located on a cape on the Aura river.[47] Archaeologists discovered here the earliest bishop's residence which was initially a timber building but was soon replaced by a stone tower with a brick floor, a large timber house with a hypocaust and a church which functioned as a cathedral, the whole cluster surrounded by an embankment and dry moat. Later, a small brick house would be added as part of the bishop's residence. Archaeologically, the site has a complex biography which makes its structures difficult to date precisely, but the uses of brick here may be one of the earliest in Finland. Large quantities of coins, particularly from Gotland, and imported ceramics have also led to suggestions there was a marketplace here too. When the episcopal seat was relocated downstream the Aura to the newly founded Åbo in the early fourteenth century, the bishop retained Koroinen as a residence and its church continued to serve the local parish.[48]

The foundation of Åbo, the first town in Finland, was a historic moment. Archaeologists have demonstrated there was in fact an existing settlement here, established some fifty years earlier. This probably functioned as a market supplying Koroinen, whose location was unsuitable for the anchorage of larger ships. The main movers of commodities across the Baltic were now German merchants, who probably resided here and developed a cohesive community. In order to retain control over maritime trade, a decision was made to formally organise the earlier settlement at Åbo into a town. A castle was built to represent royal authority and protection over trade, and to serve as an administrative centre for the crown. The bishop was also persuaded to relocate. Åbo then became the most important port in the Finnish Peninsula, with its sizeable community of German merchants populating the town council.[49]

By the time Åbo was founded, the nearby coastlines had also been settled by large numbers of Swedish migrants. Previously, it was thought these migrants were responsible for introducing villages and intensive farming techniques to coastal Finland, but in fact there is evidence of single farms developing into villages here already in the Late Iron Age.[50] In local pollen records, there is also a noticeable expansion of cultivation at this time. By the twelfth century, the areas of densest settlement were found in south-western Finland along river valleys like that of the Aura, and the region around Tampere, corresponding to what the Swedes called Tavastia. In Uusimaa (Swedish Nyland), the southern stretch of the Finnish Peninsula that faces the Estonian coastline, Swedish settlers begin to arrive in areas sparsely populated by Finns from the late twelfth or early thirteenth century onwards, with continuous waves of migration through to the mid-fourteenth century. This was driven by royal incentives, particularly in newly conquered or uninhabited areas, which included ownership rights to the land in exchange for taxes and military service. But immigration could also be more spontaneous, driven by a desire for new opportunities. This, and the fact that the number of manors established by Swedish nobles with associated estates remained low, helped create a large class of freeholding peasants who were not tied to the land. This was also a feature of the Swedish interior, which was beginning to be more intensively exploited by intrepid families of settlers at this time.

The reconfiguration of Finland's ethnic landscape has traditionally been mapped through place names, on the assumption that the language of the founders determined the name given to the new settlements. These are difficult to date, and require a fair bit of regressive thinking using later sources and maps. Individual farms or villages consisting of a handful of farms, sometimes more, were founded by both Swedes and Finns, who ended up living in close proximity to each other. We can imagine that agreements were reached over the sharing of local resources, echoes of which are found in later, better documented disputes over land. Indeed, the permanent occupation of places that had previously been used on a seasonal basis by indigenous families for activities like fishing suggests they were now settling to secure rights to the land. Territory was also reserved for royal estates – demesnes – in strategically important locations, particularly near rivers, lakes and trade routes, or in areas bordering uninhabited or sparsely populated wilderness. Here, Swedish and Finnish settlers were encouraged to clear land for farming, with royal officials present to oversee agricultural production and tax collection. Within a couple of centuries, the coastal areas of Uusimaa were largely populated by Swedish-speaking inhabitants, whose presence significantly increased the visibility of Christianity.[51] In the interior, which had a larger Finnish, Tavastian and Saami population, the new religion took longer to establish footholds.

Further to the east, Karelia remained a hazy frontier between the lands claimed by the Swedish crown and Novgorod, beyond the immediate reach of both. In the nineteenth century, the region would attract ethnographers and folklorists seeking to capture what they saw as the timeless national spirit of the Finns, untainted by Swedish Christianity.

Whilst Karelian society had not in fact remained frozen in time, during the crusading period the region was far from the epicentre of both Swedish and Rus' power, and the influence of the Catholic and Orthodox churches on customs, including burial, remained geographically limited for many centuries. Here, changes in the use of cemeteries would take the longest of any Finnish region, with earlier rites continuing in some cases into the fifteenth century.

TOWARDS LIVONIA

Scandinavian expansion across the Baltic Sea region was a continuous phenomenon from the Viking Age to the era of the crusades. What changed was not so much the adoption of Christianity in the Scandinavian regions, but the attraction of crusading, which both drove and validated the territorial ambitions of the growing Christian kingdoms. By the twelfth century, independent Churches now played a central role in Scandinavia, marked by the foundation of the archbishopric of Lund, followed by Nidaros and Uppsala. As the papacy and local prelates advocated for crusading as part of the broader Christian mission, Scandinavian rulers gradually embraced the idea of fighting for Christendom as a political and religious aspiration. Crusading culture in Scandinavia was shaped by the idea of fighting for the Holy Land, but also by local campaigns against pagans. Although traditionally viewed as motivated by territorial expansion and the desire to control trade, we can see religious elements also played an important role, from grass-roots missionary activity to the organisation of pastoral infrastructure serving both indigenous convert and migrant Christian communities.

Denmark emerges as the Scandinavian kingdom whose ruling elite became most committed to crusading. Their interest extended beyond the Holy Land and became deeply rooted in local politics, regional expansion and the Christianisation of the remaining pagan peoples of the North. Whilst the conquest of Rügen was part of a broader strategy of expanding Danish influence along the southern Baltic coast largely in competition with its Christian neighbours, the religious dimension to the aftermath of the military campaigns is inescapable. The destruction of the island's pagan religious centres served both as an act of spiritual purification and a means of breaking the political and cultural cohesion of the local population. This undermined their resistance to Danish rule and made them dependent on the Church, a supporting pillar of the state. At the same time, the missionaries who settled on the island in the wake of the conquest most probably believed they were saving the souls of the Rani. This entangled motivation can also be seen in the construction of monuments which referenced the aspirations of the crusading movement and simultaneously projected the power of the Danish crown and Church.

Swedish involvement in crusading has also been reconsidered. Traditionally, Finnish scholarship, rooted in a nationalist tradition, emphasised the expansion of the Swedish kingdom into the peninsula as a religious and cultural war. More recently, the conversion to Christianity has been regarded as a longer, more peaceful process, and one that developed alongside commercial contacts across the Baltic Sea. Cast in this light, violent confrontations have been explained away as resistance to taxation and tithe payments.[52] Despite the harsh rhetoric aimed at the pagans of Finland and their caricaturing as aggressive savages within the later cults of St Eric and St Henry, Finns were treated on equal terms with their Swedish counterparts. They could use their own language within the Church, in courts and in local administration, and they could marry without restriction. In fact, their ethnicity was rarely acknowledged and they were simply called 'Swedes'.[53] Moreover, in all historical analyses of Sweden's activities in Finland, competition with Novgorod over taxes and trade always rears its head. Given this, crusading may come across as something ephemeral, even superficial, but there is compelling evidence that it became a genuine devotional activity integrated into Swedish religious, political and social life. Papal support for these campaigns suggests that crusading in Sweden was recognised as part of the universal Christian cause. The Church's role in these campaigns, including preaching and granting indulgences, as well as some royal support for the miliary orders, also reinforces the idea that a genuine crusading culture was fostered in Sweden.

In the later decades of the twelfth century, the papacy became increasingly interested in the Christianisation of the pagans in the eastern Baltic, and more willing to sanction crusades in the region. Whilst the

Danes and Swedes remained focused on the north-eastern maritime route through the Gulf of Finland to Rus' lands, German merchants were exploring the southern route up the Daugava river through the lands of the Livs. They were soon followed by missionaries who instigated a new, transformative chapter in the history of the Baltic Crusades.

MILITARISED CHRISTIANITY IN THE NORTH

CHAPTER 5

TERRA MARIANA
Creating Livonia

On the sixth day, the Germans said: 'Do you still resist and refuse to acknowledge our Creator?; To this they [the Estonians] replied: 'We acknowledge your God to be greater than our gods. By overcoming us, He has inclined our hearts to worship Him. We beg, therefore, that you spare us and mercifully impose the yoke of Christianity upon us as you have upon the Livs and Letts.'

Henry's Chronicle of Livonia[1]

FORTIFIED MISSIONARY OUTPOSTS

When German missionaries first reached the shores of the eastern Baltic, they probably had little idea of the diverse groups they would soon encounter. Their initial contact was with the Livs who inhabited the banks of the Daugava River in what is today western Latvia and, as a result, they came to refer to their lands as Livonia in Latin, or Livland in German. In time, this name would be extended to most of what is present-day Latvia and Estonia.[2] The Daugava Livs were part of a larger Finnic group settled along the western side of the modern Latvian province of Vidzeme and along the eastern coast of Kurzeme – Curonia in Latin and Kurland in German. To the east was the vast territory of Latgale inhabited by a different linguistic group, Balts. Latgalian settlements reached the borders of the Rus' principalities of Polotsk (in modern Belarus),

Pskov and Novgorod (today in western Russia). The Curonians inhabited the rest of Kurzeme and their settlements were also found in what is modern north-west Lithuania. East of this lay Semigallia and Selonia, sandwiched between the Daugava and the northern borders of Samogitia and Lithuania. To the north, Estonia was also made up of various regional Baltic Finnic groups, with a significant cultural divide between the north-west of the region, dominated by its islands and coastline, and the south-east, with its larger expanses of woodland and uplands. None of these groups produced their own literature, so the names derive from Christian chroniclers who distinguished between them, but at times they referred to the Semigallians, Selonians and Latgalians – who all belonged to the same linguistic group – as 'Letts', and the Estonians were often grouped together, except for the Osilians who dwelt on the islands, named in chronicles after the largest, called Osilia in Latin and Ösel in German (Estonian Saaremaa). These groups were ruled over by aristocratic families who resided in strongholds, which have seen extensive archaeological investigation in both Estonia and Latvia.[3] Their varied chronology reflects a complex and uneven political landscape, as some groups extended their territorial and economic influence at the expense of others, wielding power over entire or even multiple provinces.[4]

Riga was the third outpost established by Christian missionaries in Livonia, after Üxküll (Latvian Ikšķile), the first bishopric in the region, and Holm (Latvian Mārtiņsala). The town was founded on the initiative of the third bishop of Livonia, Albert, who arrived at the mouth of the Daugava river with a crusading army in 1200. Albert was continuing the missionary work of his predecessors amongst the Livs, but the river had long been known to German merchants as it linked the Baltic Sea with trading centres in Lithuania and the lands of the Rus'. When the crusaders arrived, the power dynamics that governed the river were complex. Burials dating from between the tenth and twelfth century around the stronghold of Daugmale, which stood on the southern bank of the river, are associated with diverse groups, including Livs, Semigallians, Curonians and Osilians. The latter two had large numbers of ships and almost certainly played a role in controlling trade on the Daugava.[5] But by the end of the twelfth century, the river came under the influence of the powerful Rus' principality of Polotsk, and its ruler

Vladimir. Daugmale would be abandoned following Rus' attacks, a reflection of Vladimir's growing confidence, as he competed with Lithuania's grand dukes for control over the route. The German missionaries waded into this regional power struggle, and Riga, located in a strategically advantageous position where trading already took place, presented a fresh contender for control of the Daugava.[6]

Missions to the Livs had proven to be dangerous. Berthold had brought a crusading army with him, but had fallen in battle. Albert also petitioned the pope for a crusade, and Innocent III had urged the faithful in Saxony, Westphalia, Mecklenburg and those living east of the Elbe to participate in the venture, even permitting those who were committed to crusading in the Levant to transfer their vows to the Baltic. The papacy clearly had a vested interest in expanding its reach eastwards, but the crusades themselves were driven by individuals and groups with their own personal agendas and soon they took on a life of their own. The details of what happened were later described by someone who was close to the events at the time. We know very little about him, other than his name, Henry, that he was a member of Albert's household, and that he was well versed in Latin and German. He was most likely a priest, but opinion remains divided as to his place of birth. The chronicle he wrote and completed in 1227 – here simply referred to as Henry's *Chronicle* – is the earliest and most important account we have of how a new Christian state on the eastern shores of the Baltic Sea was forged in the fires of holy war.[7] Based extensively on his own observations, but also triumphalist and prone to exaggeration, Henry's dramatic narrative has defined how we have understood the cataclysmic events that would forever transform north-eastern Europe. It is nonetheless a polarised account, one that frames the creation of Livonia as the struggle between light and darkness, Christianity and paganism, civilisation and barbarity. This is perhaps unsurprising given not only its authorship, but also its purpose – to make the case to the papal court for the violent creation of Livonia.

Henry described how Riga was pivotal to the story of the new Catholic land. The town was 'watered by the new faith, and because through it, the peoples surrounding it are watered by the font of sacred baptism'.[8] Riga was a commercial enterprise, founded with the help of merchants and the local Livs, but it was also clearly intended as a solid anchor for Christianity in Livonia, providing a much safer haven for indigenous converts and missionaries than either Üxküll or Holm. Indeed, when Albert had first arrived with a large crusading fleet and sailed up the Daugava to visit the two outposts, he was attacked by the Livs. Two years later, the church in Holm would be burnt down by the Semigallians and in 1203 Üxküll was attacked by Rus' forces from Polotsk. With the co-operation of the Christianised Livs, the local pagan religious site was levelled (as discovered by archaeologists) and the ground prepared for the construction of the first brick church in the region – the cathedral of Riga, dedicated to the Virgin Mary. The town itself was planned from the very onset on a grid, enclosed by a timber and earth stockade, which would later be replaced by a brick wall. In time, the town would grow to absorb the two neighbouring Liv settlements within its walls.

Just over a decade ago, excavations in the south-eastern corner of the historic centre of Riga, by the junction of Audēju and Kalēju streets, uncovered the traces of the southernmost indigenous settlement. Seventeen timber buildings were discovered in this area, packed with debris and sediment which had accumulated over several centuries of dense occupation. The earliest was dated by dendrochronology to c. 1209, and it remains the oldest known wooden structure in the city dated in this way.[9] Like the other buildings on the site, it had been constructed from logs derived from largely young pine trees, placed so they crossed each other at the corners of each building – this was an unmistakably indigenous style of construction which had been used in the region for centuries. Nearly a hundred similar houses have been found in earlier excavations in Riga. The jewellery found at the Audēju/Kalēju site was of local origin and there was a virtual absence of imported objects which characterised the other parts of the town, where frame houses built from larger timbers reflected a construction technique introduced by German migrants.[10] Only twenty-four such houses have been uncovered by archaeologists in Riga, although most of the buildings in the town would later be replaced by stone and brick. Clay stoves, representing local heating technology, were found in some of these timber-framed houses. The townscape became a segregated space as migrants settled in-between the existing indigenous villages, but Riga's population did mingle and interact, not least of all within the new religious buildings that came to dominate its skyline. Indigenous labourers also invariably played a role in the construction of Riga's buildings and walls. Henry's *Chronicle* certainly paints a picture of a unified urban population, but the creation of the town quickly generated social inequality which intersected with ethnic background. The most privileged group in the town were German merchants, whose growing presence saw Riga's role in commerce flourish. Riga's population grew quickly. At the start of the thirteenth century, it was inhabited by an estimated 1,000 people, and this would double within a few decades. Soon it would become one of the most important cities in the Baltic region.

In 1205, the first monastery in Livonia began to be constructed on an islet in a branch of the Daugava flowing out to the north-east. Nearby was a harbour and trading place that had long been used by indigenous groups, particularly the Osilians. The monastery was named Dünamünde (Latvian Daugavgrīva) and Albert appointed the missionary Theoderic as its abbot, with monks arriving from the Cistercian house of Marienfeld three years later. Dünamünde was fortified and served as both a means of controlling access to the Daugava and as a centre for evangelising, but transforming the beliefs of the local Livs – and other groups who allied with the crusaders – would be a slow process.[11]

What began with a few fortified missionary outposts steadily transformed into a territorial conquest over a period of three decades, and ultimately a regional conflict that dragged on for almost a century. Riga, under the leadership of a militant episcopate, became the principal bridgehead and mustering point for the campaigns which made up the Livonian crusades. Crusading pushed the north-eastern bounds of Christendom with the creation of Livonia, which was shaped by the diverse encounters between migrants and indigenous peoples.

TERRITORIAL CHRISTIANITY

Albert travelled to the northern German provinces regularly to recruit fighters. Between 1200 and 1227 he made at least thirteen journeys, as did some of his colleagues. According to Henry's *Chronicle*, the bishop had originally enlisted crusaders from Gotland and Magdeburg, and subsequently the majority came from Saxony and Westphalia.[12] Given the competing appeal of the Holy Land, recruits for crusading in the Baltic required additional inspiration. The lands of the Baltic pagans had never been Christian territory, but the crusades authorised by Pope Innocent III justified them on the grounds of defending Christians living there, especially indigenous converts. In particular, the pope saw this as an extension of Christ's dominion when he referred to the '*plantatione novella fidei christiane*' in Livonia, literally a plantation of the Christian faith.[13] The plantation expanded at a cumulative rate. As more indigenous groups converted – or were officially recognised as such after public mass baptisms – crusading armies were brought over to protect them from their neighbours, and so the conflict also quickly came to involve the pagan Lithuanians and Samogitians, and the Orthodox Rus'. There were also internal enemies who threatened the plantation: those who had been baptised and then turned on their Catholic allies were denounced as apostates. The papacy regarded the use of force as a justifiable means of bringing these back to the true faith. This was echoed in Henry's narrative where the apostasy of indigenous converts – who, in his words, drawing inspiration from the Bible, 'like dogs, go back to their vomit' – justified the violent actions of the crusaders.[14]

From the Catholic outsider's perspective, Livonia was therefore a new Christian land that needed protection. It would become branded as 'Terra Mariana' – 'The Land of Mary'. The precedent had been set by the dedication of Livonia's first bishopric to the Blessed Virgin, but Henry's *Chronicle* framed Albert as the main promoter of her cult, with its centre in Riga. The new sacrality of the land was reinforced with the blood of martyrs – missionaries, crusaders, converts – and the deposition of relics in newly built churches, which created permanent beacons of holiness. Reports of numerous miraculous happenings in Livonia also reinforced the divine mandate for the ongoing holy war.[15] But spiritual rewards were just one part of the incentive to crusade in Livonia, and only Pope Honorius III had offered a full plenary indulgence comparable to crusading in the Holy Land. There were also material rewards to be had. Albert made his first documented grant of land in 1201 to Conrad of

Meiendorf, a German knight. At the same time, he gave land to an indigenous noble who had been christened with the name Daniel. The properties in question centred on the strongholds at Lennewarden (Latvian Lielvārde) and Üxküll. These were to be held as fiefs, in exchange for unpaid labour, which usually included military service, and a portion of any revenues generated from the land.

The expectation of being awarded land as a reward was certainly not a new concept for the Western nobility. It also seems that private property was familiar to the Livs, with evidence for family ownership of parcels of land before the crusades.[16] But with the support of crusading forces, it became possible for the new self-styled lord of Livonia to seize territory from indigenous landholders and return it to them under new terms, redefining them as vassals. This created completely new power relationships, cemented with bonds of loyalty between the incomers and the indigenous population. When Albert had received Livonia as a fief from the German emperor, this formalised his sole right to exercise secular power in the lands of his vassals. Indeed, he would rely on these individuals to govern on his behalf and maintain order in his new Christian plantation.[17] Key vassals were given judicial roles to ensure the implementation of Christian laws, although Henry complained those appointed from the laity to the post of 'advocate' were more interested in filling their own purses than upholding justice.[18] It is easy to imagine how corruption could be rife and authority, underpinned by the threat of violence, easily abused. The Livs had accepted German lordship by 1206 and the neighbouring Latgalians followed suit in 1209, after the seizure of their political centre at Jersika. Campaigns against the Estonians began in earnest in 1208 and ended in 1227 with the conquest of the islands, although there would be later region-wide insurrections. The Curonians were not conquered until 1267, and the Semigallians would resist until 1272, and then, following an uprising, they would hold out until 1290.

Alongside the new subdivisions of land, which were reconfigured several times during the first few decades of Livonia's existence, came the introduction of dioceses and parishes. From the very onset, tithes were extracted from the conquered population to support priests engaged in missionary activity and the growing Livonian Church, and this newly imposed burden had triggered hostility from the local population.[19] Following Riga, plans for new German dioceses would finally materialise in Estonia with the south-eastern episcopate of Dorpat in 1224 (Estonian Tartu), Ösel-Wiek (the Osilian islands and western Estonia) in 1228, and lastly the diocese of Curonia in 1234. Like the prelate of Riga, whose status was later elevated to that of archbishop for Livonia and Prussia, the other German bishops were granted the title of imperial prince by the emperor, and also wielded secular power on their lands. In northernmost Estonia, the Danish Church would create its own diocese. Albert had successfully established a crusading culture in the eastern Baltic, enabling him to bring seasonal armies to Livonia, and he benefited enormously from the military support provided by his indigenous allies and vassals. However, the conquest was driven by a more reliable military presence.

THE SWORD BROTHERS

The fledgling Christian outposts in Livonia encountered the same problems as had been faced by Latin rulers in the Levant following the First Crusade. Crusading armies came and went once their oath had been fulfilled, and a permanent military presence was required to provide security for this new Catholic plantation. In 1202, Theoderic, acting on behalf of Albert, recruited from Riga's aristocratic and mercantile families to form a new military order called Fratres Militiae Christi – the Brothers of the Militia of Christ. They were organised following the model of the Templars, headed up by a master, with its members dedicated to a monastic life of obedience, poverty and celibacy.[20] They also took their insignia from the Templars, a red cross set against a white field, to which they added the image of a sword. This would earn them the nickname of the Sword Brothers. As vassals of the bishop, they were given funds, lands and a residence in the east of Riga. But as an institution enshrined with the ideology of crusading, they were also encouraged to wage a defensive holy war against those neighbouring pagans perceived as a threat.

Fusing religious fervour with political ambition and economic interests, the Sword Brothers transformed the pace and intensity of Albert's crusades. As the organisation grew in size and power, it would also establish a presence in Lübeck and Visby, key recruitment centres for the Livonian crusades. The Sword Brothers' first documented engagement was in 1205, when they responded to a call for aid from the Semigallians of Terweten, who had been plagued by Lithuanian raids. Other local leaders made pacts with Bishop Albert and the Sword Brothers in exchange for protection against the Lithuanians. But allegiances could change when the opportunity presented itself. The same year, Vetseke, the indigenous lord of Koknese (rendered in German as Kokenhusen), had offered half of his lands to Albert who provided him with weapons and troops to withstand Lithuanian raids. However, Vetseke was also a vassal of Vladimir of Polotsk, and when Albert was due to depart with his crusading army for north German lands, Vetseke urged the Rus' prince to attack Riga, gathering his forces in Koknese. Albert's fleet had been held up at Dünamünde and was able to turn back and secure the city, prompting the Rus' army to set fire to Koknese and withdraw back to Polotsk, along with Vetseke. The frustrated crusaders attacked the local population instead, killing many who fled into the nearby forests.

The Sword Brothers had proven to be effective fighters, but they also developed their own territorial ambitions. When Albert was granted Livonia as a fief, the brethren demanded – and were given – a third of all the conquered territories. This division of the land, confirmed by the pope three years later, marked the beginning of a new political reality in the eastern Baltic. The brethren had their principal fortified residence in Riga, but now began to construct stone castles both to consolidate the new regime's hold on the land, and to secure their own interests against those of other territorial lords – including their liege. Their first castle was built at Segewold (Latvian Sigulda) between c. 1207 and 1209, in a strategic location on the Gauja river. Directly across the valley, at Treiden (Latvian Turaida) was the stronghold of the local Liv leader Kaupo. He had been an early convert and ally of the crusaders, and even accompanied Theoderic to Rome to meet the pope. In 1211, when the Estonians attacked Treiden, the Sword Brothers and their allies drove them off, acquiring large quantities of spoils, including ships and horses. Arguments over land and resources soon erupted.

A quarrel over fields and access to beehives (sources of wax, a very lucrative commodity) led to the Sword Brothers wounding some of the

Letts of Autine, which subsequently led to an uprising by the Letts and Livs. The bishop's vassal, Daniel of Lennewarden, arrested and imprisoned the leaders of the conspiracy and had their strongholds destroyed. Treiden was also set on fire. But accusations against the Sword Brothers' unjust behaviour continued, leading to another outbreak of war with the Livs. This time, resistance centred on the stronghold of the Liv leader Dobrel, which was largely destroyed by the Christian army, prompting the Livs to sue for peace. In 1214, under the direction of Bishop Philip of Ratzeburg (and on behalf of Albert), a castle began to be constructed in the place of the old Liv stronghold at Treiden. It was named Vredeland (Friedland – 'Land of Peace') in the hope this would bring peace to the region, although the Germanised rendering of the Liv name continued to be more commonly used. This red-brick structure was largely rebuilt in the second half of the twentieth century, when extensive archaeological investigations were conducted, but few traces of its early phase or the indigenous stronghold have been identified.

Further up the Gauja Valley, which represented the borderland between the territories of the Livs and Letts, lived a small group called Wends (no relation to those in the northern marches).[21] Little is known of them archaeologically, except for their stronghold in Cēsis. Next to the later castle, probably the best-known historical monument in Latvia outside of Riga, is an unassuming grass-covered mound known as Riekstu Hill. Excavations here uncovered the foundations of a substantial stone wall that wrapped around the top of the hill, a masonry technique associated with German migrants.[22] According to Henry, the Wends had converted to Christianity in 1206 and, a couple of years later, members of the Sword Brothers came to reside with them. They replaced the timber fortifications of their stronghold with stone walls. In 1214, the brethren began to build a castle next to the hillfort, adopting the name of the indigenous group and calling it Wenden – the Latvian name Cēsis would be used later. In 1209, the Sword Brothers had also constructed a stone castle to replace the existing stronghold of Kokenhusen, located at the confluence of the Daugava and Pērse rivers. Ownership of its territory was split with Bishop Albert, but three years later this would be handed over to him completely in exchange for the stronghold of Autine.

Having secured the Lower Daugava, Albert directed the Sword Brothers to campaign northwards into Estonian lands. These began in 1208, and transformed into a war that would last for almost two decades. The specific details of these campaigns are described in Henry's *Chronicle*, and Liv, Lett and Rus' troops fought alongside both the crusaders and Estonians. The various Estonian groups were rallied by the Saccalian elder Lembitu whose forces defeated the Sword Brothers in the same year that Treiden fell. Five years later Lembitu was killed in the battle of St Matthew's Day, fighting against the brethren and the Liv leader Kaupo, who also died. The Sword Brothers were initially successful at capturing key strongholds and when the locals had accepted baptism, they were permitted to garrison them alongside the Germans.

The impact of the Sword Brothers' campaigns is visible archaeologically. Over 200 crossbow bolts, of a type that was used in the first half of the thirteenth century, have been found during excavations of a number of strongholds in Estonia and Latvia.[23] This was the weapon of choice in Baltic Christendom at the time, and was also adopted by the indigenous defenders of these strongholds. Exceptionally preserved traces of a siege have been found in the vicinity of the castle at Viljandi, in the southern Estonian province of Saccalia. The castle was built within the remains of a indigenous timber-and-earth stronghold, which served as a regional power centre. Henry refers to 'Viliende' several times in his *Chronicle*, and it was first conquered by the Sword Brothers in 1211. On the sixth day of this siege, the Estonian defenders surrendered, acknowledging the supremacy of the Christian god. Their dialogue with the Germans, who had besieged the stronghold together with their Liv and Lett allies, quoted at the start of this chapter, was invariably wishful thinking on Henry's part. German priests were permitted into the stronghold once terms had been agreed and hostages provided by the Estonians, and they sprinkled all the buildings and people inside with holy water. They did not, however, baptise them on account of all the blood that had been spilt during the siege. Peace in Saccalia did not last long. The Estonians were able to take back the stronghold and it was besieged again and finally taken by the Sword Brothers in 1223.[24] Excavations demonstrated the settlement in the surrounding hilltops had been destroyed by fire, and the burnt-out remains of the dwellings were levelled to provide stable platforms for trebuchets. Henry describes how the German trebuchet crews were significantly hampered by the Estonian defenders firing at them with crossbows, and on one of the hills archaeologists discovered forty-one crossbow bolts, along with an iron spade.[25] The Sword Brothers were able to take and destroy the stronghold, and within a short period of time began to refortify it, constructing a stone castle named Fellin.

These castles served as centres of administration for their newly acquired lands, as well as stores for their arms, armour and the taxes they had begun to extract from their new subjects. Little is known about the design of these early fortifications, as they were expanded and rebuilt in later centuries, but as with the Teutonic Order's castles, the larger structures built by the Sword Brothers must have functioned as fortified monasteries, for the brethren lived in communities with daily routines subdivided between cycles of prayer, administrative tasks and military training. The written sources associated with their lands certainly indicate a recurring emphasis on access to natural resources, which contributed to their provisioning and income. During these years, the brethren tailored their fighting tactics to the local terrain. They discovered the most advantageous time for attacking with large numbers of cavalry was during winter, when the expansive bogs, lakes and rivers of the eastern Baltic were frozen and therefore easier to cross. This would become a regular season for crusading campaigns in both Livonia and Prussia.

Many castles built at this time would have been relatively simple structures, following the template established at Üxküll. One of the best known is Alt-Dahlen (Latvian Vecdole), built on the island of Dole within the Daugava and first mentioned in 1227. It was excavated in 1966–8 ahead of the construction of a dam across the Daugava to serve Riga's hydroelectric power station in Salaspils. Archaeologists uncovered the remains of a rectilinear structure built in two phases, representing a comparatively short period of occupation spanning much of the thirteenth century.[26] Across the threshold of the castle's main gate, the body of a calf had been laid in a pit on its back, aligned with the direction of the castle walls. The structure had been built by the Bishop of Riga's vassals, so was this evidence of a indigenous practice? Similar deposits – of animal skulls – were found under the 'Ramera tower' of Riga's north wall, associated with its rebuilding. But such deposits are also known from Christian Europe: in Germany they are referred to as *Bauopfer* and, as such, those responsible for this foundation deposit – presumably to strengthen the building through a magical act – may have been indigenous or migrant builders. Castle building was accompanied by the creation of a new religious landscape not only in Livonia's new towns, but also in the countryside. The presence of coin deposits at St Nicholas's Hill in southern Estonia, located on the road from Wenden to Dorpat, suggest the existence of a chapel here in the second quarter of the thirteenth century.[27] The chapel was located close to the crusaders' camp site mentioned in Henry's *Chronicle*, and was most probably built on the site where sermons were given to the Christian army before its campaigns into Estonian Ugaunia.

THE DANISH CRUSADE

Anticipating the conquest of Estonian lands by the Sword Brothers and their allies, Albert had appointed Theoderic as Bishop of Estonia in 1211. But indigenous resistance was too strong, and the brethren failed to conquer the northern part of the region. Conflict with various Estonian groups and their Rus' allies had continued for several years and in 1218 Albert and Theoderic travelled to the Danish court to gain King Valdemar's support in a crusade against the Estonians. Valdemar, sensing an opportunity to extend his domain, agreed and the following year asked Pope Honorius III to elevate his invasion of Estonia to the status of a crusade. Albert had also enlisted the aid of the Duke of Saxony (another Albert), which some historians have interpreted was an attempt to counter Danish territorial ambitions. Bishop Albert was of course keen to ensure the evangelisation of the eastern Baltic remained within his hands, and those of his fellow German churchmen. From the duke's perspective, his rivalry with the Danish king over lands in the northern provinces of the Holy Roman Empire would have made this an attractive proposition, as well as raising his own standing. But the duke arrived too late to make a difference and, after a slow start in Livonia, his forces were engaged with fighting around the Daugava.

King Valdemar sailed to Estonia with his army, accompanied by the Archbishop of Lund, Anders Sunesen, his chancellor, Bishop Nicholas of

Schleswig and his vassal, Wenceslaus, the Wendish lord of Rügen. However, Theoderic was slain, frustrating Albert's efforts to secure the north Estonian diocese for the Livonian Church. The Danes were able to establish a foothold on the coast and allegedly rebuilt the old indigenous stronghold on Toompea Hill at Lyndanisse, a place which soon became known as Reval (Estonian Tallinn). In time, a bishop's residence, cathedral, school and a Dominican monastery were constructed up on the hill. The intention was to create a new power centre that controlled the maritime route to Novgorod through the Gulf of Finland and acted as a counterbalance to Riga. Religion, politics and commerce were entangled as ever.[28]

What followed was a struggle between the Danish and German Livonian churches over the souls of the Estonians. German and Danish priests raced to baptise as many indigenous as they could, hoping to extend the influence of their respective churches. The Danes even gave out holy water to peasants in northern Estonia, asking them to baptise their families before the German priests arrived. These instances of rapid baptisms may be reflected in numerous finds of so-called bronze 'Hanseatic bowls' in north Estonia, which have sometimes been discovered in sets. They were probably brought over as gifts for the local nobility and may even have served as baptismal vessels.[29] It is during these competing baptisms that Henry describes how German priests destroyed the images of Estonian gods that were kept in a sacred grove in Wierland (one of the contested provinces in the north-east). This is the only explicit written reference to an attack on a pagan religious site during the crusades in Livonia, but it is evident that others – such as the Liv site in Riga – were also destroyed.

In 1223, there was a crisis in the Danish court. Valdemar and his son were abducted whilst hunting on the island of Lyø. Their captor was Valdemar's German vassal Henry, the Count of Schwerin. Whilst he'd been away on the Fifth Crusade, the Danish king had essentially appropriated a large part of the count's territories. A conflict between Danish and German forces followed, with lasting repercussions after the Battle of Mölln in January 1225 which saw the Danes defeated. Henry was able to force concessions from Valdemar which amounted to renouncing Danish claims to all German territories. Valdemar would go back on his word and attempt to conquer back the lands, but was defeated by the Count of Holstein in 1227. This saw a historical movement of the frontier to the Eider, the southern edge of the Danish duchy of Schleswig. It would not move again until the nineteenth century.

Even before the sudden loss of Danish leadership, there was an insurrection on Osilia in 1222, prompted by the construction of a Danish stronghold on the island. The rebellion spread to other Estonian provinces. The Estonians had been permitted to join the garrisons of some of the Sword Brothers' castles and at Fellin they attacked the Germans as they gathered in the church for Mass. In Jerwen, they seized the magistrate and, according to Henry, tortured him, tore out his heart, roasted it and then consumed it. They called upon Rus' mercenaries from Novgorod and Pskov to garrison the most important strongholds which they had captured from the Danes and Germans, dividing with them the spoils. There was also a distinctly anti-Christian element to the uprising. Priests were killed and those who had been buried in cemeteries were allegedly exhumed and cremated according to pagan custom. Henry also describes how the Estonians washed their strongholds, houses and themselves with water, hoping to remove what they saw as the stain of Christian baptism. They made it clear in their messages to Riga that Christianity was not welcome in their land. Warfare between the Germans and their Liv and Lettish allies against the Estonians continued into the following year, and eventually the strongholds were recaptured.

The last centre of indigenous resistance in southern Estonia was Dorpat where Vetseke, the former lord of Koknese, was holed up with soldiers from Novgorod and fighters from a number of Estonian provinces. He had been promised the lands by the Rus' princes if he could hold on to them. The Sword Brothers, along with their Liv and Lettish allies, besieged the stronghold. Vetseke turned down an amnesty which offered him and his army safe passage, hoping that reinforcements from Novgorod would arrive. When Dorpat eventually fell to the crusading army, almost everyone inside was slaughtered. Henry describes how one Rus' solider was spared, given a horse and sent to Novgorod with the news of the Vetseke's defeat. The Sword Brothers then took the opportunity to seize Danish lands in northern Estonia, but were rebuked by the papal legate and forced to hand them back. Then in 1227, the brethren were able to seize the Danish stronghold in Reval. They held it for almost a decade, during which time they constructed a new stone castle in the south-western corner of Toompea Hill. Attention now became focused on subjugating the Osilians.

THE ESTONIAN ISLANDS: A CASE STUDY IN CONQUEST AND CULTURAL CHANGE

In the winter of 1227, the Bishop of Riga set off on his campaign against the Osilians. Masterful seafarers with a reputation for raiding across the Baltic Sea, the islanders had long controlled the route through the Gulf of Finland. Osilian society was based on clans or large extended families, some of which rose to political dominance at specific times and ruled from strongholds. Contact between the islanders and Scandinavians had been ongoing for several centuries, but increased significantly in the tenth century. Episodes of violence and shifts in power dynamics resulting from this are marked by the destruction of some strongholds and the construction or refortification of others. When Christian trading and missionary outposts began to be established, first in Riga and then on the Estonian coast, the Osilian grip on trade was threatened. This prompted tit-for-tat attacks, which culminated in the crusaders' assault on the islands.

The bishop's army reached the coast of western Estonia towards the end of January. Henry's *Chronicle* provides a vivid description of the setting and the events. The snow lay thick on the ground and the sea was frozen over. It had rained the night before and the melting ice had refrozen in the morning cold. Its surface was as smooth as glass. The army must have been a sight, as thousands assembled along the shoreline with the banners of each regiment fluttering in the wind. Stepping onto the ice, the vast army began to cross the frozen strait. Many slipped and fell, shields clattering against their armour and weapons, horses flailing their legs as they struggled to keep their balance on the ice. Together, they made a noise like thunder, the ice 'singing' as it cracked and deformed under their combined weight. The army slowly rumbled across the glassy sea and reached the shore of Muhu, which the Germans called Mone or Moon.

Muhu is small and flat, and it is possible to cross from one coast to the other on foot in a few hours. Shortly before reaching the causeway across the shallow Väike Strait that connects Muhu to the far larger island of Saaremaa, earthen banks emerge from a field. The banks, overgrown in places with thick shrubs and small trees, rise up, forming a ring. They are all that remain of the stronghold built by the Osilians in the eleventh century. At the time, these earthen banks would have been formidable ramparts. Topped by a drystone wall which was crowned with a timber palisade and punctuated with wooden towers, they presented a serious obstacle to any would-be attacker. The fate of the people who were sheltering inside the stronghold was described by Henry. The bishop's army crossed the island and marched on the stronghold. The inhabitants offered to parley, even proposing to accept Christianity in exchange for peace. This gesture may have been enough for the crusaders once, and it had saved communities in the past. But this time they were unconvinced by the Osilians' sincerity, and so a fierce siege began. The stronghold's earthen ramparts were frozen, making them even more difficult to scale as the defenders rained down missiles from above. Both sides hurled boulders at each other from trebuchets, the crusaders seeking to shatter the timber walls and towers, the Osilians hoping to destroy the siege machines of the Christian army. The crusaders also sought to undermine the walls by digging tunnels underneath, and raised their own towers to use as platforms for hurling spears and firing crossbows into the stronghold below. Many centuries later, archaeologists would discover a dozen iron crossbow bolts within the stronghold.

Henry described how both sides called on their gods to grant them victory, for this was also a spiritual battle. On the morning of the sixth day of the siege, the Christians threw grappling hooks onto the stronghold's walls to try to pull them down. Then, in a dramatic moment captured in all such heroising narratives, one German crusader threw himself at the ramparts. He repeatedly scaled the walls and was forced back by the defenders each time, until at last, hacking away at their spears with his sword, he clambered onto the battlements. Thrusting his shield down, he stood his ground as his comrades scrambled onto the rampart around him, using ladders, ropes or their bare hands. Some (perhaps in hindsight) may have even felt they were being lifted up by angels, as God pushed victory into their hands. The fighting intensified and the situation became desperate for the defenders, as the crusaders poured into the stronghold. Inside, many of the Osilians were slaughtered, whilst some were taken prisoner. Any who managed to escape were caught by the Livs and Letts waiting outside, the indigenous allies of the German crusaders. Snow and muddied ice mixed with blood.

The victors looted the buildings, seized all the livestock they could find and then set the stronghold on fire. The thick black plumes of smoke rising from the shattered ruins would have been visible from the neighbouring island. News of the massacre spread as the Christian army crossed the strait. As panic swept through the Osilians, a decision was made to surrender to the crusaders to avoid further bloodshed. What followed was a ceremonial cleansing of the island. The mass baptisms of men, women and children lasted for three days, exhausting the priests who had accompanied the Christian army. Henry, describing these events, could not contain his joy. His account, of course, only provides us with one perspective, and a heavily biased one at that. How consequential was the conquest of 1227?

To better understand how society transformed as a result of the crusades, we have to turn to one of the most excavated types of archaeological site on the islands – burial grounds. In the centuries before the crusades, the Osilian elites cremated their dead upon pyres heaped with personal adornments, weapons, equestrian equipment, including harnesses and spurs, and food offerings. They then buried the ashes under or near large granite boulders, sometimes under cairns or even within stone circles. These ceremonies were accompanied by feasts, leaving behind traces of broken pots and fragmented animal bones. In this regard, the Osilians were similar to their pagan Finnish and mainland Estonian neighbours, who also practised forms of collective burial. These were not completely egalitarian societies, but they were very different to those of the crusaders.

Then, in the twelfth century, some Osilian families began inhuming their dead, the bodies laid in the ground so that their heads were pointing west and their feet east, with few or no accompanying objects. Did this reflect the early acceptance of Christian practices? A new understanding of the afterlife? A common explanation for this positioning of the body is that it would rise up on Judgment Day to face Christ, who was believed to appear in the east. Had centuries of exposure to Christianity finally prompted the Osilians to rethink how they viewed death and what lay beyond? It is difficult to say for certain but, as we have seen, similar shifts in burial rites are visible in other parts of the Baltic at a time of increasing Christian missionary activity. There are other hints that the new religion was gaining traction on the Osilian islands, but only after the crusades began. As inhumation became the prevailing burial rite here over the course of the thirteenth century, the place of burial also changed for some. These were now clustered around a wholly new type of structure – a chapel or church.

It is widely assumed that timber buildings preceded the stone churches built on the islands after 1227, but only the traces of wooden posts next to the medieval stone church at Pöide on Saaremaa have been interpreted as a pre-crusade Christian structure. These churches were built using a completely mortared stone, a technology previously unknown to the islanders. The earliest identified example, often touted as the oldest stone building in Estonia, was a chapel built at Valjala shortly after 1227. It was modelled on buildings in Saxony, with the implication that masons from that region were involved. Other churches built in subsequent decades appear to have been the work of craftsmen from Westphalia, the Rhineland and Gotland. They provide clues as to the origins of the migrants who followed in the footsteps of the crusaders. Yet if these chapels and churches were built by foreign masons and encouraged by the new regime, they were most probably commissioned and used by the indigenous elites. Their wealth and status would now be on display in buildings that reflected the new social and cosmological order.

Like in the West, those buried inside the new Osilian churches would have been the most important members of their communities. And if that's the case, then a crucial component of the Christian worldview had also been accepted here – the power of relics. We know about the early presence of relics on the Osilian islands from a remarkable wooden sculpture dated to the mid-thirteenth century – a small crucifix formerly in Kärla church (since demolished), now in Saaremaa Museum. The figure of Christ, 52 centimetres high, has been carved with the legs positioned next to each other, rather than crossed, with the result that four nails instead of the more familiar three were used to attach the body to the cross. This may seem like a trivial point, but it provides us with a specific date for the sculpture. It must have been produced in the first two decades of the thirteenth century, before it became fashionable to use three nails to crucify Christ.[30]

The rendering of Christ's face and body also provides further clues. His eyes gaze down and his mouth is slightly open. This detail is also important, for it too was popular in the early thirteenth century, at a time when hymns would be sung in front of the crucifix, which spoke of Christ directly addressing his audience. The pain of the crucifixion is visibly etched into the sculpture, as if the figure is twisting in agony – the tense posture, the arched chest with accentuated ribs, the bulging stomach, the gaping wound on his right side. The body was intended to be viewed not just from the front, but also from the side, in three dimensions, with the result that his appearance is more human, more relatable to the viewer. This reflected growing interest in the West in getting closer to Christ's humanity and suffering. The entire back of the figure, from the shoulders to the waist, was hollowed out and lined with mortar, creating a small chamber. The head also contained a tiny cavity, sealed with a plug. Inside these would have been placed relics, perhaps a small fragment of bone, wood or stone, or maybe a piece of the host (the communion bread believed to transform into Christ's body), a practice that is attested in medieval religious sculptures in the West. In the minds of believers, this would have imbued the sculpture with divine power, bringing them closer to heaven. Relics were a fundamental prerequisite of any church, and the most important were usually embedded in the altar. As a result, burial within the church, as close to the altar as possible, became highly desirable.

Changes in burial rites, the construction of churches and the presence of relics provide tangible evidence for the acceptance of Christian practices and beliefs by at least some leading Osilian families. Despite the catastrophic events of 1227, they had retained their property, social positions, even their marital and inheritance customs. But now the islanders were being asked to pay a tribute. On top of that, they had to make payments to provide for their priests. This excessive taxation was too much. Osilian uprisings would break out in the following decades, prompting further military responses from the Christian regime. In 1261, a spectacular Christian military victory was followed by a peace on harsher terms, and the new regime finally established permanent residency on the principal island in imposing castles. One of the builders of these castles was a political player who had been established in Livonia for just over two decades – the Teutonic Order.

ENTER THE TEUTONIC ORDER

Following Bishop Albert's death in January 1229, a struggle erupted between the new prelate of Riga and the Sword Brothers over the governance of Livonia. The pope's legate Baldwin of Alna took Estonia and Curonia – whose inhabitants were seeking treaties directly with the papacy in the hope of retaining their independence – under his protection. This was a sore point for the Sword Brothers, who claimed territorial rights in those regions. They gathered a coalition and drove the legate out of Livonia in 1234. Upon returning to his native land, Baldwin met the chronicler Alberic of Trois-Fontaines and complained to him about his treatment. Unsurprisingly, Alberic would go on to describe the Sword Brothers as 'all of those who have been banished from Saxony for their crimes' and as those who 'believe that they will be able to live without law nor king'.[31]

On 22 September 1236, the Sword Brothers and their allies confronted a Samogitian and Semigallian force at Saule, in north Lithuania. The crusaders, unable to manoeuvre their heavy cavalry in the marshes, were resoundingly defeated. Many of the Sword Brothers were killed, including their master Volkwin. The pagan victory sparked uprisings across southern Livonia and on the Estonian islands. The following year, with papal approval, the Teutonic Order, who had been engaged in crusading against the Prussians for six years already, incorporated what remained of the Sword Brothers into their ranks and took over their lands and castles. In fact, the Sword Brothers had approached the Order previously to discuss a possible merger, hoping it would consolidate their hold on Estonia and Curonia, and shore up their finances.[32]

The Teutonic Order sent some six hundred personnel, including sixty brother-knights, to Livonia. After taking over the Sword Brothers' holdings, the Order had to contend with the authority of the Livonian episcopates, who regarded them as vassals within their territories. It also inherited the brethren's dispute over the control of northern Estonia, but in 1238 agreed to hand this back to the Danish crown and to split any further gains from future conquests. In turn, Valdemar agreed to provide the Order with military support and granted them the district of Jerwia, which was completely independent from the authority of any Livonian bishop. The agreement to collaborate on future crusades soon bore fruit. The papal legate had been urging a crusade against Novgorod in his desire to unify the Catholic and Orthodox churches. In 1240, the crusading host, including vassals of the Danish king and a large contingent of the Order's brother-knights, took control of Pskov and from there attacked the territories of Novgorod in the winter. They only held Pskov for a short time before the Novgorodian prince Alexander Nevsky took the city and then defeated the crusading army at the 'Battle on the Ice' on the frozen Lake Peipus on 5 April 1242. This halted the Order's eastward advance, although minor clashes with Novgorod and Pskov would continue. Following this, the Livonian brethren turned their attention to the south, reoccupying Curonia and establishing a new power base at Goldingen (Latvian Kuldīga). With renewed conflict, the brethren reasserted their control over the region a decade later and divided the territory with the Curonian bishop. By this time, Semigallia had also been subdued and was carved up between the Order and the Archbishop of Riga.

In 1251, Mindaugas, the Grand Duke of Lithuania, converted to Catholicism and allied himself with the Order in Livonia, intending to crown himself king. In exchange for facilitating his baptism and supporting his coronation, the Order demanded territory and Mindaugas gave them land in Samogitia. The following year, the Order constructed a castle at Memel (Lithuanian Klaipėda), creating a foothold from which they could also support their brethren's attack on the Prussian territory of Sambia. Within a couple of years, a town had developed alongside the castle. It soon became the target for Samogitian attacks. When the Order was defeated by a Samogitian force at the Battle of Schoden in 1259, resulting in the death of thirty-three brother-knights, an emergency military tax (seven times the normal amount) was imposed on the Semigallians, who refused to pay. The Order responded by constructing castles at Doblen

(Latvian Dobele) and Karshowen to reinforce its control over the region, and the brethren besieged the indigenous stronghold of Terweten. The Samogitians came to the aid of the Semigallians, but failed to take the Order's castles. The following year, the Curonians joined the Samogitians in their conflict against the brethren. In July 1260, the Order's combined Prussian-Livonian force suffered a catastrophic defeat at the Battle of Durbe. The Livonian master Burchard of Hornhausen was killed, along with the Prussian marshal. The outcome prompted new insurrections from the Osilians, Curonians, Semigallians and Prussians, and even Mindaugas turned against the Order, expelling and killing Christians in his realm and destroying the cathedral he had commissioned. Conflict continued in southern Livonia, whilst in 1267, the Order joined the Bishop of Dorpat in fending off a Rus' attack on eastern Estonia.

In the winter of 1269/70, a Lithuanian army invaded Livonia and Otto of Lutterberg, the Order's master, led a force that included Danish troops from Estonia to confront them on the frozen sea between the mainland and Muhu. In the ensuing Battle of Karuse, the master and many brother-knights were killed. Walter of Nortecken, the new master, secured help from the Prussian brethren and captured several strongholds used by the Lithuanians to reach the coast. The following year, the Order took Terweten, forcing the Semigallians into a truce. This would be regained by the Semigallians and their Lithuanian allies in 1279. Two years later, the Order's forces encircled the stronghold, prompting the Semigallians to agree to another truce and to pay taxes. Again, peace did not last long. In the winter of 1285/6, the Order constructed the Castle of Heiligenberg across from Terweten. Both the Samogitians and Semigallians attempted to destroy this castle, but failed and eventually Terweten would be abandoned. Hostilities in Semigallia officially ended in 1290 with the surrender of the last territory of Sidrabe. The southern part of the region became depopulated as the survivors fled into Samogitia.[33] It was around this time that the second principal written source for the events of the crusades was produced – the *Livonian Rhymed Chronicle*. Composed in Middle High German, it is more imaginative in content than Henry's *Chronicle*, and was intended to inspire members of the German nobility to join the Order's ongoing crusades against Lithuania.[34]

In the latter half of the thirteenth century, the Order invested in expanding the castles built by the Sword Brothers and constructing new ones to consolidate its territorial hold. Their principal Livonian convent remained in Riga, but in 1250, a new castle was constructed in Fellin, which would become one of the strongest in the region. Within a short time, towns were laid out alongside most of these castles, and were usually surrounded by walls and moats within a short period of their foundation. They were regarded as fortified settlements by the indigenous population, as suggested by the Estonian and Latvian nouns for town – *linn* and *pilsēta*, respectively. Smaller castles also began to be constructed, such as Karkus (Estonian Karksi), where the earliest archaeological deposits date from the 1260s, with intensive building activities commencing two decades later.[35] Here, the lack of local wheel-thrown pottery and the use of stave bowls have been connected with the presence of German migrants. The discovery of exceptionally preserved tally sticks provides the earliest physical evidence from the eastern Baltic of the taxation system imposed by the new regime on the indigenous population. The notches on these sticks were records of quantities of agricultural produce that were brought to castles like Karkus by its indigenous tenants and stored for use by the castle's community or for transport to a higher-ranking centre like Fellin or Riga. The labour of the indigenous farmers is evident from the environmental record of the castle's surroundings: the local pollen record indicates the landscape here was open and cultivated at this time. We do not have any record of how many villages lay within the territories of Livonian castles in the late thirteenth century, with the exception of Danish Estonia. The royal survey of the duchy or the *Liber Census Daniae*, dating to c. 1240, lists a total of 801 *Haken* – ploughland – associated with indigenous villages from which the new lords obtained their income in the form of taxes and tithes. The Danish king was keen to know how much revenue his easternmost colony would produce.[36]

THE CREATION OF LIVONIA

The events which created the patchwork of Catholic territories that became Livonia were, without doubt, tragic. The wars led to large-scale loss of life, the subjugation of indigenous peoples and forced conversions to Christianity. The killing of men and the capture of women and children was a regular occurrence on both sides. Certain segments of the indigenous political elite, such as those of the Saccalians, were completely wiped out. The conflict drew in other regional forces, and many attacks were not directly motivated by the need to protect converts, especially as their conversion was uncertain in the first place. According to Henry's *Chronicle*, there were sixty-seven slave raids of which forty-two were conducted by Christians in the first three decades of the thirteenth century, with most of the enslaved being women and girls. Some were sent back to the Holy Roman Empire for re-education, but the effect on the indigenous population was also detrimental from the perspective of social cohesion.[37] At this time, the Church condemned the enslavement of fellow Christians, but that of pagans was often tolerated or even justified. Fields were regularly burned to deprive the enemy of food, and spoils in the form of livestock, horses, weapons and food were an anticipated bonus – even an incentive – for raids.

However, much of the indigenous population survived the onslaughts, retained its identity and would grow over the following centuries. In the early years of the Livonian crusades, the population in the region corresponding to modern Estonia has been estimated at between 150,000 and 180,000 people, and in Latvia at around 200,000. By the mid-sixteenth century, these had increased to 250,000–300,000 and 400,000, respectively.[38] The fate of the indigenous elites varied across the region. In western and northern Estonia, Curonia and large swathes of eastern Livonia, some noble families became vassals of the new regime and were permitted to reside in their strongholds. The archaeological biographies of these sites indicate a continuation of traditional lifestyles, with a noticeable absence of Western cultural elements.[39] But the families residing within them never recovered their former power: their lands had been carved up and handed out to others and so their economic bases dwindled. In time, they would abandon their ancestral homes. Most of the indigenous population continued to live in the countryside, but an increasing number migrated to the new towns.[40] Having officially accepted Christianity and the new social order, they remained free and were permitted to keep their own customs, carry weapons and inherit property. But they now had to pay taxes and tithes, and provide labour and military service for the new regime.

There was, nonetheless, a significant demographic shift in the region, as a growing number of migrants arrived from German and, to a lesser extent, Scandinavian regions, establishing a new privileged class. Their presence was limited to castles, towns and a small number of manors, resulting in a noticeable cultural divide between the bustling urban centres and the countryside. But all three types of migrant enclaves became meeting points between the colonisers and the colonised, particularly towns, which quickly developed into multi-ethnic centres. Riga's debtor's book from the end of the thirteenth century indicates the presence of merchants largely from the western and northern German provinces, as well as from England, Hungary and other parts of Livonia. There were also Rus' merchants, who had their own district with a church dedicated to St Nicholas. Livs, Letts, Estonians and Lithuanians are also documented.[41] Towns became places where intersectional differences were most clearly visible between the privileged, predominantly German, residents and the indigenous and other non-German minorities.[42]

The construction of churches and chapels, initially in towns and later in the countryside, slowly transformed the sacred landscape. With the introduction of churches came new places of burial, although indigenous village cemeteries continued to be used across Livonia. In 1214/15, the pope had demanded the Bishop of Riga and Sword Brothers allow new converts the right to choose their mode of burial, and the archaeological evidence confirms that there was little policing of indigenous funerary culture.[43] In some regions, the practice of burying the dead in richly furnished graves slowly fizzled out over the course of the thirteenth century and Christian grave orientations became the norm, while elsewhere they continued, along with elements of pre-crusade indigenous spirituality.

The creation of Livonia took place at the same time as the formation of another new Catholic polity to the south. This too would be forged by crusading, but here the Teutonic Order would take the lead and set up what would become their political heartland – Prussia.

CHAPTER 6

BLACK CROSS ASCENDANT
Conquering Prussia

At the site of that battlefield there later lived a hermit, who witnessed candles burning there on many nights; their presence clearly indicated that the men who died there had already received the crown of martyrdom from the King of Martyrs . . .

Peter of Dusburg, *Chronicle of Prussia*[1]

CRUSADING AT THE POLISH FRONTIER

An overgrown field just north of the village of Biała Góra (named Weißenberg before 1945) on the edge of the vast Forest of Sztum, located in Pomerania in northern Poland, first drew the attention of archaeologists in 1972. Over three decades later, excavations here revealed an incredible abundance of artefacts dating to the medieval period, in what would become one of the most remarkable archaeological discoveries in the country.[2] These artefacts were embedded within a thick layer of 'dark earth' spread across some 4 hectares, which contained over 100 pits filled with organic waste, ceramic fragments and metal artefacts. This density of archaeological features represented the degraded remains of an intensely occupied settlement, but the collection of artefacts also included a diverse range of military equipment: crossbow bolts, arrowheads, spearheads, caltrops (spiked devices designed to injure horses and infantry), a small fragment of armour, spurs, bridle fittings and horseshoes, as well as large quantities of horse bone, some derived from large individuals. These pointed to a military presence at the settlement, which must have included knights.

The discovery of three stacked heaps of bricks and roof tiles in the field also suggested this had once been a place of some significance. Perhaps they had derived from a brick church, which would have been the earliest construction of this type on the eastern side of the Vistula. What was even more striking was that the community at Biała Góra continued to thrive during the thirteenth century, whereas other settlements around it had been abandoned. From the perspective of its inhabitants, the location was perilous. This was the edge of Christendom and beyond lay the lands of the pagan Prussians. The archaeologists excavating the site believed it to be the Cistercian missionary outpost of Santir, which was populated by Pomerelian settlers and under the authority of the nominal Bishop of Prussia, Christian.

If this was the case, it was also most likely the base for the bishop's own military order which had been inspired by the Sword Brothers in Livonia. This group would later be referred to as the Fratres Milites Christi de Prussia or the Knights of Christ of Prussia, and they wore white cloaks emblazoned with a symbol of a red star.[3] Their existence would be short-lived. In April 1235, the pope approved the organisation's amalgamation into the Teutonic Order, although they later broke away and the Knights of Christ continued to exist as a separate group until at least 1240, after which they vanish from the written record.[4] Santir would be acquired by the Order who transformed it into one of its command centres, from which the brethren governed the lands they were seizing during their campaigns against the Prussians. The discovery of both locally produced and greyware ceramics at Biała Góra was suggestive of the presence of migrant potters working alongside the Pomerelian artisans.

The story of the Knights of Christ of Prussia encapsulates the transformation of the military campaigns against the Prussians into full-blown crusades. As in Livonia, it began with missionary activity. Cistercian monks from the abbey of Łękno in Greater Poland, inspired by the example of the martyred Adalbert, would cross over the Prussian frontier in the early thirteenth century.[5] Little is known about their activities which Pope Innocent III insisted must be peaceful, although casualties amongst their numbers were recorded, adding to the list of martyrs. The first attempted crusade against the Prussians was made by King Valdemar II, who landed with an army on the Sambian coast in 1210. The pope had urged him to convert the pagans and spread the Christian faith. Traces of Danish activity may be reflected in the large numbers of bronze 'Hanseatic bowls' found within graves in Sambian cemeteries and mostly dating to the late twelfth or early thirteenth century. Similar to those associated with later Danish presence in Estonia, they may have been offered as gifts to the Prussian nobility.[6] Yet Valdemar soon turned westwards and ended his campaign in Gdańsk, accepting a pledge of loyalty from its duke, Mestwin.[7] Polish influence over Pomerelia was reasserted the following year, effectively ending Danish involvement in Prussia. Responsibility for the Prussian mission would ultimately be given to Christian, a monk from the abbey of Oliwa near Gdańsk, who based himself at the frontier outpost of Santir. In 1215, Christian travelled to Rome with two Prussian nobles who were baptised by the pope, after which he was appointed Bishop of Prussia.

Meanwhile, the situation on the Masovian border was becoming difficult. For several years its defence had been held together by Krystyn, the Voivode of Masovia. He had distinguished himself in battle against the Rus', perhaps even crusaded in the Levant and was clearly popular amongst the Masovian nobility. Along the frontier, he had organised the construction and refortification of strongholds and may have even subjugated some of the local Prussian groups. Then in 1216, he was captured and temporarily imprisoned by the Prussians. Fearing for the safety of the Cistercian mission on the Pomerelian border and the holdings that he had been given in the Kulmerland by Conrad, Duke of Masovia, and the Bishop of Płock, Christian had appealed to the pope to raise a crusading army. This was granted in March 1217, with the proviso that Christian did not recruit those who had already committed to the Fifth Crusade in the Mediterranean. Within a few weeks, the pope had issued another bull, this time at the request of the Piast dukes and Archbishop of Gniezno. This permitted those knights in provinces directly affected by Prussian raids to exchange their existing crusading vows to the Holy Land for campaigns into Prussia. Both crusading armies failed to materialise.

Worse still, Krystyn was executed on the orders of Conrad, who probably feared him as a potential rival – historians continue to debate this enigmatic act. Whatever the reason, the result was that the borderland forces became disorganised. Bishop Christian may then have travelled to Rome to petition the pope, for in the spring of 1218 Honorius issued four bulls appealing for participation in the crusade against the Prussians, handing the responsibility for recruitment to the episcopates east of the Rhine from Denmark to the Alps. All those who took the cross would receive the same indulgences as for those taking crusading vows for the Holy Land.[8]

From the perspective of the Cistercian mission, the outcome was disappointing. One campaign to Prussia is documented in 1218, led by the Czech duke Depold and Wawrzyniec, the Bishop of Wrocław. In all likelihood, the instigator of this was Depold's father-in-law, the Duke of Silesia, Henry 'the Bearded'. His promotion of crusading against the Prussians may have had religious motivations and his wife, the Duchess Jadwiga, was also a keen supporter of the crusading movement. At the same time, given events in Livonia, he may also have been hoping for a political stake in the future of Prussian lands. The Czech-Silesian campaign almost certainly descended into a military adventure for spoils, for the pope's next bull, in May 1219, repeated his earlier prohibition against crusaders going to Prussia for personal gain. He also stressed that any crusaders required Bishop Christian's express permission to enter the lands of converts.

When papal support for the Prussian crusade was temporarily withdrawn, as it became evident that crusading forces in the Mediterranean were insufficient, Christian turned to Duke Henry and together they organised a crusading venture into Prussia. This became pressing following a Prussian raid across the borderland in 1220. Little is known about this campaign, other than a papal bull issued in January the following year which commanded the crusaders to hand over their Prussian prisoners to Christian. A few months later, a papal commission once more began to promote crusading against the Prussians, renewing Gniezno's ability to grant indulgences for this purpose. This time, the call to arms was limited to Poland and Pomerania, suggesting Polish influence was shaping the direction of the crusade. A proposal was formulated by Leszek 'the White', then High Duke of Poland, who was trying to make up for failing in his oath to participate in the Fifth Crusade. His plan involved establishing settlements in Prussia with a market in salt and iron, where missionaries could then preach to the pagans. The aim was to co-ordinate the military campaigns of Polish crusaders with Cistercian missionary activity. This is also the first time an explicit connection was made between military action and settlement in Prussia, although in the end the plan was not implemented.

Then, in the summer of 1222, Henry organised another crusade against the Prussians, this time involving brother-knights from the Teutonic Order and Templars. Again, the details of what took place are unknown, but both orders were subsequently granted land in his duchy.[9] In August of that year, Leszek met with Henry, Conrad, Bishop Christian and the Polish episcopate in Kuyavia, agreeing to work together to secure the frontier against the Prussians and rebuild the stronghold in Culm. At this point, Conrad became more invested in the crusading movement. This shift in attitude is represented on his seals. The duke's earliest seals emulated the iconic figure of the mounted armoured knight riding to battle bearing a standard in defence of his realm and the Church, popular amongst the aristocracy of Western Europe. But in 1223, the duke commissioned a new seal design which depicted an unarmoured mounted man bearing a cross and a standard with a cross. This evoked the image of a crusader and defender of the faith, a fusion of secular and spiritual knighthood. It coincided with his participation in a crusade against the Prussians in the same year, which had been sanctioned by the papal legate.[10] The campaign involved forces from Silesia, Lesser Poland, Masovia and Pomerania and is largely known from charters granted to the crusaders. The army appears to have focused its efforts on the Kulmerland, and most probably reinforced its network of strongholds.[11] When the crusaders departed, they left behind garrisons to secure the frontier, but in just over a year, internal squabbles broke down the ducal coalition and led to the withdrawal of the garrisons from Lesser Poland and Silesia.[12] The strongholds were overrun by the Prussians and what was left of their garrisons massacred. The castellany was now largely undefended. Conrad and Bishop Christian then turned to a reliable source for defending the frontiers of Christendom – the military orders.

Conrad may have initially invited the Templars to establish themselves on the frontier, but the evidence for this is sparse.[13] There were other military orders present in the Polish principalities, but the scattered distribution of their properties, the result of individual ducal initiatives, prevented their mobilisation as a cohesive force. In 1226, on Henry's suggestion, Conrad approached the Teutonic Order to ask for their help against the Prussians. The duke offered the Order the Kulmerland, but the brethren were currently focused on their military commitments in the Levant. As an added incentive, Conrad also granted the Order a village in northern Kuyavia and Bishop Christian threw in the tithe from his diocese in the frontier territory. But even this was not enough, as the Teutonic Order was focusing on its holdings in the Holy Land. The brethren had recently acquired the property of Montfort, which they began to fortify. Negotiations over their involvement in Prussia stalled.

In desperation, Conrad decided to take control of the Knights of Christ from Christian, although the exact circumstances of this are not clear. Recruits came from Lower Saxony and Mecklenburg, perhaps including knights who had responded to Christian's earlier crusading calls.[14] In 1228, Conrad, together with the Bishop of Płock, granted them lands on the Masovian–Prussian border centred on the castle at Dobrzyń, which would become their headquarters. Their role now evolved into protecting the frontier, although they were also permitted to keep half of any territory they conquered from the pagans; the rest went to Conrad. Then, sensing an opportunity, the Knights negotiated a merger with the Teutonic Order to improve their situation. This was done against Conrad's wishes as he did not want their estates to fall into the Order's hands, and in the end the duke was able to recover the territory of Dobrzyń. Not longer after, in 1237, it appears that those members who had joined the Order regretted their decision and, after being presented with another opportunity by Conrad to defend the frontier around Drohiczyn in exchange for land, they left the Order and relocated. Their subsequent fate remains a mystery.[15]

In these years, the Order's presence on the Masovian frontier came into sharp relief. The papal legate, William of Modena, met with the Order's master Herman of Salza and discussed the brethren's involvement against the Prussians. Conrad then issued two new charters to the

Order in 1230. The first, the so-called Treaty of Kruschwitz, reiterated the Order's possession of the Kulmerland, but more importantly guaranteed the brethren's independence, conferring on them the right to rule those territories they conquered from the enemies of Christ. Although historians have previously considered this document to be a forgery, most accept its authenticity.[16] It was almost certainly prepared by a notary of the Order, with the help of Salza and Modena, and then signed off by Conrad.[17] Why was the duke so eager to relinquish the Kulmerland? In the last few years before the Order's arrival, he had his eye on a much bigger prize – the throne of Cracow. He could not afford to commit his entire military resources to an attack on Prussia, and so he needed the frontier safeguarded by a reliable and neutral force. The duke's second charter granted the Order the stronghold at Nessau (Polish Mała Nieszawka), and they also received property from Bishop Christian and the Bishop of Płock. Christian still hoped to wield ecclesiastical authority over the brethren, but the Order's star was rising. The pope had been in conflict with the German emperor, and Salza had played a key role in the negotiations which resulted in peace. The pope, in turn, provided further guarantees of the Order's rights to the land granted to them in Prussia, including any obtained through conquest. The stage was set for a more sustained crusade across the war-torn frontier where the seizure of further territory was essentially preconditioned.

A priest of the Order, Peter of Dusburg, writing in the early fourteenth century, provided the earliest, most detailed sketch of the lands that were conquered during five decades of crusading. Peter subdivided Prussian lands into eleven regions, providing their names in Latin: Culm and Lubavia (two former Masovian territories which had been overrun), Pomesania, Pogesania, Warmia, Natangia, Sambia, Nadruvia, Scalovia, Sudovia, Galindia and Bartia.[18] From other sources we know that each region was subdivided further into smaller districts or groups, although we only know the details of some of these. Pomesania, for example, appears to have consisted of ten separate districts.[19] The people of Sudovia, the easternmost area named by Peter, also referred to as Jatvingians in Polish and Rus' sources, may have had their own distinct West Baltic language, and closer ties to the Lithuanians.[20] The conquest of these lands would forever transform the crusading movement in Northern Europe.

THE TEUTONIC ORDER'S CRUSADES: OCCUPYING THE KULMERLAND

As early as 1229, a handful of brother-knights of the Teutonic Order had garrisoned a stronghold called Vogelsang (Latin Cantus Avium – 'birdsong') on a hill overlooking the southern bank of the Vistula, now the boundary between pagan and Christian lands. The fortress had been built with the help of Duke Conrad's men, and served as a base for raids and reconnaissance missions into the Kulmerland. Little progress was made in that first year, and following a plea to Salza, the garrison was reinforced with a contingent of brother-knights led by the resourceful Herman Balk, who had been appointed as the master of the Order's new province of Prussia. At Salza's request, the pope issued crusading bulls which offered a full indulgence to those who would take the cross against the pagan Prussians. The recruitment campaign would be preached by the Dominicans in regions where the Prussians were considered an active threat – Masovia and Pomerania – but also in the provinces of the Holy Roman Empire where the Order had supporters – Magdeburg, Hamburg-Bremen, Moravia, Suravia and Holstein – and on Gotland, which had played an important role in the Livonian crusades. Alongside willing recruits to crusading armies, contributions would also come in the form of donations to the Teutonic Order. The Polish nobility, having ended their internal conflict, readily joined the holy war with their retinues and donations.

In 1231, the brethren established their first permanent base on the north bank of the Vistula. This was named Thorn, deriving from a Slavic term for 'worn path', most likely referring to the crossing point on the river by Nessau. Here, according to Peter of Dusburg, the brethren fortified a large oak tree, around which they built a wall. This would be later replaced by a timber-and-earth fort which provided a new military base for two years, enabling raids on Prussian settlements across the Kulmerland. There was fierce resistance, and the brethren kept boats moored nearby in case they needed to retreat across the river back to Nessau. A town was then planned alongside the stronghold at Thorn. This required a level of investment, and the Order collaborated with the Margrave of Brandenburg and Polish dukes to charter this first colony.

Its traces have recently been identified by archaeologists, with geophysical, geoarchaeological and aerial surveys revealing the presence of buildings, ditches and a protective embankment with at least two gates.[21] Very little is known of this first town, but its location made it prone to flooding and, in 1236, most of its buildings were dismantled and relocated 10 kilometres west to higher ground, where the Old Town of Toruń stands today. All that remained in the old settlement was the church dedicated to St John the Baptist (which would continue to stand there until the mid-fifteenth century) with its associated cemetery and the Order's stronghold. With its connection to the river crossing, this remained a vital mustering point for crusading armies entering the Kulmerland.

The choice of site for the relocated town which took on the name of Thorn was also deliberate. In the seventh century, a small Slavic settlement had been established here, and when the Piast state had conquered the region in the tenth century, a timber-and-earth stronghold was built, one of several intended to secure the frontier. This stronghold had been abandoned by its Masovian garrison in the mid-twelfth century, no doubt following a Prussian attack, although the settlement nearby continued to be occupied until it was finally abandoned in the early thirteenth century. The Order reused the Masovian stronghold, as its horseshoe-shaped embankment provided a ready-made defensive structure connected to the river directly to the south. The first castle would have been timber and earth, and a stone wall with a gate tower was constructed at the north-eastern foot of the embankment. Decades later, a single brick range would be added, raised on stone foundations and enclosing a courtyard with a wall that followed the line of the old earthen horseshoe. The town was laid out directly to the west of the Order's stronghold on a regular grid, and surrounded by a substantial earthen embankment with a timber stockade and moat.[22]

Thorn's location on the Vistula must have been an irresistible attraction for merchants. Here was a (relatively) secure outpost on the main artery of trade linking the Carpathians with the Baltic Sea, in a land of new opportunity. The streets of the Old Town ran straight down to the river, enabling easy access to a regular stream of cargo ships. Within a short time, Thorn developed into a buzzing commercial centre. Coins were used from the onset, firstly those from neighbouring regions and, from 1236, those minted by the Order. The Order had been given permission to produce its own coinage in Prussia by Duke Conrad the previous year, a further recognition of its sovereignty over the Kulmerland. Its earliest coins displayed an arm grasping a pennant with an equal-armed cross to the side, a reference to crusading and most probably the relic of the True Cross, which the Order carried into battle against the Prussians.[23] The brethren's early victories in western Prussian territories meant that crusading campaigns moved quickly into the more hostile eastern regions, closer to Lithuania. This must have created an atmosphere of relative stability in a town like Thorn, adding to the sense of permanence and the inevitability of reclaiming the lands taken by the pagans for Christ.

When the brethren reached the former centre of the Masovian castellany at Culm in 1232, they set about constructing a stronghold named Potterberg which archaeologists have identified as the final phase of the archaeological site of Kałdus. Decades later, this would be dismantled and the materials used to construct the stronghold at Mewe (Polish Gniew).[24] In 1233, the Order refounded Kulm (eventually Germanising its Latin name) 2 kilometres to the south at Starogród. Recent excavations uncovered traces of this settlement along with its first timber-and-earth stronghold.[25] At this time, it became clear that founding urban colonies was going to become a regular feature of securing the conquered territories. The Order created a new charter – Kulm Law, named after its second town in the region – which provided the model for most settlements in Prussia. This charter was also given to Thorn in the same year, and would be renewed for the relocated town.

The creation of the Kulm Law was designed to benefit the Order as a ruler, but also to stimulate settlement in depopulated lands, providing more attractive conditions than in the towns of the Holy Roman Empire.[26] For example, Flemish inheritance customs were incorporated in the Kulm Law, whereby both men and women could inherit property on equal terms, and sell this without any restriction. Burghers were also granted the freedom to elect their own judges (although the Order retained a say in their election and in the adjudication of serious crimes) and protection from unfair taxation and improper duty payments. They were also promised security. Naturally, the Order took its own cut. Those who owned estates in the countryside had to provide military service when called upon, with payment of 'recognition dues' (i.e. taxes) linked to the size of land (measured in *Hufen*) and fixed annual tithe payments to the local diocese. Hunting, fishing, milling and mining rights were also regulated – familiar expressions of sovereign overlordship in the West. Kulm developed for a few years before it was relocated in 1239, to where the district of Rybaki in the town of Chełmno is today. A castle was built alongside this new town by the 1240s, and a Dominican friary was constructed in the town. But, as in the case of Thorn, flooding prompted the settlement's relocation to higher ground in 1250, and this final version of the town was laid out on a regular grid using a new standardised measurement which became widely adopted by urban planners in Prussia – the *Culmer Ruthe* or 'Kulm rod', also called the 'Kulm foot'.

Thorn and Kulm served as models for how territorial gains would be secured – an incremental process of occupation and settlement. These could be dismantled and relocated as and when needed, together with their populations. The large number of crusaders who flocked to Prussia, often led by a cast of aristocratic celebrities which included kings, margraves and dukes, enabled significant military campaigns to be organised against the Prussians. Some campaigns included armies from multiple regions, as the promise of spiritual rewards closer to home proved to be highly attractive for the local Catholic nobility. The use of heavily armoured cavalry, crossbows and siege engines has often been invoked as providing the crusaders with a military advantage, but the Order succeeded in the long term by entrenching itself in former or newly built strongholds in territories that it conquered.[27] These were manned by a small number of brother-knights, soldiers and presumably indigenous converts who were obliged (and perhaps were keen) to fight against their pagan kin and neighbours. Watchtowers were also constructed to provide early warnings of incoming Prussian armies. Reinforcements could be generally relied upon to turn up on a seasonal basis.

Within a short time, planned settlements had sprung up alongside a number of the Order's castles. They became populated by migrants including merchants and artisans, as well as indigenous converts, kick-starting new micro-economies that sustained the Order's garrisons and ongoing crusades. Numerous excavations in the Kulmerland have indicated the region was particularly known for pig breeding before the crusades, and this appears to have continued in the thirteenth century. Earlier settlements may have endured the onslaught, or new rural colonies were quickly set up in the environs of towns. Peter of Dusburg described the Kulmerland as a wasteland, but in fact there is little evidence in the pollen record of the region's lakes and peat bogs of any interruption in cultivation. Each campaign pushed the frontier a little further, and then newly established strongholds created fortified points in the landscape that were hard to dislodge. The Prussians were at times successful in battle against the brethren, and captured numerous strongholds over the years, but, with the resources at its disposal, the Order was able to recover its hold over the conquered territories each time.

When did a full-blown conquest of Prussian lands become inevitable? The Order could not have foreseen five decades of conflict, but in the early years the brethren moved rapidly to conquer the regions bordering the Prussian interior. The Kulmerland was secured within a few years and the Order then campaigned north, following the Vistula, and quickly reached Pomesania. In 1233, the Order built a stronghold from pre-prepared materials on an island in the marshy fens at the edge of the Vistula floodplain, which they named Sankt Marienwerder (St Mary's Island) (Polish Kwidzyn). Not long after, the fortification was relocated further away from the floodplain to the top of the nearby escarpment. An adjacent settlement was laid out, retaining the earlier name of Marienwerder. That winter, 5,000 Prussians were killed (according to Peter) at a battle on the Dzierzgoń river by the Order and its Pomerelian allies. This figure was almost certainly exaggerated, but the event was devastating enough that it opened the way to further conquests to the north.[28] The following year, the Order refortified the burnt-out Masovian stronghold at Rehden (Polish Radzyń Chełmiński), which had previously belonged to Bishop Christian. The stronghold had guarded the northern edge of the Masovian castellany, and was situated on the edge of a lake amidst vast wetlands which were punctuated by islands of higher ground. On one such island nearby, the Order laid out a town. On the opposite edge of the Kulmerland, the Order occupied and refortified the stronghold of Graudenz (Polish Grudziądz) which overlooked the Vistula.

The Kulmerland had been secured and it became clear the Order was here to stay. In a fortuitous twist for the brethren, Bishop Christian had been abducted by the Sudovians and would be imprisoned for several years, removing a major obstacle to their territorial ambitions. In 1234, the Order's papal privileges were enshrined in the 'Golden Bull of Rieti' which also claimed the lands of the pagans as a papal fief. This was a clear endorsement of the brethren's activities and essentially legitimised future conquests. The following year, Emperor Frederick II issued the brethren with the 'Golden Bull of Rimini', backdated to 1226. This essentially granted the Order the status of an imperial prince in Prussia, and may have been an attempt to limit the pope's claim to the Order's lands.[29] In the end, neither the pope nor the German emperor would have much say in how the brethren governed the conquered territories. The cumulative effect of all these donations and confirmations was to provide the Order with a legal basis – in the eyes of Christian rulers and their subjects, some of whom would fight as crusaders or migrate and settle to live as subjects – for wielding secular power in the territories it would seize from the pagans. Indigenous Prussian converts, adapting to the new regime, its customs and legal frameworks, would also come to see the Order as rightful sovereigns. For by now it was clear the Kulmerland and all other territories secured by the Order were not an extension of Masovia, Pomerelia or Brandenburg, but were a separate territory governed by the military arm of the Holy See. From the perspective of migrating Catholics and indigenous converts, this was a new kind of holy land, watched over by the Virgin Mary as Queen of Heaven, maternal and majestic. A Christian landscape was created through the Order's strongholds, named after heavenly figures, their chapels, which contained relics, and the cathedrals and churches constructed in the new urban colonies.[30]

THE CONQUEST OF POMESANIA

From their bases in Marienwerder, Graudenz and Rehden, the brethren launched their attacks against the Prussians in Pomesania and neighbouring

Pogesania. In the winter of 1234, the Pomesanian stronghold at a place called 'Castle Hill', overlooking the Dzierzgoń river, was captured by the Order and refortified. The stronghold was named Christburg – Christ's castle. According to Peter of Dusburg, who connected this event with the first Prussian uprising (1242–9), the name derives from its capture on Christmas Eve. However, the name may in fact derive from a Prussian-German hybrid, as its variants Kirsberg/Kirsburg can be associated with the Prussian term for 'black' and the German term for 'castle'.[31] Once captured, the stronghold became the new base for mustering crusading armies for further attacks to the north and east.

Archaeologists started excavating the site in the mid-1930s, and then resumed again in the last two decades. They discovered the stronghold's earthen ramparts had been refortified three times – in the early Iron Age, the early medieval period and finally in the thirteenth century. They also found numerous arrowheads and crossbow bolts from this final phase, traces of the fierce battles over the fortification. After the Order took it, they deepened the moat, raised the height of the earthen ramparts and added a timber gatehouse. Work also began on an outer line of embankments, which remained unfinished, perhaps as a result of an indigenous insurrection. Later, the Order would establish their convent (i.e. regional command centre) in the place where the ruins of the Castle of Dzierzgoń still stand, and also named it Christburg. The stronghold at what became known as Old Christburg continued to be occupied until the early fourteenth century, and a pottery workshop was set up within its grounds – archaeologists discovered traces of a kiln and the characteristic greyware ceramics associated with German migrants. Eventually, it was abandoned, becoming overgrown and serving only as a landmark for the incomers and indigenous Pomesanians who were now subjects of the Order.

Christian's settlement and missionary base at Santir was acquired by the Order at this time, who transformed it into an administrative centre for their Pomesanian territories. Control had been regained over the Nogat river and, in 1237, a crusading army led by Count Henry of Meissen sailed from there to the Elbing river, reaching the southern edge of the Vistula Lagoon. Here, on an island in the river, the brethren constructed a timber stronghold. The following year a settlement was established nearby and named Elbing (Polish Elbląg). This was not far from abandoned Truso, although archaeologists have found no traces of continuity between the two. The advantages of these two locations were nonetheless the same, and Elbing would quickly thrive as a major trading centre. The town was laid out on a regular grid with timber streets separating tenements. It was soon populated by migrants, many of whom hailed from Lübeck. As in the other towns established in Prussia, the Dominicans quickly had a friary constructed. Feeling secure, from 1240 the brethren began to replace the timber stronghold with a castle – effectively a fortified convent – built from field stones and bricks, which a decade later would become the provincial headquarters.

Few traces of the Order's early castles have been found. They were replaced by more durable structures once the conquest was over, but one of the most exciting archaeological discoveries in Poland in the last decade took place in the grounds of the present History and Archaeology Museum in Elbląg. The museum was established after the Second World War in the remains of the Teutonic Order's fortified convent of Elbing, destroyed some four centuries earlier. Several metres below the modern ground level, in the outer ward of the north side of the castle, archaeologists discovered that the original island had been filled up and levelled to construct the new fortified complex. But more importantly, the remains of exceptionally preserved timber buildings were uncovered and dated by dendrochronology to the crusading period. The earliest, which included a partial wooden floor padded with fascines (rod bundles), was dated by dendrochronology to the 1240s, when the Order's castle began to be constructed from field stones and brick.

The largest timbers in this building consisted of whole trunks derived from massive oak trees. They measured almost a metre in diameter, and were estimated to have been around 200 years old when felled. In contrast, the earliest timber buildings and street pavings uncovered in the historic centre of the town were all constructed from much smaller planks. Such large oak trees – a species that is repeatedly associated with indigenous religion – would have been noticeable in the landscape, and may even have derived from a sacred grove. Indeed, some 20 kilometres to the south was a place named Heylgewald (holy woods), which first appears in documents in 1324 and is later rendered as Heiligenwalde, today bearing the

Polish name Święty Gaj.³² If such trees derived from a sacred indigenous site, their use as building materials by the Order would have represented a striking political and religious statement. It would be entirely in keeping with the conduct of the brethren's holy war.

Unfortunately, few other details are known about the first brick castle in Elbing, but fragments recovered during earlier excavations indicate that it was an impressive and decorated structure, as befitting a provincial centre. It included a church built in the Romanesque style, and hints of its splendour can be seen in architectural fragments uncovered during excavations on either side of the First World War. The doorway to the church was decorated with figures of the Wise and Foolish Virgins, a relatively common theme in the Christian art of Western and Central Europe, and one that would also become widely adopted for decorating the Order's castle chapels. The apocalyptic meaning of the parable of the Virgins — preparation for the Second Coming of Christ — must have resonated with how the brethren perceived their struggle against Baltic paganism. Indeed, this is the earliest evidence we have for the adoption of apocalyptic symbolism by the Order in Prussia. A relic of the True Cross which had been presented to Herman of Salza by the German emperor was deposited in the church and, as an incentive to bolster the Order's new outpost, the pope granted a ten days' indulgence to crusaders who honoured this relic.

The Kulm charter would be granted to the majority of settlements established within Prussia, but Elbing was a rare exception by adopting in 1240 the privileges of the centre of the emerging Hanse — Lübeck. This gave the Teutonic Order less control over the town — a fact the brethren clearly resented — although they did approve the town's charter six years later. However, Kulm still exerted an influence on the town's plan, which was laid out using the newly established civic measure that determined the width of streets and tenements. Communities of burghers in the major towns founded by the Order would also aspire to self-governance, and the complex relationship that emerged between the brethren and their urban subjects would be echoed across the eastern Baltic. Despite these assertions of independence, the Order would impose its authority on all the planned towns within its domains. But the relationship was not antagonistic. Settlers were attracted by the privileges and freedoms of the towns which gave them better opportunities in the conquered territories than back home. They also contributed to the crusading effort, which included donations to the Order or the provision of resources – weapons, ships, horses, military retinues. Some burghers even participated as crusaders themselves. Gifts of land, the opportunity for commerce and personal piety appear to have been the main motivators for the colonists who flocked to the conquered Prussian territories in the thirteenth century. For some individuals, all three were easily combined.

In 1242, Duke Swietopelk allied with the Prussians against the Order, as the brethren were supporting his brother's claim to Gdańsk and were also encroaching on his control over the Vistula. Historians often refer to this as the first Prussian uprising against the crusaders, although it was a multi-faceted conflict. After losing two key strongholds to the Order, Swietopelk sued for peace but, following a massacre of the brethren's army by the Sudovians on 15 June 1243, he rejoined the fray and besieged Kulm but failed to take the town. The Order gathered a coalition of allies made up of Polish dukes and Swietopelk's brothers, and the conflict would drag on for several years. Swietopelk unsuccessfully besieged Elbing, where Peter of Dusburg makes a point of noting that the women of the town, dressed as men, rushed to its ramparts – the show of force convincing the Pomerelians to retreat. His army also took Christburg, which the Order was able to later recapture. Meanwhile, the crusading armies of the margraves of Meissen and Brandenburg raided further east, subduing Pogesania and Warmia. Finally, Swietopelk agreed a truce with the Order, and the defeated Prussian nobles were obliged to accept the terms of a treaty at the brethren's new Castle of Christburg in February 1249. The treaty is one of the most valuable documents from the crusading period as it provides a rare glimpse into indigenous life, and it was already mentioned earlier in relation to indigenous religious practices. The deal was brokered by the papal chaplain, Jacob of Liège (and future pope Urban IV), whose concern was to protect Prussian converts, but also to assert Rome's authority over the conquered territories.

As such, the treaty stated the Prussian converts – referred to as 'neophytes' – could keep their personal freedom if they persevered with Christianity, whilst underlining that all land acquired in Prussia was the property of the Holy See. They were to build twenty-two churches, the majority of which were to be constructed in Pomesania to ensure that converts had access to religious services. They were to pay tithes, baptise their children in these churches, abstain from working on Sundays and during religious festivals, observe fasting and attend confession. They were also required to abandon a series of pagan practices, which included venerating Kurke, cremating the dead with horses or living people, and burying the dead with valuable objects. Two groups of indigenous priests – referred to in Latin as Tulissones and Ligaschones – who performed ritual roles at pagan funerals and claimed to see the dead riding in the sky on horses, were also banned. All future burials were to take place in Christian cemeteries. Marriages were restricted to single wives and only those who were not purchased or near relatives (i.e. stepmothers, sisters-in-law and widows) and would only be valid if conducted in a church. Those who refused baptism for themselves or their children would have their property confiscated. The Prussians also had to pay tithes and provide miliary support for the Order. In exchange, they could continue to inherit, purchase and sell property, sue in Christian courts, become priests and monks, whilst their nobles could join the Order's forces and be knighted.[33] The treaty was in fact a one-sided document, imposed on the Prussians. There was no indigenous voice within its text and the pope's representative affixed his seal on behalf of the neophytes. It would therefore come as no surprise that peace did not last.

Swietopelk would play no further role in opposing the Order, and would die in 1266. His son, Mestwin, who had spent some time as the Order's hostage, would challenge his younger brother Wratislaw and uncle Sambor for control over Gdańsk, eventually emerging as sole ruler of Pomerelia in 1273. Threatened by the territorial ambitions of the Order to the east and the margraves of Brandenburg to the west, he signed a series of treaties with the Duke of Greater Poland, Premysl II, which unified their territories in the event of the succession. After Mestwin's death in 1294, Premysl inherited Pomerelia and would be crowned king of Poland the following year. His reign was brief – less than eight months later he would be killed during a failed abduction attempt on the orders of the Margrave of Brandenburg. Although his realm fragmented upon his death, the Polish claim to Pomerelia remained and would have profound consequences for the future.

In the same year the Order constructed its stronghold at Elbing, it also became involved in Livonia, with governance of the Sword Brothers' lands given over to the Prussian master, Herman Balk. He reinforced the garrisons and negotiated the return of northern Estonia to the Danish crown. Balk left Livonia in 1238 and died the following year. After this, a separate Livonian master was appointed and the Order found itself increasingly split between investing in its growing Baltic territories and the Holy Land. On the ground, regional governance structures were developed in Prussia and Livonia as the Order rapidly evolved into a major international territorial ruler. With the appointment of separate provincial masters, the leader of the Order began to be referred to as *'magister generalis'* – 'grand master'. In 1243, following the election of Pope Innocent IV, the Order requested further crusading bulls for Livonia and Prussia. For the first time, the pope granted the brethren the ability to recruit crusaders for their ongoing war in Prussia at their own discretion, without the requirement of public preaching and with no expiration on this permission. In this respect, the Order was permitted to organise a perpetual crusade in Prussia, although it continued to ask for papal permission for future campaigns. When the Order's priests were granted the right to preach crusades in the 1260s, the brethren had gained complete control over the timing and recruitment of their campaigns.[34]

But these decades were also a dangerous time for the brethren, whose leadership became divided between supporting the German emperor or the pope in a conflict playing out in northern Italy. Since its inception, the Order had found itself caught between its two principal supporters and, under Herman of Salza's leadership, it had successfully navigated through the political maelstrom. The crisis came to a head when two grand masters were elected by the Order's opposing factions. The faction supporting the emperor elected the Prussian master, Poppo of Osterna, as grand master in 1253. Under his leadership, the conquest of eastern Prussia began in earnest.

EASTERN PRUSSIA AND INDIGENOUS RESISTANCE

The towns founded in Prussia remained vulnerable throughout the crusading period, and many were attacked and destroyed, before being rebuilt. In 1251, a large part of Thorn was destroyed by fire, perhaps as a result of a raid. This prompted the foundation of a 'new town' alongside the 'old town', both separated by their own circuits of walls. A more permanent brick wall replaced the earlier timber defences, utilising the same style of urban defences that were constructed around Riga. The town invested in formidable defences: a double wall and moat, punctuated with towers and gatehouses, two of which were later fortified with barbicans. The New Town's defensive walls and three gatehouses were constructed after the Old Town's, at which point both formed a unified, integrated circuit connected with the Order's castle. Elbing would similarly be destroyed by fire in 1288, prompting the rebuilding of the town with more formidable defences.

The war with the western Natangians lasted until 1253, and the following year the conquest was extended to the lands of Bartia and Galindia. Crusades against the Sambians, arguably the most powerful of all the Prussian groups, now came from both the north and west. In 1254, the Order's Livonian brethren launched an unsuccessful assault from Memel (Lithuanian Klaipėda) into Sambia. That winter, the largest crusading army to enter Prussian lands, which included forces from Bohemia led by King Ottokar II as well as from Brandenburg, joined the Order in a crusade against the western Sambians. Within a few days, the surviving Sambians had accepted baptism, sworn allegiance to the Order and offered up hostages. Ottokar sponsored the construction of a stronghold, overlooking the River Pregel, which was named in honour of him as Königsberg. Within a year, this had been transformed into a fortified convent and a settlement had been established alongside it. The Sambian nobility who had sworn loyalty to the Order had their lands and privileges returned, enabling the Order to turn its attention to eastern Natangia, which was finally subjugated in 1256. Although it would take a decade to fully subdue Sambia, the impact of the crusades is already visible archaeologically in the first half of the thirteenth century, when people began to be inhumed – rather than cremated – in Sambia. This is attested in at least eight cemeteries from the Kaliningrad region. The horse-cremation burial rite is abandoned and inhumations become the norm, although equestrian equipment such as horse harnesses and bridle bits continue to be deposited for several more decades, before they become replaced by spurs. They mark the transformation of the indigenous Sambian warrior class into a new knighthood – vassals of the Christian regime.[35] Many of the strongholds on the Sambian Peninsula remain poorly known archaeologically, but those that are well dated were abandoned during or before the crusading period.

The Order then began campaigns into pagan Samogitia, which was sandwiched between Livonia and Prussia. In 1257–9, a truce was arranged, enabling Livonian and Prussian merchants to travel throughout Samogitia, and pagan Samogitians to travel freely in the domains of the Order. But when the truce expired, the Samogitians attacked Christian outposts in Curonia, prompting uprisings from the Semigallians, Curonians and eventually the Lithuanians. Then in 1260, a new Prussian leader emerged who presented a serious challenge to the Order. This was Herkus Monte, a Natangian noble. Herkus had been captured during the crusade of 1240 and was taken back to Magdeburg for a Christian re-education. The Order regularly sent indigenous hostages, often young boys, for re-education in the empire, in the hope this would create a new generation of loyal Christian Prussians. Indeed, as a loyal vassal, Herkus had fought alongside the brethren against the eastern Prussians in the early 1250s. But in the process, he learned how the Order's military resources were organised and how the brethren fought. This knowledge would serve him well, as he called on the Prussians of Sambia, Natangia, Bartia and Warmia to rise up against the Christian regime. The defeat of the brethren's joint Prussian and Livonian forces at the Battle of Durbe in July 1260 – the most significant defeat suffered by the Order which saw the death of the Livonian master and Prussian land marshal – acted as a catalyst for what later became known as the Great Prussian Uprising. The insurrection began in September and German priests and settlers in the eastern Prussian regions were attacked and killed, as were those indigenous who were loyal to the Order. Some blamed the success of the rebellion on the sins of the Christians. The rebellion spread to western Prussia, prompting the pope to call for a new crusade. An army from the Rhineland came to the Order's aid and relieved the garrison of Königsberg, who were being besieged by Sambian forces. The crusaders temporarily drove off the Sambians, who returned once they had left. The garrison at Königsberg held out, but most were captured during the uprising. In 1262, the Sudovians invaded Masovia and the Lithuanians joined in attacking eastern Poland and western Prussia, with the attacks reaching the Kulmerland and Kuyavia. During a battle against the Natangians, the Master of Prussia, the marshal and many seasoned brother-knights were killed. The assaults on the Kulmerland intensified, and a large Lithuanian army attacked Masovia, Pogesania and eventually Kulm.

In the following years, crusading armies arrived from the empire and eventually the Order recovered the initiative and launched raids from its castles along the Vistula and Pregel rivers, and across the northern coast. Pogesania remained the most contested region and, in 1271, the Bartians sought to drive out the Order from here but were repelled by the garrisons at Christburg and Elbing. Shortly after, a large force of Sudovians and Lithuanians entered Kulm but failed to penetrate the town's defences, and the Bartian leader was killed after trying to storm the Order's outpost near Schönsee (Polish Kowalewo Pomorskie), which prompted his army to disperse. The following winter, refreshed by German reinforcements, the crusading armies converged on Natangia, assaulted Herkus Monte's principal stronghold and devastated the region. Monte and the leader of the Warmians were captured soon after and executed. Fighting was now concentrated on the wetlands and forests of Pogesania, where Prussian rebels had regrouped. The remaining indigenous forces were overcome at Heilsberg (Polish Lidzbark Warmiński) in 1274. A few years later, another uprising saw the Order's forces enter Pogesania and resettle part of its population, with some fleeing to Samogitia.

After this, the Order concentrated on occupying Nadruvia and Scalovia, before turning its attention to Sudovia. This region had long been the target of attacks from Rus' and Polish rulers. The latter had led a series of assaults across the frontier in the latter half of the thirteenth century, but failed to make territorial gains.[36] The Order waged a sustained war against the Sudovians which lasted a few years and, by 1283, the region had been depopulated as many of the survivors had been resettled in other parts of Prussia, with the remainder fleeing to Lithuania. Peter of Dusburg wrote that at this point the war against the Prussians was officially over, and the war with Lithuania had begun. In fact, Lithuanian armies had already been fighting alongside the Prussians against the Order, although from now the holy war would be focused against the grand duchy and Samogitia.

THE IMPACT OF CONQUEST

In Polish school textbooks, the history of the conquest of indigenous Prussian lands – and Poland's troubles with the Teutonic Order, the later Kingdom of Prussia and unified Germany – begins with Duke Conrad's decision to invite the Order into Prussia, one that can be described in hindsight, and without any exaggeration, as marking the course of European history. Most Poles relate to Conrad through the endlessly reproduced drawing by the nineteenth-century artist Jan Matejko, 'the teacher of the nation', whose paintings have provided the definitive, if highly romanticised, representations of the seminal events in Polish history. Within his famous series of illustrations of Polish rulers, Matejko rendered Conrad as a stern, hawkish, heavily armoured warrior resting a dagger on a document, an oppressive leader who solved his political problems with force.[37] Matejko had taken his source material from Jan Długosz, the quintessential chronicler of Polish history writing in the fifteenth century, who described Conrad as one who would bring the greatest defeat and misfortune to the Kingdom of Poland for his invitation to the Order to secure the Masovian frontier against the Prussians.

It is clear that Conrad's decision was one of many historical attempts to subjugate the Prussians, and to simultaneously expand the frontiers of the Piast principalities and Christendom. Crusading had become an attractive ideology for the Polish nobility and Church, and the military orders were widely perceived as suitable guardians of Christendom's borders. The Teutonic Order had been expelled from Transylvania for overreaching their remit, and perhaps for threatening missionary activities amongst the pagan Cumans which were, in turn, linked to the security and aspirations of the Hungarian kingdom. However, in Prussia, the Order was able to develop its own territorial ambitions thanks to the regular supply of crusading armies and brother-knights to maintain its garrisons. It is important to remember that spiritual rewards were significant motivators for these participants, even though around a hundred nobles were granted fiefs in Prussia, mostly in the Kulmerland. The Order facilitated this by creating a culture of crusading – installing relics in the chapels of its castles, and memorialising the death of its martyrs on the battlefield. Peter of Dusburg would fill his narrative with references to martyrdom and miracles, as quoted at the start of this chapter, contributing to the collective memory of the crusades in Prussia as a righteous spiritual war.[38]

But in terms of pragmatic efforts which consolidated territorial gains with a working economy, the Order successfully attracted large numbers of German and Polish migrants who built towns which became thriving trading centres. These were attacked, destroyed and rebuilt. Even the Kulmerland, at the southern tip of the conquered territories, remained an unstable region for many decades, suffering repeated incursions from Prussian and Lithuanian armies, the last of which was led by the Sudovians in 1277. The Prussians, aided by the Pomerelians and Lithuanians, had organised two major rebellions which failed to uproot the crusaders. Against all the odds, the Order successfully entrenched itself in the conquered territories, seeing off attacks from all sides. Its strongholds and urban colonies were the key to securing its conquest, which was underpinned by a highly effective and evolving system of territorial governance.

The Order's leadership had seen several masters come and go, and the international growth of the organisation resulted in the emergence of the office of grand master, heading an increasingly powerful international corporation. With the integration of the Sword Brothers into its ranks in 1237, the Order took full control of the military enterprises in both Prussia and Livonia. Meanwhile, the brethren's arrival heralded the end of the Cistercian mission in Prussia. When Bishop Christian was taken hostage by the Sambians in 1233, the Order raided his lands and seized the financial rights to its churches and chapels, crippling the economic basis of the Cistercian mission. With Christian held hostage for five years, the mission was completely dismantled. In 1235, the brethren of Dobrzyń were incorporated into the Teutonic Order and then came again briefly under Duke Conrad's overlordship. So, when Christian finally gained his freedom, he found that he had been outmanoeuvred and removed from any further meaningful role in Prussia. The subsequent development of ecclesiastical organisation was influenced by the Order, and the territory was subdivided into four dioceses controlled by bishops who wielded secular power on their lands. By the latter decades of the thirteenth century, the Order's domains in Prussia and Livonia were increasingly ruled as quasi-independent branches, but within a few decades Prussia would become the most politically important region for the Order.

What of the indigenous Prussians? The impact of the conquest on these groups was more severe than in Livonia. The political landscape was completely transformed as all indigenous strongholds were destroyed or appropriated by the new regime, which replaced them with a new network of fortified convents and smaller castles. Prussian communities remained socially stratified, with some noble families continuing to wield power under the new regime as vassals. But over time there was significant demographic change. An estimated 170,000 people lived in Prussia at the start of the thirteenth century. By the first decade of the fourteenth century, the indigenous population had been reduced to around 90,000, with the addition of some 30,000 Poles and 15,000 Germans.[39] The most significant ethnic transformations in the region would take place over the course of the fourteenth and fifteenth centuries, as large numbers of German, and in some areas Polish, peasants settled in the Prussian countryside.[40] In time, the indigenous language was abandoned and what it meant to identify as Prussian completely transformed.

CHAPTER 7

FORTRESSES OF HEAVEN
Religious Rule in the Medieval Baltic

> ... build a castle in their land and they will quickly come under your control ...
>
> *Livonian Rhymed Chronicle*[1]

BUILDING CASTLES

By 1284, the Teutonic Order had begun constructing a new castle in place of an existing timber-and-earthen fortress called Brandenburg on the western edge of the Prussian territory of Natangia, strategically located by the mouth of a small river that flowed into the Vistula Lagoon.[2] The name had been given by the Margrave of Brandenburg, Otto III, who came to Prussia to crusade alongside the Order and sponsored the construction of the stronghold here in 1266. Not long after, it was destroyed by the Warmians and, the following year, Otto returned with his army and had the stronghold rebuilt. This became a place of sanctity in the eyes of crusaders — one of the brothers there had witnessed an apparition of the Virgin Mary, and nearby at a place called Pokarwis, a battle had been fought against the Natangians where many Christians had perished, with one German knight who had been captured then sacrificed by being tied to a horse and burned. The fallen were regarded as martyrs in the Order's collective memory.[3]

But plans for a more substantial fortified structure remained on hold until Prussian military resistance had been finally suppressed. The conquered lands, of which the brethren controlled the lion's share, had been steadily carved up into new administrative districts called commanderies. These were widely used by the military orders to organise settlement and resources on their territories. In the eastern Baltic, the first that we know about was centred on the convent at Wenden in Livonia, shortly after the Order acquired the lands of the Sword Brothers in 1237. In Prussia, the first was formally established at Elbing in 1246. At the heart of each commandery was a fortified convent, where a group of the Order's brethren forming a 'chapter' would reside. In theory, following the Order's Rule, this consisted of a dozen brother-knights representing Christ's apostles, but in practice these became much larger communities. In Livonia, brethren would be regularly recruited from the lower nobility of what is today northern Germany, whilst in Prussia recruits largely came from southern Germany. The brother-knights formed the Order's elite fighting force, but they were also given specific duties within the convent, such as managing the storage of provisions, granaries, smithies and gardens. As such, their daily routines were divided between religious observance, military training and administrative tasks. The convent was headed by a commander, who was usually appointed for a year (sometimes longer) and would serve in a number of different houses over their career, with the more ambitious climbing the ladder to higher office. They were primarily concerned with military matters, whilst the daily business of the convent was run by their deputy and the community's spiritual needs were met by one or more priests and non-ordained clerics. Finally, there were the brother-sergeants, sometimes called 'grey mantles' on account of their prescribed garments. The wider household of the convent included administrators, servants, soldiers and artisans.

The lands of the various Prussian groups had been reorganised as the conquests progressed, and then reorganised again as the Order's provincial masters turned their attention to consolidating their territorial gains. From 1283, it was the turn of the eastern Prussian lands.[4] Brandenburg would become the centre for a newly defined commandery that stretched from the Vistula Lagoon, south-east across the wetlands and forests of the adjacent lands of Bartia and Galindia. This required a new, monumental building that symbolised the Order's unquestionable rule, a fitting residence for the commander and his chapter of brother-knights, and so, Brandenburg was transformed into a massive construction site.

The old stronghold continued to be used by the brethren as the new castle was raised in a different area, and it would take several years before they would be able to relocate and dismantle the margrave's fortification. A diverse range of building materials, some of which had not been seen before in this part of Prussia, would be assembled and replenished at seasonal intervals over the years at the construction site. Large quantities of clay, most probably extracted from the nearby river and lakes, were shaped in wooden moulds and fired in kilns to produce thousands of bricks. Each one was scored with a series of linear finger marks on their rougher side, to help the mortar adhere. Some bricks, before firing, would have been cut into moulded shapes and set aside for decorating doorways or for floor tiles. Hundreds of curved ceramic roof tiles had also been prepared. Large boulders, erratics left behind by retreating glaciers at the end of the last Ice Age, had been brought to the site, transported by wagons and dragged by horses from the surrounding meadows and forests. Smaller granite blocks had also been procured and would be used for the building's window frames and columns. Large quantities of timber obtained from the abundant woodlands in the vicinity of Brandenburg had been prepared for the castle's floors and rafters, and for any piling that needed to be driven into waterlogged ground or the riverbank to stabilise it. Thinner wooden posts were also prepared for scaffolding. Finally, vats of quicklime had been sourced for mortar.[5]

An experienced architect had been employed to head up the project, which was overseen by the castle's newly appointed commander, who, in turn, was following guidance provided by the Order's leadership. Based on the architect's preliminary sketches of the building's plan, with its proportions formulated using *ad quadrantum*, the geometry of squares, the perimeter walls were measured out with the 'Kulm rod': fourteen down one side, eleven down the other – corresponding to a modern measurement of 65.4 by 52 metres.[6] This had become the standard for planning all construction work in Prussia, from laying out new settlements to the dimensions of streets, plots and buildings. Then work began on digging the foundation trenches for the outer wall and levelling any uneven ground with sand. The workforce would have included masons, bricklayers, shingle makers and sawyers, as well as labourers drawn from the nearby indigenous Prussian villages and German migrant settlements. The new regime had commissioned locators to recruit settlers from peasant communities in Lower Saxony, North Rhine-Westphalia, Central Germany, Holland and neighbouring Polish territories. They were offered incentives to uproot and resettle in the newly conquered lands of Prussia. In return, they provided taxes, military service and labour. Christian settlers had arrived in Prussia even as the crusades were under way, but following the conquest they came in droves, bringing their livestock with them. It was a chance to start afresh, in a new land of opportunity. At Brandenburg, they probably formed the early core of the settlement that developed alongside the castle, which is otherwise poorly known except for the remains of its later fourteenth-century brick church.[7]

The indigenous population, now subjects of the Christian regime, was also being incorporated into the new system of land ownership. For example, on 14 February 1290, the Prussian Master Meinhard of Querfurt issued a charter granting the indigenous Prussians Busso and Hertwig sixty *Hufen* of land in the village of Pokarben, near Brandenburg.[8] Like other Prussians, they had been given land in exchange for their loyalty and for the value of their labour. Hertwig had also adopted a German Christian name, the start of a process of acculturation that would, over many generations, change indigenous life beyond recognition. Prussian religious beliefs and customs also persisted, but it is likely the commander of Brandenburg turned a blind eye to these. From his perspective, for all intents and purposes, the conquered Prussians were now officially Christians, certainly prone to superstition but no longer a serious threat. His immediate priorities were to get the castle built, to govern the growing population of his district, which including gathering taxes, and to organise defences against Lithuanian raids. Churchmen had complained the Teutonic Order was more concerned with exploiting their new subjects for their labour than with their spiritual wellbeing, and there may well have been some truth in this.

When work on the castle finally commenced, boulders were laid down in the narrow foundation trenches in rows to establish a solid base, held together with clay. Where they protruded above the ground level, an even pedestal of stones was created, on top of which the brick walls would be raised. With the aid of scaffolding, the outer walls were completed up to the height of four storeys, now enclosing a quadrangular space. The bricks were laid in a methodological way, with alternating single heads and stretchers referred to as the 'Wendish bond' (from its origins in the northern marches, disseminated by German builders), although within a few decades a different arrangement was being used with double stretchers.[9] Work then began on the inner walls of the south-western wing of the castle, where the principal entrance was located, including bases for vaulting and partition walls. The cellars were dug out, although these were shallow as the ground level inside the castle's courtyard would be later raised. The completion of the south-western wing and the insertion of flooring would have enabled the most important spaces in the convent to be installed – the chapel and the brethren's refectory. Glaziers would install the windows and then sculptors and painters were brought in to decorate these spaces, most probably the same group who had worked on the castles of Marienburg (Polish Malbork) and Lochstedt (Russian Pavlovo). Once completed and furnished, the chapel would house relics, including a fragment of the Holy Cross that had been brought over from the Rhine and which a few decades later would be credited with resurrecting a dead child. Only fragments of decoration have survived from the Order's castles, but they are suggestive of recurring themes. We can imagine the walls of Brandenburg's chapel and refectory were covered in paintings depicting biblical figures and episodes from the Order's history, its crusading mission and perhaps even the martyrs of Pokarwis.

Once the principal range had been completed, the two adjacent wings were gradually raised up. The north-eastern wing would not be built until a few decades later, with a tall tower raised in the northern corner. Referred to by later scholars as a *Bergfried*, this was a common feature not just in the Order's convents but of German castles more widely. Unlike a keep, it was not intended as a residence but instead served as a watchtower.[10] Vaulting and flooring was added to the interiors, supported by octagonal granite pillars in the upper levels and round ones in the cellars, and granite window frames were installed. Mistakes in the construction were also corrected as work progressed. During this time, a terrace or *Zwinger* was constructed around the outside of the castle from heaped-up soil, held in place by an outer brick wall. Some of this soil was dug out from the surrounding area, creating a moat which was then connected to the river, transforming the castle's earthen platform into a walled island. Finally, the earlier mono-pitched rooves covering the wings would be replaced by steeper gabled roofs covered in tiles, housing expansive lofts which would be used for storage.

The castle remained a building site for decades, and at various points engineers were brought in to organise massive hydraulic and earthen works. To the west, the area which had served as the builders' yard was transformed into the castle's outer ward. Several buildings were added to serve as a stable, smithy and granary, and the whole area was enclosed with a wall. It would function as a training and mustering yard. A channel was cut into the river, diverting it to create a moat around the entire complex, which now consisted of two moated, walled islands, connected by bridges and defended by the river on one side and the lagoon on the other. The castle itself, towering over the rest of the complex and the nearby settlement, would be one of the largest of its type in the eastern Baltic. Its bright red-brick fabric would have been visible from some distance, contrasting with the duller shades of the smaller timber houses belonging to the Order's subjects. The cost of its construction had been enormous, and only made possible by the Order's growing wealth, derived from its estates, supporters and, of course, newly annexed lands. Now this affluence was on display for all to see: the castle was far bigger and more majestic than any other building in the vicinity, or even within the nearest towns. But it was so many other things: a house of the Milites Christi, a representation of celestial perfection and, above all, a symbol of the new regime's unrivalled authority. The majority of the Order's convents in Prussia (and to a lesser extent in Livonia) had been constructed following a standardised design, although numerous smaller and more varied fortified structures would also be built by the brethren. Along with the castles of the other authorities in the post-crusade eastern Baltic, they became the most striking manifestations of power and affluence in the reorganised political landscape. They projected the image, legitimacy and continuing mission of the new regime.

STRUCTURES OF GOVERNANCE

The Baltic Crusades had seen decades of military campaigns, whose gains were consolidated by castles and their attached towns. This strategy was linked in the minds of contemporaries to the successful imposition of Christian rule as quoted at the start of this chapter, where the Livonian brethren were advising their master how best to suppress Semigallian resistance. Those driving the military enterprises became territorial rulers from the very onset, exercising newly invented sovereign rights. Indigenous political structures had been largely dismantled in the process, although some nobles, particularly in Livonia and Finland, retained their strongholds and lands as vassals or allies of the new Christian authorities. Following the depopulation of Sudovia in eastern Prussia and the subjugation of Semigallia in southern Livonia, the Order became the most powerful ruler in the eastern Baltic. In Prussia, its territories encompassed some 48,000 km^2 by the end of the first decade of the fourteenth century, with a further 32,100 km^2 added by the early fifteenth century, although most of these later acquisitions were only held for a short time.[11] In Livonia, the Order's territory at its greatest extent was around 67,000 km^2.

Substantial tracts of land were also controlled by bishops, and separately by the cathedral chapters (the communities of canons) that elected them. When Prussia had been subdivided into four dioceses in 1243, with a third of the conquered lands assigned to its bishops to govern, the Order moved to reorganise the cathedral chapters under its own Rule. As a result, the canons would owe their allegiance to the grand master, and thus the Order could influence the appointment of bishops. In this way, the Prussian episcopates gave the Order considerable influence in how they governed their territories. The canons served a variety of important roles for the Order – as diplomats, chaplains and notaries – and, in contrast to cathedral chapters in the West, they would also fulfil the same roles assigned to brethren in the Order's convents, including those of commanders. In the case of Warmia, the largest

Prussian diocese which encompassed the indigenous lands of Pogesania, Natangia, Bartia and Galindia, its first bishop, Anselm of Meissen, was a priest of the Order, but none of the subsequent holders of the office or canons were. Nonetheless, there was a cohesive unity in the governance of Prussia between its five territorial powers, and the Order could rely on the military support of its neighbouring religious rulers when called upon. There was also an ideological unity which supported the Order's projection of its continuing mission – to combat paganism. In contrast, in Livonia, only the Curonian chapter adopted the Order's rule, and here the brethren inherited the Sword Brothers' status as subordinates of the episcopates of Riga, Dorpat and Ösel-Wiek. This proved to be a source of political tension, especially with the archbishops of Riga, who held supreme jurisdiction over the dioceses of Livonia and Prussia from 1255.

Bishops in the two regions of the eastern Baltic that were incorporated into the kingdoms of Sweden and Denmark were not territorial lords, but still wielded extensive power. In Finland, which was subdivided into provinces governed by royal castellans, the Bishop of Åbo (Finnish Turku) became one of the most powerful landowners within what would grow into the largest diocese in the Swedish kingdom. He had authority to raise taxes and dispense justice, and served as a key advisor to the Swedish crown. In the Duchy of Estonia, the interests of the Danish crown were delegated to the governor who was based in Reval (Estonian Tallinn), the castellans of Wesenberg (Estonian Rakvere) and Narwa (Estonian Narva), a group of royal counsellors and, at the local level, vassals who had been granted hereditary fiefs. Together with the governors, the bishops of Reval also acted as colonial go-betweens for the Danish crown. Between 1332 and 1344, which included a period of interregnum in Denmark, there was no governor in Estonia, and the counsellors effectively ruled the duchy. As such, during the indigenous Estonian 'St George's Night Uprising' that took the ruling authorities by surprise, they were obliged to seek help from the Order in Livonia.[12] After the uprising was defeated, the duchy was sold to the Order in 1346 and subdivided into commanderies.

Rule by religious elites was not a novelty in the medieval Catholic world. Military orders operated as territorial lords elsewhere, most famously the Hospitallers on the Dodecanese islands in the eastern

Mediterranean and later Malta, whilst bishops wielded temporal authority in a number of regions of Christendom. Large swathes of central and northern Italy were also governed by the Holy See – the papal states – although de facto power was often in the hands of local magnates. Given the pope was the ecclesiastical overlord of the religious authorities in the eastern Baltic, there has been some debate about whether this meant the territories they governed were papal fiefs. But the lands had also been nominally granted by the German emperor, suggesting they were understood as extensions of the Holy Roman Empire. Indeed, the imperial title of 'prince bishop' would be conferred on four of the bishoprics in Livonia and one in Prussia, reinforcing the link with the empire. In practice, the religious rulers in the eastern Baltic exercised territorial governance as sovereign powers. In the early decades of crusading, their authority was underpinned by military force, and this paved the way for establishing their rule as an accepted and legal fact, recognised by their subjects and outsiders. This was reinforced not just by the continued threat of violence, but also by the process of religious conversion, which was an integral part of the conquests. For the indigenous populations who had been either voluntarily or forcibly baptised, now defined as neophytes – converted Christians – their own legal status had changed, and they were obliged to follow the laws of their new overlords and the ordinances of the Church.[13]

TERRITORIAL AMBITIONS

Although the crusades of the thirteenth century had ended, the new Christian powers in the Baltic continued to have territorial ambitions. Swedish expansion eastwards, towards the Karelian Isthmus, was marked by the construction of further castles. Following the castle at Åbo, fortifications were built in Tavastia (Finnish Häme) and Viborg (Russian Vyborg).[14] Here, on the Karelian frontier, the territorial ambitions of the Swedish crown clashed with those of Rus' Novgorod. This resulted in tit-for-tat raids throughout much of the fourteenth century, that saw the destruction of Åbo's cathedral by a Rus' army in 1318 along with the bishop's castle at Kustö (Finnish Kuusisto). From the mid-fourteenth century, more castles were built and new districts mapped out to the north in more sparsely populated areas, with the last completed in the 1470s. They would remain the principal administrative centres until the mid-sixteenth century. But in the core areas of governance, power was in the hands of Swedish nobles, encouraged to settle across the south-western coast, and then further inland. They built manors at the centres of large estates, and sponsored the construction of churches.[15]

Further south, the Teutonic Order was also focused on expanding its territory. Its lands in the Levant and Transylvania had been lost. It had scattered estates and holdings across Central Europe and parts of Italy, even some in France and Iberia, which together formed a network of provinces referred to as bailiwicks, but it was only in Prussia and Livonia where the brethren held significant territory. Their war against Lithuania became a means of extending the territory of their eastern Prussian province, with the hope this could be joined with their lands in Livonia. When Acre, the last crusader town on the Levantine coast, fell to the Mamluks in 1291, the Order's headquarters were relocated to its convent in Venice. The Order's Venetian chapter then sought to preserve its own pole position within the corporation, moving to curtail the grand master's freedom – he would need their consent to travel beyond the Alps and before making any key decisions when away from Venice. This provoked the brethren in Prussia who complained they were being sidelined. Eventually, they deposed the grand master at a meeting of the chapter in Elbing in 1303. In his place they elected Siegfried of Feuchtwangen, hoping to get better representation.

Meanwhile in Livonia, the Order was engaged in an ongoing struggle with Riga. In 1305, Archbishop Frederick of Pernstein accused the brethren of heresy. He had not been in office for long. Formerly a Franciscan friar from Moravia, he had arrived in Riga that spring and walked straight into a dispute over the Order's recent purchase of the monastery of Dünamünde (Latvian Daugavgrīva). The new acquisition meant the brethren now controlled entry to Riga itself. The town was in uproar and violence had broken out in the streets. The new archbishop had been close to the king of Bohemia, an ally of the Order, yet he sided with the citizens of Riga and wrote a letter to the pope, filled with all manner of accusations. He described how the brethren had illegally occupied episcopal castles, engaged in extortion and violence, and ignored earlier papal mediations. The letter also accused them of burning the bodies of its dead as the pagans did, carrying out mercy killings of its members, eating meat during Lent, practising witchcraft, obstructing missionary work and making commercial pacts with pagans. There may have been elements of truth woven into these accusations, but on the face of it, this seemed just like another episode in the ongoing struggle between the Teutonic Order in Livonia, the town of Riga and its archbishop. But there was a more existential threat to the Order's existence.

Following the loss of the Holy Land, the military orders were in jeopardy – they needed a new raison d'être. In the winter of 1305, Pope Clement V had sent letters to the Templars and Hospitallers, sounding out a merger of the two orders, a proposition both rejected. Then, on 13 October 1307, all the Templars in France were arrested by royal officials and soon after across other regions of Christendom, including Italy and the Holy Roman Empire. This must have alarmed the Order's leadership, who quickly realised it was essential to promote a renewed sense of purpose. The following year, when Venice occupied Ferrara, a city under papal rule, it became embroiled in a conflict with the pope who placed it under interdict, preventing religious services from being performed. When this failed to have an impact, preparations were made for a papal crusade against Venice. The city was becoming too dangerous for the Order. In 1308, events in Pomerelia presented an opportunity for further territorial expansion of the brethren's Prussian lands, with far-reaching consequences for both the future of the organisation and for Northern Europe.[16]

In order to solve their financial problems, the powerful Swienca family (Polish Święca) in Gdańsk had struck a deal with the margraves of Brandenburg, offering them control over Pomerelia which they had long coveted. Brandenburg's forces plundered the region and entered Gdańsk freely in September 1308. Bogusza, the city's governor and representative of the Polish Duke (and later king) Ladislaus I 'the Short', sought military aid from the Teutonic Order, as his lord was busy in the south. The Order's Prussian master agreed to intervene, planning to expel Brandenburg's troops and garrison the ducal castle for a year at the Order's expense, then at Ladislaus's, until stability returned, after which Polish rule would resume. However, Ladislaus later altered the agreement without consulting the Order, allowing them to occupy only half the castle for a maximum of one year.

The Order's army, which included large numbers of indigenous Prussians, reached Gdańsk in October, where it was joined by Pomeranian knights. The Brandenburgian forces in the city eventually withdrew, but when the Prussian master arrived to take charge, he was dismayed to find there was still a Polish garrison in the castle, which broke the terms of the original agreement. A violent dispute erupted, men were killed and Bogusza was seized. Soon after, the Polish garrison handed over the castle to the brethren. The gates of the town remained barred against the Order, as the burghers, many of whom remained sympathetic to Brandenburg, were also concerned about the deprivation of their liberties. On 12 November, the Order's army broke through into the town, killing many of its inhabitants, including several dozen knights, causing many others to flee and destroying a large number of buildings. Contemporaries described this as a massacre, and archaeologists have found that the ducal castle and parts of the urban area of the Old Town were severely damaged by fire at this time.[17]

When Ladislaus refused to pay the Order's expenses, the brethren purchased the territorial rights to the region for 10,000 silver marks from Margrave Waldemar of Brandenburg-Stendal on 13 September 1309. Nationalist scholars would later cast this action as the Order seeking to connect their Prussian lands with 'Germany', but in fact this was simply an opportunity to gain more territory and with it increase the brethren's revenues.[18] The region was divided into new districts, and castles built to govern them. Shortly after the acquisition of Pomerelia, Grand Master Siegfried of Feuchtwangen moved the Order's *domus principalis* from Venice to Marienburg. Prussia, where the Order ruled with impunity, seemed like the safest place for the new headquarters. The castle had been located at the western edge of the Order's lands, but it was now conveniently situated in a newly created territorial heartland – between the rest of Prussia and newly annexed Pomerelia. Following an internal struggle for power within the Order's Prussian leadership, the next grand master and his deputy were driven out, and it would only be Werner of Orseln who was able to establish Marienburg as the permanent residence of the grand master from 1324.[19]

The Order's actions in Gdańsk were condemned in a papal bull in June 1310. This also prompted an investigation into the Livonian brethren, which began a year later and resulted in their temporary excommunication, but ultimately the pope decided in the Order's favour. Archbishop Frederick would return to the papal court in Avignon in 1325, where he discredited the Order at every opportunity. Peter of Dusbug's *Chronicle*, written in Königsberg at around that time – a defence of the Order's wars against the Prussians and Lithuanians – was intended as ammunition against Frederick's continuing machinations. The Order's occupation of Pomerelia would continue to be disputed by Polish rulers, who would file lawsuits against the brethren.[20]

In 1325, in seeking an ally against a common foe, Ladislaus's son Casimir would marry Aldona, the daughter of the Lithuanian grand duke Gediminas. The following year, Polish and Lithuanian forces attacked and pillaged the Neumark, the eastern lands of the Margraviate of Brandenburg. This led to a brief war between Poland and the Order, which saw the seizure of some of its borderland territories, most notably Kuyavia in 1332 where the Order established a commandery across the Vistula centred on the convent of Nessau. Much-needed relief to the borderlands finally came with a peace treaty between the Order and Poland in 1343. Three years later, the Order acquired Danish Estonia and then in 1352 purchased the territory of Dobrzyń. During this time, the brethren and their neighbouring rulers established a new political landscape across the eastern Baltic, one defined by some of the most striking castles built in Christendom.

PROJECTING POWER AND RELIGIOUS IDEALS

In 1207, Bishop Albert of Riga had introduced the office of advocate (German *Vogt*) into Livonia as part of his plan to reshape the new colony into a feudal territory, modelled on those in the Holy Roman Empire. For the indigenous population, advocates became the public face of the new regime, responsible for managing land and property, and organising local militias, and some would be given charge of their own districts. The Teutonic Order first made use of provincial masters and commanders to govern its Baltic territories, and eventually also started using advocates.

It would develop the most complex system of territorial governance in the region and, as the wealthiest of the ruling powers, invest in the most impressive residences to project its corporate identity and authority.[21]

With the grand master's seat permanently established in Marienburg and the relocation of the Order's highest officers to nearby convents, Prussia became the most politically important region for the Order. Here, the office of procurator (German *Pfleger*) was introduced in the early fourteenth century, initially to support the grand master. These officials governed smaller districts and sent their income directly to Marienburg. This practice worked so well, that it was adopted by commanders in eastern Prussia and Pomerelia to help with the management of their territories. On the lowest rungs of the governance ladder were bailiffs (German *Kammer*), who took charge of the smallest districts made up of between fifteen and forty-five villages. Specialised offices were also created in Prussia to manage woodland and there was even an 'amber master' (German *Bernsteinmeister*), overseeing the harvesting of this luxury resource that was particularly abundant on the western coast of Sambia. This was an adaptive system of governance, designed to fit the dynamic and varied needs of administering the Order's expanding territories.

The emergence of this organisational structure was mirrored in the explosion of construction which began in the last three decades of the thirteenth century and continued intensively over the next half century. The most investment was focused on convents, some of which had been constructed during the crusading period and were now being rebuilt and expanded in both Livonia and Prussia. A number of these early castles had been irregular in shape, often reflecting the challenges and opportunities of local topography presented by hills, wetlands and the reuse of earlier earthworks. But in a short space of time, during the 1270s–80s, a new standardised design was adopted which would come to define the Order's convents, especially in Prussia. The castle at Brandenburg, described earlier, was a typical example. Built from brick and glacial boulders in Prussia, and largely from quarried dolomite and boulders in Livonia, often with brick elements, these convents consisted of four multi-storey ranges with towers enclosing a cloistered courtyard. The conventual building was encircled by a moat connected to one or more ditches, some of which were dry, others flooded with water channelled from lakes or rivers. Here, a free-standing tower could be built over the waterway and connected to the main building with an enclosed walkway. Referred to as a *Danzker* and largely confined to Prussian convents, this appears to have functioned as a fortified point which also contained latrines that emptied out into the channel below. One or more adjacent outer wards would be created as self-contained fortified islets accommodating various service buildings, stores and additional residences, connected to the main conventual building with drawbridges. Towns established next to these convents were both integrated into their outer circuit of walls, and at the same time separated by moats and inner walls. The castles towered over their adjacent towns and access to them was controlled, a clear expression of the relationship between overlord and subject.

Whilst built to impress and communicate authority through their architecture, these castles were also designed to meet the specific needs of their communities. Religious spaces were fundamentally important. The provision of a chapel was mandatory in the Order's statutes from as early as the mid-thirteenth century, but in contrast to monastic churches, these were in almost all cases tucked away on the first floor of the main wing of the conventual castle, and did not form the centrepiece of the complex.[22] The early castles were furnished with a single chapel, but more would be built in the larger convents and some were designated as churches. Their decoration (and that of other spaces) served to educate the brethren, and to remind new recruits of the main reason they were there. The most elaborate example of this can still be seen in the oldest part of the upper castle at Malbork, where the decorated doorway leading into the castle's chapel, later referred to as the 'golden gate', was built in the last quarter of the thirteenth century, within a few years of the start of building work on the castle. Its decoration represented the conflict between Good and Evil, a reminder to the brethren of both their heritage and their ongoing mission to combat paganism. They had subjugated the pagans of Prussia and Livonia, but their war against Lithuania had only just begun.[23]

These decorative schemes were educational devices, visual triggers for the memory, and their message of the ongoing spiritual struggle would be reinforced through literature. From the early fourteenth century, the Order commissioned translations of bibles and saints' lives, from which passages would be read aloud to the brethren at mealtimes. The *Livonian Rhymed Chronicle* (c. 1290) and Nicholas of Jersochin's translation of Peter of Dusburg's Latin *Chronicle of Prussia* (c. 1340) were also written in German, not just for the benefit of the brethren, but also for those German nobles who might be persuaded to support the Order in its ongoing crusading efforts. This was about promoting the Order's identity, which became closely connected with the figure of the Virgin Mary. In the fourteenth century, the Order's Prussian branch chose Mary as its principal patron, and her cult was widely disseminated throughout the organisation. The brethren presented themselves as Mary's vassals, and in turn their rule was believed to be legitimised and protected by the Queen of Heaven.[24] Representations of the crowned Virgin became incredibly popular within the Order, featuring on its seals, sculptures, wall paintings, religious manuscripts, coins and even cannons.

In keeping with the communal lifestyle of the Order's brethren, the convents also housed shared eating and sleeping areas – refectories and dormitories – along with kitchens, infirmaries, armouries, stores in their cellars and lofts, stables, granaries and other specialised spaces that varied from castle to castle. The conquests of the eastern Baltic coincided with the onset of the Little Ice Age, resulting in colder and rainier winters in Northern Europe. This prompted structural innovations within castles – pitched roofs to enable snow to slide off, and elaborate heating systems. These were essentially early storage heaters. They consisted of a small chamber filled with large stones which were heated underneath by a furnace, and the hot air would then travel through conduits to various rooms. The use of stones enabled the heat to be retained for longer, and these types of early storage heaters were adopted around the Baltic Sea region in the fourteenth century, disseminated by religious communities.[25] One of the rooms that was usually heated was the refectory, where meals were taken and meetings of the convent's chapter took place. Later German scholars, recognising these castles as a fusion between fortified and monastic designs, called them *Konventsburgen* – conventual castles. In fact, they did not resemble monasteries in terms of their layout, but their interconnected internal spaces were ideal for the needs of a militarised religious community.

It is not clear where the idea for these castles originated – there is over a century of scholarship on this topic and there have been suggestions of influences from southern Italy, Saxony, the Levant or even the castles built by the Sword Brothers in Livonia (which are poorly known).[26] We also do not know which structure provided the first model for the conventual design, although it has been suggested this was developed in the Kulmerland and then adopted for castle building further north around the Vistula Lagoon.[27] Although the largest number and best-preserved examples are found in the historical territory of Prussia (with thirty-four convents, roughly a quarter of the castles built there), it is also possible the design was pioneered in Livonia (with a dozen convents, roughly a seventh of the castles built in the region). Unfortunately, little is known of the early forms of the Order's castles here; the residence of the Livonian master at Riga, which would also come to house the largest community of brethren in any of the Order's convents, was destroyed and rebuilt several times. On the other hand, the regular form of the conventual house of Fellin (Estonian Viljandi) is well-known and likely to date from the end of the thirteenth century/early fourteenth century, as suggested by its brick bonds. Its principal building, measuring 47 by 45 metres, was one of the largest conventual structures in Livonia, along with Riga and Goldingen (Latvian Kuldīga). What is clear is that a decision was made within the Order to adopt a standardised design for its command centres in the Baltic. Providing a sense of visual unity across the Order's lands, wherever you went the corporation's power was clearly visible.

Residences were also built for lesser officials, such as advocates and procurators. These were smaller, irregular complexes consisting of one or two wings with residential spaces, a chapel and storage areas, enclosed by walls and sometimes moats. Their household was small and their function was largely administrative. A typical example from Livonia is represented by the castle first documented as Arries in 1410 (subsequently Arrasch; Latvian Āraiši), located in the southern edge of the commandery of Wenden. This was built from stone on a hill at the end of a peninsula that extended from the road into the lake, at some point in the fourteenth century.[28] It served as the residence of an advocate, and would have functioned as an administrative centre for the indigenous villages within its designated territory. It was relatively modest, consisting of a single range connected to a wall enclosing the top of the hill on three sides. The rest of the peninsula functioned as a naturally defensible outer ward, where archaeological excavations uncovered the presence of an indigenous community living in traditionally constructed cross-log buildings, and continuing to use their own dress accessories and adornments. Although the Order's houses (along with those of bishops and cathedral chapters) were predominantly masculine spaces, their extended households consisted of men and women who were employed to help with maintenance. They were drawn from a combination of migrants and indigenous and, as a result, the new regime's centres of power became meeting points between the different cultures. But these remained unequal spaces, where the balance of power was clearly defined.

Some advocates and procurators held strategically important positions, and this was reflected in the investment in their castles. One of the grandest is represented by the procurator's castle at Neidenburg (Polish Nidzica), built on the south-eastern border of the commandery of Osterode (and of the Order's Prussian lands) between 1395 and 1410. This was uniquely fitted with two large towers featuring Romanesque architectural elements, flanking a gatehouse in its heavily fortified eastern end. With a length of 64.4 metres and the width of its principal three-storeyed western wing at just over 34 metres, it was a substantial brick structure which towered over the town below. This set-up embodied the relationship between the Order and its subjects but, with its proximity to the Masovian border, also provided, as one scholar put it, a 'visual calling card' for the Order, aimed directly at its neighbours.[29]

THE LARGEST CASTLE IN CHRISTENDOM

Marienburg is by far the best-known of the Order's Baltic command centres. This is largely due to the meticulous bureaucracy of the grand master's chancellery, which produced vast quantities of documents. Paper began to supplement parchment from the mid-fourteenth century, with German increasingly replacing Latin for official correspondence. By the turn of the fifteenth century, the chancellery was using some 5,000 sheets of paper and 100 skins of parchment each year. A fraction has survived – largely from these last few decades of the Order's rule in western Prussia – but enough to provide detailed glimpses into almost every aspect of the castle's community, its layout and organisation. The castle had also become the centre of an expansive network connecting the Order's territories with Hanseatic trading routes, with a stream of regional and international imports and exports which were dutifully recorded. Progressive restoration works from the nineteenth century, and particularly after the Second World War, have also resulted in an unparalleled series of architectural and archaeological studies for any such site.[30]

The construction of the castle began at the end of the 1270s, when the convent in nearby Santir was relocated there.[31] The new location was more strategic, situated on higher ground, overlooking the floodplain of the Vistula Delta, and a more visible symbol of the Order's power on the frontier with Pomerelia. The northern range of the castle was built first, containing the chapel with its 'golden gate', as well as a vaulted refectory where meetings of the chapter were held.[32] Close examination of the early parts of the building has revealed that the builders were somewhat inexperienced, and had to correct their work as they went along. With the construction of the chapel, a different, evidently more skilful, team was hired. This has led to suggestions that Marienburg may have been the first experiment with the conventual form, at least in northern Prussia.[33] Somewhere in the vicinity would have been service buildings – a stable, armoury, stores and an infirmary. A settlement established directly south of the castle was organised as a planned town with privileges from 1286, and over the course of the fourteenth century became integrated into the convent's circuit of curtain walls and moats.

The relocation of the grand master's seat to Marienburg was followed by the rebuilding and expansion of the convent, transforming it over many decades into the largest fortified structure in Christendom. In the first half of the fourteenth century, the castle was rebuilt with the addition of a southern and eastern wing, along with four corner towers and cloistered arcades to give Marienburg its classic conventual form. The bell tower in the corner where the northern and eastern ranges met was also reconstructed, now serving the additional role of a watchtower. In the south-western corner, an imposing *Danzker* tower was connected to the castle by a 64-metre-long arcaded walkway.

The centrepiece of the rebuilding was the chapel, which was significantly expanded between 1331 and 1344 as part of the remodelling of the northern wing. The chapel was extended eastwards and redecorated in the familiar gothic style defined by foliage sprawled across its arcades, vaulting and columns. Wall paintings and sculptures of the Virgin, Christ and a range of saints important to the Order would have filled this sacred space, whilst the joints between vaulting ribs were covered by decorated roof bosses. Outside, the giant figure of the Virgin and Child, constructed from artificial gypsum stone and painted in polychrome, stood against the east end of the chapel, looking out over the conquered lands of pagan Prussia and towards Lithuania. In 1380, the entire figure would be decorated with glass mosaic tiles, most probably by artisans brought over from Venice. Underneath the convent's main chapel, another was constructed, this time dedicated to St Anne, where in 1341 Grand Master Dietrich of Altenburg – the instigator of the building works – was laid to rest inside a 6-metre-deep brick-lined crypt shaft. Eleven grand masters would be buried here, although only three of their decorated tomb slabs have survived.[34] The portals to St Anne's chapel were more elaborately decorated than the 'golden gate', with a figural scene of the discovery of the True Cross by St Helen in Jerusalem highlighting the Order's enduring connection with the holiest of Christian cities, whilst representations of heaven and hell were popular on many church tympanums as a fundamental expression of the Church's teachings. Both chapels would be further modified and redecorated in the centuries following the end of the Order's rule in Marienburg, with their final forms vividly captured in a series of photographs from the late nineteenth and early twentieth centuries, before both were almost completely destroyed in 1945.

By the end of the fourteenth century, there were seven chapels documented within Marienburg's grounds, by far the most of any of the Order's castles. With the exception of the grand master's private chapel, all were eventually designated as churches. The unusually high number attests to the size of the community in the castle complex, which would have included a substantial household alongside the brethren – by the early fifteenth century, the complex housed forty-five brothers and priests, along with several hundred servants.[35] The refectory was rebuilt up against the western wall of the chapel. It was a highly decorated space as suggested by the surviving corbels, which included a bear's head and a lion with its cubs – both symbols of resurrection. By the early fifteenth century, it was lavishly decorated with images of grand masters.[36]

The new headquarters required space for a chancellery, a residence for the grand master, more space for the growing number of brethren and, with the regular involvement of foreign knights in the Order's campaigns, quarters for visitors. To meet these needs, the lower swampy land north of the upper castle, which had served as an outer ward, was completely transformed. The entire area was levelled and, where the soil was waterlogged, stabilised with timber piles. A western range was constructed which housed the grand master's residence, later rebuilt as a four-storey tower house with decorative turrets. Expensive materials like granite and Gotlandic limestone were used for details such as portals and columns. Inside, the 'palace' (as it later became known) had rooms for the grand master, including a bedroom, chapel, chancellery, a treasury and two halls with painted vaults which were used as an audience chamber (the so-called 'summer refectory') and a private dining room (the 'winter refectory').[37] Although grand masters were elected officials, they increasingly behaved like monarchical rulers, even engaging in hunting at the nearby Castle of Stuhm (Polish Sztum), which had an enclosed park filled with game. The lifestyle of the brethren at Marienburg became quite luxurious, with high-quality food which included imported exotics and the castle's fishponds providing fresh carp. This comfort extended to other convents as well, reflecting the importance of luxury in the performance of medieval authority.

Adjoining the palace was the 'Great Refectory' – the largest enclosed space in the castle, roofed with star vaulting supported on three decorated columns. Its walls were adorned with dramatic paintings promoting the Order's ideology. These included the coronation of the Virgin as Queen of Heaven and a four-tiered frieze of mounted knights bearing heraldic banners alongside infantry, most likely representing crusading campaigns. The whole space was heated from vents in the floors and walls connected to hypocaust below.[38] It served as a feasting hall for the Order and its guests, as well as for holding numerous important meetings, including those of the general chapter which all the Order's commanders and higher officials were expected to attend.[39]

The eastern range of the outer ward was furnished with decorated rooms intended for the use of the Order's guests, additional rooms for officers such as the convent's quartermaster, whilst the north range included an infirmary with its own separate refectory and chapel, as well as bath houses.[40] Building work also extended to the plateau directly north of the outer ward, which had initially been used for storing building materials used in the construction of the rest of the complex.[41] Here, several buildings were added on the eastern side, which included an armoury, and then a western range was constructed along the riverbank which housed stores, a vast stable and a chapel dedicated to St Catherine. Excavations in-between the two ranges uncovered the remains of free-standing buildings which included a casting workshop for making canons and bells, a crossbow-maker's workshop and the residence of the castle's treasurer. Additional lodgings for the Order's guests were also located here.[42] By the mid-fourteenth century, this vast space was enclosed by a wall and moat, punctuated by towers and elaborate gatehouses, becoming a second outer ward. At some point in the 1420s, the upper castle and first outer ward became collectively referred to as the *Haus* – the castle – with the northernmost ward becoming the sole *Vorburg* or outer ward.[43] In the sixteenth century, in order to differentiate it from the upper castle, the first outer ward began to be referred to as the 'Middle Castle'.

The inner complex of Marienburg was surrounded by an impressive defensive circuit of walls and moats. Elements of these were routinely modified and rebuilt, with the eastern, southern and northern sides of the complex becoming the most heavily fortified, containing double walls with multiple towers, gatehouses and lines of wet and dry moats. The main entrance to the complex was found on the western side, where two gates, perhaps intended for different types of traffic in and out of the castle, opened onto a wooden bridge that crossed the river. On the other side, the bridge connected to an octagonal-walled barbican with two large towers and gates, constructed in the early fifteenth century. At this time, the gates were reinforced by two substantial semicircular towers and platforms for guns, as the whole complex was upgraded with the latest innovations to both counter and harness artillery. The castle proved to be impregnable, withstanding sieges in 1410 and 1454. The Order would only lose control of it in the spring of 1457 when its mercenary garrison was paid by Danzig's city council to hand over the keys, which were then passed to the Polish king. There was no more profound symbol of the steady decline of the Order's power than the loss of this castle. It signalled the end of an era.

CASTLES OF THE EPISCOPATES

The earliest stone fortifications in the eastern Baltic had been constructed under the direction of the bishops of Livonia, and subsequently by their vassals. In Finland, aside from the early fortified episcopal residence in Koroinen, the only castle built by the bishops of Åbo was located on a cape at the east end of the island of Kuusisto, some 15 kilometres south-east of the episcopal see. First mentioned in 1295 as Kustö, the early structure was made from timber and was destroyed by the Novgorodians in 1318. Construction of the stone castle began soon after, and consisted of two single-storey wings and a tower, with an attached outer ward. In the fifteenth century, the complex was significantly expanded and included a palatial residence, a timber palisade on the shoreline and two additional outer wards – its design largely determined by the constraints of its surroundings.[44]

The bishops and cathedral chapters in Prussia and Livonia would become more prolific castle builders. Since the Order's convents came to define *the* architectural vocabulary of power in the eastern Baltic, its religious co-rulers sought to emulate this brand. Often their castles were not built to the same standards – the episcopates had fewer resources at their disposal and so could not afford to employ the most qualified builders or purchase the best materials. Time was also expensive, which may explain why their castles were more hastily built, with the enclosing walls and wings raised simultaneously or within quick succession.[45] Moreover, not all features from the Order's convents were included: for example, a *Bergfried* was only found in a third of episcopal castles in Prussia, and largely those built in the second half of the fourteenth century.[46] Nonetheless, several episcopal castles were on a par with the Order's convents in projecting an image of overlordship.

The most numerous could be found in the lands of the Warmian episcopate in Prussia, where nine fortified residences were built by its bishops and four by its chapter, with a further castle built for the collegiate chapter at Guttstadt (Polish Dobre Miasto). The best-preserved episcopal residence which adopted the Order's conventual design was Heilsberg (Polish Lidzbark Warmiński). Its four-winged structure with corner towers was built from brick between 1350 and 1373, and its cloisters were added at the end of the fourteenth century, where wall paintings depicting St Catherine and the life of Christ were uncovered during recent restoration work. Gotlandic limestone was imported to decorate parts of the castle, an established marker of elite status.[47] In contrast, the fortified complex of the Warmian chapter in Frauenburg (Polish Frombork) was built and expanded in relation to the cathedral. In the late fourteenth century, a 10-metre-high statue of the Virgin was placed in the gable above the cathedral's western door, clearly emulating the sculpture in Marienburg. This not only served a religious and protective function, but also signalled the chapter's sovereignty on its lands, reinforced by the architectural language of the fortified complex.[48]

Frauenburg was one of four Prussian cathedrals, along with Kulmsee (Polish Chełmża), Königsberg (Russian Kaliningrad) and Marienwerder (Polish Kwidzyn), which were integrated into a fortified complex attached to the residence of their chapters. The castle of the Pomesanian chapter at Marienwerder was particularly striking for its design, and for the adjoining cathedral which served as the burial place for two or three of the Order's grand masters. The brick castle was built between 1320 and 1350 following the conventual design, with four ranges standing up to five and six storeys and two projecting towers which were added in the late fourteenth century – a *Danzker* tower located some 54 metres to the west and linked to the castle by an arcaded porch, and a well tower that projected 18 metres to the north. The cathedral began to be built just as the castle was being completed and the two were fully connected in the fifteenth century. The adjacent town, located directly to the south, would have been dwarfed by the entire red-brick complex, which would have been visible for miles around. The bishop resided in a separate castle, south of the town. In the early fourteenth century, the preferred episcopal residence became the castle at Reisenburg (Polish

Prabuty). This too was inspired by the conventual design, consisting of a three- or four-wing quadrangular building with a *Dansker* projecting from its north side.

The fortified residences of the Livonian bishops were equally imposing, but here there is little evidence for the emulation of the Order's castles. This may be because the conventual form was less common in Livonia and that castle forms were more influenced by local topography. The Castle of Treiden (Latvian Turaida), which belonged to the archbishops of Riga, faced off against the Order's convent at Segewold (Latvian Sigulda) across the Gauja Valley, which marked the boundary between the lands of the two powers. Unusually for Livonia, where stone was the preferred medium, it was largely built from red brick, although its present appearance is the result of a modern rebuild. The best-preserved, at least in terms of its external appearance, is Arensburg (Estonian Kuressaare), which was built from the mid-fourteenth century and later became the principal residence of the prince-bishop of Ösel-Wiek, whilst the chapter remained at Hapsal (Estonian Haapsalu). In contrast to the episcopal castle in Hapsal, Arensburg was designed with a conventual form – four ranges enclosing a cloistered courtyard, with two large towers. Its interiors contained a range of residential spaces for the bishop's extended household, warmed by an elaborate hypocaust system. Within a few years, a small settlement of artisans and merchants had developed next to the castle, first mentioned in written sources in 1427. This was typical of towns in medieval Livonia, all of which had been established alongside castles.

RULE MAKERS AND BREAKERS

The creation of new territories governed largely by religious authorities in the wake of the Baltic Crusades was not a unique phenomenon within European history, but the integration of ecclesiastical authority with military power became especially prominent in the Baltic region, and here the Teutonic Order's lands were the most expansive of any military order in Christendom. The new regime's rule had initially been secured by force, but subsequently this was reinforced by the visual trappings of authority, which were strikingly manifested in the construction of castles. Again, this was standard practice in Catholic Christendom, but the Order in particular developed a refined corporate brand that was expressed through its convents, its coinage and its insignia that became immediately recognisable from one corner of Prussia to the opposite corner of Livonia. Secular rulers and bishops elsewhere in Europe owned multiple residences, but this corporate approach to governance – at this scale – was unprecedented.

The new regimes introduced laws from the West, largely based on those from Saxony, which were even adopted in Danish Estonia. Swedish royal laws were applied to Finland. These were accompanied by Christian ordinances, which included canon law, with the establishment of separate civil and religious courts. Together, they reshaped the lives of indigenous peoples and structured them in familiar terms for incoming migrants. But at times, even the ruling authorities broke their own laws, especially in Livonia where the political history of the fourteenth and fifteenth centuries was marked by episodes of conflict between the Teutonic Order and its episcopal neighbours, particularly the archbishops of Riga, who were often allied with the town against the brethren. The most serious incidents led to full-scale warfare, but there were a number of smaller, relatively less serious conflicts. As such, the Order maintained a representative at the papal court to fight its back, more often than not against the complaints of the Livonian episcopates.

In Prussia, the religious powers happily coexisted, albeit with occasional boundary disputes, and there was a sense of a cohesive 'state', even though scholars nowadays prefer not to use this term. Here, the Order cultivated a new crusading culture, as it sought to push the eastern frontier of its lands, and of Catholic Christendom, into pagan Samogitia and Lithuania. Throughout the fourteenth century, this became the focus of a new holy war, one which drew in participants from across Europe.

CHAPTER 8

APOCALYPSE THEN?
The 'Eternal Crusade' against Lithuania

> ... many Germans and Englishmen came to Prussia ... to serve the Blessed Virgin and to obtain forgiveness for their sins ...
> Wigand of Marburg, *New Prussian Chronicle*[1]

DISCOVERING A CRUSADER'S BODY

In 1981, archaeologists made a startling discovery whilst excavating underneath the southern chancel of the church of the St Bees Priory in Cumbria, north-west England. Within an ashlar-lined vault they found the remains of two coffins that had been placed alongside each other and covered over with soil, one of which contained the skeleton of a woman, the other an anthropomorphic lead container nestled within a clay packing. The container was lifted and the lead cut open to reveal two exceptionally preserved linen shrouds. The shrouds had survived not only because they had been encased in lead, but also because they had been infused with pine-pitch, the scent of which could still be detected. Wrapped within the shrouds was one of the most exceptionally preserved bodies ever discovered by archaeologists, and it was quickly transferred to the local hospital morgue where an autopsy was performed by Edmund Tapp of the Preston Royal Infirmary. The body was that of an adult man, and his greying hair, trimmed beard and even irises were clearly visible. His hands retained fingerprints and, more astonishingly, his internal organs were also intact. Close examination indicated he had died from a deep abdominal wound, which had fractured a rib and caused a haemothorax, filling his right lung with blood. His lower jaw and hyoid bone were also fractured, most probably the result of a forceful blow to the head. His age was estimated at around 35–45 years. As evidence of a final parting gesture, a 'wreath' of dark hair had been placed on the body's chest before it was wrapped in the shrouds.[2]

What followed was an intensive search for the identity of the two bodies. Archaeologists and historians grappling with the puzzle eventually agreed the man was one Anthony de Lucy (the younger). Hailing from one of the most powerful families in Cumberland and charged with the security of the Anglo-Scottish borderland, Anthony had inherited his father's title of Warden of the West March, as well as the lordships of Cockermouth and Egremont. Shortly after his father's death in the winter of 1365, Anthony had married Joan FitzHugh, the widow of William Lord Greystoke. The marriage had gone ahead without royal consent, but the couple were quickly pardoned. Anthony provoked further anger by sanctioning raids across the border which stoked tensions at a time of relative calm, prompting Edward III to appoint new wardens to curb the impetuous marcher lord. One of these was Thomas Beauchamp, the Earl of Warwick, whose son-in-law Roger Lord Clifford was already installed as a warden in the West March. In 1365, Warwick had travelled to Prussia to participate in the Teutonic Order's ongoing crusade against Lithuania.

Inspired by the papal call of Eugenius III for crusaders to follow in the footsteps of their ancestors, crusading had become a family tradition for the European nobility, and the northern English aristocracy had been active participants; Joan's previous husband had joined Henry of Grosmont, the Duke of Lancaster, on his expedition to the pagan frontier in 1351, and Warwick's three sons would make the same journey, or 'pilgrimage' as it was framed, in 1367. This time, however, the earl appears to have persuaded Anthony de Lucy to join them, no doubt seeing this as a means of bringing stability to the western Anglo-Scottish border by distracting the hot-headed lord with a more noble endeavour. They were amongst at least twenty-four other knights who petitioned the king in 1367 and 1368 for a licence to depart the realm to fight heathens: a record season for English crusaders travelling to the Baltic.[3] With the cessation of hostilities between the English and French following the signing of the Treaty of Brétigny, the 1360s had seen English knights travelling to Prussia every year.

Anthony's licence, obtained on 20 November, was for one of the larger retinues – fifteen horsemen alongside himself – and expenditures amounting to £500 for that season (in today's money some £250,000), although this pales in comparison with the size and cost of the more famous campaigns of Henry Bolingbroke (the future English king, Henry IV) a few decades later. Anthony was accompanied by Sir John Moulton of Frampton and Sir Richard Welby, Lincolnshire knights with close family ties to the Lucys. Both John and Anthony had to borrow money from Alice Perrers, Edward III's mistress, to finance their expedition; Anthony was already in debt to her to the tune of £1,000, a sum procured to bolster his marcher lordship shortly after he acquired the title. The next and final record of Anthony is a statement of his death 'in parts beyond seas' on either 19 August or 16 September 1368, along with John Moulton. Although there is no record of Anthony's activities, he was probably one of the three Englishmen mentioned by the priest Herman of Wartberge in his *Chronicle of Livonia* as being killed during the siege of the Lithuanian stronghold of New Kaunas in September of that year.

The storming of New Kaunas was the culmination of an intensive series of campaigns or *Reysen* ('journeys'),[4] organised by the Teutonic Order, which English knights regularly participated in. These campaigns had typically followed the course of the Nemunas, which the Germans called Memel – the principal waterway connecting the political and trading centres of the Grand Duchy of Lithuania with the Baltic Sea. Some 200 kilometres up the river was Kaunas, strategically located at the confluence with the second largest river in Lithuania, the Neris, which snaked across the south-eastern territories of the duchy and flowed through the capital Kernavė. The cultural landscape around Kaunas testifies to its strategic location, studded with the earthen remains of former strongholds. Archaeological excavations have uncovered traces of daily life dating back to the medieval period in a few of these, but also crossbow bolts – remnants of the Order's relentless assaults in the latter decades of the fourteenth century. The main fortification at Kaunas had been destroyed by the Order's army during a three-week siege in April 1362, an event that would be commemorated for decades to come as a victory of Good over Evil.

The following year, the Lithuanians had hastily constructed the stronghold of New Kaunas on the nearby island of Vyrgalė, some 7 kilometres to the south. This too was destroyed. In the summer of 1368, the Order's army had built their own fortress from timber and earth on the southern bank of the Nemunas, within striking distance of Kaunas. This served as a base for attacks on the surrounding region, and it is where Anthony, his comrades and their retinue would have been quartered alongside their hosts – the brothers and sergeants of the Teutonic Order. The army eventually reached New Kaunas, noting it had been rebuilt again, and immediately began preparing for a siege. During the storming of the outer walls Anthony and his comrades most probably met their fate. Based on the wounds on the 'St Bees Man', as he became known, the historian Alexander Grant has speculated that, whilst scaling the walls of the Lithuanian stronghold on a ladder, Anthony was hit in the chest by a projectile fired by one of the defenders, and the force of the blow then knocked him to the ground, resulting in the additional injuries.

After Anthony's corpse was recovered it must have been kept cool as none of the typical post-mortem signs of bloating or decomposition were visible. Just before the body was tightly wrapped in the shrouds soaked in pine-pitch in preparation for transportation back down the Nemunas, someone close to Anthony placed the 'wreath' of hair on his chest – in all likelihood a keepsake that he had taken with him to Prussia. The body would have been transported back to either the town of Memel (Lithuanian Klaipėda) or Königsberg (Russian Kaliningrad), and a decision was made to seal it in a lead container for shipment back to England, perhaps by Lord Fitzwalter, Anthony's kinsman and a patron of St Bees Priory, who was also present in Prussia at the time. Lead containers were expensive and restricted to high-status burials in late medieval Europe, but here it also served as a suitable means of transporting the body. The sealed container locked in moisture from the body and, starved of oxygen, enabled adipocere (a waxy substance created by decomposition) to form which contributed to preventing any further decay. But such treatment of those who died on crusade was highly unusual. In 1300, Pope Boniface VIII had forbidden the practice of *Mos Teutonicus* – so called because of its popularity with German nobles in the Levant – which had involved boiling down the bodies of fallen crusaders in vinegar or wine to enable their remains to be easily transportable as bones. As a result, in the fourteenth century crusaders were typically buried in the lands where they had died. Those shipped back were exceptional cases.

But what of the woman who would later be interred alongside Anthony at St Bees? Anthony's wife Joan had remarried after his death (to her third husband) and was much older when she died than the estimated age of the female skeleton in the St Bees crypt. Historians and archaeologists concluded this was more likely to be the body of his sister, Maud de Lucy, who came to inherit the family estates and died in 1398, the last of her line. Joan and Anthony's daughter, the natural heiress, had tragically died on 30 September 1369, aged less than three years, which meant that Joan was reduced to the status of Anthony's widow, whilst his sister Maud became Lady Lucy. She was probably responsible for Anthony's internment and later made a conscious choice to be buried with her brother, whether through emotional attachment or the desire to emphasise her lineage. Isotopic analysis of both the hair wreath placed with the male corpse and the female skeleton suggested the former came from a different individual, reinforcing the interpretation of the identity of the woman as Anthony's sister.

The burials were almost certainly marked by effigies, of which one – only known from drawings made in the nineteenth century – represents a knight in armour stylistically datable to around 1360–80 and holding a chalice, an unusual object usually reserved for the funerary monuments of priests, and sometimes included within their burials. It may be that the chalice represented the holy grail, a metaphor for salvation attained through crusading. The fate of Anthony, Joan, Maud and the extinction of the Lucy line was a turning point in the history of the West March, which came under the control of the Percies and, in the following century, the Nevilles. At the same time, their biographies encapsulate the history of the frontier war. This was a tragic story of violence and loss on both sides, but also the extraordinary story of how the Teutonic Order reinvented itself as the defender of Christendom in eastern Europe, of the

APOCALYPSE THEN?

tenacious resistance of the Samogitians and Lithuanians against the military might of Latin Christendom, and the unlikely pacts made between Christians and pagans amidst brutal warfare that endured for generations.

ARMED PILGRIMS

The loss of the Holy Land in 1291 brought into question the Order's purpose, but the brethren were able to forge a new culture of crusading in north-eastern Europe, one that would define the experience of armed pilgrimage for generations. Earlier, in the late 1250s, Pope Alexander IV had issued a series of bulls allowing the Order's clerics the right to recruit crusaders, to grant crusading indulgences to all who had fulfilled their vow and even to absolve them from excommunication. These privileges, and particularly the granting of indulgences, continued to be used by the Order into the fifteenth century. Surviving examples of 'the indulgence of the *Reyse*' indicate this was a formulaic prescription. Describing how crusading in the north followed on directly from the Holy Land, the document stated – backed up by the authority of several papal grants – that the indulgence extended to those who came to Prussia and Livonia at their own expense and with true repentance, to fight against pagans, as well as those Christians supporting them.[5] The Order's officials would issue a certificate as proof of the indulgence, although only one example of this has survived. This extraordinary privilege enabled the Order to regularise crusading in the Baltic.

This crusading indulgence would have provided the likely incentive for a group of German crusaders to undertake a journey to Prussia in 1304. The Order's war with Lithuania had begun in 1283 with the destruction of the stronghold of Bisenė, but these were the first foreign knights to join the brethren in their fight against Baltic pagans for some thirty years. That winter, they accompanied the Order's armies across the frontier, targeting the strongholds of Grodno (today in Belarus) and Pograuda (Lithuanian Pagraudė). They were followed by other German knights, and eventually by English knights in the winter of 1328–9 after a cessation of hostilities with Scotland and France. Then came knights from the Netherlands, northern France and northern Italy, Scotland, southern France and southern Italy. For the English and French, these *Reysen* became a permanent fixture from the 1340s. Within a couple of decades, knights from across Christendom were travelling to Prussia, even from as far away as Iberia, although surprisingly few hailed from nearby Scandinavian regions. Despite political hostilities, Polish knights also participated until the union with Lithuania made this untenable.

The majority of named participants were drawn from the upper and lower ranks of the knightly class, as well as from urban patrician families; only occasionally did rulers make the journey to the frontier. Many participants hailed from the Order's traditional bases of support within the empire, particularly 'ministeriales' – young knights who were legally unfree and bound to their liege lords, but who also commanded their own armed vassals. Yet the popularity of the *Reysen* with the English, a realm whose principal connection with the Order was commercial, points to a broader appeal. English participants came to the Prussian frontier when the opportunity presented itself, especially during interludes of peace in the Hundred Years War, but some even undertook the journey in the midst of the Black Death. The English crown had supported the Order with an annual pension, although this was paid erratically and the last time this happened was in 1401, under Henry IV. A few years before, Grand Master Conrad of Jungingen had written to Richard II seeking to dissuade the further participation of English knights, perhaps as a result of the troublesome behaviour of the English contingent led by Henry Bolingbroke.

As we have seen with Anthony de Lucy, kinsmen regularly travelled together, as did extended noble households. The largest retinues numbered in the hundreds and, when combined with the Order's forces, these armies could be quite formidable. In the winter of 1354/5, at least a thousand combatants from the empire alone took part. There were some 300 separate campaigns against Samogitia and Lithuania organised by the Order between 1305 and 1403, and the names of around 250 French and 200 English participants are known, along with varying numbers of soldiers who joined them.[6] Participating in the Order's *Reysen* became a family tradition for some, and sometimes multiple generations made the journey. The involvement of Lords Despenser, Fitzwalter, Beaumont and Sir Simon Felbrigg in the Duke of Gloucester's expedition

1. Malbork Castle, Pomerania, north Poland, is the largest castle in Europe. Formerly known as Marienburg, it was built by the Teutonic Order in the final years of the crusades against the Prussians, and served as the organisation's headquarters from 1309 until 1457.

2. The 8-metre-tall sculpture of the Virgin and Child in the eastern end of St Mary's Church, Malbork Castle, Poland, formerly Marienburg, Prussia. Originally constructed in *c.* 1340, the Virgin was the most important patron saint of the Teutonic Order. The sculpture was destroyed in 1945 and reconstructed in 2014–16.

3. The town of Obermarsberg (formerly Eresburg) is located on an oval plateau on top of a hill overlooking the Diemel river in North Rhine-Westphalia, Germany. The hill has been identified as the site of the Saxon stronghold of Eresburg mentioned in Carolingian written sources, where the Irminsul (sacred pillar) was destroyed by Charlemagne's forces in 772. Archaeological investigations of the hilltop have been limited, although some early medieval traces have been found.

4. A depiction of the martyrdom of St Adalbert at the hands of the Prussians on the twelfth-century bronze doors of Gniezno Cathedral, Greater Poland. Adalbert's relics were housed inside. The archbishops of Gniezno would become important promoters of the crusading movement in Poland.

5. Reconstructions of early medieval Western Slavic buildings at the Archäologisches Freilichtmuseum Groß Raden, Mecklenburg-Western Pomerania, Germany. They were primarily built using horizontal log construction, a technique often referred to as 'cross-log' or 'blockhouse'. Other architectural styles included post and beam structures and wattle and daub houses.

6. An excavated late twelfth-century timber building in Gründungsviertel, Lübeck, with a sunken cellar, sill beams and posts, wall planks, floor plates and the remains of an internal well. These typified the buildings of merchants, and their architectural style was part of the reshaping of Slavic traditions. In time they would be superseded by brick.

7. A carved stone discovered in 2024 under a house in Klotzow in the eastern part of Mecklenburg-Western Pomerania, Germany. It has been dated to the twelfth century and shows what may be the missionary bishop Otto of Bamberg.

8. Horses buried (most probably alive) in the north Sambian cemetery of Kholmy, Kaliningrad Oblast, Russia, formerly Mülsen in Prussia. Dating to the twelfth century, they reflect a popular funerary rite associated with the Prussian elites before the crusades.

9. The site of the Rani's religious centre at Cape Arkona on the north-eastern tip of Rügen, destroyed by Danish crusaders in 1168. The site has been eroding into the sea for centuries, but its earthen rampart is still visible.

10. Laurits Tuxen's painting *The Taking of Arkona by Valdemar the Great and Bishop Absalon in 1169*, completed in 1894. It is based on the event described by Saxo Grammaticus which most likely took place in 1168.

11. A reconstruction of the church excavated on the hill called Ristimäki at Ravattula, south-west Finland. This is the earliest known site of its kind in Finland and the associated cemetery appears to have been in use from the mid-twelfth century through to the early thirteenth century.

12. Excavations at 33 Kalēju iela in Riga, Latvia, where an area of indigenous Liv settlement was discovered with the earliest building dating to *c.* 1209. Riga was founded in 1201 with the help of the Livs and within a decade had incorporated indigenous settlements into its expanded walls.

13. A monument inside the stronghold on the island of Muhu, Estonia, commemorating its destruction by crusaders in 1227. The stronghold's earthen walls are visible in the background.

14. Excavated greyware pots in the Museum of Archaeology and History in Elbląg (left) and the Castle Museum in Kwidzyn (right), Poland, reflecting the introduction of new kiln technology by German potters into Prussia in the thirteenth century.

15. A digital model of the Teutonic Order's castle of Brandenburg in Prussia at its full extent, and the ruined shell of the buildings in its outer ward, today in the Kaliningrad Oblast, Russia.

16. The 'golden gate' at Malbork Castle, formerly Marienburg. This is the earliest and best-preserved decorated portal from the Teutonic Order's castles and its iconography has been interpreted as symbolising the Order's mission – the ongoing struggle against paganism.

17. The castle and cathedral at Kwidzyn in Pomerania, Poland, formerly Marienwerder in Prussia. The brick castle, with its striking *Dansker* tower, was built over the course of the fourteenth century by the Pomesanian chapter, one of the territorial rulers of Prussia following the crusades.

18. Kuressaare Castle on the island of Saaremaa, Estonia, formerly Arensburg. The quadrangular castle was largely constructed in the fourteenth century from locally sourced limestone, serving as the residence of the bishops of Ösel-Wiek. It is the best-preserved castle in the Baltic states.

19. A reconstruction of one of the Teutonic Order's campaigns or *Reysen* in the frozen wetlands and forests of today's north-eastern Poland. In the fourteenth century, this would have been part of the 'Great Wilderness' separating the Order's lands from the Grand Duchy of Lithuania. The re-enactors are from Xiążęca Drużyna.

20. Lifting the wreck of the Lootsi cog in Tallinn, Estonia. The wreck, discovered near the Old Town's harbour in 2022, is one of the largest of its kind in Europe. Built in the mid-fourteenth century, it typifies the vessels that moved commodities and crusaders across the Baltic Sea, and which were crucial for the emergence of the Hanse.

21. (left and this page) The sacred oak near the village of Laumėnai in Samogitia, Lithuania. It is one of the oldest in the country and bears the marks of lightning strikes. As such it was associated with the thunder god Perkūnas, whilst a small Catholic chapel was nailed to the affected area of the trunk (and replaced several times).

22. Cēsis Castle, Vidzeme, Latvia. Formerly known as Wenden, it was built by the Sword Brothers and then expanded by the Teutonic Order. It would eventually become the preferred residence of the Order's Livonian master. The ruins of the western range destroyed during the course of the Russian siege in 1577 are visible.

23. *The Battle of Grunwald*, painted by Jan Matejko in 1878 and housed in the National Museum in Warsaw, is the most iconic depiction of the battle in 1410 (also known as Tannenberg and Žalgiris) between Poland-Lithuania and the Teutonic Order. The painting served as a symbolic act of defiance against Prussian rule and policies of Germanisation.

24. The *Alka* monument next to the earthen remains of the Curonian stronghold at Įpiltis, Klaipėda County, Lithuania. Created by Ieva Vasauskienė and Gytis Tiškus in 2007, it consists of a stone altar and posts with the symbols of Žemyna (Earth), Perkūnas (Thunder), and Saulė (Sun). The stronghold was destroyed by crusaders in 1263.

25. The Alexander Nevsky monument in Samolva, Russia, located close to the Estonian border. It was completed in 2021 and timed to coincide with the 800th anniversary of Nevsky's birth, but it was also designed to send a message to the West.

in 1391 mirrored the *Reyse* their fathers had participated in together, twenty-four years earlier.⁷ Some became regulars on the crusading circuit. The most famous was Rutger Raitz, who hailed from a patrician family in Cologne and spent thirty-two winters in Prussia and three summers in Livonia.

Most who came to fight in Lithuania returned home after completing their service, but some stayed longer or went on to join other campaigns. Dietrich of Eine, a knight from the Lower Rhine, fought against the Lithuanians on 2 February 1348, then joined the Norwegian-Swedish siege of the Rus' town of Orekhov in the summer,⁸ part of a crusade against Novgorod, then travelled back to Prussia through Livonia and returned to the frontline in Lithuania. The French knight Gadifer de La Salle, who went to Prussia in 1378, also aided the Hospitallers on Rhodes, participated in the so-called Barbary Crusade in 1390, and later would be involved in the conquests of the Canary Islands. For a few, Prussia and Livonia were just stopping points on much longer journeys, which often featured a visit to the Holy Sepulchre in Jerusalem and could last four or five years. Only the wealthiest could afford such lengthy itineraries, which combined pilgrimage with an early version of the 'Grand Tour'.

In all their various forms, the *Reysen* were serious investments and the expenses could be prodigious. Leaders of companies were responsible for paying their retinue members a daily wage, and additional costs included horses and saddles, clothing, raw fabric, tableware, weapons, armour, provisions (especially for sea voyages for both men and animals), banners and liveries. The wealthiest often brought dogs and falcons along with their handlers, turning their retinues into miniature mobile courts. To cover these expenses, upfront loans were frequently needed, as seen with Anthony de Lucy. Travelling with limited cash reserves was safer, so further loans were often sought once in Prussia. Whilst the Order as an ecclesiastical institution could not charge interest, participants still lost money due to unfavourable exchange rates, as the Order's coinage was required within its territories. Many knights returned with significant debt, though few were financially ruined by the experience. Repayments, secured by pledges of honour and other guarantees, were usually made through new loans. These transactions primarily took place in Bruges, Western Christendom's leading commercial hub, which hosted a sizeable community of Prussian merchants alongside the Order's agents. So, the *Reysen* were not just about the experience of crusading in the pagan wilderness: they were also about money, and they were only made possible with an accessible and transnational bureaucracy, defined by a regular cast of guarantors, creditors and debtors.

The knights travelling to join the Teutonic Order's campaigns were expecting to be treated well and to replicate their courtly life as best as they could – they were, after all, paying for it – but they also knew they were joining a crusading cause. Throughout the fourteenth century, the Order's Prussian brethren were regularly referred to as *cruciferi* (crusaders) by their Catholic neighbours, whilst those participating in the *Reysen* were called *perigrini* (pilgrims) as well as the Order's 'guests'.[9] The resumé of Chaucer's knight included fighting Muslims in Spain and North Africa and the Turks in the Levant, alongside the Lithuanians, demonstrating the Baltic frontier was, in the minds of contemporaries, one of the key points in the overall defence of Christendom. Even after the official Christianisation of Lithuania in 1387, the Order's promotion of holy war remained compelling for European knights.

JOURNEYING TO THE EDGE OF CHRISTENDOM

The journey to the Lithuanian frontier took a long time and was an adventure in and of itself. Knights setting out from the Netherlands took five weeks to reach Königsberg; English travellers going overland took an extra week. The French spent two months on the road, although for those coming from the south the journey lasted ten weeks. In the summer, when it was safer to travel by sea, the Prussian coast could be reached in just under three weeks from an English port, then another week to Königsberg. In the winter, with stormy weather and the Baltic Sea freezing over in places, the journey took much longer; travelling from Bruges to Danzig could take over two months, although then it was possible to continue over the frozen Vistula Lagoon directly to the Sambian Peninsula. When the return journey was added, most participants could expect to be away for four or five months, assuming they survived.

Having reached Danzig from the west, or Thorn from the south, companies could make further stops on the Vistula, which took them past the Order's headquarters at Marienburg and then Elbing, where many stopped to replenish supplies, obtain further loans and perhaps even meet with the Order's officials. The convent at Elbing was one of the most important in Prussia, functioning as the seat of the Order's grand hospitaller. From here, if companies had not gone via the lagoon directly to Königsberg, the road led through a changing landscape. Increasingly forested and hilly, the road left the Order's territory and passed through two key towns of the episcopate of Warmia: Frauenburg (Polish Frombork), where the fortified cathedral complex of the chapter was being built over much of the fourteenth century, and the Hanseatic town of Braunsberg (Polish Braniewo), where the episcopal castle remained a powerful symbol of the Warmian bishop's authority, even after their official residence was relocated from here to the south-east in 1340. Once beyond the town, the road was back in the Order's territory — this stretch governed from the coastal convent of Balga. Companies would travel up past the convent of Brandenburg and then on to Königsberg.

Visitors arriving in the fourteenth century would have experienced an urban complex consisting of three towns built on islands and patches of reclaimed land on the River Pregel, which drained into the lagoon; Königsberg would only become a single city in the eighteenth century. Each town functioned as a separate legal entity, with its own charter, parish church, market and circuits of walls studded with gatehouses, connected to the others by bridges. The oldest settlement, the Altstadt or Old Town, where the Teutonic Order's fortified convent was located, was separated by a rivulet from the town of Löbenicht to the east, which was populated by artisans. To the south, the island town of Kneiphof, settled by German merchants, had been granted its charter in 1327. The eastern side of the island had been given to the Bishop of Sambia, where visitors would have seen the gradual construction of the new red-brick cathedral — dramatically expanded in the 1350s to a three-aisled edifice. To the east another rivulet, the New Pregel, separated Kneiphof from the island of Lomse, where the Old Town burghers owned swampy grazing areas, as well as a lumberyard and warehouses clustered along its western edge. For the towns of Königsberg, the regular arrival of wealthy nobles from the West was a welcome seasonal economic boost; the cathedral, churches, civic buildings and walls were all largely built in the era of the *Reysen*. However, the towns had also joined the Hanse and trade was thriving.

The convent at Königsberg contained the largest community in the Teutonic Order's Baltic territories (some sixty-seven brethren are associated with it in 1422), and served as the seat of the Order's Prussian marshal who led the campaigns into Lithuania. Playing the role of gracious host to the visitors, he would present the most distinguished guests with gifts and, with such proximity to the 'Great Wilderness' (German *Die Große Wildnis*) that defined the landscape of the frontier, game was regularly presented – the accounts refer to gifts of deer and even bison. Residency within the convent's grounds was unusual: the majority of visitors found lodgings in the Old Town or Kneiphof. Large companies ended up spread across many hostels: in 1363, Jean de Blois's men would hire nine different lodgings; the Count of Ostrevent's company required eighteen houses and inns in 1387. Several stables were also needed, such as when the Austrian duke Leopold III brought 1,500 horses with him in the winter of 1371. The companies would quickly set themselves up: heraldic devices were painted on boards and hung up in front of lodgings for all to see and the leading nobles would have their own house where their itinerant court would be brought to life, complete with resplendent tapestries, a dining hall with fine tableware and portable chapels for private masses. Then it was a question of waiting. Sometimes for days, often weeks and perhaps even months.

During this time, nobles engaged in revelry, hosting banquets for guests from other companies as well as the Order's officials, the bishop and his canons. If delays were expected, hunting trips were organised, with some nobles bringing or borrowing falcons and hunting dogs. While there were no formal tournaments, war games between companies were sometimes organised. By the late fourteenth century, the culmination of the courtly carousel in Königsberg was the 'Table of Honour', a grand feast led by the Order's marshal or grand master. Held in the convent's refectory, the event featured speeches and the ceremonial awarding of badges of valour. In 1415, at the papal Council of Constance, the lawyer representing the Polish crown condemned the 'Table of Honour', arguing that the Order used this simply to extract money from its guests.[10] However, the guests were not complaining. This was a tangible and attractive form of gaining renown, and a feature of the ceremonial trappings of the various chivalric knightly orders that had sprung up within Christendom. Yet large sums of money could certainly be spent in Königsberg. As the weeks passed, the bills for quartering, provisioning and purchasing gifts accrued, as did gambling debts and the loans required to cover them.

At the same time, spiritual needs also had to be met: most members of the nobility were pious individuals, certainly in public if not in private. Some of the churches within the vicinity of Königsberg became popular with participants of the *Reysen*. The Church of St Anthony and the Chapel of St George attached to the leper hospital in the suburb of Haberberg became particular draws. St George was the quintessential crusader saint and an altar dedicated to him could also be found in the cathedral on Kneiphof. Foreign knights would visit his chapel in Haberberg to pray for a successful campaign and, upon returning, to thank the saint for his protection. Many left donations and had their heraldic emblems painted on boards displayed inside the chapel. Outside the city, popular sites included the Church of St Catherine in Arnau, about ten kilometers east of Königsberg, and the Church of the Blessed Virgin in Juditten, seven kilometers to the west. Here, too, knights often had their coats of arms painted on the walls. However, the cathedral was the most important stop for visitors, both at the beginning and end of their journey. Its nave became adorned with heraldic emblems of past participants, alongside the tombs of those who died fighting the pagans, their arms painted on the cathedral's windows. Many of these individuals were familiar to foreign visitors by reputation or family connections. In this respect, the cathedral became the ideal public space for promoting the ongoing holy war against the pagans.

When the call to arms came, the foreign companies set off eastwards with (or to join) the Order's army. They usually made their way to the frontier castle of Ragnit (Russian Neman), just over 100 kilometres to the north-east, although some campaigns began from outposts further south, or from Memel to the north, and travelled along the river. Ragnit had been built in 1289 on the site of a destroyed indigenous stronghold in the heart of the Prussian territory of Scalovia, following the Order's conquest. Within a few decades, it housed a convent governing a sizeable territory. But the castle remained largely a timber-and-earth fortification, one of a series of strongholds built by the Order throughout the fourteenth century along the lengthy Nemunas which cut through the Great Wilderness and into the heart of Lithuania. Their purpose was to secure territory and establish a supply chain for further attacks to the east. These were regularly attacked and damaged or destroyed by Lithuanian armies. When Ragnit was rebuilt from brick, it became the apogee of the conventual form, measuring 59 metres on each side. The adjoining ward was lined with three ranges of service buildings, and the whole complex was surrounded by a moat and wall.[11] Many foreign knights and soldiers would have passed through here on their way into the grand duchy, but few would have seen the finished brick castle. In stark contrast to the grandeur and bustle of Marienburg and Königsberg, the stronghold of Ragnit, deep within the Great Wilderness, would have felt like a distant outpost, a reminder to those coming from the West that they had reached the edge of their world.

Survival at the frontier required more than physical weapons and armour. For the Order's brethren, warfare was also a spiritual matter. The Order's devotion to the Blessed Virgin was woven into the conduct of the *Reysen*. When the armies set out, they often did so on her feast days – on 15 August, the Feast of the Assumption; on 8 September, the Feast of the Nativity; and on 2 February, the Feast of the Purification (Candlemas). They would carry the Queen of Heaven's banner in front of them along with that of St George; some also had images of the Virgin painted on their own banners. The *Reysen* were carried out under her spiritual protection, and its participants believed that her intervention would grant them victory over the pagans. Wigand of Marburg, a herald of the Order and one of our main sources for the *Reysen*, wrote a retrospective account of the battle between the Order's army and Lithuanians on the frozen Strėva river in February 1348. He described how Mary came to the aid of the crusaders who were ultimately victorious, prompting the grand master to subsequently establish two monasteries in her honour. The identification of the wars against Lithuania with the Virgin was promoted externally: in letters to foreign rulers written by the Order's officials referring to the Order's lands and its wars against the pagans, the connection with Mary was repeatedly emphasised.[12]

APOCALYPSE THEN?

To meet the army's spiritual needs, portable altars would be carried, along with wax candles. Participants would have also brought their own religious artefacts, and even their weapons would have served an amuletic function. Several swords, dating to the fourteenth century, have been found in rivers along the well-trodden route of the *Reysen*. They are typified by the hand-and-a-half sword, dating to c. 1350–1400, found in the River Tina which flows into Lake Drużno near Elbląg, today on display in the Castle Museum in Malbork. Its pommel was decorated with the Jerusalem cross (representing the five wounds of Christ) and smaller crosses inlaid with a non-ferrous metal, as well as letters inscribed into the blade that most likely refer to Christ. One cross-decorated sword in the collection of the Deutsches Historisches Museum in Berlin includes heraldic devices of a cross and a lion within shields inscribed on the blade, and has been interpreted as a gift from the Teutonic Order to John of Luxembourg, the King of Bohemia, during his *Reyse* in 1329.[13] Irrespective of whether such weapons belonged to visiting nobles or brethren of the Order, they exemplify how the physical and spiritual nature of warfare were fused together.

INTO THE WILDERNESS

Today, if you drive through north-eastern Poland towards Lithuania, you can get an impression of what the medieval Prussian frontier must have been like. The Forest of Augustów, part of a vast corridor of woodland that stretches up towards Vilnius, is a remnant of the Great Wilderness.[14] Although plantations of trees have become more prevalent, the national park still has pockets where human disturbance is barely visible, where dead trees have been allowed to fall and decay, where the creation of beaver dams has flooded woodlands and then slowly transformed them into meadows to then be recolonised by new trees, and marked throughout by a diverse abundance of plant and animal life. Here there are few archaeological traces of human presence in the medieval period, whilst pollen records point to minimal human impact on the local vegetation until the seventeenth century. Written sources indicate that armies would occasionally encounter traces of habitation – the huts of fishermen, trappers or those harvesting honey and wax from wild hives in the forests. Contemporary chroniclers referred to this region as *desertum* and *solitudinem* – terms that were commonly used to describe the biblical wilderness.[15] Indeed, for Western Christians this frontier was both a physical and spiritual desert, a fitting backdrop for the Order's continuing holy war.

Continuing from Augustów on the road heading north-east across the modern Lithuanian border, you pass by another fragment of the Great Wilderness, today the Meteliai Regional Park, before reaching Alytus, where the fortified outpost became a regular target for the Order's attacks. The belt of wilderness stretched to the north-west across Sudovia and the Nemunas, where it separated the lands of the convents at Ragnit and Memel from the region of Samogitia. The historical reputation of the Samogitians as fiercely independent persists into the present day. Modern Samogitia (Lithuanian Žemaitija) is situated in north-western Lithuania, bordering with Latvia, slightly reduced in size from its extent in the Middle Ages. It is the only Lithuanian region where the local dialect, which is more of a separate language, is still used by the provincial government. By the late thirteenth century, Samogitia had become sandwiched between the Order's lands in Prussia and Livonia, and Lithuania, and whilst the grand dukes were nominally its overlords, in practice the region's leaders maintained a strong degree of independence. Samogitia's nobles also influenced the decisions of grand dukes to endorse pagan practices, essentially a means of supporting the local status quo, where political and religious identities were intertwined. Alongside their attacks on the heartland of the grand duchy, the Order was intent on bringing the region fully into the Catholic fold.

The logistics of campaigns had to be tailored to the season. Winter was ideal, as frozen lakes, marshes and rivers made travel easier, and snow provided traction for infantry and cavalry. If a mild winter made the wetlands difficult to cross, or conversely one that was dangerously cold with deep snow, knights and their retinues would sometimes move on to Livonia to join campaigns against the Rus' or Lithuanians. In summer, travel along rivers was easier, whilst the wetlands at this time were plagued by biting insects. Pack horses handled the terrain better than wagons, and sledges were used in the winter. They formed slow-moving convoys which could stretch for kilometres. Crucial to the success of a campaign was provisioning, and since hunting was unreliable, food had to be brought along. In the summer, livestock was taken as 'meat on the hoof', whilst winter supplies included dried, smoked and salted meats, flour and a variety of condiments, including expensive imports like saffron and pepper. Food caches and horse fodder were left at strategic points for the return journey, and folding tables were brought for preparing meals.

Local guides were essential. They would not only navigate through the wilderness, relying on landmarks and the stars, but also provide accurate appraisals of the thickness of the ice on the frozen rivers, as well as the suitability of crossings and routes at different times of the year. Sudden changes in weather prompted quick retreats as the thawing ice was dangerous, and written accounts tell of horses drowning as they fell through into the freezing water. When it was not possible to follow rivers or streams, fallen trees and vegetation would have to be hacked away with hatchets and axes to open up a route for the convoy. Men and animals were crushed against each other in the narrow paths through the thickets, horses at times standing up to their saddles in swampy mud or swirling snow drifts, and the howling of wolf packs would have been an ever-present sound.

As they approached Lithuanian settlements and strongholds, the companies would switch into their military formations, hoping to use the element of surprise when launching the assault, desperate to avoid ambushes. Pitched battles were rare – the norm was a carefully planned raid or siege, with the aim of causing as much devastation as possible and to demoralise the enemy. When attacking strongholds, siege engines such as battering rams, towers and trebuchets were assembled, and by the 1380s and 1390s, guns were being used by both sides.[16]

BRUTALITY AND COMPROMISE IN THE FRONTIER WAR

The chronicles neither hold back on, nor apologise for, the killing of women, children and elderly men, their enslavement, the seizure of their livestock or the burning of their villages and grain stores. Rarely were spoils of gold or silver taken: prisoners and animals were the principal material rewards. Written accounts paint a distressing and grim picture of captives with their hands bound, strung to horses and forced to walk back to the Order's lands. If the crusaders had to retreat quickly, they would kill their prisoners. For English and French veterans of the ongoing Hundred Years War, this would have been all too familiar: the English had become known for their *chevauchées* intended to terrorise French towns and villages through systematic acts of burning, pillaging and rape. In October 1346, Henry of Grosmont, then Earl of Lancaster, had led a brutal *chevauchée* against Poitiers and its surroundings: after successfully capturing the town, his army spent over a week sacking it. Five years later, now with a ducal title, Grosmont would make the journey to the Lithuanian frontier, where his experiences of raiding would be highly valued by the Order. Following his return, he led another *chevauchée* in Normandy.

Whilst the English became famed and hated for their actions in France, violence against civilians was found across the war zones of medieval Europe. The Samogitians and Lithuanians did likewise when raiding in order to seize goods, livestock and slaves. Like the Order, they preferred to attack in winter, and were as well equipped and armed. German settlements established on the fringes of eastern Prussia were swallowed up by the wilderness; women and children were killed or seized as captives and the Order's officials were captured and imprisoned or sacrificed by immolation – the fear of the latter continued to haunt combatants, even after Lithuania's official Christianisation. Lithuanian armies were also able to strike deep into Prussia and Livonia. Archaeological excavations near Barczewko in north-east Poland have uncovered the most dramatic example of the devastation caused by such a raid within the heart of the Warmian episcopate – the destroyed remains of the small town of Wartenburg, which has been linked to the documented Lithuanian attack in the winter of 1354.[17]

The town was one of several that had been founded in the early decades of the fourteenth century, part of a deliberate policy of encouraging German migrants to settle; 10 kilometres to the south, the castle and town of Allenstein (Polish Olsztyn) would see significant investment from the Warmian chapter. Wartenburg was typical of such planned colonies, which archaeological excavations revealed consisted of several rows of timber houses and a central market square, where more prestigious buildings were also found, perhaps one of which served as a town hall. There was also a church and cemetery, and the town's perimeter was protected by a timber palisade, with a substantial moated rampart and gate complex on its more vulnerable western side. The space within the walls was not yet crowded with buildings, and there was plenty of open land that must have been used for cultivation. Yet this was not a community of peasant farmers: the burghers, many of whom were merchants and artisans, were doing well for themselves, sporting the latest fashionable jewellery and using ceramic vessels imported from the empire.

The townspeople appear to have been taken by surprise and Wartenburg's defences must have been quickly breached. Once the Lithuanians were inside, a massacre took place – numerous crossbow bolts and arrowheads were found throughout the town, and some of the inhabitants had tried to hide in cellars. The skeleton of a young woman, aged eighteen to twenty, was found face down, her arms folded in front of her, a bronze ring on the finger of her right hand, and her head shattered by falling beams. In another cellar the remains of a one-year-old toddler were found; nearby were two silver rings, most probably hidden by the mother together with her child. The distribution of projectiles suggests that a desperate last stand took place in the market square as the Lithuanians swept through the town. The timber houses were set on fire and collapsed, burying their cellars together with their contents. After the Lithuanians departed, the bodies of the townspeople must have been recovered and reburied, except for those hidden deep within the collapsed debris, but the burnt-out town was not rebuilt and its remnants became gradually overgrown earthworks. Wigand, who described the attack, added that the entire population of the town was killed. Two years later, Allenstein would repel a Lithuanian attack, but seventeen villages in the vicinity would be destroyed.

Archaeologists have similarly discovered traces of destruction at a number of Lithuanian strongholds targeted by the *Reysen*, such as at Mitkiškės, Kernavė and Maišiagala, which they have connected with the Order's attacks in the later fourteenth century. It is difficult to know the true number of communities obliterated during the frontier war, but figures of casualties are scattered throughout the chronicles and, inevitably, there were particularly tragic episodes. For example, in 1336, a crusading army had besieged the stronghold at Pilėnai, nestled amidst forests on an outcrop overlooking the Nemunas. The crusaders set fire to the timber walls of the castle and, rather than surrender, the Lithuanian men killed their children and wives, before finally turning their blades on themselves. The mass suicide at Pilėnai horrified the Germans, who withdrew in shock. This episode was clearly disturbing even for the Order's own chronicler, but other accounts of campaigns have celebratory tones. In 1377, the herald Peter Suchenwirt accompanied Duke Albert III of Austria to the Prussian frontier. In his account, lavishly praising the actions of the ducal company, the Lithuanians are dehumanised, described as savage animals to be hunted down, and the victorious crusaders bind them and lead them away as if they were their dogs. A surprise attack on a Lithuanian wedding is framed as a lethal dance with the crusaders, resulting in the slaughter of sixty pagans.[18] In contrast, several French accounts treat the Lithuanians as honourable and worthy opponents.

But the frontier conflict was not a merciless war of annihilation, for it also involved compromise, conditional surrenders and even friendships with the enemy.[19] There were regular treaties between the opposing sides, enabling periods of peace and commerce.[20] Whilst this contrasts with the confrontational ideology promoted by the Order, a closer scrutiny of its own narratives reveals a consistent respect for the enemy, in some instances verging on admiration. Before the crusades began in earnest in the Baltic, there had already been several papal prohibitions against the sale of arms and military resources to Saracens, on pain of excommunication. This was repeated by Pope Honorius III in 1218 when referring to the sale of arms to Prussians to prevent them using these against Christians, and complaints about Christian merchants selling weapons to pagans would be subsequently repeated. However, the Order included provisions for trading with pagan Samogitians and Lithuanians in its treaties, as a means of sustaining its political and military assets. The brethren had petitioned the pope for permission to trade in all places on account of their 'poverty', at a time when a peace treaty had been negotiated with the Samogitians. This was granted and then reaffirmed in 1263, on condition that it did not become the normal way of conducting business.

The Order held on to this privilege to justify their economic dealings with their pagan opponents throughout the fourteenth century. In 1312, a delegation from Riga complained to the papal legate that the Livonian brethren were selling weapons to pagan Lithuanians, and that the Order had made a specific truce to facilitate this. The Rigans were, of course, looking out for their own commercial interests, and were furious the Order had sidestepped its merchants and made exclusive deals with the Lithuanians. The Order, in response, presented its papal privilege, adding that not only were its members not selling contraband (iron, arms, food or drink) to the Lithuanians, but in fact it was the merchants of Riga who were engaged in this forbidden trade with 'infidels making war on Christians'. Yet the Order was also prepared to compromise its ideological stance when prudent. One truce with the Lithuanians included a stipulation the Order's brethren refrain from burning sacred pine woods, which were noted as the locations of cremation funerals – the dwelling places of ancestors.[21]

Lithuanian rulers also became well-versed political players, forging alliances with their Rus' and Polish neighbours. Gediminas's lengthy reign (c. 1316–41) exemplifies this, his careful political negotiations including a truce with the Order's Livonian branch, a petition to the papacy for protection and an invitation to Catholic migrants to settle in Lithuania with financial incentives and the promise of guaranteeing freedom of religion. German artisans and merchants from Livonia came and settled close to the castle in Vilnius, alongside a community of Franciscan friars to minster to them. Some archaeologists have argued the remains of the timber building found under Vilnius Cathedral represent the earliest Franciscan church here. A Rus' Eastern Orthodox community is also attested at Vilnius, as at Kernavė.[22] Gediminas went as far as asking for a papal legate to baptise him and drew up a contract to the effect, which a Christian delegation witnessed in Vilnius. Denounced by the Prussian synod of Elbing, as well as succumbing to pressure from his Orthodox allies and pagan subjects, he revoked his early pledge, whilst secretly reiterating the promise of a future baptism to the Archbishop of Riga, resulting in the continuation of peace with Livonia.

In 1325, the truce was broken when the grand duke's representative was assassinated in Riga. Yet just over a decade later, in 1338, another treaty between Gediminas and the Order's Livonian branch included provisions for safe passage for German merchants through ducal lands. Lithuanian merchants were permitted within a spear's throw of the Daugava, enough for them to gain access to Riga's trading network. Astonishingly, the treaty was sealed by the swearing of sacred oaths that crossed all the religious divides – the Catholic delegates from Livonia, as well as the Orthodox Rus' vassals from Lithuania, kissed a cross, whilst the pagan Lithuanians conducted their own religious rites which were deemed valid and binding. Lithuanian merchants were amongst the first to convert during these exchanges, with Riga's records mentioning several who had adopted Christian names. Tensions nonetheless remained, and three years later two Franciscan friars in Vilnius were killed for denouncing the indigenous religion. In December of that year, Gediminas would die a pagan, his body burnt on a funeral pyre along with the customary human and animal sacrifices. He also established a dynasty that would define Lithuanian politics into the sixteenth century.

The subsequent decline in trade agreements between the Order and Lithuania from the mid-fourteenth century coincided with an intensification of attacks. In 1363, the crusaders destroyed Kaunas, then several strongholds in Kernavė and two years later reached Vilnius, where they burned down large parts of the town, having failed to take the castle. They would do so again in 1383. During these two decades, the frontier had been consolidated with the construction of castles on the banks of the Nemunas – Georgenburg, near the mouth of Mituva; New Marienburg by the mouth of Dubysa; Bayerburg; Gotteswerder on an island at the confluence of the Nemunas and Nevėžis rivers; and lastly in 1384, Marienwerder, on an island at the confluence of the Neris and Nemunas. This final castle would be rapidly constructed from brick and stone, with materials shipped in from Prussia. Intending this as a new permanent base for further attacks against Samogitia and Lithuania, the Order established a substantial garrison of forty brother-knights headed by a commander, several hundred soldiers and supplies of gunpowder and small cannons. Supply lines and routes were mapped out from Ragnit for future *Reysen*.[23]

The timing of Marienwerder's construction coincided with a tumultuous period in Lithuanian politics. The death of Grand Duke Algirdas had left the grand duchy in the hands of his son Jogaila. After he made a secret pact with the Order to protect his own western lands but not those of his uncle Kęstutis, the latter seized the throne in a short-lived civil war. In August 1382, Kęstutis and his son Vytautas were captured and imprisoned. Kęstutis died under mysterious circumstances and Vytautas escaped and allied with the Order against Jogaila. The following year he converted to Catholicism and, in January 1384, in exchange for help in recovering the lands he claimed and recognising him as grand duke, Vytautas promised to cede a part of Samogitia to the Order. Yet only a few months later, Vytautas entered into an alliance with Jogaila, burning the strongholds of Georgenburg and New Marienburg. Then, forces led by Jogaila, his brother Skirgaila and Vytautas besiged Marienwerder for almost seven weeks before its garisson surrendered. The castle was demolished, and although it would be partially rebuilt in 1402, the Order never succeeded in establishing a foothold deeper into Lithuanian territory.

With the grand duchy's official adoption of Catholicism, a new agreement would give merchants from Vilnius and Polotsk access to Riga. Then in January 1390, Vytautas made a secret pact with the Order, agreeing to cede them a portion of Samogitia in exchange for a military alliance against Jogaila and Skirgaila. Four months later, this was reaffirmed in a treaty signed in Königsberg by thirty Samogitian nobles who acknowledged Vytautas's lordship. In the winter of that year, the Order's army stormed the walls of Vilnius along with a Lithuanian contingent, in an unlikely alliance forced by the civil war. Two years later, when Vytautas and Jogaila were reconciled, the pact with the Order was broken and once again the *Reysen* faced a united Samogitian and Lithuanian front. The historian Stephen Rowell summed it up best when he described the dealings between the opposing powers in the late medieval eastern Baltic as 'the harshest *realpolitik*'.[24]

RENOWN

Some historians have viewed the *Reysen* as overindulgent chivalric adventures pursued by macho glory-seekers, cynically manipulated into filling the Teutonic Order's coffers, lured by offers of extravagant feasts and hunts of exotic beasts.[25] Yet the experience in the Great Wilderness was a far cry from the glamour of tournaments and staged hunts in Western Europe that marked the masculine chivalric lifestyle. Travelling from bustling Königsberg into the heart of the untamed wilderness brought participants closer to the imagined experience of errant knights, popular figures in courtly literature. Like the earlier crusades, the *Reyse* was itself a journey with a spiritual goal, reminiscent of Percival's quest for the grail, which in the empire had become popularised by Wolfram of Eschenbach's poem *Parzival*. Here, as in other Arthurian romances, courtly life was starkly juxtaposed with the ominous and perilous wilderness of the quest. Sometimes the Order recreated chivalric ceremonial in the pagan realm by staging the 'Table of Honour' on campaign, as at Kaunas in 1391, but this was probably an infrequent occurrence reserved for particularly distinguished participants.

There was an evident synergy with crusading: Anthony de Lucy, as we saw, was seemingly memorialised with a representation of the grail. Enmeshed within the horror and violence of the frontier war was the elusive reward of spiritual reawakening, of personal redemption; the crusading indulgence provided by the Order must have reinforced this. The earlier crusades to the Holy Land had reinvented the ideal of Catholic knighthood, and in the fourteenth century the *Reysen* offered a tangible door to that ideal for aristocratic men. Yet, as Wolfram's retelling of *Parzival* also reveals, spirituality was just one facet of knighthood. Equally, if not more important, was courting aristocratic women, building a lineage and gaining renown. From the twelfth century, a young knight's reputation was based on accruing experiences of service within a noble household, jousting, fighting in battles and ultimately by going on crusade. In the fourteenth century, the *Reyse* also provided an ideal opportunity to invest in reputation and, as we have seen, participation could become a family tradition. It is therefore clear that renown, lineage and spirituality were inseparable in the world of fourteenth-century crusading, even as the driving motivations varied from one individual to the next.

A colourful example of these entangled motivations is provided by the exploits of Henry Bolingbroke. Henry's behaviour continues to divide his biographers, and much has been written on his journeys to

Prussia in 1390 and 1392, for which detailed documentation survives. By participating in the *Reysen*, Henry was continuing a family tradition: his grandfather and father-in-law had both fought alongside the Teutonic Order against the Lithuanians. Henry's father, John of Gaunt, the richest and most powerful nobleman in England, a son of Edward III and uncle of the ill-fated Richard II, encouraged his son to go and funded his expeditions. This was particularly crucial for building Henry's own reputation, for despite his celebrated and larger-than-life status, John's own crusading efforts had been fruitless.[26] Henry, on the other hand, would have first-hand experience of crusading at the age of twenty-five. In May 1390, he declared his intention to campaign in both Barbary and Prussia.[27]

However, Henry was denied safe passage through France and so instead that summer he headed to Prussia to aid the Order amidst the ongoing civil war in Lithuania between Vytautas, Jogaila and Skirgaila – by then all converts to Christianity. This fact did not seem to bother him, nor was this how the campaign was perceived by outsiders. The *Westminster Chronicle*, which documented Henry's exploits, described this as a conflict between Christians and pagans.[28] The crusading host initially confronted Skirgaila's forces near Kaunas, where the English longbow lived up to its reputation with the result that some 300 Lithuanians were killed. Skirgaila retreated to Vilnius and the crusaders pursued him, besieging the town. Vilnius had developed into a crowded, bustling and cosmopolitan metropolis by this time, and its expansive castle complex was the principal residence of the grand duke. The Teutonic Order had besieged the castle on several occasions, with no success. By 1390, Vilnius was formally a Catholic city with its own Polish bishop. This did not stop the assault, which must be viewed not only within the context of the dynastic conflict the Order was actively involving itself in, but also in the disregard of the validity of Lithuanian conversions. When Grand Master Conrad of Jungingen wrote to the pope in 1403 to defend the Order's wars, he described them in the familiar language of earlier crusades: these were divine wars against infidels and schismatics and their purpose was to expand the Lord's vineyard. The siege lasted for five weeks, after which the crusaders were forced to retreat to Königsberg before winter set in. There they waited for the wetlands of the frontier to freeze over, but no new campaign was organised, and Henry and his company remained in the city over Christmas until February before relocating to Danzig. Henry finally set sail for England at the end of March.

His subsequent attempt to join the Order's campaign in the summer of 1392 also became embroiled in dynastic politics. Vytautas and Jogaila made peace, and the Order informed Henry (and other English knights) his services would not be required. Henry had even got as far as Königsberg before having to turn back and return to Danzig. From there, he decided to head to the Holy Land and took the route through some of the most important courts in Europe, travelling with his retinue through Pomerania into the heart of the empire, down to Prague, then wended his way to Vienna and Venice, from where he sailed to Jaffa and then took the well-trodden pilgrimage road to Jerusalem, reaching the holy city in late January. Again, the journey was largely funded by his father. To reach Jerusalem was the dream of every Christian pilgrim, and this too enhanced his reputation significantly. His return journey to Venice included Cyprus and Rhodes, both bulwarks of Christendom's frontier against the Turks. Nonetheless, reminiscing in later years, Henry described himself as a 'child of Prussia' – the experience in the Baltic had evidently been a very fulfilling one.[29]

Henry's expeditions almost certainly had several entangled motivations. In 1389, Richard II had reasserted his authority following the seizure of power by the Lords Appellant, who had counted Henry amongst their number, which had resulted in a deadly purge of the king's allies and advisors. It would have been prudent for Henry to distance himself from the court as Richard had come back into the spotlight; indeed, this is the explanation given by the Austin friar John Capgrave who provides the principal account of Henry's 1392 journey. Richard, no doubt happy to have Henry outside his realm, had granted permission for him to leave. The crusade had cost a staggering £4,383 (the equivalent of almost £3 million today) and the second 'tour' £4,195, of which the bulk had been paid by Henry's father – a clear investment in building his son's reputation, perhaps with the intention of eventually replacing Richard II on the throne, and Henry made sure his exploits were regularly documented in newsletters.[30] The publicity paid off. Chroniclers emphasised both Henry's piety in fighting for the cross and his manliness: writing many decades later in the reign of Henry's grandson, Capgrave emphasised Bolingbroke's achievements, above all, as a crusader, a chivalric paragon of the Lancastrian line. In stark contrast to Richard, who had not fought in battle let alone participated in a 'righteous war', Henry had followed in the footsteps of legendary kings such as Richard the Lionheart and Edward I.

There was also a more unsettling side to the first campaign Henry participated in, which typified the long war against paganism in the eastern Baltic. It was not uncommon to capture indigenous people during *Reyse*, often children, and send them for re-education. This practice was not restricted to this frontier of Catholic Europe, but the Order had actively done this since the start of crusading in the eastern Baltic. Some of the Order's guests did likewise in the fourteenth century, reinforcing the promotion of the *Reysen* as a form of missionary warfare. Thomas Beauchamp, the Earl of Warwick and one of the founding members of the Order of the Garter, had brought back a son of the Lithuanian grand duke to London, where he was baptised and given the Christian name Thomas. The *Westminster Chronicle* describes how, after the siege of Vilnius in 1390, 11,500 Lithuanian prisoners had been taken – 8,000 to Prussia by the Order's marshal and 3,500 to Livonia by the provincial master. Their fate was not specified, but religious re-education would have certainly been on the minds of the captors. Wigand of Marburg noted that some 7,000 pagans were killed by the crusaders during this campaign. Medieval chroniclers notoriously exaggerated numbers, but the details are nonetheless disturbing. Amidst the ostentatious and glory-seeking elements of Henry's expeditions, amidst the deadly game of *realpolitik* being played out between the Order and the grand duchy, and between members of Lithuania's ruling dynasty, it reminds us of the goal of the *Reysen* promoted by the brethren – the eradication of paganism, whether through conversion or death.

THE END OF THE 'ETERNAL CRUSADE'

By the summer of 1394, the participation of foreign knights in the Order's *Reysen* declined, as attention shifted to the Ottoman threat in the Balkans. By the early fifteenth century, this had dropped to single figures.³¹ The Order continued to argue the Lithuanians were still pagans and the Poles were heretics for aiding them, and this certainly convinced some of its guest knights and foreign observers: the French chronicler Enguerrand of Monstrelet framed the war between the Order and Poland-Lithuania in these terms. He described the outcome of the battle of Grunwald in 1410, where foreign knights fought alongside the Order, as 'lost by the Christians', whilst celebrating the Order 'finally drove the infidels' out of Prussia in its aftermath. Yet English chroniclers were increasingly critical of the brethren, condemning them for attacking Jogaila after his conversion to Catholicism.³² For English knights, the renewed war with France, especially under Henry V's leadership, took precedence over crusading as the ultimate expression of chivalric duty.

It was not until the Council of Constance, which began in 1414 and lasted three years, that the Order's mandate to wage holy war against Lithuania was publicly questioned. Clerics and delegates from across Christendom attended, and the Order presented a detailed defence of its mission, reiterating its old arguments against Lithuania and Poland. From the Order's viewpoint, Christians aiding pagans were legitimate targets, a position supported by the Dominican John of Falkenburg, who condemned the Poles as idolaters and infidels, even claiming the Polish king deserved death. In response, Paweł Włodkowic, representing the Polish crown, argued that the Order's war and their intended occupation of Samogitia were unjust, criticising the forced conversion of pagans. Both sides framed themselves as defenders of the Catholic faith. Ultimately, Falkenburg's writings were condemned as libel by the papal commissioners and his own monastic order. While Pope Martin V hesitated to directly sanction the Order, in the end the responsibility for evangelising the Samogitians was given to the union. The last contingent of German knights intending to participate in a *Reyse* arrived in Prussia in the winter of 1422, just as a peace treaty was concluded where the Order renounced its claim on Samogitia once and for all. But peace would not last indefinitely, as trouble was brewing for the Order amongst its own subjects.

WORLDS IN TRANSITION

CHAPTER 9

THE HANSEATIC WORLD
Migrants and Indigenes in the Medieval Baltic

> We will also assign to the inhabitants of this town the rights that Lübeck has, on the condition that whatever is committed against God and our Order, town and country, will be completely excluded [from its jurisdiction] . . .
>
> Excerpt from the charter of privileges granted to the town of Elbing by Henry of Hohenlohe, Grand Master of the Teutonic Order, 10 April 1246[1]

CROSSING THE FREEZING SEA

In 2022, archaeologists in Tallinn unearthed the remains of one of the largest medieval ships ever found in Northern Europe. Measuring 24.5 metres long and 9 metres at its widest, the exceptionally preserved hull was found in the vicinity of Lootsi Street where, until the nineteenth century, the mouth of the Härjapea river had flowed out into the Baltic. Although parts of the bow were missing, much of the vessel was intact, having been preserved under nineteenth- and twentieth-century landfill, with its stern lying some 5 metres below the present-day ground surface. As more of the sand-filled hull was revealed, the overlapping clinker planks on its sides gave way to flush-laid timbers in its flat bottom. The seams of both sets of planks were caulked with pitch-soaked animal hair and moss, and covered with wooden laths fastened with iron sintels (staples that secured caulking), ensuring a watertight seal. These could be dated to the mid-fourteenth century, and this was broadly confirmed by dendrochronological dating of some of the ship's timbers. The use of animal hair in the caulking in addition to moss, an unusual choice, also suggested the vessel was manufactured in Scandinavia. The reason for the ship's sinking remains unknown, but part of the keel had been torn off and the vessel may have been caught in one of the river's sandbanks. The crew must have escaped the sinking ship, as no bodies were found in the wreckage.[2]

This design identified the ship as a cog – a single-mast, flat-bottomed vessel – of which forty wrecked examples have been found in Northern Europe so far.[3] The earliest known are Scandinavian in origin, leading to suggestions the cog was the legacy of late Viking Age shipbuilding traditions, after which the design became adopted in what would become its heartland – what is today northern Germany – exemplified by the wreck discovered in Bremen in 1962.[4] In its later form, the addition of aft and fore galleys or 'castles' adapted cogs for naval warfare. These wrecks date to the thirteenth and fourteenth centuries, exhibiting a number of design variants, and they reflect the close relationship between shipping, commerce and crusading in the North.[5] The first definitive written reference to a cog in the Baltic region is found in Henry's *Chronicle of Livonia*,[6] and such ships were regularly used during the crusading era in the Baltic by Danes, Swedes and Germans. They were supplied by merchants, particularly Gotlanders, but also burghers from north German ports such as Lübeck, who played a key role in moving people, animals and materials across the sea to the newly established towns in the east.[7]

Above all, they were used to transport goods for sale. By the end of the fourteenth century, most cogs had the capacity to carry cargo weighing between 40 and 120 tonnes, although a few larger ships could carry more than 200 tonnes. Commodities moved by ship from the eastern Baltic were dominated by wax, fur, timber and grain. These were transported in bulk to meet the insatiable demands of Western European markets. Documentary records provide some idea of the quantities. In 1368, Reval exported around 75,000–80,000 pelts and 18.5 tonnes of wax, and in 1406, English pirates seized three ships from Riga and discovered almost 400,000 pieces of fur in their holds. At this time, an estimated 1.5 million pelts were being exported annually from the eastern Baltic, the majority deriving from Rus' lands, although by the end of the fifteenth century, the source of furs had shifted to Livonia.[8] Sea journeys did not take a huge amount of time: the journey from Lübeck to Reval could be done in a couple of weeks, less if the wind was favourable. But then it would take several more weeks to unload all the cargo. This meant that return trips took around two months, and so only two trips were possible during the sailing season, which lasted from April through to October. During the winter the Baltic's waters became frozen and impassable in places, particularly in the Gulf of Bothnia (between Sweden and Finland) and the Gulf of Finland (between Finland and Estonia).[9]

Merchants had been trading across the Baltic Sea during the Viking Age, and those sharing a common homeland and language began to band together, forming discrete communities. Their presence was highly sought after by local rulers – they brought with them a wide range of goods and raw materials that were not locally available, stimulated local economies and facilitated political alliances. As a result, they were often given privileges and the freedom to govern their own enclaves. Scandinavians had dominated trade in the Baltic Sea region during the Viking Age but, by the mid-twelfth century, German expansion into the northern marches resulted in the foundation of planned towns, later referred to as the 'Wendish towns', whose merchant communities formed a trade consortium – the Hanse. The term itself, which had been more widely used to refer to groups of foreign traders, became associated with companies of merchants engaged in long-distance trade and, by the late thirteenth century, it was being used to refer to the organisation of German trading groups transporting goods in the Baltic and North Sea regions. The towns where these merchants were burghers began issuing privileges to secure trading rights, and the Hanse became influential enough to organise both guarantees of free trade and embargos. Traditionally, the Hanse was viewed as a top-down hierarchical structure, governed from its mother city, Lübeck, but more recently it has been understood as a community of interest, with individuals and groups of equal status variously involved, as and when it suited them.[10]

In each town, merchants and traders formed guilds, with their own internal administration, jurisdiction and identity, and the Hanse relied on these – and town councils – to function. The growth of maritime trade demanded investment in harbours but also ship construction on a huge scale, with the result that the cog has been referred to as the 'Hanseatic workhorse'.

The story of the Hanse is inextricably bound to the export of the urban ideal to the new Catholic 'plantations' in the east Baltic. In the eleventh century, towns had begun to introduce law codes to cater for their distinctive and privileged communities, separating them from the broader laws of the land. These, in turn, emerged from earlier sets of privileges that had been granted by rulers, which governed the life of town dwellers and clearly separated their legal status from those living in the countryside. In the twelfth century, these laws would be codified as a charter, and those of the German towns of Lübeck and Magdeburg – which outlined the details of self-governance, trade, access to resources and even the dimensions of tenements – came to represent an urban ideal. These charters, variously referred to as town laws or privileges, would become the standard for organising towns in vast swathes of Central-Eastern Europe, particularly Magdeburg's Law which would be adopted by a thousand towns. The paradigm was exported to the eastern side of the Baltic during the crusades, where the new urban colonies became dominated by communities of German-speaking merchants, even in Danish Estonia and Swedish Finland. In time, a number of their towns became key partners in the rapidly growing Hanseatic network.

Like the towns of the north German marches, the urban colonies established during the Baltic Crusades became multi-cultural communities. The military campaigns were followed by substantial and regular influxes of migrants from the West, who came to settle in the new towns – former crusaders who decided to stay on having fulfilled their vow, but most often as families of merchants and artisans who were looking for new opportunities and a fresh start. Other groups of foreign merchants would also establish diasporas. Indigenous people were drawn to the new towns for similar reasons, forming growing components of the urban population. These towns depended on good connections with the surrounding countryside for their provisions and tradable commodities and, as a result, new economic ties were created, which connected the most remote farms at the frontiers of the Catholic world to the major ports of the Baltic, and from there to the rest of Europe. In Prussia and southern Finland, as in the north German marches, migrating peasants were encouraged to settle the countryside in large numbers, slowly changing the ethnic composition of the conquered territories. In contrast, in Livonia, migrants generally kept to towns, castles and manors, with little demographic impact on the indigenous rural population.

The story of the Baltic Crusades is therefore not just one of conquest and regime change, but also of the creation of a vast commercial network which came to be dominated by German merchants. This was itself dependent on the web of connections between towns and the countryside, where cultural encounters between migrants and indigenous played out to shape new, composite societies for centuries to come.

RISE OF THE HANSE

The seeds of mercantile success in the southern Baltic, the future core region of the Hanse, were first sown in the conquest of Wendish lands in the twelfth century, giving rise to a number of trading towns which fostered ambitious merchant communities. Then the crusades which created Livonia and Prussia provided the springboard for the organisation with the creation of more towns that became home to sizeable communities of German merchants, retaining strong connections with their homelands. Of these, the two most important groups, who at times competed with each other, were the merchants of Lübeck, who became the dominant group within the Hanse, and the German merchants of Visby on Gotland, whose economic fortunes took a downturn in the fourteenth century. The rise of the Hanse is a complex story of numerous treaties between towns that brought a level of stability to the Baltic Sea region, of the mass production of cogs that enabled large numbers of people, animals and goods to be transported over long distances, and of growing urban markets creating demand for new luxury commodities, staples and raw materials.[11] But it was the merchants of Lübeck and Visby whose commercial interests became enveloped with the Baltic Crusades and shaped the settlements that followed in their wake.

Burghers from Lübeck and Bremen had participated in the Third Crusade and established the field hospital during the siege of Acre in 1190 which developed into the Teutonic Order. In years to come, the Order would define the crusading movement in the Baltic and would continue to receive support from Lübeck's patricians. The Order acquired property in the city, as did the Livonian Sword Brothers. These became points of recruitment for the ongoing war against the pagans. The army of the first crusade to Livonia set sail from Lübeck in 1198, which, according to the chronicler Arnold of Lübeck, included German merchants, and the town would remain a mustering point for future campaigns.[12] Indeed, merchants regularly appear to have participated as combatants, which is not surprising given that wealthy trading families in north German towns frequently married into those of ministerial knights, resulting in a class of lower noble burghers who were actively involved in crusading campaigns, and whose sons would join the Sword Brothers and the Teutonic Order. Merchants and nobles also contributed funds for equipping and transporting armies as a means of redeeming a crusading vow, and the town's trade network helped in the collection of tithes and donations designated for the cause.

In 1219, during the height of active crusading in Livonia, the Danish king Valdemar briefly took control of Lübeck and subsequently blockaded its harbour to try to bring the city back under Danish authority, with the aim of preventing crusaders and supplies reaching the eastern Baltic. The Sword Brothers complained to the pope who intervened, even permitting the citizens of Lübeck to take up arms against the Danes to lift the blockade. After shaking off Danish authority in 1226, the town council of Lübeck moved to ensure theirs would be a free city. The town sent a delegation to the court of Emperor Frederick II at Parma to petition for the status of a free imperial city, which was granted. They also represented their allies, the Sword Brothers, and obtained an imperial privilege for the order.[13]

Lübeck's elevation gave its council the right to make its own by-laws. The council then issued a document that codified the freedoms and privileges of Lübeck's inhabitants. This became known as the Lübeck Law and it was not just a list of rights and rules – including family, inheritance and criminal laws: it was the birth of a new idea of the town rooted in commercial prosperity. Lübeck's victory against the Danes resonated across the Baltic, inspiring nascent urban communities and, in time, some hundred towns in Northern Europe would adopt the Lübeck Law. Valdemar would attempt a second blockade of the city in 1234, failing again. Lübeck's rapid ascent to self-determination took place during the formative decades of the Livonian crusades. Its merchants shipped crusaders, artisans, settlers and a range of luxury commodities, and brought back raw materials from the eastern Baltic. In the process, they accumulated considerable wealth, which they poured into their gabled town houses and the city's religious and civic buildings. But they were not the only group of merchants profiting from the crusades.

In the second half of the twelfth century, north German merchants began to permanently settle in Visby on Gotland, encouraged by the local nobility who sought to realign their political interests away from Sweden, and German marcher lords like Henry the Lion, who saw opportunities to extend their influence.[14] Visby's German merchants started using the eastern shipping route to the Gulf of Finland and from there to Lake Ladoga and the Neva river, which provided a means of reaching Novgorod, the principal commercial distributor for the entire western Rus' arable and hunting regions. In exchange for supplying commodities like wax and fur to the Westerners, Novgorodians gained access to fine cloths, metal goods, glassware, salt, wine and fish. Relations between Gotland and Novgorod were formalised in treaties, and a Rus' trade court was set up in Visby and its German equivalent in Novgorod.[15]

German merchants were also sailing up the Daugava with the aim of reaching the Rus' markets of Polotsk, Vitebsk and Smolensk, and in 1201 arrived in Novgorod using this route.[16] When the missionary Meinhard joined them, it must have been a mutually beneficial arrangement: the conversion of the Livs would have aided their efforts to establish a trading base on the Daugava by introducing Christian norms and, with them, protection for merchants. Gotland was evidently an important stopping point for these voyages, and Meinhard brought masons from the island to build the first stone fortification in Livonia. When the mission floundered, the merchants active in Gotland – German, Danish and Norwegian – offered to provide Meinhard with armed men to protect him. Clearly, their commercial interests in the region were also under threat. Then in 1196, the first documented joint miliary venture involving churchmen and merchants took place. With the aid of the Swedish earl Birger Brosa, an army raised in Gotland led by either Meinhard or Theodoric set sail to attack the Curonian coast with the aim of converting the indigenous population by force, but ended up being diverted to Estonia.

The merchants of Visby must have been involved in providing financing and ships for the venture. The Curonians were a well-known threat to trade, but the establishment of a Christian outpost on their land would have also benefited the commercial interests of Visby's merchants. When Albert took over as Bishop of Livonia in 1199, he sailed to Gotland where, according to Henry's *Chronicle*, he recruited 500 crusaders.[17] Again, the aid of the merchants of Visby for a successful military venture to Livonia would have been indispensable, and they clearly saw in him a charismatic leader who would establish a secure foothold on the eastern Baltic. Albert had a church in Visby dedicated to St James, and we can imagine it would have served as a place of worship for crusaders en route to Livonia, and no doubt a venue for the preaching of future crusades.

The foundation of Riga in 1201 must have been a commercial decision. It was clearly too dangerous for cogs to sail up the river to the missionary base at Holm, so a location closer to the sea would have provided safer anchorage. Merchants settled in Riga and their numbers increased over the coming years. The creation of a monetary standard in Visby, on the island of Gotland, meant that value was no longer exclusively tethered to the weight of silver, but to individual coins. These soon reached the eastern Baltic, where the earliest coins in Riga were struck by Gotlanders in imitation of their own money. A few years before, the coins on Gotland had begun to be struck with the design of a cross pattée on their reverse face, a symbol widely used by crusaders. If this new coinage had been issued at the instigation of Visby's merchants, perhaps it signalled their support for the crusades?[18] Around the same time as the coins started to be produced, the Danish archbishop, Anders Sunesen, who played a leading role in the conquest of Estonia, visited Gotland a number of times, and may have been involved in the construction of the Church of the Holy Sepulchre (later renamed the Holy Ghost) with its octagonal nave referencing the heavenly Jerusalem.[19] But when the papal legate William of Modena preached a crusade against the Osilians in Visby in July 1226, only the German merchants responded to the call, while the Gotlanders themselves showed little interest. This one event has been taken by some historians to mean the islanders became detached from the crusading movement.

In fact, both town and country on Gotland were actively profiting from the crusades, and they were pouring their surplus cash into buildings. The boom in construction activity, which peaked in the mid-thirteenth century, is reflected in the raising of sixteen churches within or close to Visby, and an astonishing ninety-five in the countryside. In the latter half of the thirteenth century, the burghers of Visby also invested heavily in large stone houses and the town's circuit of walls and towers. By then, they had essentially taken control of trade from the island's old nobility. The Gotlanders appear to have been manufacturing and exporting large quantities of weapons. A glimpse of the scale of industrial activity is provided by a find of 7,500m^3 of slag – the waste product of smithing – at Smedjegatan in Visby, corresponding to 10,000 tonnes of iron, and has been linked to the production of sword blades. The deposit was dated to c. 1150–1250.[20] The islanders had no qualms about selling weapons, horses and provisions to all sides, pagan or Christian – in 1229 and 1230, they were rebuked by Pope Gregory IX for trading with pagans.

In 1280, Lübeck and Visby entered into a contract to protect trade across the Baltic Sea, and Riga joined two years later. This was a pivotal moment, for it signified for the very first time that maritime trade routes would be protected by towns rather than individual rulers. But tensions were brewing on Gotland as the war economy of the crusades wound down. A conflict between Visby's burghers and the island's farmers broke out in 1288 over the imposition of duty on products from the countryside. This was ultimately about access to the shrinking international market, and in the countryside, investments in churches – into which wealthy farmers had poured their financial surplus – appear to have been misguided, at least economically. By the fourteenth century, there were fewer churches and stone houses being built in Visby, and Gotland pivoted to exporting limestone, which became a highly desirable material for baptismal fonts, architectural details and grave slabs around the Baltic. But the island's economic fortunes were on the downturn, even before the Danish invasion of 1361.

We can therefore see how the rise and fall of Gotland's affluence broadly aligns with the tempo of the Baltic Crusades, and with the emerging Hanseatic monopoly on trade with the Rus' which became dominated by Lübeck and Riga.[21] Over the course of the thirteenth century, Low German became the lingua franca of the Baltic, as its principal speakers flocked to the new towns established in the wake of crusading campaigns. These communities of German merchants provided the critical mass that enabled the Hanse to become a transnational organisation.

URBAN PARADIGMS IN THE EAST BALTIC

Towns established in the conquered territories during the Baltic Crusades should be understood as collaborative ventures between secular or religious rulers, merchants, the Church and indigenous groups. They served as economic pillars supporting the military outposts established in the conquered territories, as outposts for trade with access to new markets and as footholds for the Catholic faith. After the original spate of Christian plantations, more urban centres would be founded, particularly in Prussia, where they were used to bolster the Teutonic Order's rapidly developing economy. Across the conquered territories governed by different authorities, there were differences both in the intensity of urbanisation and how towns were run. Up until the mid-sixteenth century, nineteen towns were founded in Livonia. With the exception of Riga, all had been established alongside castles, of which ten were located within the Teutonic Order's lands. In Danish Estonia, Reval was granted the use of the Lübeck Law, whilst in the rest of Livonia, Riga's Law was applied, initially derived from Gotland with its revision informed by Hamburg's ordinances.[22] In Finland, the process of urbanisation was much slower, and only six towns were founded before the mid-fifteenth century, two of which developed around monasteries. Here, Swedish laws prevailed, and only two medieval towns with sizeable populations of German burghers adopted the Lübeck Law – Åbo and Viborg – and this was relatively late. The situation was also different in Prussia, largely due to the influence of the main landowner, the Order. This region experienced the highest rate of urbanisation in the wake of the crusades, with ninety-six towns established, the majority on the Order's lands. Of these, only seven were granted the Lübeck Law, with most organised under the Order's own Kulm Law, itself derived from the widely used Magdeburg Law. In Livonia and Prussia, German laws were new to urban communities, but when the Order annexed Pomerelia, it adjusted the legal systems of existing towns, many of which had begun adopting German frameworks for trade and governance. In Prussia, the Order also extended the use of such protocols to organise rural settlements. The bureaucracy of exploiting the conquered lands became a well-oiled machine.

Like the Wendish towns, the towns established in the east Baltic became multi-ethnic centres where migrants and indigenes cohabited. Over time, many towns outgrew their walls and some had expansive suburbs which, in some cases, developed into separate settlements. The most important would become fully integrated into the trading networks that connected them with the rest of Catholic Christendom; a dozen Livonian towns would become members of the Hanse, nine in Prussia (at its greatest extent) and three in Finland. Our knowledge of life in these towns and the reach of their networks varies from one place to the next. One of the best-known is Elbing. Its historic centre was completely destroyed in 1945, although its medieval layout survived and, now part of Poland again with its official name Elbląg (as it had been in 1466–1772), began to be documented in the 1950s, after which intensive archaeological excavations took place in the 1980s–1990s. Thanks to the incredible preservation of organic material in the town's waterlogged soils, it has become one of the most important medieval urban archaeological sites in Europe.[23]

The initial settlement was not organised in a systematic way, and dwellings were built with little attention to their relative alignment. But there was a focus – the market street, which divided the settlement in two and where the main civic buildings were raised. In the centre, a town hall was built for the merchant oligarchy that came to represent the town and in front of it a pillory, symbol of civic justice. Across from this was the parish church of St Nicholas, where a cemetery was laid out and began to be used from the mid-thirteenth century. A trading post was also constructed which would later develop into a so-called *Artushof*, a communal guild house, along with a Dominican monastery in the northwestern corner of the town, with a church dedicated to the Virgin Mary.

All other buildings in the early settlement consisted of detached, single-storey timber-framed structures filled with wattle and daub, and heated by stone hearths. They sat on plots separated by narrow streets which ran off the long market towards the river. These were the dwellings of artisans and labourers, perhaps even the Pomerelians and Prussians who provided crockery and tableware for the settlers. There were certainly indigenous villages in the vicinity, and they must have become regular suppliers of provisions, which otherwise had to be shipped in. It is around this time that the oldest known German-Prussian dictionary was compiled in Elbing. The earliest surviving copy of the so-called *Elbinger Vokabular* dates from the end of the fourteenth century, although it appears to have gone through several iterations. It consists of a list of 802 Old Prussian words alongside their German counterparts, organised into thematic sections, and represents one of the few written sources for the indigenous Prussian language.[24] It was most likely compiled early on by the colony's merchants who were engaged in local trade, for, as in the case of the Rus', communicating with the local market would have given them a strong competitive edge.[25]

Indeed, the Order was keen to promote trade in all the towns founded by its castles, as they provided a solid basis for its own 'crusading economy'. Elbing became a crucial point on the Order's supply chain, as its armies pushed further east into Prussia. By the mid-thirteenth century, this had become the most important political centre in the conquered territories, and the town was rapidly developing into a major Baltic port. Suburbs soon emerged which contained hospitals, inns, taverns, brothels, mills and manufacturing areas. In 1246, the Order officially confirmed that Elbing would be governed by Lübeck's Law, with the stipulation of loyalty to the town's overlord, as quoted at the start of this chapter. A good measure of the town's mercantile growth is indicated by how its codex rapidly developed, from an initial 82 articles to 256 within fifty years.[26]

During this time, large quantities of stoneware vessels, particulary from the Rhineland and Saxony, as well as from Saintonge (in West-

Central France), and glazed ceramics produced in Flemish-Dutch, Danish and north German workshops were imported into the town. They are a solid measure of the purchasing power of Elbing's burghers and the town's integration into the emerging Hanseatic network – these sought-after wares are found in all the major towns of the Baltic.[27] As elsewhere, indigenous pottery was soon replaced by the greyware brought in by migrant potters who constructed new kilns. By the 1280s, greyware pots were being manufactured en masse. This is evident from the excavation of a potter's workshop, where archaeologists discovered over 80,000 shards of wheel-thrown greyware, derived from a range of vessels, including pots, bowls, jugs, lamps and even spindle whorls and fishing weights. The specific design of the pots has led to suggestions the potter originated from Thuringia or Upper Saxony.[28]

The workshop was exceptionally preserved because it had been destroyed in a fire in 1288, which also wiped out most of the town. It is not known whether this was the result of an accident or a Lithuanian raid. However, this gave the town's leaders the opportunity to replan and impose a more regular layout over the next few decades, one that would remain fixed into the eighteenth century. A new brick wall was constructed, and the town hall was rebuilt in grander style, with the addition of a 36-metre-long 'cloth hall', where archaeologists discovered large quantities of imported ceramics.[29] Timber was gradually phased out as the principal building material and, by 1360, there were over a hundred brick buildings in the town. Many would have had step-gables, characteristic of late medieval civic and religious buildings across the Hanseatic world. As street levels were built up, the entrances of these houses were also elevated, and eventually these ended up being located on first floors, with cellars occupying the lower level. Their interiors became split between residential, administrative and storage spaces, with outbuildings, wells and one or more latrines in their yards, where animals might also be kept. Heating was now more likely to be produced by stoves with glazed tiles, manufactured locally but sporting German designs. Almost every house was furnished with pipes made from hollowed-out oak trunks, which provided water for cooking and for bathing in wooden tubs. Sewage, in turn, was channelled out through log-lined ditches.[30]

Most of the tableware and kitchenware found inside these buildings, wells and latrines were locally manufactured, but in the fourteenth century there was a dramatic increase in imported goods, as the port became crowded with granaries, warehouses and shipyards. Cogs dropped off regular cargos of stoneware jugs and glass drinking vessels – over a thousand fragments of glassware have been found during excavations in Elbing, originating from across Europe, especially Bohemia and southern Germany – barrels of wine, cod and herring, the staples of the stock fish trade, and exotic spices and foods such as black pepper, nutmeg and figs.[31] The quantities of imported ceramics are particularly striking, as they are in the other ports of the east Baltic, leading some to argue the decision to purchase stoneware vessels was not just about seeking to emulate aristocratic dining culture, but also about expressing a common 'Hanseatic identity'.[32] Finds of a small bowl, two plates and fragments of an *albarello* – a majolica earthenware jar – all decorated in the *mudéjar* style are rare imports from Andalusia and Valencia, most likely gifts or personal purchases, and testify to the reach of the Hanse's network.[33] Some 50 per cent of Elbing's clothing was also imported, with the most luxurious represented by Flemish and Italian silk. The cogs then filled their holds with the staple exports of the east Baltic ports – grain, timber (Elbing was one of three ports in Prussia exporting timber, along with Gdańsk and Königsberg), furs and wax, although the full range of commodities exported from the town was incredibly diverse.[34]

The majority of Elbing's original inhabitants hailed from Westphalia, the Rhineland and Thuringia, but there were also burghers from Pomerelia and other parts of Prussia.[35] Written sources indicate that indigenous Prussians made up around 3 per cent of the population of the Old Town; however, there is no archaeological evidence to date of distinctive indigenous material culture in the town's later phases.[36] This probably reflects the relatively rapid 'Germanisation' of indigenous communities here and in other Prussian towns. Indigenous people would have invariably formed part of Elbing's poor, who are largely invisible in both the written and archaeological record, but would have been an ever-present part of the population. Whilst the urban landscape, as in other towns, came to reflect the disparities between rich and poor, the great social levellers became the town's bath houses.[37] Here Elbingers from across all walks of life could meet, where social barriers were temporarily suspended. Hospitals were also set up for the town's residents, and there were three in Elbing, the earliest constructed by the Order in 1277, which later became passed into the hands of the town council and also served as a refuge for lepers.

As the town grew, its central cemetery was relocated outside the walls, and the land around the church was built up with artisanal workshops. This growth spilled out into a nearby suburb, which became the focus for a new settlement in the early fourteenth century. Within a few decades, it had been structured by the Order into Elbing's 'New Town', with a parish church dedicated to the Three Kings, and in 1347 it was granted a modified version of the Lübeck Law. By the early fifteenth century, both towns had an estimated population of around 8,500 residents and represented one of the largest urban complexes in medieval Prussia. The growth of the town was sustained not only by imports but by the development of its rural hinterland. Elbing's *patrimonium* – land owned by its residents which could be rented out or used for farming, pasture and forestry – was the largest out of all the Prussian towns, covering an area of 200 km^2.

The Order's castle at Elbing remained a construction site for several decades as it was expanded, and would eventually dominate the town's skyline. Although the convent officially lost its status as the provincial centre in 1309, it remained one of the most important in the Order's Baltic territories. It became the residence of the grand hospitaller and one of the Order's Prussian mints was also located here. The castle's chapel, dedicated to St Andrew, contained numerous relics including a piece of the True Cross and a fragment of the Virgin Mary's robes. It served as an important centre for local pilgrimage, but pilgrim badges found in the town also demonstrated that some of its residents took long penitential journeys, visiting shrines in Maastricht, Cologne, Compostela and Rome.

The Order's military strength derived, in part, from the obligations of its urban tenants, and Elbing's burghers were no different. They participated in campaigns against the Prussians and subsequently against the Lithuanians – the *Elbinger Kriegsbuch* (*Elbing's 'War Book'*) documents this for the years 1321, 1360 and 1377. In 1410, Elbing's burghers contributed to the Order's forces at Tannenberg. Although relations between the town and its overlord had been generally good up to that point, the war with Poland saw this deteriorate, as Elbing's burghers felt increasingly alienated by the Order's style of governance and what they saw as the infringement of their rights. In 1440, the town joined the Prussian Confederation – a coalition which sought to end the Order's dominance and align with the Kingdom of Poland, hoping for a better economic deal. When the Polish king signalled his support early in 1454, the townspeople rose up and destroyed the Order's castle. This moment symbolised the town's break from the over two centuries of rule by the Order, and, just over a decade later, Elbing was formally incorporated into Poland.

COHABITING URBAN CULTURES

In contrast to Prussian towns, the indigenous urban population in Livonia is much more visible.[38] The best example is provided by Reval, today Tallinn, the modern capital of Estonia, which has some exceptionally preserved late medieval archives and has also seen bursts of excavations particularly in the decades after the Second World War, with more than eighty carried out within the town's walls by 2024.[39] Its Old Town was first defined as a protected area in 1951, and it has been on UNESCO's world heritage list since 1998 as an exemplar of a medieval North European trading city. There were changes to its appearance in the nineteenth century, and in March 1944 Soviet bombing destroyed the southern areas of the Old Town, but large parts have survived intact, including the layout and its medieval fortifications.

Archaeologists have demonstrated the earliest settlement here dates to the pre-crusade period, located on the eastern side of the Tõnismäe hillock. Some have argued this was also a place of trade, making it an attractive location for establishing a Danish foothold in Estonia.[40] The Danes built their castle on nearby Toompea Hill in 1219, where there are also traces of an earlier indigenous settlement and perhaps a pagan religious site.[41] Later on, the Sword Brothers would build their castle in the south-western corner of the hilltop. This would become the residence of the Danish governor again between 1238 and 1346, after which it was rebuilt by the Teutonic Order for use as a convent. Toompea Hill developed into an elite settlement – the 'upper town' – where the episcopate and vassals also resided. Down the eastern slope there is evidence for buildings dating to the first half of the thirteenth century, and here a three-aisled church was built and dedicated to St Nicholas. Its design suggests that Gotlanders were involved in its construction. Burials excavated near the church were recently dated to the eleventh and twelfth centuries, indicating the presence of a pagan burial ground, and it is possible St Nicholas's may have served as the first parish church for the local Christianised Estonians.[42]

To the north-east, closer to the harbour, settlement clusters emerged around two churches: St Olaf's, most likely intended for Scandinavian traders, and St Nicholas's for Rus' merchants, although the earliest phases of both are difficult to date.[43] In time, the settlement areas between the harbour and Toompea Hill would form the 'lower town'. The growing port attracted significant numbers of Germans, which included burghers from Lübeck, and cooking vessels appear to have been brought over from what is today western Germany.[44] Many were involved in trade, but there were also artisans, and their presence helped foster close economic and cultural ties with their hometown. This was, of course, part of the story of the Hanse, and so when the Danish king granted the town the Lübeck Law in 1248, it was a strategic move to promote commerce and integrate Reval into the growing Hanseatic network, acknowledging the advantage that German merchants had in trading with Novgorod. This move, in turn, attracted more German settlers and strengthened Lübeck's influence – by the end of the fourteenth century, Lübeck's share in the maritime trade of Reval was around one-fifth or one-sixth of its total volume.[45]

Archaeologists have discovered that the earliest houses in the town were timber cross-log houses with heating stoves in their corners, identical to those found in rural settlements. These would have been built by Estonians but used by all ethnic groups until enough Scandinavian and German builders were present for timber-framed and stone architecture to become the norm. Mixed building traditions are evident, where for example timber-framed buildings included stoves associated with Estonian dwellings.[46] As Reval's population increased over the second half of the thirteenth century, larger stone and timber-framed buildings were constructed, following the same German architectural trends evident in the other Livonian towns. These would be later rebuilt and enlarged into multi-room, step-gabled houses with residential and storage spaces. As plot boundaries stabilised, an internal street plan emerged, along with a fixed location for the market square and town hall, the core of the 'lower town'. Monastic institutions represented by the Dominicans and Cistercians clustered around the edges of this core, particularly on its eastern side. Whilst the 'upper town' was fortified early on, the first wall around the 'lower town' was only constructed in 1265 and then expanded to enclose the built-up area to the north around 1310. Like the walls of other Baltic towns, it played a defensive role, but it was equally important for defining the town's boundary. This contributed to a visual sharpening of difference between the rural population, which was almost entirely indigenous Estonian, and the urban population, which was heterogenous but lived in a Germanised environment.

Reval grew to become the second biggest town in Livonia after Riga, and by the mid-fourteenth century, it had an estimated population of between 4,000 to 5,500 residents. It is difficult to judge the relative representation of different ethnic groups at this time, but sixteenth-century records indicate around half of the population was Estonian, some 30–40 per cent were German, with smaller numbers of Scandinavians, Finns and Rus'.[47] Reval's town books, guild statutes and legal documents made clear distinctions between the German burghers, Estonians, Swedes and Rus'. The most privileged and affluent group were German merchants and artisans, who continued to emigrate from the northern provinces of the Holy Roman Empire throughout the later thirteenth and fourteenth centuries. For example, Germans dominated the most prestigious metal-working professions in the town – in the fourteenth century, they accounted for thirty-eight out of forty-six known goldsmiths, silver-smiths and minters in Reval, with only three Estonians or Scandinavians, and two Rus', and from 1393, membership of the guild of goldsmiths would only be permitted to Germans.[48] German burghers dominated the town council and principal 'Great Guild', and distinguished themselves by their clothes – sewn from imported fine woollen fabrics trimmed with lace, silk and broidery or outerwear coats, hats and removable collars lined and trimmed with furs. They also sported the latest trends in Western footwear. The wealth of these burghers is attested in their wills, which list various luxuries in the late fourteenth and fifteenth centuries, but also in the large multi-room houses they built, predominantly in the central parts of the town. These were warmed by heat-storage hypocausts, of which over fifty examples have been identified in medieval buildings in Tallinn, although this represents just a small percentage of the original number. They have also been found in other Livonian towns, castles and monasteries, and over the course of the fifteenth century they were replaced by glazed-tile stoves.[49]

Estonians represented the other major ethnic group in Reval. Whether migrating from nearby villages in search of employment or born in the town, they worked as artisans and labourers and preserved elements of their traditional dress, as commented on by contemporaries and indicated by finds of indigenous jewellery in different plots across the town. As in Riga's 'Liv quarter', relative poverty intersected to a large degree with ethnic identity. In comparison to the finer clothes of wealthier German burghers, those worn by Estonians were distinguished by cheaper, homespun linen and coarse wools. Their diet was similar to that of indigenous rural communities with its reliance on wheat, rye and barley, although those who could afford to also consumed millet, imported from the southern Baltic.[50] Many Estonians continued to live in timber houses, not having the financial means to replace them in stone. But by the end of the fourteenth century, the town council forbade the construction of wooden houses within the walls, and in some cases ordered their Estonian owners to build stone houses in their place as a condition for the legal rights to claim ownership of those plots. This type of ordinance was intended to prevent fires and was enacted in towns across the Baltic Sea region at various times, but it also resulted in pushing out those who could not afford to upgrade their houses, reshaping the town's landscape according to affluence and, by association, German and Germanised identities.[51]

At the same time, Estonians (like indigenous urban dwellers elsewhere in Livonia) clearly rubbed shoulders with those from other ethnic groups of the same social class. This is most visible within workshops or guilds that were multi-lingual environments and explains how foreign fashions and technologies were adopted. For example, the manufacture of bone combs appears to have been introduced by migrating artisans, as such objects are rarely found in Estonian rural settlements and those produced in Reval are similar in design to those found in the late medieval phases of Scandinavian towns. Indigenous metalworkers also adopted the use of imported German-style crucibles, which became the norm in the fourteenth century. Leatherworkers and cobblers emulated contemporary footwear fashions in Scandinavia and northern Germany; however, indigenous potters continued to produce largely unglazed earthenware vessels, which differed noticeably from imported stonewares favoured by the wealthier burghers. Although there was some early experimentation with glazes, indigenous potters only appear to have started imitating Western imports in the fifteenth and sixteenth centuries.[52]

The third distinct group in Reval was the Rus' community, which was clustered in the area of today's Sulevimägi in the northern part of the Old Town. Their known occupations were more diverse, and they worked as furriers, goldsmiths, shoemakers, smiths, masons and carpenters. However, as Orthodox Christians, they remained outsiders, with no possibility to become official citizens of the town, which required swearing an oath and joining guilds that followed Catholic traditions. In order to do so, they had to convert and assimilate, that is Germanise.[53] Part of the area associated with the Rus' community has been excavated, revealing little imported tableware in contrast to the households of German burghers. The majority of ceramics were locally produced vessels, resembling those from Novgorod and Pskov. Residues of melted glass inside ceramic crucibles have been found here, as well as in the Rus' district in Riga, suggesting that glassworking was one of the occupations of Rus' artisans.[54]

In the second half of the fourteenth century, the term 'non-German' (German *Undeutsche*) entered legal discourse in Livonia. This was a social category rather than a strictly ethnic one, and recently it has been argued that it was largely applied to indigenous peasants and foreigners migrating to the region's towns.[55] Its use coincides with the replacement of Latin by Low German as the prevalent language of administration, and it was adopted to restrict membership of urban guilds, land ownership and participation in town councils. Traditionally, this has been understood as reflecting ethnic tensions within Livonia, but a more compelling interpretation has been related to urban demographic changes and economic decline in the later fourteenth and fifteenth centuries. The prohibition on non-Germans was predominantly used to protect economically important groups of merchants and artisans from the growing numbers of rural immigrants flocking to towns at this time. As a result, migrating rural Estonians hoping to improve the quality of their lives were pushed into low-income professions such as boatmen, servants, quarry workers and fishermen.[56] Similar responses are evident in Prussia in the second half of the fifteenth century, when small towns passed legislation restricting access to 'non-Germans' as a way of protecting the economic interests of urban artisans.[57]

Summarising cohabitation in medieval Reval and in other Livonian towns, the power dynamics that rapidly emerged after the crusades encouraged the definition of group identities and boundaries. These were expressed through distinct customs, language, diet and material culture and intersected with levels of affluence; in this respect, ethnicity played both a conscious and unconscious role in shaping group identity. But boundaries could also blur and there were pathways for indigenous people to adopt select elements (or the entire package) of the Germanised identity of the privileged social group.[58] In the case of Reval, most cross-group interaction would have been between Estonian, Finnish and Scandinavian inhabitants, who resided in the same neighbourhoods and socialised together. German merchants, in turn, would have engaged with indigenous Estonian servants in their households, and with those involved in the transport of goods from ships to warehouses. All groups would have met in public spaces such as the market, although there were evidently restricted private spaces where cultural conservatism could flourish.

The narrative of cohabitation differed from town to town and across regions, with the contrasts becoming most evident when examined through their material culture. In Prussia, as we have seen, the locals soon vanished into the Germanised urban environment. In Finland, indigenous people were treated on a more equal footing in the eyes of the law and both Swedes and Finns could participate in trade and urban life more freely. While certain professions or positions might have been dominated by Swedish settlers or other foreigners (like Germans), Finnish and Swedish cultures coexisted more fluidly across the Swedish realm and, over time, Finnish elites, in particular, were able to integrate into Swedish-speaking society.[59] In Livonia, the dynamics of cohabitation in medieval Reval and other towns serve as microcosms of the broader societal shifts following the crusades. Western migrants, particularly Germans, inhabited towns and castles and were largely absent from the countryside until the fifteenth and sixteenth centuries, when more began to acquire manors and engage in rural landownership.[60] Up until this point the sharpest cultural contrasts existed between towns and villages, and in the political struggles between the townspeople of Riga and the Order, both German and non-German were united. When the Order surrendered its castle in Riga to the townspeople on 8 May 1484, the town council issued a statement that everyone – rich and poor, old and young, German and non-German – had the right to take part in razing the castle to the ground. The demolition of the castle proceeded smoothly and was completed by mid-August.[61] It would only be many decades later, during the Reformation, that vernacular religious services resulted in the more pronounced ethnic segregation of congregations, which in turn influenced the composition of guilds and civic life.[62]

EXPLOITING THE COUNTRYSIDE

From the very onset of the Baltic Crusades, the exploitation of natural resources within the conquered territories became essential for sustaining military campaigns, garrisons and urban colonies. This developed into cohesive systems of land management, behind which lay an ideology that justified Christian rule. Pagan lands were perceived as abundant in natural resources but underdeveloped due to the perceived ignorance and chaos of their indigenous societies. Farming, at the heart of the colonisation practices adopted across the conquered lands, was to replace pagan disorder with a Christian paradise.[63] The reality was, of course, somewhat different. Cultivation, woodland management and animal husbandry had long been practised across the southern and eastern Baltic, and in some regions, such as the Polish-Prussian borderlands and north-west Estonia, there is evidence for intensive rotational farming before the crusades. The political and military power of indigenous elites residing in strongholds across the eastern Baltic had been underpinned by economies driven by trade in slaves, furs, honey, horses and rye, and the environmental records from the Late Iron Age indicate that the expansion of cultivated land within their territories was accompanied by deforestation, alongside intensive hunting and fishing. Following the crusades, levels of biodiversity continued to decrease, accentuating these earlier ecological trends and most visible in parts of Prussia and Livonia.[64]

The impact of regime change on the countryside was transformative in different ways in Livonia, Prussia and Finland. In the former, there were now taxes and tithes, but otherwise little appears to have changed in the daily experience of rural life. Laws governing Latgalian, Curonian and Semigallian peasants were established early on and permitted them to remain free and mobile, alongside the right to bear arms, own and inherit property, and trade.[65] As the indigenous population grew, new villages were established in a process sometimes referred to as 'internal colonisation', which saw marginal areas increasingly cultivated. Earlier husbandry regimes continued: for example, a genetic study of Estonian sheep indicated no changes in the population structure before the eighteenth century.[66] The same agricultural equipment continued to be used. The situation worsened for the peasantry in Livonia in the late fourteenth and fifteenth centuries, with the reshaping of the manorial economy intended to maximise profits through the imposition of serfdom.

In Prussia, migrating peasant families established over 1,000 new villages east of the Vistula between the last decades of the thirteenth century and the early fifteenth century, organised under the Kulm Law. They brought new ploughs, rotational farming, the cultivation of a broader range of crop species and new husbandry regimes. Improvements in fodder enabled farmers to increase the size of their livestock, maximising quantities of meat and wool. Grain production, which can be tracked in regional pollen records, became concentrated in the Kulmerland, then around the Lower Vistula and only later in the Prussian interior, mapping onto the documented waves of migrating peasants. In eastern Prussia, which had the highest density of rural indigenous communities, intensification in farming is only evident with the arrival of German and Polish settlers along with the creation of new, regulated settlements. Although Prussian communities had been conquered and taxed, in some areas where settlements were dispersed and the new authorities only had a limited presence, they proved to be more difficult to govern and perhaps even resisted demands to maximise their productivity. Accompanying rural colonisation was investment in new infrastructure for cereal processing, with the widespread construction of mills and granaries. The former were built close to villages, and channels were also dug to form mill runs – significant feats of hydraulic engineering which connected kilometres of waterways and lakes.[67]

But significant belts of woodland endured, managed as a resource by the new authorities. They provided habitats for beehives, which produced one of the most sought-after commodities transported along the Hanse's network – wax. They were also home to wild game and fur-bearers, but their most commercially valuable elements were hardwood species of tree such as hornbeam and oak. These were exported as lumber, shipped down major rivers like the Vistula and Daugava, whilst conifers served local construction needs and became the dominant feature of managed forests. This also explains why extensive woodland endured in regions which were densely settled. Woodland in eastern Prussia and parts of Livonia was more difficult to access, and would only be exploited more intensively in later centuries. In these regions there is evidence for continuity in cultivation, livestock husbandry, hunting and fishing, as indigenous communities continued to practise their traditional farming methods.

Similar trends are visible in Finland, where intensification in farming in the southern coastal regions coincides with the arrival of Swedish migrants, whilst the international market for furs drove the exploitation of the interior by indigenous hunters and trappers. At the Saami settlement in Geahcevainjarga, on a peninsula in Arctic east Finnmark, evidence for intensive hunting of reindeer in the late medieval period has been linked to Hanseatic commercial demands and the tributary requirements of the rulers of Norway and Novgorod. These external pressures created tensions within the Saami community, who nonetheless clung to their conservative lifestyles. The discovery here of a coin minted by the Teutonic Order in Reval in the first half of the fifteenth century indicates that even the distant Arctic, where the Saami lived at the edges of the Catholic and Orthodox spheres of influence, was not beyond the Hanse's reach.[68]

THE HANSE'S WORLD

The Hanse has been regarded by some as synonymous with the rise of capitalism, colonialism and proto-globalisation, and the urbanisation of the east Baltic – part of Catholic Christendom's expansion – played a key role in this.[69] From the very start, the leaders of the Baltic Crusades founded towns as a means to consolidate their military conquests, establishing footholds in pagan lands. These were set up in collaboration with merchants, who formed communities in the newly established towns which became connected to each other across the Baltic through shared business interests and kinship, contributing to the development of an expansive network across which money, commodities, information and ideas moved freely. This movement was made possible by the cog, which transported large numbers of crusaders and cargo across the Baltic. Visby's German merchants played an important role in the early decades of the crusades but, over time, the centre of gravity for the newly emerging network – the Hanse – shifted to Lübeck. Even as this town's role as the singular birthplace of the Hanse has been demythologised, its influence on the urban centres established around the Baltic rim is difficult to overstate. It not only played a pivotal role in the establishment of regular trade between Western and Eastern markets, but also served as a model for key towns in the conquered territories to which many Lübeckers flocked. Once these regions had been militarily subjugated, there was further investment in urbanisation, a deliberate policy from the new rulers which went in step with the economic reorganisation of the countryside. With the simultaneous growth in urbanisation, resource exploitation and commerce came a dramatic increase in the complexity of bureaucracy, as paper came to replace parchment in the second half of the fourteenth century and Middle Low German became *the* written language for keeping records, managing territory and its natural resources.

As elsewhere, towns were reliant on produce from the countryside for their own sustenance. Large quantities of cattle bones excavated in all the major east Baltic urban centres indicate their populations became reliant on good-quality beef as a staple, along with grain which was now available in increasing quantities from the surrounding countryside and beyond. This grain also became sought after in Western Europe following shortages in the fourteenth and fifteenth centuries, a demand met by Prussia and to a lesser extent by Livonia. The towns of these regions, particularly the major ports, became the principal collection and redistribution centres of the surplus, its movement facilitated by the Hanse. Grain was, of course, produced by local peasants — the real drivers of change on the ground — who were obligated to provide a portion of their harvest as rent or tax to their lords. Some might be kept for local use, but a significant portion was then destined for sale in nearby markets or for export. Rural communities were therefore not segregated from towns in a fundamental economic sense, even if there were stark differences in the rhythm and character of daily life, and in this respect the Baltic Sea region shaped by the crusades very much became 'the Hanse's world'.

CHAPTER 10

OLD GODS, NEW GODS
Religion and Indigenous Resilience

> The German brothers have not allowed new converts to be baptised, claiming that they can be stronger as lords of pagans than of those who believe in God . . .
>
> Complaint of Christian, Bishop of Prussia, to Pope Gregory IX against the Teutonic Order[1]

SPIRITUAL ANXIETIES

In 1425, the synod of the Prussian diocese of Sambia gathered in the cathedral quarter on the island town of Kneiphof in Königsberg (Russian Kaliningrad). Headed by the charismatic bishop Michael Junge, the assembled churchmen noted with alarm how pagan practices were still widespread amongst the indigenous population in the diocese. Michael issued a decree urging the Prussians not to perform any pagan rituals in forests and groves, to refrain from baptising their children a second time in rivers and giving them names other than those officially given at their christening. This would be punished with a whipping or a fine of three pounds of wax, a valuable commodity. He also called on the Prussians to abandon performing heathen rites for their dead, to avoid gathering by burial mounds and graves according to pagan customs, not to invoke demons in forests or in their houses, to end sacrificial feasts and the offering of animals to demons. By demons, Michael, and his predecessors, had meant the local deities and ancestral spirits whom they regarded as misguiding and deceiving the indigenous peoples of the eastern Baltic.[2]

The recurring mention of forests in the synodical documents referred to one of many sacred natural sites that remained spiritually important for indigenous communities. Sacred groves were places where the dead had been cremated and ancestors honoured, and where the gods could be contacted and venerated. The synod decreed the punishment for any obstinance would be the deprivation of a proper burial.[3] From a medieval Christian perspective, a proper burial within consecrated ground and attended by a priest was an essential prerequisite for the soul's salvation, as well as a moral duty for the living. To be denied this, a punishment meted out to certain criminals and outcasts, including those who had been excommunicated, was to suffer the soul's damnation. By this time, Christian eschatology – beliefs concerning the fate of the soul after death – was more clearly defined. In 1179, the Third Lateran Council emphasised the importance of a proper burial, and conversely its denial as a sanction. Within a few decades, the concept of Purgatory was also formalised in Church doctrine. Whilst theologians continued to debate the importance of the integrity of the deceased body for salvation, preparations for death and the treatment of the body were believed to have an impact on the soul after death, along with the spiritual benefits of indulgences. In this respect, the denial of proper burial would have represented a fearful punishment – at least for those devoutly subscribing to a Catholic vision of the afterlife.

Three years after the decrees issued by Samland's religious authorities, the synod of Riga followed suit and condemned burials in unconsecrated places in the wilderness 'where their ancestors and relatives were buried in the times of heathendom'. Feasting in cemeteries was also forbidden.[4] Although the Church had recognised early on that new converts to Catholicism – or neophytes, as they were called – should be given some leeway and gradually weaned off their earlier beliefs, the synodical decrees in Prussia and Livonia suggested this was an uphill struggle. But what, in fact, do we know of indigenous spirituality after the crusades? Why did the Baltic Church seemingly fail to standardise religious practices? The prevailing narrative was for many centuries formulated by external observers – initially churchmen, then later on by mythologists and ethnographers. The principal chroniclers of the Baltic Crusades were clerics, and their brief descriptions of indigenous religious practices served as commentaries on pagan exoticism. The more elaborate accounts produced by the Polish priest Jan Długosz in the later fifteenth century and the Prussian Dominican Simon Grunau in the early sixteenth century were influenced by a resurging interest in Classical paganism, prompting the creation of pantheons for the pagan Balts.[5] A more critical approach came with the integration of archaeological evidence and a gradual rejection of a universal and timeless pagan Baltic culture.

Careful consideration of the fragmented written sources – not simply the chronicles but also episcopal regulations and correspondence, as well as legal and economic documents – has yielded valuable glimpses of the struggle to evangelise as well as the character of indigenous resilience in the face of the cultural upheavals following the crusades. From the late sixteenth century, Jesuits – who spearheaded the Counter Reformation as missionaries in parts of Prussia, Livonia and Lithuania – also encountered and documented what they regarded as enduring pagan practices, describing them in detail. Lutheran pastors did likewise. Settlement charters and boundary descriptions from the late medieval period through to the eighteenth century preserved numerous references to sacred natural sites. Folklore collected in the nineteenth and twentieth centuries, though very much a product of its time, contained echoes of earlier practices and beliefs, and scholars have remarked on similarities across neighbouring Balt and Finnic societies. All of these sources have to be considered together, and whilst noting that no culture is frozen in time, some elements of indigenous spiritual practices endured in a recognisable form, such as the continuing sacred role of certain natural sites.

But if a general impression for the adoption of Christianity across the eastern Baltic is difficult to grasp, this is because the tempo and character of religious transformation varied from place to place. The complaints of clerical authorities paint a confrontational picture of religious polarisation, especially between towns and the countryside, and this dichotomy has remained influential. Indigenous religious practices did, nonetheless, change into forms that were neither wholly Catholic, from the perspective of religious authorities, nor a replication of pre-Christian religion. A comparison can be drawn with the religious practices that emerged after the Spanish and Portuguese conquests of Central and South America, as well as those developed by enslaved African communities in the Caribbean. These were not straightforward adoptions of colonial Christianity, but rather a composite blend of beliefs and practices resulting in new expressions of spirituality.

THE STRUGGLE FOR SOULS

Christianity did not arrive in the eastern Baltic with crusading armies, as there had already been contact with both the Catholic and Orthodox worlds. Nonetheless, the violence of crusading campaigns was accompanied by mass baptisms, the imposition of tithes to support priests and the creation of dioceses. Some pagan sacred sites were destroyed during the crusades and in the decades that followed, but these were relatively infrequent incidents. Since most of the indigenous population resided in rural areas, successful evangelisation required a strong pastoral infrastructure that extended well beyond the towns. In Prussia and Finland, this would appear with the arrival of Catholic migrants, who sponsored the construction of rural churches. With them came an established Christian worldview, marking the cycle of life – birth, baptism, adulthood (the ability to 'reason', recognised at twelve years of age), marriage and death.[6] This worldview also included an understanding of prayer, the importance of confession, penance and absolution, the miracle of transubstantiation and the sacred nature of the Host, an appreciation of indulgences, the value of pilgrimage and the power of relics, a fear of excommunication, the observance of fasting, as well as weekly church attendance, participation in feast days and proper funerary rites. The statutes of the Pomesanian diocese from 1411 indicate the faithful were expected to attend at least a hundred masses in a year connected with feast days, of which fifty-two took place on Sundays.[7] Evangelising indigenous communities was, therefore, not just a question of introducing a new deity with a set of prayers and buildings for worship: it was a fundamentally different way of living, thinking and relating to other people.

But if there were problems with enforcing correct religious observances in regions with the densest populations of Catholic migrants after the crusades, such as the dioceses of Kulm and Pomesania in western Prussia, which episcopal documents suggest there were, the situation further east must have seemed almost insurmountable. In Warmia, indigenous Prussians made up some 50–75 per cent of the population, further east in Natangia they accounted for as much as 90 per cent, whilst the population of Sambia was almost entirely Prussian, with a few scattered migrant enclaves. The slow pace of introducing a pastoral infrastructure can be seen at a glance in the western swathes of the Prussian territory of Bartia, where governance was split between the Teutonic Order and the Warmian episcopate following the crusades. The region remained a frontier into the mid-fourteenth century, the target of devastating Lithuanian raids which saw the destruction of castles and prompted the fortification of urban colonies. Here, the earliest chapels are documented in the Order's castles at Leunenburg (Polish Sątoczno) and Rastenburg (Polish Kętrzyn) in the 1320s, but parish churches would only be built from the late fourteenth or early fifteenth century. By the time the pastoral infrastructure had been established here the region had become another frontier: between Catholic Warmia and Lutheran Ducal Prussia. In Livonia, the demographic differences were as extreme as in easternmost Prussia, with the German-speaking population essentially confined to towns, castles and manors. The construction of churches and chapels beyond the towns varied across the region, and here it depended on investment from the various religious authorities who governed the conquered territories, as well as the relative density of the population. This was most intensive on the lands of the episcopates, particularly in the Lower Daugava and parts of Estonia. In contrast, there were very few in Curonia, Semigallia and large swathes of south-eastern Livonia.[8]

Building churches for the use of indigenous communities was a start, but church attendance was another matter. The Bishop of Warmia, Henry Sorbom, was appalled when indigenous Prussian villages selected two people to attend churches and feast days, as representatives of the whole community. This was, after all, missing the whole point. Sorbom demanded that all adults attend to hear the Word of God on pain of a fine of one shilling, unless there was a good reason — such as fighting in defence of their homeland or working for their lords.⁹ In fact, the Teutonic Order was accused several times of obliging its indigenous subjects to do just that, rather than attend Mass, and certainly the laws issued by grand masters in the fifteenth century permitted their subjects to work on Sundays and feast days.¹⁰ The brethren were not alone in trying to maximise the labour from their subjects: some bishops did the same. Erratic church attendance was also compounded by a lack of priests who spoke the indigenous language, making the communication of the Church's teachings through a crucial part of the Mass, the sermon, almost impossible. Eventually, this became a requirement of episcopal decrees, particularly teaching the three fundamental prayers to indigenous congregants in their own language.

In Prussia, the greatest challenges lay in the Sambian diocese. Here in the early fourteenth century, Bishop Siegfried of Regenstein ordered church altars to be decorated with crucifixes and biblical images – the standard means of communicating the teachings of the Church. A century later, this demand would be repeated by Bishop Junge, who also clarified that all Prussians from the age of twelve had to attend their parish church on Sundays and religious feast days. Those who did not fulfil their obligations had to report to the Order's bailiffs and receive instruction from their parish priest. Junge demanded priests to preach in Prussian, but also referred to the use of interpreters, if required. Incentives were provided. The Pomesanian statutes of 1411 offered ten-day indulgences to those who made confession, took part in masses, witnessed the elevation of the Host, listened to the Gospel and participated in Christian burials. Those who attended the Mass for the patron saint of the diocese of Pomesania, St John the Evangelist, and recited the Our Father and Hail Mary three times would obtain a forty-day indulgence; in Sambia, the patron who was honoured in this way was St Adalbert, the missionary martyr.¹¹ Of course, the effectiveness of these incentives depended on an understanding of the concept of Purgatory and the spiritual value of an indulgence.

The problem of church attendance was also evident in parts of northern and eastern Finland. Here, the few churches were located significant distances from many communities, and, in 1504, Bishop Laurentius Suurpää of Åbo complained to the Swedish royal council that the people of Savonia and Karelia attended church services once every three or four years, and that children died without being baptised. Some inhabitants had never even seen a church, let alone stepped inside one. The bishop received support for creating more chapels in the east to enable priests to reach these communities. Most criticism fell on the Saami, who were regularly described as obstinate pagans.[12]

A further challenge to evangelising the population was the sparse number of monasteries established in the eastern Baltic. These institutions had played a vital role in supplying intrepid missionaries, and they were a ubiquitous feature of western Catholic societies where they provided not only pastoral support but also essential welfare services ranging from hospitals to orphanages and regularly played the role of powerful landowner. In Finland, Livonia and Prussia, relatively few monastic communities were established, the majority being Dominican or Franciscan houses in large towns. Foundations in sparsely populated areas, even within the safe confines of a migrant community, were difficult to sustain. Friars certainly contributed to promoting the Church's teachings in towns and, as indigenes had joined some of the orders, they were able to preach to their own. In the countryside, there were invariably attempts to evangelise indigenous communities, but as the Dominican Simon Grunau noted from experience, this could be dangerous – when he visited a indigenous Prussian village the people wanted to kill him, and he was only spared by appealing to their *waidlott* (vaidelot – an officiant) using the few words of Prussian he knew. He then had to swear by the pagan thunder god that he would not say anything to the bishop (the territorial ruler) and was obliged to witness the ritualistic sacrifice of a goat. Simon, confused by what he saw, tried to interpret the events through his Christian mindset.[13]

It is clear the Church was battling more than just enduring paganism in the eastern Baltic. From the recurring attempts at enforcing correct Christian instruction amongst the clergy, as well as Catholic congregants, the prevention of heretical beliefs and practices was as pressing a concern as the evangelisation of pagans and neophytes. Religious standards were also variable within the Teutonic Order's ranks. The politics of the Christian elites, especially in Livonia, were punctuated by intrigue, coercion, abductions, assassinations and sometimes full-blown military conflict; the Order was even known to ignore the sacred rule of sanctuary, killing its enemies sheltering inside churches – an offence usually punishable by death.[14] If the religious authorities could not even lead by example, it is not surprising that religious conformity across the indigenous population was difficult to achieve. But this population was also far from being passive subjects.

INDIGENOUS RESILIENCE

On 18 October 1252, the Bishop of Courland and a representative of the Teutonic Order issued a joint document concerning the ownership of woodland within the newly formed parishes, which specified that woods previously referred to as 'holy' were exempt from felling.[15] This sentiment was repeated the following year as the bishop and the Order were subdividing the governance of Curonian lands, singling out indigenous religious sites as exempt from economic transactions and land division. Instead, sacred woods and trees would come to feature as boundary markers in numerous later charters. This was not out of any concern to preserve local traditions, but co-opting indigenous sacred sites into the new regime's administration of its territories may have represented the path of least resistance towards the effective governance of the conquered population. The effect of this approach is visible on a much larger scale in southern Estonia, which was split between the governance of the Bishop of Dorpat and the Teutonic Order. Here, the limits of religious authority were clearly defined by the proliferation of sacred natural sites which existed alongside the Christianised landscape of churches and chapels.[16] At the same time, they overwhelmingly reflect indigenous agency. The proliferation of new sacred trees, lakes, hills and stones, which are recorded much later, can be connected with the growing indigenous population, with younger generations establishing new villages along with new sacred sites. Unlike the construction of a chapel or church, the designation of a natural feature in the landscape was relatively quick and simple.

This process is evident in other parts of the eastern Baltic and the type of ritual that may have been involved was described by the cleric Matthaeus Praetorius in the seventeenth century, here in the case of 'creating' sacred trees in Samogitia.[17] The officiant would summon a 'god' (*Gott*) into a designated tree over the course of a three-day ceremony that involved prayers and fasting. The presence of the god would be indicated by a strong shaking of the tree's branches, which would often also be accompanied by an inhuman mumbling. If the ritual failed, it could be attempted again after a short time, and if it failed again the officiant would be required to smear the tree with his own blood or, if that did not have the desired result, with that of his child. A successful ritual concluded with further offerings and a festival celebrated by the local community. In this respect, if the tree was cut down by a zealous cleric, another could be selected and the ritual repeated. This made it virtually impossible to suppress sacred natural sites within communities that were actively intent on using them. When it came to immovable features such as lakes, the only thing religious authorities could do to mitigate the supernatural powers attributed to them was to perform exorcism rituals, as Jesuits would do in south-eastern Estonia after the Livonian War. Relatively few sacred natural sites in the eastern Baltic have been investigated by archaeologists, and so the long-term chronology of their use has been difficult to pin down. The most detailed studies have been conducted in Estonia, indicating that some sites only began to attract ritual activity in the nineteenth or twentieth centuries.[18]

More is known of the emergence of a Christian sacred landscape in the countryside of the eastern Baltic. Alongside the construction of parish churches, a larger number of chapels were also built, initially as relatively simple timber structures. Some of these were built during or soon after the crusades, as demonstrated by excavations at the Chapel of Helme in southern Estonia where the discovery of coin deposits dated the first timber building to the mid-thirteenth century.[19] These became places where the worlds of Catholicism and indigenous spirituality overlapped. Whilst some pre-Christian sacred sites were replaced with such chapels, the majority were not. Their contemporaneous presence has often been interpreted as evidence for parallel religious systems, which occasionally intersected.[20] This is also how the process of religious transformation has been viewed in other parts of Europe. The term 'syncretism' has been confusingly used to refer to both two separate religions existing side by side as well as to a blending of different elements to create a hybrid set of religious beliefs and practices. Religion, as experienced by indigenous communities in the post-crusade period, can perhaps be more cautiously described as increasingly composite, with noticeable differences between towns and the countryside, and across regions.[21]

A new religious calendar was introduced, mapped in part onto existing seasonal festivities. Amongst the most important feast days introduced by the Church was that of St John. Celebrated on 24 June, this was important in the liturgical calendar as it preceded the birth of Christ six months later, whilst its seasonal significance, marking the end of crop sowing, and embedded with apotropaic customs to purge malevolent forces, ensured it also became the most important feast day for rural communities after Christmas. In Livonia, it became merged with the existing symbolism of the summer solstice, and in turn with sacred sites connected with the sun such as Sauleskalns (Hill of the Sun) in Krāslava, Latvia, but more often these were renamed 'Jana kalni' ('John's hills'), with over seventy-five such sites documented.[22] In fact, a broad range of sacred natural sites, from springs to boulders, were renamed after John and became the focus for the saint's feast day celebrations. In this way, the memory of earlier sacred places was in one way preserved, and in another transformed. It is unclear if the lighting of bonfires was a continuation of an indigenous tradition – the use of fire on this day is documented earlier in other parts of Europe, which some have connected with pre-Christian roots, others with the Christian symbolism of light and John the Baptist. Irrespective of whether clerics or farmers led the way in popularising the feast of St John in the countryside, it was enthusiastically perpetuated by subsequent generations. The association of midsummer festivities with St John was also mirrored in Prussia and Finland.

More evidence for grassroots adoption of Christian elements can be seen with the rural cult of St Anthony in Livonia, and particularly in Estonia. Here, the saint's popularity is reflected in large numbers of rural chapels and in the widespread celebration of his feast day on 17 January, when gifts were left at these chapels, as well as by specific trees and stones that, as in the case of St John, became attached to St Anthony. These are largely known from the seventeenth century, indicating their persistence amongst rural communities after the Reformation. Tõnis, the Estonian rendering of the saint's name, also became a popular choice for male names, and pendants associated with his distinctive Tau cross were produced by local artisans. Whilst St Anthony was also venerated in Livonia's towns, in 1428, the condemnation of the saint's rural chapels and images by Riga's synod suggests a separation between the spirituality promoted by Livonia's religious authorities and that of the indigenous peasantry. The saint was invoked to protect against ergotism (poisoning from consuming rye contaminated with the ergot fungus) and plague, but his popularity in the countryside most likely reflected his association with pigs, which extended to the supernatural protection of herds and farmers. Seventeenth-century observers described rituals in Estonia involving the sacrifice of pigs on St Anthony's Day, and in 1681 the Lutheran pastor of Võnnu complained that the saint was revered as a *Schweingötze* — a god of pigs.[23] Indeed, the particular and enduring focus on St Anthony, compared to other saints, has led to suggestions that he was syncretised with an indigenous deity connected with fertility and animals.[24]

In Prussia, the steady influx of Catholic migrants into the countryside resulted in a more developed Christian sacred landscape, although this was slow to emerge in the eastern regions dominated by indigenous communities. Here too, the encounter between indigenous and imported beliefs also resulted in the emergence of grassroots pilgrimage centres. The most important was the site of Heiligelinde (Polish Święta Lipka), part of a cluster of indigenous sacred sites whose memory had become fossilised as their toponyms were written down. The place name Heiligelinde refers to a sacred linden tree, a species that was associated with spiritual qualities in other parts of Prussia, Livonia and Lithuania; in the later folk traditions of Latvia and Lithuania such trees were associated with Laima, goddess of fate and childbirth.[25] Nearby, the toponym of Lake Denow (Polish Denjowa) connected it with ritualistic singing and dancing and also within the vicinity was Ramboten (Polish Ramty), a sacred grove. At some point in the fourteenth century, the tree at Heiligelinde became associated with the Virgin Mary, and by 1473 the site was attracting pilgrims hoping to be healed. Two decades later, the shrine would be endorsed by religious authorities, and a brick chapel was constructed around the linden tree. There are other instances where linden trees were directly connected with the Virgin Mary, not only in the eastern Baltic but also in neighbouring Poland, perhaps also mapping onto indigenous pre-Christian female deities. When the Reformation swept through eastern Prussia, the chapel at Heiligelinde was destroyed by local Protestants who cut down the tree and threw the sculpture of the Virgin into a nearby lake. The site was repurposed for executions with the construction of a gallows, but pilgrims continued to visit in secret. A century later, the Jesuits would oversee the building of a lavish baroque church here and revive the pilgrimage site which became a beacon of the Counter Reformation, and for which Święta Lipka is still known today.[26]

In Livonia, several examples of so-called 'folk pilgrimage' sites which are documented after the Reformation also appear to have had their origins in the late medieval period.[27] A seventeenth-century account describes how gatherings to offer coins at a spring called Uduallikas, near Viljandi in southern Estonia, associated with St Bridget involved a local, self-appointed female 'priest'; in 1836, coins found at the site were dated to between the late medieval period to the nineteenth century. One of the largest assemblages of deposited offerings has been found in coastal Vidzeme, in Latvia, where 628 coins were discovered, dating to between the fourteenth and nineteenth centuries, along with pieces of jewellery and clothing, fragments of clay pipes and other objects in the 'Cave of Offerings' (Latvian Lībiešu upurala) which had crosses and other symbols engraved into its sandstone walls, one of twenty-seven sacred caves documented in Kurzeme and Vidzeme.[28] Yet these examples, without a clear connection with a non-Christian deity, are better understood as composites of Catholicism and the memories of earlier religious sites.

Depositing artefacts such as coins in sacred places can be understood as examples of magical acts – attempts at connecting with supernatural forces for help, to influence events and avert crises, that took place at the margins of the Church's officially sanctioned devotional activities. Even in the heartlands of Catholic Europe, people engaged in a variety of colourful ritual acts which involved depositing objects, including coins, as well as animals within the foundations of buildings and bridges.[29]

These were not so much remnants of prehistoric religion as magical practices that existed within the context of a Catholic worldview, and whilst some were conducted in private, others were clearly very public acts, tolerated if not endorsed by the local clergy. In the eastern Baltic, the fading memory of earlier pagan practices appears to have been preserved in the places where these offerings were deposited, but archaeologists have demonstrated such activities began at least a century or two after the crusades. Then again, rituals such as the consecration of a sacred tree would not have left tangible traces and so the evidence for continuity largely rests on the documented creation of later sacred natural sites and the estimated antiquity of their toponyms.[30]

Some of these magical practices took place in churches or chapels and were clearly acceptable to local clerics, even if they diverged from the standard liturgical use of such spaces. Christian religious objects, such as the Bible, crosses (including the representation of the cross on a coin, perhaps the principal reason why coins became used as offerings), the consecrated Host, altar candles or even soil from a churchyard became part of the repertoire of symbols that were believed to be magically efficacious. Over a thousand coin finds are known from Estonian churches alone, the largest collection deriving from Harju-Risti where the earliest coins are dated to the fifteenth century, although most were deposited in the seventeenth and eighteenth centuries.[31] In Finland, over 13,500 coins have been found within churches, of which some 2,000 date to the medieval period.[32] The new religious buildings came to be regarded as places of spiritual power, alongside trees, stones and lakes. At the same time, people recognised a world of supernatural entities that was not endorsed by the religious authorities.

Clerics readily dismissed these as superstition at best or manifestations of the infernal at worst, and framed their observations of 'superstitious' or 'pagan' practices in the language of Classical religion. Jesuits engaged in missionary work in Livonia documented household rituals to appease domestic spirits which were referred to in Latin terms that were familiar from Roman paganism – Lares and Penates. Behind these rebrandings, there was clearly a thriving culture of ritual practices amongst rural communities. People would spill beverages such as beer and milk, as well as food, in certain parts of the house as offerings. Other rituals governed everything from choosing the location of a dwelling to protecting agricultural produce in barns.[33] The sauna, of central importance to indigenous village life in Finland, Livonia, Lithuania and Prussia, was regarded as a spiritually powerful place where women gave birth and the health of the newly born was protected, where people could be healed and curses lifted, and with distinctive objects such as the birch whisk, charms and songs, all of which are only recorded much later. At the same time, the sauna became associated with Christian notions of purification.[34]

More worrying for the Christian authorities was the enduring practice of animal sacrifice. In the sixteenth and seventeenth centuries, some ten episodes of animal sacrifice are documented in eastern Prussia and Lithuania.[35] The earliest of these is a fascinating account provided by the chronicler Lucas David, who described the ritual killing of a black bull in 1520 to protect the Sambian coast from Danzig's fleet in the midst of the war between the Teutonic Order and Poland. The presiding indigenous officiant, one Valtin Supplit, had even been given consent from the grand master himself to proceed. The event took place on the northern shore of the peninsula at Rantau,[36] where the bull was slaughtered and his bones and entrails were burnt, Valtin praying in the Prussian language to the gods whilst making strange gestures with his hands and feet, after which the meat, along with two specially selected barrels of good-quality beer, were served to men from the surrounding villages at a special feast – women were excluded from attending. This was reported to have had the desired effect and the hostile fleet moved away from the peninsula, although the ritual also appears to have driven off the local fish. Six or seven years later, following complaints from the local fishermen, Valtin performed a similar ceremony with the aim of restoring fish to the local waters. This time it involved the sacrifice of a black sow, again with a feast involving two barrels of beer and seventy-three men from eight villages in attendance. But times had changed, and the Reformation had begun to transform eastern Prussia. The celebrants were sanctioned by the reformed Church, and later retellings of the event were creatively exaggerated. Even before the Reformation, the Bishop of Sambia, George of Polentz, had been continuing the efforts of his forebears to instruct the indigenous congregants of his diocese in their own language and suppress the worship of the thunder god Perkun. In his new role as the first Protestant bishop of the duchy, he would double his efforts with pastoral provision, condemning the veneration of pagan deities by the Sudovians in his diocese.[37]

The Sudovians in Sambia were also singled out for sacrificing goats. Later accounts of sacrifices sought to link them to specific deities, at a time when a structured Baltic pantheon was being created on paper with the resurgent interest in Classical pagan religions. Hence in 1582, the chronicler Matthew Stryjkowski described how white piglets were sacrificed to a river god to purify the water, whilst the Jesuit Yearbook of 1605 specifies how a goat was killed and its blood poured into a river for the god Nosolum to bless the community with a bountiful harvest.[38] Yet there were recurring elements, such as the role of water, which also feature in accounts from Livonia. The sacrifice of children and cattle at lakes in south-eastern Estonia was reported by local Jesuits in 1583 who exorcised the lakes with holy water and the placement of crosses. Two years later, the papal legate Antonio Possevino, on a short visit to Dorpat after the end of the Livonian War, elaborated on this practice, describing how people abducted children and threw them into a certain lake, or shed the blood of an infant who would subsequently die, in order to prevent bad weather and destructive storms. He went on to write the Jesuits performed an exorcism of the lake which involved sprinkling holy water over it. Subsequently, the memory of this practice was preserved in a folkloric motif where children would be given to supernatural beings within lakes in exchange for money.[39] In Lithuania and Latvia, this is also echoed in a folklore motif of 'offering-requesting lakes', some of which required the forfeit of a life every year.[40]

Taking these accounts together, they draw on an indigenous repertoire of symbols, rituals and deities and are connected with a broader sacred landscape. They almost certainly preserved the memory of earlier religious sites, if not practices, associated with bodies of water but, by the time they were documented, they were closer to magical rather than devotional acts, intended to help the community at a time of crisis, or to prevent misfortune. In the same way that magical practices in the West drew on, and functioned within, a Christian cosmology, in the Baltic they operated within a composite and regionally varied worldview which selectively incorporated elements from indigenous spirituality, Catholicism and, in some regions, also Orthodox Christianity.

THE FATE OF SOULS

Indigenous Balt conceptions of the soul as a life force within every person had absorbed Slavic notions represented by the addition of the term *dusi* into the local languages from at least the tenth century, but this diverged from Christian thought by recognising the transformation of the soul after the death of the body into multiple forms. First, the *vėlė* that departed to the otherworld, a realm which mirrored the organisation of mortal society: those of high rank would retain their status in death and vice versa – this was not an egalitarian afterlife. Second, the soul known as the *siela* remained connected to the mortal world by inhabiting a tree, an animal – often a snake or toad, animals that could then be brought into the household – or even a newly born child.[41] A pluralistic understanding of the soul was also shared by Finnic societies, where it too could assume the form of an animal.

Following the crusades, the introduction of a new vision of the afterlife, centred on Purgatory and divine judgment, competed with existing beliefs recognising the spiritual potency of ancestral souls, connected with specific places in the landscape that were also recognised as sacred. Archaeologists have demonstrated that many indigenous cemeteries continued to be used after the crusades, and so they became places of cultural resilience where local identities, kinship structures and political allegiances, alongside beliefs in an afterlife diverging from mainstream Christian thought, were maintained. Over time, the treatment of the dead within these sites changed, and eventually these cemeteries were abandoned in favour of consecrated churchyards. In some regions, this was a rapid process; in others, it did not happen until the seventeenth or eighteenth centuries. The earliest surviving wooden grave markers in Lithuania date to the nineteenth century, and whilst the use of the cross is ubiquitous in both Catholic and Protestant cemeteries, some markers are decorated with zoomorphic shapes reminiscent of creatures such as toads, perhaps visual echoes of the pluralist soul that also endured in folklore and language.[42]

One of the most vivid examples of a persistent, if highly localised, ancestral custom is associated with a privileged group of indigenous vassals in Curonia who were 'free', called *koniņi* (which translates to 'kings'), living in a cluster of seven villages within the Teutonic Order's commandery of Goldingen (Latvian Kuldīga). Close to the villages were three sacred groves, identifiable in property documents and place names. In 1414, Guillebert de Lannoy, a French diplomat travelling through the region, appears to have witnessed the cremation of one of these 'kings' within a grove on a pyre of oak wood, the body dressed and adorned with the finest ornaments. He added the participants believed if the smoke rose up to the sky, the soul was saved; if it was blown to the side, it was lost. A later account sheds light on how such groves were perceived as spaces reserved for the dead. Reinhold Lubena, an apothecary from Königsberg, described his journey through Curonia in late December 1585, where the Curonian 'king' went hunting in the sacred forest in preparation for the feast of the dead. This was the one time such activities were permitted, as hunting and cutting timber in this forest was otherwise forbidden throughout the year. The catch of the hunt, roe deer, red deer and hares, were cooked and placed on a table with a large number of wax candles for the souls of the departed family members. Feasting and dancing around the table followed throughout the night, and any leftover food which the guests could not finish had to be fed to the dogs. Since these sacred forests were used for funerals, where the dead would travel to the otherworld through the medium of fire, these territories became reserved for the souls of the departed and, in this respect, whatever was inside them – plants and animals – also belonged to the dead. Subsequently, the sacred groves were reinterpreted in Christian terms, as later folklore connected them with the presence of legendary churches, the use of a stone as an altar and a linden tree carved with a cross where God was venerated. Given that some clerics regarded these ancestral souls as demons, the construction of crosses or chapels within such groves may also have reflected attempts to exorcise them. Nonetheless, taboos against breaking branches or lighting fires in the groves were documented amongst local villagers even two decades ago, faint memories of what had been the single permitted use of fire in the groves – for funerals.[43]

The continued practice of cremating high-ranking deceased individuals in natural places is also evident in eastern Prussia, where a funerary urn packed with burnt human bone was discovered in 1703 inside a barrow within the Forest of Eylau near Stablack (Polish Stabławki), along with a hoard of thirty coins dating to the early fifteenth century.[44] Burning the dead in sacred groves was exactly the type of pagan ritual the Baltic Church was hoping to suppress. These groves were at the heart of indigenous identity for they were connected with ancestral memory. In the same way that indigenous Prussians organised a 'second baptism', they were also accused of organising a 'second funeral', where pagan rather than Christian rites would be enacted. The recurring episcopal complaints concerning the use of unconsecrated cemeteries suggest this was widely practised in regions with substantial indigenous populations into the fifteenth century. Some groves also continued to be used for inhumation burials. At Aseri in northeast Estonia, the cemetery founded in the first century AD continued to be used after the crusades, with one grave containing a Tau cross depicting the crucifixion and dated to the fifteenth century. Such groves clearly had long ancestral histories.[45]

But archaeological excavations of indigenous cemeteries, particularly in the historical territory of Livonia, have also demonstrated gradual shifts in burial practices over time, with significant differences between towns, dominated by migrants and their descendants, and indigenous villages. When compared with contemporary customs in Western Europe, there are also striking differences. Here, priests and rulers were buried with their regalia, whilst most people were buried in shrouds. When archaeologists have excavated these graves, the majority of objects they have found typically represent the remnants of the shroud's fastenings. Crosses and crucifixes that were worn in life are rarely found in graves, as they were usually donated to churches or kept within the family as heirlooms.[46] However, additional objects were sometimes included, such as lead papal bullae, the only surviving traces of an indulgence document, as well as more elaborate artefacts such as medical trusses.[47]

In the eastern Baltic, burials in shrouds also appear during the crusading period and those inside churches are the most reminiscent of

Western practices; however, clothed burials, furnished with additional objects, remained prevalent amongst indigenous communities. Whilst some clerics urged shrouding the deceased, in imitation of Christ's own burial, clothing the dead body did not contradict the teachings of the Church. Both types were simultaneously practised in the same churchyards, perhaps reflecting the burials of migrants and indigenes, or at least those indigenes who had not adopted German cultural practices: both were clearly acceptable in the eyes of observing priests. Where indigenous people continued to be buried in richly furnished graves, the maintenance of social identity (perhaps even ethnic identity) through the use of traditional dress and bodily adornments is visible alongside the increasing acceptance of Christian funerary norms.[48]

Whilst the eschatology behind the contrasting rites may have differed, Catholic and indigenous pagan conceptions of the fate of the soul gradually converged, resulting in a composite set of beliefs and practices. At the end of the sixteenth century, Peter Culesius, an intrepid Jesuit who would become an active missionary in south-eastern Livonia, described beliefs in a parallel world of the dead, observed amongst indigenous peasants and one that would endure in later folklore.[49] In this otherworld, the dead had similar needs to the living and required food, clothing and items to function. Tools connected with the occupation of the deceased had to be included in the grave to enable them to continue to work in the afterlife. In Livonia, the practice of depositing grave goods was abandoned in towns in the fourteenth and fifteenth centuries, no doubt hastened by the incorporation of indigenous artisans into guilds which regulated religious life as well as funerals. In the countryside, indigenous funerary rites remained predictably conservative and women, men and children continued to be buried in clothing with accompanying objects into the nineteenth century; but, by the sixteenth century, large objects, including equestrian equipment, agricultural tools and weapons, as well as large pectoral jewellery pieces and neck rings, were no longer being deposited. The cessation of weapon deposits also coincided with the decreasing involvement of the indigenous population in military activities, as the authorities switched to relying more on professional soldiers and passed edicts forbidding the peasantry from bearing arms. By this time, essentially all rural burials had become standardised inhumations, aligned east–west and organised into rows, emulating cemeteries attached to churches, with their consecrated space defined by a visible boundary.[50] This trend is also visible in eastern Prussia, although here the incorporation of ceramic fragments into the burials of indigenous individuals has been interpreted as a transitional rite, marking their status as neophytes.[51]

Christian objects became more popular additions to graves, particularly medallions of saints and rosary beads; by the sixteenth century, rosaries were described as the preferred gifts for brides and women's necklaces. Some objects became attached to a distinctly Christian vision of the afterlife: placing shoes in a grave was believed to enable the dead to walk to heaven more easily, whilst coins, which became popular deposits in graves across the eastern Baltic, were necessary to pay St Peter. At the same time, some evidently non-Christian beliefs continued to affect funerary deposits. Objects the dead had come into contact with during their life were placed in the grave to appease their souls, as suggested by later folklore, and failure to do so would incur misfortune amongst their living relatives. In some parishes of southern Estonia, it became customary for mourners to carve crosses into trees during a funeral, on the way to the cemetery.[52] This practice is largely documented from the nineteenth century, although crosses carved into trees are attested in medieval documents where they also serve as boundary markers.

All these variants can be interpreted as a blend of funerary fashion, variable notions of the afterlife and the fate of not just current souls but also ancestral ones, as well as magical acts aimed at either protecting the dead from malevolent supernatural forces or to protect the living from the dead. These had parallels in other parts of Catholic Europe – the distinctive features in the eastern Baltic reflected the variable incorporation of earlier practices and the meanings attached to them, including the sacrifice of people and animals for the benefit of the deceased, the role of fire for transitioning to the otherworld and, connected to this, the dwelling place for the earthbound souls: for those cremated in groves, their souls could remain ever-present, and Lannoy's description of the soul being lost in the event of smoke from the pyre blowing to the side echoes later-documented Lithuanian beliefs that the dead ascended up a spectral mountain following the trail of smoke from the pyre, some on horseback, others on foot. Whilst cremation burials and the custom of raising earthen mounds or barrows over the dead were eventually abandoned, funerary feasts and the consumption of food by the graveside continued, and this type of practice was also found in neighbouring Russian, Polish and Pomeranian regions. The reappearance of grave goods in urban cemeteries in Livonia in the sixteenth and seventeenth centuries has been connected with the influx of rural migrants, but it may have reflected the impact of the Reformation, which, in the West, prompted a fashion for burying the dead in everyday clothing rather than in shrouds. It is therefore also conceivable that German Lutherans popularised this rite amongst indigenous communities in eastern Baltic towns.[53]

LITHUANIAN CHRISTIANITY

Throughout much of the fourteenth century, the changing relationship between politics and religion can be tracked in the funerals of Lithuania's grand dukes. Those of pagan rulers featured large numbers of animal sacrifices and food offerings that were burnt in spectacular public ceremonies. In 1364, Philippe de Mézières, who travelled to the Order's Baltic lands as the ambassador of the King of Cyprus, described such a funeral in detail. The dead Lithuanian grand duke would be mounted, armed, on a living horse, of good stock, in the centre of a pyre made of fir trees. Nearby, the grand duke's closest companion would willingly enter a wooden cage and, together with his lord and horse, he would be burnt alive in order to join him in the afterlife.[54] The last grand duke to be cremated was Algirdas in 1377, after which Jogaila, later christened Władysław shortly before his marriage to the Polish monarch Jadwiga, would be buried in the Wawel cathedral in Cracow. His cousin Vytautas, rebaptised as Alexander and subsequently assuming the title of grand duke, would be buried in Vilnius cathedral, whilst Jogaila's brother Skirgaila was christened into the Eastern Orthodox faith as Ivan (John) and would be buried in Pechersk Lavra monastery in Kyiv. The abandonment of ancestral burial rites at the highest levels of Lithuanian society was simultaneously a political and religious act.

With the establishment of the diocese of Vilnius, missionaries were sent out to the corners of the realm. Jerome of Prague, a Camaldolese monk, visited Samogitia where he reported encountering the sorts of pagan activities that would be documented elsewhere in Lithuania: sacred groves, grass snakes kept in houses, a sacred fire maintained by priests within a temple, and worship of the sun. However, it is also evident from his account that some communities had incorporated elements of Christian monotheism into their cosmologies.[55] The presence of missionary Franciscans – and specifically those belonging to the so-called 'third order' or tertiaries, whose lifestyle was less strictly organised – is attested by finds of their distinctive metal badges in the form of birds and rosettes that decorated their leather pouches. These have been uncovered within inhumation burials in Samogitia and Lithuania dating from the end of the fourteenth and into the fifteenth century.[56]

Clearer evidence of the dissemination of Christian material culture is represented by ring brooches decorated with grapevines, seven doves (representing the seven gifts of the Holy Spirit) and perhaps a stylised crown of thorns. Fewer than a dozen of these brooches have been found in southern Livonia, whilst the majority – some 176 examples – have been recovered in Lithuania from both cremation burials dating to the fourteenth century and later inhumation burials dating through to the second half of the fifteenth century, where they are found with women, children and men. Interestingly, large numbers have also been discovered in substantial pits within major ancestral cemeteries such as Marvelė and Obeliai, containing the traces of what have been interpreted as ritual bonfires, where various objects, including such brooches, were thrown in at different times. Some of these pits have been radiocarbon dated to the late fourteenth century. Twenty-five intact brooches were also found in the lake at Obeliai, some deformed by intense heat, alongside substantial remains of cremated bone. These brooches have been interpreted as badges of Christian allegiance, distributed by the Franciscans as part of their missionary activities. Their deposition on cremation pyres and bonfires can be tentatively interpreted as a meeting between contrasting religious worlds during the period of Lithuania's conversion: the pagan otherworld and the evangelical symbolism of baptism by fire.[57] Cremation would be finally abandoned by the mid-fifteenth century.

In 1417, the diocese of Samogitia was officially created and the seat of its bishops was established in Medėninkā (later called Varniai), where Grand Duke Vytautas sponsored the construction of a cathedral. Major pagan religious centres such as Šatrija Hill (Telšiai district) were abandoned and, as with some other natural sacred sites in Lithuania, would later become associated with witches and devils. Some of the larger ancestral cemeteries were also abandoned and new ones established, where cremations, ritual pits and animal deposits were absent. However, later church documents indicate rural communities continued to bury their dead in groves and meadows, without the presence of a priest or the correct funerary rite. The Order's officials duly noted down sacred sites as they began to reorganise the annexed territory, and whilst the Polish-Lithuanian union took over the governance of Samogitia shortly after, in 1422, the pastoral infrastructure remained limited; few priests spoke the local language and later sources point to increasingly composite beliefs. A late sixteenth-century account described how a priest in Kaunas demonstrated the flagellation of Christ on Good Friday by striking a crucifix with a rod. A Samogitian peasant witnessing this asked who he was striking, to which the reply was 'The Lord God', whereupon the peasant asked if it was the one responsible for a bad harvest the previous year, and was therefore pleased *this god* was being punished.[58]

In 1587, the Bishop of Samogitia, Merkelis Giedraitis, complained the local people 'sacrifice to the thunder collectively, worship grass snakes and regard oaks as sacred'. Giedraitis was an industrious evangelist, investing in the Samogitian priesthood, encouraging the Jesuits to undertake missionary activity in the diocese and sponsoring the translation of the Catechism and the Postil (a collection of Catholic sermons and commentaries) into Lithuanian, amongst the first books published in the language.[59] Jesuits would actively seek out and destroy sites of pagan worship in the wilderness; one such example, within the peat bogs near Šilalė, consisted of a large boulder marked with depressions, next to which lay a hearth with a continually burning fire.[60] At the same time, the invigorated Samogitian Church was fighting the Reformation, which intensified in the last decades of the sixteenth century. A few decades later, the Swedish invasion of the Polish-Lithuanian Commonwealth, branded later as the 'Deluge' (Polish *Potop*), would have a devastating impact on the Samogitian population, and the pastoral system would have to be rebuilt. Given the religious and political turmoil in the region, it is not surprising that a standardised form of Christianity was difficult to enforce.

Of the 2,500 ancient sacred sites documented in modern Lithuania, the best-preserved composite examples, where Catholic practices were merged with the use of sacred natural sites, are found in Samogitia. Timber chapels with images of saints and crosses are found within groves of trees, in many cases surrounded by a stone wall or wooden fence. The trees in the grove themselves are not venerated or attributed with supernatural power, but elsewhere individual trees are associated with a history going back a century or more of ritual activities, such as offerings of coins and prayers. Samogitia has the largest number of documented sacred pine trees which, given their relatively short lifespan, could only represent a memory of a former sacred site and were fully integrated with Catholic devotional practices. Its hills with the sacred place-name element '*alka*' are consistently associated with recurring folktale motifs of sacrifices, continuously lit sacred fires and virgins (i.e. unmarried women) serving pagan priests. More widely distributed across Lithuania, although rare in occurrence, are folktales of priestesses and priests committing suicide by drowning in a river or spring near a sacred site following the introduction of Christianity.[61] Are these the product of nineteenth-century reimaginings? In the absence of contemporary indigenous sources or archaeological data, it is entirely possible, but the biographies of sacred sites are complex and require more archaeological investigation on a case-by-case basis to map their prehistory.

THE TEMPO OF RELIGIOUS TRANSFORMATION

With the foundation of the Samogitian diocese, the process of incorporating the eastern Baltic lands into Catholic Christendom was officially complete. At least on paper. On the ground, the Church continued to struggle with evangelising the indigenous population. There had been numerous obstacles from different sides of the cultural divide. The Teutonic Order, standard bearer of the crusading movement in north-eastern Europe, was repeatedly criticised for ignoring the spiritual welfare of its subjects. The most effective missionaries, friars, were too few in number and, despite the repeated efforts of bishops, many priests lacked the skills or willingness to preach in the local languages and were prohibited from translating key texts into the vernacular to avoid the pitfall of heretical misunderstandings. There were, of course, German priests who spoke the indigenous language, and indigenous speakers who had become ordained priests, but the episcopal statutes that hammered away at the importance of multi-lingual preaching suggest these were not enough. The foundation of a school in Heilsberg (Polish Lidzbark Warmiński) in 1426 for training Prussian boys as priests was the first concerted attempt to overcome this problem, but this would not happen in Livonia until the following century and Finland until even later.[62]

It is, therefore, not surprising that mainstream Catholicism, in a form that would have been recognisable in Western Europe, flourished where migrant communities had become established. This was most pronounced in Prussia, where the abandonment of indigenous sacred sites followed the pace of migrant settlement. Already in the fourteenth century, fishing in lakes with sacred names, such as Schwentein and Perkun, had been permitted in Pomesania, the heartland of the Order's Prussian lands. By the fifteenth century, this was happening on the eastern frontier: the commander of the convent of Ragnit permitted trees to be felled in the woods called Schwentai (Sacred). In the following century, clerics documented the last vestiges of lingering paganism. In 1595, the Lutheran pastor Kaspar Hennenberger described the vanishing practice of self-blinding with the removal of one eye as an offering to the River Golbe near the east Prussian town of Insterburg, considered a mark of honour amongst the older generation of Lithuanian Prussians. The pastor likened this to the spiritual blindness caused by the Devil and noted, no doubt with relief, that younger generations were not self-harming in this way as they had abandoned such beliefs.[63] Indigenous spirituality had incorporated elements of Catholicism but, as eastern Prussia became increasingly Germanised and Polonised, as well as being subjected to renewed attempts at evangelisation with the Reformation and the Counter Reformation, the connections with ancestral souls and deities, as well as their sacred places in the landscape, faded into memory, becoming fossilised in toponyms and echoing increasingly faintly in cycles of folktales. The influence of a Christian worldview is evident where some former sacred sites were branded with names such as Teufelstein (Devil's Stone) or Teuffeltsche Eiche (Devil's Oak), as well as in the local languages where terms for 'soul' were recontextualised as 'demon', as with Lithuanian Velniabala (Devil's Swamp) and Latvian Velnezers (Devil's Lake).

In rural Livonia and the interior of Finland, on the other hand, where migrants were few and far between, a large part of the sacred landscape not only remained intact after the crusades but, with the growing indigenous population now increasingly adopting the various elements of the new religion, it continued to develop and transform in previously unforeseen ways. Here, archaeologists and historians have argued for the existence of parallel worldviews which, at specific places and times, overlapped, blended and ultimately transformed into new, composite forms. The devastation of the Livonian War curtailed the influence of religious authorities in the midst of the Reformation and saw a resurgence in visits to rural chapels by indigenous peasants to make offerings. But what this also demonstrates is the popularity of Catholic elements amongst rural communities in the form of chapels, images and pilgrimages.

Baltic Lutheran clergy disapproved of Catholics and idolatry, but particularly condemned peasant religion which, in their eyes, continued to be tainted by both Catholicism and paganism. In Finland, the Lutheran Church took a more active role in educating and disciplining the rural population, and pastors were particularly opposed to *Tietäjät* ('those who know') – Finnish seers, who were prominent figures in rural communities known for their magical incantations.[64] In Estonia, the Lutheran struggle against Catholicism and paganism is captured in a catechism published in the indigenous language in 1694, which stated, in relation to the First Commandment, that 'if a man gives worship, which is meant only for God, to those who are not worthy of it, if idols are worshipped, dead saints appealed to, gifts brought in special times, the Earth Mother or *Maa-alused* [subterranean supernatural beings in Estonian folklore] worshipped, some places, hills, stones, springs, the steam of the sauna, groves or trees in a forest are considered holy, sacrifice is made to them or in other ways idols are served . . .'⁶⁵ Other Lutheran texts make the same clear distinction between true faith and superstition. What may be seen as a final act of resistance is documented in the south-eastern Estonian parish of Urvaste in 1642. Here, the indigenous peasants destroyed a newly constructed mill that had been built on the River Võhandu, considered sacred and the abode of the thunder god.⁶⁶

The establishment of the Moravian Church (or the so-called 'Herrnhut movement', named after its place of origin) in eighteenth-century Livonia had a further impact on religious practices. Its preachers, who noted lingering superstitions from what they called Catholic and pagan times, gave their sermons in the local languages, promoting a new level of social and intellectual confidence amongst the indigenous population. For the indigenous peasantry this finally saw the abandonment of many sacred natural sites, at a scale medieval religious authorities had never been able to achieve. Numerous sites were destroyed by Latvian and Estonian peasants, although not all, as folklorists observed the continued presence of offerings at some into the early twentieth century, particularly those associated with healing, as well as folklore that has endured within modern communities. With the national awakenings of the Baltic countries came a revival of interest in pagan religion and, as elsewhere, reimagining by neo-pagan movements.

CHAPTER 11

HOLY WAR IN CRISIS
Rebellion and Reformation

> Furthermore, such warring against infidels, especially without just cause, is not compatible with love of one's neighbour . . . and according to the Truth, both faithful and infidels are our neighbours . . .
> Paweł Włodkowic, *Saevientibus olim Pruthenis*, 1416[1]

THE PATH TO RUIN

The dramatic ruins of the castle in Cēsis in northern Latvia – formerly called Wenden – still preserve the main form of the conventual building and, with three outer wards, it was one of the largest of the Teutonic Order's castles. But its appearance largely dates to the reign of the Livonian master, Walter of Plettenberg, and the final decades of the Order's rule in the eastern Baltic. In Livonia's political history, Plettenberg is widely considered as the greatest of the provincial masters. Hailing from a noble Westphalian family, he had joined the Order in his teens, and was elected as Marshal of Livonia in 1489. Two years later, he had faced and defeated Riga's army, which essentially guaranteed his elevation to the master's office. For many decades, the Livonian masters had been acting increasingly independently of the Order's Prussian leadership and, although their power was, in theory, checked by an inner circle of officials, Plettenberg aspired to rule in his own right.[2] From the mid-fifteenth century, Livonian masters had been adding their own family arms to the coins minted in the name of the Order, but Plettenberg issued gold ducats which were decorated with a full-figure portrait of himself, in plate armour, holding an upright sword in his right hand, and the arms of the Order quartered with his own in the other. The reverse was decorated with a figure of the crowned Virgin and child, emanating rays, with the legend reading 'Mary, save your people'. What was this, if not a declaration that he was the most powerful de facto ruler in Livonia?

Already in 1413, the castle at Wenden served as an occasional residence for the Livonian master and became the centre of a newly created district designed to bolster his resources, providing a generous annual income. When the Order's Livonian castles were inventoried during a region-wide visitation in 1451, Wenden turned out to be the best-supplied after Riga, with more than a third of the grain in the entire country found within its stores, of which half was set aside for mercenaries. This is evidence of the castle's growing significance, and whilst the convent in Riga remained the most important centre for the Order in Livonia, after relations with the town broke down (again), the master's seat was permanently relocated to Wenden. The Order's castle in Riga would be destroyed in 1484 and, even after it was rebuilt by the townspeople in 1515 (for the third time), future masters remained in Wenden.[3]

Under Plettenberg, there was significant investment in Wenden Castle. The crowning jewel was the reconstruction of the master's chamber on the first floor of the western tower of the main convent building. It was furnished with a reticulated vault, built from brick and supported by corbels made from artificial stone (i.e. large blocks of plaster) decorated with vine leaves. Its panels were painted blue to resemble the night sky and gold stars on wooden pallets were attached to the keystones at the intersections of the vault's ribs. Restoration work in the 1980s discovered the walls were also painted with floral motifs and animals, which included a hunting scene depicting a man with a crossbow and squirrel in a tree. Perhaps this was a reminder of one of the main sources for the Order's wealth at the time – squirrel pelts, when the supply of luxury fur for the Hanseatic market had shifted from Novgorod to Livonia.

The chamber was also furnished with a latrine, a fireplace and a niche widely interpreted as a space for a bed. It would have been a spectacular sight, and it survives today as a unique example of the luxurious quality of life in the Order's Livonian castles. In the adjoining range, there would have been a chancellery and a library, and excavations at the castle have uncovered around sixty book fittings, deriving from at least twenty-two books made in north Germany and the Netherlands between the early fourteenth century and the 1520s.[4] Even one of the towers added to the outer ward with clear defensive capabilities was furnished with a luxury chamber containing a large fireplace, sleeping niche and latrine, most probably for one of the convent's officials. The brethren of Wenden, and by all accounts in the other houses belonging to the Order in Livonia, were living the good life. But less than three decades after Plettenberg's death in 1535, the Order's Livonian branch would be dissolved by its last master who, in the face of a catastrophic Russian invasion that became known as the Livonian War, converted to Lutheranism and declared his allegiance to the Polish king.

The story of Wenden's 'old castle' does not end with the dissolution of the Order in 1561, but with a more poignant episode in the final stage of the Livonian War. The castle had been given over to a Polish garrison, headed up by a former brother-knight of the Order. But when, in the summer of 1577, the Russian tsar, Ivan IV 'the Terrible', declared that he would conquer the rest of Livonia, the townspeople of Wenden, in fear for their lives, drove out the garrison and submitted to the tsar's vassal, Duke Magnus, the former Danish Bishop of Ösel-Wiek who had been proclaimed 'King of Livonia'.[5] Magnus took up residence in the town as his new seat of power, which infuriated Ivan. The tsar arrived at Wenden with his vast army in September and Magnus was forced to grovel for mercy. The story goes that Ivan was about to take pity on the cowering duke, when a shot from the castle narrowly missed his head, at which point his blood rose and he swore that no one in Wenden would be spared. The bombardment of the castle began. Some 300 men, women and children had taken shelter inside. Fragments of the south tower and lead cannon balls were found during archaeological excavations in the moat below the south tower. This had been rebuilt in the 1540s as a central point in the castle's defensive system, with numerous gun ports, and would have drawn significant fire from the besiegers.[6]

After five days and nights of shelling, the people inside decide to commit suicide en masse, rather than fall into the hands of the Russians.

They gathered in the castle's western range on 6 September which they then blew up with gunpowder. The upper two storeys and loft of the range collapsed, burying the bodies. Archaeologists excavating the ruins in the 1974 discovered skeletal remains in the basement together with fragments of brocaded textiles, amidst collapsed beams, fragments of vaulting, painted plaster and stove tiles. During the same excavations, the largest hoard of silverware in the eastern Baltic was found in the rubble, consisting of 965 coins (the majority minted in Estonia, Curonia and Riga) and various women's clothing items and accessories, including a silver girdle and purse fastener. The plate on the girdle was engraved with the name Walter Strick, leading to suggestions that the woman who hid the hoard was his wife. Strick, whose family hailed from Ösel, may have been a member of Magnus's retinue and was most probably captured and killed along with Magnus when the Russians took Wenden. His wife, on the other hand, after hiding away her precious possessions, may well have been one of the people who died in the explosion.[7] Also discovered in the basement of the western range was one of the largest archaeological deposits of medieval armour in Europe – some 300 pieces consisting of helmets, gauntlets, vambraces (forearm guards), breast and back plates, which had originally been manufactured in southern Germany. The basement had evidently served as an armoury, but what was striking about the finds was that much of the armour was seventy to ninety years old, and therefore outdated. It provides us with an oblique glimpse into the Order's declining finances in its final decades of rule.[8]

The tragedy at Wenden sent shockwaves through both Catholic and Protestant Europe. The Lutheran pastor, Balthasar Russow, wrote in his chronicle of the Livonian War that those who remained alive in the castle were tortured to death by the Russians with great cruelty.[9] Later writers would elaborate on the details, and by then, the Muscovites were, along with the Turks, widely proclaimed as an apocalyptic threat to Christendom. The Russians had already taken the place of the Lithuanians as the main perceived danger to Livonia – and by extension, the 'civilised world' – in the fifteenth century, and this was ratcheted up to another level during the Livonian War. The events at Wenden would remain in the public consciousness in Livonia for several generations to come, although eventually the fact that the castle even had a western range was forgotten, until its rediscovery by archaeologists in the twentieth century.

The Russians did not hold Wenden for long. In December 1577, the town and castle were recaptured by the castellan of Treiden (Latvian Turaida), Johann Biering, leading an army of Polish, German and Latvian soldiers.[10] Muscovite troops would attempt sieges of Wenden the following year, but were repelled, the first of a string of defeats that eventually forced the tsar to cede Russian-occupied eastern Livonia to the Polish-Lithuanian Commonwealth. After the war, the castle would become the property of the Swedish Oxenstierna family, and then home to a royal garrison who vandalised and partially dismantled the buildings. During the Great Northern War (1700–21), the Russians continued to demolish the castle, having also destroyed other castles in Livonia to prevent them from being refortified. The rubble and standing remains were taken apart and used for building material. Over time, wind and rain eroded the remaining walls and towers, now standing roofless. In the later eighteenth century, the former gatehouse of the outer ward would be rebuilt as a manor house – the 'new castle' – which saw further demolition of the old fortifications to provide building materials. By that time, the old castle, like many others in Livonia, was a hollowed-out shell and the world it represented was long gone.

The story of the last crusades in the east Baltic is also that of the downfall of the Teutonic Order, the region's most powerful ruler and the fading embodiment of Catholic holy war in the North. It is dominated by political and military events – those are inescapable for understanding the cultural transformations that marked the end of the crusading world in the Baltic. But the impact of the Reformation was ultimately decisive in severing the ties that linked societies around the Baltic Sea to the papacy, when the world forged and sustained by the crusades in the North finally came to an end.

THE LAST CRUSADES IN THE BALTIC

In the thirteenth century, the territorial expansion of Norway and Sweden northwards and eastwards, with the aim of controlling trade and access to natural resources, encountered the westward growth of

Novgorod. Caught between these opposing Christian powers were indigenous pagan groups – principally Finns, Saami (also referred to as Finns in contemporary sources, or Lapps) and Karelians. Although the colonising regimes were largely concerned about defining which of these groups paid them taxes – the focus of various treaties demarcating borders – crusading ideology became enmeshed within their territorial policies. This continued in the fourteenth and fifteenth centuries, when the northernmost edge of Christendom was routinely described as under constant threat from pagans, schismatics and infidels. These simplistic dichotomies – a clash of cultures between the Norse and Saami, or between the Swedes and Karelians – were deliberately created to serve political ends. The reality was, of course, much more complex, and interactions across religious and ethnic lines were varied.[11] Indeed, each 'crusade' had a context relating to specific events on the ground, the details of which are often lost to us. One episode where we know more relates to the Swedish frontier in Karelia in the mid-fourteenth century and the activities of Magnus Eriksson, King of Sweden and Norway.

The pretext was by then well established for, in the eyes of Swedish rulers, Catholicism in Karelia – and its resources – were permanently under threat. In 1328, Magnus had written to the pope to ask that half of the money collected as 'Peter's Pence' (a papal tax) in his realm should be used to wage war against the pagans and schismatics who threatened Sweden on its eastern frontier. No campaigns are recorded but, in 1346, Magnus confirmed in the will made out jointly with his wife, Queen Blanche, that he had taken a crusading vow and, if he died before fulfilling it, the will's executors were obliged to send out a hundred armed men against the enemies of the Catholic faith.[12] The vow was probably made in relation to the crusade planned by the French king Philip VI in 1331, which in the end never took place. Perhaps Magnus had been contemplating another military venture to Karelia, most probably intended to fend off Novgorod's influence. He may have been persuaded to portray this as a crusade under the influence of Bridget, the Swedish mystic who founded her own monastic order and was later canonised.

Bridget claimed to have received a series of visions of Christ, the Virgin Mary and various saints, which she recorded and compiled into a multi-volume work, initially in Old Swedish and then translated into

Latin as *Revelationes Caelestes* (*Celestial Revelations*). One of the political figures addressed in these revelations was King Magnus, who was urged to return to a more pious way of ruling. Bridget pitched herself as a messenger sent by God to influence the actions of earthly leaders, and she was recognised by the Church as a religious authority. Her revelations outlined in some detail the duties of an ideal Christian ruler, which would bring about the spiritual renewal of their kingdom. High on the list was crusading, which she described as the physical equivalent of the spiritual fight for one's own soul, an opportunity for penance. The fact that Magnus and Blanche had left a donation to Bridget's new monastery in Vadstena in their will, after which Bridget started having visions about crusading, has led some to suggest the king actively approached the mystic to lend support for a planned campaign in the east.[13]

Bridget's revelations provided detailed instructions to Magnus on how a crusade ought to be organised. Its participants should be motivated by spiritual virtue, rather than by personal gain, and their goal was the conversion of pagans. Bishops and monks should accompany the crusaders in order to facilitate peaceful conversion, offering the pagans salvation. Those who refused should be immediately killed, for the longer they lived the more they would suffer in the afterlife.[14] Bridget's vision of a crusade was different to previous ones. Rather than stressing the need to defend Christendom, its benefit was for the kingdom and, as such, papal approval and the accompanying crusading indulgence were not required. Yet a crusading bull would have made it easier to raise an army, and Magnus may have procured one. He evidently needed to draw on the military resources of both of his kingdoms and, according to the *Icelandic Annals*, the Norwegians were unconvinced, until he demonstrated to them that he had the pope's support.[15] It is also probable that Bridget's words of encouragement, likening crusading to the imitation of Christ, along with its spiritual rewards, were read out across the realm to inspire participation in the campaign. As with all the 'Swedish Crusades', historians are divided on the driving motives. Many have argued this was just another war of territorial expansion, others that it was also driven by genuine religious sentiments.

According to Rus' chronicles, Magnus did attempt to follow Bridget's instructions. He sent envoys to Novgorod to debate the virtues of

Catholicism and Orthodoxy, although some historians have suggested their real purpose was to deliver an ultimatum regarding Swedish control of Karelia. The Rus' refused to engage and sent their own delegates to Viborg to listen to the king's grievances, whereupon they were told that Novgorod must adopt Catholicism. At this point, talks broke down and the Swedish army marched on the Vod district, where they began forcibly baptising the local Izhorians (a neighbouring Finnic group) and killed those who resisted. The Swedes captured the town of Orekhov on the Neva river, which served as the entry point to Lake Ladoga. Most of the army then departed, leaving behind a small garrison, and the Novgorodians were able to recapture the town after a six-month siege. Magnus returned with a fleet in 1350, but a storm on the Neva sank many of the ships and the campaign was called off.

The following year, the pope threw his weight behind the campaign against Novgorod. He prohibited the trading of weapons, horses and ships with the Rus', granted Magnus half of all the tithe collected over the next four years, asked the Teutonic Order to aid the king and then ordered the three Scandinavian archdioceses – Lund, Uppsala and Nidaros – to preach the crusade in defence of the new converts in Karelia against the Rus', with the same indulgences as for the Holy Land. When the pope died in December 1352, his successor Innocent VI reissued the crusading bulls.[16] But as a result of the devastation caused by the Black Death in Sweden and Norway, the campaign never materialised. By 1355, the pope had lost patience, demanding the return of the tithe money. When Magnus failed to do this, he was excommunicated. Bridget, perhaps seeking to safeguard her own credibility, wrote a lengthy rebuke, chastising the king for ignoring the advice of God, and following instead the counsel of worldly men who had prevented him from completing his task of converting the pagans. Magnus's popularity waned, and eventually he lost his throne to his nephew, then drowned when his ship sank in 1374.

There were further conflicts between the Swedes and the Rus' on the Karelian frontier in the late fourteenth and early fifteenth centuries, but as the *Chronicle of Novgorod* notes, they met with little success.[17] During this time, Scandinavian political history is marked by the rise of the Kalmar Union in 1397, which unified the three Scandinavian kingdoms and their dependencies. Danish monarchs dominated the union, and so the eastern frontier now once again became their concern. In 1401, the founder of the union and its de facto ruler, Queen Margaret of Denmark, requested a crusading bull from the pope, arguing that her lands needed defending from constant attacks. In response, Pope Boniface IX demanded the Scandinavian archbishops preach the crusade against the Union's enemies, 'be they Christian or pagan', with the same indulgences granted to those going to the Holy Land. This was unusual as Christian targets of crusades had previously been condemned as heretics or schismatics, but Boniface, the pope in Rome, was facing off rival popes in Avignon, and this was evidently a way of garnering support for his position.

With the sacking of Constantinople in 1453, all attention now shifted to the eastern Mediterranean, along with efforts to organise future crusades. However, some northern rulers, including the Teutonic Order, were claiming they were still too preoccupied with their own corner of Christendom to join the war against the Turks. The most insistent was Christian I, who ruled the Kalmar Union from 1457, having acquired all three Scandinavian crowns. In various letters to the papacy, Christian repeatedly made excuses for why he could not join crusades against the Turks, on account of how the frontiers of Sweden and Norway were constantly being attacked by pagans, who desecrated the holy places and enslaved Christians. Worse, they were being encouraged by his rival for the throne, Karl Knutsson, who had made a pact with the Rus'. Knutsson had even threatened to hand over Viborg to Novgorod. In the end, the pope sided with Christian, and would go on to accuse Knutsson of tyranny and heresy.[18]

The principal target of crusading changed in 1471, following the victory of Moscow's forces over Novgorod. The city became formally incorporated into Muscovy seven years later, and now Moscow was deemed the principal threat. When the Rus' raided the district around Viborg, the Swedish royal council conscripted soldiers, invoking saints Eric and Henry, who had 'won' the land to the glory of God and for the expansion of Christendom and Sweden.[19] By now, crusading heritage was firmly embedded in the religious culture of the Swedish kingdom. Scenes of St Eric of Sweden and Bishop Henry travelling to Finland decorated church walls, and Henry's tomb in Nousiainen church in

Finland had been decorated in the 1420s with brass plates depicting the Swedish crusades, which included scenes of the arrival of the Swedish army in cogs, its landfall and the baptism of pagans.

When Innocent VIII became pope, he renewed calls for crusading in all corners of Christendom. In February 1485, he commanded the Archbishop of Uppsala to persuade King John (aka Hans), the ruler of the Kalmar Union, to wage war on the schismatics, and then worked to promote peace in his lands to enable John to organise a joint campaign with the Teutonic Order against the Rus'. Those Swedish princes who would not respect the peace were threatened with excommunication, with the result that John would be able to crusade against them. Sweden had been a problematic partner in the Kalmar Union, and its nobles had struggled against Danish rule. This is perhaps why, in the 1490s, John began negotiating with Ivan III of Moscow, hoping to gain his support against his Swedish rival Sten Sture and the Teutonic Order. As a result, Sten Sture would receive a crusading bull from the pope in 1496, authorising a holy war against the Rus' and their Danish allies. In the end, this had little impact. Sture lost a significant battle against John the following year, who was then officially recognised as King of Sweden.

The last crusades against the Rus' were organised by the Livonian master, Walter of Plettenberg, in the early years of the sixteenth century. By this time, the term crusading was connected more broadly to the defence of Christendom, and military orders like the Teutonic Order and Hospitallers justified their actions in this way.[20] Nonetheless, Plettenberg tried to persuade the pope to supply him with a crusading bull with the support of the Archbishop of Riga and the grand master in Prussia. No indulgence was initially forthcoming. Despite this, Plettenberg won significant victories against Rus' forces which eventually led to a truce. In 1503, the pope finally granted a crusading indulgence to Plettenberg for a period of three years. The indulgence was to be offered in all towns around the Baltic Sea, all those belonging to the Hanse and in the dioceses of Riga, and Reval (Estonian Tallinn), Magdeburg, Bremen and Kammin (Polish Kamień Pomorski). So much money was raised that Plettenberg applied for a second indulgence in 1506. This, too, was granted, and preaching and collecting funds continued until 1510. But there would be no further crusades, and peace with Moscow held for half a century.

THE TEUTONIC ORDER'S DOWNFALL IN PRUSSIA

By the end of the fourteenth century, the Teutonic Order was suffering an identity crisis, its role as *the* crusading institution in the North terminally undermined. Despite the baptism of Grand Duke Jogaila – now Ladislaus II Jagiello – in 1386, the brethren continued to argue that Lithuanians remained pagans and Poles were either liars or heretics for aiding them, pressing their claims to Samogitia – a means to extend their territory and validate their fading crusading mantle. Grand Master Conrad of Jungingen had justified the Order's territorial intentions in the familiar language of expanding and defending Christendom.[21] However, it became clear the papacy now recognised the rulers of the Polish-Lithuanian union as the most important defenders of the faith in Eastern Europe.

But the union was on rocky ground. Grand Duke Vytautas was striving for Lithuania's independence, which included his own territorial ambitions in Ruthenia (corresponding to large parts of modern-day Ukraine and Belarus). To further this, in 1398, he ceded Samogitia to the Order in exchange for military aid against the Mongols. Its ruler, Tokhtamysh, had been fighting Timur (also known as Tamerlane), who had created a new Mongol empire in Central Asia and was expanding his territory westwards through a series of conquests. In 1395, the Golden Horde's capital, Sarai, had been destroyed and its population killed or enslaved. Tokhtamysh was deposed and fled to Crimea, and from there to Lithuania. After being welcomed in the grand duke's court, he made a deal with Vytautas, offering him lordship over those Ruthenian lands that had been under the Golden Horde's control, in exchange for military help to regain his throne. Vytautas's forays were initially successful, and he received papal backing to declare his war a crusade. On 12 August 1399, Vytautas, accompanied by a contingent of brother-knights from the Teutonic Order, as well as his Rus' vassals and Mongol allies, faced off against the army of the new khan of the Golden Horde – Temur Qutlugh – at the Vorskla river. The battle ended with a disastrous defeat for the 'crusaders' (which, as one historian has pointed out, was a coalition of Catholics, 'schismatics' and 'pagans')[22] and Vytautas barely escaped with his life. Temur's army went on to besiege Kyiv, whilst

Tokhtamysh went into hiding and was assassinated a few years later. Vytautas's territorial ambitions in Ruthenia were crushed, and he made peace with his cousin, formally reaffirming the Polish-Lithuanian union.

The period of peace between the Order and Lithuania led to the flourishing of trade, but Marienburg's coffers soon began to empty. In 1402, the Order purchased the Neumark from the Margraviate of Brandenburg, and after expelling the piratical Vitalian Brothers from Gotland a few years earlier following a costly military campaign, it bought the island. The Order then had to defend it against the forces of Queen Margaret of Denmark in the winter of 1403/04, another costly venture. The conflict ended in stalemate, and when Ulrich of Jungingen succeeded his brother as grand master in 1407, he decided to at least remove one antagonist and ceded Gotland to Margaret.[23]

The 'Great War' with Poland-Lithuania, as it became known, had been brewing for some time, and the spark would be Samogitia. The brethren's rule was not popular there and, following the reconciliation of Vytautas and the Polish king Jagiello, the Samogitians rebelled against the Order in March 1401, attacking and destroying two castles the brethren had recently built. Vytautas had supported the uprising in secret, but when his brother Švitrigaila allied with the Order, keen to seize the ducal throne for himself, the grand duke openly joined the conflict. During the fighting, both sides appealed to the pope for support, and eventually a peace was concluded in 1404. Under its terms, the brethren retained control of Samogitia and Vytautas was to aid them in suppressing any dissent, which he did. He even helped the Order construct a new castle on the Šušvė river, which was manned by a joint garrison of brother-knights and Poles. The Order's rule was, once more, oppressive, aimed at maximising the profit from the yields of Samogitian farms, and brutally punishing any resistance.

Tensions remained, and relations between the Order and Vytautas became strained once again. The Lithuanian grand duke and Polish king discussed support for another Samogitian rebellion, as a means of provoking the Order into declaring war. The plan worked. Following a devastating famine, the Samogitians rebelled again in May 1409, destroying several of the Order's castles and reaching as far as the town of Memel. Once more, Vytautas declared his support for the rebels, and when the Order threatened to attack Lithuania, Poland, in turn, stated that it would retaliate against Prussia. The grand master had been prepared for this, and declared war on Poland, sending his armies across the southern border. An initial truce was signed, but the following year Polish and Lithuanian forces attacked Prussia.

On 15 July 1410, both sides met on a field between the villages of Grünfelde (Grunwald) and Tannenberg (Stębark), in what became known as one of the most famous battles of the Middle Ages – Tannenberg for Germans, Grunwald for Poles and Žalgiris for Lithuanians. An entire sub-genre of scholarship exists dedicated to this battle and the broader conflict.[24] Archaeologists have also scoured the battlefield, with new finds reported on a regular basis – most recently fragments of swords, dozens of arrowheads, spearheads, axes, spurs and parts of belts belonging to knights. Earlier discoveries included a clasp for fastening a coat with the inscription 'Ave Maria', and a seal bearing the image of a pelican feeding her young with her blood – a familiar Christian symbol of martyrdom used by the Order. The Order's army, which included foreign 'guest knights', suffered a catastrophic defeat. Jungingen was slain, together with several of the Order's leading officials, over 200 brother-knights and thousands of soldiers. The bodies of men and horses, piled on top of each other in a gory mess of bloodied and broken limbs, were buried where they lay. A few years later, the Order would commission a chapel that was built directly on top of the spot where the grand master fell. The remains of this building would later be uncovered by archaeologists, together with the bones of some 300 men.[25]

Tannenberg looms large in the history of European battles, but its significance was more symbolic. The Order had been weakened, not destroyed. Its corporate structure enabled a new grand master to be quickly elected and Henry of Plauen would be given the role in recognition of his defence of Marienburg. The Polish-Lithuanian army had marched on the Order's headquarters, arriving on 25 July, only to discover that much of the town south of the castle had been deliberately razed to deny them shelter. They positioned cannons around the castle and began bombarding it, causing damage to a number of towers and buildings. As the weeks passed, the castle's defenders began to launch effective counterattacks, leading skirmishes against the artillery crews. Both sides weakened as supplies ran low. With news of the arrival of reinforcements from Livonia, the leaders of the Polish-Lithuanian contingent began to leave, starting with Vytautas. Eventually, on 19 September, Jagiello ordered the lifting of the siege although, had they stayed for a couple more weeks, the defenders would have run out of food. The Order then took back most of the castles that had been captured, but faced another defeat by a Polish-Lithuanian army at Koronowo on 10 October. Finally, both parties came to terms and signed a peace treaty in Thorn in February 1411. The Order agreed to withdraw from Samogitia for as long as Vytautas and Jagiello lived, return the Dobrzyń Land to Poland, and pay a vast sum in war reparations – 6 million Prague *Groschen*. If each coin contained 3.5 grams of silver, that would equate to a silver bullion value today of around $12.6 million.

Fortunately for the Order, it could be paid in instalments, but the effect on its finances was debilitating. In fact, income sources from its Baltic commanderies and European bailiwicks were also in decline and, as grand masters sought to mitigate their financial problems, they turned to debasing their currency, reducing the amount of silver in the coinage. Unpopular tax rises and inflation followed, straining relations with their subjects. To make matters worse, the brethren were also suffering from a recruitment shortage. There had been a general decline of interest in religious life within the organisation, and standards had been falling. Getting new recruits through the door was proving increasingly difficult. By the start of the fifteenth century, there were around 700 brother-knights, brother-sergeants and brother-priests in Prussia, and some 250 in Livonia. Tannenberg dealt a significant blow to the existing membership which, by 1437, had dropped to below 400 in Prussia. By 1525, there were only 55 brethren left. It was the same story in Livonia and in the Order's imperial bailiwicks, where membership had fallen by two-thirds by the end of the fifteenth century. This meant the Order was having to increasingly rely on mercenaries to garrison its castles and, as its finances dwindled, so too did its ability to retain their services.[26]

Control over Samogitia remained a pressing issue for the Order, and Polish-Lithuanian armies once again raided Prussia, prompting another truce in October 1414. That year, attempts were made to finally resolve the conflict at the papal Council of Constance. This was one of the most pivotal events in Church history, for it restored a single pope as the head of the Catholic faith, ending the schism that had seen multiple claimants to the throne of St Peter. The council also condemned the teachings of John Wycliffe (posthumously) and the Bohemian reformer Jan Hus as heretical. Hus, along with his supporter Jerome of Prague, was burnt at the stake, an act that provoked the 'Hussite Wars' in Bohemia and is widely regarded as the start of a chain reaction which led to the Reformation. Then there was the issue of the conflict between Poland-Lithuania and the Order. Representatives from both sides presented their arguments, blaming each other. The lawyer heading up the Polish delegation, Paweł Włodkowic, presented a detailed case against the Order, which was expanded to defending the rights of pagan nations and challenging the practice of forced Christianisation, arguing this was both immoral and invalid. His argument, an excerpt of which is quoted at the start of this chapter, helped to shift the tone of debates on the use of force in religious matters and laid early groundwork for later discussions on tolerance. The Order, it was argued, would be better suited to defending Christendom against the Mongols and Turks. On the other hand, the Order's supporters, especially King (and later Emperor) Sigismund, recognised the legitimacy of the brethren's role in Prussia for the defence of Christendom. The two sides would continue to throw these arguments at each other in the coming decades.[27] In the end, responsibility for the conversion of Samogitia was handed to Poland-Lithuania. With the establishment of the diocese of Samogitia in 1417, the entirety of the grand duchy was now officially Catholic in the eyes of the Church.

There were further confrontations across the border in Prussia, as Polish-Lithuanian forces attacked the Order's lands in a short-lived conflict in 1422. A treaty was agreed on the shores of Lake Melno, which reaffirmed Lithuanian authority over Samogitia and fixed the eastern border of the Order's Prussian lands, with the River Lyck serving as a major demarcation line.[28] This finally ended the war between the Order and Lithuania, and the brethren gave up their former accusations of fake conversion, and started pointing out that the grand duchy had more schismatics than Catholics.[29] With this peace, the brethren were encouraged by King Sigismund to become involved in the defence of eastern Hungary against the Ottomans, but the death of Vytautas in 1430 provided a further opportunity to drive a wedge between the Polish-Lithuanian union. His successor Švitrigaila sought to make Lithuania independent, and when Jagiello sent troops into Lithuania to confront him, the Order rallied to support him, attacking and burning the Polish town of Inowrocław. But when Jagiello and Švitrigaila agreed a truce, the Order became isolated and suffered a further defeat at Dąbki. A short peace followed as diplomatic efforts resumed, and the Poles joined an alliance with the Hussites the following year.

The conflict between the Hussites and Catholics had become a religious war, with the pope calling for crusades against them. The Hussites, in turn, had also embraced the concept of martyrdom on the battlefield. They had a number of victories against crusading armies, and then began raiding the territories of their enemies. Since the Order supported the war on the Hussites, the latter became natural allies for the Poles, even though the Polish Church was vehemently opposed to their reformist ideology. In 1433, a Polish-Hussite force invaded the Order's lands in Pomerelia and the Neumark, seizing the town of Dirschau (Polish Tczew), but failed to take Danzig. Again, the Order sued for peace. When warfare broke out between Švitrigaila and Vytautas's brother Sigismund Kęstutaitis, the Order's Livonian brethren provided military support. Sigismund triumphed at the Battle of Ukmergė (also known as Vilkomir) on 1 September 1435, forcing the brethren to the negotiating table in December. At this point, the Order swore not to interfere in Lithuanian affairs again, and its resources were stretched too thin to provide meaningful support in Hungary. Trouble was also brewing for the Order amongst its own subjects in Prussia.

By the early fifteenth century, town burghers and the nobility had emerged as powerful social groups in Prussia with political and economic agency, which historians have referred to as the 'estates' (German *Landstände*).[30] As the Order raised taxes and imposed trade restrictions to restore its depleted finances, resentment began to build, particularly in the leading towns. Repeated military losses steadily weakened the Order's control, and this emboldened the nobility of the Kulmerland and the major Prussian towns to establish the Prussian Confederation in

February 1440. Its purpose was to resist the Order's rule and regain economic autonomy. When the Order's grand master challenged the validity of the Confederation in the imperial court (which declared it illegal), its members began to secretly plot a revolt against the Order with the support of Poland. On 4 February 1454, the members of the Confederation renounced their loyalty to the Order and their armies attacked its castles in Thorn, Graudenz and Elbing. The garrisons quickly surrendered and the castles were then blown up with gunpowder. Other towns also saw rebellions – in Rastenburg, the Order's procurator was drowned by the burghers. The Confederation's envoys were warmly received at the Polish court in Cracow, and on 6 March Casimir IV Jagiellon proclaimed all of Prussia to be part of the Kingdom of Poland, declaring war on the Order.

This became the 'Thirteen Years War' which was marked by numerous conflicts and short-lived truces. Some towns were attacked multiple times: for example, Frauenburg, where the Warmia chapter had declared its allegiance to the Polish king, was attacked by the Order's armies in 1454, then recaptured by Polish forces in 1455, then attacked again by the Order in 1456, 1461 and 1462. The Order's victories were attributed by its chroniclers to divine intervention, often featuring the Virgin Mary – proof the organisation still had a heavenly mandate.[31] In the end, a string of defeats and a reliance on underpaid mercenaries lost the Order its prized headquarters of Marienburg. The great castle was purchased from its mercenary garrison by the city of Danzig, which then handed it over to the Polish king who rode in triumphantly on 8 June 1457. The grand master was forced to relocate his seat to Königsberg, far from the front line. The town of Marienburg, however, refused to capitulate, and the Poles began a lengthy siege. In March 1460, Danzig's army joined the besieging Polish forces and the town surrendered after several months. Marienburg's defiant mayor was executed and Danzig's role in the conquest was memorialised two decades later in a painting of the siege, which was hung in its Artus Court. The painting was photographed before it was lost in 1945 and represents the earliest known artistic representation of the castle and town.

In 1466, the Order ceded its western Prussian territories to the Polish crown, and would now only rule over the eastern half of its lands (corresponding roughly to the territory of later East Prussia) for another six decades. The grand master was obliged to take an oath of loyalty to every Polish monarch, and to provide military assistance when called upon. The ceded territories in the west became known as Royal Prussia, and were given a degree of autonomy within the Polish kingdom. Meanwhile, in eastern Prussia, the Order's leadership set about encouraging a new wave of migration to develop its sparsely populated territories, dominated by forests and lakes. The settlement of the Prussian territories of Galindia and Bartia had already begun in the fourteenth century, but after 1466, large numbers of Polish settlers from neighbouring Masovia created new villages, mills and foundries and built parish churches. Here they encountered and cohabited alongside Germans and indigenous Prussians, resulting in the emergence of a new hybrid culture – Masurian. This saw the development of a new Polish dialect, which incorporated German and Old Prussian words.

The Order's leadership sought to renew the organisation's purpose and revive its spirituality, but to no avail. When Frederick, the younger son of the duke of Saxony, was elected grand master in September 1498, he governed as if he were ruling over a secular princely court.[32] His successor, Albert, the third son of the Margrave of Brandenburg-Ansbach, a cadet branch of the powerful House of Hohenzollern, would change everything. When elected in 1511 at the age of twenty-one, he became the youngest to hold the title, continuing his predecessor's style of secular governance and refusal to recognise Poland's overlordship. Eight years later, Albert finally demanded the return of territories lost in 1466, which led to another war with Poland. In December of that year, the Order's forces attacked Warmia, the start of a conflict that dragged on for fourteen months. Despite recruiting a substantial army of mercenaries, Albert failed to capture key towns and, when Ottoman troops invaded Hungary, Emperor Charles V demanded an end to the war, leading to a truce signed on 5 April 1521.

After a temporary end to the hostilities, Albert sought new allies in the empire against Poland-Lithuania, where he encountered key figures of the Reformation.[33] In 1522, he travelled to Wittenberg and met with Martin Luther. Luther, who was opposed to the whole concept of crusading, ultimately persuaded Albert to secularise the Order's territories in Prussia and sever ties with the Catholic Church. In March 1523, Luther published an open letter to the Order's leaders, urging them to abandon celibacy and become a true order of knighthood. Luther's associates visited Königsberg, where their preaching greatly influenced the Bishop of Sambia, who would embrace reformist ideas and aid Albert in organising Lutheran preaching throughout his lands. On 8 April 1525 in Cracow, Albert signed a peace treaty with the Polish king Sigismund, swore allegiance and symbolically handed over his robe of office, ending the long-standing conflict between them. The new duke renounced his loyalty to the papacy, a move soon echoed by most of the remaining Prussian brethren. Eastern Prussia became a vassal state of the Polish crown under the secular governance of the Hohenzollerns. Sigismund did not demand that the Order's territory be transformed into a secular duchy: this was Albert's initiative. The Polish king feared the spread of Lutheranism in his realm and hoped that it would be easier to restore Catholicism in Prussia as a Polish fief. In a significant move, the Bishop of Sambia transferred his secular authority over the diocese to the duke, reflecting Lutheran views on state power; the diocese of Pomesania would follow suit two years later.

The East Prussian Church was reorganised and Lutheranism spread quickly in the towns, but was slow to reach rural areas, particularly along the Polish and Lithuanian borderlands where migration intensified.[34] Nonetheless, as it did, it contributed to the further Germanisation of the remnants of the Old Prussian population. As in other Protestant states, Catholic elements in churches were removed, wall paintings limewashed, and religious sculptures destroyed. The ducal court in Königsberg became a hub for arts and sciences, leading to the establishment of a university there in 1544. Despite bordering Catholic Polish and Lithuanian territories, there is no evidence of significant religious conflict between Lutherans and Catholics, although Jesuits later arrived as part of the Counter Reformation, supported by the rulers of Poland-Lithuania.[35] The Order's territorial administration was replaced by new divisions, and its castles, no longer centres for corporate rule, were repurposed. Efforts were made to integrate Ducal Prussia's monetary system with that of Poland and Royal Prussia, leading to the Order's coinage being declared invalid in June 1530.[36] Across the duchy, the black cross was replaced by a black eagle with a gold crown and the letter 'S' (for Sigismund), symbolising both ties to the Holy Roman Empire and allegiance to the Polish crown. It marked the end of an era.

THE END OF OLD LIVONIA

In the late fourteenth and fifteenth centuries, the Teutonic Order in Livonia promoted itself as the only capable defender of Christendom against the threat of the schismatic Rus'. This, as we saw earlier, echoed similar statements from Scandinavian rulers. But in Livonia, the Order used this to justify its continuous attempts to become the dominant power in the region. In a letter to the pope in 1392, the Livonian master defended the occupation of Riga's archbishopric by the Order's army on the grounds that the archbishop and chapter had been allied to pagans, Rus', infidels and other enemies of the Order, and therefore the brethren were acting in the best interests of Catholic Livonia. Similar accusations were thrown at the Bishop of Dorpat, and the Order repeatedly sought to promote itself as the episcopate's 'protector', again citing the need for Catholic unity against the Rus'.[37] Tensions with the episcopates were further elevated in 1428 when the Order's advocate of Grobin intercepted a delegation bound for Rome intending to complain about the brethren directly to the pope. The delegates were robbed of their valuables and clothes, and murdered. The advocate fled and was condemned, but in secret some of the Order's higher-ranking members protected and supported him financially.[38]

The Order in Livonia took care of its own but, within the upper echelons of its ranks, there was an ongoing power struggle between two factions – Rhinelanders (which also included the Order's Dutch bailiwick of Utrecht) and Westphalians (corresponding to modern northwestern Germany). The Rhinelanders, who dominated the leadership for the first three decades of the fifteenth century, were in favour of the status quo, whilst the Westphalians sought more independence. As in Prussia, the Order in Livonia had been hit by a drop in membership. With numbers further depleted by an outbreak of plague in 1433, Master Cisse van den Rutenberg started to recruit new members from the Order's Utrecht bailiwick and, by 1435, a sixth of the Livonian brethren were Dutch.[39] Then, the Battle of Ukmergė, mentioned earlier, was a disaster for the Rhinelanders. The Livonian master and many of his leading officials were killed. This was, in many respects, a 'Tannenberg' for the Livonian brethren, and contributed to the Order vowing to end its involvement in Lithuania. This also meant the Westphalians would now come to the fore, eventually appointing a new master from their ranks. They would steer the Order in Livonia towards increasing autonomy from Prussia.

The battle marked a significant turning point in Livonia's power dynamics. The brethren found themselves unable to dominate the region militarily or politically as they once had. The need for a new political structure became apparent, and so the Order, together with the other territorial powers in Livonia, including all the episcopates and leading towns, created the Livonian Confederation. As in Prussia, the Order in Livonia was having to increasingly rely on mercenaries to garrison many of its castles. This, in turn, threatened the region's security, and so the Confederation was intended as a mutual defence pact against all external enemies. The Confederation also sought to redress the balance of power in Livonia, to ensure that no one group could dominate the region. A *Landtag*, or regional diet, would be created, where the various political stakeholders grouped into 'estates' were represented, essentially forcing the Order to share power with both secular and ecclesiastical authorities.[40] A manorial system had already begun to develop in Livonia, first on episcopal lands but eventually within the Order's commanderies, and by the fifteenth century the manors of the descendants of crusaders and German immigrants were more numerous than those of indigenous vassals, becoming a stronger political force.[41] In the end, the Livonian bishops and the Order would continue to clash over the division of power in the Confederation, tensions that occasionally erupted into armed conflict. During Walter of Plettenberg's reign, the process of summoning regular assemblies saw the *Landtag* gradually transform into a regular forum for discussing Livonia's domestic and foreign policies. This would eventually lead to a regulated assembly in the early decades of the sixteenth century.

During this time, the Order continued its long-standing feud with the burghers of Riga, which erupted into open conflict in the 1480s and pitched battles between the two sides. The usual justification was wheeled out. The Livonian master declared that, if the Order had secular authority over Riga's archbishopric, it would be able to better protect Livonia against the Rus'. Evidently, no one was buying into the Order's propaganda. In 1485, the Order's army was defeated by Riga's, but six years later, the tables were turned, as the brethren triumphed under Plettenberg's leadership of its army – then acting as the Livonian marshal. On 31 March 1491, the two sides finally came to a lasting agreement in Wolmar. All in all, the brethren in Livonia got off lightly. Riga was the only town that truly challenged their rule, even if Reval proved to be a difficult political partner, and there was no equivalent of the Prussian Confederation, no co-ordinated uprisings. This is almost certainly because the economic situation in Livonia was not so drastic (even though the Order had debased the coinage here too), but also because the balance of power had depended on consensus since the crusading era, reiterated in the various agreements between the region's powers in the fifteenth century.[42] At the same time, Livonia's territorial divisions limited the development of a cohesive union of towns and nobles, as the general assemblies became places for negotiations between representatives from different territories, rather than places of solidarity.[43] The lack of a unified state would eventually prove fatal.

Then, the Reformation started taking root in Livonia, first in Riga and Curonia, and then in the other major towns.[44] Interest in Lutheranism within the Order grew slowly, with William of Balen, the commander of Windau, becoming the first high-ranking member to join the reformers. While he was demoted and transferred, reformist tendencies were generally tolerated as the dominant Westphalian faction prioritised autonomy from Prussia over religious division. Although Plettenberg was a committed Catholic, his successors were more receptive to Lutheran ideas and encouraged preachers in Livonia. After the death of Master John of Recke in 1551, both the emperor and the Order's grand master sought a more committed Catholic leader, but the next master, Henry of Galen, supported Lutheranism and even participated in evangelical services. Reformist ideas were not seen as a threat to the Order's integrity, reflecting its transformation from a Catholic corporation into an aristocratic, chivalric organisation accommodating different religious denominations.[45]

At the start of the sixteenth century, tensions between Livonia and Muscovy were at an all-time high following Ivan III's sacking of Novgorod, and his closure of its Hanseatic kontor (trading post). Plettenberg's war and the truce that followed resulted in decades of peace, until the ascension of Ivan IV 'the Terrible'. As the first tsar of a Russia unified under Moscow, Ivan was eager to secure access to the Baltic Sea for trade purposes and to expand Russian influence in the region. Livonia, politically fragmented, economically weak and militarily outdated, was an easy target. When Livonian tribute payments to the Russians were halted, this was used as a pretext for war. In January 1558, Ivan's armies quickly overran much of the region, defeating the forces of the Confederation. The war escalated into a larger conflict as Poland-Lithuania, Sweden, and Denmark-Norway became involved, each seeking to assert their own influence over Livonia and contain Russian expansion.

The war had a devastating impact on Livonia's population, with many towns and villages destroyed. Later audits listed numerous vacant farmsteads, as many fled from war-torn areas to escape the violence, resulting in significant population displacement. Refugees often moved to safer areas, including Poland and Lithuania, but also those parts of Livonia largely unaffected, such as Ösel. The disruption caused by the conflict led to famine and outbreaks of disease, whilst the destruction and neglect of agricultural land and the collapse of local economies made it difficult for the population to sustain itself. But its lasting effects were to bring the old political order crashing down. Gotthard Kettler, who had risen up the ranks of the Order in Livonia to commander of Fellin, forced the Livonian master to resign and took his place, hoping for military aid from Poland-Lithuania against Moscow. With northern Estonia submitting to Sweden, Kettler — now also a convert to Lutheranism — saw the only way to preserve his own power was to make a formal alliance with Poland.[46] In 1561, he entered into negotiations with the Polish king who agreed to the creation of the Duchy of Courland and Semigallia from the Order's southern lands in Livonia. The Order's old vassals then declared their allegiance to the new duke, affirming the creation of the new political order. Kettler would later invite prominent Lutherans to his lands and ordered the translation of confessional texts into the

Latvian language. This contributed to establishing its status as a written language, and laid the foundations for Latvian literature.[47]

By the end of the war, the bishoprics of Dorpat, Courland, Ösel-Wiek and Riga had been secularised, and their territories redivided between the new powers. The Polish-Lithuanian Commonwealth, led by King Stephen Báthory, launched successful military campaigns against Russia, gradually reclaiming territory in Livonia. The war ended with treaties between Russia and Poland-Lithuania, and between Russia and Sweden. Russia was forced to relinquish its claims to Livonia, and Poland-Lithuania and Sweden solidified their control over the region. Nonetheless, the war marked the beginning of Russia's long struggle to gain influence in the Baltic and transformed the balance of power in Northern Europe.

THE END OF THE CRUSADING WORLD IN THE NORTH

The final crusade in the North was an attempt to reconquer Greenland by the Kalmar Union's monarch, Christian II. Greenland's Norse colonies had been abandoned in previous decades, and the intended targets of the crusade were the indigenous Inuit, who were savage pagans in the eyes of the Church. In 1514, the pope provided a crusading bull which offered indulgences to all participants in the campaign, but after two failed attempts to launch the expedition, the plan was eventually abandoned.[48] Within a few years, the Reformation had swept through Northern Europe, and in time the Scandinavian kingdoms, Prussia and Livonia – for centuries pitched as the frontier of Catholic Christendom – all adopted Lutheranism. Protestants dismissed the pope's authority to declare wars, along with the value of indulgences. Paweł Włodkowic's arguments, which emphasised the rights of non-Christians and questioned the moral and legal grounds of conversion by force, resonated with the reformers. When the brethren of the Teutonic Order in Livonia discarded their monastic robes in 1561, all connections with the crusading movement in the Baltic were finally severed. Nonetheless, the concept of a 'just war' remained significant in Protestant thought, particularly in the conflict with Catholic states.[49]

Lutheranism spread rapidly across the northern provinces of the Holy Roman Empire and, by the mid-sixteenth century, it was adopted in the duchies of Pomerania and Mecklenburg, both areas which still had significant Wendish populations. Whilst in Finland and Livonia, the Reformation had resulted in the production of the first texts in the indigenous languages as a means of reaching the broader population, here it accelerated the Germanisation of the Wends. As German-speaking Protestant clergy began to replace Catholic priests in Wendish areas, the use of the German language increased. Limited efforts were made to translate some religious materials into the Wendish language but, as Protestant churches promoted the use of German-language Bibles and hymns, the Wendish language declined, even as literacy rates increased with the Protestant focus on education. As a result, the Wends, who were already a minority group within a predominantly German-speaking society, experienced further cultural marginalisation during the sixteenth century. In contrast, the efforts of Protestant clerics in the eastern Baltic saw the beginnings of written Latvian, Estonian, Lithuanian and Finnish literature – the foundations for the later national awakenings of these countries.

The Catholic Church did not take all this lying down. Backed by the Habsburg dynasty, it threw its energies into fighting Protestantism through the Counter Reformation. This saw the rise of Baroque art and architecture, which was designed to reflect the glory and power of the Catholic faith, and to inspire congregants with grander visions of heaven. New religious orders also emerged, who would play a critical role in revitalising Catholic spirituality, most famously the Jesuits. In the North, they were especially active on the territories of Poland-Lithuania, which became the main centre for the Counter Reformation in the Baltic. Here, the Catholic Church waged a battle not only on Protestantism, but also on what it considered to be lingering traces of indigenous paganism. This became particularly focused on southern Livonia, where Jesuits were active in promoting Catholicism and winning back converts from Lutheranism but, while some success was achieved in towns like Riga, the majority of the population remained Protestant.

The Counter Reformation was cut short by Sweden's seizure of much of Livonia from the Commonwealth. Under the leadership of King Gustavus Adolphus (reigning 1611–32), Sweden became a major player in European politics, particularly as a result of its military victories during the Thirty Years War (1618–48), which resulted in the occupation of parts of the Holy Roman Empire, Royal Prussia, Poland and Livonia. The conflict that followed – the Great Northern War – saw Sweden pitted against a coalition that included Russia, Denmark-Norway and the Polish-Lithuanian Commonwealth. The war ended with the Treaty of Nystad in 1721, which resulted in substantial territorial gains for Russia, including northern Estonia, Livonia and parts of Finland. Sweden lost its status as a major power, while Russia emerged as a dominant force in Northern Europe. Meanwhile, Ducal Prussia transformed from a former vassal state of Poland into a new, independent kingdom. This brought with it new reflections on its past that would eventually shape how the Baltic Crusades would be reimagined.

FROM BLACK CROSS
TO IRON CROSS

CHAPTER 12

ANCESTRAL STRUGGLES
Reimagining the Baltic Crusades

Humanity shudders at the blood that was spilt here in long and savage wars, until the ancient Prussians were nearly extirpated, and the Courlanders and Latvians reduced to a state of slavery, under the yoke of which they still languish. Perhaps centuries will pass before it is removed, and these peaceful people are recompensed for the barbarities, with which they were deprived of land and liberty, by being humanely formed anew to the use and enjoyment of an improved freedom.

> Johann Gottfried Herder, *Outlines of a Philosophy of the History of Man*, 1803[1]

THE EMPEROR AT MARIENBURG

In 1902, an extraordinary event took place at the Castle of Marienburg in West Prussia (Polish Malbork), once the headquarters of the Teutonic Order.[2] The German emperor, William II, was visiting on one of his official '*Kaisertage*' or 'Emperor's Days'. William had taken a personal interest in the restoration of Marienburg, visiting the castle almost forty times over the course of his reign, usually twice a year. On three occasions, these visits coincided with lavish and highly politicised celebrations that glorified the German Empire and his family, the Hohenzollerns, whose lineage included the last grand master of the Teutonic Order in Prussia.

On each occasion, William gave a speech praising Marienburg as a resplendent symbol of German civilisation. The celebrations in 1902 went a step further. The event had been meticulously planned for two years, with the upper castle's two-decadal restoration to be completed for the occasion and crowned with the consecration of the Church of the Blessed Virgin. Accommodation within the castle had to be prepared for a long list of distinguished guests, which included German royals, high-ranking nobles and members of the imperial court, as well as delegates from the Brandenburgian Protestant Order of St John, of which the Hohenzollerns were protectors, and high-ranking delegates from the Catholic Teutonic Order, now headquartered in Vienna.

The celebrations, which included numerous processions, speeches and a lavish banquet, had been planned for the autumn of 1901 but, with the death of William's mother Victoria in August, they were postponed until Thursday 5 and Friday 6 June the following year, the latter marking the provincial holiday of West Prussia. The elaborate pageantry blended the splendour of William's court with the re-enactment of the medieval Teutonic Order – soldiers from the local 152nd infantry regiment stationed across the castle complex were dressed as knights of the Order in full battle gear, complete with chainmail, helmets, shields, spears and swords. William himself would wear the robes of the Brandenburgian Hospitallers, with a broad collar of ermine and a black hat with a white feather. The castle was awash with the banners of the German Empire, the Kingdom of Prussia, the Teutonic Order and the heraldic arms of eleven grand masters, the Order of St John and the most famous of all crusading saints, St George. Even the breakfast menu provided for the guests was lavishly branded with the arms of both military orders, as well as the eagle of the Hohenzollerns, with the restored red-brick castle pictured in the background.

The inaugural service at the Church of the Blessed Virgin was marked by a sermon from the imperial court's preacher Ernst Dryander, who had accompanied William and his wife Augusta Victoria to Jerusalem in 1898 for the equally dramatic inauguration of the Lutheran Church of the Redeemer. Dryander highlighted the importance of Marienburg for the Teutonic Order's history and, crucially, for the German future of Prussia, as well as referring to the connection with the Order of St John, invoking the shared past of the two medieval military orders. William had decreed the church was to serve both Catholics and Protestants, a sign of religious reconciliation in the service of German unity, vividly represented by the presence of the Brandenburgian Hospitallers and the Teutonic Order. That evening, during the course of a lavish banquet, the emperor gave speeches where he praised both orders, reminiscing about the Middle Ages and the German achievement represented by Marienburg, stating that it should remain a permanent symbol of German undertaking. He then went on, in typical form, to evoke the threat to Germanness posed by Poland, and called on the German nation to defend its customs. The highest-ranking member of the Order present at the feast, Baron Anton of Mauchenheim, the general of the Austrian cavalry, publicly thanked the emperor for restoring Marienburg, highlighting it as a symbol of German loyalty. William II was a colourful, buffoonish figure, a traditional autocrat, prone to diplomatic gaffs, regularly lampooned by his opponents and increasingly alienated from his subjects, but his provocative speech infuriated the Polish press, and even shocked some of his own entourage.

Yet he was not alone in his sentiments. Like the battlefield of Tannenberg, the Castle of Marienburg had been transformed into a nationalist symbol within a growing climate of ethnic tensions driven by the political upheavals of the nineteenth century. During William's reign, the remodelling of the castle was directed by one of the great pioneers of architectural restoration – Conrad Steinbrecht. He had begun his work during the ascendancy of the German Empire, a superstate that had been brought together by the 'Iron Chancellor' Bismarck and led by the indomitable 'Iron Kingdom' of Prussia.[3] Steinbrecht's approach to Marienburg Castle sought to capture the historical spirit of a monument which rivalled the great fortresses of medieval Europe. It also defined the conquest and taming of 'the East', a bastion of the civilising influence from Western Europe which had reached its apogee in the German Empire. This point had been repeatedly made by William in his speeches.

But this was a recent historical creation, and its genesis was a process of myth-making, where the fragmented conquests and migrations of the Middle Ages were brought together to provide a new history for the unified German nation. The notion of German cultural supremacy was met with a counter-narrative from Polish nationalists living under Prussian, Austrian and Russian rule, which emphasised the historical victory over the Teutonic Order, and thus over German civilisation. Meanwhile, Lithuanians, Estonians, Latvians and Finns sought to assert their independence from Russian control, and in the process constructed their own national histories. Smaller groups such as the Masurians and Saami came under renewed pressure to integrate within the newly defined nation states. The Baltic Crusades became central to these politicised narratives, where they were reimagined to create new and competing historical memories.

REIMAGINING MEDIEVAL PRUSSIA

In 1525, nearly three centuries of rule by the Teutonic Order in Prussia ended. The former grand master, Albert, became ruler of both the duchy and his hereditary lands in Brandenburg, a political union that was formalised under his son and which subsequent Hohenzollerns inherited. In 1657, the electors of Brandenburg gained full hereditary sovereignty over Prussia in a treaty with the Polish-Lithuanian Commonwealth mediated by the Habsburgs. This would embolden the elector Frederick III to declare his candidacy for the office of 'King of Prussia' in 1700. Supported by Emperor Leopold I, Frederick sought to enhance his prestige with a royal title; although facing opposition from the pope, the Teutonic Order (which continued to claim ownership of its former Prussian lands) and the Polish parliament, Frederick's claim required further legitimation. This was to be found in Prussia's past, but it was not the crusading past.[4] The Brandenburgian diplomat Frederick Werner had allegedly found proof in old historical documents that pagan Prussia had been a kingdom under a powerful and wise sovereign called Waidewutus. The Hohenzollerns embraced this mythology which not only legitimised Frederick's claim to the 're-established' Prussian throne, but also extended the family's territorial claims to the ancient bounds of Prussia. Henceforth, the name 'Kingdom of Prussia' would be used to refer to all the Hohenzollern lands, including Brandenburg.

Pro-Hohenzollern scholars then began to focus on the idea of a distinct Prussian identity, one that stressed freedom, wisdom and nobility, separate to that of the German-speaking migrants who had colonised the region after the Order's conquest; from their perspective, it was the foreign Germans, rather than the indigenous Prussians (the so-called *National-Preussen*), who had given Prussia a bad reputation. Therefore, the newly founded kingdom at the turn of the eighteenth century was legitimised by the rejection of an enslaving and oppressive German past, whilst embracing a mythical realm of freedom-loving people governed by a wise and just ruler. Frederick, in identifying with Waidewutus, was throwing off the shackles of enslavement by the 'foreign' Teutonic Order. His coronation in Königsberg in January 1701 as Frederick I of Prussia was accompanied by the inauguration of the Order of the Black Eagle. This chivalric order headed by the Hohenzollerns, whose badge depicted black eagles wearing gold crowns, was part of the ceremonial package of kingship. The coronation took place inside the church of the ducal castle which was redecorated with the insignia of the new knighthood.

The Grand Master of the Teutonic Order at the time, Count Palatine Franz Ludwig of Neuburg, protested against Frederick's coronation before the Imperial Diet in Regensburg in 1703. Polish Prussian historians, alarmed by the prospect of a Hohenzollern monarchy, also waded into the debate, emphasising the fragmented nature of Prussian history and the legitimacy of the Polish-Lithuanian Commonwealth's governance.[5] But this did not put the brakes on the ascendancy of the new Prussian kingdom which, by the end of the eighteenth century, had grown to become the most powerful state in the Holy Roman Empire, and had increasingly annexed land from the Commonwealth in a series of partitions with Russia and Austria. As the French Revolution inspired political change across Europe, nationalism began to emerge as a powerful force. The dissolution of the Holy Roman Empire in 1806, following Napoleon's victory at Austerlitz, fuelled the rise of German nationalism as a reaction to French domination, which included aspirations to unify the fragmented German polities into a nation state. Romantic nationalist poets, artists and thinkers played a key role in shaping the cultural discourse on unification, and looked to the Middle Ages for the defining characteristics of what it meant to be German – a time before the divisive damage inflicted by the Reformation, the Enlightenment and French imperialism. This was accompanied by a drive to restore medieval buildings, as well as inspiring an architectural revival of primarily gothic styles at a time of rapid industrialisation and urban growth.

Within Prussia, the medievalist revival focused on the heritage of the Teutonic Order, whose lands historically lay in the easternmost provinces of the Iron Kingdom, which included the recently annexed lands of Polish Prussia. The first significant moment in this revival was the creation of the *Eisernes Kreuz* or Iron Cross in 1813 after the decisive battle of Leipzig, by order of Prussian King Frederick William III to decorate soldiers who had fought against Napoleon.[6] The original design by Karl Frederick Schinkel was based on the Order's black cross. The link between the Iron Cross and medieval German crusaders was made explicit for the public not long after the medal's inauguration, when Max von Schenkendorf celebrated it as the renewal of the Order's emblem and spirit in his poem *Eisernes Kreuz*.[7] The cross quickly became more than just a military award. It was added to the kingdom's war flag a few years after the medal's inauguration and eventually onto other military flags and the royal standard. By the time of German unification, the flared black cross had become as much an emblem of the Iron Kingdom as the black eagle and, as such, both became the principal symbols of imperial Germany.

In his poem, Schenkendorf had also referred to the other iconic symbol of the medieval Order – Marienburg Castle. During the reigns of the first two Prussian kings, little value had been placed on the Order's crumbling castles, and some were even readily dismantled. The Hohenzollern rulers had acquired Marienburg Castle after annexing Polish Prussia and transformed it into a barracks, demolishing and modifying many parts of the structure to fulfil modern military needs. Friedrich Gilly's drawings of Marienburg after a visit in 1794, followed by Friedrich Frick's etchings, drew public attention to the castle, and more broadly to the Order's monuments in Prussia. When Schenkendorf protested against the demolition of the castle in an article published by a Berlin newspaper in 1803, it prompted the royal cabinet to order the preservation of the fortified complex the following year. Active restoration began in 1817, initially focusing on the so-called Middle Castle. The Grand Master's Palace and Great Refectory were cleared and their interiors elaborately redecorated, including a series of idealised paintings of eight grand masters and two Prussian masters in the summer refectory of the palace. At times, conservation was trumped by practicality. The railway cut through the castle's outer ward, where a train station was set up – one that Emperor William would later use for his regular visits.[8]

The most important period of restoration began in 1882 under the direction of Conrad Steinbrecht. A native of Tangermünde, a picturesque town on the Elbe, Conrad had fought in the short-lived Franco-Prussian War in 1870–1, which had concluded with the unification of Germany, before joining a German archaeological team excavating and restoring the ruins of Olympia in Greece. Upon his return, he became involved in the restoration of medieval buildings at Thorn, the first urban colony established during the thirteenth-century crusades which had quickly developed into a major Hanseatic centre. Impressing his peers, he was granted the directorship of the restoration programme at Marienburg. Steinbrecht's colleague Bernhard Schmidt, who had been introduced to medieval Prussian architecture by Steinbrecht's own brother, a teacher in Kolberg, would in turn take over as director of building works at Marienburg in 1922. By this time, the castle had been restored to its medieval appearance – or at least how Steinbrecht imagined it – stripping away subsequent centuries of alterations, replacing elements that had been demolished in the early nineteenth century and restoring the complex to invoke the spirit of Marienburg's heyday under the Order. The task was immense, and his achievement was, by any standards, impressive.[9]

Steinbrecht's approach to restoring Marienburg was methodical and academic, and reflected a genuine interest in conservation as a means of capturing the authentic character of medieval buildings. His programme of restoration, which sought to turn back the clock to the pre-Polish ownership of the castle, emphasised military architecture externally, whilst the internal appearance, which did in places maintain visibly surviving decoration, evoked an imagined German chivalric court, complete with suits of armour and antler chandeliers. The work involved a complete overhaul of the complex and, in the process, resulted in the first systematic architectural and archaeological study of Marienburg Castle. Although striving for authenticity, Steinbrecht replicated the nationalist link between the Teutonic Order and the Kingdom of Prussia, emphasising German militarism over monasticism. The adjacent town was furnished with a spate of Gothic Revival buildings, which continued to be constructed into the 1920s. The route to Marienburg was also lavishly decorated with a series of neo-gothic bridges across the Vistula floodplain for the new railway that ran from Danzig through to East Prussia. The portals of these bridges were decorated with figures of the Teutonic Order, including Herman of Salza, who had brought the Order to Prussia, and Albert, the last Prussian grand master and first duke, ancestor of the Hohenzollern kings. These framed the Order as the forebears of German civilisation in the East who had tamed the indigenous Prussians. Over the course of the nineteenth century, historians also began to take a serious interest in the Order. Between 1827 and 1839 Johannes Voigt published his monumental nine-volume work on the history of the Order in Prussia, but the true milestone was reached in the last decade of the nineteenth century, when the extant written sources began to be assembled in the formidable *Preußisches Urkundenbuch* (*Prussian Records Book*) series, with the first volume published in Königsberg in 1882.

Yet the conquest and religious conversion of Prussia by Catholic forces was at odds with the *Kulturkampf* (cultural struggle) which saw intensive state-sponsored hostility towards Catholicism in late nineteenth-century Protestant Prussia. Here, the Order's connection to crusading and the papacy was quietly sidelined, and instead a shared Christian heritage was invoked. This theme dominated German literature on the conquest of Prussia. In 1806, Zacharias Werner, who had been born in Königsberg, published *Das Kreuz an der Ostsee* (*A Cross on the Baltic*), a novel which celebrated the acceptance of Christianity by the Prussians, who were depicted as primitive and warlike. Later writers such as Franz Lubojatzky continued this theme, but focused on the figure of Herkus Monte, the ill-fated leader of the Prussian uprising of 1260.[10] Here, the indigenous Prussians were depicted as courageous freedom fighters, whilst the Order's brethren were pious Christian Germans whose conquests were presented as inevitable.[11] The influential conservative and Reichstag member Heinrich von Treitschke's *Das deutsche Ordensland Preußen* (*The Teutonic Order's Prussia*), written in 1862, went further, drawing on the vocabulary of colonialism to pitch the thirteenth-century conquerors and colonists as an early manifestation of the enduring 'German spirit'.[12] In his mind, the Order's Baltic conquests and German colonialism in Africa were analogous: the pagan lands were eulogised as the German nation's early colonies.

For nationalists promoting unification, Prussia's provincial history became part of Germany's history, and Prussian museums were designed to distil and highlight the contribution of the local German culture towards a common national identity. The varied eastward migrations of German-speaking merchants, peasants and knightly families in the Middle Ages were merged into a continuous and unified diaspora with a shared destiny. As a result, the Order's German and military characteristics were brought to the fore, just as their Catholic crusading role faded into the background. The origin of the notorious phrase *Drang nach Osten* or the 'Push to the East' can be traced to the Polish historian Julian Klaczko in 1849, who linked contemporary German nationalism with historical expansion, referring in particular to the Order.[13] The phrase was subsequently adopted by Russian journalists attacking German speakers in the Baltic provinces, and ultimately found its way into German nationalist discourse.[14]

This promotion of German Christian colonialism did not, however, detract from interest in the regional distinctiveness of Prussia. Within the multitude of expressions of German nationalism, one grassroots movement emerged in the second half of the nineteenth century which looked to a more intimate sense of belonging. This was the '*Heimat*' movement, often translated as 'homeland', although there is no real equivalent term in English.[15] Broadly speaking, the concept of *Heimat* was expressed on a sliding scale, from identifying with one's personal home, locality and region, through to a sense of national solidarity. It was also deeply embedded in nostalgia for the pre-modern agrarian world: a world that was being transformed by agricultural mechanisation and urban industrialisation.[16] As such, its adherents became focused on preserving and celebrating everything encompassed by the term *Volkskultur* – local customs and festivals, oral histories, artefacts, especially locally found archaeological objects, historical buildings, particularly farmhouses, and even landscapes – the physical and mental sum of belonging to a particular place. *Heimat* societies and museums sprang up across the thirty-seven German states, and *Heimatkunde*, or the study of the homeland, would become a staple of school textbooks. This included those regions historically occupied by German speakers beyond the bounds of the Holy Roman Empire, where provincial identities were articulated through the historical encounters between Germans, Balts and Slavs. Still dominated by substantial tracts of woodland, as well as its lakes and marshes, the province of East Prussia had not industrialised to the same extent as other German regions, and this strengthened its image as a bastion of rural life, unspoilt by modernity. It was the picture-perfect *Heimatland*.

As elsewhere, intellectuals set out to record and preserve the indigenous *Volkskultur*, and in 1837, Jodocus Dedatus Hubertus Temme and Wilhelm Johann Albert Tettau coauthored *Die Volkssagen Ostpreussens, Litthauens und Westpreussens*, a rich compendium of folklore from across Prussia. Old Prussian may have vanished as a living language, but Lithuanians living in East Prussia were recognised as the natural inheritors of indigenous culture.[17] With the formation of the Prussian Antiquity Society (Altertumsgesellschaft Prussia) in 1844, scholars set out to systematically record the diversity of Prussian culture, which included archaeological excavations of prehistoric sites and surveys of medieval structures. This also led to the creation of the first regional museums, including the Prussia Museum in Königsberg which became the principal repository for all archaeological materials associated with the pre-German past. Local amateurs also conducted their own excavations and handed over large quantities of materials to these museums. Richard Jepsen Dethlefsen, the restorer of Königsberg Cathedral, stands out as the promoter par excellence of Prussia's composite heritage in the early twentieth century. He argued for East Prussia's unique cultural value, describing it as a multicultural society, and this was clearly embodied in the *Heimat* museum he later cofounded, where Old Prussian, Lithuanian, German and Masurian cultures were all represented. But the celebration of the medieval past in Prussia also prompted the development of a cultural war against the 'historical enemy' of Germanness – Poles.

THE CULTURAL WAR WITH POLES

In 1864, a monument was erected in Marienburg to a local historical celebrity. This was Bartholomäus Blume, the town's major who had led the resistance against Polish forces during the Thirteen Years War and was eventually captured and executed in 1460. This seemingly obscure memorial, in fact, epitomised the ethnic struggle that had become associated with the medieval Teutonic Order in the nineteenth century, eclipsing the conquest and Christianisation of the indigenous Prussians. For nationalists, the Order's (and by extension German nation's) greatest foes were not the extinct indigenous Prussians, who had been conquered and subdued, but the Poles, who had antagonised, eroded and finally (along with the Lithuanians) cowed the Order's power. Prussia itself was, therefore, the quintessential historical battlefield between the Germans and Slavs, and it was this reframed ethnic conflict that came to overshadow popular retellings of the region's history.

Following the shrinkage and dissolution of the Polish-Lithuanian Commonwealth in the late decades of the eighteenth century, Lithuania had been annexed by Russia, whilst northern and western Polish territories were incrementally taken by Prussia, with Austria occupying the south. The Prussian Protestant regime was openly hostile to Polish Catholics, who faced social, religious and economic discrimination, alongside policies of Germanisation, which included the redistribution of land to German settlers. This became more intensive following the unification of Germany, when Bismarck led the *Kulturkampf* – the state's attack on the Catholic Church. Nationalist societies like the Deutscher Ostmarkenverein (German Eastern Marches Society) sought the obliteration of a distinctive Polish national identity within German lands, and even the physical replacement of Poles with Germans. Similar sentiments were also expressed in the popular genre of *Ostmarkenromane* or East March romance literature, some of which evoked fears of racial contamination in what was imagined as a German colonial space.[18] This perspective would be endorsed by William II's recurring verbal attacks on Poles throughout his reign. The Polish press responded by ridiculing William and there were regular boycotts of his visits to Polish towns, although his invocation of the Teutonic Order and its civilising mission in the East during his 1902 visit to Marienburg drew particular condemnation: oppressive German colonialism in Cameroon was compared to the subjugation of Poles in Pomerania and Greater Poland by the 'bloodthirsty Teutonic Order'.

Poland's partition and occupation by foreign states, as well as the suppression of Polish identity, fostered in turn a nationalist movement built on resistance and patriotism, which also looked to the past. Here, too, the Middle Ages became a major focus, and for those Poles living under German rule, historical tensions with the Teutonic Order were invoked as a mirror of contemporary struggles. These tensions had also brought the Poles and Lithuanians together in a historically profound union. So, whilst indigenous pagan Prussians were often represented in nineteenth-century Polish literature as the barbaric 'other', whose aggression against their Christian neighbours was to blame for the ensuing conflicts, Lithuanian pagans could be sympathetic and heroic figures. This is particularly evident in the work of Adam Mickiewicz, the founder of Polish Romanticism. Several of his poems were set in Lithuania, and two in particular referred to the historical conflict with the Order. In 1823, he published *Grażyna*, which centres on a tragic Lithuanian heroine married to one prince Litawor who has made a pact with the Order, and in 1828, *Konrad Wallenrod* told the story of a pagan Lithuanian who, as a boy, is captured and re-educated as a Christian by the Order in Marienburg, but whose sense of national identity is later awoken, leading him to take revenge against the brethren. Mickiewicz, like the other great Polish Romantic poet Juliusz Słowacki, had no problem with the pagan elements of either Balt or Slavic culture, which were regarded as the source of the national soul.

The shared struggle against the Order was also emblematised in the paintings of Jan Matejko, which came to define how key moments in Polish history were imagined and represented. Two in particular were concerned with the triumph over the Teutonic Order – *The Battle of Grunwald* (1878), depicting the death of the Grand Master Ulrich of Jungingen at Tannenberg in 1410, and *The Prussian Homage* (1880–2), which showed the supplication of Albert of Hohenzollern to King Sigismund.[19] Unsurprisingly, both were negatively received by the Prussian authorities, as unpleasant reminders of the defeat of German civilisation which called into question its alleged superiority over the Slavs. Matejko had lived and painted his *Grunwald* in Cracow, which had emerged as the centre of the Polish national revival in the partially autonomous Austrian province of Galicia. On Friday 15 July 1910, during the culmination of the 500th anniversary celebrations of the battle of Grunwald, an evocative equestrian monument of Jagiello dedicated to the victory over the Order was unveiled in Cracow. Below, the figure of Lithuanian grand duke Vytautas stood over the sprawling body of the fallen grand master Ulrich of Jungingen.[20]

Equally influential was Henryk Sienkiewicz – the second Polish Nobel laureate after Maria Skłodowska Curie – who remains particularly known for his epic work *Krzyżacy* (commonly translated into English as *Knights of the Cross*). This was initially published in weekly instalments between 1897 and 1900 and then as a book. It had taken a decade to prepare, and Sienkiewicz drew on a diverse range of scholarly works and primary sources, including Długosz's text, but also an earlier (and far less popular) novel on the conflict with the Order by Józef Ignacy Kraszewski. Matejko's *Grunwald* would have provided visual inspiration but, in Sienkiewicz's rendition of the battle, the Vytautas is only given a modest role, in contrast to how he is depicted in the painting. Nonetheless, Sienkiewicz continued and firmly established the trope of the Teutonic Order's brethren as cruel, nefarious Germans, in a conflict with the morally superior union of Poland and Lithuania. Sienkiewicz stated that one of the reasons for writing *Krzyżacy* was to bolster Polish national confidence in the face of continuing occupation by foreign powers, although the setting was also specifically chosen to make it acceptable to Russian censors who had banned or heavily edited Mickiewicz's works for much of the nineteenth century. Sienkiewicz was an outspoken critic of Prussia's policy of Germanisation, and his portrayal of the Order, now firmly ingrained in both nationalist camps as the ancestors of the German Empire in the East, reflected his political views and resonated widely with Poles living under occupation.

The identity politics of Prussia were not confined to the cultural war with Poles, but also involved the Slavic Kashubs in Pomerelia and the Masurians in East Prussia. These minority groups experienced their own national revivals, which emphasised their distinctive languages, customs and histories; some aligned their identity politics with Polish nationalism and, indeed, Prussian nationalists grouped all of them under the label of undesirable Poles or Slavs. In Masuria, where the Order had invited German and later Masovian settlers, a dialect (some have called it a distinct language) developed from the late fifteenth century. Masurian became a composite of Polish and German, and had also absorbed some Old Prussian words. In the 1870s, the policy of Germanisation within eastern Prussia targeted Masurians in the same way as Poles. The 'success' of this policy resulted in a widespread perception of Masurian as a secondary dialect, with most of the population identifying themselves as German in 1925; the number of Masurian speakers had dropped to less than 30 percent of the total documented in 1900. However, the process of homogenisation had also fostered a vocal minority who sought to preserve their distinct identity: the Masurenbund or Masurian Federation, founded by Gustaw Sawicki in Lyck in 1923, lobbied the German government for recognition.[21] Germanisation of non-German-speaking populations residing within the Iron Kingdom was, therefore, not only seen as a means of purifying the Prussian nation – it was also historical vengeance.

REVIVING THE GRAND DUCHY

Most of the lands of the Grand Duchy of Lithuania came under Russian control with the disintegration of the Commonwealth and, in the first half of the nineteenth century, a sense of an ethnically defined Lithuania began to emerge, connected to the duchy's historical bounds. Initially, Lithuanian nationalists, all members of the bilingual aristocracy, argued for close ties with Poland, emphasising the historical importance of the shared Commonwealth in the development of Lithuanian culture – Mickiewicz was equally important to Polish and Lithuanian intellectuals. This relationship ended with the bloody suppression of the so-called 'January Uprising' in 1864, an insurrection led by Polish officers in which Lithuanian gentry and peasants also become involved, intended to overthrow Russian rule and restore the Commonwealth. The reprisals that followed the crushing of the rebellion included the suppression of national languages, with a ban on all publications in the Lithuanian language unless it was rendered in Cyrillic.

In the 1880s, a new form of nationalism emerged which promoted ethno-linguistic rather than cultural identity, a response to the Russian state's suppression of the Lithuanian language. The cultural map of the

Commonwealth was replaced by a Lithuanian national space defined by indigenous speakers living on lands under the thrall of Prussia, Russia and, historically, Poland. Lithuanian political sovereignty, in turn, became projected onto this space – the reimagined grand duchy. As a result, the rulers of the pre-Polish 'golden age' in the grand duchy became framed as national heroes, particularly Gediminas, his son Kęstutis and, above all, Vytautas. As a convert to Catholicism, Vytautas bridged the pagan and Christian worlds, but without the shadow of Polish rule associated with his cousin Jogaila (Jagiello). In geographic terms, nationalist impulses also coalesced around Samogitia more than Polish-dominated Vilnius, where the Russian census of 1897 indicates Lithuanians formed as little as 2 per cent of the population.[22] This region, which had also been on the front line in the wars against the Order, became regarded as the bastion of the Lithuanian national spirit. The country's vibrant peasant heritage had also been swept up in the folk revival of the nineteenth century that sought to capture the essence of being Lithuanian. The memory of the state and of the Lithuanian peasant were woven together by novelists, poets and artists to evoke a Romantic image of a pagan realm where people lived in harmony with nature and successfully resisted historical German aggression. But most anti-German sentiments coalesced around territorial claims to the adjacent German Memelland, the north-eastern part of Prussia which included a substantial population of Prussian Lithuanians, in a nationalist bid to attain ethnic unity. This saw the framing of Germans and Lithuanian Prussians as two diametrically opposed groups – brutal crusaders and their victims, respectively.[23] Yet here there was no internal discussion of nationhood associated with linguistic purity, no ambition to detach from Germany: the bilingual and socially conservative Lithuanian Prussians were happy with their dual identity and even shared a sense of *Heimat* with the Germans. In the Memelland, one's place of birth was more important than ethnicity.[24] Neighbouring Lithuanian nationalists regarded this group as Germanised and in need of re-Lithuanisation and their later efforts focused on promoting the Lithuanian identity of the towns of Memel and Tilsit. However, their energy was largely directed at the Poles. Inspired by Latvian nationalists in the early twentieth century, Lithuanian nationalists saw clear similarities between the Latvian conflict with the local Germans and their own conflict with the Polish elite who still dominated land ownership in the core of ethnically defined Lithuania. The synergies between Latvian and Lithuanian cultural movements in the early twentieth century even sidestepped religious differences, and a common Latvian-Lithuanian state began to be discussed in opposition to the former union with Poland which continued to preoccupy the dreams of Polish intellectuals.[25]

This finally came to a head in the short-lived Polish-Lithuanian War in 1919, which resulted in the seizure of Vilnius by Poland as part of Chief of State József Piłsudski's vision of resurrecting the old union. The act of independence in February of the previous year had defined the Lithuanian state as the re-established grand duchy with Vilnius as its capital. In the following two decades, the medieval vision of Lithuanian national identity was widely disseminated through currency, postage stamps and art commissioned by the new government. In 1923, this culminated in the celebration of the 600th anniversary of the founding of Lithuania's historic capital Vilnius, then still under Polish control. Historical grand dukes, depicted as armoured warriors, appeared on everything from playing cards to hotel lobby décor for the mass consumption of the new republic. On 31 December 1929, the government created the Jubilee Year of Vytautas the Great, leading to an array of celebrations for this national hero, and the following year the Order of Vytautas the Great would be established as the Republic's highest award.[26] The jubilee year was marked by celebrations across Lithuania and the construction of monuments dedicated to Vytautas in town squares around the country. These sculptures, some figural, some more abstract, would be destroyed by the Soviets and then rebuilt in the late 1980s and 1990s, as Soviet monuments were, in turn, demolished.

REMEMBERING OLD LIVONIA

The promotion of the Teutonic Order's link with the German Empire did not extend to its other former eastern Baltic domain – Livonia. In the eighteenth century, Russia had incrementally wrested control of the region from Swedish and Commonwealth rule, subdividing it into the governates of Estonia, Livonia and Curonia. The German aristocracy, who made up less than 10 per cent of the population, were permitted to retain their privileges and continued to dominate the upper echelons of society, including landownership, education and administration, whilst the majority of those who lived in the countryside – ethnic Estonians and Latvians – remained serfs. Ties with Germany were largely cultural and many of the so-called 'Baltic German' elite studied in German universities, which also meant that Enlightenment thinking influenced reflections on their history as colonisers and promoted a growing interest in the plight of the indigenous peasantry.[27] This resulted in the first detailed critiques of the German impact – framed as it was in ethnic terms – on Livonia.

One of the first to write about medieval Livonia in this way, although better known for his work on the Balkans, was Ludwig Albrecht Gebhardi. He attributed the success of the crusades, which created Livonia, to the superiority of German military technology and the strategies of its leading proponents, particularly Bishop Albert, whilst dismissing the role of religion. Following the tendency of Enlightenment historians, he also criticised the crusaders for their brutal and hypocritical treatment of the indigenous population. Gebhardi had plenty of material to work with and his critique of the German regime in Livonia extended right up to the Reformation, including the selling of indulgences by the Teutonic Order at the start of the sixteenth century. The only real hero in his narrative was Gotthard, whom Gebhardi considered to be both competent and truly pious. Yet from his perspective the stifling legacy of the crusades was represented by the German landed nobility, who resisted attempts to reform the peasantry as well as the opportunity to create a strong, centralised government. With the advent of Lutheranism, the indigenous peasantry faded into the background of Gebhardi's history, no longer relevant to the events he saw unfolding before him. Focusing solely on the failure and fate of the German ruling class in Livonia, it did not even occur to him that the next century would be defined by the rise of Latvian and Estonian national movements.[28] Similar sentiments were echoed by the far more influential German Enlightenment philosopher Johann Gottfried Herder, who reflected more broadly on the moral and cultural legitimacy of German dominance over indigenous peoples in both Prussia and Livonia, as quoted at the start of this chapter.[29]

Ideas associated with 'Popular Enlightenment' were also adopted directly from Germany. This saw the idealisation of Latvian and Estonian peasants, whose social status was regarded as synonymous with their ethnicity, as the embodiments of the natural, raw state of society, coupled with the desire to educate and modernise them (albeit with some restraint to avoid 'too much enlightenment'). This, in turn, led to discussions regarding serfdom and aristocratic privileges, whose advocates and opponents both looked to the crusading period to support their arguments. The indigenous peasants were very much perceived through a colonial lens, where the 'discovery' of the eastern Baltic with its 'exotic' and 'primitive' populations was compared to that of North America. Yet the stereotypes drew attention to the problems of serfdom, and the practice was eventually abolished in all three Baltic governates.[30]

In the nineteenth century, the intellectual and political climate shifted, influenced by Romanticism and emerging nationalistic ideologies. German Baltic intellectuals increasingly sought to justify and glorify the role of German settlers in Livonia, presenting their colonisation as a 'civilising mission'. Where Gebhardi and Herder saw oppression and loss, writers now saw progress and salvation.[31] In 1874, the incorporation of Henry's *Chronicle of Livonia* into the *Monumenta Germaniae Historicae* made Livonia an essential part of German history, and the text itself would be a foundational narrative for Baltic German identity. The events described in the *Chronicle* had been illustrated in earlier decades by the engraver Friedrich Ludwig von Maydell, and the images conveyed a sense of German cultural superiority. One of the leading Baltic German scholars on Livonia whose impact resonated more widely was Theodor Schiemann. Born in Curonia, he had studied in Dorpat (Estonian Tartu) and relocated to Berlin with his family in response to the Russification policies of Tsar Alexander III. Here, he became professor of Eastern European history and regional studies in 1892. Under the influence of Heinrich von Treitschke, his work would come to define German scholarship on the eastern Baltic, and also inspired Emperor William, who sought his advice on matters relating to the region. Schiemann, ferociously opposed to Russian hegemony, promoted the idea of the eastern Baltic as an integral cultural element of the German Empire – he would describe the region as the 'first

German colony'. At the same time, Schiemann and his disciples advocated the special status of the Baltic Germans in the Russian governates, opposing their assimilation into a greater Germany.

Baltic Germans also participated in the Gothic Revival which, as elsewhere, became twinned with the conservation and restoration of medieval buildings.[32] Monuments were raised to celebrate key German figures from Livonian history. In Latvia, representations of Bishop Albert were erected, most famously in Riga's cathedral, where he was depicted on a stained-glass window, and a copper statue on the southern wall.[33] An eighteenth-century portrait of Walter of Plettenberg in Nordkirchen also served as a model for later sculptures and representations of the Livonian master, which became popular in both Latvia and Estonia. In 1834, the Riga Society for Antiquities was founded, serving as the inspiration for later Baltic scholarly societies. It produced numerous publications relating to local archaeology and the acquisition of antiquities. However, the focus remained very much on German heritage and, even when conservationist societies were established towards the end of the nineteenth century, they were primarily concerned with medieval buildings and art – the material culture of the Livonian elites.[34] The castle at Wenden (Latvian Cēsis) was the first in the region to open to visitors in the 1840s, and subsequently attracted enough interest to kick-start restoration work funded by antiquarians. In 1913, when the Riga Society led the way in creating the first post of provincial archaeologist for the Baltic provinces of Russia, the appointee was a German – Max Ebert from Berlin – although the outbreak of the First World War cut short his investiture. The first state-sponsored archaeology would come with independence.

The Baltic German monopoly on the past would be challenged by the national awakenings of the Latvians and Estonians in the 1850s: the first clear recognitions of national identities in the eastern Baltic. At this time, a spatial sense of 'Latvia' began to form, albeit separately from the region of Latgale (which was Catholic rather than Lutheran); a more clearly defined geography would not be shaped until the end of the century, along with the earliest attempt at producing a map of Estonia in the Estonian language. Nationalist intellectuals also looked nostalgically to the past but, influenced by Enlightenment views of crusading as barbaric and strong anti-German sentiment, challenged the idea of the crusades as a civilising force. New histories were written which also drew on Henry's *Chronicle*, but which characterised the crusades as ushering in a period of oppression and slavery, ending an indigenous 'golden age'. Not all nationalists agreed everything about pre-crusade culture was admirable: for example, in Estonia the notion of pagan brutality posed a moral dilemma, whereas in Latvia (and also Finland) it did not.[35]

Nonetheless, the crusades became an enduring chronological marker for national historical memory. In 1868, the Estonian historian Carl Robert Jakobson divided Estonian history into three eras – light, darkness and dawn – and framed the notion of '700 years of slavery' following the crusades. Jakobson, as a Protestant, like other Estonian Enlightenment writers, was critical of Catholicism rather than Christianity per se. But this division would dominate Baltic historiography into the twentieth century, reinforcing the idea of the crusades as the start of centuries of oppression by German rulers.[36] This would be mirrored in the writings of Latvian historians, such as Jānis Krodzinieks, which stressed that German crusaders hindered the natural historical trajectory of the Latvian nation.[37] Novelists also popularised the indigenous struggle. The Estonian writer Eduard Bornhöhe published *Tasuja* (*Avenger*) in 1880 and *Villu võimisemed* (*Battles of Villu*) in 1890, both centred on the St George's Night Uprising, which embedded the event in the public consciousness. Industrialisation resulted in further tensions between the wealthy German elites, who still ruled the Baltic governates on behalf of the Russian state, and the largely indigenous workers in Estonia and Latvia, for whom the ancient struggle reverberated in the newly exacerbated inequalities of urban life.

Yet the dichotomy between Germans and Latvians and Estonians was not always so clearly defined, and there was a burgeoning interest amongst German intellectuals in indigenous folk culture; some have argued this empathy had already been present for a long time, particularly amongst humanists. This became embodied by organisations such as the Gelehrte Estnische Gesellschaft (Learned Estonian Society), which was dedicated to the study and promotion of Estonia's historical culture. In the absence of any indigenous chronicles related to the ancestral past and its struggle with foreign invaders, new ones had to be compiled, drawing on Estonian and Latvian folklore. As in Prussia and elsewhere, folklore was avidly collected from peasants by scholars such as Jakob Hurt, Matthias Johann Eisen and Jaan Jung, who perceived this body of knowledge as a record of the unblemished pre-industrial – and, in this case, specifically pre-Christian – past. One of the Learned Estonian Society's achievements was the publication of *Kalevipoeg* (*Kalev's Son*) – an epic poem inspired by Estonian folklore and written by Friedrich Reinhold Kreutzwald, a leading figure in the country's national awakening. The Latvian national epic *Lāčplēsis* ('Bear Slayer', the name of the heroic protagonist) was written by Andrejs Pumpurs under similar circumstances, with the theme of the struggle against the invading Germans running throughout the poem.[38] National indigenous folk revivals at the time bypassed the German elements of post-crusade society and sought their roots in prehistoric culture.

The sidelining of German heritage eventually also came from the Russian authorities, who were increasingly intent on restricting the political autonomy of the Baltic Germans in the governates.[39] At the same time, there were attempts to align eastern Baltic indigenous heritage with that of Slavic Russia. This led to narratives highlighting how indigenous people first encountered a peaceful form of Christianity through the Russian Orthodox Church, before the oppressive Catholicism of the German and Scandinavian crusaders. In this respect, the value of Christianity had already been known in Estonia and Latvia, and contributed to a notion of a shared Baltic-Russian heritage in opposition to that of Catholic Europe. This narrative, unsurprisingly, would become very dominant during the Soviet era when anti-German sentiments were widely promoted by the authorities. Cast in this light, Henry's *Chronicle* became regarded as the biased document of a foreign agent complicit in the subjugation of the indigenous Baltic peoples. Some, however, sought to reclaim Henry's text by suggesting he was a well-educated local – Henry 'the Lett'. Those indigenes who had sided with the crusaders and had been lauded by Baltic Germans, such as Kaupo, were branded as traitors to the nation. Others, in particular Lembitu, were regarded as courageous freedom fighters. This reading of the events of the crusades that created Livonia filtered into the national awakenings of Estonia and

Latvia. Whilst both Germanisation and Russification were resisted, the indigenous struggle against Western crusaders defined the popular narrative which connected the past with the present.

The events following the Bolshevik Revolution and the collapse of Tsarist Russia cemented this negative impression of Germans in the eastern Baltic. German forces occupied Estonia in October 1917 and, whilst initially allied with the Latvians against the Bolsheviks, it became clear their intent was to establish a new German duchy here. The flag of the 'United Baltic Duchy' was, of course, none other than a black cross on a white background. The German Catholic nobility hoped to recolonise the eastern Baltic with Catholic settlers in the name of the Virgin Mary, echoing the events of the crusades.[40] This plan was scrapped following the downfall of William's imperial regime in 1918; however, over the next two years, Latvia and Estonia fought what would become wars of independence, firstly against the Russian Bolsheviks and then eventually against Baltic German forces. Ancestral heroes were invoked during the war, for example Lembitu's name was given to an Estonian gunboat and several armoured cars. Contemporary battles became associated with those against crusaders, in particular St Matthew's Day when both Kaupo and Lembitu were defeated, and the revived memory of the Estonian St George's Night Uprising in 1343 resonated with the conflict against both the Russians and Germans. Even the Latvian Bolsheviks had a regiment of volunteers named after Ymanta, a Liv chieftain who had resisted the German crusaders, whose legend had been forged a century earlier by the Baltic German Lettophile Garlieb Helvig Merkel in his poem *Wannem Ymanta*.[41] The signing of the armistice on 11 November 1918 would subsequently be commemorated in Latvia annually as 'Lāčplēsis Day', a direct reference to the 'Bear Slayer' who by then embodied the defence of the nation against foreign invaders.

The two decades following the end of the Estonian and Latvian wars of independence saw the assertion of the identities of the new nation states in relation to the past. Comprehensive inventories of archaeological and ethnographic monuments were drawn up and heritage conservation laws were passed in 1923 in Latvia and in 1925 in Estonia, with the aim of recognising and protecting both prehistoric and medieval sites, as well as sacred natural sites. There was a flourishing of archaeological investigations, museum foundations and exhibitions and, whilst the remits of the national heritage bodies and scholarly societies encompassed the entirety of the past, in practice preferential treatment was given to prehistoric monuments rather than the 'foreign' medieval period. This went hand in hand with state-sponsored programmes of Estonianising and Latvianising the minority German and Russian populations, alongside replacing street names and toponyms. In this respect, the historical conflict between crusaders and indigenous took centre stage in the cultural programmes of national assertion.

This was expressed, in part, by the construction of monuments which celebrated resistance to the German conquerors in key locations picked from Henry's *Chronicle*. These were unveiled with great ceremonial and folk pageantry, bridging contemporary and reimagined ancestral identities. One such memorial was placed at the centre of the earthen stronghold on the Estonian island of Muhu. According to Henry's *Chronicle*, the stronghold had been besieged in 1227 by German crusaders, who eventually breached its defences and slaughtered everyone inside. The unveiling of the memorial pillar, which was dedicated to the defenders and their 'ancient fight for freedom', in 1928 was accompanied by a lavish folk-costumed ceremony.[42] Two years earlier, a monument dedicated to the Estonian War of Independence had been unveiled in Suure-Jaani. It had a sculpture of Lembitu by Amandus Adamson, armour-clad and fallen but raising his sword in defiance, with his name engraved on the plinth together with the dates 1217 and 1918–20, thus making a direct connection between the modern and ancestral struggle for freedom against foreign oppression. The monument would be demolished in 1941, restored, removed again in 1949 following the loss of independence, and finally reinstated in 1990 with the regaining of sovereignty.[43]

FINNISH ORIGINS

The Great Northern War had resulted in a part of south-eastern Finland being transferred from Swedish to Russian control, reorganised by the new authorities as the Vyborg Governate and subsequently also referred to as *Staraya Finlyandiya* – 'Old Finland'. The remainder of Swedish-controlled Finland passed to Russia in 1809 and, whilst indigenous Finns had resisted Russian incursions, the region, reconstituted as a grand duchy within the empire, attained a significant level of autonomy. Although politically acquiescent, nationalism in Finland would take the form of the Fennoman movement, with roots already in the late eighteenth century, which stressed the primacy of Finnish language and customs. This was driven by Finnish nationalists, engaging in a culture war against the minority Swedish elite, as well as opposing attempts at Russification. It was opposed by the pro-Swedish Svekoman movement in the late nineteenth century which later evolved into the modern Svenska folkpartiet i Finland – the Swedish People's Party in Finland. The Svekomans, much like the Baltic Germans, promoted their own ancestral heritage to stake their historical claim to Finland, which they traced not only back to the crusades but to an earlier, romanticised Viking Age. At the heart of their argument was the idea that Swedish Vikings had settled the Finnish littoral before the Finns, and the movement even adopted the Vikings as its emblem. Figures from the crusading era were also celebrated as colonial heroes, such as Tyrgils Knutsson who was associated with the 'Third Swedish Crusade' and the foundation of Viborg – Finnish Viipuri.[44] By the early twentieth century, the Swedish language had retained a place in Finnish society, but its importance was dramatically reduced, and opposing nationalist tensions would rise following Finland's declaration of independence.

Finnophiles also looked back to the pre-crusader period for their source of national identity and pride. A new national history was created as an integral part of Finland's national awakening.[45] This narrative would draw on familiar materials – select archaeological monuments and artefacts, fragmentary historical sources and, most of all, folklore, which survived primarily in oral form and was perceived as timeless. Antiquarians and early archaeologists focused their attention on the Late Iron Age, the centuries preceding the Swedish conquest. Other periods of prehistory were deemed far less important because they were considered to pre-date the origin story of the Finns. In the new narrative, the Finns were thought to have migrated to Finland during the Iron Age and established a powerful warlike society that resisted the recurring threat of foreign invaders, most of all the Vikings – the ancestors of the Swedish crusaders – whilst simultaneously being culturally superior to the neighbouring Saami, who were regarded as exotic primitives. Opinion was divided over whether the Finns were originally Germanic or Finno-Ugrian, a distinction that had explicit political overtones.[46] But where to find the essence of Finnishness? As elsewhere, Romantic nationalists turned to the peasants, whom they regarded as the faithful custodians of the national soul.

Finnish intellectuals would capture this essence by transcribing the intangible, orally transmitted songs and folklore of peasants onto paper for the burgeoning national market; centuries of Lutheran insistence on reading the Bible in the vernacular had ensured the majority of the population was literate by the mid-nineteenth century. The Finnish Literature Society collected and published over thirty volumes of folk poetry in its series *Suomen Kansan Vanhat Runot* (*Ancient Poems of the Finns*), and the region of Karelia, like Samogitia for the Lithuanians, became regarded as the principal source of Finnish indigineity, drawing Romantic artists alongside ethnographers and folklorists. Historically a frontier region between Swedish and Russian spheres of political and religious influence, Karelia became an integral part of the ethno-nationalist map of Greater Finland. The zenith of nationalist literature was Elias Lönnrot's epic *Kalevala*, first published in two volumes in 1835–6, which synthesised large numbers of folk songs recorded during visits to Karelia; a subsequent edition incorporated new material from additional trips. This final text became the foundation of Finland's national literature, even serving as a primary source for Finnish history, and was later immortalised in the paintings of Akseli Gallen-Kallela and the music of Sibelius. The *Kalevala* and other folk poems celebrated the heroic pre-Christian past with a colourful array of characters inhabiting a prehistoric national environment, one that archaeologists populated with Iron Age monuments and artefacts. With the publication of Väinö Voionmaa's influential history of Karelia in 1915, Finnish peasants became idealised as culturally sophisticated, rational and integral to societal development.

By the early twentieth century, and particularly following the creation of an independent Finland in 1917, the narrative became more confrontational. Whilst the ancestral Iron Age Finns were perceived as powerful warriors governing an independent state, centuries of oppression and cultural degradation had reduced the population to the status of servile peasants. The sparse documents from the crusading period provided the details for the narrative of the heroic, but ultimately tragic, struggle against the Swedish crusaders and the Church. Archaeologists working on the Late Iron Age searched for Finnish pagan survivals that could be dated to the twelfth and thirteenth centuries, examples of cultural endurance, even resistance against Swedish rule and colonial Christianity. The narrative of a violent cultural confrontation was underlined by illustrated reconstructions, including the forced baptisms of indigenous peoples conducted under the watch of sinister churchmen.[47] But whilst Catholicism had certainly transformed indigenous religion, the nation's spiritual revival (along with the promotion of the Finnish language) was framed as beginning with Lutheranism and, in this respect, the introduction of Christianity was perceived as ultimately beneficial. Although the first history of Finnish art, published in 1891, omitted medieval castles – in part, because they had been built by Swedes – antiquarian interest in ruined medieval monuments developed into a more profound appreciation of cultural heritage. With the professionalisation of archaeology in Finland, including the appointment of a state archaeologist and the foundation of a state museum, medieval monuments became officially part of the nation's cultural heritage.

REIMAGINING THE CRUSADING PAST

If there was ever a time when the past was reinvented to serve the contemporary needs of entire societies, it was during the period between the rise of Napoleon's empire and the aftermath of the First World War, marked by political turmoil and societal transformations across Europe. In the Baltic Sea region, the emergence of nationalist movements would eventually result in the creation of independent states, the birth of modern Germany, Estonia, Latvia and Finland, and the re-emergence of sovereign Poland and Lithuania. National identity was defined, above all, by language, which was gradually mapped onto territory, although the geopolitical situation would continue to fluctuate. Ethno-linguistic identities were framed in reference to a reimagined past, visually marked by revivalist architecture, the restoration or reconstruction of select historical and prehistoric monuments, alongside canonical works of literature and art, all reinforcing national historical narratives with dramatic effect.

From the Prussian littoral to Finland, the crusades were regarded as the defining moment for ancestral histories, whether from the perspective of the conquerors and 'civilisers' or that of the 'true indigenous' who looked back to an earlier time of freedom, before the cascade of German, Swedish, Polish and Russian rule. The inheritors of the medieval conquests, whether German-speaking or Swedish in the case of Finland, constructed narratives revolving around their historical civilising influences to legitimise their continuing political and economic privileges. Indigenous nationalists, in turn, variously promoted elements of the pagan past, not always rejecting the impact of the conquests, including the long-term role of Christianity in shaping their societies. Minorities like the Sorbs and Masurians also drew on the past to assert a distinct identity in the face of intensified Germanisation.

Learned societies of historians and archaeologists began to seriously and systematically research this period, generating a vast corpus of data, but all too often their work was filtered through a nationalist lens. Together with museums, schools, the press and eventually film makers, they disseminated the new historical narratives to receptive public audiences. By the early decades of the twentieth century, the Baltic Crusades were widely regarded as the first episode in a protracted ethnic struggle between indigenous and migrant cultures. The rise of the Kingdom of Prussia, the German Empire and subsequently the Third Reich ensured that the dominant narrative, twinned with the history of the Baltic Crusades, would become the German 'Push to the East', where contemporary colonial aspirations were projected onto the past. The notion of crusading, already distasteful to Enlightenment thinking, became replaced with an ethnic military history that encompassed the historical conflicts with Poland and Lithuania. The leading role of Prussia in the unification of Germany elevated the Iron Cross to a symbol of the two regimes that followed, echoing the black cross of the Teutonic Order, and ingrained the ethnic struggle between Germans and Slavs in political ideologies with catastrophic consequences in the Second World War, ones that continue to resonate into the present.

CHAPTER 13

FROM ARYAN CRUSADERS TO EUROPEAN HERITAGE
The Baltic Crusades Rehabilitated

Malbork Castle, a symbol of power and cultural tradition, is the most important monument to the monastic state of the Teutonic Order, a unique phenomenon in the history of Western civilization. The Castle is at the same time the major material manifestation of the Crusades in eastern Europe, the compulsory conversion to Christianity of the Baltic peoples, and the colonization of their tribal territories, which played a vital role in the history of Europe.
Statement on the inscription of Malbork Castle on UNESCO's World Heritage List, 1997[1]

UNEARTHING THE CONQUEROR OF THE WENDS

On 17 July 1935, Adolf Hitler arrived at the city of Brunswick in Lower Saxony, a bastion of Nazi support. His itinerary included a visit to the recently opened tomb of Henry the Lion, the Duke of Saxony and conqueror of the pagan Wends. The excavation, conducted in secrecy, had been organised by Dietrich Klagges, the Nazi leader of the short-lived Free State of Brunswick, in an attempt to raise his own political profile and that of his 'fiefdom' within the Third Reich. As a prominent figure in northern Germany's medieval history, Henry was a focal point for Saxon identity, but the cathedral and ducal tomb were to be converted into a national shrine celebrating the German colonisation of Slavic lands.

Except the unearthed skeletal remains identified as Henry's were much smaller than expected and had an abnormal hip joint, with one leg being shorter than the other. Confused by the discovery (and lacking any osteological skills), experts concluded that Henry was short and deformed. Investigations in the later twentieth century would determine the skeleton most probably belonged to Henry's wife Matilda who had been buried alongside him. A second body, identified at the time as Matilda, is now thought to have been Henry's. But the initial discovery was a massive disappointment for the Nazi leadership, and the archaeologist's report was not published at the time.[2] Moreover, Hitler's own opinion of the duke was far from positive, as he idolised the Holy Roman Emperor, Frederick Barbarossa, who had been 'betrayed' by Henry. The stunt backfired for Klagges and he had his control over the cathedral and tomb rescinded. Hitler then ordered the design of a new crypt for the ducal couple, and this would be completed in 1938 and decorated with heraldic emblems and a swastika. The tombs were illuminated by bowls of fire, and a lock of Henry's alleged hair was also on display in the manner of a relic. The cathedral interior would also be remodelled to turn back the clock to Henry's time, or at least how the Nazis imagined it. It included new paintings in the nave that illustrated Henry's conquest of the Wends. By 1940, the cathedral had been rebranded as a 'sacred German pilgrimage site', although Hitler had lost interest by then and did not attend the rededication ceremony. The elevation of Henry to the status of national hero was nonetheless popular amongst Nazis, and it was underpinned by an ideology that influenced the Third Reich's expansionist and genocidal policies.

This was *Völkisch* nationalism, which had emerged in the nineteenth century and emphasised the racial purity and superiority of the 'Aryan' or German people. Deeply tied to anti-Semitism, it promoted an ideal of a racially homogeneous, agrarian society based on a romanticised view of rural German life, largely rooted in an imagined version of the Middle Ages. Here, the medieval German peasantry was idealised as the purest expression of the *Volk*. The movement's ideologues were deeply critical of modernity, urbanisation and industrialisation, which they saw as forces that disrupted the 'natural' way of life of the German people. *Völkisch* thought shaped, and in turn was given intellectual support by, Ostforschung ('Eastern research') – a group of German scholars and academic institutions, whose studies of

Central-Eastern Europe claimed that 'Germanic' peoples had historically settled and 'civilised' these regions.[3] The *Völkisch* movement's interest in the restoration of an ethnically pure German state aligned with Ostforschung's academic interests, where the reclaiming of Germany's historical territories became framed not only as a matter of survival but also of racial destiny. This idea was closely tied to the concept of *Lebensraum* ('living space'), the belief that the German people needed to expand territorially to fulfil this national destiny. *Lebensraum* had already been accepted into nationalist political discourse to justify imperial expansion leading up to the First World War, and would notoriously become a principal foreign policy of the Third Reich. For propagandists like Dietrich Klagges, who represented the intersection between *Völkisch* and Nazi thought, Henry the Lion embodied the spirit of *Lebensraum* – a model of leadership for German territorial expansion. Klagges had even compared Hitler's policies as a continuation of Henry's, in a speech given the month before the Führer's visit to Brunswick. Klagges was also one of those *Völkisch* thinkers who reinterpreted Christian history and symbolism to fit the ideological mould of a struggle for racial purity.[4] The Baltic Crusades, now well-established in German nationalist histories as a civilising mission to 'barbaric' societies, were framed as a dichotomous conflict between 'Aryan' crusaders and 'non-Aryan' pagans.

The descendants of those Wendish groups targeted by Henry and other marcher lords were still living in Germany. They were the Sorbs, a largely rural population inhabiting the region of Lusatia. They had also had their national revival and actively resisted attempts at further Germanisation, which had intensified with the rise of nationalist policies. Following the end of the First World War, Sorbian and Czech activists had petitioned to include Lusatia within the new Czechoslovak Republic, arguing from the standpoint of their common Slavic roots. The proposal was rejected on practical grounds but, as a result of such attempts, suspicion of the Sorbs grew within German nationalist circles.[5] 'The Wendish Danger' was adopted as a journalistic slogan for describing this perceived internal threat to Germanness. Historians and archaeologists of the Ostforschung had long emphasised the primitivism of Slavic societies, and German leaders who had confronted the Wends, like Henry the Lion, became important in the historical narrative of German expansion.

Tensions between the Sorbs and the German state increased during the Weimar era, particularly as nationalist sentiments grew. In 1920, a 'Wendish Department' was set up in Bautzen with the aim of Germanising the Sorbs. By the time the Nazis came to power in 1933, the number of Sorbish speakers had fallen by 50 per cent. Within a few years, Sorb organisations, publications and the use of the language in public were banned, whilst Slavic place names were Germanised.[6] The scholars of the Ostforschung declared the Sorbs had no history, and so their 'disappearance into Germandom' was regarded as inevitable although, to speed up the process, Slavic-sounding place names were replaced with German ones.[7] But far greater fears of the threat to Germanness became focused on the province of East Prussia. It was here that historical events connected with, and adjacent to, the Baltic Crusades were most vividly invoked, in an escalating culture war. Whereas the medieval German margraves had limited propaganda value for the Nazis, the standard bearer of the crusading movement in the North – the Teutonic Order – would come to symbolise German expansion for both the Nazi regime and for those it conquered and occupied.

The historical memories of the Baltic Crusades were appropriated by the Third Reich within, and especially at, the borders of German territory, and they were also invoked in the propaganda that accompanied the horrors of the conquests of Central-Eastern Europe and the oppressive rule of both Nazi and Soviet regimes. The association between German crusaders and Nazi aggression endured for decades following the end of the Second World War and continued to play a role in the propaganda of the Cold War. It would only be with the dissolution of the Soviet Union, the reunification of Germany and the restoration of full sovereignty to Poland, Lithuania, Belarus, Latvia and Estonia that new histories of the crusades began to be created. They now became a recognised part of European history, even as shadows of their nationalist past did not completely recede.

HISTORICAL MEMORY AT THE 'BLEEDING BORDER'

After the end of the First World War, the province of East Prussia became part of the Free State of Prussia which replaced the former kingdom following the dissolution of the German Empire. Containing less than 4 per cent of the population of Germany, the region was sparsely populated and of little economic importance, still dominated by rural holdings controlled by aristocratic families, but it came to play a disproportionately large ideological role in foreign relations with Poland and Lithuania. Under the terms of the Treaty of Versailles, a substantial part of Pomerelia in former West Prussia, the region of the Lower Vistula, was incorporated into the Republic of Poland as the Pomeranian voivodeship. The earlier policy of Germanisation, which had seen hundreds of thousands of German migrants settle in West Prussia during the nineteenth century as well as the confiscation of land from Polish nobles, was replaced by a reverse exodus driven as much by economic as political motives, followed up by the expropriation of the remaining German-owned estates within Polish territory. In Germany, right-wing hard-liners denounced the loss of Pomerelia in the familiar *Völkisch* language of cultural degeneration, especially as Germans were emigrating from the region in their hundreds of thousands.[8]

The free city of Danzig (Polish Gdańsk), separated from both Germany and Poland, remained largely populated by those identifying as ethnic Germans. The Prussian districts bordering the redefined Republic in the north-east, Marienwerder and Allenstein, with varying proportions of Polish- and German-speaking populations, were placed under the command of Inter-Allied Commissions to oversee a plebiscite determining which country they would be incorporated into. On 11 July 1920, in the midst of Poland's war with Bolshevik Russia and with preceding weeks of German-led activist violence and intimidation, the plebiscite took place. The relentless propaganda campaign had targeted Masurian communities in particular, and included references to an ethnically defined history of Prussia stretching back to the crusading period. Posters for a German vote included striking images of Teutonic Knights which were intended to symbolise continuity with East Prussia's past.[9] With the exception of a few borderland villages, the population in both districts voted overwhelmingly to remain part of Germany. The district of Marienwerder was then split between the Polish and Weimar republics – the German part would be incorporated into East Prussia, where its regional name Regierungsbezirk Westpreußen, which also included the districts of Elbing, Marienburg, Rosenberg and Stuhm, served as a reminder of the lost territory of West Prussia.

The province of East Prussia, truncated from the rest of Germany, then became the focus of national and regional campaigns to protect its German identity, in particular its borderlands. Polish communities within the province were marginalised and intimidated, particularly with the rise of local paramilitary and Nazi organisations, but they remained a noticeable element, closely tied to the Catholic culture of Warmia (German Ermland). Investment poured into conserving those distinctive architectural features of the province's *Heimat* deemed quintessentially German, especially historical rural buildings such as farms and mills, regarded as embodying the spirit of generations of German settlers.[10] The forests and lakes of Masuria, as well as the fenlands of the Vistula Delta, were also regarded as an integral part of the East Prussian cultural landscape, infused with German history. However, this went beyond nostalgic pride, this was *Heimatschutz* – defending the cultural property and identity of the German homeland.

The Lower Vistula, a borderland once more between 1920 and 1939, was studded with the remains of some of the most spectacular castles built in the wake of the crusades against the indigenous Prussians, not least of all the castle-cathedral at Marienwerder which had been constructed for the Pomesanian chapter in the first half of the fourteenth century. In 1551, the castle had passed to Albert of Hohenzollern, the former grand master and, after serving as a secular residence for two centuries, it was converted into a court and prison, partially dismantled in the process, then restored in the second half of the nineteenth century. In 1926, Waldemar Heym, a local schoolteacher and First World War veteran, opened the Heimatmuseum Westpreußen in the town, where he built up a photographic archive and collection of historical artefacts from neighbouring districts. Archaeological excavations had been taking place here since the late 1870s, but the new museum prompted a renewal of investigations within the castle and town, as well as excavations of prehistoric cemeteries along the Lower Vistula, and the collections of artefacts steadily grew. By the inter-war period, antiquarian societies were well established across Prussia and these years saw extensive excavations which filled museum storerooms, particularly those of the

Prussia Museum in Königsberg. Between 1934 and 1939, there was an increasing nationalist emphasis on the interpretation of the Prussian borderland's history, which included the denial or demeaning of any past 'foreign' presence or influence, particularly from Poland and Lithuania. This also saw the replacement of over 2,000 place names of Polish, Lithuanian and Old Prussian origin.[11]

The role of so-called 'borderland museums' (*Grenzlandmuseen*) like the ones in Marienwerder, Marienburg and Elbing, as well as scholarly societies in these towns, was to promote the historical German identity of the region. With the Nazis in power, the castle at Marienwerder was procured for ideological purposes, serving as a school for the Hitlerjugend. The town also became the base for the East Prussian Tourist Propaganda office. Tourism had long focused on the region's castles, where visitors could 'follow in the footsteps of the Teutonic Knights', but this was part of a new trend of appropriating castles with symbolic connections to German colonisation for inspiring the new generation of Nazi loyalists.[12] Tours from Germany, especially for youth groups, to this 'bleeding border' intensified in the 1930s, when the need to defend German lands from the threat of Poland was emphasised in pointed speeches and visits to historical monuments. In this respect, the complex history of conquest, settlement and religious transformation across the southern and eastern Baltic became subordinated to the nationalist narrative of an ethnic conflict, one that was mirrored in the present.

Fresh ammunition to bolster the territorial claims of the Third Reich was provided by the foundation of the Deutsche Ahnenerbe, a Nazi research institute dedicated to the study of the heritage of the 'Indo-Germanic Nordic race'.[13] Although several of its members were competent archaeologists, their findings were intended to serve as propaganda. East Prussia became one of the most important regions for their research, where Polish and Lithuanian historical claims to territory could be disputed and cast aside.[14] The first and largest excavations conducted by the Ahnenerbe took place at the stronghold of Old Christburg between 1935 and 1937, initiated by Heinrich Himmler after a visit to the site, and directed by Hans Schleif. The location was, of course, highly significant, not just because it was associated with the Teutonic Order's conquest of Prussian lands, but also because it was near the contemporary Polish border. The excavations were extensive, and initially focused on the stronghold's rampart, but then extended to the central area where numerous 'Germanic' pottery sherds were found. In his final report, Schleif concluded the site had been created by early Germanic settlers, and when the Order had taken the stronghold from the Prussians, they had regained lands that had always been German. Crucially, the absence of Slavic pottery clearly ruled out any historical basis for Poland's claims to Prussia and Pomerania. A field museum was set up, and local schools, youth organisations and Nazi dignitaries dropped by to visit. When excavations in the neighbouring Old Town of Christburg did not produce similar evidence for early Germanic presence, they were quickly discontinued.[15]

The Nazis also presented themselves in relation to this racialised vision of the past. The party's elite were envisaged as a new, quasi-medieval German knightly order, one that would follow in the path of the Teutonic Order with a reconquest of the East. Alfred Rosenberg, an enthusiastic Nazi ideologue, even regarded the Third Reich as a revived Teutonic Order state, an idea he promoted in his own polemical work on National Socialism, *Der deutsche Ordensstaat*, published in 1934. From 1936, special training centres were established at three purpose-built Nazi *Ordensburgen* or 'Order castles', at Krössinsee, Sonthofen and Vogelsang, with the aim of preparing the next generation of party leaders. Yet within the Nazi's ideological mishmash, the connections with the Order were not always explicit. Where visual comparisons were made between Nazis and medieval knights in art created for propaganda purposes, they were depicted as secular warriors, albeit with an air of sacrality: instead of crosses marking them as Teutonic Knights or medieval crusaders, there were swastikas. Where a cross was occasionally used, it was the Iron Cross.[16] For the SS, the Teutonic Order and other figures from the *Drang nach Osten* ('Push to the East') provided role models of Aryan knights. At Wewelsburg Castle near Paderborn in north Germany, which was intended as a place of assembly and inspiration for SS group leaders, some rooms were named after Marienburg, the Teutonic Knights (this room to be decorated with a painting of Marienburg) and, of course, Henry the Lion.[17]

A fourth Nazi *Ordensburg* was in fact intended at Marienburg and, whilst this plan was never implemented, the castle would serve as one of the most important symbols for the regime. Following the death of

Conrad Steinbrecht in 1922, Bernhard Schmid had taken over directing the castle's restoration until his retirement in 1941. Both men's legacy extended beyond conservation and restoration to a systematic and serious study of the historical monuments of Prussia, especially its castles. A few years before his retirement, Schmid had joined the Nazi Party during a time of increasing political tension over the so-called 'Polish Corridor'. The castle had been well-established as a nationalist symbol by Emperor William and this continued in the inter-war period and under the Nazis. As early as 1920, Marienburg had become a burgeoning centre for nationalist groups, including numerous paramilitary organisations, hosting various congresses including a visit from Marshal Hindenburg in May of that year. In the 1930s, the castle was used as the backdrop for the consecration ceremonies of the Hitlerjugend and its younger division, the Deutsches Jungvolk, as well as for political speeches by Nazi ministers. Propaganda films of 'German power in the East' showcased the vast and photogenic fortress, which must have left a profound impression on school groups and youth organisations during their *Heimat* visits. In 1931, the 700th anniversary of the arrival of the Teutonic Order was celebrated in East Prussia, focused on the castle at Marienburg and attended by high-ranking government officials, including President Hindenburg. The festivities and speeches were laced with German nationalist and anti-Polish sentiment.[18] In April 1934, Rosenberg gave an impassioned speech in Marienburg Castle, where he urged East Prussians to follow the example of the Teutonic Order, reiterating the *Drang nach Osten* and the creation of living space for German settlers, with the Nazis as the inheritors of the Order's legacy.

In the conditioning educational culture of the Hitlerjugend, a substantial part of the syllabus featured Prussia. Livonia – Livland – featured as well, although very much in the background. Compared to Prussia, it lacked the same depth of historical significance in German national memory. Moreover, Nazi racial ideology concentrated on demonising Slavic peoples, and Baltic and Finnic groups were less central to this racialised narrative. But the medieval heritage of the Baltic states would eventually become the focus of a renewed propaganda campaign, starting with the annexation of the Memelland. The population of this former region of East Prussia was split between Germans and Prussian Lithuanians. Following the region's incorporation into Lithuania in 1923, tensions with Germany simmered and flared up in incidents such as the Kovno trial in the spring of 1935, where 126 Memel Nazis were accused of committing high treason against the Lithuanian state. The commentary surrounding German claims to the region was embedded in its history which, for sympathisers and Memel Nazi organisations, only began with the Teutonic Order's conquest. In the meantime, Tilsit (later Russian Sovetsk), with its substantial Lithuanian population and which had remained within East Prussia, was rebranded as a German stronghold in the East, where the Order's heritage was emphasised.[19] The Memel Territory, as it was named in the Treaty of Versailles, became a key target for Nazi revanchist politics – the regaining of lost territories and reunification of the German *Volk*. When Germany reacquired the region in March 1939, the use of the Lithuanian language and symbols in public was suppressed.

Yet while the Nazi regime found it useful to celebrate the medieval Teutonic Order's militaristic role in the Baltic, especially in its confrontations with those perceived as lesser races, attitudes to the contemporary Order, as a Catholic organisation, were frosty and then openly hostile. In 1938, the Order was dissolved in Germany and Austria, and in the following year in Czechoslovakia – part of a broader campaign against religious organisations, aligned with the Nazi government's goal of reducing the influence of the Catholic Church. The Order's properties were seized and its priests and nuns persecuted: thirty-three members were murdered in Hartheim Castle in Austria as part of the Nazis' notorious euthanasia programme Aktion T4. The Nazis were perfectly content with discarding the modern, charitable incarnation of the Order, while simultaneously appropriating aspects of its medieval past for propaganda that glorified German militarism and expansionism. The Protestant Hospitallers of Brandenburg, previously under the protection of the Hohenzollerns, were not suppressed but continued to play a role in German society, including the provision of both welfare and military services. Although they endorsed the Nazi war against Bolshevism, their members also became actively involved in resistance against Hitler's rule.[20]

RELIVING OLD CONFLICTS

In August 1914, when the German army annihilated the Russian Second Army near Allenstein in what became one of the pivotal battles of the First World War on the Eastern Front, Field Marshal Hindenburg named the event the 'Battle of Tannenberg'. The site of the medieval battle was far from there, but his direct reference to the Order's defeat in 1410 underlined this as the latest retributive chapter in the historical German–Slavic conflict, whether against Poles or Russians, and it was celebrated as such in a slew of triumphalist poetry and press commentary.[21] Just over a decade later, the memorial dedicated to the victory was designed as an octagonal fortress built from brick and crowned with eight towers, a stark, modernist castle. Its architects (who would go on to redesign Henry the Lion's crypt in Brunswick) insisted that it was inspired by a stone circle. But this fooled no one, and for both Germans and Poles it was an explicit symbolic act that echoed the familiar monuments of the Order's rule. Situated close to the Polish border, its purpose was to bolster German steadfastness against the fear of Polish expansionism. When Hindenburg died in August 1934, the Tannenberg monument came once again to the foreground, as Hitler's orchestration of the president's state funeral at the memorial transformed it into pure political theatre. Hitler glorified Hindenburg's achievements and Germany's military past, and the German press covering the event referred to the Order's return. The site quickly became a place of pilgrimage, another marker in the cultural landscape of the *Drang nach Osten*.

In Poland, the 1930s were marked by an escalation in the war of historical symbols, in response to the Tannenberg memorial.[22] This became particularly acute on the border with Prussia, close to the site of the original battlefield. Activists from Działdowo, the only part of Masuria incorporated within the reborn Polish state, were especially involved in this. A museum opened in the town which included a room dedicated to the battle of Grunwald, as the Poles called it, and a few years later a monument to Ladislaus Jagiello, the victor of the battle, was raised. Another monument was built in the nearby village of Uzdowo, located right on the border with East Prussia. In comparison to the more dramatic Grunwald memorial in Cracow these were humble structures, but their location was far more provocative. In 1936, new copies of the Order's banners captured during the battle were made and hung in Wawel Castle in Cracow as the earlier set had been lost. Three years later, the Polish pavilion at the World Fair in New York flaunted an equestrian monument dedicated to Jagiello made by Stanisław Ostrowski.

In the summer of 1939, as Poles were anticipating war with Germany, the anniversary of the battle on 15 July provided an occasion for bolstering morale. Celebratory masses were held in Warsaw and Cracow, rallies took place around Grunwald monuments and nationalists reminded onlookers of the old glory days. There was even talk of a 'new Grunwald' in the expected conflict with Germany, as there had been in earlier decades. Lithuanians too invested in monuments celebrating Žalgiris, as they referred to the battle, centred on the figure of Vytautas. A copy of Matejko's *Grunwald* was bought in 1937 for the collection of the Vytautas the Great War Museum which had been built as the centrepiece of the jubilee celebrations. From the Lithuanian perspective, this painting – and especially Vytautas's prominent positioning – spoke of freedom from oppression and of an independent sovereign state. This promotion would continue on the global stage. Mirroring the Polish promotion of Jagiello at the World Fair, the centrepiece of the Lithuanian pavilion was a statue of Vytautas by Vytautas Kasuba, whilst one of seven large accompanying paintings depicted the Order's brethren laying down their banners before Vytautas following their defeat.

On 1 September 1939, German tanks and planes, branded with the Iron Cross in a manner reminiscent of latter-day Teutonic Knights, swept into Poland in what soon became a joint invasion with the Soviet Union that quickly overwhelmed the Polish state. The Iron Cross medal, held by many First World War veterans, had come to symbolise German pride in the face of national humiliation, and the transformed military, the *Wehrmacht*. The invasion of Poland saw the renewal of the various classes of the Iron Cross, with the new medals branded with a swastika on their obverse side, connecting the ideology of National Socialism with the earlier wars that had resulted in German unification. A brand-new version of the Iron Cross was also created – the Knight's Cross or *Ritterkreuz*. This was the Nazis' own black cross, intended to celebrate the new German knighthood which was reclaiming its ancestral legacy as the conquerors of the East. This vivid association between the medieval Teutonic Order and modern German military power was also bitterly clear to the Poles.

In his speech relating to the attack on Poland, Hitler referred to the struggles down the centuries between Germans and Poles – the knights of the Teutonic Order and the activities of medieval German settlers on Polish lands. This set the tone for the occupation. In October, the governor of the newly created *Reichsgau* Danzig-West Prussia, Albert Forster, urged the Germans who had been invited to occupy properties and lands confiscated from Poles to cast themselves 'into the spirit of the *Ordensritter*' – the Teutonic Knights. Forster sought nothing less than the eradication of non-Germans within his new governate, especially Poles and Jews.[23] A policy of population replacement was implemented which saw the removal of Polish citizens from West Prussian towns, including Marienburg, and their replacement with German settlers. Meanwhile, the newly created Nazi administration in Poland, the General Government, engaged in a systematic policy of destroying Polish national symbols, with Grunwald monuments topping the list – particularly the one in Uzdowo and the more elaborate memorial in Cracow. The replicas of the Order's banners were taken from Wawel Castle to Marienburg. On 19 May 1940, they were paraded in a solemn procession from the town hall to the castle in a symbolic reassertion of German power over Poland, made very clear in the accompanying speech by Hans Frank, the new head of the General Government.[24] The Nazi authorities were particularly keen to get their hands on Matejko's *Battle of Grunwald* and *The Prussian Homage* for obvious reasons, but failed to locate their hiding places. Meanwhile, all street names connected in any way with the Polish defeat of the Order, whether that be Grunwald or Sienkiewicz, were to be replaced.

Although the division of Poland and the eastern Baltic countries had been agreed by Germany and the Soviet Union shortly before they invaded, both shared a deep-seated mutual distrust of each other. In 1938, a milestone in Soviet cinema appeared with the release of *Alexander Nevsky*, directed by Sergei Eisenstein. It told the story of the heroic duke of Novgorod and his defeat of the Teutonic Order's army on the famous 'battle on the ice' which saved the city and halted the eastward advance of Catholic crusaders. The characters, of course, were filtered through the lens of Soviet nationalism, meaning that references to Christianity were toned down, Nevsky took on the persona of a Bolshevik peasant hero and the German characters bore the insignia of the Reich's eagle and swastika.[25] The analogy being drawn with fears of Germany's expansionist policies could not have been clearer. The film, released in November 1938, was put on hold the following year with the Soviet–Nazi pact, and then shown again as German armies began their assault on Russia.

In June 1941, Hitler launched 'Operation Barbarossa' (aptly, in his mind, named after the Holy Roman Emperor) – the invasion of the Soviet Union. German forces swiftly occupied the Baltic states, replacing the oppressive Soviet occupation with an equally brutal Nazi regime. The offensive resulted in extensive damage to the historical centres of Liepāja and Riga. Along with economic exploitation and the suppression of resistance, the new civilian administration, the Reichskommissariat Ostland, was charged with implementing Nazi racial ideology. This would soon include the ghettoisation and systematic extermination of the Baltic Jews and Roma, along with the promotion of pro-German propaganda as preparation for the resettlement of the region by Germans. Unsurprisingly, the crusades and the Order's legacy were invoked throughout. The 11th SS Panzer battalion, which fought on the Eastern Front and included foreign volunteers from Scandinavia and the Baltic states, was even named after the Order's famous leader, Herman of Salza. The war on Russia was itself framed as an extension of the Order's crusades, as made clear by Hitler in a speech on 30 January 1943: 'In earlier times, German knights set out for distant lands in order to fight for the ideals of their faith; today, our soldiers fight in the vastness of the east in order to save Europe from destruction.'[26] Hitler would later refer to the military successes of the Teutonic Order as a model to follow for the warriors of National Socialism.[27]

In Latvia, the Nazi governors sought to highlight German heritage and connect it to the legitimacy of their occupation. An article published in the Reichskommissariat's newspaper, *Deutsche Zeitung im Ostland*, by Erwin Aßmann, focused on his alleged excavation of the first stone building in Latvia (and the eastern Baltic) – the castle at Ikšķile. As the 'first castle', this was seen to legitimise German presence in the Baltic states, and symbolised the *'real'* causes of the Second World War – the historical battle between the West and East. At the same time, the Nazis sought to highlight how Germans and Latvians had always been historical allies against the Russians. An exhibition in Riga called *Nākotnei pretī* or *Towards the Future* included huge frescoes depicting ancient Latvian warriors and the Order's knights, both setting out to battle in the East. A map showed an imagined line of hillforts organised to defend against the Russians, and archaeological evidence presented at the exhibition was used to demonstrate how the eastern Latvian region of Latgale had never been touched by Slavic culture, in a complete reversal of how the Soviets promoted it. Just to make the analogies clear, the exhibition included photomontages showing the contemporary battle against Bolshevism.[28] There is no evidence anyone was taken in by this propaganda, and Latvian scholars fought for the independence of their republic against both the Soviet Union and Nazi Germany.

In Estonia, there was a similar attempt to revive interest in medieval German heritage. The German art historian Konrad Strauss, who took a particular interest in ceramics, had visited the eastern Baltic several times before the war to carry out research, studying museum collections in Riga and Tallinn. Under the Nazi occupation, he organised excavations inside Narva Castle, hoping to find traces of the first German (or Danish) colonists. Again, Narva was framed in his research and by the press as a bastion of Western civilisation against Russian barbarism. The idea of the eastern Baltic as a fortress against 'Asian bandits' featured widely in the propaganda of both German and Estonian institutions. Here too, an exhibition entitled *Eesti rahva eluvõitlus* or *The Struggle for the Existence of the Estonian Nation* connected the historical struggle for freedom with the conflict against the Soviet Union. From the Estonian perspective, any collaboration with the Germans against the Soviets was regarded as a necessary evil – a pathway to restoring Estonia's national independence.[29] Ultimately, the Estonian intelligentsia found itself caught between two oppressive forces. Some chose to resist or at least withdraw from active support of the Nazis, while others prioritised resistance to the Soviet threat, as the prospect of a renewed Russian occupation loomed large.

In the same way, Finland aligned with Germany not to advance Nazi goals but to regain its independence and territory from the Soviets, although there were sympathisers on both sides. Here, references to Finland's long-standing role as a buffer against incursions from the East, which occasionally included the medieval period, framed the collaborative fight against the Soviet Union as part of a historical struggle. Fears of Russia became particularly centred on Karelia, that enduring frontier region whose cultural significance had been elevated in nationalist thought. When Finland joined Operation Barbarossa, its Lutheran clergy promoted the campaign as a crusade (despite its Catholic association) and framed the Finnish army as soldiers of Christ. Bishop Aleksi Lehtonen (later Archbishop of Turku) invoked the Swedish crusades in particular, which he claimed had rescued Finland from obscurity. The Finnish flag – the blue cross – was in turn envisaged as a crusading banner. When the offensive against the Soviets stalled, this rhetoric was replaced by lamentations of the Finns' sinfulness.[30]

THE DESTRUCTION OF CITIES

In the summer of 1944, the Red Army began its counteroffensive, breaking through German defensive lines across the eastern Baltic. Soviet air raids, demolitions by retreating German forces and artillery battles destroyed the historical centres of many Estonian and Latvian towns. The worst affected were Narva and Jelgava, but significant damage was also done to Tallinn, Tartu, Pärnu, Rēzekne, Valmiera and Liepāja.[31] Within a few months, German forces had been pushed into the tip of Curonia, where they were encircled and pinned down until the end of the war. Further south, the Soviet assault concentrated on German lines in Belarus and rapidly advanced westwards towards East Prussia. Before and during the counteroffensive, Soviet propagandists sought to foster a sense of historical continuity in resisting German aggression, framing the Red Army as a natural protector of Baltic lands. Leaflets and broadcasts referred to the Nazis as the 'new Teutonic invaders', likening their brutality and territorial ambitions to those of the medieval crusaders. Posters depicted Nazi soldiers alongside images evoking the Teutonic Knights – armoured, faceless and brutal – contrasted with heroic Soviet soldiers and Baltic partisans. The visual connection was intended to remind locals of the historical cycle of German invasions and indigenous resistance. The memory of the usual historical episodes was revived – in Estonia, the St George's Night Uprising, and in Lithuania and later particularly in Poland, the victory over the Order in 1410.

During the Nazi occupation of Lithuania (1941–4), the Reichskommissariat had actively suppressed Lithuanian nationalism and undermined any symbols that could inspire resistance. This included a ban on the public promotion of historical Lithuanian leaders who had fought against the Order, especially Vytautas. The memory of Lithuania's grand dukes was then (briefly and cynically) utilised by Soviet Lithuanian propagandists during the pushback against the German army. In pro-Soviet Lithuanian history books, published in Moscow in 1942 and 1944, the Germans were represented as the eternal enemies of the Lithuanian nation – and the union of Balts and Slavs was therefore a natural one against this ancient common enemy. This included titles such as *Lithuania in the Time of Grunwald*, written by the Lithuanian poet Liudas Gira at the behest of the Soviet government. The cover depicted the Teutonic Order's knights fleeing from Lithuanian horsemen, above which a Soviet tank crushed German infantry, and underneath flew a red flag bearing the hammer and sickle. The Soviet fight mirrored the historical Lithuanian fight. Gira, who had enthusiastically supported the Soviet occupation, wrote in Lithuanian and Polish, hoping to inspire both with their collaborative historical defeat of the Germans.[32]

The historical centres of Germany, including East Prussia, became targets for allied bombing. The most important, Königsberg, was hit first by the Soviet air force several times between 1941 and 1943, and then by RAF bombers in the summer of 1944, which destroyed most of its historical centre. This was followed by a Soviet ground assault in the spring of 1945 with the city now far behind the front line. One by one, the old centres of Prussia were besieged, their historical districts obliterated. In the wake of the Soviet advance, thousands of refugees fled westwards towards Germany in one of the most desperate evacuations of the war; almost all who stayed either died when the towns were taken or were subsequently deported; many also died fleeing. Marienburg, with its strategic location on the principal route across the Vistula's floodplain, had been declared a fortress by Hitler in the summer of 1944. When Soviet tanks rolled in to the town on 23 January 1945, they faced only a couple of thousand German defenders. Most of the civilian population of 25,000 had been evacuated west, although some chose to remain behind. Within a few days, the town had been reduced to rubble and the Soviets started to shell the eastern side of the castle.[33] Soon there was a gaping hole where the church had once stood, the giant figure of the Virgin Mary reduced to rubble in the moat. The German defenders held out for two months then, on 9 March, they slipped away under cover of darkness and retreated west, blowing up the bridge over the Nogat as they left.

In the winter of 2008, archaeologists uncovered a mass grave just outside the castle's eastern wall, ahead of a proposed hotel development. Almost 2,000 individuals were identified as primarily women and children – the civilian victims of the Red Army's siege. In late March and April in 1945, a Soviet army division had been ordered to 'clean up' the town, recovering bodies from destroyed buildings and streets and collectively dumping them in a pit, along with decomposing animal carcasses. The aim was to stop the spread of disease.[34] In the following months, the entire district of Marienburg was 'cleansed' of Germans, although a few families who could speak Polish were permitted to stay. The town was now a deserted shell, although incredibly the town hall survived, today one of the best-preserved examples of medieval Prussian civic architecture. The Church of St George was destroyed along with Conrad Steinbrecht's grave, the man who had dedicated a large part of his life to restoring the castle. Bricks would be taken from the rubble of the town for the rebuilding of Warsaw.

Over the next decade, Polish migrants would settle in towns like Marienburg. Many hailed from former Polish territories which had been incorporated into the Soviet Union after the war – parts of Ukraine, Belarus and Lithuania. Some settlers also came from central Poland, looking for new opportunities as towns like Marienburg – now officially Malbork – and other former German territories needed rebuilding and resettlement. The castle remained largely intact and a decision was made by the Polish authorities not to dismantle it for rebuilding Warsaw. The plan was to restore it as the residence of the Polish kings (1457–1772), a way of reclaiming this profoundly symbolic structure from Germany.

CHANGES IN TERRITORY AND HISTORICAL MEMORY

The 'liberation' of Estonia, Latvia, Lithuania and Poland came with a terrible price. The three Baltic states were incorporated into the Soviet Union, and further human tragedies would follow with the mass deportation and execution of anyone who was deemed a political threat. Estonians and Latvians became minorities in their own capitals, after the Soviet authorities encouraged the immigration of large numbers of Russians, part of a deliberate process of Russifying the occupied countries. The same policy was applied to much of Karelia, which had been ceded to the Soviet Union. The post-war environment, where the demographic landscape had been completely reconfigured, was accompanied by a flurry of propaganda which sought to emphasise historical Slavic associations with the land.

In Estonia, the first excavations in Tallinn after the war, in 1952–3, were focused on Toompea Hill and the square in front of the town hall. The aim was to demonstrate early contacts between Estonians and Slavs (i.e. Russians), and to prove that Tallinn existed as a town before the arrival of the crusaders.[35] While the Soviet authorities sought to censor aspects of national history that deviated from their own approved version, they were willing to celebrate figures who could be reinterpreted to serve Soviet goals. The best example is provided by Lembitu, who continued to be an acceptable symbol of the struggle against German – and now Western – imperialism, providing he was not used to reference Estonian sovereignty.[36] Hence, the War of Independence monument featuring Lembitu in Suure-Jaani was destroyed twice by the Soviets, in 1942 and 1950. On the other hand, that raised by the hillfort of Lõhavere in 1969, consisting of upright slabs of red granite with excerpts from Henry's *Chronicle* in both Latin and Estonian, was permitted. Ideologues could happily interpret this as an anti-imperialist monument, whilst patriots would understand the reference to a broader struggle against foreign invaders.

Russia's leading historical role was also emphasised in Lithuania and Belarus. After the short-lived propaganda war against the German occupation, the positive image of the grand duchy was suppressed by the Soviet government in both the public and academic domains. All monuments to Vytautas, the most important figure associated with Lithuanian statehood, were destroyed, and his name was removed from public places. Lithuanian historians were discouraged from studying the period of the grand duchy, especially the reigns of rulers like Algirdas who had conquered Rus' territories, although some work was completed in exile. When a new history of Lithuania's origins was published in 1959 by the Marxist Russian historian Vladimir Pashuto, he interpreted the grand duchy as forming in response to the threat posed by the Order, whilst stressing the Russian contribution to both the state's development and the fight against the crusaders.[37] In the same year the Lithuanian novelist Juozas Grušas published *Herkus Mantas* (*Herkus Monte*), which centred on the Natangian leader who led the Great Prussian Uprising against the Order. Herkus is presented as a doomed freedom fighter, and appears to have evoked the tragic uprising in Lithuania against Soviet occupation in the early 1950s.[38] His sculpture would later be unveiled in Klaipėda in 1987, at a time when censorship of Lithuanian history was beginning to ease. In neighbouring Belarus, before it became a founding republic of the Soviet Union, historians had emphasised its prominent role in the history of the grand duchy, which they described as a Lithuanian-Belarusian state. This notion would be suppressed during the Soviet era when the eastward expansion of Lithuania was framed in aggressive terms. Cast in this light, Belarus was 'liberated' by Russia from Lithuania's (and the Commonwealth's) oppression.[39]

Marxist historians in the German Democratic Republic (East Germany) also turned their attention to the history of the Slavs, in this case the Wends, arguing they were the victims of German feudal oppression which they regarded as an early expression of capitalism. 'Slavic archaeology' in the GDR became tethered to this narrative, as excavations of Wendish strongholds and trading centres sought to overturn the earlier negative perceptions of Slavs.[40] The Sorbs themselves saw a brief resurgence in cultural rights after the war, although the population declined over the second half of the twentieth century due to further assimilation, urbanisation and migration.[41] German colonisation remained a vivid feature of historical writing across the Soviet Eastern Bloc, as the newly formed German Federal Republic (West Germany) was still considered a threat. On 10 March 1958, Konrad Adenauer, the Chancellor of the Federal Republic, had been made an honorary member of the Teutonic Order in Cologne, in a widely publicised event. Donning the white robe emblazoned with the black cross, he became the poster boy for the enduring German threat in Soviet propaganda. It did not help that the surviving members of the Ostforschung still harked on about superior German cultural achievements, having now reframed German colonisation in the Baltic as part of the flowering of Western Europe. For one leading scholar, Erich Weise, writing in the mid-1950s, the Teutonic Order represented the concentrated energy of European culture and served as a bulwark against the 'threat from the East'. The *Drang nach Osten* had been repurposed for the Cold War.[42]

In Poland, which received the lion's share of Prussia in 1945, the annexation of lands referred to as the 'Recovered Territories' was accompanied by the dismantling of the German cultural landscape, some of it centuries-old, some the product of more recent policies of Germanisation.[43] To this end, every German place name was replaced by its Polish equivalent, although some were completely renamed, such as Rastenberg which became Kętrzyn, adopting the name of the Masurian-Polish patriotic historian Wojciech Kętrzyński. The rebranding of the cultural landscape was accompanied by the removal and destruction of the majority of visibly German symbols, including the Iron Cross and the black eagle. They were replaced by a landscape of new memorials to the war dead and the victims of Nazi crimes, with some also converted into Catholic shrines. In keeping with history writing across the Eastern Bloc, the Teutonic Order continued to be presented as the earliest agent of German imperialism.[44] Sienkiewicz's *Krzyżacy* now become more timely than ever, and was effectively read as popular history. In the post-war era, it became part of the widespread promotion of the historical memory of Grunwald in Poland, which was connected to the defeat of Nazi Germany in what was described as a 'Second Grunwald'.[45] The name was widely reapplied to streets, landmarks and bridges in the newly defined Polish state and several Grunwald monuments would be restored, including the most famous one in Cracow. However, the primary emphasis of memorialisation would be directed at the battlefield itself.

In 1960, the festivities surrounding the 550th anniversary of the battle included a showing of Aleksander Ford's new film adaptation of *Krzyżacy*. This had become an overnight hit and, like the novel before it, would define the attitudes of an entire generation. The celebrations were also about emphasising the immutability of Poland's post-war borders. Reflecting on how the Teutonic Order's legacy could be rekindled in West Germany, the journalist Eugeniusz Paukszta framed the celebrations in Grunwald as a 'warning to those descendants of the Teutonic Knights'.[46] Throughout the latter half of the twentieth century, the cultural deployment of Grunwald remained a mirror of Polish–German relations, and more widely of Soviet–Western relations.[47]

Neighbouring Sambia, which was annexed by Russia, became the Kaliningrad Oblast after Königsberg was renamed in honour of Mikhail Kalinin, the late head of state of the Soviet Union.[48] In 1945, Russian town planners began to reconstruct the city of Kaliningrad following the established template of building quick and cheap communal housing. In a climate discouraging the expression of individualism within architecture, there was no interest in reviving the character of the historic centre, which by then was a melange of medieval, baroque and later-period buildings. The surviving historical monuments, including the ruined cathedral, some churches and suburban houses, were left. The castle, however, suffered the fate that Marienburg narrowly avoided. The Russian authorities had no qualms about destroying this symbol of Prussia and in 1949 the entire structure was demolished with explosives. In its place, one of the brutalist eyesores of post-war Europe was constructed – the House of the Soviets. The rest of the peninsula was treated in a similar fashion. Historical buildings were largely left alone; a number had already been partially dismantled in the nineteenth century such as the castle at Balga, and they provided readily accessible quarries for the new wave of settlers from across the Soviet Union who almost entirely replaced the German population. German place names were replaced with Russian ones and Kaliningrad itself became a city for Red Army veteran families, memorialised in countless monuments that now defined the numerous public spaces emerging from the rubble.

REHABILITATING THE HERITAGE OF THE BALTIC CRUSADES

Malbork Castle Museum opened on 1 January 1961, heralding a new era in the history of the monument, one which would see a gradual disentanglement of the Teutonic Order from the identity of German imperialism. As testimony to the efforts of the Polish conservators, the castle was designated a UNESCO World Heritage Site in 1997. In the official statement justifying the designation, as quoted at the start of this chapter, the Order's contribution is explicitly acknowledged, along with the place of the crusades and their impact on indigenous populations. Reconstructed buildings have been added periodically to the vast complex which has become a symbol of local, regional and national pride, and one of the biggest tourist attractions in the country, drawing over 700,000 visitors annually. Since the 1990s, the museum has also fostered an interdisciplinary research centre with international reach, including Polish–German partnerships, and has been at the forefront of rehabilitating the Order's image as a medieval religious corporation – one engaged in crusading, rather than ethnic warfare.

More broadly, Poland's accession to the European Union in 2004 encouraged a more conciliatory approach to historical memory, shifting the narrative towards emphasising shared heritage rather than conflict. Polish historians, archaeologists and art historians have led the way in critical reappraisals of the Order's historical role as a major player in the Baltic Crusades, alongside its interactions with Poland, Lithuania and other medieval states. In Malbork, this was encapsulated by the recent exhibition *Nigra Crux, Mala Crux: The Black and White Legend of the Teutonic Order*, which opened in the Castle Museum on 28 September 2023. Featuring artefacts from Poland, Germany, Lithuania, France, Austria and Belgium, it encompassed the entirety of the Order's history, presenting and challenging the nationalist myths and stereotypes that had developed over the last two centuries.[49]

Although the castle was saved, the adjacent town was rebuilt with no attempt to recreate its former architectural character, although the town hall, surviving gate towers and fragments of the defensive walls were preserved, rather than dismantled. There was also no attempt to excavate the historic centre ahead of construction, and a great opportunity was lost, one still lamented by archaeologists today. The story of the rebuilding of the Old Town of Elbląg is very different. Its ruins were not fully cleared until the 1960s, and since there were not enough funds to rebuild in the centre, this became a long-term archaeological site which has enriched our understanding of life in one of the most important Hanseatic towns in the Baltic. In the 1980s, it was decided that tenements would be rebuilt in such a way so as to represent medieval buildings following the concept of 'retroversion', whereby the character of the new buildings referenced their historical form.[50] As such, neo-medieval townhouses now crowd the Old Town with their distinctive and modernised stepped gables. This approach also inspired efforts in other towns, and signifies a conscious effort to connect with the troubled medieval past which is still in the process of being rehabilitated. Since the 1990s, the castles built by the Order have been reframed as part of Poland's and Europe's shared cultural heritage, and are a major attraction for local and international tourists. At the same time, there has been a growing interest in indigenous Prussian cultural heritage, driven by both scholars and local enthusiasts.

Public memory remains attached to Grunwald, with a re-enactment of the battle every year since 1998, alongside the enduring place of Sienkiewicz's *Krzyżacy* in school curricula, reinforced by the cult status of Ford's cinematic rendition. The 600th anniversary of Grunwald in 2010 was marked by the raising of various monuments, including in Malbork. Their purpose was to serve as reminders of the 'Polishness' of historical Prussia. More recently, celebrations in April 2025 in some Polish towns marked the 500th anniversary of the 'Prussian Homage' – the act of submission of the Order's last Prussian grand master to the Polish king. This has caused some controversy in Olsztyn, where a sculpture based on Matejko's famous painting was to be unveiled. Local government officials have opposed it, but the reasoning of its supporters shows that the historical opposition between Poles and Germans remains attached to the Order. The visual motifs established by Matejko crop up in pop art and urban murals every so often.

A similar process of rehabilitation was evident in the neighbouring Kaliningrad Oblast until fairly recently. Here, increasing detachment from Soviet narratives also came in the 1990s, when leading members of the reconstituted Prussia Museum publicly called for the remaining historical heritage to be preserved. The cathedral was restored, although not without controversy, and plans were openly discussed for revitalising the castle district. These included suggestions to rebuild the entire structure, which, whilst financially unrealistic, demonstrate just how far attitudes had shifted. A small group of scholars is now dedicated to the history and archaeology of the region, and local enthusiasts have been documenting and restoring its historical monuments. Yet in the poorer parts of the oblast, in the south and east, historical buildings continue to be dismantled for raw materials. Recent events have derailed the oblast's reconciliation with its European neighbours.

In Vladimir Putin's Russia, the narrative of the historical struggle with the West has been revived for political purposes, and has once again included the figure of Alexander Nevsky. In 2021, Russia celebrated the 800th anniversary of Nevsky's birth. The Russian Military Historical Society, with the support of the Ministry of Defence and the Orthodox Church, raised a monument to Nevsky on the shore of Lake Chudskoe (Lake Peipus) celebrating the 'Battle on the Ice' against the Order. The battle itself is depicted on a religious triptych at the back of the monument, which doubles up as an altar. In a speech given at the unveiling ceremony, Putin invoked the defeat of the West all those centuries ago. The monument depicts Nevsky and an armed retinue of knights, holding banners marked with the faces of saints and Russian Orthodox crosses. The monument's placing makes it largely inaccessible to Russian viewers, but its location close to the Estonian border sends a clear message to 'the West' that draws parallels between Nevsky and Putin as defenders of Russia.[51] In neighbouring Belarus, the opportunity to reclaim a place in Europe through the heritage of the grand duchy has been derailed by its anti-Western regime. Indeed, Lithuanians also largely remember Belarus as a Soviet republic rather than as an 'equal partner' in the grand duchy.[52]

In Estonia and Latvia, which saw a flowering of scholarship on the Baltic Crusades in the 1990s, the celebration of indigenous resistance to the crusaders endures on a more subdued level, linked to discreet memorials placed in some of the Late Iron Age monuments destroyed by crusading armies in the thirteenth century. Yet, at the same time, those monuments most associated with the regime established by the crusades – castles – are also widely appreciated. In Lithuania, the dissolution of the Soviet Union revived interest in the grand duchy. Numerous monuments to Vytautas would be rebuilt from the end of the 1980s, and other memorials have been raised celebrating indigenous resistance in places of historical memory. In 2013, a large battle axe was placed at the site of the Battle of Strėva in south-eastern Lithuania, which took place in 1348. This commemorated the Lithuanian forces who fought against the Order, marking 665 years since the battle. On the opposite side of the country, by the dramatic earthen remains of the Curonian stronghold of Įpiltis, destroyed by the Order in 1263, wooden sculptures were installed in 2003 to celebrate the indigenous identity of the site, and in 2007 to mark a sacred space with the symbols of the pagan gods of the Balts.

The celebration of pre-crusade culture is also evident in the historical territories of the Western Slavs. During the years of the German Democratic Republic, which saw increasing interest in Wendish heritage, a wooden statute of the four-headed god Svantovit was installed at Arkona on Rügen. It was destroyed by a storm in 2013, along with parts of the cliff around the archaeological site of the Rani's former religious centre. In 2021, a new sculpture of the deity was created for the site by Polish artist Patrycja Kujawowicz (collaborating with her former teacher Tadeusz Golinczak) who lives in nearby Putgarten. It consists of four metal faces bolted onto a trunk of locally sourced oak. Representations of this deity can also be found in other sites associated with Wendish heritage in northern Germany and Poland, such as the archaeological open-air museum at Groß Raden which opened in 1987. No longer branded as something 'other', Wendish cultural heritage is increasingly seen as an essential part of Central European history. Museums and historical societies, particularly in Brandenburg, Saxony and Mecklenburg-Western Pomerania, showcase Wendish history as an integral part of their regional identity. Despite this, Wendish language and identity continue to decline, the legacy of centuries of Germanisation.

The first complete histories of the Baltic Crusades were created by nationalists during a time when new identities were being forged in Europe, and they have proven to be incredibly influential, even now. Today, we understand the crusades in Northern Europe as expressions of territorialised Christianity, involving diverse actors with varying agendas. The *Drang nach Osten* paradigm is dead and buried, and it has been replaced by a more critical understanding of the collective identities of the groups involved. Nationalist framings of ethnic colonialism have been replaced by more nuanced understandings of medieval colonisation, enabling the impact of conquest and societal transformation to be contextualised within a European and even a global historical framework.

Since the Baltic countries joined the European Union, the historical conquests of pagan lands have been seen through the lens of Europeanisation. Yet modern political and linguistic borders still exert a strong influence on interpretations, and the past continues to be recycled and reimagined to meet the emotional needs of the present. This is not surprising given that all history and archaeology is informed by its present-day cultural context, but that national sentiments continue to play an influential role here is particularly striking. Within the persistent grand historical narratives, small or extinct groups – like the indigenous Prussians – have been sidelined.[53] Depending on how the geopolitical situation unfolds around the Baltic Sea region, which is difficult to predict, nationalism may finally loosen its grip on 'future pasts'. Many scholars have already begun to contribute to this process, and this book has been an attempt to amplify their voices more widely.

ENDNOTES

INTRODUCTION

1. *Livonian Rhymed Chronicle* 10041.
2. For the most recent overview of the structure's complete history see Mentzel-Reuters and Samerski 2019.
3. I use the word 'German' here and in later chapters as the equivalent of the Latin exonym used in contemporary sources, whilst recognising that groups with this collective identity were also defined by their region of origin (e.g. Saxons, Westphalians etc.).
4. Markowski 1984. This term is adopted by the end of the twelfth century, before then crusaders are commonly referred to as pilgrims.
5. For a recent discussion of how these states were formed see Barber 2012.
6. I use the term Catholic throughout this book as a shorthand for Roman Catholic, i.e. the Christian community under the leadership of the pope in Rome.
7. Ousterhout 2003.
8. Latham 2011.
9. Bernard of Clairvaux, Letter to Eastern France and Bavaria Promoting the Second Crusade, 1146.
10. Gilchrist and Sloane 2005, 94–6.
11. Brundage 1969, 155.
12. For the use of the term pagan in relation to Northern Europe see Hofstra, Houwen and MacDonald 1995.
13. Palmer 2007; Janson 2010. I have opted to use the term 'indigenous' to describe those populations which inhabited a geographical region at the time of conquest or colonisation, following the UN's ILO Convention 169, after Wang 2023, 4–5.
14. https://sourcebooks.fordham.edu/source/urban2-5vers.asp
15. Robert the Monk, *Historia Iherosolimitana* I: 1.
16. Ottewill-Soulsby 2016.
17. Ottewill-Soulsby 2016, 410; for a good overview of medieval Christian perceptions of Islam see Tolan 1994.

18. Bartlett 1993.
19. For general histories on the Templars see Barber 1995; for the Hospitallers see Riley-Smith 1999; for the Teutonic Order see Urban 2003, Militzer 2005, Pluskowski 2024. The most comprehensive work on the archaeology of the military orders is Boas 2006.
20. Boas 2006, 84–8, 93–4.
21. For a comprehensive study of the Teutonic Order in the Levant see Morton 2009.
22. *The Rule and Statutes of the Teutonic Order*, Prologue 3; Sterns 1969, 203–04.
23. Hunyadi 2008.
24. Fonnesberg-Schmidt 2007, 27.
25. Dragnea 2020.
26. Tamm 2013.
27. *Henry's Chronicle of Livonia* II: 2
28. *Henry's Chronicle of Livonia* II: 7
29. Rowell 2014; Christiansen 1997; Urban 2003, 2019.

CHAPTER 1 CONFRONTING PAGANISM

1. Scholz and Rogers 1970, 51.
2. *Charlemagne and Pope Leo*; Dutton 1993, no. 1 Jot 2.
3. Coupland 2005, 223–6.
4. The most recent work on the Carolingian conquest of the Saxons is Cragle 2024.
5. Reynolds 2016, 91–2.
6. Karras 1986, 556
7. Dümmler 1881, pp. 380–1.
8. Rembold 2017.
9. Hines 2003, 306–07
10. McKitterick 2008, 105.
11. Saxony in this chapter refers to Old Saxony, rather than the later German state of Saxony whose origins lie in the eastern subdivision of Henry the Lion's duchy in the late-twelfth century.
12. Rembold 2017, 39–40.
13. Einhard, *Life of Charlemagne*, Holder-Egger, ch. 7, 10.
14. Flierman 2017, 1111–12.
15. Groenewoudt, Van Beek and Groothedde 2014, 1–3.
16. The most concise discussion of interpreting early medieval burials in terms of social identity, ethnicity and religious change remains Halsall 1995.
17. Rembold 2017, 191–7.
18. Wood 1995, 259–60.
19. Müller-Wille 2003.
20. Flierman 2017, 130–1.
21. Rembold 2017, 183.
22. Flierman 2017, 136.
23. In northern Germany similar cases of reuse stretched into the High Middle Ages, see Sopp 1999.
24. Cusack 2011.
25. Maraschi 2019
26. *Chronicle of the Slavs* I: 47.
27. Palmer 2007.
28. An excellent recent overview of the Wends in English is Dragnea 2021.

29. A good overview in English is Fehring 2016.
30. Dragnea 2021, 13–14.
31. For a detailed case study see Friedland 2013.
32. For a recent overview see Biermann 2015.
33. These territories are also referred to as the Saxon marches. The term Nordmark ('Northern March') specifically referred to a distinct territory created in 965 as a partition of the larger Saxon Eastern March or Gero's March. It encompassed areas that would later become part of Brandenburg.
34. Adam of Bremen, *History of the Archbishops*, III: 22.
35. Blough 2016.
36. Pederson 2006.
37. Jensen 2017, 59–60.
38. Henning 2002.
39. Janson 2010.
40. Mieszko is a later rendering of various names.
41. The most accessible work in English is Buko 2008; for discussions on the complexity of the origins of the Polish state see Urbańczyk 2008a and the sections on Poland in Berend, Urbańczyk and Wiszewski 2013. For the most recent synthesis see Buko 2021.
42. Buko 2008, 316.
43. For a recent discussion on the origins of the Piast's miliary elites see Gardeła 2024.
44. On Giecz see Kara, Krysztofiak and Wyrwa 2016.
45. Urbańczyk 2012; Kajkowski 2021.
46. Roach 2020.
47. *Deeds of the Princes of the Poles* I: 4.
48. *Deeds of the Saxons* III: 69.
49. For a recent study on the Christianisation of Poland see Dobosz, Matla and Strzelczyk 2017.
50. Kotecki, Jensen and Bennett 2021, 11.
51. Bukowska 2012.
52. Buko 2008, 311–12.
53. Shephard 2005, 267.
54. The dating and architectural identification of the church at Kałdus have been disputed; Rodzińska-Chorąży 2011.
55. Paner 2001.
56. Kuczkowski and Kajkowski 2011, 35.
57. Gołembnik 2004.
58. Kalaga, 2006
59. Michałowski 2016.
60. This is thoroughly discussed in Michałowski 2016.
61. Shepard 2005, 272–4.
62. Urbańczyk 2008a, 357–9.
63. Güttner-Sporzyński 2014, 170.
64. McKitterick 2008.
65. Gabriele 2011, 30–31.
66. Stuckey 2008.
67. For the latest work on the connection between Christianity and warfare see Kotecki, Jensen and Bennett 2021.

CHAPTER 2 THE FIRST CRUSADE IN THE NORTH

1. *Epistolae et privilegia*, col. 1203, no. 166.
2. Constable 2008, 197–214.
3. Anonymous, *A Letter of Support against the Pagans (Slavs)*; Riley-Smith and Riley-Smith 1981, 74–7.
4. Bysted et al. 2012, 29.
5. Barber 2012.
6. Słupecki 2004.
7. *History of the Archbishops* II: 21.
8. *Chronicle of the Slavs* I: 52.
9. The best synthesis remains Słupecki 1994.
10. Lübke 2008.
11. Słupecki 1994, 57–8.
12. *History of the First Crusade*, chapter 1.
13. See chapters 3 and 4.
14. Fonnesberg-Schmidt 2007, 30–31.
15. Bysted 2009, 11.
16. Güttner-Sporzyński 2015, 137–43.
17. Lees 2015.
18. Bysted 2009, 13.
19. Stuckey 2008, 143–6.
20. Hoffmann 2012.
21. *History of the Archbishops* I: 84.
22. Chernyshov 2008.
23. Partenheimer 1994.
24. Kluge 2009.
25. Wünsch 2008, 25.
26. For a good discussion of the application of the term to medieval frontier societies see Bartlett 1993 and West 1999.
27. Zientara 2013.
28. For more detailed studies see Piskorski 2004.
29. Spanuth 1985.
30. Koebner 2012.
31. *History of the Archbishops* I: 89.
32. Wieckowska-Lüth 2013, 134.
33. Rüdiger 2009.
34. Kempke 1995; see papers in Wesse 1998 and especially Biermann and Mangelsdorf 2005; Brather 2005.
35. Larsen 2019; Shroeder 2022.
36. For a recent summary of the archaeology of the Western Slavs see Brather 2008.
37. For a recent summary see Lübke 2013.
38. Leciejewicz 1995.
39. Hill 1995.
40. For a recent summary of the city's development see Gläser 2015.
41. *Chronicle of the Slavs* 84.
42. See chapter 4.
43. Wiwjora 1996, 176.
44. Reiger 2019.

45. Biermann 2015, 72–4.
46. Wünsch 2008.
47. Stone 2016, 42–3.
48. Hoffmann 1991.
49. Stone 2016, 79.
50. Leciejewicz 1995.
51. Bryda 2022.
52. Jensen 2013, 222–3.

CHAPTER 3 PRECARIOUS FRONTIERS

1. *Deeds of the Princes of the Poles* I: Introduction: Bisson 2003, 12–13. It is not clear what Selencia refers to, but most probably a Wendish region adjacent to Pomerania. The 'vipers' references Matthew 3:7 and Luke 3:7.
2. For recent synthesis on the Christianisation of Pomerania see Rębkowski 2007; see also Rosik 2020.
3. The aim of the First Crusade, though, was not to convert Muslims, but rather to bring Jerusalem under Christian control.
4. For Otto of Bamberg's life see Lyon 2017, 98–149.
5. Rębkowski 2007.
6. Rębkowski 2017.
7. Migdalski 2020.
8. *Deeds of the Princes of the Poles* II: 42.
9. Since I'm largely referring to its archaeology in this chapter, the Polish name is used.
10. Bartlett 1985.
11. See previous chapter.
12. Urbańczyk 2012, 256.
13. Kajkowski 2011; Makowiecki and Makowiecka 2014.
14. Kuczkowski and Kajkowski 2011.
15. The best discussion of the character of this frontier is Jamroziak 2011.
16. See chapter 4.
17. I discuss German town laws in more detail in chapter 9.
18. Jabłoński 2019.
19. Śliwiński and Możejko 2017, 17; I use the Polish name until the fourteenth century, when the official documented use of Danzig starts and remains dominant until after the Second World War.
20. Jagodziński 2010; Bogucki and Jurkiewicz 2012.
21. Makowiecki et al. 2022.
22. Śliwiński and Możejko 2017.
23. Ceynowa and Paszkiewicz 2015.
24. Paner 2001.
25. Ossowski 2016.
26. Latałowa, Święta-Musznicka and Pędziszewska 2009.
27. Paner 1997, 277–9.
28. Jagodziński 2004.
29. For synthetic works on the indigenous Prussians see Okulicz-Kozaryn 1983 and 1997. For recent work on religion see Kawiński and Szczepański 2016, and Kawiński 2018.
30. Długokęcki 2009, 43; Nowakiewicz 2010.
31. Shiroukhov 2015, 266, 270.

32. *Chronicle of Prussia* III: 5.
33. Vėlius 1996, 319.
34. Okulicz-Kozaryn 1983, 32.
35. Although similarly carved figures are known from the Wendish area.
36. Szczepański 2015, 320.
37. For Prussian religion see Kawiński and Szczepański 2016; Kawiński 2018.
38. Białuński 1993.
39. Kawiński and Szczepański 2016, 37–8.
40. Kawiński 2018, 199.
41. Zinoviev 2009; Karczewski 2011, 161–91.
42. French et al. 2024.
43. *Chronicle of Prussia* III: 5.
44. *Chronicle of Prussia* III: 3.
45. Haftka 1987, 37–41; Haftka and Wadyl 2015, 180–1.
46. For a full discussion of Polish wars against the Prussians in a crusading milieu see Gładysz 2012 and Güttner-Sporzyński 2014.
47. Güttner-Sporzyński 2022.
48. Güttner-Sporzyński 2014, 70.
49. Güttner-Sporzyński 2014, 72.
50. Białuński 1999, 8.
51. Kalaga 2006
52. Gogosz 2020.
53. Powierski 2001, 171–2, 192.
54. Güttner-Sporzyński 2014, 170.
55. Borchardt 2008.
56. Gładysz 2012, 118–20.

CHAPTER 4 FROM PAGANS TO CRUSADERS

1. *History of the Danes* XIV: 39.34.
2. Ibsen and Frenzel 2010.
3. Mägi 2018.
4. For a recent summary of the Christianisation of Scandinavian regions see Brink and Price 2008, part III.
5. Blöndal and Benedikz 2009.
6. Jensen 2017, 77–8.
7. Jensen 2017, 68–9.
8. Doxey 1996.
9. Jensen 2017, 115.
10. Svenungsen 2016.
11. Lindkvist 2001.
12. Markus 2020, 18.
13. For a comprehensive summary in English see Bysted et al. 2012.
14. Bysted et al. 2012, 30–1.
15. Jensen 2002.
16. Roslund 2007, 509–10.
17. Jensen 2002, 191.
18. Naum 2013, 87.
19. Jensen 2002.

20. Skaarup 1994–5, 157.
21. This is unlikely to have been the original Slavic name.
22. *History of the Danes* XIV: 39.32
23. *History of the Danes* XVI: 5.1 The term used here is *scelestorum*, meaning wicked or impious.
24. For a digestible summary see Tummuscheit 2006.
25. Fonnesberg-Schmidt 2007, 46–7.
26. Roslund 2007, 216–23; Naum 2012.
27. Biermann and Herrmann 2014, 53; Gabriel and Muhl 2014, 410.
28. e.g. Jensen 2007; Bysted et al. 2012.
29. Markus 2020.
30. Jensen 2018.
31. Jürgensen 2021.
32. Markus 2020, 84.
33. See the chapters in Bandlien 2023.
34. Sonne De Torrens 2024.
35. Jensen 2002, 192.
36. Poulsen 2011, 287–8.
37. Lind 2015. The 'crusading period' in Finnish archaeology traditionally starts in c. 1025, based on finds of Byzantine coins in graves, and reflects the period when external powers were thought to begin to influence Finnish society.
38. Line 2009; see also Korpela 2008.
39. Waśko 2013; Heikkilä 2016.
40. Line 2009, 81.
41. I've retained 'Finns' for the sake of simplicity, but in Scandinavian sources *Finnar/Finni* referred to the Saami, and those living in the south-west of the Finnish Peninsula were called *Finlander* (Line 2009, 74; see also Wang 2023)
42. Jensen 2022, 149.
43. Lind 2015; Lindkvist 2001.
44. Johansen 2008, 53; Korpela 2008, 47.
45. Wessman 2010; Moilanen 2021.
46. Mäntylä 2007.
47. There is some dispute over whether Nousiainen was the first bishopric, as the evidence for this is much later and connected with the promotion of Henry's cult.
48. Ratilainen et al. 2016.
49. Immonen, Kinnunen and Harjula 2021.
50. See papers in Poutanen 2011.
51. Heinonen 2023.
52. Fewster 2000.
53. Lamberg 2006.

CHAPTER 5 TERRA MARIANA

1. *Chronicle of Livonia* 4, XV.1.
2. Bojtár 1999, 129; Tamm 2011.
3. Valk 2014.
4. Valk 2018.
5. Mägi 2024.
6. For an excellent discussion of the regional power dynamics see Selart 2015.

7. The best discussion of Henry's *Chronicle* is Tamm, Kaljundi and Jensen 2011.
8. *Chronicle of Livonia* 3, IV.5.
9. Banerjea et al. 2017.
10. Caune 2007, 77–8.
11. Tamm 2009.
12. Mänd 2009, 195; Tamm 2020.
13. Fonnesberg-Schmidt 2007, 93.
14. *Chronicle of Livonia* 3, IX.8.
15. Tamm 2013.
16. Blūzma and Lazdiņš 1998; Šnē *2006*.
17. Tamm 2013, 454.
18. *Chronicle of Livonia* 2, X.15
19. Kala 2001, 10–12.
20. Benninghoven 1965, 420–68.
21. Murray 2013.
22. Apala and Apals 2014.
23. Lang and Valk 2011.
24. *Chronicle of Livonia* 4, XXVII: 2.
25. Lang and Valk 2011, 296–301.
26. Atgāzis 1999.
27. Valk et al. 2013a, 121–2, 125–7.
28. For an excellent summary see Markus 2020, 304ff.
29. Tamla and Valk 2017.
30. Andreson 2014.
31. Alberic de Trois-Fontaines, *Chronica Albrici monachi Trium Fontium, a monacho Novi Monasterii Hoiensis interpolata*, 1874, 930.
32. Kreem 2001, 217–18.
33. Jarockis 1998, 52; Šnē 2008, 92–3.
34. Murray 2001.
35. Valk et al. 2013b.
36. Olesen 2013.
37. Nielsen 2013, 146.
38. Šterns 1997 and 2002.
39. Šnē 2009a, 67; Šnē 2009b, 131–2.
40. Brown 2019.
41. Šterns 1998; Selart 2009, 38–41.
42. Kalling 1997, 55–7.
43. Arbusow 1928, 296–7, 323.

CHAPTER 6 BLACK CROSS ASCENDANT

1. *Chronicle of Prussia* III: 123.
2. Sawicki et al. 2015.
3. Peter of Dusburg wrote they wore a symbol of a sword and star, but this was a mistake resulting from his identifying them with the Sword Brothers (Dorna 2024, 16).
4. Dorna 2024, 31.
5. Gładysz 2012, 182–3.
6. Tamla and Valk 2017, 106.

7. Szacherska 1988; Fonnesberg-Schmidt 2007, 103.
8. Gładysz 2012, 185ff.
9. Pósán 2014, 439–41.
10. Kuczyński 1978, 130–1.
11. Gładysz 2012, 200–02.
12. Gładysz 2012, 177ff.
13. Jusupović 2006.
14. Güttner-Sporzyński 2014, 207–08.
15. Dorna 2024, 20–22.
16. Dorna 2008.
17. Gouguenheim 2012, 120–4.
18. *Chronicle of Prussia* III: 3. Other sources also refer to the territory of Sasna, located between Lubavia and Galindia.
19. Szczepański 2019.
20. See Bojtár 1999 and Powierski 2003 for detailed discussion of the various Prussian groups.
21. Wroniecki, Molewski and Uziembło 2021.
22. Wasik 2017, 245–6.
23. Paszkiewicz 2009, 69–70.
24. Poliński 2003, 179.
25. Wiewióra 2018, 247–50. I have used Kulm to distinguish it from the Masovian centre.
26. Zdrójkowski 1983; Pósán 2010.
27. Ekdahl 1998.
28. *Chronicle of Prussia* III: 11.
29. Gouguenheim 2012, 129–31.
30. Leighton 2022.
31. Szczepański 2018, 40–43.
32. Fonferek 2019.
33. Szczepański 2013, 20.
34. Ehlers 2001, 29.
35. Shiroukhov 2012.
36. Białuński 1999, 119.
37. Łysiak 1999.
38. Leighton 2022.
39. Okulicz-Kozaryn 1983, 70–85; Hoffmann 2002, 11–12.
40. Biskup 2002, 133.

CHAPTER 7 FORTRESSES OF HEAVEN

1. *Livonian Rhymed Chronicle* 5291–2.
2. Today Ushakovo in the Kaliningrad Oblast, Russia.
3. Leighton 2022, 82.
4. The revised dating of Brandenburg's commandery is discussed in Jóźwiak and Trupinda 2019.
5. On the building of the Order's castles see Arszyński 1995 and 2005; Wasik 2018.
6. The interpretation of the building phases of Brandenburg are summarised in Herrmann 2007, 371–2; for a more detailed analysis see Torbus 1998, 369–72. The measurements are an approximation, as the Kulm rod was 4.35 metres.
7. Herrmann 2007, 372–3.

8. 1 *Hufe* = 16.8 hectares.
9. Herrmann 2007, 112.
10. Reconstructions of Brandenburg also include a latrine tower or *Danzker*. Most convents had this structure, but not all and there is no clear evidence it was present at Brandenburg.
11. Tandecki 2009, 109.
12. On Danish governance in Estonia see Olesen 2013.
13. A good discussion of this changing status can be found in Nielsen 2013.
14. For Finnish medieval castles see Knuutinen and Haggrén 2023.
15. Haggrén 2018.
16. Militzer 2011 on the politics of the Order after 1291.
17. Paner 1997, 282.
18. For the image of the Order in Polish historiography see Kożuchowski 2019.
19. Vercamer 2007.
20. Śliwiński 2003. On Pomerania and the Teutonic Order see Milliman 2013.
21. For a recent English overview of the Teutonic Order's administrative structure see Czaja and Radzimiński 2016.
22. Herrmann 2009, 213.
23. Jakubowska 2016; Leighton 2022, 51.
24. Dygo 1989.
25. Tvauri 2009.
26. Arszyński 2010, 44.
27. Wasik 2021, 140.
28. Apals 2012.
29. Herrmann 2007, 613–15.
30. Jóźwiak and Trupinda 2007; Mentzel-Reuters and Samerski 2019. The Castle Museum in Malbork has also published detailed studies of individual parts of the castle.
31. Petrographic analyses of the bricks from the site of Biała Góra connected them to the same clay source as used in the earliest phase of Marienburg's upper castle (Hayward 2019).
32. For a summary of Marienburg's origins see Jóźwiak and Trupinda 2007, chapter 3.
33. Wasik 2021, 140.
34. Jurkowlaniec 2010, 213–14.
35. Jóźwiak and Trupinda 2007, 333–7.
36. Trupinda 2004.
37. For the latest work on the 'palace' see Herrmann 2019.
38. Pospieszna 2002.
39. Jóźwiak and Trupinda 2010, 33.
40. Pospieszna 2002, 20–21.
41. Dąbrowska 2007.
42. Dąbrowska 2007.
43. For the development of the castle's topography and its changing terminology see Jóźwiak and Trupinda 2012, 65–89.
44. For a detailed summary see Uotila 1998, 87–112.
45. Wasik 2021.
46. Herrmann 2007, 83.
47. Wółkowski 2016.
48. Dygo 1989, 69.

CHAPTER 8 APOCALYPSE THEN?

1. *New Prussian Chronicle* VII: 30–1.
2. See Knüsel et al. 2010.
3. Grant 2013.
4. Jensen 2007, 19.
5. Ehlers 2007, 50–76, 532–7; Ehlers 2008.
6. The most important work on the Lithuanian *Reysen* (modern German *Reisen*) is Paravicini 1989–95, 2020, 2024.
7. Guard 2016.
8. Oreshek, today Shlisselburg in the Leningrad Oblast, Russia.
9. Milliman 2013, appendix 3.
10. Cook 1915, 377.
11. Jóźwiak and *Trupinda* 2009.
12. *New Prussian Chronicle* VIII: 25.
13. Żabiński 2017
14. On the Great Wilderness see Striegler 2018, 61–158.
15. On the biblical wilderness see Saunders 1993; numerous examples of these terms used to describe the frontier can be found in the *New Prussian Chronicle*.
16. The best summary of siege engines in the medieval Baltic is Ekdahl 2007.
17. Biermann et al. 2019.
18. Lazda-Cazers 2009.
19. This is based on analysis of the Order's own chronicles, e.g. Kwiatkowski 2017.
20. See Mažeika 1994 and Rowell 2014.
21. See chapter 10.
22. For a summary of Christian presence in medieval Lithuania see Baronas 2014.
23. Almonaitis 2017.
24. Rowell 2014, 229.
25. Murray 2019.
26. Bell 2012.
27. Tyerman 1996, 278–80.
28. Hector and Harvey 1982, 444–9; Smith 2015.
29. More detailed descriptions of Henry's expeditions can be found in Given-Wilson 2016, especially chapter 5, and Guard 2016.
30. As calculated in Smith 2015.
31. Mažeika and Chollet 2016, 48.
32. Manion 2018, 79–80.

CHAPTER 9 THE HANSEATIC WORLD

1. *PrUB* 1, 31-133, no. 181.
2. Tammet, Lätti and Heikkilä 2023.
3. Roio 2006.
4. Crumlin-Pedersen 2000.
5. Paulsen 2016; Zwik 2017.
6. *Chronicle of Livonia* XIV: 1; XIX: 2, 5, 11; XXIV: 7.
7. Cogs were also used in the Mediterranean, and may have been identified on the basis of their regional 'brands'.
8. Maltby et al. 2019.
9. Kreem 2011; Mänd and Leimus 2017, 284.

10. Wubs-Mrozewicz and Jenks 2012.
11. For a good summary see the introduction in Wubs-Mrozewicz and Jenks 2012, and also Harreld 2015.
12. *Chronicle of the Slavs* (Arnold of Lübeck) V: 30.
13. Benninghoven 1965, 208.
14. Myberg 2010a.
15. Мельникова 2019.
16. Munzinger 2012.
17. *Chronicle of Livonia* III: 2–5.
18. Myberg 2010b; Jonsson 2017; Leimus 2022.
19. Markus 2020.
20. Magnusson 1995.
21. Wienberg 2004.
22. Frankot 2007, 154.
23. For a recent summary see Nawrolska 2016.
24. The final part of the *Codex Neumannianus*.
25. Lemeškin 2018.
26. Domagała 2004, 92.
27. Nawrolska 2013, 88–95.
28. Nawrolska 2006, 396–400.
29. Nawrolska 2004, 307–8.
30. Nawrolska 2004, 316–17.
31. Latałowa, Jarosińska and Badura 1998; Badura and Możejko 2019.
32. Gaimster 2005, 2014.
33. Nawrolska 2008.
34. Pelech 1987, 65.
35. Nawrolska 2008, 510.
36. Czaja 2009, 447.
37. Kubicki 2010.
38. Haak 2015 and 2022; Naum 2014 and 2016.
39. Russow 2024, 75.
40. For a recent summary see Markus 2020, 261–2, 304–30, and Russow 2020 and 2024.
41. Mägi 2015.
42. Markus 2020, 321; Russow 2024, 75.
43. Markus 2020, 322–3; Russow 2024, 89.
44. Russow 2024, 92.
45. Mänd and Leimus 2017, 280.
46. Russow 2024, 85–6.
47. Naum 2014, 659.
48. Saage and Russow 2020, 334.
49. Tvauri 2009.
50. Lightfoot et al. 2016.
51. Naum 2014.
52. Russow 2007.
53. Selart 2009.
54. Caune and Ose 2004, 461.
55. Kala 2012; Strenga 2020.
56. Kala 2009, 189.
57. Czaja and Stevens 2022.

58. Naum 2014, 656.
59. Immonen 2007.
60. Mugurēvičs 1990.
61. *Das rothe Buch inter Archiepiscopalia*; Fuchs 1853, 780, 790, 792.
62. Strenga 2020.
63. Tamm 2009.
64. Pluskowski 2019.
65. Šnē 2008.
66. Rannamäe et al. 2016.
67. Kubicki 2012.
68. Odner 2001.
69. Gaimster 2014.

CHAPTER 10 OLD GODS, NEW GODS

1. *PrUB* 1, no. 134.
2. Radzimiński 2006a, 84–5.
3. Radzimiński 2006b, 95–100.
4. *LUB* VII, 690; Rand 2015.
5. Young 2022.
6. Radzimiński 2006a, 73.
7. Radzimiński 2006b, 217.
8. Pluskowski, Valk and Szczepański 2018.
9. Radzimiński 2006a, 75–7.
10. German *Landesordnungen*.
11. Radzimiński 2006a, 77.
12. Lavery 2017. On medieval churches in Finland see Hiekkanen 2023.
13. Możdżeń 2013.
14. Simiński 2013, 301–02.
15. *LUB* I, 240, 304.
16. Pluskowski, Valk and Szczepański 2018.
17. *Deliciae Prussicae* III: 140–42.
18. Jonuks, Oras and Veldi 2018, 96.
19. Valk and Kiudsoo 2018.
20. E.g. as consistently argued by Heiki Valk.
21. For a recent discussion of the term see Ščavinskas 2017.
22. Vaitkevičius 2004, 12.
23. Põltsam-Jürjo 2021.
24. Jonuks and Joosu 2013; Valk 2009, 54–5.
25. Białuński 1993.
26. Klimek 2016.
27. The terms 'folk religion' or 'popular religion' are still widely used in the Anglophone literature, although both are vague and have been variously defined.
28. Urtāns 1977, 87, 92.
29. Merrifield 1988.
30. Pluskowski, Valk and Szczepański 2018.
31. Johanson and Jonuks 2015, 136.
32. Ehrnsten 2018.

33. For various Baltic examples, as well as a broader treatment of household spirits, see Lecouteaux 2013.
34. Jezierski 2020, 414ff.
35. Balsys 2015; Kawiński 2018, 225.
36. Today Zaostrov'ye in the Kaliningrad Oblast.
37. For sixteenth-century reports of pagan practices see Vėlius 2001.
38. Vaitkevičius 2004, 37.
39. Valk 2015; Heiki Valk has identified the lake as Kauru.
40. Vaitkevičius 2004, 38–9.
41. Here the Lithuanian terms are used, with related Balt and Finnic appellatives. See Kawiński 2018, 308ff.
42. For interpretations of Lithuanian folk art see Richardson 2003.
43. Laime 2009.
44. Chmielewski 1963. Today Eylau (or Preußisch Eylau) is called Bagrationovsk.
45. Jonuks 2007, 25.
46. Gilchrist 2012, 211–12.
47. See Gilchrist and Sloane 2005 for the best-surveyed range of examples.
48. Muižnieks 2015.
49. Muižnieks 2015.
50. On burial rites in historical Estonia see Valk 2001 and 2004; for Latvia see Muižnieks 2015.
51. Koperkiewicz 2020.
52. Torp-Kõivupuu 1996.
53. Muižnieks 2015.
54. Mažeika and Chollet 2016, 44.
55. Baronas 2014, 71–5.
56. Svetikas 2002.
57. Svetikas 2006.
58. Described by Maciej Stryjkowski in 1582, see Baronas 2014, 74.
59. Rephrased from Vaitkevičius 2004, 24.
60. Kosman 1989, 113.
61. For Lithuanian natural sacred sites see Vaitkevičius 2004; for a recent work on Lithuanian paganism see Ščavinskas 2024.
62. Radzimiński 2006a, 80.
63. Kawiński 2018, 263.
64. These chants were preserved in oral poetry, later referred to as 'Kalevala' after the nineteenth-century national epic.
65. Rephrased from Jonuks, Oras and Veldi 2018, 93.
66. Valk 2009, 59.

CHAPTER 11 HOLY WAR IN CRISIS

1. *Saevientibus olim Pruthenis*, 141 (*Paweł Włodkowic, Writings*).
2. Kreem 2001.
3. Neitmann 1993.
4. Taimiņa 2018.
5. During this period the terms Russia and Russian began to be used more frequently and gradually replaced Rus' in reference to the Muscovite state. I have opted to use this to refer to the tsardom and later incarnations of the Russian state.

6. Lapiņš 2018.
7. Dzenis 2017.
8. Chęć 2017.
9. *Chronicle of Livonia*, 125.
10. By the sixteenth century, the Latvian language, which evolved from Latgalian, began to emerge as a distinct linguistic identity.
11. For the complexity of Norse-Saami relations see Wang 2023.
12. Waśko 2013, 276.
13. Johansen 2008, 82–3.
14. *Revelations* VIII: 40.
15. Johansen 2008, 67–8.
16. Jensen 2022, 151.
17. *Chronicle of Novgorod* 1348, 141.
18. Jensen 2007, 84–5.
19. Jensen 2007, 135.
20. Sarnowsky 2017, 124.
21. Sarnowsky 2017, 125–6.
22. Sarnowsky 2017, 139.
23. Etting 2004, 134–5.
24. On the 'Great War' see Jóźwiak et al. 2010.
25. Wolski 2008, 75, 79–81.
26. Arnold 1994.
27. Sarnowsky 2017, 127.
28. Białuński 2002, 10.
29. Selart 2009, 67.
30. Jóźwiak 2009, 455.
31. Sarnowsky 2017, 128–9.
32. Jähnig 2013.
33. Arnold 2006.
34. Rowell 1999, 191.
35. Rowell 1999, 195
36. Paszkiewicz 2009, 240–48.
37. Selart 2017.
38. Mol 2023.
39. Mol 2015.
40. Raudkivi 2018.
41. Šnē 2008, 94.
42. Kreem 2002, 159.
43. Piirimäe 2013.
44. Kreem 2006.
45. Kreem 2013.
46. Arnold 2006, 24.
47. Schoenborn 2017.
48. Jensen 2007, 158–89.
49. For a discussion of this transition and the secularisation of 'just war' see Johnson 1975.

CHAPTER 12 ANCESTRAL STRUGGLES

1. Herder, *Outlines of a Philosophy of the History of Man* II, 338–9.
2. Dobry 2018.
3. The German Empire was named the Second Empire or *Reich* by the Nazis, as a means of legitimising their own 'Third Reich' as the direct successor of the Holy Roman Empire.
4. Clark 2006, 73–4.
5. Friedrich 2000, 161, 164–6.
6. For a recent history of the symbol see Heinemann 2019.
7. Schenkendorf 1872, 103–05.
8. Lijka and Herrmann 2024.
9. Steinbrecht 1896.
10. Franz Lubojatzky *Herkus Monte* 1840 or Heinrich's *Herkus Monte. Aus Altpreussens Vergangenheit* (1865).
11. Kuzborska 2020.
12. Confino 1997, 154.
13. Klaczko used '*Drang nach dem Osten*', and the *dem* was dropped by Mikhail Katkov in 1863; Leuschner 2012.
14. Wippermann 1981.
15. For good summaries of *Heimat* see Confino 1997, especially chapter 6, and Boa and Palfreyman 2000.
16. Later expressions of *Heimat* included urban spaces and cities.
17. Strakauskaitė 2015.
18. Kopp 2012.
19. For recent commentary on Matejko's *Grunwald* see Kiełczewska 2010.
20. Michalski 2008, 118.
21. Today Ełk in Poland.
22. Based on language rather than nationality: Srebrakowski 2020, 47.
23. Safronovas 2016, 173–85.
24. Vareikis 2001, 62–3.
25. Pivoras 2021.
26. Mickūnaitė 2006.
27. Initially referred to as Balts or German Balts in the 1860s and Baltic Germans after 1918; Topij 2011, 63.
28. For a detailed commentary see Jennison 1971.
29. Melliņa-Flood 2019, 23.
30. Daija 2017.
31. Plakans 1998.
32. Jõekalda 2020.
33. The sculpture vanished after the First World War and was replaced by a bronze replica in 2001, sponsored by Baltic Germans for Riga's eighth centenary.
34. Tvauri 2006.
35. Kukk 2013.
36. A good summary is provided by Jensen 2017.
37. Plakans 1998.
38. Kruks 2004.
39. Kļaviņš 2006.
40. Jõekalda 2024, 58.
41. Kļaviņš 1998.
42. A new monument was raised at the site in 1967.

43. Selart 2021.
44. Ripatti 2024.
45. Fewster 1999 and 2006.
46. On Finnish archaeology see Immonen and Taavitsainen 2011.
47. Fewster 2000.

CHAPTER 13 FROM ARYAN CRUSADERS TO EUROPEAN HERITAGE

1. https://whc.unesco.org/en/list/847/
2. It would only be published in 1978; see Menzel 2021.
3. Burleigh 1988.
4. Germann 1995.
5. Maxwell 2014.
6. Stone 2016, 306–07.
7. Burleigh 1988, 118–19.
8. Chu 2012, 54
9. Derda 2020.
10. Prarat 2014.
11. Kozłowski 2008.
12. Harvey 2005, plate 6.
13. Arnold 2006, 19–20; Panfil 2016.
14. Arnold 2006, 19–20.
15. Szczepański 2014.
16. Heinen 2011.
17. John-Stucke 2022.
18. Fiedor 1967, 494.
19. Safronovas 2016, 280–81.
20. Bertrand 2004.
21. Vermeiren 2018, 780–82.
22. On comparisons between Tannenberg in 1410 and 1914, see Goebel 2016.
23. Harvey 2005, 89.
24. Burleigh 1988, 194–5; Vermeiren 2018.
25. Merritt 1994–5, 36–49.
26. Domarus 2004, 2748.
27. Borejsza 2017, 136.
28. Broka-Lāce 2023, 327–9.
29. Russow 2023, 356.
30. Tilli 2017.
31. Fülberth 2019.
32. Jankevičiūtė 2010.
33. Biskup 1986.
34. Tomkiewicz 2024.
35. Russow 2023.
36. Selart 2021.
37. Gudavičius 1997, 12-13; Мерем 2020.
38. Kuzborska 2020.
39. Marozava 2019.
40. Kilger 1998; Fehring 2016; Roslund 2007.
41. Panayi 2001, 220, 225, 229–30.

42. Burleigh 1988, 315–16.
43. Grzechnik 2017.
44. Kożuchowski 2019.
45. Gałęziowska 2010.
46. Grzechnik 2017, 354.
47. Ekdahl 1991; Schenk 2001, 452.
48. For a recent study of the exclave see Modzelewski and Żukowski 2021.
49. Trupinda 2023.
50. Lubocka-Hoffmann 2019; Urban 2000.
51. Prout 2022, 37.
52. Dementavičius 2016, 243.
53. Mägi 2018, 430.

BIBLIOGRAPHY

ABBREVIATIONS

LUB   Liv-, Est- und Kurländisches Urkundenbuch nebst Regesten (*Book of Certificates and Register for Livonia, Estonia and Courland*)
PrUB Preußisches Urkundenbuch (*Prussian Records Book*)

PRIMARY SOURCES

Arbusow, L. (1928) 'Römischer Arbeitsbericht, I', *Acta Universitatis Latviensis* 17, pp. 285–422.

Bernard of Clairvaux, Letter to Eastern France and Bavaria promoting the Second Crusade, 1146: Robinson, J. H. (1904) *Readings in European History I*. Boston: Ginn and Company, pp. 330–33.

Carolingian Chronicles: Royal Frankish Annals and Nithard's Histories: Scholz, B. W. and Rogers, B. (1970). Ann Arbor: University of Michigan Press.

Chronica Albrici monachi Trium Fontium, a monacho Novi Monasterii Hoiensis interpolata / Alberic de Trois-Fontaines: Scheffer-Boichorst, P. (1874), Hanover.

The Chronicle of Livonia, Balthasar Rüssow: Smith, J. C., Eichhoff, J. and Urban, W. (1988) *The Chronicle of Balthasar Russow*. Madison: Baltic Studies Center.

The Chronicle of Novgorod, 1066–1471: Michell, R., Forbes, N., Beazley, R. C. and Shakhmatov, A. A. (1914). London: Royal Historical Society.

The Chronicle of Prussia / Peter of Dusburg. Wenta, J. and Wyszomirski, S. (2011). *Kronika ziemi Pruskiej*. Toruń: University of Nicolaus Copernicus.

The Chronicle of the Slavs / Arnold of Lübeck: Loud, G. A. (2019) *Chronica Slavorum*. London: Routledge.

Deeds of the Princes of the Poles / Gallus Anonymous: Knoll, P. W., Schaer, F. and Bisson, T. (2003) *Gesta Principum Polonorum*. Budapest: Central European University Press.

Deeds of the Saxons / Widukind of Corvey. Bachrach, B. S. and Bachrach, D. S. (2014) Washington, DC: The Catholic University of America Press.

BIBLIOGRAPHY

Deliciae Prussicae, oder, Preussische Schaubühne / Matthaeus Praetorius: Lukšaitė, I. Gerulaitienė, V. and Ulčinaitė, E. (1999) *Prūsijos įdomybės, arba, Prūsijos regykla* / Matas Pretorijus. Vilnius: Lithuanian Institute of History.

Dutton, P. E. (1993) *Carolingian Civilization: A Reader*. Peterborough: ONT.

Epistolae et privilegia / Eugenius III: Migne, J-P. (1902) *Patrologia Latina cursus completus* 180. Paris: Garnier Fratres.

Henry's Chronicle of Livonia / Henry: Brundage, J. A. (2003) *The Chronicle of Henry of Livonia*. New York: Columbia University Press.

History of the Archbishops of Hamburg-Bremen / Adam of Bremen: Tschan, F. J. (2002) New York: Columbia University Press.

The History of the Danes / Saxo Grammaticus: Friis-Jensen, K. and Fisher, P. (2014) Oxford: Oxford University Press.

The History of the First Crusade: Historia Iherosolimitana / Robert the Monk: Sweetenham, C. (2005) Aldershot: Ashgate.

Life of Charlemagne / Einhard: Holder-Egger, O. (1911) *Vita Karoli Magni*. Hanover: Hahn.

The Livonian Rhymed Chronicle. Smith, J. C. and Urban, W. L. (2001) Chicago: Lithuanian Research and Studies Center.

Max von Schenkendorf (1872) *Gedichte*. Leipzig: Reclam.

The New Prussian Chronicle / Wigand of Marburg: Zonenberg, S. and Kwiatkowski, K. (2017) *Nowa kronika pruska*. Toruń: Towarzystwo Naukowe.

Outlines of a Philosophy of the History of Man / J. G. Herder: Churchill, T. (1803) London: Luke Hansard.

Paweł Włodkowic, Writings. Thompson, E., Knoll, P. W. and Kraszewski, C. S. (2023) Rome, Warsaw: Angelicum University Press; Fundacja Świętego Mikołaja.

Poem Concerning the Conversion of the Saxons. Dümmler, E. (1881) *Carmen de conversione Saxonum* in *Monumenta Germaniae Historica, Poetae* 1. Berlin: Weidemann, pp. 380–81.

Revelations / St Birgitta of Sweden: Searby, D. and Morris, B. (2006–09) *The Revelations of St Birgitta of Sweden*. Oxford: Oxford University Press, 3 volumes.

Das rothe Buch inter Archiepiscopalia / *Scriptores Rerum Livonicarum* (2 volumes): Fuchs, M. (1853) Riga, Leipzig: E. Frantzen's Verlag-comptoir.

The Rule and Statutes of the Teutonic Order: Sterns I. (1969) *The Statutes of the Teutonic Knights: A Study of Religious Chivalry*. Publicly Accessible Penn Dissertations 1181. http://repository.upenn.edu/edissertations/1181

The Westminster Chronicle, 1381–1394. Hector, L. C. and Harvey, B. F. (1982) Oxford: Clarendon Press.

SECONDARY SOURCES

Abenheim, D. (1988) *Reforging the Iron Cross: The Search for Tradition in the West German Armed Forces*. Princeton: Princeton University Press.

Almonaitis, V. (2017) 'The capture of the Marienwerder Castle, or where the Teutonic Order's expansion to the East was stopped,' *Acta Baltico-Slavica* 41, pp. 1–30.

Andreson, K. (2014) 'The presence of the sacred: A 13th-century cult image from Saaremaa (Estonia),' *Baltic Journal of Art History* 8, pp. 7–43.

Apala, Z. and Apals, J. (2014) 'The Vendic hill fort on Riekstu Kalns in Cēsis', in H. Valk (ed.) *Strongholds and Power Centres East of the Baltic Sea in the 11th–13th Centuries*. Tartu: Institute of History and Archaeology at the University of Tartu, Department of Archaeology at the Institute of History of Tallinn University, pp. 115–38.

BIBLIOGRAPHY

Apals, J. (2012) *Āraišu ezerpils: rakstu izlase un draugu atmiņas*. Riga: LU Latvijas vēstures institūts.

Arnold, B. (2006) '"Arierdämmerung" : Race and archaeology in Nazi Germany', *World Archaeology* 38 (1), pp. 8–31.

Arnold, U. (1994) 'Eight hundred years of the Teutonic Order', in M. Barber (ed.) *The Military Orders: Fighting for the Faith and Caring for the Sick*. Aldershot: Ashgate, pp. 223–35.

Arnold, U. (2006) 'Hochmeister Albrecht von Brandenburg-Ansbach und Landmeister Gotthard Kettler. Ordensritter und Territorialherren am Scheideweg in Preußen und Livland', in J. A. Mol, K. Militzer and H. J. Nicholson (eds) *The Military Orders and the Reformation: Choices, State Building, and the Weight of Tradition*. Hilversum: Verloren, pp. 11–29.

Arszyński, M. (1995) *Budownictwo warowne zakonu krzyżackiego w Prusach (1230–1454)*. Toruń: Wydawnictwo Uniwersytetu Mikołaja Kopernika.

Arszyński, M. (2005) 'Budownictwo', in A. Radzimiński (ed.) *Zakon Krzyżacki: wybór tekstów źródłowych*. Toruń: Wydawnictwo Uniwersytetu Mikołaja Kopernika, pp. 123–44.

Arszyński, M. (2010) 'Architektura warowna Zakonu Krzyżackiego w Prusach', in B. Pospieszna (ed.) *Fundacje artystyczne na terenie państwa krzyżackiego w prusach*. Pelplin: Wydawnictwo Bernardinum, pp. 7–45.

Atgāzis, M. (1999) 'Vecdoles pils nocietinājumi un apbūve,' *Latvijas Viduslaiku Pilis* 1, pp. 312–48.

Badura, M. and Możejko, B. (2019) 'The plant element in the diet of the inhabitants of Gdańsk, Elbląg and Malbork during the rule of the Teutonic Order: The historical and archaeobotanical perspective', in A. G. Pluskowski (ed.) *Ecologies of Crusading, Colonisation and Religious Conversion in the Medieval Baltic*. Turnhout: Brepols, pp. 95–110.

Balsys, R. (2015) 'Pagoniškieji lietuvių ir prūsų aukojimai prie vandens ir per vandenį', *Res Humanitariae* 18, pp. 167–77.

Bandlien, B. (ed.) (2023) *Jerusalem in Viken: Crusading Ideology, Church-Building and Monasticism in South-Eastern Norway in the Twelfth Century*. Oslo: Cappelen Damm Akademisk/NOASP.

Banerjea, R. Y., Badura, M., Kalejs, U., Cerina, A., Gos, K., Hamilton-Dyer, S., Maltby, M., Seetah, K. and Pluskowski, A. (2017) 'A multi-proxy, diachronic and spatial perspective on the urban activities within an indigenous community in medieval Riga, Latvia,' *Quaternary International* 460, pp. 3–21.

Barber, M. (1995) *The New Knighthood: A History of the Order of the Temple*. Cambridge: Cambridge University Press.

Barber, M. (2012) *The Crusader States*. New Haven and London: Yale University Press.

Baronas, D. (2014) 'Christians in late pagan, and pagans in early Christian Lithuania: The fourteenth and fifteenth centuries,' *Lithuanian Historical Studies* 19, pp. 51–81.

Bartlett, R. (1985) 'The conversion of a pagan society in the Middle Ages', *History* 70 (229), pp. 185–201.

Bartlett, R. (1993) *The Making of Europe: Conquest, Colonization and Cultural Change, 950–1350*. London: BCA.

Bell, A. (2012) 'English members of the Order of the Passion: Their political, diplomatic and military significance', in *Philippe de Mézièrs and his Age*. Leiden: Brill, pp. 321–46.

Benninghoven, F. (1965) *Der Orden der Schwertbrüder: Fratres Milicie Christi de Livonia*. Cologne: Böhlau.

BIBLIOGRAPHY

Berend, N., Urbańczyk, P. and Wiszewski, P. (2013) *Central Europe in the High Middle Ages*. Cambridge: Cambridge University Press.

Bertrand, S. (2004) 'The Order of St John in Germany and the Second World War', *Guerres Mondiales et Conflits Contemporains* 215, pp. 91–106.

Białuński, G. (1993) 'Bogini Kurko – główny kult Galindii', *Komunikaty Mazursko-Warmińskie* 1, pp. 3–10.

Białuński, G. (1999) *Studia z dziejów plemion pruskich i jaćwieskich*. Olsztyn: Ośrodek Badań Nauk. im. Wojchiecha Kętrzyńskiego.

Białuński, G. (2002) *Kolonizacja 'Wielkiej Puszczy' (do 1568 roku) – starostwa piskie, ełckie, straduńskie, zelkowskie i węgoborskie (węgorzeweskie)*. Olsztyn: Ośrodek Badań Nauk. im. Wojchiecha Kętrzyńskiego.

Biermann, F. (2015) 'Central place and periphery in early and high medieval north-eastern German territory', in A. Wilkin, J. Naylor, D. Keene and A.-J. Bijsterveld (eds) *Town and Country in North Western Europe: Dynamic Interactions*. Turnhout: Brepols, pp. 49–86.

Biermann, F. and Herrmann, C. (2014) 'The origin and rise of brick technology and use in medieval Pomerania, Pomerelia and Lower Silesia', in T. Ratilainen, R. Bernotas and C. Herrmann (eds) *Fresh Approaches to Brick Production and Use in the Middle Ages*. Oxford: Archaeopress, pp. 51–61.

Biermann, F., Herrmann, C., Koperkiewicz, A. and Ubis, E. (2019) 'Burning Alt-Wartenburg. Archaeological evidence for the conflicts between the Teutonic Order and the grand duchy of Lithuania from a deserted medieval town near Barczewko (Warmia, Poland),' *Lietuvos Archeologija* 45, pp. 265–93.

Biermann, F. and Mangelsdorf, G. (eds) (2005) *Die bäuerliche Ostsiedlung des Mittelalters in Nordostdeutschland: Untersuchungen zum Landesausbau des 12. bis 14. Jahrhunderts im ländlichen Raum*. Frankfurt am Main: Peter Lang.

Biskup, H. (1986) 'Malbork podczas działań wojennych w 1945 roku', *Komunikaty Warmińsko-Mazurskie* 1–2, pp. 63–75.

Biskup, M. (2002) 'Etniczno-demograficzne przemiany Prus Krzyżackich w rozwoju osadnictwa w średniowieczu', in M. Biskup, *Opera Minora: Studia z dziejów zakonu Krzyżackiego*. Toruń: Towarzystwo Naukowe w Toruniu, pp. 129–50.

Blöndal, S. and Benedikz, B. S. (trans.) (2009) *The Varangians of Byzantium: An Aspect of Byzantine Military History*. Cambridge: Cambridge University Press.

Blough, K. (2016) 'The Lance of St Maurice as a component of the early Ottonian campaign against paganism', *Early Medieval Europe* 24 (3), pp. 338–61.

Blūzma, V. and Lazdiņš, J. (1998) 'Paražu tiesības Latvijas teritorijā līdz XIII gs.', in E. Meļķisis (ed.) *Latvijas tiesību avoti. Teksti un komentāri. 1. sējums. Seno paražu un Livonijas tiesību avoti 10.gs.–16.gs.* Riga: Fonds Latvijas Vēsture, pp. 19–25.

Boa, E. and Palfreyman, R. (2000) *Heimat: A German Dream. Regional Loyalties and National Identity in German Culture 1890–1990*. Oxford: Oxford University Press.

Boas, A. (2006) *Archaeology of the Military Orders: A Survey of the Urban Centres, Rural Settlement and Castles of the Military Orders in the Latin East*. London: Routledge.

Bogucki, M. and Jurkiewicz, B. (eds) (2012) *Janów Pomorski, stan. 1. Wyniki ratowniczych badań archeologicznych w latach 2007–2008, Elbląg*, 3 volumes. Elbląg: Muzeum Archeologiczno-Historyczne w Elblągu.

Bojtár, E. (1999) *Foreword to the Past: A Cultural History of the Baltic People*. Budapest: Central European University Press.

Borchardt, K. (2008) 'Competition between the military-religious orders in central Europe, c. 1140–c. 1270', in J. Upton-Ward (ed.) *The Military Orders: On Land and by Sea*. Aldershot: Ashgate, pp. 29–34.

BIBLIOGRAPHY

Borejsza, J. W. (2017) (trans. D. French) *A Ridiculous Hundred Million Slavs: Concerning Adolf Hitler's World View*. Warsaw: PAN.

Brather, S. (2005) 'Hochmittelalterliche Siedlungsentwicklung und ethnische Identitäten –Slawen und Deutsche östlich der Elbe in archäologischer und siedlungsgeographischer Perspektive', in F. Biermann and G. Mangelsdorf (eds) *Die bäuerliche Ostsiedlung des Mittelalters in Nordostdeutschland: Untersuchungen zum Landesausbau des 12. bis 14. Jahrhunderts im ländlichen Raum*. Frankfurt am Main: Peter Lang, pp. 29–38.

Brather, S. (2008) *Archäologie der westlichen Slawen: Siedlung, Wirtschaft und Gesellschaft im früh- und hochmittelalterlichen Ostmitteleuropa*. Berlin: De Gruyter.

Brink, S. and Price, N. (eds) (2008) *The Viking World*. London: Routledge.

Broka-Lāce, Z. (2023) 'The struggle to survive and work: Archaeology in Latvia during the German occupation (1941–1945)', in M. Eickhoff, D. Modl, K. Meheux and E. Nuijten (eds) *National-Socialist Archaeology in Europe and its Legacies*. Cham: Springer, pp. 315–35.

Brown, A. (2019) 'Vegetation changes in Livonia: The palynological data', in A. G. Pluskowski (ed.) *Environment, Colonization and the Baltic Crusader States*. Turnout: Brepols, pp. 105–36.

Brundage, J. A. (1969) *Medieval Canon Law and the Crusader*. Madison: University of Wisconsin Press.

Bryda, G. C. (2022) 'Tainted trees: Uncovering the long shadow over Germany's medieval maypoles and ancient tree cults', *Zeitschrift für Kunstgeschichte* 85 (3), pp. 337–62.

Buko, A. (2008) *The Archaeology of Early Medieval Poland: Discoveries – Hypotheses Interpretations*. Leiden: Brill.

Buko, A. (2021) *Świt państwa polskiego*. Warsaw: Wydawnictwo Instytutu Archeologii i Etnologii PAN, Muzeum Historii Polski.

Bukowska, A. (2012) 'The origins of Christianity in Poland. Actual research on the church archaeology', in O. Heinrich-Tamaska, N. Krohn and S. Ristow (eds) *Die Christianisierung Europas: Entstehung, Entwicklung und Konsolidierung im archäologischen Befund*. Regensburg: Schnell + Steiner, pp. 449–68.

Burleigh, M. (1988) *Germany Turns Eastwards: A Study of* Ostforschung *in the Third Reich*. Cambridge: Cambridge University Press.

Bysted, A. (2009) 'The ideology of mission and the Wendish Crusade of 1147', in B. F. Jensen and D. Wille-Jørgensen (eds) *Expansion-Integration, Danish-Baltic contacts 1147–1410 AD*. Vordingborg: Danmarks Borgcenter, pp. 9–14.

Bysted, A., Jensen, C. S., Jensen, K. V. and Lind, J. H. (2012) *Jerusalem in the North: Denmark and the Baltic Crusade, 1100–1552*. Turnhout: Brepols.

Caune, A. (2007) *Pētījumi Rīgas archeoloģijā*. Riga: LVIA.

Caune, A. and Ose, I. (2004) *Latvijas 12. gadsimta beigu – 17. gadsimta vācu piļu leksikons*. Riga: Latvijas vēstures institūta apgāds.

Ceynowa, B. and Paszkiewicz, B. (2015) 'Sambor I and Otto of Bamberg on early Gdańsk coins', *Wiadomości Numizmatyczne* 59 (1–2), pp. 199–200.

Chęć, A. (2017) 'Ieskats Cēsu pils izrakumos iegūto viduslaiku bruņu kolekcijā', in G. Kalniņš (ed.) *Cēsu pils raksti: 1: archeoloģija, architektūra*. Cēsis: Cēsu pils saglabāšanas fonds, pp. 143–65.

Chernyshov, K. (2008) 'The first Brandenburg coins (12th century) in the Hermitage Collection', *Reports of the State Hermitage Museum* 66, pp. 57–64.

Chmielewski, S. (1963) 'Czy pruski grób ciałopalny z XV wieku? (Próba interpretacji opisu znaleziska z 1703 r.)', *Rocznik Olsztyński* 5, pp. 295–319.

Christiansen, E. (1997) *The Northern Crusades*. London: Penguin.

BIBLIOGRAPHY

Chu, W. (2012) *The German Minority in Interwar Poland*. Cambridge: Cambridge University Press.

Clark, C. (2006) *Iron Kingdom: The Rise and Downfall of Prussia, 1600–1947*. London: Penguin.

Confino, A. (1997) *The Nation as a Local Metaphor: Württemberg, Imperial Germany and National Memory, 1871–1918*. Chapel Hill: University of North Carolina Press.

Constable, G. (2008) *Crusaders and Crusading in the Twelfth Century*. Farnham: Ashgate.

Cook, A. S. (1915) 'Beginning the board in Prussia', *Journal of English and Germanic Philology* 14 (3), pp. 375–88.

Coupland, S. (2005) 'Charlemagne's coinage: ideology and economy', in J. Story (ed). *Charlemagne. Empire and Society*. Manchester: Manchester University Press, pp. 211–29.

Cragle, J. M. (2024) *Converting the Saxons: A Study of Violence and Religion in Early Medieval Germany*. London: Routledge.

Crumlin-Pedersen, O. (2000) 'To be or not to be a cog: The Bremen cog in perspective', *International Journal of Nautical Archaeology* 29 (2), pp. 230–46.

Cusack, C. (2011) 'Pagan Saxon resistance to Charlemagne's mission: "Indigenous" religion and "world" religion in the Early Middle Ages', *The Pomegranate* 13 (1), pp. 33–51.

Czaja, R. (2009) 'Rozwój osadnictwa miejskiego', in M. Biskup et al. (eds) *Państwo zakonu krzyżackiego w Prusach: Władza i społeczeństwo*. Warsaw: Wydawnictwo Naukowe PWN, pp. 370–83.

Czaja, R. and Radzimiński, A. (eds) (2016) *The Teutonic Order in Prussia and Livonia: The Political and Ecclesiastical Structures 13th–16th century*. Toruń: Towarzystwo Naukowe w Toruniu.

Czaja, R. and Stevens, M. F. (2022) 'The place of native populations in the chartered towns of conquered regions. Wales and Prussia as a comparative case study', in M. F. Stevens and R. Czaja (eds) *Towns on the Edge in Medieval Europe: The Social and Political Order of Peripheral Urban Communities from the Twelfth to Sixteenth Centuries*. Oxford: Oxford University Press, pp. 21–45.

Dąbrowska, M. (2007) 'Badania archeologiczno-architektoniczne na terenie zamku niskiego w Malborku w latach 1998–2004', in G. Nawrolska (ed.) *XV Sesja Pomorzoznawcza*. Elbląg: Muzeum Archeologiczno-Historyczne w Elblągu, pp. 303–16.

Daija, P. (2017) *Literary History and Popular Enlightenment in Latvian Culture*. Newcastle: Cambridge Scholars.

Dementavičius, J. (2016) 'Baltarusijos istorijos politika kaip Lietuvos istorijos politikos subjektas ir aporija', in R. Lopata and I. Vinogradnaitė (eds), *Lietuvos ir Baltarusijos istorijos politika*. Vilnius: VU leidykla, pp. 235–57.

Derda, A. (2020) 'Kampania i przebieg plebiscytu z 11 lipca 1920 roku na Warmii i Mazurach w świetle materiałów tekstowych oraz ikonograficznych zamieszczonych w lokalnej prasie niemieckojęzycznej', *Echa Przeszłości* 21 (1), pp. 239–60.

Długokęcki, W. (2009) 'Prusy w starożytności i we wczesnym średniowieczu', in M. Biskup et al. (eds) *Państwo zakonu krzyżackiego w Prusach: Władza i społeczeństwo*. Warsaw: Wydawnictwo Naukowe PWN, pp. 25–50.

Dobosz, J., Matla, M. and Strzelczyk, J. (eds) (2017) *Chrzest Mieszka I i chrystianizacja państwa Piastów*. Poznań: Wydawnictwo Naukowe Uniwersytetu im. Adama Mickiewicza w Poznaniu.

Dobry, A. (2018) 'Dni Cesarskie i poświęcenie kościoła na Zamku Wysokim w Malborku w 1902 r.', *Historia Slavorum Occidentis* 1 (16), pp. 56–71.

BIBLIOGRAPHY

Domagała, T. (2004) 'Zagubiony Elbląski kodeks prawa lubeckiego z 1240 roku. Próba identyfikacji i rekonstrukcji tekstu', in R. Czaja, G. Nawrolska, M. Rębkowski and J. Tandecki (eds) *Archaeologia et historia urbana*. Elbląg: Muzeum w Elblągu, pp. 89–93.

Domarus, M. (2004) *Hitler: Speeches and Proclamations, 1932–1945: The Chronicle of a Dictatorship*, vol. 4: *The Years 1941–1945*. London: I.B. Tauris.

Dorna, M. (2008) 'Przywilej kruszwicki Konrada Mazowieckiego z czerwca 1230 roku. Przyczynek do genezy państwa krzyżackiego w Prusach', *Zapiski Historyczne* 73 (1), pp. 7–35.

Dorna, M. (2024) *Knights of Christ of Prussia: A Forgotten 13th Century Military Order*. Tallinn: Eostre.

Doxey, G. B. (1996) 'Norwegian crusaders and the Balearic Islands', *Scandinavian Studies* 68 (2), pp. 139–60.

Dragnea, M. (2020) *The Wendish Crusade, 1147: The Development of Crusading Ideology in the Twelfth Century*. London: Routledge.

Dragnea, M. (2021) *Christian Identity Formation across the Elbe in the Tenth and Eleventh Centuries*. New York: Peter Lang.

Dygo, M. (1989) 'The political role of the cult of the Virgin Mary in Teutonic Prussia in the fourteenth and fifteenth centuries', *Journal of Medieval History* 15 (1), pp. 63–81.

Dzenis, A. (2017) 'Cēsu Pils "voltera Štrika depozīts": izcelsme un priekšmetu identificēšanas problēmas', in G. Kalniņš (ed.) *Cēsu pils raksti: 1: archeoloģija, architektūra*. Cēsis: Cēsu pils saglabāšanas fonds, pp, 189–205.

Ehlers, A. (2001) 'The crusade against Lithuania reconsidered', in A. V. Murray (ed.) *Crusade and Conversion on the Baltic Frontier 1150–1500*. Aldershot: Ashgate, pp. 21–44.

Ehlers, A. (2007) *Die Ablasspraxis des Deutschen Ordens im Mittelalter*. Marburg: N. G. Elwert.

Ehlers, A. (2008) 'The use of indulgences by the Teutonic Order in the Middle Ages', in V. Mallia-Milanes (ed.) *The Military Orders*, vol. 3: *History and Heritage*. Aldershot: Ashgate, pp. 139–45.

Ehrnsten, F. (2018) 'A cheap salvation? Post-Reformation offerings in Finnish churches', in N. M. Burström and G. T. Ingvardson (eds) *Divina Moneta: Coins in Religion and Ritual*. Abingdon: Routledge, pp. 228–48.

Ekdahl, S. (1991) 'Tannenberg/Grunwald – ein politisches Symbol in Deutschland und Polen', *Journal of Baltic Studies* 22 (4), pp. 271–324.

Ekdahl, S. (1998) 'Horses and crossbows: Two important warfare advantages of the Teutonic Order in Prussia', in H. Nicholson (ed.) *The Military Orders: Welfare and Warfare*. Aldershot: Ashgate, pp. 119–51.

Ekdahl, S. (2007) 'The siege machines during the Baltic Crusades', *Fasciuli Archaeologiae Historicae* 20, pp. 29–51.

Etting, V. (2004) *Queen Margrete I (1352–1412) and the Founding of the Nordic Union*. Leiden: Brill.

Fehring, G. P. (2016) *The Archaeology of Medieval Germany: An Introduction*. London: Routledge.

Fewster, D. (1999) 'The invention of the Finnish Stone Age: politics, ethnicity and archaeology', in M. Huurre (ed.) *Dig it All: Papers Dedicated to Ari Siiriäinen*. Helsinki: The Archaeological Society of Finland, pp. 13–20.

Fewster, D. (2000) 'Approaches to the conversion of the Finns: Ideologies, symbols, and archaeological features', in G. Armstrong and I. N. Wood (eds) *Christianizing Peoples and Converting Individuals*. Turnhout: Brepos, pp. 89–102.

BIBLIOGRAPHY

Fewster, D. (2006) *Visions of Past Glory: Nationalism and the Construction of Early Finnish History*. Helsinki: Finnish Literature Society.

Fiedor, K. (1967) 'Formy antypolskiej działalności w Prusach Wschodnich w latach 1918–1939', *Komunikaty Mazursko-Warmińskie* 4, pp. 485–517.

Flierman, R. (2017) *Saxon Identities, AD 150–900*. London: Bloomsbury.

Fonferek, J. (2019) 'The environmental setting of the earliest Teutonic Order stronghold in Elbąg', in A. G. Pluskowski (ed.) *Ecologies of Crusading, Colonisation and Religious Conversion in the Medieval Baltic*. Turnhout: Brepols, pp. 16–23.

Fonnesberg-Schmidt, I. M. (2007) *The Popes and the Baltic Crusades, 1147–1254*. Leiden: Brill.

Frankot, E. (2007) 'Medieval maritime law from Oléron to Wisby: Jurisdictions in the Law of the Sea', in J. Pan-Montojo and F. Pedersen (eds) *Communities in European History: Representations, Jurisdictions, Conflicts*. Pisa: Pisa University Press, pp. 151–72.

French, K. M., Musiał, A. D., Karczewski, M. et al. (2024) 'Biomolecular evidence reveals mares and long-distance imported horses sacrificed by the last pagans in temperate Europe', *Science Advances* 10, eado3529.

Friedland, S. N. (2013) 'Network analysis in Slavic archaeology: An example from the Plon area in Wagria (Schleswig-Holstein)', in S. Kleingärtner, T. P. Newfield, S. Rossignol and D. Wehner (eds) *Landscapes and Societies in Medieval Europe East of the Elbe*. Toronto: Pontifical Institute, pp. 139–70.

Friedrich, K. (2000) *The Other Prussia: Royal Prussia, Poland and Liberty, 1569–1772*. Cambridge: Cambridge University Press.

Fülberth, A. (2019) 'Further destruction as a result of too much confidence in Communism? Baltic cities after World War II', in S. Michonneau et al. (eds) *Paisajes de Guerra*. Madrid: Casa de Velázquez, pp. 95–105.

Gabriel, I. and Muhl, A. (2014) 'Der slawische Trinkhornmann von Seehausen, Lkr. Börde – Präsentation und Interpretation einer frühmittelalterlichen Kleinskulptur', *Jahresschrift für mitteldeutsche Vorgeschichte* 94, pp. 399–416.

Gabriele, M. (2011) *An Empire of Memory: The Legend of Charlemagne*. Oxford, Oxford University Press.

Gaimster, D. (2005) 'A parallel history: The archaeology of Hanseatic urban culture in the Baltic c. 1200–1600', *World Archaeology* 37 (3), pp. 408–23.

Gaimster, D. (2014) 'The Hanseatic cultural signature: Exploring globalization on the micro-scale in late medieval Northern Europe', *European Journal of Archaeology* 17 (1), pp. 60–81.

Gałęziowska, M. (2010) 'Grunwald i idea – celoworacjonalność 535. i 550. rocznicy obchodów bitwy', *Komunikaty Mazursko-Warmińskie* 3, pp. 339–58.

Gardeła, L. (2024) *The Vikings in Poland*. London: Routledge.

Germann, H. (1995) *Die politische Religion des Nationalsozialisten Dietrich Klagges: Ein Beitrag zur Phaenomenologie der Ns-Ideologie*. Frankfurt: Peter Lang.

Gilchrist, R. (2012) *Medieval Life: Archaeology and the Life Course*. Woodbridge: Boydell.

Gilchrist, R. and Sloane, B. (2005) *Requiem: The Medieval Monastic Cemetery in Britain*. London: Museum of London Archaeology Service.

Given-Wilson, C. (2016) *Henry IV*. New Haven and London: Yale University Press.

Gładysz, M. (2012) *The Forgotten Crusades: Poland and the Crusader Movement in the Twelfth and Thirteenth Centuries*. Leiden: Brill.

Gläser, M. (2015) 'The development of Lübeck into a medieval metropolis', in M. S. Kristiansen, E. Roesdahl and J. Graham-Campbell (eds) *Medieval Archaeology in Scandinavia and Beyond: History, Trends and Tomorrow*. Aarhus: Aarhus University Press, pp. 335–54.

BIBLIOGRAPHY

Goebel, S. (2016) 'The German crusade: The battle of Tannenberg 1410 and 1914', in K. Stevenson and B. Gribling (eds) *Chivalry and the Medieval Past*. Woodbridge: Boydell, pp. 169–86.

Gogosz, R. (2020) *Od ziemi swietej do ziemi Prusów*. Połomia: Inforteditions.

Gołembnik, A. (2004) 'Early medieval Plock', in P. Urbańczyk (ed.) *Polish Lands at the Turn of the First and Second Millennia*. Warsaw: Institute of Archaeology and Ethnology, Polish Academy of Sciences, pp. 241–70.

Gouguenheim, S. (2012) *Krzyżacy*. Malbork: Muzeum Zamkowe w Malborku (original French edn publ. 2007).

Grant, A. (2013) 'The St Bees Lord and Lady, and their Lineage'. Lancaster: University of Lancaster.

Groenewoudt, B., van Beek, R. and Groothedde, M. (2014) 'Christianisation and the afterlife of pagan open-air cult sites: Evidence from the northern Frankish frontier', *Medieval and Modern Matters* 5, pp. 1–28.

Grzechnik, M. (2017) '"Recovering" territories: The use of history in the integration of the new Polish western borderland after World War II', *Europe–Asia Studies* 69 (4), pp. 668–92.

Guard, T. (2016) *Chivalry, Kingship and Crusade: The English Experience in the Fourteenth Century*. Woodbridge: Boydell.

Gudavičius, E. (1997) 'Ar pasistūmėta sovietinėje istoriografijoje po Henryko Lowmianskio "Studijų apie Lietuvos valstybės ir visuomenės 3 genezę"', *Lietuvos istorijos studijos* 5, pp. 7–22.

Güttner-Sporzyński, D. von (2014) *Poland, Holy War and the Piast Monarchy, 1100–1230*. Turnhout: Brepols.

Güttner-Sporzyński, D. von (2015) 'Poland and the second crusade', in J. T. Roche and J. M. Jensen (eds) *The Second Crusade: Holy War on the Periphery of Latin Christendom*. Turnhout: Brepols, pp. 115–54.

Güttner-Sporzyński, D. von (2022) 'The periphery of Europe and the idea of crusade: Adaptation and evolution of crusader ideology in Poland under the Piast dynasty (1100–47)', in P. Srodecki and N. Kersken (eds) *The Expansion of the Faith: Crusading on the Frontiers of Latin Christendom in the High Middle Ages*. Turnhout: Brepols, pp. 69–88.

Haak, A. (2015) 'Problems in defining ethnic identity in medieval towns of Estonia on the basis of archaeological sources', in A. Haak, V. Lang and M. Lavento (eds) *Today I Am Not the One I Was Yesterday: Archaeology, Identity, and Change*. Tartu: University of Tartu, pp. 13–27.

Haak, A. (2022) '"Local" characteristics of the medieval Livonian town', in A. Selart (ed.) *Baltic Crusades and Societal Innovation in Medieval Livonia, 1200–1350*. Leiden: Brill, pp. 232–60.

Haftka, M. (1987) 'Mikroregion osadniczy Węgry-Gościszewo-Malbork w świetle kilkunastoletnich obserwacji terenowych', in A. Pawłowski (ed.) *Badanaia archeologiczne w woj, elbląskim w latach 1980–83*. Malbork: Muzeum Zamkowe w Malborku, pp. 27–42.

Haftka, M. and Wadyl, S. (2015) *Węgry. Zespół osadniczy na pograniczu Pomorsko-Pruskim w XI–XII w*. Malbork: Muzeum Zamkowe w Malborku.

Haggrén, G. (2018) 'Six estate landscapes: Traces of medieval feudalisation in Finland?', in P. Kouki and T. Kirkinen (eds) *Landscapes of the Past and Future: Current Finnish Research in Landscape Archaeology*. Turku: Archaeological Society of Finland, pp. 69–86.

BIBLIOGRAPHY

Halsall, G. (1995) *Early Medieval Cemeteries: An Introduction to Burial Archaeology in the post-Roman West*. Skelmorlie: Cruithne Press.

Harreld, D. J. (2015) *A Companion to the Hanseatic League*. Leiden: Brill.

Harvey, E. (2005) *Women and the Nazi East: Agents and Witnesses of Germanisation*. New Haven and London: Yale University Press.

Hayward, K. (2019) 'Resources for castle construction medieval Prussia and Livonia', in A.G. Pluskowski (ed.) *Ecologies of Crusading, Colonisation and Religious Conversion in the Medieval Baltic*. Turnhout: Brepols, pp. 35–58.

Heikkilä, T. (2016) 'An imaginary saint for an imagined community: St. Henry and the creation of Christian identity in Finland, thirteenth–fifteenth centuries', in W. Jezierski and L. Hermanson (eds) *Imagined Communities on the Baltic Rim, from the Eleventh to Fifteenth Centuries*. Amsterdam: Amsterdam University Press, pp. 223–52.

Heinemann, W. (2019) *Das Eiserne Kreuz: Die Geschichte eines Symbols im Wandel der Zeit*. Potsdam: Militärgeschichtliches Forschungsamt.

Heinen, F. A. (2011) *NS-Ordensburgen: Vogelsang, Sonthofen, Krössinsee*. Berlin: Ch. Links.

Heinonen, T. (2023) 'Development of the medieval villages in Southern Finland', in M. Ødegaard and I. Ystgaard (eds), *Complexity and Dynamics: Settlement and Landscape from the Bronze Age to the Renaissance in the Nordic Countries (1700 BC–AD 1600)*. Leiden: Sidestone Press, pp. 201–10.

Henning, J. (2002) 'Der slawische Siedlungsraum und die ottonische Expansion östlich der Elbe. Ereignisgeschichte – Archäologie – Dendrochronologie', in J. Henning (ed.) *Europa im 10. Jahrhundert. Archäologie einer Aufbruchszeit*. Mainz: P. von Zabern, pp. 131–46.

Herrmann, C. (2007) *Mittelalterliche Architektur in Preussenland: Untersuchungen zur Frage der Kunstlandschaft und -geographie*. Petersberg: Michael Imhof.

Herrmann, C. (2009) 'Kloster und Burg – die Architektur des Deutschen Ordens in Preußen und Livland', in O. Auge, F. Biermann und C. Herrmann (eds) *Glaube, Macht und Pracht. Geistliche Gemeinschaften des Ostseeraums im Zeitalter der Backsteingotik*. Rahden: VML, pp. 209–20.

Herrmann, C. (2019) *Der Hochmeisterpalast auf der Marienburg. Konzeption, Bau und Nutzung der modernsten europäischen Fürstenresidenz um 1400*. Petersberg: Michael Imhof.

Hiekkanen, M. (2023) *Suomen keskiajan kivikirkot*. Helsinki: Suomen Kirjallisuuden Seura.

Hill, T. (1995) 'Von der Konfrontation zur Assimilation: Das Ende der Slawen in Ostholstein, Lauenburg und Lübeck vom 12. bis zum 15. Jahrhundert', in M. Müller-Wille, D. Meier and H. Unverhau (eds), *Slawen und Deutsche im südlichen Ostseeraum vom 11. bis 16. Jahrhundert*. Neumünster: Wachholtz, pp. 79–104.

Hines, J. (2003) 'Converting the Old Saxons', in D. H. Green and F. Siegmund (eds) *The Continental Saxons from the Migration Period to the Tenth Century: An Ethnographic Perspective*. Woodbridge: Boydell, pp. 299–328.

Hoffmann, J. (2012) *Die mittelalterliche Baugeschichte des Havelberger Domes*. Berlin: Lukas.

Hoffmann, L. (1991) 'Das "Volk". Zur ideologischen Struktur eines unvermeidbaren Begriffs', *Zeitschrift für Soziologie* 20 (3), pp. 191–208.

Hoffmann, M. (2002) 'Struktury społeczne i gospodarka Prusów w VII–XIII wieku', *Masovia* 5, pp. 5–16.

Hofstra, T., Houwen, L. A. J. R. and MacDonald, A. A. (eds) (1995) *Pagans and Christians: The Interplay between Christian Latin and Traditional German Cultures in Early Medieval Europe*. Groningen: University of Groningen.

BIBLIOGRAPHY

Hunyadi, Z. (2008) 'The Teutonic Order in Burzenland (1211–1225): New reconsiderations', in H. Houben and K. Toomaspoeg (eds) *L'Ordine Teutonico tra Mediterraneo e Baltico. Incontri e scontri tra religioni, popoli e culture*. Galatina: M. Congedo, pp. 151–62.

Ibsen, T. and Frenzel, J. (2010) 'In search of the early medieval settlement of Wiskiauten/Mohovoe in the Kaliningrad region,' *Lietuvos archeologija* 36, pp. 47–58.

Immonen, V. (2007) 'Defining a culture: the meaning of Hanseatic in medieval Turku', *Antiquity* 83 (313), pp. 720–32.

Immonen, V., Kinnunen, J. and Harjula, J. (2021) 'At the fringes of urbanisation: A socio-economic model of founding of the town of Turku, Finland, c. 1300', *Zeitschrift für Archäologie des Mittelalters* 49, pp. 217–34.

Immonen, V. and Taavitsainen, J. P. (2011) 'Oscillating between the national and the international: The case of Finnish archaeology', in Ludomir R. Lozny (ed.) *Comparative Archaeologies: A Sociological View of the Science of the Past*. New York: Springer, pp. 137–78.

Jabłoński, A. (2019) 'Język kaszubski jako element narodowotwórczy,' *Postcritum Polonistyczne* 1, pp. 45–56.

Jagodziński, M. (2004) 'Podstawy źródłowe – analiza. Przekazy pisane – odkrycia archeologiczne', in J. Trupinda (ed.) *Pacifica Terra: Prusowie-Słowianie-Wikingowie u ujścia Wisły*. Malbork: Muzeum Zamkowe w Malborku, pp. 21–40.

Jagodziński, M. F. (2010) *Truso. Między Weonodlandem a Witlandem*. Elbląg: Muzeum Archeologiczno-Historyczne w Elblągu.

Jähnig, B. (2013) 'Albert de Brandebourg-Ansbach et la sécularisation de l'Ordre Teutonique en Prusse', *Histoire, économie & société* 2013 (2), pp. 19–27.

Jakubowska, B. (2016) *Magiczna przestrzeń Złotej Bramy w Malborku: progres badawczy czy regres?* Malbork: Muzeum Zamkowe w Malborku.

Jamroziak, E. (2011) *Survival and Success on Medieval Borders: Cistercian Houses in Medieval Scotland and Pomerania from the Twelfth to the Late Fourteenth Century*. Turnhout: Brepols.

Jankevičiūtė, G. (2010) 'Constructing national identity: The image of the medieval Grand Duchy of Lithuania in Lithuanian art from the 1920s to the 1990s', *Central Europe* 8 (2), pp. 158–80.

Janson, H. (2010) 'What made the pagans pagans?', in T. Stepanov and G. Kazakov (eds) *Medieval Christianitas: Different Regions, 'Faces', Approaches*. Sofia: Voenno, pp. 11–30.

Jarockis, R. (1998) 'Semigallia 1100–1400: A review of archaeological and historical sources', in N. Blomkvist (ed.) *Culture, Clash or Compromise? The Europeanisation of the Baltic Sea Area 1100–1400 AD*. Visby: Gotland Centre for Baltic Studies, pp. 45–53.

Jennison, E. W. (1971) 'An eighteenth century appraisal of Germany's Baltic Crusade: Gebhardi's History of Livonia in the "Allgemeine Welthistorie"', *Bulletin of Baltic Studies* 2 (7), pp. 3–12.

Jensen, C. S. (2017) 'Appropriating history: Remembering the crusades in Latvia and Estonia', in M. Cassidy-Welch (ed.) *Remembering the Crusades and Crusading*. London: Routledge, pp. 231–46.

Jensen, J. M. (2007) *Denmark and the Crusades, 1400–1750*. Leiden: Brill.

Jensen, J. M. (2018) 'Martyrs for the faith: Denmark, the Third Crusade and the fall of Acre in 1191', in J. France (ed.) *Acre and its Falls: Studies in the History of a Crusader City*. Leiden: Brill, pp. 49–68.

Jensen, K. V. (2002) 'The blue Baltic border of Denmark in the High Middle Ages: Danes, Wends and Saxo Grammaticus', in D. Abulafia and N. Berend (eds) *Medieval Frontier Concepts and Practices*. London: Routledge, pp. 173–93.

BIBLIOGRAPHY

Jensen, K. V. (2013) 'Crusading and Christian penetration into the landscape: The new Jerusalem in the desert after c.1100', in S. W. Nordeide and S. Brink (eds) *Sacred Sites and Holy Places: Exploring the Sacralization of Landscape through Time and Space*. Turnhout: Brepols, pp. 215–36.

Jensen, K. V. (2017) *Crusading at the Edges of Europe: Denmark and Portugal, c. 1000–c. 1250*. London: Routledge.

Jensen, K. V. (2022) 'Papal crusade bulls and preaching to Scandinavia', in K. Salonen, A.-S. Hägglund and C. Gejrot (eds) *Scandinavia and the Vatican Archives: Papers from a Conference in Stockholm, 14–15 October 2016*. Stockholm: The Royal Swedish Academy of Letters, History and Antiquities, pp. 141–56.

Jezierski, W. (2020) 'Livonian hospitality: The "Livonian Rhymed Chronicle" and the formation of identities on the thirteenth-century Baltic frontier', *Frühmittelalterliche Studien* 54, 395–427.

Jõekalda, K. (2020) 'German Monuments in the Baltic Heimat? A Historiography of Heritage in the "Long Nineteenth Century"'. PhD thesis, Estonian Academy of Arts, Tallinn.

Jõekalda, K. (2024) 'Mothers of the land: Baltic German and Estonian personifications from the Virgin Mary to the Epic Linda', in C. Heß and G. Strenga (eds) *Doing Memory: Medieval Saints and Heroes and their Afterlives in the Baltic Sea Region (19th–20th Centuries)*. Berlin: De Gruyter, pp. 43–80.

Johansen, R. (2008) 'The Political Impact of Crusading Ideology in Sweden 1150–1350'. Master's thesis, University of Oslo.

Johanson, K. and Jonuks, T. (2015) 'Superstition in the House of God? Some Estonian case studies of vernacular practices', *Mirator* 16 (1), pp. 118–40.

John-Stucke, K. (2022) 'Himmler's plans and activities in Wewelsburg', in K. John-Stucke and D. Siepe (eds) *Myths of Wewelsburg Castle: Facts and Fiction*. Leiden: Brill, pp. xiv–32.

Johnson, J. T. (1975) *Ideology, Reason and the Limitation of War: Religious and Secular Concepts 1200–1740*. Princeton: Princeton University Press.

Jonsson, K. (2017) 'The earliest coinage on Gotland and in the Baltic countries', in M. C. Caltabiano (ed.) *Proceedings – XV International Numismatic Congress Taormina 2015*. Rome: Arbor Sapientiae editore, pp. 1128–32.

Jonuks, T. (2007) 'Holy groves in Estonian religion', *Estonian Journal of Archaeology* 11 (1), pp. 3–35.

Jonuks, T. and Joosu, L. (2013) 'Pendants of St. Anthony cross with the crucifixion from Estonia: Possible badges of a folk pilgrimage', *Estonian Journal of Archaeology* 17 (2), pp. 123–38.

Jonuks, T., Oras, E. and Veldi, M. (2018) 'Mix and match, old and new: Material remains of religious practices by Estonian pagans', in J. Leskovar and R. Karl (eds) *Archaeological Sites as Space for Modern Spiritual Practice*. Newcastle: Cambridge Scholars, pp. 90–109.

Jóźwiak, S. (2009) 'Rycerstwo-szlachta', in M. Biskup et al. (eds) *Państwo zakonu krzyżackiego w Prusach. Władza i społeczeństwo*. Warsaw: Wydawnictwo Naukowe PWN, pp. 450–59.

Jóźwiak, S., Kwiatkowski, K., Szweda, A. and Szybkowski, S. (2010) *Wojna Polski i Litwy z zakonem krzyżackim w latach 1409–1411*. Malbork: Muzeum Zamkowe w Malborku.

Jóźwiak, S. and Trupinda, J. (2007) *Organizacja życia na zamku krzyżackim w Malborku w czasach wielkich mistrzów (1309–1457)*. Malbork: Muzeum Zamkowe w Malborku.

Jóźwiak, S. and Trupinda, J. (2009) 'Budowa krzyżackiego zamku komturskiego w Ragnecie w końcu XIV–na początku XV wieku i jego układ przestrzenny', *Kwartalnik Historii Kultury Materialnej* 57 (3–4), pp. 339–68.

BIBLIOGRAPHY

Jóźwiak, S. and Trupinda, J. (2010) 'Funkcjonowanie wielkiego refektarza w czasach krzyżackich (do 1457 r.)', in J. Trupinda (ed.), *Wielki refektarz na zamku średnim w Malborku: dzieje – wstrój – konserwacja*. Malbork: Muzeum Zamkowe w Malborku, pp. 31–9.

Jóźwiak, S. and Trupinda, J. (2012) *Krzyżackie zamki komturskie w Prusach. Topografia i układ przestrzenny na podstawie średniowiecznych źródeł pisanych*. Toruń: Wydawnictwo Naukowe Uniwersytetu Mikołaja Kopernika.

Jóźwiak, S. and Trupinda, J. (2019) 'Czas powstania krzyżackiego komturstwa w Pokarminie (Brandenburg) a kwestia chronologii wznoszenia tamtejszego zamku', *Studia z Dziejów Średniowiecza* 23, pp. 100–13.

Jürgensen, M. W. (2021) 'Depictions of violence in late Romanesque mural paintings in Denmark', in R. Kotecki, C. S. Jensen and S. Bennett (eds) *Christianity and War in Medieval East Central Europe and Scandinavia*. Amsterdam: Amsterdam University Press, pp. 117–38.

Jurkowlaniec, T. (2010) 'Z Prus do wieczności . . . o nagrobkach', in B. Pospieszna (ed.) *Fundacje artystyczne na terenie Państwa Krzyżackiego w Prusach*. Pelplin: Wydawnictwo Bernardinum, pp. 213–22.

Jusupović, A. (2006) '"Domus quondam Dobrinensis": Przyczynek do dziejów templariuszy Na ziemiach Konrada Mazowieckiego', *Zapiski Historyczne* 71 (1), pp. 1–12.

Kajkowski, K. (2011) 'Wyspy jako symboliczne centra wczesnośredniowiecznych mikroregionów osadniczych Pomorza Środkowego', *Nasze Pomorze* 13, pp. 23–42.

Kajkowski, K. (2021) '"Kryzys monarchi piastowskiej" i problem tzw. reakcji pogańskiej okiem archeologa', *Slavia Antiqua* 62, pp. 193–216.

Kala, T. (2001) 'The incorporation of the northern Baltic lands into the western Christian world', in A. V. Murray (ed.) *Crusade and Conversion on the Baltic Frontier, 1150–1500*. Aldershot: Ashgate, pp. 3–20.

Kala, T. (2009) 'Rural society and religious innovation: Acceptance and rejection of Catholicism among the native inhabitants of medieval Livonia', in A. V. Murray (ed.) *The Clash of Cultures on the Medieval Baltic Frontier*. Farnham: Ashgate, pp. 168–90.

Kala, T. (2012) 'Gab es eine "Nationale Frage" in mittelalterlichen Reval?', *Forschungen zur baltischen Geschichte* 7, pp. 11–34.

Kalaga, J. (2006) 'Formy i etapy rozwoju ciałopalnego obrządku pogrzebowego w miedzyrzeczu Liwca, Bugu i Krzny we wczesnym średniowieczu', in H. Karwowska (ed.) *Stan Badań Archeologicznych na pograniu*. Białystok: Muzeum Podlaskie, pp. 113–25.

Kalling, K. (1997) 'Uusi paleoantropoloogilisi andmeid Tartu Jaani kirikumatuste kohta – Arheoloogilisi uurimusi', *Tartu Ülikooli Arheoloogia Kabineti Toimetised* 9, pp. 54–70.

Kara, M., Krzysztofiak, T. and Wyrwa, A. M. (2016) *Gród Piastowski w Gieczu. Geneza – Funkcja – Kontekst*. Poznań: Poznańskie Towarzystwo Przyjaciół Nauk.

Karczewski, M. (2011) *Archeologia środowiska zachodniobałtyjskiego kręgu kulturowego na pojezierzach*. Poznań-Białystok: Bogucki Wydawnictow Naukowe.

Karras, R. M. (1986) 'Pagan survivals and syncretism in the conversion of Saxony', *Catholic Historical Review* 72 (4), pp. 553–72.

Kawiński, P. (2018) *Sacrum w wyobrażeniach pogańskich Prusów Próba interpretacji na pograniczu historii i etnologii religii*. Olsztyn: Pruthenia.

Kawiński, P. and Szczepański, S. (2016) *Szkice o religii Prusów*. Olsztyn: Pruthenia.

Kempke, T. (1995) 'Slawen und Deutsche in Ostholstein bis zum frühen 13. Jahrhundert aus archäologischer Sicht', in M. Müller-Wille, D. Meier and H. Unverhau (eds)

Slawen und Deutsche im südlichen Ostseeraum vom 11. bis 16. Jahrhundert. Neumünster: Wachholtz, pp. 9–28.

Kiełczewska, A. (ed.) (2010) *Jan Matejko's Battle of Grunwald: New Approaches*. Warsaw: National Museum in Warsaw.

Kilger, C. (1998) 'The Slavs yesterday and today: Different perspectives on Slavic ethnicity in German archaeology', *Current Swedish Archaeology* 6 (1), pp. 99–114.

Kļaviņš, K. (1998) 'The Baltic Enlightenment and perceptions of medieval Latvian history', *Journal of Baltic Studies* 29 (3) pp. 213–24.

Kļaviņš, K. (2006) 'Eastern Prussia and Livonia: Interactions of power and culture from the 13th to the 18th century', in A. Cimdina and J. Osmond (eds) *Power and Culture: Hegemony, Interaction and Dissent*. Pisa: Pisa University Press, pp. 53–67.

Klimek, R. (2016) 'Od pogańskiego miejsca kultu do chrześcijańskiego sanktuarium: Święta Lipka i Gietrzwałd na tle krajobrazu sakralnego Warmii', *Komunikaty Mazursko-Warmińskie* 3 (293), pp. 431–44.

Kluge, B. (2009) 'Jacza de Copnic und seine Brakteaten. Fakten, Thesen und Theorien zum ältesten Thema der brandenburgischen Numismatik', *Beiträge zur brandenburgisch / preußischen Numismatik* 17, pp. 14–42.

Knüsel, C. J., Batt, C. M., Cook, G., Montgomery, J., Müldner, G., Ogden, A. R., Palmer, C., Stern, B., Todd, J. and Wilson, A. S. (2010) 'The identity of the St Bees Lady, Cumbria: An osteobiographical approach', *Medieval Archaeology* 54 (1), pp. 271–311.

Knuutinen, T. and Haggrén, G. (2023) 'Medieval castles and castle studies in Finland', in T. Heinonen, M. Holappa, T. Knuutinen, J. Harjula and G. Haggrén (eds) *Reconsidering Raseborg: New Approaches to a Medieval Castle in Finland*. Turku: The Society for Medieval Archaeology in Finland, pp. 9–26.

Koebner, R. (2012) 'The settlement and colonisation of Europe', in N. Berend (ed.) *The Expansion of Central Europe in the Middle Ages*. Ashgate: Variorum, pp. 39–60.

Koperkiewicz, A. (2020) '"Zmartwychwstanie neofity" czyli pierwsi chrześcijanie w okolicach Świętej Lipki', in A. Jacyniak and E. Sukiennik (eds) *Święta Lipka: perła na pograniczu ziem, kultur i wyznań, Part 2*. Kętryzn: Labrita, pp. 28–61.

Kopp, K. (2012) *Germany's Wild East: Constructing Poland as Colonial Space*. Ann Arbor: University of Michigan Press.

Korpela, J. (2008) *The World of Ladoga: Society, Trade, Transformation and State Building in the Eastern Fennoscandian Boreal Forest Zone c. 1000–1555*. Münster: LIT.

Kosman, M. (1989) *Litwa pierwotna: Mity, legendy, fakty*. Warsaw: Iskry.

Kotecki, R., Jensen, C. S. and Bennett, S. (2021) 'Introduction' in R. Kotecki, C. S. Jensen and S. Bennett (eds.) *Christianity and War in Medieval East Central Europe and Scandinavia*. York: Arc Humanities Press, pp. 1–22.

Kozłowski, J. B. (2008) 'Germanizacja nazw', in W. Mierzwa (ed.) *Mazury – słownik stronniczy, ilustrowany*. Dąbrówno: Retman, pp. 46–57.

Kożuchowski, A. (2019) 'The devil wears white: Teutonic Knights and the problem of evil in Polish historiography', *East Central Europe* 46 (1), pp. 135–55.

Kreem, J. (2001) 'The Teutonic Order as a secular ruler in Livonia: The privileges and oath of Reval', in A. V. Murray (ed.) *Crusade and Conversion on the Baltic Frontier 1150–1500*. Aldershot: Ashgate, pp. 215–32.

Kreem, J. (2002) *The Town and its Lord: Reval and the Teutonic Order (in the Fifteenth Century)*. Tallinn: Tallinna linnaarhiiv.

Kreem, J. (2006) 'Der Deutsche Orden und die Reformation in Livland', in J. A. Mol, K. Militzer and H. J. Nicholson (eds) *The Military Orders and the Reformation: Choices, State Building, and the Weight of Tradition*. Hilversum: Verloren, pp. 43–57.

BIBLIOGRAPHY

Kreem, J. (2011) 'Seasonality of transport network in the Eastern Baltic', in H. Houben and K. Toomaspoeg (eds) *Towns and Communication*, vol. 2. Galatina: M. Congedo, pp. 259–69.

Kreem, J. (2013) 'Crusading traditions and chivalric ideals: The mentality of the Teutonic Order in Livonia at the beginning of the sixteenth century', *Crusades* 12 (1), pp. 233–50.

Kruks, S. (2004) 'The Latvian epic *Lāčplēsis*: Passe-partout ideology, traumatic imagination of community', *Journal of Folklore Research* 41 (1), pp. 1–32.

Kubicki, R. (2010) 'Problem utrzymywania czystości w średniowiecznym mieście – funkcje i znaczenie łaźni publicznych na przykładzie Elbląga', *Studia Historica Gedanensia* 1, pp. 35–46.

Kubicki, R. (2012) *Młynarstwo w państwie zakonu krzyżackiego w Prusach w XIII–XV wieku (do 1454 r.)*. Gdańsk: Wydawnictwo Uniwersytetu Gdańskiego.

Kuczkowski, A. and Kajkowski, K. (2011) 'Nourishment for the soul – nourishment for the body: Animal remains in early medieval Pomeranian cemeteries', in A. G. Pluskowski (ed.) *The Ritual Killing and Burial of Animals: European Perspectives*. Oxford: Oxbow, pp. 34–50.

Kuczyński, S. K. (1978) *Pieczęcie książąt mazowieckich*. Wrocław–Warsaw: Wydawnictwo Polskiej Akademii Nauk.

Kukk, K. (2013) 'Stubborn histories', *Scandinavian Journal of History* 38 (2), pp. 135–53.

Kuzborska, A. (2020) 'Das Bild von Herkus Monte in der deutschen und litauischen Literatur und Kultur', *Przegląd Wschodnioeuropejski* 11 (2), pp. 251–64.

Kwiatkowski, K. (2017) 'Kapitulacje załóg punktów umocnionych w wojnach pruskiej gałęzi zakonu niemieckiego z Litwą od końca XIII do początku XV stulecia', in A. Niewiński (ed.) *Kapitulacje w dziejach wojen: z dziejów wojskowości polskiej i powszechnej*. Oświęcim: Wydawnictwo Napoleon V, pp. 117–59.

Laime, S. (2009) 'The sacred groves of the Curonian Ķoniņi: Past and present,' *Folklore* 42, pp. 67–80.

Lamberg, M. (2006) 'Finns as aliens and compatriots in the late medieval Kingdom of Sweden', in O. Merisalo (ed.) *Frontiers in the Middle Ages: Proceedings of the Third European Congress of the Medieval Studies*. Louvain-la-Neuve: Fédération internationale des instituts d'études médiévales, pp. 121–32.

Lang, V. and Valk, H. (2011) 'An archaeological reading of the Chronicle of Henry of Livonia: Events, traces, contexts and interpretations', in M. Tamm, L. Kaljundi and C. S. Jensen (eds) *Crusading and Chronicle Writing on the Medieval Baltic Frontier*. Aldershot: Ashgate, pp. 291–316.

Lapiņš, A. (2018) 'Cēsu pils aizsardzības spējas 16, gadsimta pirmajā pusē', in G. Kalniņš (ed.) *Cēsu pils raksti: 2: archeoloģija, architektūra*. Cēsis: Cēsu pils saglabāšanas fonds, pp. 37–55.

Larsen, L. A. (2019) 'The early introduction of the moldboard plow in Denmark', in B. Poulsen, H. Vogt and J. V. Sigurðsson (eds) *Nordic Elites in Transformation, c. 1050–1250*, vol. 1. New York: Routledge, pp. 80–106.

Latałowa, M., Święta-Musznicka, J. and Pędziszewska, A. (2009) 'Źródła paleobotaniczne do rekonstrukcji wczesnych etapórozwoju Gdańska', in L. Domańska, P. Kittel and J. Forysik (eds), *Środowisko–Człowiek–Cywilizacja*, 2. Poznań: Bogucki Wydawnictwo Naukowe, pp. 175–85.

Latałowa, M., Jarosińska, J. and Badura M. (1998) 'Elbląg średniowieczny w świetle dotychczasowych materiałów archeobotanicznych', *Archeologia Polski* 43, pp. 147–66.

Latham, A. A. (2011) 'Theorizing the Crusades: identity, institutions and religious war in medieval Latin Christendom', *International Studies Quarterly* 55, pp. 223–43.

Lavery, J. (2017) *Reforming Finland: The Diocese of Turku in the Age of Gustav Vasa 1523–1560*. Leiden: Brill.

Lazda-Cazers, R. (2009) 'Landscape as other in the *Livlandische Reimchronik*', *Amsterdamer Beiträge zur älteren Germanistik* 65, pp. 183–209.

Leciejewicz, L. (1995) 'Slawen und Deutsche in Pommern', in M. Müller-Wille, D. Meier and H. Unverhau (eds) *Slawen und Deutsche im südlichen Ostseeraum vom 11. bis 16. Jahrhundert*. Neumünster: Wachholtz, pp. 43–57.

Lecouteaux, C. (2013) *The Tradition of Household Spirits: Ancestral Lore and Practices*. Rochester, VT: Inner Traditions.

Lees, J. T. (2015) '"Why have you come with weapons drawn?" The leaders of the Wendish Campaign of 1147', in J. T. Roche (ed.) *The Second Crusade: Holy War on the Periphery of Latin Christendom*. Turnhout: Brepols, pp. 273–301.

Leighton, G. (2022) *Ideology and Holy Landscape in the Baltic Crusades*. York: ARC Humanities.

Leimus, I. (2022) 'Money in Livonia in the thirteenth century', in A. Selart (ed.) *Baltic Crusades and Societal Innovation in Medieval Livonia, 1200–1350*. Leiden: Brill, pp. 164–88.

Lemeškin, I. (2018) 'Senoji baltų leksikografija Hanzos pirklių tarnyboje. Rankraštinių žodynų paskirtis bei sudarymo laikas', *Acta Linguistica Lithuanica* 78, pp. 9–52.

Leuschner, T. (2012) 'The German *Drang nach Osten*: Linguistic perspectives on historical stereotyping', *German Life and Letters* 65 (1), pp. 94–108.

Lightfoot, E., Naum, M., Kadakas, V. and Russow, E. (2016) 'The influence of social status and ethnicity on diet in mediaeval Tallinn as seen through stable isotope analyses', *Estonian Journal of Archaeology* 20 (1), pp. 81–107.

Lijka, J. and Herrmann, C. (eds) (2024) *Malbork około 1800*. Malbork: Muzeum Zamkowe w Malborku.

Lind, J. (2015) 'The "First Swedish Crusade" against the Finns: A part of the Second Crusade?', in J. T. Roche and J. M. Jensen (eds) *The Second Crusade: Holy War on the Periphery of Latin Christendom*. Turnhout: Brepols, pp. 303–322.

Lindkvist, T. (2001) 'Crusades and crusading ideology in the political history of Sweden, 1140–1500', in A. V. Murray (ed.) *Crusade and Conversion on the Baltic Frontier, 1150–1500*. Aldershot: Ashgate, pp. 119–30.

Line, P. (2009) 'Sweden's conquest of Finland: A clash of cultures?', in A. V. Murray (ed.) *The Clash of Cultures on the Medieval Baltic Frontier*. London: Routledge, pp. 73–99.

Lübke, C. (2008) 'Christianity and paganism as elements of gentile identities to the east of the Elbe and Saale rivers', in I. H. Garipzanov, P. Geary and P. Urbanczyk (eds) *Franks, Northmen and Slavs: Identities and State Formation in Early Medieval Europe*. Turnhout, Brepols, pp. 189–203.

Lübke, C. (2013) 'Eastern Europe: medieval era colonizations and reclamation of land', in *The Encyclopedia of Global Human Migration*. doi.org/10.1002/9781444351071.wbeghm189

Lubocka-Hoffmann, M. (2019) 'Powojenna odbudowa miast w Polsce a retrowersja Starego Miasta w Elblągu,' *Ochrona Zabytków* 1, pp. 35–71.

Lyon, J. R. (2017) *Noble Society: Five Lives from Twelfth-century Germany*. Manchester: Manchester University Press.

Łysiak, W. (1999) *Album królów polskich*. Warsaw: Wydawnictwo Andrzej Frukacz.

Mägi, M. (2015) *Rafala. Idateest ja Tallinna algusest*. Tallinn: Argo.

Mägi, M. (2018) *In Austrvegr: The Role of the Eastern Baltic in Viking Age Communication across the Baltic Sea*. Leiden: Brill.

Mägi, M. (2024) 'Ports for whom? Harbors in the early thirteenth-century Eastern Baltic', *Journal of Baltic Studies* 56 (1), pp. 147–64.

Magnusson, G. (1995) 'Iron production, smithing and iron trade in the Baltic during the Late Iron Age and Early Middle Ages (c. 5th–13th centuries)', in I. Jansson (ed.) *Archaeology East and West of the Baltic*. Stockholm: Department of Archaeology, Stockholm University, pp. 61–70.

Makowiecki, D., Janeczek, M., Pasicka, E. et al. (2022) 'Pathologies of a horse skeleton from the early medieval stronghold in Gdańsk (Poland)', *International Journal of Osteoarchaeology* 32 (4), pp. 866–77.

Makowiecki, D. and Makowiecka, M. (2014) 'Faunal remains', in W. Chudziak and R. Kaźmierczak (eds) *The Island in Żółte on Lake Zarańskie, Early Medieval Gateway into West Pomerania*. Toruń: Nicolaus Copernicus University, pp. 311–66.

Maltby, M., Pluskowski, A., Rannamäe, E. and Seetah, K. (2019) 'Farming, hunting, and fishing in medieval Livonia: The zooarchaeological data', in A. G. Pluskowski (ed.) *Environment, Colonization and the Baltic Crusader States*. Turnhout: Brepols, pp. 137–74.

Mänd, A. (2009) 'Saints' cults in medieval Livonia', in A. V. Murray (ed.) *The Clash of Cultures on the Medieval Baltic Frontier*. Farnham: Ashgate, pp. 191–223.

Mänd, A. and Leimus, I. (2017) 'Reval (Tallinn): A city emerging from maritime trade', in W. Blockmans, M. Krom, and J. Wubs-Mrozewicz (eds) *The Routledge Handbook of Maritime Trade around Europe 1300–1600*. London: Routledge, pp. 273–91.

Manion, L. (2018) 'Thinking through the English crusading romance: *Sir Gowther* and the Baltic', in K. C. Little and N. McDonald (eds) *Thinking Medieval Romance*. Oxford: Oxford University Press, pp. 68–90.

Mäntylä, S. (2007) 'The meaning of weapons as grave goods: Examples from two south-west Finnish Crusade Period cemeteries', *Archaeologia Baltica* 8, pp. 302–09.

Maraschi, A. (2019) 'There is more than meets the eye: Undead, ghosts and spirits in the *Decretum* of Burchard of Worms', *Thanatos* 8 (1), pp. 29–61.

Markowski, M. (1984) '*Crucesignatus*: Its origins and early usage,' *Journal of Medieval History* 10 (3), pp. 157–65.

Markus, K. (2020) *Visual Culture and Politics in the Baltic Sea Region, 1100–1250*. Leiden: Brill.

Marozava, S. (2019) 'Establishment of the Grand Duchy of Lithuania (mid XIII–third quarter of XIV centuries): A view from Belarus', in O. B. Keller (ed.) *Opere et Veritate*. Minsk: RIVSH, pp. 114–25.

Maxwell, A. (2014) 'Edvard Beneš and the soft sell: Czechoslovak diplomacy toward Lusatia, 1918–1919', *Bohemia* 54 (2), pp. 348–67.

Mažeika, R. (1994) 'Of cabbages and knights: Trade and trade treaties with the infidel on the northern frontier, 1200–1390', *Journal of Medieval History* 20 (1), pp. 63–76.

Mažeika, R. and Chollet, L. (2016) 'Familiar marvels? French and German crusaders and chroniclers confront Baltic pagan religions', *Francia* 43, pp. 41–6.

McKitterick, R. (2008) *Charlemagne: The Formation of a European Identity*. Cambridge: Cambridge University Press.

Мегем, М. Е. (2020) 'Советская историография средневекового литовского прошлого', Изв. Сарат. ун-та. Нов. сер. Сер. История. Международные отношения 20 (3), pp. 318–25.

Melliṇa-Flood, B. (2019) 'Reconstituting the fatherland in early modern Livonia', *Proceedings of the Latvian Academy of Sciences*, Section A (2), pp. 21–41.

Мельникова, Е. А. (2019) 'Существовал ли двусторонний новгородско-готландский договор доганзейского времени?', *Петербургский исторический журнал* 4, pp. 26–40.
Mentzel-Reuters, A. and Samerski, S. (eds) (2019) *Castrum sanctae Mariae: Die Marienburg als Burg, Residenz und Museum*. Göttingen: V&R Unipress.
Menzel, U. (2021) *Zwischen Deutschen Christen und Neuen Heiden. Hitlers überraschender Besuch vom Juli 1935 in Braunschweig, die Umwidmung des Braunschweiger Doms und die Neukonzipierung der 'Gemeinschaftssiedlung Lehndorf' und deren Kirche*. Wolfenbüttel: Evangelisch-lutherische Landeskirche in Braunschweig.
Merrifield, R. (1988) *The Archaeology of Ritual and Magic*. London: Batsford.
Merritt, R. (1994–5) 'Recharging Alexander Nevsky: Tracking the Eisenstein-Prokofiev war horse', *Film Quarterly* 48 (2), pp. 34–47.
Michałowski, R. (2016) *The Gniezno Summit*. Leiden: Brill.
Michalski, M. (2008) 'The two swords: using the symbol of the battle of Grunwald (1410) in the 19th and 20th century Poland', in P. Wiszewski (ed.) *Meetings with Emotions: Human Past between Anthropology and History*. Wrocław: Chronicon, pp. 109–28.
Mickūnaitė, G. (2006) *Making a Great Ruler: Grand Duke Vytautas of Lithuania*. Budapest: CEU Press.
Migdalski, P. (2020) 'Early-medieval Slavdom as a factor legitimizing the Polish presence westward as exemplified by Western Pomerania', *Quaestiones Medii Aevi Novae* 25, pp. 163–79.
Militzer, K. (2005) *Die Geschichte des Deutschen Ordens*. Stuttgart: Kohlhammer.
Militzer, K. (2011) 'Die Übersiedlung Siegfrieds von Feuchtwangen in die Marienburg', *Ordines Militares* 16, pp. 47–61.
Milliman, P. (2013) *The Slippery Memory of Men: The Place of Pomerania in the Medieval Kingdom of Poland*. Leiden: Brill.
Modzelewski, W. T. and Żukowski, A. (eds) (2021) *The Kaliningrad Region: A Specific Enclave in Contemporary Europe*. Leiden: Brill.
Moilanen, U. (2021) 'Variations in Inhumation Burial Customs in Southern Finland (AD 900–1400): Case Studies from Häme and Upper Satakunta'. PhD thesis, University of Turku.
Mol, J. (2015) 'The knight brothers from the Low Countries in the conflict between the Westphalians and the Rhinelanders in the Livonian branch of the Teutonic Order', *Ordines Militares* 20, pp. 123–44.
Mol, J. (2023) 'The murder of the Rome legation of the Livonian bishops in 1428 and the subsequent career of the chief perpetrator, Goswin von Ascheberg,' in U. Arnold, R. Czaja and J. Sarnowsky (eds) *Zwischen Mittelmeer und Baltikum. Festschrift für Hubert Houben zum 70. Geburtstag*. Ilmtal-Weinstraße: VDG Verlag im Jonas Verlag, pp. 343–59.
Morton, N. (2009) *The Teutonic Knights in the Holy Land: 1190–1291*. Woodbridge: Boydell.
Możdżeń, J. (2013) '"Von ihrem irtumb und seltzam wan noch heutt in tagk": The role of real life experience in the records of the Prussians made by Szymon Grunau (mid-15th century – 1529/30)', in L. Słupecki and R. Simek (eds) *Conversions: Looking for Ideological Change in the Early Middle Ages*. Vienna: Fassbaender, pp. 223–64.
Mugurēvičs, Ē. (1990) 'Interactions between indigenous and western culture in Livonia in the 13th to 16th centuries', in D. Austin and L. Alcock (eds) *From the Baltic to the Black Sea*. London: Routledge, pp. 168–78.

BIBLIOGRAPHY

Muižnieks, V. (2015) 'The co-existence of two traditions in the territory of present-day Latvia in the 13th–18th centuries: Burial in dress and in a shroud', in S. Tarlow (ed.) *The Archaeology of Death in Post-Medieval Europe*. Berlin: Walter de Gruyter, pp. 88–110.

Müller-Wille, M. (2003) 'The cross goes north: Carolingian times between the Rhine and Elbe', in M. Carver (ed.) *The Cross Goes North: Processes of Conversion in Northern Europe, AD 300–1300*. Woodbridge: Boydell, pp. 443–62.

Munzinger, M. R. (2012) 'The profits of the Cross: Merchant involvement in the Baltic Crusade (c. 1180–1230)', *Journal of Medieval History* 32 (2), pp. 163–85.

Murray, A. V. (2001) 'The structure, genre and intended audience of the Livonian Rhymed Chronicle', in A. V. Murray (ed.) *Crusade and Conversion on the Baltic Frontier, 1150–1500*. Aldershot: Ashgate, pp. 235–51.

Murray, A. V. (2013) 'Henry of Livonia and the Wends of the Eastern Baltic: Ethnography and biography in the thirteenth-century Livonian Mission', *Studi Medievali* 54 (6), pp. 807–33.

Murray, A. V. (2019) 'Contrasting masculinities in the Baltic crusades: Teutonic Knights and secular crusaders at war and peace in late medieval Prussia', in N. R. Hodgson, K. J. Lewis and M. M. Mesley (eds) *Crusading and Masculinities*. London: Routledge, pp. 113–28.

Myberg, N. (2010a) 'A worth of their own: On Gotland in the Baltic Sea, and its 12th-century coinage', *Medieval Archaeology* 54, pp. 157–81.

Myberg, N. (2010b) 'The colour of money: Crusaders and coins in the thirteenth century Baltic Sea', in F. Fahlander and A. Kjellström (eds) *Making Sense of Things: Archaeologies of Sensory Perception*. Stockholm: Dept. of Archaeology and Classical History, Stockholm University, pp. 83–102.

Naum, M. (2012) 'Difficult middles, hybridity and ambivalence of a medieval frontier: The cultural landscape of Lolland and Falster (Denmark)', *Journal of Medieval History* 38 (1), pp. 56–75.

Naum, M. (2013) 'Convivencia in a borderland: The Danish-Slavic border in the Middle Ages', *Archaeological Review from Cambridge* 28 (1), pp. 75–93.

Naum, M. (2014) 'Multi-ethnicity and material exchanges in late medieval Tallinn', *European Journal of Archaeology* 17 (4), pp. 656–77.

Naum, M. (2016) 'Migration, identity and material culture: Hanseatic translocality in the medieval Baltic Sea', in L. Melheim, H. Glørstad and Z. Tsigaridas Glørstad (eds) *Comparative Perspectives on Past Colonisation, Maritime Interaction and Cultural Integration*. Sheffield: Equinox, pp. 129–48.

Nawrolska, G. (2004) 'Remarks on infrastructure of the Old Town of Elbląg', in R. Dunckel, M. Gläser, U. Oltmanns and J. Scheschkewitz (eds) *Lübecker Kolloquium zur Stadtarchäologie im Hanseraum IV: Die Infrastruktur*. Lübeck: Schmidt-Römhild, pp. 303–22.

Nawrolska, G. (2006) 'Handicrafts in medieval Elbląg', in I. Hillenstedt, C. Kimminus-Schneider, D. Mührenberg and M. Schneider (eds) *Lübecker Kolloquium zur Stadtarchäologie im Hanseraum V: Das Handwerk*. Lübeck: Schmidt-Römhild, pp. 393–416.

Nawrolska, G. (2008) 'A way of life: Luxury in a medieval town', in C. Kimminus-Schneider, D. Mührenberg, M. Schneider and C. Sheehan (eds) *Lübecker Kolloquium zur Stadtarchäologie im Hanseraum VI: Luxus und Lifestyle*. Lübeck: Schmidt-Römhild, pp. 509–27.

Nawrolska, G. (2013) 'Przemiany kulturowe w XIII–wiecznym Elblągu efektem spotkania tradycji i obcych wpływów', *Archaeologia Historica Polona* 21, pp. 79–99.

Nawrolska, G. (2016) 'The first hundred years of Elbląg', in M. Gläser and M. Schneider (eds) *Lübecker Kolloquium zur Stadtarchäologie im Hanseraum X: Vorbesiedlung, Gründung und Entwicklung*. Lübeck: Schmidt-Römhild, pp. 427–40.

Neitmann, K. (1993) 'Riga und Wenden als Residenzen des livländischen Landmeisters im 15. Jahrhundert', in U. Arnold (ed.) *Stadt und Orden. Das Verhältnis des Deutschen Ordens zu den Städten in Livland, Preussen und im Deutschen Reich*. Marburg: Elwert, pp. 59–93.

Nielsen, T. (2013) 'The making of new cultural landscapes in the medieval Baltic', in K. Salonen, K. V. Jensen and T. Jørgensen (eds) *Medieval Christianity in the North: New Studies*. Turnhout: Brepols, pp. 121–53.

Nowakiewicz, T. (2010) 'Some remarks on settlement systems of early medieval Prussians: The case of northern Galindia', in U. L. Hansen and A. Bitner-Wróblewska (eds) *Worlds Apart? Contacts across the Baltic Sea in the Iron Age*. Copenhagen: Det kgl. Nordiske Oldskriftselskab, pp. 487–504.

Odner, K. (2001) 'Trade, tribute and household responses', *Acta Borealia* 18 (1), pp. 25–50.

Okulicz-Kozaryn, Ł. (1983) *Życie codzienne Prusów i Jaćwięgów w wiekach średnich (IX–XIII w.)*. Warsaw: Państwowy Instytut Wydawniczy.

Okulicz-Kozaryn, Ł. (1997) *Dzieje Prusów*. Wrocław: Fundacja na Rzecz Nauki Polskiej.

Olesen, J. E. (2013) 'Danish law and government in medieval Estonia', in J. Steinar (ed.) *Legislation and State Formation: Norway and its Neighbours in the Middle Ages*. Trondheim: Akademika, pp. 101–14.

Ossowski, W. (2016) 'Pierwsze bałtyckie statki handlowe i ich użytkownicy', in B. Możejko and E. Bojaruniec-Król (eds) *W epoce żaglowców. Morze od antyku do XVIII wieku*. Gdańsk: Muzeum Archeologiczne w Gdańsku, pp. 45–57.

Ottewill-Soulsby, S (2016) 'Those same cursed Saracens': Charlemagne's campaigns in the Iberian Peninsula as religious warfare', *Journal of Medieval History* 42 (4), pp. 405–28.

Ousterhout, R. (2003) 'Architecture as relic and the construction of sanctity: The stones of the Holy Sepulchre', *Journal of the Society of Architectural Historians* 62 (1), pp. 4–23.

Palmer, J. (2007) 'Defining paganism in the Carolingian world', *Early Medieval Europe* 15 (4), pp. 402–25.

Panayi, P. (2001) 'Continuities and discontinuities in race: Jews, Gypsies and Slavs under the Weimar Republic and the Third Reich', in P. Panayi (ed.) *Weimar and Nazi Germany: Continuities and Discontinuities*. Harlow: Pearson, pp. 218–45.

Paner, H. (1997) 'The archaeology of Danzig (Gdańsk)', in D. Mührenberg (ed.), *Lübecker Kolloquium zur Stadtarchäologie im Hanseraum I: Stand, Aufgaben und Perspektiven*. Lübeck: Schmidt-Römhild, pp. 277–89.

Paner, H. (2001) '10th- to 17th-century domestic architecture in Gdańsk', in B. Dahmen, M. Gläser, U. Oltmanns and S. Schindel (eds) *Lübecker Kolloquium zur Stadtarchäologie im Hanseraum III: Der Hausbau*. Lübeck: Schmidt-Römhild, pp. 491–509.

Panfil, R. (2016) 'Wątki nacjonalistyczne w działalności niemieckiego stowarzyszenia naukowego Elbinger Altertumsgesellschaft', *Zapiski z Pogranicza* 4, pp. 99–111.

Paravicini, W. (1989–95, 2020, 2024) *Die Preußenreisen des europäischen Adels* (4 vols). Sigmaringen: J. Thorbecke; Göttingen: V&R Unipress.

Partenheimer, L. (1994) 'Albrecht der Bär, Jaxa von Köpenick und der Kampf um die Brandenburg in der Mitte des 12. Jahrhunderts', *Forschungen zur brandenburgischen und preußischen Geschichte: Neue Folge* 4, pp. 151–93.

Paszkiewicz, B. (2009) *Brakteaty – pieniądz średniowiecznych Prus*. Wrocław: Wydawnicto Uniwersytetu Wrocławskiego.

BIBLIOGRAPHY

Paulsen, R. (2016) *Schifffahrt, Hanse und Europa im Mittelalter: Schiffe am Beispiel Hamburgs, europäische Entwicklungslinien und die Forschung in Deutschland*. Cologne: Böhlau.

Pedersen, A. (2006) 'The Jelling monuments: Ancient royal memorial and modern world heritage site', in M. Lerche Nielsen, M. and G. Fellows-Jensen (eds) *Runes and Their Secrets: Studies in Runology*. Copenhagen: Museum Tusculanum Press, pp. 283–313.

Pelech, M. (1987) 'Die Teilnahme der Altstadt Elbing am Großen Krieg (1409–1411) und ihre während des Krieges erlittenen Schäden', *Beiträge zur Geschichte Westpreußens* 10, pp. 49–66.

Piirimäe, P. (2013) 'Staatenbund oder Ständestaat? Der livländische Landtag im Zeitalter Wolters von Plettenberg (1494–1535)', *Forschungen zur Baltischen Geschichte* 8, pp. 40–80.

Piskorski, J. M. (2004) 'The medieval colonization of Central Europe as a problem of world history and historiography', *German History* 22 (3), pp. 323–43.

Pivoras, S. (2021) 'The role of Latvian nationalism in the transformation of Lithuanian nationalism during the long 19th century', *Nations and Nationalism* 27 (2), pp. 566–79.

Plakans, A. (1998) 'Latvian historiography', in D. R. Woolf (ed.) *A Global Encyclopedia of Historical Writing*, vol. 2. London: Garland, pp. 545–6.

Pluskowski, A. (ed.) (2019) *Environment, Colonization and the Baltic Crusader States*. Turnhout: Brepols.

Pluskowski, A. G. (2024) *The Teutonic Knights: Rise and Fall of a Religious Corporation*. London: Reaktion.

Pluskowski, A. G., Valk, H. and Szczepański, S. (2018) 'Theocratic rule, native agency and transformation: Post-crusade sacred landscapes in the Eastern Baltic', *Landscapes* 19 (1), pp. 4–24.

Poliński, D. (2003) *Późnośredniowieczne osadnictwo wiejskie w ziemi chełmińskiej*. Toruń: Wydawnictwo Uniwersytetu Mikołaja Kopernika.

Põltsam-Jürjo, I. (2021) 'The cult of Saint Anthony in medieval and early modern Estonia', *Acta Historica Tallinnensia* 1, pp. 39–68.

Pósán, L. (2010) 'The Kulmian letters patent of the Teutonic Order of 1233', *Acta Classica Univ. Scient. Debrecen* 146, pp. 205–32.

Pósán, L. (2014) 'Prussian missions and the invitation of the Teutonic Order into Kulmerland', in A. V. Murray (ed.) *The North-Eastern Frontiers of Medieval Europe*. London: Routledge, pp. 429–48.

Pósán, L. (2021) *Hungary and the Teutonic Order in the Middle Ages*. Budapest: Research Centre for the Humanities.

Pospieszna, B. (2002) *Ogrzewanie w Zamku Malborksim w dawnych wiekach*. Malbork: Muzeum Zakowe w Malborku.

Poulsen, B. (2011) 'Tribute as part of the financial system of the medieval Danish king', in S. Imsen (ed.) *Taxes, Tributes and Tributary Lands in the Making of the Scandinavian Kingdoms in the Middle Ages*. Trondheim: TAPIR Akademisk Forlag, pp. 279–92.

Poutanen, M. (ed.) (2011) *Colonists on the Shores of the Gulf of Finland: Medieval Settlement in the Coastal Regions of Estonia and Finland*. Vantaa: Vantaa City Museum.

Powierski, J. (2001) *Prusowie, Mazowsze i sprowadzenie Krzyżaków do Polski: Vols I, II/1, II/2*. Malbork: Muzeum Zamkowe w Malborku.

Powierski, J. (2003) *Prussica 1*. Malbork: Muzeum Zamkowe w Malborku.

Prarat, M. (2014) 'Architektura wiejska w granicach Prus Zachodnich jako przedmiot zainteresowań naukowych i konserwatorskich do lat 40. XX w.', *Acta Universitatis Nicolai Copernici Zabytkoznawstwo i Konserwatorstwo* 45, pp. 185–221.

BIBLIOGRAPHY

Prout, C. (2022) 'Constructing a usable past in Putin's Russia: St. Alexander Nevsky from screen to stone'. Undergraduate Honors thesis, William & Mary, Paper 1767.

Radzimiński, A. (2006a) 'The contribution of the Teutonic Order to the evangelisation of Prussia: Some remarks based on synod legislation', *Lithuanian Historical Studies* 11, pp. 67–88.

Radzimiński, A. (2006b) *Kościół w państwie zakonu krzyżackiego w Prusach 1243–1525*. Malbork: Muzeum Zamkowe w Malborku.

Rand, N. (2015) 'Die livländische Bauernschaft in den Statuten der Rigaer Provinzialsynoden', in K.-R. Hahn, M. Thumser and E. Winkler (eds) *Estnisches Mittelalter. Sprache – Gesellschaft – Kirche*. Berlin: LIT-Verlag, pp. 167–92.

Rannamäe, E., Lõugas, L., Speller, C. F., Valk, H., Maldre, L., Wilczyński, J., Mikhailov, A., and Saarma, U. (2016) 'Three thousand years of continuity in the maternal lineages of ancient sheep (Ovis aries) in Estonia', *PLoS ONE* 11(10): e0163676.

Ratilainen, T., Immonen, V., Salonen, K. and Harjula, J. (2016) 'The bishop's brick house remains of medieval buildings on the river bank of Koroinen, Finland', *Lund Archaeological Review* 22, pp. 61–87.

Raudkivi, P. (2018) *Der livländische Landtag. Zur Entstehung einer mittelalterlichen Institution*. Berlin: LIT-Verlag.

Rębkowski, M. (2007) *Chrystianizacja Pomorza Zachodniego. Studium archeologiczne*. Warsaw: Wydawnictwo Instytutu Archeologii i Etnologii PAN.

Rębkowski, M. (2017) 'Badania milenijne na Pomorzu Zachodnim. Przebieg, znaczenie, skutki', *Przegląd Archeologiczny* 65, pp. 117–31.

Reiger, D. (2019) 'Twelfth century timber buildings in Lübeck's oldest quarter', in C. Jahnke (ed.) *A Companion to Medieval Lübeck*. Leiden: Brill, pp. 36–65.

Rembold, I. (2017) *Conquest and Christianization: Saxony and the Carolingian World, 772–888*. Cambridge: Cambridge University Press.

Reynolds, B. W (2016) *The Prehistory of the Crusades: Missionary War and the Baltic Crusades*. London: Bloomsbury.

Richardson, M. B. (2003) 'The Metamorphosis of the Lithuanian Wayside Shrine, 1850–1990'. PhD thesis, Boston University.

Riley-Smith, J. (1999) *Hospitallers: The History of the Order of St John*. London: Hambledon.

Riley-Smith, L. and Riley-Smith, J. (1981) *The Crusades: Idea and Reality, 1095–1274*. London: Edward Arnold.

Ripatti, A. (2024) 'State, race, and colonization: Tyrgils Knutsson's controversial monuments in 19th-century Finland', in C. Heß and G. Strenga (eds) *Doing Memory: Medieval Saints and Heroes and their Afterlives in the Baltic Sea Region (19th–20th Centuries)*. Berlin: De Gruyter, pp. 161–88.

Roach, A. (2020) 'The people trafficking princes: Slaves, silver and state formation in Poland', *Slavonica* 25 (2), pp. 132–56.

Rodzińska-Chorąży, T. (2011) 'Kilka uwag w sprawie metody prezentacji i interpretacji reliktów budowli sakralnej w Kałdusie', *Forum Architecturae Poloniae Medievalis* 23 (108), pp. 369–79.

Roio, M. (2006) 'The Investigation of Underwater Heritage in Estonia', in V. Lang and M. Laneman (eds) *Archaeological Research in Estonia 1865–2005*. Tartu: University of Tartu Press, pp. 301–10.

Rosik, S. (2020) *The Slavic Religion in the Light of 11th- and 12th-Century German Chronicles (Thietmar of Merseburg, Adam of Bremen, Helmold of Bosau): Studies on the Christian Interpretation of pre-Christian Cults and Beliefs in the Middle Ages*. Leiden: Brill.

BIBLIOGRAPHY

Roslund, M. (2007) *Guests in the House: Cultural Transmission between Slavs and Scandinavians*. Leiden: Brill.

Rowell, S. (1999) 'The Lithuano-Prussian forest frontier, c. 1422–1600', in D. Power and N. Standen (eds) *Frontiers in Question: Eurasian Borderlands, 700–1700*. Basingstoke: Macmillan, pp. 182–208.

Rowell, S. C. (2014) *Lithuania Ascending: A Pagan Empire within East-Central Europe 1295–1345*. Cambridge: Cambridge University Press.

Rüdiger, J. (2009) 'Framing the frontier: The Green Ithmic border of the Danish Baltic', in B. F. Jensen and D. Wille-Jørgensen (eds) *Expansion–Integration, Danish–Baltic contacts 1147–1410 AD*. Vordingborg: Danmarks Borgcenter, pp. 15–26.

Russow, E. (2007) 'Joitakin huomioita punasavikeramiikasta keskiajan ja uuden ajan Tallinnassa', in K. Majantie (ed.) *Ruukkuja ja ruhtinaita: saviastioita ja uunikaakeleita ajalta 1400–1700*. Turku: Aboa Vetus & Ars Nova, pp. 69–80.

Russow, E. (2020) *Lood ja leiud Tallinna algusest*. Tallinn: Stilus.

Russow, E. (2023) 'Between the rock and a hard place: Estonian archaeology at the times of National, Socialist, and National Socialist ideologies', in M. Eickhoff, D. Modl, K. Meheux and E. Nuijten (eds) *National-Socialist Archaeology in Europe and its Legacies*. Cham: Springer, pp. 337–65.

Russow, E. (2024) 'Unearthing the origins of Medieval Tallinn', in R. Atzbach and M. Ebert (eds) *Town and Castle: Early Urban Formation Processes in the Southern Baltics*. Weimar/Rostock: Grünberg Verlag, pp. 67–100.

Saage, R. and Russow, R. (2020) 'Urban casting tools as evidence for transfer of technology across the Baltic Sea in 13th- to 17th-century Estonia', *Medieval Archaeology* 64 (2), pp. 330–53.

Safronovas, V. (2016) *The Creation of National Spaces in a Pluricultural Region: The Case of Prussian Lithuania*. Boston: Academic Studies Press.

Sarnowsky, J. (2017) 'The military orders and crusading in the fifteenth century: Perception and influence', in N. Housley (ed.) *Reconfiguring the Fifteenth-Century Crusade*. London: Palgrave Macmillan, pp. 123–60.

Saunders, C. J. (1993) *The Forest of Medieval Romance: Avernus, Broceliande, Arden*. Cambridge: D. S. Brewer.

Sawicki, Z., Pluskowski, A., Brown, A. et al. (2015) 'Survival at the frontier of holy war: Political expansion, crusading, environmental exploitation and the medieval colonizing settlement at Biała Góra, North Poland,' *European Journal of Archaeology* 18 (2), pp. 282–311.

Ščavinskas, M. (2017) 'A few remarks on the so called first stage of Christianization of the eastern coast of the Baltic region', *Tabularium Historiae* 2, pp. 57–76.

Ščavinskas, M. (2024) *Kristus prieš Belialą. Lietuvių pagonybės dialektika Viduramžiais* (2 vols). Klaipėda: Klaipėdos universiteto leidykla.

Schenk, F. B. (2001) 'Tannenberg/Grunwald', in E. François and H. Schulze (eds) *Deutsche Erinnerungsorte*. Munich: Beck, pp. 438–54.

Schoenborn, U. (2017) 'Kurland im Horizont der Reformation: Resonanz – Korrelation – Interaktion', *Acta Historica Universitatis Klaipedensis* 35, pp. 45–82.

Selart, A. (2009) 'Russians in Livonian towns in the thirteenth and fourteenth centuries', in D. Keene, B. Nagy and K. Szende (eds) *Segregation–Integration–Assimilation: Religious and Ethnic Groups in the Medieval Towns of Central and Eastern Europe*. Farnham: Ashgate, pp. 33–50.

Selart, A. (2015) *Livonia, Rus' and the Baltic Crusades in the Thirteenth Century*. Leiden: Brill.

Selart, A. (2017) 'Switching the tracks: Baltic crusades against Russia in the fifteenth century', in N. J. Housley (ed.) *The Crusade in the Fifteenth Century: Converging and Competing Cultures*. London: Routledge, pp. 90–105.

Selart, A. (2021) 'Lembitu: A medieval warlord in Estonian culture', *Studia Slavica et Balcanica Petropolitana* 1, pp. 3–14.

Shephard, J. (2005) 'Conversion and regimes compared: The Rus' and the Poles, ca. 1000', in F. Curta (ed.) *East Central and Eastern Europe in the Early Middle Ages*. Ann Arbor: University of Michigan Press, pp. 254–82.

Shiroukhov, R. (2012) 'Prussian graves in the Sambian peninsula, with imports, weapons and horse harnesses, from the tenth to the thirteenth century: The question of the warrior elite', *Archaeologia Baltica*, 18, pp. 224–55.

Shiroukhov, R. (2015) 'Contacts between Prussians and Curonians in the 11th–early 13th centuries, according to the archaeological data', in M. Hoffmann, M. Karczewski and S. Wadyl (eds) *Materiały do Archeologii Warmii i Mazur 1*. Warsaw-Białystok: Instytut Archeologii Uniwersytetu Warszawskiego/Instytut Historii i Nauk Politycznych Uniwersytetu w Białymstoku, pp. 255–73.

Shroeder, N. (2022) 'The "cerealization" of continental north-west Europe, c.800–1200', in M. McKerracher and H. Hamerow (eds) *New Perspectives on the Medieval 'Agricultural Revolution', Crop, Stock and Furrow*. Liverpool: Liverpool University Press, pp. 199–210.

Simiński, R. (2013) 'Church as sacred space in the light of thirteenth and fifteenth century Livonian and Prussian sources', in J. Wenta (ed.) *Sacred Space in the State of the Teutonic Order in Prussia*. Toruń: Wydawnictwo Naukowe Uniwersytetu Mikołaja Kopernika, pp. 291–307.

Skaarup, J. (1994–5) 'Medieval castles and castle mounds on the islands south of Fyn', *Journal of Danish Archaeology* 12, pp. 151–69.

Śliwiński, B. (2003) *Pomorze Wschodnie w okresie rządów księcia polskiego Władysława Łokietka w latach 1306–1309*. Gdańsk: Muzeum Archeologicne w Gdańsku.

Śliwiński, B. and Możejko, B. (2017) 'The political history of Gdansk from the town beginnings to the sixteenth century', in B. Możejko (ed.) *New Studies in Medieval and Renaissance Gdańsk, Poland and Prussia*. London: Routledge, pp. 17–47.

Słupecki, L. (1994) *Slavonic Pagan Sanctuaries*. Warsaw: Institute of Archaeology and Ethnology, Polish Academy of Sciences.

Słupecki, L. (2004) 'West Slavic pagan ritual as described at the beginning of the eleventh century', in A. Andrén, K. Jennbert and C. Raudvere (eds) *Old Norse Religion in Long-Term Perspectives: Origins, Changes, and Interactions*. Lund: Nordic Academic Press, pp. 224–7.

Smith, L. T. (2015) *Expeditions to Prussia and the Holy Land: Made by Henry, Earl of Derby (afterwards King Henry IV) in the Years 1390–1 and 1392–3: Being the Accounts Kept by his Treasurer for Two Years*. Burlington: TannerRitchie Publishing.

Šnē, A. (2006) 'The economy and social power in the late prehistoric chiefdoms in eastern Lativa', *Archaeologia Baltica* 6, pp. 68–78.

Šnē, A. (2008) 'The medieval peasantry: On the social and religious position of the rural natives in southern Livonia (13th–15th centuries)', *Ajalooline Ajakiri* 1 (2), pp. 89–100.

Šnē, A. (2009a) 'The early town in late prehistoric Latvia', in J. Staecker (ed.) *The Reception of Medieval Europe in the Baltic Sea Region*. Visby: Gotland University Press, pp. 127–36.

Šnē, A. (2009b) 'The emergence of Livonia: The transformation of social and political structures in the territory of Latvia during the twelfth and thirteenth centuries', in A. V. Murray (ed.) *The Clash of Cultures on the Medieval Baltic Frontier*. Farnham: Ashgate, pp. 53–71.

BIBLIOGRAPHY

Sonne De Torrens, H. M. (2024) *Crusader Rhetoric and the Infancy Cycles on Medieval Baptismal Fonts in the Baltic Region*. Turnhout: Brepols.

Sopp, M. (1999) *Die Wiederaufnahme älterer Bestattungsplätze in den nachfolgenden vor- und frühgeschichtlichen Perioden in Norddeutschland*. Bonn: Rudolf Habelt.

Spanuth, H. (1985) *Der Rattenfänger von Hameln: Vom Werden und Sinn einer alten Sage*. Hemeln: Niemeyer.

Srebrakowski, A. (2020) 'The nationality panorama of Vilnius', *Studia z Dziejów Rosji i Europy Środkowo-Wschodniej* 55, pp. 33–56.

Steinbrecht, C. (1896) *Die Wiederherstellung des Marienburger Schlosses*. Berlin: Wilhelm Ernst & Sohn.

Šterns, I. (1997) *Latvijas vēsture, 1290–1500*. Riga: Daugava.

Šterns, I. (1998) 'Viduslaiku *Rīgas Krievu ciema* plans', *Senā Rīga* 1, pp. 22–54.

Šterns, I. (2002) *Latvijas vēsture 1180–1290: Krustakari*. Riga: Latvijas Vēstures Institūta Apgāds.

Stone, G. (2016) *Slav Outposts in Central European History: The Wends, Sorbs and Kashubs*. London: Bloomsbury.

Strakauskaitė, N. (2015) 'The interest in East Prussian ethnic culture in the second half of the 19th century and its impact on the activities of Richard Dethlefsen', *Acta Historica Universitatis Klaipedensis* 30, pp. 74–83.

Strenga, G. (2020) 'Turning transport workers into Latvians? Ethnicity and transport workers' guilds in Riga before and after the Reformation', *Journal of Baltic Studies* 52 (1), pp. 61–83.

Striegler, S. (2018) *Raumwahrnehmung und Orientierung im südöstlichen Ostseeraum vom 10. bis 16. Jahrhundert: Von der kognitiven zur physischen Karte*. Stuttgart: J. B. Metzler.

Stuckey, J. (2008) 'Charlemagne as crusader? Memory, propaganda and the many uses of Charlemagne's legendary expedition to Spain', in M. Gabriele and J. Stuckey (eds) *The Legend of Charlemagne in the Middle Ages: Power, Faith and Crusade*. New York: Palgrave Macmillan, pp. 137–52.

Svenungsen, P. B. (2016) 'Norway and the Fifth Crusade: The crusade movement on the outskirts of Europe', in E. J. Mylod, G. Perry, T. Smith and J. Vandeburie (eds) *The Fifth Crusade in Context: The Crusading Movement in the Early Thirteenth Century*. London: Routledge, pp. 218–30.

Svetikas, E. (2002) 'The Tertiaries in the early stages of Christianity in Lithuania: Their attributes in the light of archaeology', in G. Helmig, B. Scholkmann and M. Untermann (eds) *Centre, Region, Periphery: Medieval Europe Basel, 2*. Basel: Archäologische Bodenforschung Basel-Stadt, pp. 411–14.

Svetikas, E. (2006) 'Burial and sacrifice in Lithuania during the late fourteenth–fifteenth century: Religious confrontation or a unique conversion phenomenon – baptism by fire?', *Lithuanian Historical Studies* 11, pp. 107–35.

Szacherska, S. M. (1988) 'Valdemar II's expedition to Pruthenia and the mission of Bishop Christian', *Mediaeval Scandinavia* 12, pp. 44–75.

Szczepański, S. (2013) 'Chomor sancti adalberti (1249) a możliwości lokalizacji terenowej wybranych kościołów pomezanii', *Komunikaty Mazursko-Warmińskie* 1 (279), pp. 19–45.

Szczepański, S. (2014) 'Archeologia w służbie nazistów – czyli rzecz o działalności "Wydziału Wykopalisk" SS-Ahnenerbe na stanowiskach w Starym Dzierzgoniu i Starym Mieście (1935–1937)', in H. Paner and M. Fudziński (eds) *Z dziejów badań archeologicznych na Pomorzu Wschodnim*. Muzeum Archeologiczne w Gdańsku, pp. 223–46.

Szczepański, S. (2015) 'Old Prussian "Baba" stones: An overview of the history of research and reception. Pomesanian-Sasinian case', *Analecta Archaeologica Ressoviensia* 10, pp. 313–63.

Szczepański, S. (2018) 'Osadnictwo średniowieczne wokół Starego Dzierzgonia', in D. Gazda (ed.) *Wielokulturowy obiekt warowny na Górze Zamkowej oraz gród cyplowy w Starym Dzierzgoniu. Studia i materiały*. Warsaw: Trzecia Strona, pp. 57–88.

Szczepański, S. (2019) *Pomezania: Na styku świata pogańskiego i chrześcijańskiego*. Olsztyn: Instytut Północny w Olsztynie.

Taimiņa, A. (2018) 'Cēsu pils gramatu apkalumi', in G. Kalniņš (ed.) Cēsu pils raksti: 2: archeoloģija, architektūra. Cēsis: Cēsu pils saglabāšanas fonds, pp. 111–27.

Tamla, T. and Valk, H. (2017) 'Gifts of the king. "Hanseatic" bronze bowls in thirteenth-century Estonia: Signs of Danish crusades?', *Archaeologia Baltica* 24, pp. 93–109.

Tamm, M. (2009) 'A new world into old words: The eastern Baltic region and the cultural geography of medieval Europe', in A. V. Murray (ed.) *The Clash of Cultures on the Medieval Baltic Frontier*. Farnham: Ashgate, pp. 11–36.

Tamm, M. (2011) 'Inventing Livonia: The name and fame of a new Christian colony on the medieval Baltic frontier,' *Zeitschrift für Ostforschung* 60, pp. 186–209.

Tamm, M. (2013) 'How to justify a crusade? The conquest of Livonia and new crusade rhetoric in the early thirteenth century', *Journal of Medieval History* 39 (4), pp. 431–55.

Tamm, M. (2020) 'Mission and mobility: The travels and networking of Bishop Albert of Riga (c. 1165–1229)', in A. Mänd and M. Tamm (eds), *Making Livonia: Actors and Networks in the Medieval and Early Modern Baltic Sea Region*. London: Routledge, pp. 17–47.

Tamm, M., Kaljundi, L. and Jensen, C. S. (eds) (2011) *Crusading and Chronicle Writing on the Medieval Baltic Frontier: A Companion to the Chronicle of Henry of Livonia*. Farnham: Ashgate.

Tammet, M., Lätti, P. and Heikkilä, R. K. (2023) 'A 14th-century wreck discovered at Lootsi Street 8 in Tallinn', *Archaeological Fieldwork in Estonia* 2022, pp. 115–28.

Tandecki, J. (2009) 'Rozwój terytorialny państwa zakonnego w Prusach', in M. Biskup et al. (eds) *Państwo zakonu krzyżackiego w Prusach. Władza i społeczeństwo*. Warsaw: Wydawnictwo Naukowe PWN, pp. 105–09.

Tilli, J. (2017) '"Deus Vult!" The idea of crusading in Finnish clerical war rhetoric, 1941–1944', *War in History* 24 (3), pp. 362–85.

Tolan, J. C. (ed.) (1994) *Medieval Christian Perceptions of Islam*. London: Garland.

Tomkiewicz, M. (2024) 'Działania wojenne na terenie Malborka w 1945 r. i kwestia masowego grobu ponad dwóch tysięcy cywilnych ofiar wojny', *Gdański Notatnik Historyczny* 3, pp. 66–78.

Topij, A. (2011) 'The role of the *Deutschbalten* in the cultural and economic development of Russia's Baltic provinces in the 19th century,' *Zapiski Historyczne* 76 (4), pp. 63–94.

Torbus, T. (1998) *Die Konventsburgen im Deutschordensland Preußen*. Munich: R. Oldenbourg.

Torp-Kõivupuu, M. (1996) 'Ristipuud lõuna-eesti matusekombestikus', *Mäetagused* 1–2, pp. 55–74.

Trupinda, J. (2004) 'Średniowieczne dzieje i wstrój Kapitularza', in J. Trupinda (ed.) *Malborski Kapitularz: dzieje – wyposażenie – konserwacja*. Malbork: Muzeum Zamkowe w Malborku, pp. 29–51.

BIBLIOGRAPHY

Trupinda, J. (ed.) (2023) *Nigra crux mala crux: Czarna i biała legenda zakonu krzyżackiego*. Malbork: Muzeum Zamkowe w Malborku.

Tummuscheit, A. (2006) 'Pre-Christian cult at Arkona: A short summary of the archaeological evidence', in A. Andrén, K. Jennbert and C. Raudvere (eds) *Old Norse Religion in Long-Term Perspectives: Origins, Changes, and Interactions*. Lund: Nordic Academic Press, pp. 234–7.

Tvauri, A. (2006) 'The conservation of archaeological heritage in Estonia', in V. Lang and M. Laneman (eds) *Estonian Archaeology 1: Archaeological Research in Estonia 1865–2005*. Tartu: University of Tartu Press, pp. 247–92.

Tvauri, A. (2009) 'Late medieval hypocausts with heat storage in Estonia', *Baltic Journal of Art History*, Autumn, pp. 49–78.

Tyerman, C. (1996) *England and the Crusades, 1095–1588*. Chicago: University of Chicago Press.

Uotila, K. (1998) *Medieval Outer Baileys in Finland: With Special Reference to Turku Castle*. Turku: Society for Medieval Archaeology in Finland.

Urban, F. (2020) 'Postmodern reconciliation: Reinventing the Old Town of Elbląg', *Architectural Histories* 8 (1), p. 16.

Urban, W. (2003) *The Teutonic Knights: A Military History*. London: Greenhill.

Urban, W. (2019) *The Last Years of the Teutonic Knights: Lithuania, Poland and the Teutonic Order*. London: Greenhill.

Urbańczyk, P. (2008) *Trudne początki Polski*. Wrocław: Wydawnictwo Uniwersytetu Wrocławskiego.

Urbańczyk, P. (2012) *Mieszko Pierwszy Tajemniczy*. Toruń: Wydawnictwo Naukowe Uniwersytetu Mikołaja Kopernika.

Urtāns, J. (1977) 'Senās kulta alas Latvijā', *Latvijas PSR Zinātņu Akadēmijas Vēstis* 2, pp. 85–94.

Vaitkevičius, V. (2004) *Studies into the Balts' Sacred Places*. Oxford: Archaeopress.

Valk, H. (2001) *Rural Cemeteries of Southern Estonia: 1225–1800 AD*. Tartu: Archaeology Centre, University of Tartu.

Valk, H. (2009) 'Sacred and natural places of Estonia: regional aspects,' *Folklore* 42, pp. 45–66.

Valk, H. (ed.) (2014) *Strongholds and Power Centres East of the Baltic Sea in the 11th–13th Centuries*. Tartu: Institute of History and Archaeology at the University of Tartu, Department of Archaeology at the Institute of History of Tallinn University.

Valk, H. (2015) 'Pühast Võhandust, Pühalättest ja ohvrijärvest Otepää lähistel', *Ajalooline Ajakiri* 1/2 (151/152), pp. 3–37.

Valk, H. (2018) 'Estonia in the 12th and early 13th centuries: Territorial structures, power centres and administration', *Revue d'histoire nordique* 26, pp. 89–117.

Valk, H., Kama, P., Rammo, R., Malve, M. and Kiudsoo, M. (2013a) 'The Iron Age and 13th–18th century cemetery and chapel site of Niklusmägi: Grave looting and archaeology', *Archaeological Fieldwork in Estonia* 2012, pp. 109–32.

Valk, H. and Kiudsoo, M. (2018) 'Trial excavations in Helme: Medieval stone chapel and earlier wooden sanctuary with 13th–14th century coin offerings', *Archaeological Fieldwork in Estonia*, December, pp. 139–54.

Valk, H., Rannamäe, E., Brown, A., Pluskowski, A., Badura, M. and Lõugas, L. (2013b), 'Thirteenth century cultural deposits at the castle of the Teutonic Order in Karksi', *Archaeological Field Work in Estonia* 2012, pp. 73–92.

Vareikis, V. (2001) 'Memellander/Klaipėdiškiai identity and German-Lithuanian relations in Lithuania Minor in the nineteenth and twentieth centuries', *Sociologija. Mintis ir veiksmas* 7 (1–2), pp. 54–65.

BIBLIOGRAPHY

Vėlius, N. (1996/2001) *Baltų religijos ir mitologijos šaltiniai* (2 vols). Vilnius: Mokslo ir enciklopedijų leidykla.

Vercamer, G. (2007) 'Politische Machtstrukturen im Ordensstaat Preußen zu Anfang des 14. Jahrhunderts am Beispiel des Obersten Marschalls Heinrich von Plotzke', *Zeitschrift für Ostmitteleuropa-Forschung* 56 (1), pp. 91–104.

Vermeiren, J. (2018) 'The Tannenberg myth in history and literature, 1914–1945', *European Review of History* 25 (5), pp. 778–802.

Wang, S. M. (2023) *Decolonising Medieval Fennoscandia: An Interdisciplinary Study of Norse-Saami Relations in the Medieval Period.* Berlin: De Gruyter.

Wasik, B. (2017) 'Początki krzyżackich zamków na ziemi chełmińskiej. Pierwsze warownie i obiekty murowane', *Archaeologia Historica Polona* 24, pp. 233–360.

Wasik, B. (2018) 'Techniki budowy zamków w typie kasztelu w państwie krzyżackim w Prusach', *Ochrona Zabytków* 2, pp. 33–60.

Wasik, B. (2021) 'Castles in the Teutonic Order state in Prussia as medium of ideology and manifestation of power', *Światowit* 60 (2), pp. 133–55.

Waśko, A. (2013) 'Crusades in Finland and the crusade ideology in Sweden from the 12th to 14th centuries', *Quaestiones Medii Aevi Novae* 18, pp. 257–80.

Wesse, A. (ed.) (1998) *Studien zur Archäologie des Ostseeraums. Von der Eisenzeit zum Mittelalter: Festschrift für Michael Müller-Wille.* Neumünster: Wachholtz.

Wessman, A. (2010) *Death, Destruction and Commemoration: Tracing Ritual Activities in Finnish Late Iron Age Cemeteries (AD 550–1150).* Helsinki: Finnish Antiquarian Society.

West, F. J. (1999) 'The colonial history of the Norman Conquest?', *History* 84 (274), pp. 215–398.

Wieckowska-Lüth, M. (2013) 'The settlement history of the Ostholstein lakeland area in the Middle Ages, as revealed by palynological records', in S. Kleingärtner, T. P. Newfield, S. Rossignol and D. Wehner (eds) *Landscapes and Societies in Medieval Europe East of the Elbe.* Toronto: Pontifical Institute, pp. 117–38.

Wienberg, J. (2004) Medieval Gotland churches, chronologies and crusades', in J. Staecker (ed.) *The European Frontier.* Lund: Almqvist & Wiksell, pp. 285–98.

Wiewióra, M. (2018) 'Najstarsze fazy osadnictwa krzyżackiego na zamkach w Unisławiu, Zamku Bierzgłowskim i Starogrodzie. Studia nad osadnictwem obronnym na ziemi chełmińskiej w XIII wieku', *Archaeologia Historica Polona* 26, pp. 239–64.

Wippermann, W. (1981) *Der 'Deutsche Drang nach Osten': Ideologie und Wirklichkeit eines politischen Schlagwortes.* Darmstadt: Wissenschaftliche Buchgesellschaft.

Wiwjora, I. (1996) 'German archaeology and its relation to nationalism and racism', in J. A. Atkinson, I. Banks and J. O'Sullivan (eds) *Nationalism and Archaeology in Europe.* Glasgow: Cruithne Press, pp. 164–88.

Wółkowski, W. (2016) *Zamek biskupów warmińskich w Lidzbarku Warmińskim – dzieje budowlane i problemy konserwatorskie.* Olsztyn: Muzeum Warmii i Mazur.

Wolski, K. (2008) *Polskie pola bitew w świetle archeologii.* Racibórz: WAW.

Wood, I. A. (1995) 'Pagan religions and superstitions east of the Rhine from the fifth to the ninth century', in G. Ausenda (ed.) *After Empire: Towards an Ethnology of Europe's Barbarians.* Woodbridge: Boydell, pp. 253–68.

Wroniecki, P., Molewski, P. and Uziembło, R. (2021) 'Revealing the first location of abandoned medieval town Toruń, Poland, with the use of integrated noninvasive research', *Archaeological Prospection* 29 (2), pp. 275–92.

Wubs-Mrozewicz, J. and Jenks, S. (eds) 2012. *The Hanse in Medieval and Early Modern Europe.* Leiden: Brill.

BIBLIOGRAPHY

Wünsch, T. (2008) *Deutsche und Slawen im Mittelalter*. Munich: R. Oldenbourg.

Young, F. (2022) *Pagans in the Early Modern Baltic: Sixteenth-Century Ethnographic Accounts of Baltic Paganism*. Leeds: ARC Humanities Press.

Żabiński, G. (2017) 'A late medieval sword from the River Wisła near Gniew (Mewe) in Pomerelia', *Fasciculi Archaeologiae Historicae* 30, pp. 163–79.

Zdrójkowski, Z. (1983) *Zarys dziejów prawa chełmińskiego 1233–1862*. Toruń: Wydawnictwo Naukowe Uniwersytetu Mikołaja Kopernika.

Zientara, B. (2013) 'The sources and origins of the "German Law" (*Ius Teutonicum*) in the context of the settlement movement in Western and Central Europe (eleventh to twelfth century)', *Acta Poloniae Historica* 107, pp. 179–216.

Zinoviev, A. V. (2009) 'Horses from two burials in Samland and Natangen (second century, Kaliningradskaia province, Russia)', *Archaeologia Baltica* 11, pp. 50–55.

Zwik, D. (2017) 'Maritime Logistics in the Age of the Northern Crusades'. PhD thesis, University of Kiel.

INDEX

Aachen 28, 51
Åbo (Turku)
  bishops 125, 130, 195, 210, 274
  castle 196
  foundation 130
  Lübeck Law 252
Absalon, Archbishop of Lund 115, 117–18, 122, plate 10
Acre 4, 11–12, 14, 112, 122, 197, 248
Adalbero, Archbishop of Bremen 61
Adalbert, Archbishop of Hamburg-Bremen 56
Adalbert, Archbishop of Magdeburg 42–3
Adalbert, Bishop of West Pomerania 90
Adalbert, St 50–1, 63, 94, 164, 274, plate 4
  churches 88
  relics 83, 86, 51
Adam of Bremen 39–40, 55–6, 109, 381
Adelgoz, Archbishop of Magdeburg 54
Adenauer, Konrad 371
Adolf II, Count of Holstein 72–3
Adolf III, Count of Holstein 71
Adolphus, Gustavus 320
advocates
  Livonia 143, 200, 204–5, 315
  Prussia 200, 205
Akseli Gallen-Kallela 349
Alberic of Trois-Fontaines 157, 386
Albert III, Duke of Austria 232

Albert, Bishop of Riga 17, 138–47, 149, 200, 250, 341, 343
Albert the Bear 59, 61, 64–5, 68, 106
Albert of Hohenzollern, grand master 313–14, 328, 332, 336, 357
Aldona, Princess of Lithuania 200
Alexander III, tsar 342
Alexander of Malonne, Bishop of Płock 103
Algirdas, Grand Duke 289, 234, 371
Allenstein (Olsztyn) 230–1, 356, 362, 375
Altenkirchen, Rügen 120
Altertumsgesellschaft Prussia (Prussian Antiquity Society) 334
Alytus 228
Andrew II, King of Hungary 13–14
Anselm, Bishop of Havelberg 61
Anselm of Meissen, Bishop of Ermland 195
Anton of Mauchenheim 327
apiculture 227–8
apostasy 42–3, 60, 104, 105, 142
archbishops
  Gniezno 51, 87, 104, 107, 165
  Hamburg-Bremen 41, 56, 67, 110
  Lund 57, 113, 114, 115, 118, 149, 250, 303
  Magdeburg 42, 54, 57, 62, 82, 87, 114
  Nidaros 113, 303

INDEX

Riga 144, 158, 195, 197–8, 212, 213, 233, 315
Uppsala 126, 303, 305
Arensburg (Kuressaare) 212
Arkona 58, 90, 108, 117–20, 124, 377, plates 9, 10
armour 12–13, 55, 64, 65, 98, 100, 148, 152, 163, 218, 221, 226, 297, 299, 331
Arnold of Lübeck 248, 390
Arrasch (Āraiši) 204–5
artisans 38, 66, 71, 73–5, 84–5, 93, 95, 97, 103, 108, 115, 164, 174, 189, 212, 223, 231, 233, 246, 249, 254, 259, 260–3, 279, 287
  blacksmiths 85, 189, 251, 262
  carpenters 75, 262
  cobblers 262
  comb producers 262
  furriers 262
  glass makers 207
  goldsmiths 260, 262
  leatherworkers 262
  metalworkers 260, 262
  minters 260
  potters 73, 115, 164, 255
  silversmiths 260
Aßmann, Erwin 265
Aura (river) 129–30
aurochs 22
Autine 146
Avignon 200, 304

badges, pilgrim 257
Baldwin I, King of Jerusalem 112
Baldwin of Alna 157
Balga 223, 373
Balk, Herman, master 170, 181
Baltic Germans 340, 341–3, 345–6, 348, 394
Baltic Sea 8, 38, 58, 74, 84, 86, 90, 96, 152, 159, 221, 244–5
  freezing in winter 152, 159, 222, 245
baptism 10, 16–17, 52, 59, 86, 102, 123, 139, 147, 151, 180, 182, 272, 286, 305
  bowls 150, 165
  fonts 123, 252
  of leaders 31, 41, 42, 46, 158, 233, 306

Barczewko (Wartenburg) 230–2
Bardy-Świelubie 109
Bartia 169, 182–4, 190, 195, 273, 313
Belarus 9, 18, 111, 137, 219, 306, 355, 367, 369, 370–1, 376
bells 47, 128, 206, 209,
Bergen (Rügen) 120
Berlin 2, 18, 227, 330, 342–3
Bernard II, Duke of Saxony 56
Bernard of Clairvaux 5, 10, 15, 60
Berthold of Loccum, Bishop of Livonia 16–17, 139
Biała Góra (Weißenberg) 163–4, 388
Biebrza (river) 103
Biering, Johann 300
Birka 110, 125
Bisenė 219
bishoprics
  Finland 129–30, 385
  Frisia 28
  Holy Roman Empire 42, 63, 65, 68–9, 73
  Lithuania 289, 291, 310
  Livonia 138, 140, 142, 144, 150
  Poland 49–50, 103
  Pomerania 49, 86, 89
  Prussia 194–5, 223, 269, 272, 274
Bismarck, Otto von 327, 335
bison 22, 224
Black Sea 111
Blanche of Namur 301–2
blockhouse style of building 71; *see also* buildings, cross-log
Blume, Bartholomäus 334–5
Bogislaw, Duke of Pomerania 124
Bogislaw, Duke of Szczecin 90
Bogusza 198–9
Boleslaus I 'the Cruel', Duke of Bohemia 46
Boleslaus II 'the Bold', King of Poland 93
Boleslaus III 'Wrymouth', Duke of Poland 45, 59, 82, 87, 89, 93, 96, 101
Boleslaus IV 'the Curly', Duke of Poland 102, 104–5
Boleslaus 'the Brave', King of Poland 45, 47–51

INDEX

Boleslaus 'the Tall', Duke of Wrocław 102
Bolingbroke, Henry 216, 220, 236–9
Bolshevik Revolution 346, 356
Bonaparte, Napoleon 118, 329, 330, 350
bonfires 278, 290
Boniface, St 29
Bornhöhe, Eduard 344
Bornholm 116
Borrebjerg 116
boundary markers 98, 99, 276, 288
Brandenburg (Germany) 39, 64, 68–9, 73, 76, 78, 79, 91, 119, 175, 200, 307, 328, 377, 381
   bishops 58, 68
   Hospitallers 361
   margraves 90, 94–5, 106, 170, 179, 180, 198, 199, 313
   participation in crusades 58, 61, 170, 179, 182
Brandenburg (Prussia) 188–94, 201, 223, 387, 388, plate 15
Braunsberg (Braniewo) 223
Bretislav I, Duke of Bohemia 50–1
brooches with religious symbolism
   Lithuania 290
   Saxony 34
Brosa, Birger 250
Bruno of Querfurt 43
Brunswick 352–4, 362
buildings
   brick 2–3, 72, 75, 79, 95, 120, 129–30, 140, 146, 164, 171, 177, 178, 182, 190–3, 201, 204–7, 211–12, 223, 226, 234, 255, 279, 297, 326, 362, 369, 388
   cross-log 71, 91, 205, 259
   stone 129, 140, 145, 146, 148, 152, 155, 171, 204, 210, 212, 234, 249, 251, 259, 260–1, 365
   timber-framed 71, 74, 91, 140, 254, 259, 260
bullae, papal (seals) 6, 286
Burchard, Bishop of Worms 37
Burchard II, Bishop of Haberstadt 57
Burchard of Hornhausen, Livonian master 159
burial rites
   agricultural tools 287
   animal deposits 88, 101, 291
   ceramics 88, 288
   coins 288
   cremation 33, 49, 50, 88, 100–1, 127–8, 151, 154, 182, 233, 270, 285, 288–91
   Curonian 285
   Danish 41
   feasting 88, 154, 270, 285, 289
   Finnish 127–9
   Holstein 69
   horses 88, 100–1, 180, 289, plate 8
   inhumation 33, 88, 100, 127–8, 155, 182, 286–7, 290
   jewellery 98, 100, 287
   Karelian 132
   Lithuanian 233, 284, 289–91
   Lithuanian grand dukes' 234, 289
   Livonia 162, 259, 286–9, 392
   Masovian 50
   mound burial 33, 41
   orientation 33, 129, 162, 287–8
   Osilian 154–6
   Pomeranian 48–9, 88–9
   Prussian 98, 100–1, 182–3, 269–70
   Reformation 289
   rosaries 288
   saint medallions 288
   Saxon 33–4
   second funeral 286
   scales 98
   shrouds 214–15, 217, 286, 289
   Teutonic Order 211
   trees 288
   weapons 100–1, 128, 154, 287

caltrops 163
canals 3, 67
candles 163, 227, 281, 285
Canute I, King of Sweden 126
Canute V, King of Denmark 61
Canute VI, King of Denmark 41, 71, 124
Capgrave, John 238–9
Capitulary for the Saxon Regions 32–3
Carolingians 8, 9, 21, 28–39, 52, 59, 70, 76
Casimir I 'the Restorer', Duke of Poland 93, 104
Casimir II 'the Just', Duke of Poland 105

INDEX

Casimir III 'the Great', King of Poland 200
Casimir IV Jagiellon, King of Poland 312
castellanies 103, 167, 172, 174
castles
   Bergfried (tower) 192, 210
   chapels 192, 202, 204, 206–9, 257
   communal spaces 192, 203, 206, 207–9, 224
   construction methods 188–94, 204
   Danzker 202, 206, 211, 388
   decoration 202–3
   episcopal 210–12
   Finland *see* Åbo; Kustö; Tavastia; Viborg
   Levant *see* Montfort
   Lithuania *see* Pilėnai; Vilnius
   Livonia *see* Arensberg; Arrasch; Fellin; Hapsal; Heiligenberg; Karkus; Reval; Riga; Segewold; Treiden; Wenden
   Lübeck 72
   moats 2–3, 130, 171, 176, 193, 201, 204, 209, 226, 298, 369
   Poland *see* Dobrzyń; Gdańsk
   Prussia *see* Allenstein; Brandenburg; Braunsberg; Christburg; Elbing; Graudenz; Guttstadt; Heilsberg; Königsberg; Kulm; Leunenburg; Marienburg; Marienwerder; Memel; Neidenburg; Ragnit; Rastenburg; Rehden; Reisenburg; Stuhm; Thorn; Vogelsang
   Teutonic Order 201–10
   Zwinger (terrace) 193
catechism 291, 294
cathedral chapters
   Livonia 195, 212, 315
   Prussia 211, 223, 230, 312, 357
cathedrals
   Åbo 196
   Brandenburg 65
   Brunswick 352–3
   Cracow 289
   Frauenburg 211, 223
   Gniezno 50, 52, 107, plate 4
   Havelberg 63
   Königsberg 223, 225, 269, 334, 373, 375
   Koroinen 129
   Magdeburg 42
   Marienwerder 211, 357, plate 17
   Nidaros 113
   Płock 50, 103
   Reval 150
   Ribe 122
   Riga 140, 343
   Vilnius 159, 233, 289, 291
   Wrocław 49
cattle 114, 119, 267, 282, 283
Celestial Revelations, St Bridget 301–2
cemeteries
   Denmark 41
   Finland 127–9
   Holstein 69
   Karelia 132
   Lithuania 284, 289–91
   Livonia 16, 151, 154, 162, 259, 270, 284, 286, 288
   Pomerania 49, 88–9
   Prussia 100–1, 165, 171, 180, 182, 231, 253, 257, 286, 357
   Saxony 33–4
ceramics
   burials 88, 288
   ethnicity 359
   Finland 6, 130
   floor tiles 190
   German stoneware 95, 160, 231, 254–6
   greyware 73–4, 164, 176, 255, plate 14
   kilns 72, 176, 190, 255
   Reval 262
   roof tiles 164, 190, 193
   Saintonge stoneware 254
   stove tiles 255, 299
   Wendish 73–4, 115, 119–20
chapels *see also* castles
   Estonian islands 155
   Estonian mainland 149, 277
   Frankish 28
   Grunwald 308
   Heiligelinde 279–80
   Helme 277
   Königsberg 225
   Lübeck 75
   Piast 47, 49
Charlemagne

INDEX

Frankish ruler 27–38, 52, 76
  imagined crusader 8, 52, 62
Chełmno 173; *see also* Culm; Kulm
Christburg (Dzierzgoń) 176, 179, 184, 359; *see also* Old Christburg
Christian, Bishop of Prussia 166–9, 174–5, 186
Christian I, Kalmar Union 304
Christian II, Kalmar Union 319
Chronicle of Livonia, Henry 137, 139, 141–2, 149, 152, 159, 161, 244, 250, 342, 344, 345, 347, 370, 380, 385, 386, 389, 390, 393
Chronicle of Livonia, Herman of Wartberge 216
Chronicle of Novgorod 303, 393
Chronicle of Prussia, Peter of Dusburg 163, 200, 203, 384, 386, 387
church attendance 272–4
churches *see also* round churches
  Altenkirchen, Rügen 120
  Blessed Virgin, Brandenburg 65
  Blessed Virgin, Juditten 225
  Blessed Virgin, Marienburg 326
  Holy Sepulchre, Jerusalem 10, 121, 221
  Holy Sepulchre, Visby (later Holy Ghost) 250–1
  Nativity, Bethlehem 113
  St Adalbert, Aachen 51
  St Adalbert, Szczecin 88
  St Anthony, Königsberg 225
  St Catherine, Arnau 225
  St George, Marienburg 369
  St James, Visby 250
  St John the Baptist, Thorn 171
  St Nicholas, Elbing 253
  St Nicholas, Gdańsk 95
  St Nicholas, Reval 259
  St Nicholas, Riga 162
  St Olaf, Reval 259
  St Olaf, Tønsberg 123
  Three Kings, Elbing New Town 257
churchyards 34, 281; *see also* cemeteries
Cistercians 5, 10, 16, 66, 79, 94, 106, 119, 123, 141, 164–7, 186, 260
cogs (ships) 74, 122, 244–7, 250, 256, 267, 305, 389
  found in Bremen 244
  found in Tallinn 243–4, plate 20
coins
  Albert the Bear 65
  Arkona 119
  Boleslaus I 51
  Boleslaus III 51
  Charlemagne 28
  deposits 280–1, 286, 288, 292, 385
  Gdańsk 95
  Gotlandic 129–130, 250
  Harald Gormsson 41
  Jaxa of Köpenick 65
  Pribislav 64
  Rügen 124
  Sambor 94
  Szczecin 86
  Teutonic Order 171–2, 203
  Thorn 171–2
  Valdemar I 121
  Walter of Plettenberg 297
  Wenden hoard 299
colonialism 9, 36, 40, 66, 78, 109, 195, 267, 272, 332, 333, 335, 342, 348, 350, 351, 378
colonisation 19, 48, 58, 66, 70, 77, 78, 179, 264–6, 332, 342, 352, 358, 371, 372, 378
condemnation of pagan practices/superstition/disregard of Christian praxis
  Finland 126, 274–5, 294
  Livonia 270, 279, 291, 294
  Prussia 180, 269–70
  Rhineland 37
  Saxony 32–4
Conrad of Burgundy 42
Conrad of Jungingen, grand master 220, 237, 306
Conrad of Masovia, Duke of Poland 14, 165–9, 172, 185
Conrad of Meiendorf 142–3
Constantinople 51, 111–12
  sacking in 1453 304
convents of Teutonic Order *see* castles
converts (neophytes) 32, 87–8, 97, 105, 107, 140, 142, 161–2, 166, 173–5, 179–80, 196, 237, 269, 270, 275, 288, 303

INDEX

Corrector, Burchard of Worms 37
Council of Constance 224, 240, 310
Counter Reformation 271, 280, 293, 314, 320
Cracow (Kraków) 14, 49, 94, 96, 105, 169, 289, 312, 314, 336–7, 362–4, 372
cross and crucifixion pendants 34, 128, 279
cross-marked trees 288
cross-shaped brooches 34
crossbows 147–8, 153, 163, 173, 176, 209, 216, 231, 297
crusades
  Estonia 149ff
  Greenland 319
  Kalmar Union's enemies 304
  Lithuania 214ff
  Livonian 17, 137ff
  Magnus Eriksson's 301–3
  Novgorod 158
  Prussian 165ff
  Swedish 124–32
  Vytautas' 306
  Wendish 15, 58–62, 79, 102
Culesius, Peter 387
Culm (Masovian) 103, 167, 169, 172; *see also* Kulm
Cumans 13–14, 185
Curonia (Kurzeme) 137, 144, 157–8, 161, 183, 273, 285, 299, 317, 341, 342, 367
Curonian *koniņi* (kings) 285
Curonians 108, 138, 143, 149, 183, 250

Dąbki 311
Danevirke 68
Danish islands 115–17, 120
Danzig *see* Gdańsk
Danzig-West Prussia (*Reichsgau*) 364
Dargun 119
Das deutsche Ordensland Preußen, Heinrich von Treitschke 332
Das Kreuz an der Ostsee, Zacharias Werner 332
Daugava (river) 15, 134, 137–41, 146–9, 234, 249, 266, 273
Daugmale 138–9
David, Lucas 282

Deeds of the Princes of the Poles, The, Gallus 81, 381, 383
deer 224, 285
deforestation 69–70, 96, 265
Deluge (*Potop*, Swedish invasion) 292
Demmin 61
dendrochronology 44, 72, 140, 177
Denmark (as crusader state) 113, 120–4
Der deutsche Ordensstaat, Alfred Rosenberg 359
Dethlefsen, Richard Jepsen 334
Deutsche Ahnenerbe 358
Deutscher Ostmarkenverein (German Eastern Marches Society) 335
diabolical toponyms 294
Die Volkssagen Ostpreussens, Litthauens und Westpreussens, Temme and Tettau 334
Dietrich of Altenburg, grand master 207
Dietrich of Eine 221
Dirschau (Tczew) 311
Długosz, Jan 91, 185, 271, 337
Dobin 61
Doblen (Dobele) 159–60
Dobrel 146
Dobrzyń, military order 168, 186
Dobrzyń Land 103, 200
Dominicans 96, 99, 150, 170, 173, 177, 240, 254, 260, 271, 275
Dorpat (Tartu) 144, 149, 151, 159, 195, 276, 283, 315, 319, 342
Doubravka of Bohemia 46
Drang nach Osten
Drohiczyn 168
Dryander, Ernst 326
Duchy of Courland and Semigallia 318
Duchy of Estonia 195
Duchy of Prussia 314, 321
Dünamünde (Daugavgrīva) 141, 145, 197
Durbe (battle) 159, 183
Dutch migrants 67–9
Działdowo 362

eagle (emblem)
  black 314, 326, 329, 330, 365, 372
  white 44–5
Ebert, Max 343
Edith of England 42
Einhard 31, 380

Eisernes Kreuz, Max von Schenkendorf 330
Elbe (river) 15, 32, 35, 38, 39, 42, 43, 54, 55, 57, 61, 68, 71, 139, 331
Elbing (Elbląg)
  bath houses 256–7
  castle 177–8, 223, 257, 312
  cemeteries 257
  ceramics 254–5
  churches 253
  destruction in 1288 182
  excavations 253ff, 374–5
  foundation 176–7
  glassware 256
  houses 254
  Lübeck's Law 178, 243, 254
  New Town 257
  population 257–8
  rebuilding 374–5
  siege 179
  town hall 255
  walls 257
Elbinger Kriegsbuch 257
Elbinger Vokabular 254
Eldena 119
Enguerrand of Monstrelet 240
Enlightenment 329, 341–4, 351
Eresburg 29–30
Eric I 'the Good', King of Denmark 112, 117
Eric II 'the Memorable', King of Denmark 59
Eriksson, Magnus, King of Sweden 301–3
Eskil, Archbishop of Lund 113, 118, 121
Estonia (*see also* Reval)
  Danish rule 149–52, 160, 181, 195, 252
  dioceses 144
  heritage 376
  independence 346–7
  islands *see* Muhu; Osilia
  literature 343–4
  Nazi occupation 366–7
  population 161
  Russian rule 341
  Soviet occupation 370
  strongholds 147
  Swedish rule 318

Viking Age 125
  War of Independence 346
Estonians 138
ethnic conflict 335, 341, 351, 358, 374
ethnicity 51, 58, 71, 74, 78, 131, 133, 141, 162, 187, 247, 253, 259–64, 263, 287, 301, 339, 342
European Union 19, 374, 378
Europeanisation 9, 378

fasting 32, 180, 272, 277
feast days 272–4
  Marian 226
  St Anthony (17 January) 278
  St John (24 June) 278
  St Maurice (21 September) 42
Fellin (Viljandi) 148, 151, 160, 204, 318
Fennoman movement 348
Fifth Crusade 13–14, 113, 150, 165, 167
Finland
  archaeology 348, 350, 385
  heritage 348
  independence 348
  literature 349
  Russian rule 347
  Second World War 366–7
Finnish Literature Society 320
Finns 124–32, 260, 263, 301, 347–50, 385
First Crusade 4–5, 8, 9, 21, 51, 52, 54, 55, 65, 82, 105, 111–12, 121, 144
First World War 343, 350, 354, 355, 357, 362, 363, 394
fishing 85, 131, 173, 255, 265, 266, 293
Flemish inheritance customs 172
Flemish migrants 66–8
Flemish silk 256
folklore 271
  Estonian 294, 295, 345
  Finnish 348, 349
  German 57
  Latvian 279, 283, 284, 287, 288, 345
  Lithuanian 279, 283, 284, 292
  Prussian 294, 334
Forest of Augustów 227–8
Forest of Eylau 286
Forest of Sztum 163
Forster, Albert 364
Franciscan tertiaries 290
Franciscans 197, 233, 234, 275, 290

INDEX

Franz Ludwig of Neuburg, grand master 329
Frauenburg (Frombork) 211, 223, 312
Frederick II, emperor 90, 175, 248
Frederick III (I), King of Prussia 328–9
Frederick Barbarossa, emperor 41, 64, 73, 124, 353
Frederick of Pernstein, Archbishop of Riga 197
Frederick of Saxony, grand master 313
Frederick William III 330
Frick, Friedrich 330
Frisia 28, 34, 36
Fritzlar 30

Galindia 99, 103–5, 169, 182, 190, 195, 313, 387
Gallus 45–6, 81, 82
Gauja (river) 16, 145, 146, 212, 179
Gdańsk (Danzig) 1, 48, 92–6, 106, 180, 222, 238, 311, 312, 332, 356
  Brandenburgian takeover 198–9
  Danish influence 165
  churches 95–6
  ducal stronghold 95, 198–9
  Old Town 95
  Piast conquest 48
  Teutonic Order's takeover 199–200
  trade 256
Geahcevainjarga 266
Gebhardi, Ludwig Albrecht 341–2
Gediminas 200, 233–4, 339
Gelehrte Estnische Gesellschaft (Learned Estonian Society) 344
Georgenburg 234, 235
Gerhard of Augsburg 47
German Democratic Republic 78, 371, 377
German Empire 325, 326–7, 337, 340, 342, 351, 356, 394
German Federal Republic 371
German language 320
Germanisation 346
  Masurians 338, 351
  Poles 335, 337, 356, 372
  Prussians 256
  Sorbs 351, 354
  Wends 58, 76, 78, 91, 314, 320, 377

Gero, margrave 46
Giecz 44, 47, 48
Giedraitis, Merkelis, Bishop of Samogitia 291
Gilly, Friedrich 330
Gira, Liudas 368
Gniezno 44–52, 86, 87, 89, 102, 104, 107, 165, plate 4
Golbe (river) 293
Golden Bull of Rieti 175
Golden Bull of Rimini 175
Golden Horde 306
Goldingen (Kuldīga) 158, 204, 285
Gorm 40–1
Gormsson, Harald (Bluetooth) 40, 109–10
Gothic revival 329–32, 343
Gotland 108; *see also* Visby
  churches 250–1
  coins 129–30, 250
  cross pendants 128
  crusaders 142, 170
  fonts 123
  law 252
  limestone 208, 211, 251
  manufacturing weapons 251
  masons 155
  merchants 74, 125, 247, 249–52
  Teutonic Order 307
  Viking Age 109
  Vitalian Brothers 307
Gotteswerder 234
Göttin 73
Gottschalk 56, 110
grain 22, 38, 70, 75, 99, 229, 244, 256, 265, 267–8, 297
Graudenz (Grudziądz) 175, 312
grave markers 284
Grażyna, Adam Mickiewicz 336
Great Northern War 18, 300, 321, 347
Great Wilderness 224, 226–8, 236, 389
Greenland 108, 109, 110, 319
Griffins (family) 81, 85, 89, 90–1
Grobiņa 108–9
Grodno 219
Grudusk 104
Grunau, Simon 99–100, 271, 275
Grunwald (Tanneberg, Žalgiris, battle)
  aftermath 308

INDEX

anniversaries 336, 363, 372–3, 375
archaeology 308
banners 363
battle 240, 308
chapel 308
monuments 362–4
museum 362
painting 336, 337, 363, 364, plate 23
Second World War 372
Grušas, Juozas 371
guilds 246, 254, 260–2, 264, 287
Guldborg 116
Guttstadt (Dobre Miasto) 211

Habsburgs 320, 328
Haken (ploughland) 160
Hakoinen 127
Hamburg 56, 71
Hanse 22, 178, 224, 245–7, 252–3, 259, 267–8, 305; *see also* Lübeck; Visby
Hapsal (Haapsalu) 212
Hartbert, Bishop of Brandenburg 58
Hartwig II, Archbishop of Hamburg-Bremen 16
Havelberg 58, 62–3, 65, 68–9
heating systems 140, 203, 255, 259; *see also* hypocausts
Heiland 36
Heiligelinde (Święta Lipka) 279–80
Heiligenberg, Livonia 159
Heiligenwalde (Święty Gaj) 177
Heilsberg (Lidzbark Warmiński) 184, 211, 293
Heimat
  concept 333, 339, 394
  Heimatmuseum Westpreußen 357
  museums 334
  Prussia 357, 360
Helmold of Bossau 37, 56, 63, 68, 72, 73
Hennenberger, Kaspar 293
Henry (Nakonid) 57
Henry, Bishop of Uppsala 125, 304–5
Henry, Count of Schwerin 150
Henry I 'the Fowler' 39
Henry 'the Bearded', Duke of Poland 166–8
Henry of Galen, master 317
Henry of Grosmont 215, 230
Henry the Lion

conquests 59, 61, 69, 90
crusading 62, 75, 106
Gotland 249
Lübeck 73
nationalism 354, 359
Rügen 117
tomb 352–4
Henry of Meissen 176
Henry of Plauen, grand master 308
Henry of Sandomierz 104
heraldry 81, 208, 224–5, 227, 326, 353
Herder, Johann Gottfried 325, 341
Herkus Mantas, Juozas Grušas 371
Herman of Salza, master 13, 168–70, 178, 332, 365
Herman of Wartberge 216
Hevelli 38–9, 63
Heym, Waldemar 357
Hindenburg, Paul von 360, 362
History of the Danes, Saxo Grammaticus 108, 117, 124, 384, 385
Hitler, Adolf 352–3, 362, 364–5, 368
Hohenzollerns 313, 328–30, 332, 336, 357
Holm (Martinsala) 16–17, 138, 140, 250
Holstein 35, 38, 63, 68, 69, 71, 72, 80, 123, 151, 170
Holy Roman Empire 9, 12, 15, 58, 65, 71, 77, 81, 106, 121, 149, 161, 170, 172, 196, 198, 200, 260, 315, 319, 321, 329, 334, 353, 365
horses 164, 229, 230, 251, 264, 303
  pack animals 228
  ritual use 49, 55, 57, 93, 88, 100, 101, 119, 180, 182, 188, 289; plate 8
  warfare 17, 145, 152, 161, 163, 179, 221, 224, 229, 308
Hospitallers 11–14, 75, 106, 120–1, 195, 198, 221, 305
  of Brandenburg 326–7, 361
House of the Soviets, Kaliningrad 373
household rituals 281
Hufen 173, 191
Hugo Butyr 105
Hungary 13–14, 66, 162, 311, 313

434

INDEX

hunting 125, 150, 173, 208, 224, 229, 249, 265, 266, 285, 297
Hussites 310–11
hypocausts 129, 208, 212

Iberia 5, 7, 8, 30, 52, 59, 66, 110, 114, 197, 220
Iceland 108, 109
indulgences 5, 15, 142, 170, 178, 219, 236, 274, 286, 302, 305
and *Reyse* 219
Ipiltis 377
Irminsul 29, 32
Iron Cross 19, 23, 330, 351, 359, 372
Nazi variants 363
Ivan III, Grand Prince of Moscow 305, 318
Ivan IV 'the Terrible', tsar 298, 318
Izhorians 303

Jacob of Liège 179
Jadwiga, King of Poland 289
Jadwiga of Silesia 166
Jakobson, Carol Robert 344
Janów Pomorski 92, 109; *see also* Truso
January Uprising, 1864 338
Jaromar 119
Jaxa of Köpenick 64–5
Jedvardsson, Eric, King of Sweden (St Eric) 124–5
Jelling 41–2
Jerome of Prague 289–90, 310
Jersika 143
Jerusalem 4–5, 8, 10–11, 12, 13, 15, 52, 55, 57, 82, 122, 326, 383
cross 227
kingdom 112
pilgrimage 121, 221, 238
symbolism 28, 41, 54, 114, 122–3, 207, 251
Jerwia 158
Jesuits 271, 277, 280, 281, 283, 287, 291, 314, 320
Jogaila (Ladislaus II Jagiello) 235, 237–8, 240, 289, 306, 339
John, Bishop of Mecklenburg 57
John of Falkenburg 240
John of Luxembourg, King of Bohemia 227

John of Recke, master 317
Junge, Michael, Bishop of Samland 269, 274

Kaisertage 325
Kałdus (*see also* Culm) 48, 103, 172, 381
Kalevala, Elias Lönnrot 349, 392
Kalevipoeg (*Kalev's Son*), Friedrich Reinhold Kreutzwald 345
Kaliningrad 373; *see also* Königsberg
Kaliningrad Oblast 9, 17, 182, 373, 375
Kalmar Union 303–5
Kalundborg 123
Karelia 18, 126–7, 131, 275, 301, 303, 349, 367, 370
Karenz 117, 119
Karkus (Karksi) 160
Kärla 155
Karshowen 159
Karuse 159
Kashubs 91–2, 337
Kaunas 216–17, 234, 236, 237, 291
Kaupo 16, 145, 147, 345, 346
Kernavė 216, 231, 233, 234
Kęstutaitis, Sigismund 311
Kęstutis 235, 339
Kętrzyński, Wojciech 372
Kettler, Gotthard, master 318, 341
Klaczko, Julian 333, 394
Klagges, Dietrich 352, 354
Klak, Harald 41, 109
Knight's Cross 363
Knights of Christ of Prussia 164, 168, 186
Knutsson, Karl 304
Knutsson, Tyrgils 348
Koknese (Kokenhusen) 145, 151
Kolbatz (Kołbacz) 94
Kolberg (Kołobrzeg) 49, 84, 86, 331
Konghelle 112
Königsberg 2, 200, 235, 285, 332; *see also* Kaliningrad
base for *Reysen* 217, 222–6, 236, 237, 238
cathedral 211, 269, 334
foundation 182
Frederick I 329
grand master's seat 312
Lutheranism 314

INDEX

Prussian attacks 183–4
Prussia Museum 334, 358
trade 256
university 314
Second World War 368, 373
Konrad Wallenrod, Adam Mickiewicz 336
Koroinen 129–30, 210
Koronowo (battle) 309
Kossina, Gustaf 74
Kraszewski, Józef Ignacy 337
Krodzinieks, Jānis 344
Kruto 57
Krystyn, Voivode of Masovia 165–6
Krzyżacy (Knights of the Cross)
    Aleksander Ford's 372–3
    Henryk Sienkiewicz's 337, 372, 375
Kulm 172–3, 179, 184, 273; *see also*
    Chełmno; Culm
Kulm Law 172, 178, 253, 265
Kulm rod/foot 173, 190, 387
Kulmerland (Ziemia Chełmińska) 48, 97,
    103, 105, 165, 167, 168–75, 184,
    186, 204, 265, 311
Kulmsee (Chełmża) 211
Kulturkampf 332, 335
Kurke 99, 100, 180
Kurzeme (Curonia, Kurland, Courland)
    137–8, 280
Kustö (Kuusisto) 196
Kuyavia 97, 102, 167, 168, 184, 200
Kyiv 9, 43, 45, 49–51, 102, 109, 111, 289,
    306

La Salle, Gadifer de 221
Lāčplēsis (*Bear Slayer*), Andrejs Pumpurs
    345, 346
Ladislaus I 'the Short', King of Poland
    198–9
Ladislaus II 'the Exile', Duke of Poland
    104
Ladislaus II Jagiello, King of Poland 306,
    307, 309, 311, 337, 339, 362, 363
Ladislaus Herman, Duke of Poland 93,
    103
Ladoga, Lake 126, 249, 303
Laima 279
Langeland 116
Lannoy, Guillebert de 285
Lateran councils 6, 58, 107, 270

Latgale 137, 265, 343, 363
Latvia 9, 15, 18, 108, 161, 228, 343
    folk traditions 279, 283
    heritage 146, 296, 343, 376
    independence 346, 350, 355
    language 320, 393
    literature 318–20
    national history 344–6
    Nazi occupation 365
    Soviet occupation 370
    strongholds 138, 147
Laurentius Suurpää, Bishop of Åbo 274
Lavard, Canute 59, 114
laws
    canon 37, 60, 213
    Danish 123
    Flemish and Dutch settlements 67
    German 67, 70, 76
    Kulm 172–3, 253, 265
    Lübeck 95, 243, 246, 248–9, 252–4,
        257, 259
    Magdeburg 91, 246, 253
    Riga 252
Lebensraum ('living space') 354
Lebuinus 29
Lehnin Abbey 79
Lembitu 147
    modern uses 345–7, 370
Lennewarden (Lielvārde) 143, 146
Leopold I, emperor 328
Leopold III, Duke of Austria 224
Leszek 'the White', Duke of Poland 94,
    167
Letts 137, 138, 146, 154, 162
Leunenburg (Sątoczno) 273
Levant 4, 5, 7, 9, 11, 14, 18, 55, 65, 66,
    105, 106, 112, 113, 121, 139, 144,
    165, 168, 197, 204, 218, 222, 380
Liber Census Daniae 160
Liepāja 365, 367
Lithuania 9, 18, 22, 138, 157; *see also*
    Polish-Lithuanian Commonwealth
    animal sacrifice 282
    Christianisation 289–92
    folk traditions 279, 283–4, 292
    grand duchy 9, 18, 185, 216, 226, 228,
        235, 239, 310, 338–40, 370–1, 376
    heritage 340, 377
    independence 350

436

INDEX

Jesuits 271
literature 336
migration 184, 318
nationalism 338–40, 368
Nazi occupation 368
relations with Germany 358, 361
Russian rule 335, 338
Soviet occupation 370–1
trade 138
Viking Age 98
war with Poland, 1919 340
war with Teutonic Order 184, 197, 202, 213, 214ff, 307–8
Little Ice Age 203
livestock 56, 76, 154, 161, 191, 229, 230, 265, 266; *see also* cattle; horses; pigs; sheep
Livonia
   early crusades 17–18, 19, 137ff
   Landtag (Diet) 316
   manors 162, 247, 264, 273, 316
   murder of episcopal representatives 315
   political tensions 315–17
   Russian governates 340–5
Livonian Confederation 316
Livonian Rhymed Chronicle 1, 19, 159, 188, 230, 379, 387
Livonian War 277, 283, 294, 298–300
Livs 15–17, 107, 134, 137–43, 146, 154, 162, 249
located settlements 67–8
locators 67–8, 191
Lochstedt (Pavlovo) 192
Lothar II, emperor 62
Lothar of Saxony 58
Lubavia 103, 169, 387
Lübeck *see also* laws
   bishopric 69, 73
   ceramics 73–4
   crusaders 11, 145, 248
   Danish rule 75, 123, 248
   excavations 72, plate 6
   foundation 72
   Hanse 245, 247ff, 267
   harbour 74
   merchants 72ff, 95, 247ff
   migrants 95, 177
   Slavs 64, 72ff

town council 75, 248
trade 244, 245, 251–2
walls 75
Lubena, Reinhold 285
Lubojatzky, Franz 332
Lucy, Anthony de 215–18, 220–1, 236
Lucy, Maud de 218
Lund 41, 57, 113–18, 132, 149, 303
Lusatia 59, 77–8, 354
Luther, Martin 313–14
Lutheran clergy 271, 279, 293, 294–5, 299, 314, 317, 367
Lutheranism 23, 273, 298, 314, 317–20, 326, 341, 349, 350
Lutici 38–9, 43, 55–7, 61, 82
Lyck (Ełk) 338
Lyck (river) 310

Maa-alused 294
Magdeburg 42–3, 54, 57, 61–3, 65, 79, 82, 87, 89, 103, 142, 170, 183, 246, 305; *see also* laws
magic 36, 37, 38, 93, 110, 149, 280–1, 283, 288, 294
Magnus, Duke 298
Magnusson, Birger, King of Sweden 127
Malbork *see* Marienburg
Margaret of Denmark 304, 307
Marienburg (Prussia) 1–4, 18, 205ff, plates 1, 2
   adaptation to artillery 209–10
   armoury 209
   barbican 209
   barracks 330
   bridge 209, 369
   Castle Museum 1–4, 227, 373–4
   chancellery 205, 208
   Chapel of St Anne 207
   Chapel of St Catherine 209
   Chapel of the Virgin 207
   construction 206–8
   excavations 209
   fishponds 208
   'golden gate' 206, 207, plate 16
   Grand Master's Chapel 207
   Grand Master's Palace 208
   Great Refectory 208
   infirmary 209
   moats 2, 209

INDEX

outer wards 209
restoration 327–32
sale by mercenaries 312
sculpture of Virgin 3, 207, 211
seat of grand master 199, 201, 206
Second World War 18, 364, 368–9
siege of 1410 308–9
stables 209
town 18, 206, 312, 334–5
train line 2
UNESCO status 352, 374
use by Nazis 359–60, 364
walls 209
William II's visits 325–7, 335
Marienburg (Transylvania) 14
Marienwerder (Kwidzyn)
   castle and town 174, 175, 211, 357, plate 17
   district in Prussia 356
   museum 358
Marienwerder (Lithuania) 234–5
Martel, Charles 29
martyrdom 17, 42, 43, 52, 62, 83, 89, 107, 110, 113, 114, 122, 123, 125, 142, 163, 164, 165, 186, 188, 192, 274, 308, 311, plate 4
Marvelė 290
Maschenholt 121
Masovia 14, 50, 84, 96–7, 101–4, 165–7, 170, 175, 184, 313,
Masuria 100, 337, 357, 362
Masurians 313, 334, 338, 356, 372
Matejko, Jan 185, 336, 337, 363, 364, 375, 394, plate 23
Matilda, Duchess of Saxony 62, 90
Matilda of England 353
Maydell, Friedrich Ludwig von 342
Mecklenburg 31, 57, 90, 106, 139, 168, 320
Medėninkā (Varniai) 291
Meinhard, Bishop of Livonia 15–16, 249–50
Meinhard of Querfurt, master 191
Memel (Klaipėda) 158, 182, 216, 217, 225, 228, 307, 339, 361
Memelland 339, 360–1
merchants 25, 38, 66, 71, 125, 174, 243ff
   Arensburg 212
   Christian–pagan trade 232, 233–5
   Elbing 254
   Gdańsk 92, 93, 95
   German 15, 130, 134, 138, 267, 333
   Gotland 74, 244, 249–52
   Königsberg 223
   Lithuanian 233–5
   Lübeck 75, 95, 247–9, 251
   Pomerania 84
   Prussian 92, 97–8
   Reval 259–63
   Riga 139–41, 162, 250
   Rus' 74, 162, 259
   Samogitia 183
   Scandinavian 108, 111
   Szczecin 85, 87, 91
   Thorn 171
   Wartenburg 231
   Wendish 117
Mestwin I, Duke of Pomerelia 165
Mestwin II, Duke of Pomerelia 95, 180
Meteliai Regional Park 228
Mickiewicz, Adam 336
midsummer festivities 278
Mieclaw 104
Mieszko, Duke of Poland 43–7, 49, 51, 381
Miesko II, King of Poland 104
Mieszko III 'the Old', Duke of Poland 61, 102
Millennium Programme (Poland) 83
mills 11, 70, 254, 266, 295, 313, 357
Mindaugas, grand duke 158–9
ministeriales 220, 248
missionaries *see* Anselm of Havelberg; Boniface; Franciscan tertiaries; Jesuits; Lebuinus; Meinhard; Otto of Bamberg; St Adalbert; Vicelin
monasteries 4, 7, 203, 226, 261, 275
   Dünamünde 141, 197
   Elbing 254
   Finland 252
   Frankish 27, 32
   Fulda 36
   Holstein 69
   Magdeburg 42
   Oliwa 94
   Pechersk Lavra 289
   Reval 150
   Rügen 118–20

INDEX

Saxony 35
Stolpe 89
Usedom 89
Vadstena 302
Mongols 306, 310
Monte, Herkus 183–4
  in literature 332, 371
  memorials 371
Montfort (Starkenberg) 14, 168
Monumenta Germaniae Historicae 342
Moravian Church 295
mortar 156, 190
Moscow, Muscovy 18, 304–5, 318, 368
mouldboard 69–70
Mucha, Alphonse 118
Muhu (Moon) 159
  monument 347, plate 13
  siege of 1227 152–4
museums 347, 351
  Art History Museum (Vienna) 40
  borderland 358
  Castle Museum (Malbork) 227, 373–4, 388
  Estonia 366
  Ethnological Museum (Berlin) 118
  Finland 350
  German (modern) 227, 377
  Groß Raden 377, plate 5
  Heimat 333, 357
  History and Archaeology Museum, Elbląg 177
  Latvia 366
  Lithuania 363
  Museum of Western Pomerania (Szczecin) 83
  Poland 83, 362
  Prussia 333, 334, 358, 359, 375
  Prussia Museum (Königsberg) 334, 358
  Saaremaa Museum (Kuressaare) 155

Nadruvia 169, 184
Nakonids 56–7
Narwa (Narva) 195, 366, 367
Natangia 169, 182, 183, 184, 188, 185, 273
national awakenings 23, 92, 295, 320, 343, 345, 348
nationalism 66, 329, 350, 351, 374, 378
  Danish 118
  Estonian 344
  Finnish 133, 348–9, 367
  German 74, 327–9, 333–5, 353–5, 358–60
  Latvian 344
  Lithuanian 338–9, 368
  Polish 199, 336–7
  Russian 376
  Soviet 19, 23, 365
Nazis 18, 19, 23, 78, 352ff
  appropriation of Teutonic Order 355ff
  General Government 364
  Ordensburgen 359–60
  persecution of Teutonic Order 361
  Reichskommissariat Ostland 365–8
  SS 359, 365
Neidenburg (Nidzica) 205
Neris (river) 216, 234
Nessau (Mała Nieszawka) 169, 170, 200
Neumark (New March) 79, 89, 200, 307, 311
Nevsky, Alexander
  'Battle on the Ice' 158
  monuments 376, plate 25
  Sergei Eistenstein's film 364–5
New Kaunas 216–17
New Marienburg 234–5
New Prussian Chronicle (Wigand of Marburg)
Nicholas, Bishop of Schleswig 149–50
Nicholas of Jersochin 203
Nidaros (Trondheim) 113, 132, 303
Niels, King of Denmark 82, 114
Nogat (river) 1–2, 101, 176, 369,
Norbert, Archbishop of Magdeburg 62–3
Nordkirchen 343
Nordmark (Northern March) 79, 381
northern marches 39, 43, 55ff, 85, 106, 146, 192, 245
Nosolum 383
Nousiainen 304, 385
Novgorod 9, 18, 109, 126, 131, 133, 138, 150, 151, 158, 196, 221, 249, 259, 262, 266, 297, 301, 302–4, 318, 364
Nyklot 59, 61

Obeliai 290
Obotrites 31–2, 38–40, 56–9, 61, 90, 110, 114–15
Oder (river) 15, 43, 48, 70, 71, 79, 84–6

INDEX

Old Christburg 176, 358
Oldenburg 37, 69, 73
Oliwa 94, 165
Olsborg 68–9
Operation Barbarossa 365, 367
Order of the Black Eagle 329
Order of Calatrava 106
Orekhov (Nöteborg) 221, 303
Orthodox Christianity
Ösel-Wiek 144, 195, 212, 298, 319
Osilia (Ösel, Saaremaa) 138, 151–7
Osilians 138, 141, 152–7, 159, 251
Osterode (Ostróda) 205
Ostforschung ('Eastern research') 353–5, 372
Ostmarkenromane (East March romance literature) 335
Ostrów Lednicki 44, 47
Ostrów Tumski 47
otherworld beliefs 80, 284–8, 290
Otto I, emperor 40–2, 76
Otto III, emperor 50–1
Otto III, Margrave of Brandenburg 188
Otto of Bamberg, St 82, 87–8, 94, 383, plate 7
Otto of Lutterberg, master 159
Ottokar II 182
Ottoman Turks 239, 299, 304, 310, 311, 313
Outlines of a Philosophy of the History of Man 325, 393
Oxenstierna (family) 300

Paderborn 34–5, 359
pagan *see also* sacred natural sites
 burial rites *see* burial rites
 deities 55, 96, 99–100, 118, 150, 153, 282, 377
 fires 278, 285, 288, 290–2
 idols 55, 57, 58, 63, 73, 87, 88, 99, 111, 117–18, 294–5
 priests 55, 63, 85, 86, 99, 120, 180, 290, 292
 temples 29, 55–6, 57–8, 65, 85–6, 108, 117–19, 290
 terminology 7–8
 rituals 56, 88, 93, 99, 118–9, 180, 276–7, 280–2, 286, 290–2
 snake symbolism 284, 290–1
partition, of Polish-Lithuanian Commonwealth 329, 335–6
Parzival 236
Peace of Thorn 1466 312–13
Peipus, Lake 158, 376
Pepin III 29
Perkun/Perkuno 100, 283, 293
personal names
 Estonian 279
 Lithuanian 234, 239
 Liv 143
 Prussian 191, 269
 Slavic 63, 76, 78, 119
Peter of Dusburg 98–9, 101, 104, 105, 163, 169, 170, 174, 176, 179, 184, 186, 200, 203, 386
Peter the Venerable 114
Peter's Pence 301
Petrissa 64
Philip, Bishop of Ratzeburg 146
Philip of Mézières 289
Piasts 43ff
 Christianity 46–52
 crusading 82, 105
 expansion of state 47–52
 foundation myth 44–5
 Pomerania 85ff
 Pomerelia 92ff
pigs 119, 174, 279
Pilénai 232
pilgrimage 5, 106, 120, 121–2, 219, 221, 238, 257, 279–80
piracy 98, 115, 126, 244
plebiscite, 1920 (East Prussia) 256–7
Płock 50, 102–3, 165, 168, 169
ploughs 69–70, 76, 98, 124, 265
Poem Concerning the Conversion of the Saxons 30
Pogesania 100, 169, 176, 179, 184, 195
Pograuda (Pagraudė) 219
Pöide 155
Pokarben 191
Pokarwis 192
Poland
 Deluge (*Potop*) 291–2
 Greater Poland 44, 164, 180, 335,
 Lesser Poland 46, 167
 partitions 336

INDEX

Second Republic 356
Third Republic 83, 91, 253
Poland-Lithuania 18, 23, 240, 307, 310, 313, 314, 318, 319, 320
Polish-Lithuanian Commonwealth 18, 291, 300, 319–21, 328–9, 335, 338–9, 340
Polish-Lithuanian War, 1919 340
pollen records 69–70, 130, 160, 174, 227, 240, 265
polonisation 293
Polotsk 9, 16, 137–8, 140, 145, 235, 249
Pomerania 1, 31, 38, 46, 48–9, 59, 81ff, 124, 163, 166–7, 170, 238, 320, 335, 359, 383, 388
Pomerelia 83–4, 92ff, 165, 175, 180, 198–9, 200, 201, 206, 253, 256, 311, 337, 356
Pomesania 84, 169, 174–81, 273, 274, 293, 314,
Pomesanian statutes 272–4
popes
   Alexander III 122, 126
   Alexander IV 219
   Boniface VIII 218
   Boniface IX 304
   Calixtus II 58–9
   Clement V 198
   Eugenius III 54, 60, 61, 215
   Gregory IX 6, 251, 269
   Honorius III 142, 149, 166, 232
   Innocent III 6, 106, 122, 126, 139, 142, 165
   Innocent VI 303
   Martin V 240
   Urban II 4, 8, 52, 55, 57
   Urban IV 179
Poppo of Osterna, grand master 181
Possevino, Antonio 283
Potterberg 172
potters *see* ceramics
Poznań 48
Praetorius, Matthaeus 276
Prątnica 99
Pregel (river) 182, 184, 223
Premonstratensians (Norbertines) 62–3, 66, 89, 123
Premysl II, Duke of Greater Poland 180
Preußisches Urkundenbuch 332

Pribislav of Brandenburg 58, 59, 63, 64–5
Pribislava 89
Prussia
   duchy 314
   early crusades 163ff
   estates 311–12
   free state 355–6
   Heimat 334, 357, 360
   kingdom 19, 92, 185, 326–7, 328–9, 331
   museum 334, 358
   peasant settlement 265–6
   Reformation 280, 282, 313–15
   Royal Prussia 313, 314, 321
Prussian Confederation 258, 311, 317
Prussians (indigenous) 14, 21, 43, 50–1, 59, 63, 83, 96–103, 104–7, 109, 157, 163ff, 191, 199, 200, 232, 254, 256, 257, 269, 273–4, 286, 313, 314, 325, 329, 332, 335, 336, 357, 359, 378
   first uprising 176, 179
   Great Uprising 159, 183–4, 332, 371
   language 254, 313, 334, 338, 358
   Lithuanian Prussians 293, 339
Przemyśl 49
Pskov 9, 138, 151, 158, 262
Purgatory 6, 270, 274, 284

Ragnit (Neman) 225–6, 228, 234, 293
Raitz, Rutger 221
Rani 38, 58, 59, 61, 117, 133
Rastenburg (Kętrzyn) 273, 312
Ratibor 89
Recovered Territories (Poland) 83, 372
Reformation 22, 300, 310, 319
   Finland 294, 320
   Holy Roman Empire 319–20
   Livonia 264, 279, 280, 289, 294, 317–18, 320, 341
   Pomerania 91–2
   Prussia 280, 282, 293, 313–14
   Samogitia 291
Rehden (Radzyń Chełmiński) 174, 175
Reinbern, Bishop of Kolberg 86
Reisenburg (Prabuty) 211–12
relics 34, 36, 40, 42, 51, 112, 142, 155–6, 172, 175, 178, 186, 192, 257, 272

INDEX

retroversion 375
Reval (Tallinn) 150, 152, 195, 258ff, 266, 305, 317
  castle 258–9
  cathedral 150
  cemeteries 259
  cog 243–4, plate 20
  Estonians 261–2
  Germans 260–1
  excavations 258ff, 370
  guilds 260
  harbour 259
  houses 259–62
  Lübeck Law 252
  monasteries 150, 260
  museums 366
  Old Town 258, 262
  population 260
  Rus' 262
  Toompea Hill 150, 152, 258–9, 370
  trade 244–5, 259
  walls 258, 260, 261
  Second World War 258, 367
Reysen (campaigns against Lithuania) 214ff, plate 19
  captives 230, 239
  composition of retinues 220–1
  financing 216, 221–2
  Great Wilderness 227–9
  guides 229
  Henry Bolingbroke 236–9
  horses 221, 224, 228–9
  religious symbolism 226–7
  renown 235–9
  role of English knights 214ff, 220ff
  siege of Vilnius 1390 237, 239
  stay in Königsberg 223–5
Ribe 121
Richard II, King of England 220, 237–8
Riedegost (Rethra) 55–8
Riga
  archdiocese 144
  cathedral 140
  conflict with Teutonic Order 197–8, 264, 316–17
  crusading 141
  earliest buildings 140
  excavations 140, plate 12
  foundation 15, 138–40, 250
  Livs 140–1, 150, 162
  merchants 233, 235, 250
  museums 366
  Nazi occupation 365–6
  population 141, 162
  Reformation 317, 320
  Rus' 262
  Society for Antiquities 343
  Sword Brothers 144–5
  symbolism 139, 142
  Teutonic Order's castle 160, 204, 264, 297
  trade 235, 244, 251–2
  Second World War 365
  walls 18
Rikalanmäki 128
Ristimäki 129, plate 11
Rolandslied 61–2
Romanticism 329, 336, 339, 342, 349
Rosenberg, Alfred 359–60
Roskilde 42, 115, 119
rotational farming 70, 264–5
round churches 121–3
Royal Frankish Annals 27, 30
Rugard 119
Rügen 58–9, 71, 90, 108, 115, 117–21, 124, 132, 150, 377, plates 10, 11
Rus' merchants 74, 162, 259
Russia 18, 23, 111, 138, 318, 319, 321, 329, 335–6, 339, 340; *see also* Kaliningrad Oblast
  governates 340–5, 347
  heritage 340, 345, 376
  Soviet 19, 23, 78, 346, 355, 356, 363–73, 375–6
Russification 342, 346, 348
Russow, Balthasar 299
Rutenberg Cisse van den, grand master 315
Rye 261, 265, 279

Saami 110, 126, 131, 266, 275, 301, 328, 349, 385, 393
Saccalia 147
sacred natural sites
  Alka 292, plate 24
  caves 280
  destruction 63, 99, 150
  groves 63, 150, 177, 269, 270, 279, 285–6, 288, 290–2, 294

INDEX

hills 88, 98, 276, 278, 291–2, 294
lakes 88, 98, 276, 277, 281, 283, 293
rivers 98, 283
solar 98, 278, 290
springs 278, 280, 292, 294
stones 48, 99, 276, 278, 281, 291, 294
trees 29, 63, 79, 98–9, 177–8, 276–81, 288, 292–3, plate 21
woods 276, 285
sacrifice/ritual killing
  animals (general) 88, 109, 234, 269, 282, 288, 289
  cattle 282, 283
  children 100, 283
  goats 275, 283
  horses 49, 55, 57, 93, 88, 100, 101, 119, 180, 182, 188, 289, plate 8
  people 56, 57, 119, 188, 230, 234, 288
  pigs 279, 282–3
Saevientibus olim Pruthenis, Paweł Włodkowic 296, 392
St Bees Priory burials 214–19
St George's Night Uprising 195, 344, 346, 368
St Matthew's Day (battle) 147, 346
St Nicholas's Hill 149
saints
  Adalbert 50, 51, 63, 83, 86, 88, 94, 164, 274, plate 4
  Andrew 257
  Anthony 225, 278–9
  Bridget 280, 301–3
  Canute 113, 122
  Eric 124–5
  George 225, 226, 282, 326, 269
  John the Baptist 171, 278
  John the Evangelist 274
  Maurice 40, 42, 65, 79
  Nicholas 95, 162, 253, 259
  Olaf 113, 123
  Otto *see* Otto of Bamberg
  Ulrich of Augsburg 47
Sambia 100, 158, 169, 182, 183, 201, 273, 274
Samborides 94–5
Samogitia (see also *Reysen*) 22, 138, 158, 159, 183–5, 228, 306–10, 339

diocese 291
paganism 277, 289–92
uprisings 307
sanctuary, rule of 276
Santir 164–5, 176, 206
Šatrija Hill 291
Saule (battle) 157
saunas 282, 294
Sawicki, Gustaw 33
Saxo Grammaticus 59, 108, 115, 116, 117, 124
Saxons 8, 15, 27ff, 54, 55, 59, 64, 114, 121
Scalovia 169, 184, 225
Scania 115
Schenkendorf, Max von 330
Schiemann, Theodor 342
Schinkel, Karl Frederick 330
Schlamesdorf 123
Schleif, Hans 358–9
Schleswig 39, 114, 121–2, 150–1
Schmidt, Bernhard 331
Schoden (battle) 158
Schönsee (Kowalewo Pomorskie) 184
Second Crusade 5, 60, 102
Second World War 366
  bombing of Lübeck 72
  destruction of towns in Estonia 358, 367
  destruction of towns in Latvia 367
  destruction of towns in Prussia 368–9
  East Prussian offensive 2, 368–9
  Finland 367
  invasion of Poland 363–4
  invasion of Soviet Union 365
  Nazi propaganda 355
  Soviet propaganda 23, 355
Segewold (Sigulda) 145, 212
Selonia 138
Semigallia 138, 157, 158, 159, 194, 265, 273, 318
serfdom 265, 341–2
Serock 105
ships 17, 74, 114, 130, 138, 145, 171, 179, 243, 244, 250, 263, 303; *see also* cogs
Sibelius 349
Sidrabe 159
siege engines 108, 117, 148, 153, 173, 229, 389

INDEX

Siegfried of Feuchtwangen, grand master 197, 199
Siegfried of Regenstein, Bishop of Sambia 274
Sienkiewicz, Henryk 337, 364
Sigismund I 'the Old', King of Poland 314, 315, 336
Sigismund of Luxembourg, emperor 310–11
Sigurdsson, Haakon 42
Silesia 38, 46, 49, 166, 167
Skirgaila 235, 237, 289
Skötkonung, Olof, King of Sweden 109
slavery 45, 64, 7, 98, 104, 115, 117, 123, 161, 229, 230, 264, 272, 304, 306, 325, 329, 344
Słowacki, Juliusz 336
Småland 114
Sorbom, Henry, Bishop of Warmia 273
Sorbs 351, 354, 355, 371
soul (belief) 270, 284, 285, 287, 288, 294
Spear of Longinus 40
spearheads 44, 163, 308
Sprevani 38
Starogród 172
Steinbrecht, Conrad 327, 331, 360, 369
Sten Sture 305
Stettin *see* Szczecin
stone (in buildings) 129, 140, 145, 146, 148, 152, 155, 171, 204, 210, 212, 234, 249, 251, 259, 260–1, 365
  Dolomite 201
  glacial erratics 190
  Gotlandic limestone 208, 211, 251
  granite 190, 193, 208
Strauss, Konrad 366
Strėva (battle) 226, 377
Strick, Walter 299
strongholds (timber and earth)
  Curonian 377
  Danish 116, 151–2
  Estonian 147–51, 152–4, 347, 370, plate 13
  Finnish 126, 127–8, 194
  Frankish 29
  German marcher 73, 79
  Lithuanian 216–17, 219, 229, 231, 232
  Livonia 138, 143, 145–6, 159, 161, 194, 264, 366
  Masovian 103, 165, 167, 169, 171, 174
  Ottonian 42
  Piast 44–5, 47–8, 50, 83, 104
  Pomeranian 86–7, 90
  Pomerelian 92, 93, 95, 96, 101, 179
  Prussian 97–8, 176, 183, 184, 187, 225, 264, 358
  Saxon 29–30, 39
  Swedish in Finland 127
  Teutonic Order in Lithuania 226, 235
  Teutonic Order in Prussia 170ff, 186, 188, 225–6, 358–9
  Wendish 38, 57, 61, 64, 65, 68, 73, 118, 119, 371
Stryjkowski, Maciej 392
Stuhm (Sztum) 163, 208, 357
Sudovia (Jatvingia) 103, 105, 169, 184, 194, 228
Sudovians 175, 179, 184, 186, 283
Sunesen, Anders, Archbishop of Lund 113, 149, 250
Suomen Kansan Vanhat Runot (*Ancient Poems of the Finns*) 349
Svantovit 117–19, 120, plate 10
Svekoman movement 348
Švitrigaila 307, 311
Sweden 18, 23, 108–10, 115, 124ff, 133, 195, 245, 249, 300, 301, 303, 318–21
Swedish crusades 124ff, 133, 302–5, 348
Sweyn II, King of Denmark 110, 112
Sweyn III, King of Denmark 61
Sweyn 'Forkbeard' 42
Swienca family 198
Swietopelk II, Duke of Pomerelia 94, 96, 179, 180
Sword Brothers 107, 144ff, 157, 160, 162, 164, 181, 186, 189, 195, 204, 248, 258
swords 44, 100, 128, 227, 308, 326
syncretism 277, 279
Szczecin (Stettin) 61, 81ff

'Table of Honour' 224, 236
Tallinn *see* Reval
tally sticks 160
Tannenberg *see also* Grunwald
  1914 battle and memorial 362

INDEX

Tasuja (*Avenger*), Eduard Bornhöhe 344
Tau cross 279, 286
Tavastia 126, 130–1
Tavastia castle (Häme) 196
taxation 34, 45, 70, 76, 117, 122, 124, 126, 131, 133, 148, 156, 159, 160, 161, 172, 173, 191, 195, 265, 301, 311
Templars 11–14, 75, 106, 120, 121, 144, 167–8, 198
temple rings 117
Temur Qutlugh 306
Terra Mariana 142
Terweten (Tērvete) 145, 159
Teutonic Order *see also* castles; *Reysen*
  accusations of heresy 197
  acquisition of Duchy of Estonia 195
  annexation of Pomerelia 198–200
  advocates 200
  amber master 201
  bailiffs 201
  bailiwicks 197, 309
  chapters 189
  commanders 189–90, 191, 194, 200–2, 209, 234, 293, 317, 318
  commanderies 189, 200, 204, 205, 385, 387
  conflict with Poland 200, 307ff
  conflict with Riga 197–8, 264, 297, 316–17
  convent design 188ff
  cross emblem 4, 12, 19, 314, 330, 351, 372
  crusading in Livonia 157ff
  crusading in Prussia 17, 99, 167ff, 186
  Fifth Crusade 13
  foundation 4, 11–12
  Gotland 307
  grand hospitaller 223, 257
  grand master 181, 186, 194, 197, 199, 201, 207, 208, 220, 224, 226, 237, 243, 305–8, 312–13, 317, 325, 328, 329, 332, 336, 337, 375
  literacy 19, 98
  Lutheranism 313–14, 317–19
  marshals 159, 183, 184, 224, 239, 296, 317
  masters 13–14, 168
  masters of Livonia 159, 181, 183, 194, 204, 239, 296–8, 305, 315–18, 343
  masters of Prussia 170, 181, 184, 191, 198–9
  numbers in decline 309
  persecution by Nazis 361
  procurators 201
  reimagined 19, 359ff
  Rhinelanders 315–16
  rule in Livonia 198, 213
  rule in Prussia 20, 167ff
  secularisation in Livonia 22, 318–19
  secularisation in Prussia 22, 314–15
  Transylvania 13–14, 185
  Utrecht bailiwick 315
  Venice 197
  war against Lithuania 18
  Westphalians 315–16
Tezlaw 119
Theoderic, Cistercian missionary 16, 141, 144, 145, 149–50
Thietmar, Bishop of Meresburg 55–6
Third Crusade 11, 12, 105, 248
Thirteen Years War 312, 335
Thirty Years War 321
Thorn (Toruń) 222, 309
  castle 171, 312
  charter 172
  fire of 1251 182
  first foundation 170
  merchants 171–2
  New Town 182
  restoration 331
  second foundation 171, 173
  walls 182
thunder (worship) 98, 100, 275, 283, 291, 293, 295
Tietäjät 294
Tilsit (Sovetsk) 361, 339
Tina (river) 227
tithes 34, 56, 57, 63, 67, 68, 70, 76, 126, 143, 160, 161, 180, 248, 265, 272
Tokhtamysh 306–7
toponyms 281
  Finnish 131
  German 91, 279, 294
  Latvian 285, 294
  Lithuanian 292, 294
  Prussian 98, 99, 279

replacement 91, 347, 372, 355, 358, 373, 446
Swedish 131
Wendish 78, 115
trade 21, 32, 38, 39, 45, 47, 74, 84, 86, 87, 90, 92, 95, 114, 125, 128, 130, 131, 312, 133, 138, 152, 171, 224, 245–6, 248ff, 265, 267, 300, 307, 311, 318; see also *Hanse*; merchants
  amber 90, 95, 98, 201
  between Christians and pagans 110–11, 232–4, 234, 251
  fur 22, 98, 111, 125, 244–5, 249, 256, 261, 264, 266, 297
  honey 99, 111, 227, 264
  timber (lumber) 22, 74, 244, 256, 266
  wax 22, 111, 145, 228, 244, 249, 256, 266, 269
treaties
  Christburg 99, 101, 179–80
  Kruschwitz 169
  Melno 310
  Nystad 321
  Versailles 356, 361
Treiden (Turaida) 16, 145, 146, 147, 212, 300
Treitschke, Heinrich von 342
Triglav 65, 85, 86
Transylvania 14, 185, 197
Truso 48, 84, 92, 98, 109, 177
Tryggvason, Olaf, King of Norway 109
Tuxen, Laurits 118, plate 10

Ugaunia 149
Ukmergė (Vilkomir) (battle) 311, 315
Ulrich of Jungingen, grand master 307–8, 336–7
Undeutsche (non-German) 262
United Baltic Duchy 346
Uppsala 110, 125, 126, 132, 303, 305
Urvaste 295
Utrecht 28–9, 315
Uusimaa (Nyland) 130, 131
Üxküll (Ikšķile) 15, 17, 138, 140, 143, 148, 365
Uzdowo 362, 364

Vadstena 302
Väinö Voionmaa 349

Valdemar I 'the Great', King of Denmark 90, 114, 117–19, 120, 121, 122
Valdemar II, King of Denmark 71, 123–4, 149–50, 158, 165, 248, 249
Valjala 155
Valtin Supplit 282
Vanhalinna 127
Varangians 111–13
Västergötland 112
Vecdole (Alt Dahlen) 148
Veleti 31
Venice 197, 198, 199, 207, 238
Verden 31
Vetseke 145, 151
Viborg (Vyborg) 127, 196, 252, 303, 304, 347, 348
Vidzeme 137, 280
Viljandi (Fellin) 147–8, 151, 160, 204, 280, 318
Villu võimisemed (*Battles of Villu*), Eduard Bornhöhe 344
Vilnius 227
  castle 233
  cathedral 233, 289
  census 1897 339
  Franciscans 234
  merchants 235
  Polish annexation 340
  Rus' 233
  sieges 235, 237, 239
Vincentius, Bishop of Cracow 94, 105
Virgin Mary (in art) 3, 203, 207–8, 211, 226, 280–1, 297, 369, plate 2
Visby 145, 247, 249–51, 267
Vistula
  border 1920–39 357
  delta/fenlands 1, 84, 92, 102, 206, 332, 357
  lagoon 176, 188, 189, 204, 222
  river 38, 48, 50, 70, 84, 92, 96, 97, 106, 164, 170, 171, 174, 175, 179, 184, 200, 265, 266
Vitalian Brothers 307
Vladimir 'the Great', Grand Prince of Kyiv 111
Vladimir of Polotsk 16, 139, 145
Vogelsang 170, 359
Võhandu (river) 295
Voigt, Johannes 332

INDEX

Völkisch nationalism 353–6
Volkskultur 333–4
Volkwin 157
Vytautas 'the Great' 235, 237–9, 291, 306–9, 311
  censorship 368, 370–1
  Jubilee Year 340
  memorials 337, 339, 340, 363, 370–1, 376
  order 340
  war museum 363

Waidewutus 328–9
Waidlott 275
Waldemar, Margrave of Brandenburg-Stendal 199
wall paintings 207–8, 211, 314, 330
Walter of Nortecken, master 159
Walter of Plettenberg, master 159, 296–7, 305, 316–18, 343
Wannem Ymanta, Garlieb Helvig Merkel 346
Warmia (Ermland) 99, 169, 179, 183, 194, 211, 223, 230, 273, 312, 313, 357
Wartislaw 87, 89
watchtowers 192, 206
Wawrzyniec, Bishop of Wrocław 166
Węgry 101
Weise, Erich 372
Wenceslaus of Rügen 150
Wenden (Cēsis) 296ff, plate 22
  armour 299
  chancellery 298
  commandery 204
  construction 146, 189
  excavations 299
  grain supply 297
  library 298
  master's chamber 297–8
  master's residence 297
  museum 343
  new castle 300
  siege of 1577 298–9
Wendish Crusade 15, 58–62, 64, 79, 89, 102, 114
Wendish Department, Bautzen 355
Wendish language 320
Wends (Livonia) 146
Wends (Western Slavs) 15, 38–9, 43, 47, 54, 82; *see also* Hevelli; Kashubs; Lutici; Obotrites; Pomeralia; Pomerania; Rani; Veleti; Wendish Crusade
  Christianisation 42, 61, 63–4, 117–20
  conquest 39–40, 57, 59–61, 66–9, 79, 110ff, 121, 122, 124, 353–4
  Germanisation 76–8, 320
  historiography 371
  legal status 76
  perceptions 55–6, 110, 115
  towns 71, 72–4
werewolves 37
Werner, Zacharias 332
Werner of Orseln, grand master 199
Wesenberg (Rakvere) 195
Westminster Chronicle 237, 239
Wewelsburg Castle 359
Wichman 46
Widukind of Corvey 41, 46
Widukind of Havelberg 58
Wieczorowski, Tadeusz 83
Wigand of Marburg 214, 226, 231, 239
Wigmodia 32
William II, emperor 325–7, 346
William of Balen 317
William of Modena 168, 251
Windau (Ventspils) 317
winter campaigns 148, 152, 158, 159, 174, 176, 182, 184, 219–20, 222, 224, 228–30, 235, 240
Wise and Foolish Virgins (in art) 178
Wiskiauten 98, 109
Witslaw 124
Wittekind (Widukind) 30–1, 36
Witzan 31
Wizna 103
Włodkowic, Paweł 240, 296, 310
Wolin 46, 48, 83, 84, 90, 109
Wolmar (Valmiera) 317
woodland management 201, 264, 266, 276
World Fair 363
Wrocław 49, 102, 166

Ymanta 346

Žalgiris (battle) *see* Grunwald; Tannenberg
Zealand 120–1